MUSIC FOR PIANO

To Emily

F. E. KIRBY

MUSIC FOR PIANO

A Short History

Foreword by Maurice Hinson

Amadeus Press
Reinhard G. Pauly, General Editor
Portland, Oregon

Jacket front: The Alma-Tadema Steinway piano, which is among the world's most valuable musical instruments. Auctioned at Sotheby's during the early 1980s for $390,000, it is currently exhibited at the Boston Museum of Fine Arts. Courtesy Steinway & Sons.

Jacket back: An excerpt from Liszt's "Harmonies du soir" from *Transcendental Etudes*.

ISBN 0-931340-86-1

Printed in Singapore

Amadeus Press
The Haseltine Building
133 S.W. Second Avenue, Suite 450
Portland, Oregon 97204, U.S.A.

Library of Congress Cataloging-in-Publication Data

Kirby, F. E.
        Music for piano: a short history / F. E. Kirby; foreword by
    Maurice Hinson.
                p.   cm.
        Includes bibliographical references (p.   ) and index.
        ISBN 0-931340-86-1
        1. Piano music—History and criticism. I. Title.
    ML700.K   1995
    786.2´09—dc20   94-42642
                                                         CIP
                                                         MN

Contents

Foreword

What a joy to welcome *Music for Piano: A Short History*. Many readers will recall with pleasure Dr. Kirby's earlier book, *A Short History of Keyboard Music*, which unfortunately has been out of print for a number of years.

A few earlier books in English have examined the development of piano music in a historical, chronological manner. Ernest Hutcheson's *The Literature of the Piano* (1948, revised by Rudolph Ganz, 1964) was of interest because of that distinguished Australian pianist's penetrating views. Willi Apel's *Masters of the Keyboard* (1952) provided a brief survey from 1300 to 1940, included a few complete works that were discussed, and was clothed in musicological garb. *Music for the Piano* (1954) by James Friskin and Irwin Freundlich covered the period from 1590 to 1952 by focusing on periods and style groupings. This volume also included music for piano duet (four hands), music for two pianos and concertos. John Gillespie's *Five Centuries of Keyboard Music* (1965) provided broad coverage of the subject to around 1960. My own *Guide to the Pianist's Repertoire* (1973, second edition 1987) is devoted only to solo piano music and is arranged alphabetically by composer.

Dr. Kirby's new volume focuses solely on piano music and is concerned with the development of style, historically and chronologically. The earlier volume has been rewritten, expanded, and updated to include works for piano duet and two pianos, and organ music is dropped. Chapter Nine is almost entirely new and provides an exciting overview of this most recent and multifaceted period. The copious bibliography will take the reader into many fascinating related areas and provide even more detail. Kirby writes in a clear and creative style that flows easily and makes the manuscript difficult to lay down.

This book will not only be extremely useful to the piano student and teacher, but will also provide an outstanding introduction to the field for anyone interested in this great repertoire and its development. The volume will be ideal to use as a text for any course on piano literature.

Maurice Hinson
Louisville, Kentucky

Maurice Hinson, internationally known pianist, educator, editor, and author of standard bibliographical works in the field of piano music, received his B.A. from the University of Florida and his doctorate from the University of Michigan, with other studies at the Juilliard School and the conservatory at Nancy (France). Since 1957 he has been on the faculty of the Southern Baptist Theological Seminary in Louisville.

Preface

This book presents a history of music for the piano. While I emphasize music for piano solo, I also consider important compositions for piano duet and two pianos. Music for piano with orchestra (concertos and the like) has been excluded, because its inclusion would have greatly enlarged the book and because such music is dealt with elsewhere, mostly in books on symphonic music in general. Similarly, chamber music with piano has also been omitted. Some attention, however, is given to the historical development of the piano as an instrument.

The book relies on standard editions of music and the standard scholarly literature and references in the field. The aim has been to provide a comprehensive overview of the field, drawing, as far as possible, on the results of the most recent research. I hope that my historical interpretations drawn from this study of the entire repertory of solo piano music will be suggestive and will stimulate further investigations. Any interpretation of this sort requires selection, and here opinions will differ on what ought to be included and what not, and on what ought to be emphasized and what subordinated. I have tried to be objective and fair and to follow where the evidence seemed to lead.

This book, therefore, is the successor of *A Short History of Keyboard Music* (1966). But it is not a second edition of that book: it differs in content, because it does not survey music for all the keyboard instruments but rather restricts itself to music for the piano—music, that is to say, in the fine-art or classical tradition. Not only has the coverage been brought up to date but more attention has been given to music by women composers, black composers, and composers in Latin America and Asia.

Some points concerning the use of the book:

1. Works are identified by numbers from thematic catalogs; for example, D (Deutsch) numbers for Schubert, K (Koechel) numbers for Mozart. Should a work be well known under its opus number, this number follows the identification from the thematic catalog, separated from it by a slash (/).

9

Where the thematic catalog identification has been revised, as in Mozart, the new number appears first, with the older—and often more familiar—number second, the two, again, separated by a slash.

2. Titles of works appear mostly in the original language, followed where appropriate by translations. For sets of pieces, the number of pieces in the set is given as an arabic number enclosed in parentheses immediately after the title, followed by the date of composition and/or of first publication. When mentioned in the text, individual pieces within a set are identified by lowercase roman numbers. Two examples: Impromptus (4, D. 935/op. 142, composed 1827, published 1839), and Sonata in D major (op. 10 iii). Thus in this book lowercase roman numerals do not refer to movements.

3. With very few exceptions, the notes serve to document information given in the text. They are not intended to provide a bibliography of the field. This appears at the end in the extensive bibliography that—unlike the one in the earlier version of the book—is topically organized to make it easy to locate books and articles on a particular topic.

There remains the pleasant task of acknowledging assistance of all kinds. Advice and encouragement came from J. Bunker Clark (University of Kansas), Maurice Hinson (Southern Baptist Theological Seminary), Franklin S. Miller (University of Wisconsin–Milwaukee), William S. Newman (University of North Carolina, Chapel Hill), the late Paul Amadeus Pisk (University of Texas and Washington University, St. Louis), Virginia Raad (Salem College), the late Paul J. Revitt (University of Missouri, Kansas City), Robert J. Silverman (former editor-publisher of the *Piano Quarterly*), and James Ure (Lake Forest College). Nathaniel B. Kirby, skilled in the arcane world of computer programming, facilitated the task no end; at a late stage other help came from Dr. Russell S. Kirby. Some traces of the competent and untiring work of William C. Watson (Washington State University) on the original version of the book survive in the present one. I offer thanks to the libraries where the work was done: Boston Public Library, Harvard University, Lake Forest College, Northwestern University (particularly), the University of Chicago, University of New Hampshire, and Yale University. Preparation of the typescript was materially advanced by a grant from Lake Forest College. I am grateful to the publishers of *Encyclopaedia Britannica* for generously permitting us once more to reproduce their drawings of piano actions, as well as to Belmont Music Publishers, Pacific Palisades, California; Alphonse LeDuc, Paris; and Music Associates of America, New York. Other permission to reprint music under copyright was granted by Boosey & Hawkes, Inc., New York; European American Music Corporation, Valley Forge, Pennsylvania; C. F. Peters, New York; Theodore Presser and Co., Bryn Mawr, Pennsylvania; and G. Schirmer, New York. For the fine photographs reproduced on the jacket and throughout this book, we thank Leo Spellman of Steinway & Sons, New York. Historic music title pages are courtesy of Dover Publications, Inc. Finally, the book owes more than I can say to the informed, skillful, and careful editing by Reinhard Pauly and Eve S. Goodman of Amadeus Press.

List of Examples

CHAPTER ONE

The Repertory of Keyboard Music to ca. 1750

Before we can deal with the literature of early keyboard music, we should consider the instruments themselves. We divide the acoustic keyboard instruments into four types: first, the various kinds of organs, instruments whose tone is produced by air columns vibrating in pipes; second, the clavichord, where the strings are struck by tangents; third, the harpsichord family, whose strings are plucked; and, finally, the piano, whose strings are struck by hammers. The organ is by far the oldest, having existed since Antiquity; the harpsichord and clavichord can be documented from the fourteenth century but are undoubtedly older; the piano, however, dates from the early eighteenth century but came into general use in the last decades of that century. While the incisive sound of the harpsichord's plucked strings has become familiar, the subdued, almost muffled, sound of the clavichord has not. The harpsichord's sound rendered it suitable for use in public performances, while the softer, more subtle, sound of the clavichord made it fit only for domestic use. Neither was readily capable of much variation in dynamics and color: that capability insured the success of the piano (see Chapter Two).

Therefore virtually no music before the latter part of the eighteenth century can properly be described as piano music. Yet the forms, styles, and techniques of this earlier music established the traditions that govern much piano music: the great unifier here is the keyboard, so that in a general way the basic playing technique of one such instrument holds for all. Thus much of this earlier music can satisfactorily be played on the piano. The following survey of early keyboard music, which will proceed by genres and will emphasize those most important for piano music, is intended to provide a general introduction to this field.

In music of the Middle Ages and Renaissance, it is often difficult, if not impossible, to tell what instrument or combination of instruments was intended. Polyphonic ensemble music in which keyboard instruments participated was notated in parts, either on one large page (choirbook format) or in part-books, but with no specification as to the instrument or instruments to be used. On the other hand, polyphonic music for a single instrument was ordinarily notated either in two-staff score or in tablature. Tablature is a specifically instrumental notation which differs from the normal notation of the time in that it employs letters and numerals, which refer to pitches and scale steps or fingerings. The problem is that composers not infrequently used the same tablature notation for lute as for keyboard music, so that it is often difficult to tell what was intended. Moreover, since many organs in the period prior to approximately 1700, particularly in Italy, were two-manual instruments, i.e., without pedals, organ music was often notated in two staves like music for the other keyboard instruments. Therefore, once one has decided in favor of a keyboard instrument, there remains the question of which: organ on the one hand, harpsichord or clavichord on the other.

This is a difficult question. In most cases a distinction cannot be made on the basis of musical style. Much of the secular music for keyboard from the time up to the late eighteenth century, therefore, must be regarded as for keyboard instruments generally, equally suited to any of them, with no specific traits that would allow an association with one or the other. Yet a classification based on whether a piece is sacred or secular, with the corresponding use of the organ for the former and the harpsichord or clavichord for the latter, holds in a general way and can serve as a general principle despite the many important exceptions.

The repertory of the time includes the following types, which we will consider below: intabulations; settings of and variations on secular songs; pieces in toccata style; imitative-contrapuntal pieces; dances and dance-related pieces; and sonatas. Then we will turn to the keyboard music of J. S. Bach, one of the greatest composers—if not the greatest—of all time and the only composer of the Baroque whose music looms large in the current repertory of the piano.

THE REPERTORY TO THE EARLY EIGHTEENTH CENTURY

Intabulations

Intabulations, also known as intavolaturas, are transcriptions or arrangements of polyphonic ensemble pieces for a keyboard instrument (also lute or guitar). The capacity for rendering polyphony on a single instrument has long been perceived as a principal advantage of keyboard instruments. Intabulations are present in the earliest sources of keyboard music: the Robertsbridge, Faenza, and Reina manuscripts from the fourteenth century and the Buxheim manuscript from the fifteenth century. Of the fourteenth-century manuscripts, the Faenza manuscript (written ca. 1400 and containing a fourteenth-century repertory) is the largest: almost half of it consists of intabulations, some of music by important composers of the time (Francesco Landini and Guillaume de Machaut). Intabulations continue to dominate the repertory of fifteenth-century keyboard music as well, particularly the important and very large Buxheim manuscript (ca. 1470), the contents of which again comprise primarily intabulations of works by leading composers of the time (John Dunstable, Gilles Binchois, Walter Frye, Guillaume Dufay, and others). The type remains dominant in keyboard music up to around 1600. In the sixteenth century, in fact, as we will see, it gave rise to other important genres of keyboard music. After 1600 the term fell out of use even though the practice of such transcriptions continued.

Settings of Songs and Their Variations

The practice in the earliest polyphony was to add new melodic lines (parts) to a pre-existent melody. This is known as cantus firmus–setting. While this procedure usually appears in sacred music, most early sources of keyboard music, such as the Faenza manuscript and the German manuscripts of the fifteenth century, have such settings of secular music. Examples also appear in the *Fundamentum organisandi* (1452) of Conrad Paumann (ca. 1413–1473) and in the *Lochamer Song Book*.

Related to this is variation form, in which the melody (the theme) is restated a number of times, each statement in a different setting. Again there are models in sacred music and also, as we will see, in dance music. In the sixteenth century this genre was cultivated particularly in Spain and England. From Spain, where the type was known as *diferencias*, we can refer among others to two pieces by Antonio Cabezón (1510–1566), *Diferencias sobra la pavana italiana* and *Diferencias sobre el canto del Caballero*. For the figurative ornamentation so prominent in such compositions they used the term *glosa*.

In England the type was prominent in the so-called virginal music,[1] which dates mostly from the late sixteenth and early seventeenth centuries. These English variations are of the cantus firmus type, so that the melody used as the basis for the piece is repeated over and over again in ostinato fashion. Should it appear in the bass part, it becomes a basso ostinato, or as the English called it, a ground (or ground bass). Since the melody was usually a popular song of the time, it was not stated in simple form at the beginning: the work just begins with the first variation. The principle of variation used here involves altering the character of the accompanying parts in such a way that contrast between the sections is achieved. Common devices are the operation with small motives that are worked out in the accompanying voices and the employment of extremely rapid scale passage-work punctuated with sharp chords. Among the many examples of this type of composition are "The Carman's Whistle" by William Byrd (1543–1623), "Loth to Depart" by Giles Farnaby (ca. 1653–1640), and "Goe from my Windoe" by John Mundy (ca. 1555–1630). Sometimes these are large and important pieces, as evidenced by "The Woods so Wilde" by Orlando Gibbons (1583–1625). Another type of variation is the *dump* or *domp*, based on an ostinato and associated with lamentation. In Italy variation form appears in the work of Antonio Valente (fl. 1565–1580) who composed five sets (published 1576), all based on dances.

This type continued throughout the seventeenth century. The Dutch composer Jan Pieterszoon Sweelinck (1562–1621) was important here, but his sets seem primarily intended for the organ. In the work of Girolamo Frescobaldi (1583–1643), large sets of variations on popular dance melodies of the time, such sets known as partitas, are more characteristic. There are sets on the two versions of the *Passamezzo*, the *antico*, and the *moderno*, along with *Romanesca*, *La Monachina*, *Ruggiero*, and the famous *La Folia*, in each of which the characteristic melody appears in the bass. Later examples appear in Alessandro Poglietti (d. 1683).

Two types have become better known, the chaconne (ciaccona) and passacaglia.[2] Apart from the circumstance that the passacaglia seems to have originated as the ripreso or ritornello in songs used as promenading music (*pasar la calle*), while the chaconne was a dance, there does not seem to have been any general distinction between the two in the Baroque. Both came to show the same features: slow triple meter, dotted rhythms, and the link to variation (ostinato) form. In Italy the chaconne was more closely associated with the ostinato than was the passacaglia, and there was also a difference in modality, the chaconne being minor and the passacaglia major. In France, on the other hand, the passacaglia most often appeared with variation form, the chaconne usually appearing in combination with the rondeau. We find both traditions in Germany.

Variation form is prominent in German composers of the time; for example in sets by Johann Jakob Froberger (1616–1667) on "Die Mayerin," Jan Adam Reincken (1623–1722) on "Schweiget mir vom Weibernehmen," and Dietrich Buxtehude (ca. 1637–1707). Yet the principal set is doubtless by Johann Pachelbel (1653–1706), the *Hexachordum Apollinis* (1699). The English composers John Blow (1649–1708) and Henry Purcell (ca. 1659–1695) continued the tradition.

The Toccata

This term refers to music that consists primarily of elements of figuration, which involves mostly scale passages and arpeggios, often with full chords and sudden and unexpected changes in harmony, tempo, and dynamics. The style seems based on improvisation, emphasizing figurative elements that are well adapted to the keyboard instruments; referred to as idiomatic, this way of writing exploits a particular instrument's individual qualities. However, because such pieces came to serve an introductory or preludial role in different contexts, sacred as well as secular, it is often impossible to tell whether their composers intended them for the organ or the stringed keyboard instruments.

The earliest examples, short pieces in free rhythm intended to precede the performance of a motet or other piece in the church service, date from the fifteenth century; they are by Adam Ileborgh (manuscript of ca. 1448) and Paumann. Originally mostly for organ and often specifically identified as to key, these pieces served to establish the pitch for the performers of the larger work and for this reason were referred to as intonations and later as preludes.

While this short and rather simple type continued in the sixteenth century, as evidenced by the *intonazioni* of Andrea Gabrieli (ca. 1510–1586) and by examples from England, particularly by John Bull (ca. 1562–1628, see Ex. 1-1), more characteristic is the toccata itself. Here, while the quasi-improvisational style is clearly dominant, the whole composition has been greatly enlarged. The alternation between sections contrasting in character remains the basis, but the sections have become longer, and episodic passages involving imitative counterpoint have been introduced. The most prominent composer here was Claudio Merulo (1533–1604), in whose toccatas (see Ex. 1-2) a ternary formal scheme prevails: first a section employing massive chords and brilliant scales, then a middle part featuring imitative counterpoint, and finally a concluding section in which the virtuoso character of the beginning returns. Still other toccatas have five sections, with three parts in the toccata style separated by two in imitative counterpoint. Other examples come from Andrea Gabrieli, Sperindio Bertoldo (ca. 1530–1570), Ercole Pasquini (ca. 1550–ca. 1613), and Andrea Gabrieli's nephew Giovanni (ca. 1555–1612), among others. It has been discovered that since the early sixteenth century many toccatas, particularly those associated with Venice, in fact either originated as elaborations upon or contain passages that are elaborations upon psalm tones.[3]

The genre was continued in seventeenth-century Italy, first by Giovanni Maria Trabaci (ca. 1575–1647) and others of the Neapolitan group of the time, and then by Frescobaldi, whose twenty-odd toccatas use the same external form as those of Merulo. The difference is rather one of quality, due largely to the use of extreme chromaticism and sudden contrasts, both evidently

Example 1-1. BULL: Prelude from *Fitzwilliam Virginal Book*—Excerpt (mm. 1–3)

Example 1-2. Merulo: Toccata—Excerpt (mm. 21–24)

derived from the madrigal of the time; psalm-tone formulas are less prominent. Frequently, however, the counterpoint operates with short motives that
are treated quasi-imitatively among the various parts and accompanied with
figurational material, so that instead of having the two strictly separated, as in
Merulo, we find them combined (see Ex. 1-3). In other works, such as Frescobaldi's Toccata IX (1637), several shorter and contrasting sections produce
a restless discontinuity. An accumulation near the end forms an impressive
conclusion, and in the score we find the remark, "the end will not be reached
without difficulty." While most of Frescobaldi's toccatas contain chromaticism, a few capitalize on it. The best known of these is the *Toccata di durezze
e ligature* (1637, see Ex. 1-4), related to similar pieces by Giovanni de Macque
(ca. 1548–1614), Ascanio Mayone (ca. 1565–1627), Rocco Rodio (ca. 1535–ca.

Example 1-3. Frescobaldi: Toccata (Book I, No. 6)—Excerpt (mm. 5–6)

Example 1-4. Frescobaldi: *Toccata di durezze e ligature* (1637, No. 8)—Excerpt (mm. 6–10)

1615), and Trabaci; the term refers to dissonances and tied notes. Entirely different, however, are the serene toccatas for organ in his *Fiori musicali*.

The toccata continued as a main form—perhaps the main form—of Italian keyboard music of the Baroque. In the seventeenth century it is prominent in the work of Michelangelo Rossi (ca. 1602–1656), Scipione Giovanni (fl. 1650), and Alessandro Poglietti. In the first half of the eighteenth century we find toccatas by Bernardo Pasquini (1637–1710) and Alessandro Scarlatti (1660–1725), the latter formerly considered spurious, but authenticity of which has been established. Some of Scarlatti's reveal a feature that came to have great importance for the keyboard music of the time—the employment of a specifically orchestral style. In the fast sections this seems evident from the relentlessly driving rhythms of the themes, in which figuration is important, and in the form, which resembles the ritornello scheme common in contemporary orchestral music. In this scheme, contrasting sections intervene between statements of the opening passage (the ritornello).

The style also appears in French preludes of the seventeenth century. Most of these carry on the old tradition without bringing in the elements added by Italian composers of the latter part of the sixteenth century. In Louis Couperin (ca. 1626–1661) and Jean-Henri d'Anglebert (1635–1691), for example, the prelude remained a small form in a quasi-improvisational manner exhibiting great freedom of rhythm. Often such pieces do not even have time signatures; rather, all notes are written as being equal in value (the whole-note is used exclusively), so that meter and rhythm are at the discretion of the player. The melodic material consists largely of arpeggios. Some of Louis Couperin's preludes, however, are in two parts: the first is as just described, but the second, with the designation *changement du mouvement,* is fugal, so that there we see a relation to the orchestral French overture.

In seventeenth-century Germany Merulo's larger form of the toccata was continued in the work of Jacob Praetorius (1586–1651) and Ferdinand Tobias Richter (1651–1711). It was particularly emphasized by composers in Vienna: Froberger, Johann Kaspar Kerll (1627–1693), and Georg Muffat (1653–1704). The latter's *Apparatus musico-organisticus* (1690) consists largely of toccatas. While Froberger favored a tripartite structure, a fugal section preceded and followed by passages in the toccata style, Kerll and Muffat employed a larger number of shorter sections. Kerll's, however, like Frescobaldi's, make little use of imitative counterpoint.

Imitative Contrapuntal Forms

The first keyboard music printed in Italy by Antico in Rome in 1517 was a collection of intabulations: frottolas, polyphonic songs in a popular style. The intabulation of such popular songs lies back of the earliest imitative contrapuntal type, the *canzona francese* or simply canzona. At first works with this title were simply keyboard intabulations (transcriptions) of popular French chansons. Since such a chanson was a modest polyphonic piece, generally of light character but employing the principle of contrapuntal imitation, its keyboard intabulation shows the same features. Thus, we find these keyboard canzonas to be sectional, with each section employing its own theme which is treated in imitative counterpoint; the only change lies in the addition of idiomatic keyboard figuration. Two examples are Thomas Crecquillon's "Pour ung plaisir," which was made into a canzona by Andrea Gabrieli, and Josquin's famous "Faulte d'argent," which was worked out as a canzona by Girolamo da Cavazzoni (ca. 1525–ca. 1577). But the type was common in Italian keyboard music of the time.

The next step in the development finds the keyboard canzona breaking away from its source: now it is a freely composed and independent composition called canzona that resembles what we have just described. Thus the vocal model gave rise to a new and idiomatic category of keyboard music, the first imitative contrapuntal genre for keyboard. Its original source, however, continued to be reflected in the stereotyped thematic forms used in canzonas, particularly in their opening sections. Such themes generally are sharply defined rhythmically and make use of repeated notes and ascending leaps of a fourth or fifth; figuration continues to play an important role (see Ex. 1-5). Among Italian composers who emphasized the canzona were A. Gabrieli, Mayone, Trabaci, Frescobaldi, and Giovanni Salvatore (ca. 1620–ca. 1688); among the Germans were Froberger, Kerll, and Muffat.

Two important subgroups consist of the variation canzona and the capriccio. In the variation canzona the themes of the succeeding sections are variants of that of the opening, a procedure that fosters overall consistency. Among many composers are A. Gabrieli, Mayone, Frescobaldi, Froberger, and Kerll. The capriccio is an imitative contrapuntal type that indulges in sud-

Example 1-5. A. GABRIELI: *Canzona francese* on *Petit Jacquet*—Excerpt (mm. 1-5)

den contrasts and makes much use of chromaticism. Mayone was an early exponent of this genre, and his lead was followed by Frescobaldi and Viennese composers of the seventeenth century: Froberger, Kerll, and Poglietti. Froberger's in particular emphasize the surprising and striking, with unusual and characteristic themes. The capriccio, moreover, became the vehicle for program music, expressive of an explicit and extra-musical content. This is already clear in some of Frescobaldi's capriccios and it continues in pieces like Kerll's "Capriccio Cucu," his battaglia (a piece conveying the tumult of a battle), and his "Halter. Der steyrische Hirt." A better-known example is Poglietti's "Capriccio über das Henner und Hennengeschrey" (Capriccio on Hens and their Cackling), the musical description of a barnyard scene.

The situation is much less clear with another form frequently associated with the canzona—the ricercar. The term comes from the Italian meaning "to search" or "seek out." Composers applied it to different kinds of instrumental music of the early sixteenth century, first to lute music and then to keyboard and ensemble music. Since most compositions bearing the name *ricercar* are composed in imitative counterpoint, the ricercar used to be considered an instrumental motet, the "serious" counterpart to the canzona. The main difficulty is that no ricercars were found to be intabulations of motets, although in the earliest source that contains them, a collection of music by Marco Antonio (da Bologna) Cavazzoni (ca. 1490–ca. 1560), published 1523, they are placed before the intabulations of motets. Moreover, these early ricercars are not in imitative counterpoint but, in common with the earlier ricercars for lute, show the figurative style characteristic of the prelude (what we have been calling the toccata style). In a more recent interpretation[4] ricercars in general are regarded as preludial in function, but their style over time changed from the toccata-like figuration to imitative counterpoint. The first keyboard ricercars composed in imitative counterpoint—and hence the first to employ the term in the sense in which we generally understand it—appear in a collection of music by Marco Antonio's nephew, Girolamo Cavazzoni, published 1543, intended for organ.

The decisive shaping of the form, stamping it with the features generally associated with the category; appears in the work of Venetian composers. While there are some ricercars by Adrian Willaert (ca. 1490–1562), these are actually ensemble pieces not intended for keyboard. It is rather the work of Andrea Gabrieli that has the greatest importance here (see Ex. 1-6). In his seventeen ricercars (published posthumously in 1595 and 1596) we find both the contrapuntal approach and the sectional organization. But the number of sections has been reduced, so that the number of themes used is correspondingly less: seven of them are monothematic, while several others employ but two or three themes. At the same time, an increase in complexity takes place: the contrapuntal procedures become more involved; the theme, for instance, is broken up and its second part used to accompany the entrance of the theme in another voice, thus a countersubject. Furthermore, the devices of learned counterpoint—inversion, diminution, and augmentation of the theme, as well as stretto, closely staggered entries of the theme—also appear.

From the latter part of the sixteenth century there are ricercars by Jacques Buus (ca. 1500–1565), Annibale Padovano (1527–1575), and Merulo. Two of those by Padovano, both found in the posthumous collection published in 1604, employ four and five themes respectively. The interesting point here is that Padovano introduced the principle of thematic variation into the category; the subject of the first imitative section is varied to form the subjects of the subsequent sections, thus promoting monothematicism. Merulo, on the other hand, best known for his toccatas, published three volumes of ricercars that represent the earlier type with a multiplicity of sections and themes, some also incorporating variation. Other Italian composers of ricercars include Bertoldo, Valente, Trabaci, and Frescobaldi.

Another imitative contrapuntal type of early keyboard music is the fantasia, which developed in the sixteenth century. Like *ricercar*, the term *fantasia*—often *fancy* in England—is current in lute tablatures of the time. Its first application to keyboard music occurs in Germany (tablature of Hans Kotter, written ca. 1513–1514). The sixteenth-century fantasia has nothing resembling a "free flight of fancy"—the rhapsodic elements appear later—but rather is a work in strict imitative counterpoint. Thus in the sixteenth century, par-

Example 1-6. A. GABRIELI: Ricercar arioso—Beginning (mm. 1–5)

ticularly in Italy, there does not seem to have been any real difference between the fantasia and the ricercar. Composers important in the early history of the fantasia are Sweelinck and Gibbons. In Spain such imitative contrapuntal compositions were known as *tientos*, particularly important in the work of Cabezón.

The historical process by which these forms came together to create what we know as the fugue remains unclear. While the various species we have identified did not completely die out, they declined in importance, particularly toward the end of the seventeenth century, to be replaced by the fugue, which we may regard as a sort of combination form.

The designation *fugue* had been in use since the late fifteenth century with several meanings all related to contrapuntal imitation, but often implying canon. In the seventeenth century the term came to designate a composition, often but not exclusively for keyboard, employing contrapuntal imitation. The first important publication to use the term *fugue* in this sense this was a set of organ pieces by Samuel Scheidt (1587–1654), *Tabulatura nova*, Part Three (1624). Other examples come from the *Harmonia organica* (1645) by Johann Erasmus Kindermann (1616–1655), and the work of Pachelbel.

Features found in Pachelbel's fugues become typical of the genre: first the formulation of the theme itself, especially the use of figurative elements, and then the breaking down of the theme into component motives as the composition unfolds. The learned devices are generally absent, but Johann Krieger (1652–1735) produced a set of four fugues with themes combined into one quadruple fugue.

The combination of the two types, the toccata and the fugue, into a single genre took place in the Venetian toccata of the sixteenth century. Yet another tradition of simply combining a prelude or toccata with a fugue in the same key developed in the seventeenth century, as can be seen in a modest way in a prelude and fugue for organ in D major, by Heinrich Scheidemann (ca.

1595–1663). This approach was continued by Krieger, Pachelbel, Franz Xaver Murschhauser (1663–1738), and Johann Caspar Ferdinand Fischer (ca. 1670–1746). While the idea of associating the two seems clear, we find cases in which the order is reversed, the piece in toccata style coming after the fugue. In Murschhauser, while the pieces are in the same key, the order has not been fixed by the composer, so that the performer has to choose which pieces to play—to choose, for instance, out of a group consisting of an *intonatio*, a *praeambulum*, three fugues, and another *praeambulum*, all in the same key. Fischer's collection, *Ariadne musica* (1702), is a forerunner of Bach's *Well-Tempered Clavier* in its assumption of some form of equal temperament.

Moreover, the fantasia, which had been a strictly imitative contrapuntal type, came to alter its character completely: it became similar to the toccata. Therefore, it is often not possible to distinguish between the toccata, the prelude and fugue, and the fantasia.

Dances and Suites

The largest part of the repertory of early keyboard music is related to dance. Even the earliest source containing keyboard music, the Robertsbridge manuscript (fourteenth century), contains three *estampies*. But dance is not emphasized again in sources of keyboard music until the sixteenth century, when we find it particularly in German tablatures. Here that of Hans Kotter is important; it contains, for example, among much else, a dance attributed to Hans Weck, "Il re di Spagna," a basse danse. The original melodies for the basse danse are monophonic and appear in notes of equal value. These melodies served as cantus firmi for polyphonic settings. In Weck's piece, for example, one of them appears ornamented in the upper part.

Other dances are found in France, especially in the publications of the Parisian printer Pierre Attaingnant which appeared ca. 1530, and Italy, in three printed collections, one anonymous, the others by Marco Facoli (1588) and Giovanni Maria Radino (1592). The dances represented include the passamezzo, an extended dance in variation form employing either of two forms of a basic melody, the *antico* and the *nuovo* or *moderno*; the saltarello, a leaping dance; the pavane; and the galliard.

From England we find dances in the extensive repertory of virginal music, almans (allemandes), corantos (correntes), jigs, and branles. Other dances of the sixteenth century include the tourdion, hornpipe, and sarabande. The minuet, gavotte, and bourrée date from the seventeenth century.

In the fifteenth century the practice was to have the slow and dignified basse danse followed by a quick dance in triple time. This custom of linking dances in pairs continued through the sixteenth century. In Germany the second dance was known either as the *Nachtantz* (the dance after or following) or the *Proportz*. The latter name may be explained by another aspect of these dance pairs: the second dance often is a variation of the first, presenting the same musical material but in triple time. Thus it involves the system of proportional notation. The practice of variation among dance pairs is common;

other standard pairings are the French pavane and galliard and the Italian passamezzo and saltarello.

In general these dances are short and, with the exception of the basse danse, simple. But individual examples can be artistically more elaborate, as, for instance, the pavane and galliard that bears the title "Lord of Salisbury," by Orlando Gibbons; the title relates to the person to whom the piece is dedicated and not to a specific dance melody. Here the pavane in particular has been transformed. We find long and irregular phrases and long ascending sequences, much use of chromaticism with unusual expressive intervals, and considerable contrapuntal detail, all of which combine to make this a masterpiece of early keyboard music (see Ex. 1-7). Such a treatment of a dance is known as stylization, a practice that continued to play an important part in the history of keyboard music. Gibbons' galliard is a variation of the pavane.

In the seventeenth-century dance and dance-related forms, which in some cases are intabulations of lute pieces, dominate the repertory of French keyboard music. The three most important composers are Jacques Champion de Chambonnières (ca. 1602–1672), Louis Couperin, and d'Anglebert; apart from their printed collections a large repertory has been preserved in the Bauyn manuscript. The forms and types represent dances popular at the time. We have considered the sixteenth-century custom of grouping dances in pairs. In this lies the origin of the practice of having a group of dances in the same key, a form known as the suite or dance suite. Another influence may stem from the *ballet de cour.* Producing cyclic form by means of thematic variation, however, is not a characteristic of the seventeenth-century French

Example 1-7. GIBBONS: Pavane, Lord of Salisbury from *Parthenia*—Excerpt from the third part (mm. 46–52)

repertory. The inclusion of three or more numbers in the suite seems to have been the achievement of French keyboard composers of the time, although, as we will see, there were contributions from elsewhere. In any case, the form quickly attained international standing. The most prominent dances are:

Allemande: moderate duple time
Courante: moderate triple time
Sarabande: slow triple time
Gigue: fast compound triple time (generally 6/8).

The designation *suite* with reference to keyboard (harpsichord) music appeared infrequently in seventeenth-century France and meant nothing more than a succession or set of pieces, mostly dances, and carried no implication of a particular genre. Three different kinds of arrangements have been found in this music, all based on the use of one key throughout: first, the "loose" form, consisting of a number of dances arranged by type, any number of dances in each group; second, the opposite of this, a series of single dances, one of each kind; and third, a combination form, some dances represented by single pieces and others by groups.[5] In some cases the dances are preceded by a prelude in the toccata style (see above).

While the suites of Chambonnières are of the third variety—for instance, with an allemande, one or more courantes, and a sarabande followed by an indefinite number of other dances, those of Louis Couperin are of the first kind, the dances being arranged by key and then by type. In Couperin, first there is a group in C major, then one in D minor, followed by groups in D major, E minor, F major, G major, and so on, and within each group, or suite, all the allemandes are together, then all the courantes, and then the sarabandes, along with occasional other dances. Much the same situation is found in the music of d'Anglebert and Nicolas-Antoine Lebègue (ca. 1631–1702). It was not until the end of the century, in suites by Charles Dieupart (ca. 1667–ca. 1740), who lived in England, Elisabeth-Claude Jachet de La Guerre (1667–1729), and Louis Marchand (1670–1732), that the succession allemande–courante–sarabande–gigue appeared with any regularity. It therefore seems evident that in the seventeenth century the player was to make a selection of pieces in the same key and to play these as a suite; the emphasis went to the dances as individual compositions and not to the larger form to which they belonged.

In most of these individual dances the form comprises two parts each to be repeated, thus the term *binary form.* This may be represented as ‖:a:‖ ‖:b:‖. A modulation from tonic to dominant (or relative major) takes place in the first section with a return to the tonic, often after passing through other keys, in the second. In many cases the second section employs essentially the same thematic material as the first (thus ‖:a:‖ ‖:a′:‖), or it commences differently and then restates, with changes, the first; this last is often called rounded binary form, ‖:a:‖ ‖:b a:‖. Often found, especially with the courante and minuet, is the double, a variation of the dance.

Then there are dances whose form differs principally from these. Important here is the rondeau, which has a refrain that like a ritornello is repeated throughout and separates sections of contrasting character that were called couplets. (The number of couplets was not fixed.) The passacaille and chaconne, as we have seen, are both variation forms based on short ostinato patterns. At times we find the *chaconne en rondeau*, a chaconne serving as the refrain element in a rondeau.

Composers often gave descriptive or characteristic titles to such dances and other pieces. While in some cases the titles are dedicatory, in others they indicate the affect that the music is to express. Examples in the work of Chambonnières are the "Allemande dit l'afflige," "La drollerie," "Les barricades," representing a battle scene, and the gigue "La villageoise," among many others. D'Anglebert's pieces, on the other hand, bear no descriptive titles.

Serious lyric expression will be found in the sarabandes, especially those of Louis Couperin. But another highly characteristic genre was taken over from lute music—the tombeau, literally a tomb. Such works are restrained lamentations. All the leading composers of the time composed tombeaus: noteworthy are Louis Couperin's for Monsieur Blanchecroucher and d'Anglebert's for Chambonnières (see Ex. 1-8).

On the whole, however, these pieces are simple and of light character, except, of course, for the sarabandes and tombeaus. Usually a simple melody is presented in the upper part and accompanied by basic harmonies in the others. The relationship to lute music can easily be noted, on the one hand in the extensive ornamentation, chiefly of the melodic part and, on the other, in the frequent use of broken-chord patterns, associated with the *style brisé* of lute music—the term refers to the breaking up of chords so as to create the impression of contrapuntal part-writing. Extreme delicacy, lightness, and clarity prevail here. An exception may be seen in the work of d'Anglebert, who had been associated with Lully and carried features of the orchestral style

Example 1-8. L. Couperin: Sarabande in D minor—Beginning (mm. 1–5)

into keyboard music. He imparted an orchestral massiveness and power to his music through the use of full chords with much doubling, driving and insistent rhythms, and avoidance of the lute-like quality. We can recall d'Anglebert's transcriptions for keyboard of orchestral pieces of Lully. Although few pieces here make extensive use of contrapuntal imitation, there is a canonic gigue by Chambonnières and a similar sarabande by Louis Couperin.

The role played by ornamentation, the adding of trills, turns, mordents, and so on, in this music was of great importance. The simplicity of the melodies as they are written is deceptive—their ornamentation must be considered fundamental. This is not a peculiarity of French harpsichord music, but is a regular feature of Baroque music and derives from vocal music. So important was ornamentation at the time that Chambonnières, d'Anglebert, Lebègue, and others in their several publications gave full instructions for the execution of the various ornaments. Yet there are many details concerning which we find no agreement among the various sources. This lack of agreement involves not only what the different symbols stand for but also in what the various ornaments actually consist. The most important ornaments are shown in Ex. 1-9.

In seventeenth-century Germany the keyboard suite shows a move toward a fixed form. The process involved several steps. The most important figure for the German harpsichord suite was Froberger, who alone composed thirty suites. These are preserved in two versions, one in manuscript (1649), the other in a posthumous publication *Suites de clavecin* (Amsterdam, 1690s). From the manuscripts it seems that Froberger began with the three-dance sequence, allemande–courante–sarabande, that had been common in France, later adding a gigue between the allemande and courante—we also find this sequence in suites by Pachelbel and Matthias Weckmann (ca. 1619–1674). But in the print, which appeared almost thirty years after Froberger's death, we find the annotation on the title page "mis en meilleur ordre" (put in better order) and the succession allemande–courante–sarabande–gigue. Two suites by Kindermann, preserved in manuscript, have the same order. This arrangement became the standard and can be observed in most suites published in late seventeenth-century Germany: for instance, in those of Buxtehude (published ca. 1680), Krieger (published 1697), Johann Kuhnau (1660–1722, two sets published 1689 and 1692), Poglietti (published 1698–1699), Georg Böhm (1661–1733), and Fischer (published in the 1690s).

Yet we do not find the succession in all German keyboard suites of the time; substitutions, additions, and omissions are common. Other dances that were involved in suites are the minuet, the bourrée, and the gavotte, as well as the variation forms (chaconne and passacaille) and sometimes the aria. Later, one of these was regularly inserted between the sarabande and the gigue. We often find doubles. Many suites, such as those in Kuhnau's *Clavier-Übung*, have preludes, a practice followed by Fischer and many others in the eighteenth century.

Interesting is the tombeau or lament, which Froberger at times used in place of the allemande. In the four that he composed we find elements tra-

Name	Written	Performed

Appoggiatura
    French: *port de voix* or *coulé*
    German: *Vorschlag*		

*Mordent French: *pincé*		

Turn
    French: *double cadence* or *brisé*
    German: *Doppelschlag*		

Slide (also slur or double appoggiatura)
    French: *coulé sur un tierce*
    German: *Schleifer*		

† Trill (also shake)
    French: *cadence* or *tremblement*
    German: *Triller*
    Italian: *trillo*		

* The inverted mordent (*Schneller*) was of German origin.

† The trill could be prefixed with an appogiatura, producing the *tremblement appuyé* or *vorbereitete Triller*, and terminated with a turn-like figure (the *Nachschlag*). The short trill consisting of but four notes (the *Pralltriller*) went out of use at the end of the eighteenth century.

Example 1-9. Common Ornaments

ditional in the expression of sadness: chromaticism, unusual chord progressions, expressive arpeggios, sudden pauses, outbursts, and irregular rhythms. He wanted them to be played "avec discrétion" (with care), and, in the lament for Emperor Ferdinand IV of Hapsburg, the player is enjoined to play "sans observer aucune mesure" (without observing any meter), thus revealing a link to Frescobaldi and Monteverdi (see Ex. 1-10).

In sum, the German suite differs from the French in several regards: it has a fixed order of dances, not found in the French; and the characteristic French delicacy and clarity are lacking—the phrase-lengths become more regular or "square" and the harmonies fuller, and there is less emphasis on the ornaments. The main point, however, has to do with the conception of the suite as a unified whole, a large form consisting of component parts. The German insistence on the designation *parthien*, related to partita with its implication of variation, is important. The term *suite* was not used in Germany until the *Musicalische Clavier-Kunst und Vorrathskammer* (1713) of Johann Heinrich

Example 1-10. Froberger: Lament on the Death of Ferdinand IV from Suite in
C major—Beginning (mm. 1–4)

Buttstett (1666–1727). We have previously observed that in the old dance-
pairs the second (fast) dance often was a variation of the first (slow). This pattern was now and then incorporated into the suite, most often involving only
the allemande and the courante. The thematic relationship is easily observed,
for example, in suites of Froberger, Pachelbel, and Kuhnau. In some cases the
cyclic relationship governs the entire piece.

In England, where suites were known as lessons or airs, the general
arrangement was a succession of three or four dances—the alman (allemande), coranto (courante), and a sarabande (or, as some sources have it,
"sarabrand"). At times an "ayre" (air, a moderate piece with regular accentuations), a minuet, a "Round-O" (the English equivalent of the rondeau, usually with two couplets or episodes), or a hornpipe appeared in addition to or
instead of a more common dance. Such are the suites of Matthew Locke (ca.
1622–1677), John Blow, and Jeremiah Clarke (ca. 1674–1707), as can be seen
in the latter's *Choice Lessons for the Harpsichord or Spinet* (1711). Several
suites of William Croft (1678–1727), on the other hand, add a prelude (sometimes rather elaborate) in the figurational style we have noted. The individual
dances tend to be simple in form and compositional technique, most of the
interest devoted to the uppermost part which, in the French fashion, is highly
ornamented. The alman is usually the most highly stylized of the dances, the
corante is of the Italian variety with its simpler rhythms, and the sarabande as
usual forms the slow movement.

The greatest figure in seventeenth-century English music, however, was
Henry Purcell, the celebrated "Orpheus Britannicus." While keyboard music
was relatively unimportant in his work as a composer, his eight suites for
harpsichord, a toccata, a few independent preludes, a number of individual

dances, and several sets of variations on a ground are worthy of attention. But few of these appeared in print during his lifetime—some in John Playford's *Musick's Hand-Maide*, Part II (1663), and in Purcell's own *A Choice Collection of Lessons*, a set of suites published posthumously (1696).

Purcell's suites are similar to those already described. There are usually three or four dances: the allemande, the corrente, and the sarabande are the most common, but the minuet and the hornpipe also appear. All but one of the suites have a prelude. As elsewhere the allemande is the most stylized, an approach particularly evident in that of the Suite in G minor (No. 2), or the highly figured melodic line in that of the Suite in D major (No. 7).

The Sonata

An important development in seventeenth-century German keyboard music involves the solo sonata. This genre is usually associated with one composer, Johann Kuhnau, since it makes its first appearance in the second part of his *Neue Clavier-Übung* (1692). This collection is devoted mainly to suites (*Partien*), but the last work is his Sonata in B-flat major. This piece is in four sections (they seem too brief to be called movements) in the order Slow–Fast–Slow–Fast, with the first section repeated at the end, da capo. The fast sections are fugal while the third is aria-like in the slow triple meter characteristic of the *bel canto* style. This order suggests that the Italian *sonata da chiesa* is in the background. Further indication is the strong influence from the trio-sonata style of part-writing. In several sections Kuhnau's sonata could be a keyboard arrangement of such a composition: the bass clearly resembles a continuo line while the upper parts are like solo voices that often move in parallel thirds and sixths (see Ex. 1-11). The fast fugal second section exhibits violinistic figuration.

This composition has attracted a great deal of attention, especially from early German historians of music eager to claim it as the first solo keyboard sonata. Actually there are Italian pieces called sonata for keyboard instruments by Gioanpietro Del Buono (fl. 1641) and Gregorio Strozzi (ca. 1615–ca. 1687), but these resemble canzonas. Apparently the first use of the term in reference to keyboard music occurs in a harpsichord suite by Johann Heinrich Schmelzer (ca. 1623–1680), the first movement of which bears the diminutive name sonatina.[6] Other early examples of keyboard pieces called sonatas are by Sybrandus van Noordt (d. 1702) of Amsterdam (published 1690); like those of Kuhnau these show the influence of the ensemble *sonata da chiesa*.

But these sonatas are isolated, so that Kuhnau's distinction is to have made a number of contributions to the new genre. He produced two collections devoted entirely to the keyboard sonata: the *Frische Clavier-Früchte* (1696) and the celebrated *Musicalische Vorstellung einiger biblischen Historien* (known in English as Biblical Sonatas, 1700, with several other editions, including one in Italian, 1710). In all he composed fourteen sonatas.

In the seven sonatas of the *Frische Clavier-Früchte* there is much variety. All we can say is that they consist of a succession of movements (three to six),

Title pages from Johann Kuhnau's *Neue Clavier-Übung*, published by the composer, Leipzig, c. 1692–1695. British Museum (first part); Deutsche Staatsbibliothek, Berlin (second part). The first part contains seven suites (*Partien*). The title background probably represents Kuhnau's native town of Geising. The second part consists of seven more suites and a sonata, believed to comprise the first appearance in Germany of the term *sonata* in a printed work for clavier: the Sonata in B-flat major (see Ex. 1-11.)

From *Decorative Music Title Pages*, G. S. Fraenkel, ed., Dover Publications, Inc., 1968.

Example 1-11. KUHNAU: Sonata in B-flat major—Excerpt (mm. 12–15)

contrasting in key, tempo, thematic material, and affect. While the overall form is similar to that of the earlier Sonata in B-flat, the four-movement works present several different formal schemes (including Moderato–Fast–Fast–Slow, and one incorporating a chaconne). In the five-movement works Kuhnau has added a fast movement at the beginning, producing the succession Fast–Slow–Fast–Slow–Fast. Once again the part-writing recalls the ensemble sonata.

More attention has been aroused by the six Biblical Sonatas. These are virtual program sonatas in the nineteenth-century sense. They take their subjects from stories of the Old Testament. Kuhnau regarded them as similar to the oratorio. In each case the sonata as a whole embodies the story, each movement portraying an episode or situation, thus representing a single affect, as was traditional in Baroque music. The number of movements varies from three to eight, so that these sonatas resemble the others by Kuhnau. The *battaglia* appears in "Il combattimento tra David e Goliath" (No. 1) and "Gideon salvadore del populo d'Israel" (No. 5), with the fugue in both cases representing the headlong retreat of the opposition (in which case *fuga* here literally also means "flight"). Finally, Kuhnau has used hymn melodies symbolically: "Aus tiefer Not" for the prayer of the Israelites before the confrontation between David and Goliath and "O Haupt voll Blut und Wunden" in the "Hezekiah" sonata, so that these movements are related to the chorale prelude.

BACH

None of the music of Johann Sebastian Bach (1685–1750), strictly speaking, was intended for the piano, an instrument that was a novelty in his lifetime—it did not come into general use until after his death. He is only known to have performed one of his pieces on a piano: the first number of the *Musical Offering*. Nonetheless his music has become an important part of the repertory of the piano, particularly what was primarily intended for harpsichord and/or clavichord, but also in some cases music for the organ, the latter through transcriptions. The distinction that we drew earlier between sacred and secular music, the organ associated mostly with the former and the harpsichord or clavichord with the latter, holds generally for Bach, although there are some important exceptions.

Today's view of Bach's character and work has become radically different since the task of editing and producing the new critical edition of his works began in the 1950s, also yielding the new chronology of his vocal works. While this work has had less effect on the dating of his instrumental music, some new dates have nevertheless been established; they will be used here.

While there is no question about Bach's fundamental commitment to the church and liturgical music, the new chronology of his works clearly shows that his involvement with secular music over time grew increasingly important, particularly after the late 1720s. Thus, those periods in his earlier career when he emphasized secular and instrumental music, the years at Weimar (1708–1717) and Cöthen (1717–1723), now appear as less exceptional than they did previously and to have more in common with the later years at Leipzig.

But few of Bach's keyboard compositions were published during his lifetime. This lag applies particularly to the organ works as well as to what became his most famous and influential composition, the one upon which his reputation in the late eighteenth and early nineteenth centuries was based, *The Well-Tempered Clavier* (BWV 846–893),[7] which remained in manuscript until 1800. It also applies to the French and English Suites. The most comprehensive publication personally undertaken by Bach himself of any of his music is the *Clavier-Übung* (Keyboard Practice) which he brought out in four installments. The first (1731) contains the six partitas (BWV 825–830); the second (1735) has diverse harpsichord compositions, the *Concerto nach italienischem Gusto* (Italian Concerto, BWV 971), the *Ouverture nach französischer Art* (Suite in B minor, or French Overture, BWV 831), and several toccatas; the third (1739) contains organ music; and the fourth (1741) consists of the *Aria mit dreissig Veränderungen* (Aria with Thirty Variations or the Goldberg variations, BWV 988). The title *Clavier-Übung*, as we have seen, had been used by both Krieger and Kuhnau.

The Well-Tempered Clavier (BWV 846–893)

Bach's most influential composition, this set, in two parts, contains preludes and fugues in all the major and minor keys, arranged consecutively in ascending order, first the major and then the minor, making a total of forty-eight. While the first part dates from the period 1722–1723 when Bach was in Cöthen, the second dates from around 1744 and thus belongs to his late phase. The title does not appear on the original manuscript of the second book but is popularly used since the plan is the same as that of the first book which does bear the title. The second book, moreover, contains pieces that Bach composed much earlier which he arranged and in some cases transposed to accord with the plan of the work. The practice of adapting and reusing earlier pieces is characteristic of Bach's work in the 1730s and later.

Title page from the fourth part of Bach's *Clavier Übung*, the Goldberg variations. Nuremberg: Balthasar Schmid, 1741. British Museum, London.
From *Decorative Music Title Pages*, G. S. Fraenkel, ed., Dover Publications, Inc., 1968.

That *The Well-Tempered Clavier* is a didactic work is made clear from its title statement: it is intended not only to assist young people in learning music but also for the diversion of those already accomplished in the art.[8] The designation "well-tempered" has to do with Bach's interest in some form of equal temperament, in which the octave is divided into twelve equal parts or semitones, in place of the mean-tone system which had been in use since the Renaissance. The latter worked well as long as the signatures of the keys used did not exceed two sharps or flats (assuming the instrument to have been tuned in C). The medium intended by Bach is not expressly stated beyond *clavier*, a term denoting keyboard instruments in general. There has been much discussion on this subject, with both the harpsichord and clavichord and even the organ having had their supporters. For Bach *clavier* was sufficient—the pieces were simply for keyboard: they were realizable on whatever instrument was at hand. Therefore there can be no objection to the use of the piano.

We have seen that the history of the prelude and fugue lies primarily in organ music, that the genre is an outgrowth of what we have been calling the toccata. As treated here by Bach it differs from its counterpart in organ music in that the pieces are shorter—the preludes are for the most part cast as continuous wholes and not divided into sections—and the fugues are both more concise and stricter.

The preludes maintain the essential character of the genre. They are short, highly unified pieces; each has its own sharply drawn character that is maintained throughout. The tendency is to operate with a short theme or motive—a phrase, a characteristic texture, rhythm, or type of figuration—that at once establishes the piece's character or affect and provides its basic thematic material. Most often this thematic material consists of figuration; for example, scale patterns in the D major prelude of Part I and the F major prelude of Part II, arpeggio patterns in the D minor and G minor preludes of Part I, and broken chords in the F major and B-flat major preludes of Part I and the D minor of Part II.

At the same time, some of the preludes fall into clearly defined sections. The largest, in E-flat major (Part I), with its three sections and characteristic mixture of imitation and figuration, is related to the old toccata. Others employ changes in tempo (the C minor and E minor preludes in Part I; the C-sharp minor in Part II). Binary form with each part to be repeated appears once in the preludes of Part I (B minor, the last one), but nine times in Part II (C minor, D-sharp minor, E major, E minor, F minor, G major, G-sharp minor, A minor, and B-flat major). In several preludes the thematic material of the beginning reappears in the original key toward the end, thus producing the effect of a recapitulation, as in Part I (preludes in C-sharp minor, D major—in the subdominant instead of the tonic—and A major) and Part II (F major, F minor, F-sharp minor, and B-flat major). When this comes together with the use of binary form, as in the Prelude in F major (Part II), we can speak of rounded binary form, common in dances of the time, as we have seen.

We have noticed that forms and procedures of other types of instrumental music have an effect on keyboard music, for example, in Alessandro Scarlatti, Louis Couperin, and d'Anglebert. This influence appears in the preludes of *The Well-Tempered Clavier* (and the fugues as well but to a lesser extent). In the preludes we can find, for example:

- the *style brisé*, the broken chords of lute music, in Part I (C major) and Part II (E-flat major)
- the important chamber-music medium of the trio sonata, in Part I (C-sharp minor, G-sharp minor, A major, and B major) and Part II (C-sharp minor, E major, A major, and B-flat minor)
- the sonata for solo violin with continuo accompaniment with concertato relationship (concerto-like alternation) between the two parts, in Part I (E minor and A-flat major, the latter complete with double-stops, see Ex. 1-12) and Part II (G-sharp minor)
- orchestral form, in Part II (D major, with its "trumpet tune")
- the arioso, associated with the recitative of *opera seria*, in three preludes of Part I (E-flat minor, the E minor in its first section only, and B-flat minor)
- the pastoral, often related to the siciliano dance, in Part I (E major) and Part II (C-sharp minor, E-flat major, and A major).

Other preludes suggest dances:

- the allemande, in Part I (F-sharp minor and B major)
- the corrente, in Part II (E major)
- the gigue, in Part I (F-sharp minor) and Part II (B-flat major), both in 12/16 meter
- the sarabande, in Part I (E-flat minor, also an example of the arioso).

Bach frequently works out the thematic material in contrapuntal imitation, as in Part I (E-flat major, F-sharp major, G-sharp minor, and A major, the last with invertible counterpoint) and in Part II (D-sharp minor, E minor, A minor, also with invertible counterpoint, and B minor). The Prelude in A minor is noted for its intense chromaticism.

The fugues in *The Well-Tempered Clavier* tend to be either three-voice or four-voice. Part I contains eleven in three voices and ten in four, with but one

Example 1-12. BACH: Prelude in A-flat major (BWV 862) from *The Well-Tempered Clavier*, Part I—Beginning (mm. 1–6)

in two-voices and two in five. Part II contains fifteen three-voice fugues and nine in four. (In Part I, the two-voice fugue is in E minor and the two five-voice fugues are those in C-sharp minor and B-flat minor.) No specific musical form appears here consistently beyond the rather general consideration that all exhibit the technique of imitative counterpoint. Usually, straightforward presentations of the subject (principal theme) in each voice (the expositions) alternate with passages that use elements derived either from the subject or from its countersubject or from free material (the episodes). The countersubject comprises subordinate thematic material used to accompany the subject in its subsequent entrances. Often the episodes are motivic or sequential rather than imitative, as in Part I (fugues in C minor, C-sharp minor, D major, and A major) and in Part II (D minor, F-sharp major, G major, G minor, A minor, and A-flat minor). One fugue, the C major in Part I, lacks such episodes. Toccata-like passages near the endings are also common.

In most cases a fugue in *The Well-Tempered Clavier* has a subject and along with it a countersubject. Two countersubjects appear in both of the fugues in C-sharp major. But we also find double and triple fugues, that is, two or three different subjects exposed independently of one another and then all presented together in contrapuntal combination, as in Part II (F-sharp minor and G-sharp minor). There are also cases in which the countersubject proves to be the inversion of the subject, so that the fugue is rigorously monothematic, as in the G minor fugue in Part I. In most cases, however, the fugues of *The Well-Tempered Clavier* employ one subject and one countersubject.

There has been much discussion of the idea that the uniqueness of Bach's fugues stems from his ability to invent suitable subjects that in themselves are inherently adaptable for use in fugues. While we may find this in any of Bach's fugues, its plainest manifestation is here in *The Well-Tempered Clavier*. Many elements are involved: continuously driving rhythms, figuration patterns, sequential phrase structures, the use of arresting combinations of intervals, and so on. We may identify some characteristic types of fugue subjects:

- subjects in the long, slow notes in the tradition of the ricercar, as in Part I (C-sharp minor, E-flat minor, F minor, F-sharp minor, and B-flat minor) and Part II (E-flat major, E major and B-flat minor)
- subjects related to the old canzona, as in Part II (D major)
- subjects associated with types of ornaments, the turn, the slide (*Schleifer*), or the appoggiatura, as in Part I (C minor, D major, E-flat major, F-sharp major, and B minor) and Part II (C minor)
- subjects related to dances, for instance, the passepied, a lively dance in 3/8 or 6/8, in Part I (F major) and the gigue in Part II (C-sharp minor and B minor).

Some subjects are short, as in the A-flat major fugue in Part I and the C-sharp minor, only four notes, in Part II. Others are long, incorporating several rhythms and motives, as in Part I (G major, B-flat major, and B major) and Part

II (D minor, E minor, and G minor). Some fugue subjects are divided into two distinct parts, as in Part I (D major, E-flat major, E major, G minor, and A minor) and Part II (C major). An unusual instance of this occurs in the G minor fugue (Part II). After detached statements of a motive employing the upward leap of a fourth and a downward one of a third, there comes a phrase with a note repeated no fewer than seven times. Some fugue subjects move in even notes, as in Part I (F minor, A-flat major, A major, and B minor) and Part II (B-flat major).

In connection with the fugal working-out, the devices of learned counterpoint are less prominent in *The Well-Tempered Clavier* than one may be inclined to believe. To be sure, stretto and inversion occur frequently. We find stretto in Part I (C major, C-sharp minor, D minor, E minor, E-flat minor, F major, G major, A major, and A minor) and in Part II (C-sharp major, D major, D-sharp minor, E-flat major, and B-flat minor), and inversion in Part I (D minor, E-flat minor, F-sharp minor, G major, and B major) and Part II (C minor, C-sharp minor, D minor, and B-flat minor). On the other hand diminution appears not at all in Part I and only three times in Part II (C-sharp major, E major, and A minor). In the A minor the second part of the subject is the diminution of the first. Augmentation appears but three times: in Part I (E-flat minor) and Part II (C minor and C-sharp minor); retrograde comes but once, in Part II (C-sharp minor). Thus the most learned fugue in the whole set, C-sharp minor (Part II), which employs all the learned devices including retrograde motion, has the shortest subject. In three other fugues learned aspects predominate: Part I, E-flat minor; Part II, C minor and E major. Two of these have subjects related to the old ricercar as previously noted. By contrast the least learned fugues are those in D major and F minor (Part I), the first because its subject is motivic—as Bach has emphasized at the expense of imitation in the working-out—while the second, the only two-voice fugue in the set, even contains parallel octaves. Thus, as strict as these fugues for the most part are, their "learnedness" may have been exaggerated in the literature.

These compositions, the fugues as well as the preludes, generally share the central aim of Baroque music: the expression of affections. This term refers to the various passions (such as joy, anger, love, hate) and other aspects of human feeling and experience (the pastoral, the pathétique, the military, the mimicry of national phenomena, among others), conceived at the time as essentially static states of mind. Such expression is intimately bound up with the keys, meters, rhythms, and melodic types, as well as with the various genres that are suggested. While such expression of the affects cannot be demonstrated in all cases, we can single out some obvious instances: joy (Part I, G major); *passionato* (Part I, E minor); solemnity (Part II, F-sharp minor); *maestoso* (Part II, E major, a ricercar). The expression of affects frequently involves dance rhythms: the bourrée (Part I, C-sharp minor and F minor); the gavotte (Part I, F-sharp major); the allemande (Part II, A-flat major); and the gigue (Part I, G major and A major). Finally, the fugues associated with the ricercar provide examples of the *fuga patetica*—serious, learned, and intense. These are, in Part I, the C-sharp minor, D-sharp minor, F minor, F-sharp minor, G minor, and B-flat minor; and in Part II, the E major, G minor, A minor, and F-sharp minor.

Many have investigated the extent to which Bach specifically related the members of a pair of preludes and fugues of *The Well-Tempered Clavier* to one another. Various answers have been given, some in the negative and others in the positive. It is generally agreed that with but few exceptions Bach has not used the same thematic material in both prelude and fugue of a pair. The most frequently alleged exceptions to this are the pairs in B major and D major, both in Part I. Yet in neither of the two fugues can we find the characteristic downward leap of a fifth that appears in the corresponding preludes.

Other didactic pieces are contained chiefly in the manuscript collection Bach prepared for his oldest son Wilhelm Friedemann, the *Clavierbüchlein* (1720–1721, original at Yale University) and two manuscript notebooks for his wife Anna Magdalena (1722 and 1725). These contain a variety of short pieces —preludes, contrapuntal works, dances, chorale settings for organ, and so on. . The *Clavierbüchlein* also contains the well-known two-part Inventions (BWV 772–786) and the three-part Sinfonias (BWV 787–801), short imitative pieces designed to teach a beginner to play two or three contrapuntal voices preparatory to studying larger and more elaborate compositions. As with many of the titles used for musical genres, the term *invention* is derived from rhetoric.[9] Some of these pieces, particularly in the three-part sinfonias, are elaborate contrapuntal works, as, for instance, the F minor, which has three important themes, and the G minor. The *Clavierbüchlein* also includes preludes that appear in *The Well-Tempered Clavier* as well, and a set of little preludes.

In the two books for Anna Magdalena we find, among others, five of the French Suites. There are also two other sets of Little Preludes for harpsichord (BWV 933–938 and 939–943), also intended for teaching.

The large form of the fantasia (or prelude) and fugue also appears in Bach's harpsichord music. The chief work here is the Chromatic Fantasia and Fugue in D minor (BWV 903, first composed presumably in Weimar and Cöthen, ca. 1714–1722, and then reworked, ca. 1730). In this piece Bach has manifested the fantasia type on a grand scale: there are many sections involving changes of tempo and key, as well as passages marked *recitativ*, confirming a relation to vocal music. The fugue, more freely treated in *The Well-Tempered Clavier*, has the expected chromatic subject. Along with this large work are the fantasias in A minor (BWV 904) and C minor (BWV 906), as well as independent preludes, fantasias, and fugues, all composed for clavier.

Related to the fantasias are the seven toccatas for clavier (BWV 910–916). These resemble the larger organ toccatas except that in some the individual sections have become so large that they stand almost as separate movements, as in the toccatas in D major (BWV 912), D minor (BWV 913), and E minor (BWV 914). The others are long multisectional works, usually three or four sections, opening in the traditional toccata style and culminating in a long fugue. The toccatas in F-sharp minor (BWV 910) and C minor (BWV 911) each have several fugal sections. Dynamic indications and inversion of the fugue subjects appear in the Toccata in G minor (BWV 915).

The Suites

The most important are the English Suites (6, BWV 806–811), the French Suites (6, BWV 812–817), and the Partitas (6, BWV 825–830). The chronology is uncertain, the latest estimates putting the English and French Suites in the late Cöthen and early Leipzig years (ca. 1722–1726, with the French Suites known to have been composed between 1722 and 1724), and the partitas a little later (1726–1730); the partitas, as we have seen, represent Bach's first publication of any of his works.

The English Suites are in A major, A minor, G minor, F major, E minor, and D minor, and the French Suites in D minor, C minor, B minor, E-flat major, G major, and E major. The designations English and French associated with these suites are not Bach's; they are confusing and misleading. Both sets are "French" to the extent that the dances used are French, but the order—allemande, courante, sarabande, and gigue, with other dances inserted between the sarabande and gigue—as we have seen, is mostly, but not entirely, German. Furthermore, the stylization of the dances—the degree of elaboration and the emphasis on counterpoint that characterizes Bach's suites—goes far beyond that of other suites of the time regardless of the composer's nationality.

With few exceptions a single external form is common to all these dances: binary form, with double-bar near the middle, each part to be repeated. In general the two parts parallel one another and present the same or similar material in much the same sequence. But they are distinguished by key, the first part moving from the tonic to the dominant or relative major, the second with some excursions back to the tonic.

In the allemandes Bach has retained only the slow tempo and duple meter of the original dance and not its characteristic rhythm. Instead the thematic material involves short motives made up of figurational elements—scale-runs, broken chords, or standard patterns derived from ornamentation—which Bach has treated sequentially and contrapuntally. Frequently the motion goes in constant eighth-notes. The dance has become generalized: its specific features have been lost in the process of stylization (Ex. 1-13A). While this type of allemande may be found in any of the French or English Suites, particularly good examples are in the French Suite in C minor (where the part-writing suggests the trio sonata), and the English Suite in A major.

In the courantes Bach made a careful distinction between the French courante and the Italian corrente, even preserving the terminology, but some later editions, including that of the Bachgesellschaft, have suppressed the distinction, labeling all of them *courante*. The corrente, found in four of the French Suites (C minor, E-flat major, G major, and E major), but in none of the English Suites, is in quick triple time (3/4); like the allemande, while it shows

A.

B.

C.

Example 1-13. BACH: Dances from the Suites—Excerpts
    A. Allemande from French Suite 2 in C minor (BWV 813)—Beginning
       (mm. 1–2)
    B. Corrente from French Suite 2 in C minor (BWV 815)—Beginning (mm. 1–4)
    C. Courante from English Suite 2 in A minor (BWV 807)—Beginning
       (mm. 1–4)

no characteristic rhythmic patterns, it makes use of motives made up of figurative elements (Ex. 1-13B). On the other hand, the courante, found in all the other suites, is a more elaborate and refined affair, moving in compound meter (6/2 or 3/2) with frequent oscillation between two beats each subdivided by three and three beats subdivided by two, a phenomenon known as hemiola (see especially that of the English Suite in A minor, Ex. 1-13C).

The sarabande, the slow dance in triple time, although stylized in much the same way, still retains rhythmic patterns characteristic of the dance. The process of stylization, in other words, had not progressed as far as in the case of the allemande and courante (corrente). The basic rhythmic pattern of the dance and some of Bach's variants of it are shown in Ex. 1-14.

While the gigue, like the courante, exists in both French and Italian types, in these suites Bach uses only the more elaborate French variety.[10] The dance retains the fast tempo and compound triple meter (frequently dotted) but the technique is imitative counterpoint involving two or three voices, often with the theme presented in inversion after the double-bar. This form of the gigue may be seen in all the French Suites except the B minor and in all the English Suites except the A minor. Noteworthy is the elaborate subject in the gigue of the French Suite in D minor and the chromatic gigues of the English Suites in E minor and D minor.

Among the "optional" dances the three most prominent are the minuet which appears in the French Suites in D minor, C minor, B minor, and E major, but only in one English suite, the F major; the bourrée, a sturdy dance in duple time, in the French Suites in G major and E major, and the English Suites in A major and A minor; and the gavotte, moderate and in duple time, with half a bar as upbeat, in the French Suites in E-flat major, G major, and E major, and the English Suites in G minor and D minor. Dances used less frequently are the anglaise in fast duple time (French Suite in B minor); the loure, a dance in moderate tempo in 6/4 time, often dotted (French Suite in G major); the polonaise (French Suite in E major); the passepied (English Suite in E minor, here in the form of a rondeau with three couplets); and the air, a short songlike piece (French Suites in C minor and E-flat major). Doubles appear in the English Suites in A major and D minor, the courante and sarabande respectively.

The English Suites are larger than the French Suites. Not only are the individual movements longer, but each of the English Suites has a prelude as the opening movement. Except for the first movement of the English Suite in A major (the prelude of which is built on a single motive and thus resembles most of those in *The Well-Tempered Clavier*), these preludes have a similar scheme. A large sectional structure alternates a fugal passage with one or two episodes in a way that suggests the ritornello form seen in the Allegro movement of an Italian orchestral concerto of the time; moreover the types of themes and figuration patterns employed also suggest Italian writing for strings. This resemblance is clear in the first movement of the English Suite in D minor: first a slow section, then a fast one in the orchestral style. The first movement of the English Suite in F major displays violinistic figuration. These

A. "Normal" sarabande rhythm

B. English Suite in A minor and French
   Suite in D minor

C. English Suite in G minor

D. English Suite in D minor

E. French Suite in C minor

F. Partita in D major

G. Partita in B-flat major

Example 1-14. Variants of the Sarabande Rhythm in Bach's Suites

movements recall not only the organ toccatas of the Arnstadt and Weimar
periods but also the numerous transcriptions for keyboard Bach made of Italian concertos of this period (some of which are spurious).

The partitas are also six in number: B-flat major, C minor, A minor, D
major, G major, and E minor. As we have seen, they were composed later
than the English and French Suites. Like the English Suites they contain introductory movements. While the more traditional short prelude appears in the
partitas in B-flat major and A minor, the others have more elaborate compositions. The first piece in the Partita in D major is a full French overture with
concerto-like episodes in its brilliant fugue; the sinfonia of the Partita in C
minor is in much the same style as the prelude to the English Suite in D
minor; and the brilliant toccata of the Partita in E minor has a slow part full of
arpeggios, full chords, and scale figuration followed by an extended solemn
fugue, after which the first part returns.

In other respects, the partitas resemble Bach's other suites. The set order
of dances is for the most part maintained, the chief exception begin the Partita in C minor, which substitutes a capriccio for the gigue as the concluding
movement. The allemandes continue to be highly stylized; consider especially the long-phrased example in the Partita in D major. The elegant French
courante appears in the partitas in C minor and D major, while the simpler
corrente is used in the others. The sarabande, as usual, appears as the slow
movement. The simple Italian giga appears in the Partita in B-flat major, the
French gigue in the others, with inversions of the theme in the partitas in A

minor and E minor. Of optional dances and other pieces we find the minuet in the partitas in B-flat major, D major, and G major; the rondeau in the Partita in C minor; the burlesca, a piece of playful character, and the scherzo, a piece of light character, in the Partita in A minor; the passepied in the Partita in G major; the gavotte in the Partita in E minor; and the aria in the partitas in D major and E minor.

Rather different is the *Ouverture nach französischer Art* or Suite in B minor (the French Overture, BWV 831, composed 1833–1834) that appears in the *Clavier-Übung* along with the partitas. Here as elsewhere we may note the adaptation of orchestral styles and types to the keyboard, so that this work is closer to Bach's orchestral suites (or overtures) than to the suites for keyboard. A large French overture stands at the beginning, with Italianate "orchestral" episodes in its fugal section; it is followed by a number of dances that do not correspond to what one would expect in a suite for keyboard. From the usual dances come the courante (the French type), sarabande, and gigue, with the allemande absent; between them come two gavottes, two passepieds, two bourrées, and, at the end, an echo (see Ex. 1-15). The frequent dynamic markings not only underline the orchestral quality of the piece but would also have required a large two-manual harpsichord; these dynamic changes, however, are easily realizable on the piano. The movements themselves, as we might expect, are simpler than what we find in the keyboard suites: the phrases are shorter and balanced, the rhythms less elaborate; there

Example 1-15. BACH: "Echo" from Suite in B minor (BWV 831)—Beginning (mm. 1–9)

is less use of figuration; and the harmonies are less complex. Noteworthy are the drone-bass passages in the courante and the dense chordal part-writing in the sarabande.

Two other traditional types of keyboard music that appear in Bach's work are the capriccio and the sonata. Of the capriccio there are two examples, both composed in Arnstadt (1704). One is an extended imitative work in E major (BWV 993) in the Italian manner, and the other is the famous *Capriccio sopra la lontananza del suo fratello dilettissimo* (Capriccio on the Departure of His Beloved Brother) in B-flat major (BWV 992) that depicts the departure of Bach's brother for Sweden. This last is a programmatic work in the same spirit as Kuhnau's Biblical Sonatas: an introductory slow movement, Arioso, expressive of the friends' trying to keep him from making the journey; a fugal representation of the reasons he wants to make the trip; the lament of his friends, complete with chromatic ostinato; the parting; the short fanfare-like "Aria di postiglione" (Song of the Driver of the Post-cart); and, as finale, "Fuga all'imitazione della cornetta in postiglione," with horn-call figures. While Kerll and Poglietti preceded Bach in the composition of program capriccios, theirs were not on such a large scale.

Of the five sonatas for clavier, four are of doubtful authenticity. All are transcriptions, one of a sonata for unaccompanied violin by Bach himself, two of trio sonatas for violins and continuo from Reincken's *Hortus musicus*, and a fragment (a movement from an anonymous trio sonata), derivations that confirm the association between keyboard and ensemble music mentioned earlier. This relationship also informs the one bona fide sonata, in D major (BWV 963, composed 1704 in Arnstadt). It consists of three movements, the first in the Italian homophonic manner and the others fugal (the last imitative of birds); at the beginning and in between come slow transitional passages.

An important keyboard composition by Bach for the larger harpsichord but eminently realizable on the piano is the popular *Concerto nach italienischem Gusto* in F major (the Italian Concerto, BWV 971, composed ca. 1735), which is also included in the *Clavier-Übung*. Bach deliberately cast this work in the style of an Italian orchestral concerto, specifically Vivaldi's, as he did in other pieces referred to above. Thus, in the Italian Concerto we find three movements in the succession Fast–Slow–Fast. In the first movement there are two themes corresponding, respectively, to those of the ripieno and solo portions of an orchestral concerto movement, and the same holds for the finale; the point is underlined by frequent use of dynamic markings. The slow movement, Andante, resembles an aria.

Another group of keyboard works comprises the sets of variations: the *Aria variata alla maniera italiana* in A minor (BWV 989, composed in Weimar, 1709), with ten variations, and the celebrated *Aria mit dreissig Veränderungen* in G major (BWV 988, the Goldberg variations), published in 1741[11] as Part IV of the *Clavier-Übung*, composed for Johann Gottlieb Goldberg, one of Bach's pupils. A third set of variations, the *Sarabande con partite* in C major (BWV 990), is of doubtful authenticity.

The outstanding work here is the Goldberg variations. The theme is called simply "aria": it is a melody in the sarabande rhythm, highly embellished and cast in binary form. This aria appears in the early collection Bach compiled for his wife Anna Magdalena and may not be of his composition. The melody—the upper part—of the aria, however, is not the subject of the variations; rather the aria's bass part, characterized by descending stepwise motion, remains the constant throughout, sometimes ornamented, sometimes not. This melodic line appears in the bass in all variations except the sixth and the eighteenth where Bach has moved it to the uppermost part. Thus the Goldberg variations are allied to the standard variation procedures of the Baroque and earlier—the ostinato or variations on a ground. As the title indicates, there are thirty variations on this melody, each different in character. The work as a whole is divided into two parts, the break coming at the fifteenth variation; suitably enough the sixteenth variation which commences the second half is a small French overture. At the very end the aria is restated in its original form.

Canon also plays an important role in the Goldberg variations. Every third variation is a canon and in each a different interval is used for the imitation, so that a full cycle of canons results. The third variation is a canon at the unison, the sixth a canon at the second, the ninth a canon at the third, and so on; the twenty-fourth is a canon at the octave, and the twenty-seventh variation and final canon is at the ninth. All but one of these canonic variations involve three parts, the two canonic parts and the supporting bass; the exception is the last, which is in two parts.

Finally, Bach imparted to each variation a specific character and used forms and types common in Baroque music in the definition and expression of these characters or affects. For example, the tenth variation is a fughetta, and the sixteenth, as already indicated, is a French overture; variations five, eight, fourteen, sixteen, twenty-three, twenty-eight, and twenty-nine are virtuoso pieces emphasizing fast tempos and brilliant figuration and require crossing the hands (*pièces croisées*). The seventeenth and twenty-fourth variations show the rhythm of the siciliano; three variations are in the minor (*minore*)—the fifteenth, twenty-first, and twenty-fifth, the first two canonic and the third in the character of an *aria patetica*. The last variation is a quodlibet, an old type that involves making a piece out of existing melodies; Bach combines two old and well-known German songs, "Ich bin so lang bei dir gewest" and "Kraut und Rüben."

In addition to the oscillation between the sacred and secular that characterized Bach's career, we can also note the free and full exploitation of stylistic elements from different countries, a circumstance that led Bukofzer to qualify Bach's art as the "fusion of national styles."[12] In drawing together such elements Bach added much that was his own, intensifying the music largely by combining counterpoint with harmonic richness in a way that exceeded the capacities of his contemporaries.

This emphasis on counterpoint became pronounced in Bach's last works, in which he not only composed a large cycle of fugues on a single theme, *Die Kunst der Fuge* (The Art of Fugue, BWV 1080), but also occupied himself with the strictest of contrapuntal forms, canon, in *Das musikalische Opfer*

(The Musical Offering, BWV 1079). During this time he also organized the second volume of *The Well-Tempered Clavier.*

The Art of Fugue evolved in two stages, the first from the late 1730s to 1748, the second in 1748–1749, the work being published posthumously in 1751. It consists for the most part of fugues on the same subject that incrementally increase in degree of complexity (in this set Bach used the term *contrapunctus* for fugue). In its original form the work began with simple fugues, progressed through counterfugues (in which the subject is combined with its inversion), double fugues, triple fugues, a quadruple fugue, and canons, and concluded with a canon in augmentation and inversion.[13] In the final (published) version Bach added more pieces and planned a large quadruple fugue in which the fourth subject was based on the letters of his name, B-A-C-H, the letters of which in German correspond to the notes B-flat, A, C, B (natural), but left this fugue unfinished. The progressive organization of *The Art of Fugue* has occasioned many interpretations, some of them involving allegory. At all events it seems clear that Bach envisioned a compendium of fugal composition, exhausting the possibilities of the technique. Since Bach notated the work in open score, a manner of notation used for keyboard music at the time, that seems to be the appropriate medium for it, even though in a few cases one player cannot play all the notes; arrangements for instrumental ensembles of various kinds, however, have been made and are often used.

The other late contrapuntal work involving the keyboard, *The Musical Offering*, has an unusual history. It is the souvenir of a visit Bach made to the court of Frederick the Great in Berlin in 1747. There the king gave Bach a theme to improvise upon (a standard practice at the time) and Bach did so, employing the Silbermann piano that was at the court. The king then asked him to improvise a six-part fugue on the theme; Bach did this the following day but was not satisfied with the result. Upon his return to Leipzig Bach set about the composition of a group of works based on this theme given him by the king, the whole then presented to the king in manuscript as a "musical offering"; it was subsequently published. In its title statement we see an acrostic in Latin:

Regis
Iussu
Cantio
Et
Reliqua
Canonica
Arte
Resoluta

Thus, *ricercar*, translated: "At the King's command, the theme and the rest worked out in canonic form."

The work consists mostly of canons and a trio sonata that are not for solo keyboard. But the two ricercars, the first in three parts that opens the cycle and the other in six parts the position of which is uncertain but which is usually put at the end, are clearly keyboard music. The first is apparently close to what Bach improvised at the king's court in Potsdam, while the second represents his response to the king's challenge. Thus the first represents Bach's sole piece known to have been associated with the piano. The layout of the whole cycle has been connected with Quintillian's *Institutio oratorio*.[14]

In conclusion, Bach's influence on composers of the late-eighteenth and nineteenth centuries was exercised through the small number of his works that were circulated first in manuscript and later in printed form. The bulk of his music remained unknown until the appearance of the Bachgesellschaft edition in the second half of the nineteenth century. The best known was the first book of *The Well-Tempered Clavier* which established Bach as the model for fugue writing, the learned style as it was called at the time—to the admiration, aspiration, and often despair of his successors. Here, and in Bach's music generally, the complexity of the counterpoint vies with that of the harmony. Beethoven spoke for many when he put the matter in the form of a pithy pun: he should not be called Bach, which in German means "brook," but rather Meer, "ocean."

NOTES FOR CHAPTER ONE

1. Virginal is the name used in England at the time for the small, often rectangular, form of harpsichord with a single manual, the strings running parallel to the keyboard. The term appears to have been derived from the soft, sweet, and mild quality of their tone, like the voice of a young lady (*vox virginalis*), but other etymologies have been suggested.

2. See T. Walker, "Ciaccona and Passacaglia," *Journal of the American Musicological Society* 21 (1968): 300–320, and R. Hudson, *Passacaglia and Ciaccona* (Ann Arbor: UMI, 1981).

3. M. Bradshaw, *The Origin of the Toccata* (Rome: American Institute of Musicology, 1972).

4. W. Kirkendale, "Ciceronians versus Aristotelians on the Ricercar as Exordium, from Bembo to Bach," *Journal of the American Musicological Society* 23 (1979): 1–44.

5. M. Reimann, *Untersuchungen zur Formgeschichte der französischen Klaviersuite* (1941; reprint, Regensburg: Bosse, 1968), 16–17.

6. See W. Newman, *The Sonata in the Baroque Era*, 2nd ed. (New York: Norton, 1966), 281.

7. BWV (= *Bach Werk-Verzeichnis*) numbers assigned to Bach's compositions in W. Schmieder, *Thematisch-systematisches Verzeichnis der musikalischen Werke von Johann Sebastian Bach*, 2nd ed. (Wiesbaden: Breitkopf & Härtel, 1990).

8. The title in the original: *Das wohltemperierte Clavier oder Praeludia und Fugen durch alle Töne und Semitonia sowohl tertiam majorem oder Ut re mi anlangend als*

durch tertiam minorem oder Re mi fa anlangend: Zum Nutzen und Gebrauch der Lehrbegierigen Musicalischen Jugend als auch deren in diesem Studio schon habil seyender besonderen Zeitvertreib aufgesetzet und verfertiget von J. S. Bach.

9. See E. Flindell, "A propos Bach's Inventions," *Bach*, vol. 14, no. 4 (October 1983): 3–14; 15, no. 1 (January 1984): 3–16; 15, no. 2 (April 1984): 3–17.

10. The Italian type (*giga*), less common in Bach, is a much simpler affair that does not make use of imitative counterpoint.

11. Date according to G. Butler, "Neues zur Datierung der Goldberg-Variationen," *Bach-Jahrbuch* 74 (1988): 219–222.

12. M. Bukofzer, *Music in the Baroque Era* (New York: Norton, 1947), 260.

13. See G. Butler, "Ordering Problems in Bach's *Art of Fugue* Resolved," *Musical Quarterly* 69 (1983): 44–61.

14. U. Kirkendale, "The Source for Bach's *Musical Offering*: The *Institutio oratorio* of Quintillian," *Journal of the American Musicological Society* 33 (1980): 88–141.

CHAPTER TWO

The Time of Change (ca. 1720–1790)

It is a commonplace to regard the work of Johann Sebastian Bach as the culmination of Baroque music. But this generally accepted assertion becomes ironic in some respects when we realize that in his lifetime Bach's oeuvre received neither wide currency nor general acceptance: indeed his way of composing caused him considerable difficulties with the authorities in Leipzig from the 1730s on. Decisive and far-reaching changes were taking place, changes as profound as any that had ever occurred in any period of the history of music, changes that made Bach's music sound needlessly involved, erudite ("learned" was the qualification used at the time), and old-fashioned. Perhaps the crowning irony with respect to Bach himself was that his sons became important in the development of the new musical style, and one of them, Carl Philipp Emanuel, supposedly went to the point of calling his father, affectionately one hopes, "the old wig." On the other hand, analytical interpretations since the 1970s suggest that some of Bach's music from the 1730s and after gives evidence of his adoption of the new style.[1]

It is always difficult to survey a period of historical change. That of the eighteenth century is particularly difficult in view of the great mass of material involved, and of the many crosscurrents, here the lingering on of the old, there the early appearance of the new, often with combinations of the two. But in spite of the immense amount of music that is available, there is still not enough to gain a truly accurate picture, since at the time much important music—and we have seen that this was true of Bach's—was circulated only in manuscript copies and even now has yet to be published. Although the last few decades have witnessed much activity in this field, much remains to be done.

The changes went beyond musical style; they affected all aspects of musical life. Put in the most general way, they involved the decline of the Italian vocal art of Baroque music and the rise of a predominantly instrumental art in which Germanic musicians took the lead. But the new emphasis on instrumental music appears also in the work of Italian composers, several of whom exerted an influence on their German contemporaries. This new instrumental music brought with it new genres of keyboard music; or, to put it another way, a new emphasis was given to certain older types so that they were transformed into something new and different. Generally we can note the decline of the organ and its music and at the end of the century the rise of the piano. The old types—cantus firmus settings, imitative contrapuntal types, the toccata, the suite, and so forth—gave way to new genres, in particular one created around 1700 and capable of encompassing great variety: the sonata.

Apart from repertory the changes affected the social position and role of music and the musician. The main aspect here, of course, involved the decline of the aristocracy and aristocratic patronage of music and the subsequent support of musical life by the middle class. Hitherto the main genre of secular music intended for a large audience had been opera. In the eighteenth century, through the *collegia musica* in Leipzig and Hamburg and similar institutions elsewhere, public concerts aimed at the middle class and featuring instrumental music became ever more prominent. Related to this change was a gain in the importance of the amateur and the dilettante, to whom composers began to address their efforts, so that music became a vehicle for entertainment, diversion, and pleasure. At the same time the aim of music as the delectation of the senses that had been patent in the seventeenth century continued in the eighteenth. Johann Kellner described his *Manipules musices* (1753) as "a handful of pleasant amusement to pass the time away" (ein Hand voll kurzweiliger Zeitvertreib), a sentiment that also figured in Valentin Rathgeber's collection, *Musikalischer Zeitvertreib* (first published 1733). In the first part of one of his sets of *Partien* (1733), Christoph Graupner claimed as his purpose the pleasure ("Vergnügen") of the player as well as the development of his skill, an intent contrasting with the traditional end of music, "for the glorification of God and the edification of man." In this spirit there came a new genre of music, emphasizing sonatas and other works, intended specifically for women. From around the middle of the century we can note Giuseppe Paganelli's *Divertissement de le beau sexe* [sic], Christoph Nichelmann's *Brevi sonate da cembalo massime all'uso delle dame* (first published 1745), and later C. P. E. Bach's sonatas *à l'usage des dames* (1770). Easy sonatas intended as teaching pieces were also common.

This new environment for music, with strong domestic overtones, went hand in hand with the changes in musical style. The public taste had to be satisfied; music had to be agreeable, easy, graceful, directly perceptible, and enjoyable. In the parlance of the time, it had to be galant. The older way, with its long melodic phrases and its emphasis on counterpoint, came to be called learned. As the famous German theorist and writer on music Johann Mattheson put it in his *Grosse General-Bass Schule* (1731), "as the end of the orator is to persuade his listeners, that of the musician is to please the multitude."[2]

Another contemporary theorist and critic, Johann Adolf Scheibe, stated in his *Der Critische Musikus*, "the beauty and naturalness of this manner of writing may really be said to exist when the melody is always clear, lively, flowing, and also witty [clever, *scharfsinnig*, characterized by sharpness of sense], when it makes free and natural use of all sorts of well-conceived embellishments, when it is free, easy and ever new."[3] Note here the emphasis placed on melody, which is to be cantabile, ingratiating, with an accompaniment that is simple and unobtrusive. This is the age of the Alberti and Murky basses, in which simple stereotyped patterns of figuration, broken chords in the former, octave leaps in the latter, are prominent. This turn to simplicity particularly victimized J. S. Bach.

Finally, a new aesthetic idea made itself felt with regard to music, an ideal closely connected to a purely instrumental kind of music existing apart from any text. In the Baroque the ideal for a musical work was to express a single affect all the way through—*d'un teneur*; the musical materials and procedures were selected in accordance with the emotional or affective character of the composition. While this had been especially true of the operatic aria, it applied to other genres of composition as well: keyboard suites, fugues, individual movements of sonatas, and so on. But as the eighteenth century wore on, the ideal changed; it was now felt that many different characters and emotional qualities should be embodied in a single work. We can see this new attitude in a statement by Marpurg: "We know how fast emotions change, since they themselves are nothing but motion and restlessness. . . . The composer then must in alternation play a hundred roles, he must take on a thousand characters."[4]

This attitude brought with it a striking change in the conception of the musical composition. While such contrasts were not unknown in the music of the seventeenth and early eighteenth centuries (many of Handel's arias and oratorio choruses, for example, represent contrasting affects), they remained by and large the exception. By the middle of the eighteenth century, however, the new ideal of emotional contrast in a musical work has become the accepted one. Carl Philipp Emanuel Bach, for instance, was famous for the extraordinary variety of his keyboard playing—the wide range of emotional contrasts he could produce in one and the same work.

Furthermore, this new aesthetic ideal, with its decisive influence on the procedures of musical composition, was equally decisive in regard to the instrument itself. For the constant changing of character, in which dynamics are especially important, required an instrumental medium capable of registering such changes easily and rapidly. While the harpsichord was capable of some dynamic variation (particularly with the aid of elaborate additions like the celebrated Venetian swell), this clearly was not the instrument's strong point. Thus the piano, which responded readily to such changes in dynamics, inevitably came to be the instrument *par excellence* of the new music.

THE PIANO

This youngest member of the family of keyboard instruments like the harpsichord and clavichord was descended from the dulcimer, an instrument common in medieval Europe. While similar to the psaltery, in which the strings were plucked, the dulcimer was played with blunt clobbers with which its strings were literally struck. In a piano, then, the tone is produced by hammers striking against the strings—thus the term *hammer action*. The piano then is unique among keyboard instruments in that the volume (loudness) of sound depends on the force with which the hammer strikes the strings and thus on the force with which the player strikes the keys. This is the significance of the designation *pianoforte*, or *fortepiano* as it was often called in the eighteenth century, the instrument that plays either soft or loud, with dynamic shadings possible.

While isolated references to stringed keyboard instruments using some sort of hammer action have come down from the Renaissance and Baroque (in the fifteenth century Henri Arnault de Zwolle mentioned keyboard instruments with *ictus* [Latin for stroke]), and in 1673 Kircher referred to a similar instrument with *marculi* [little hammers]), the earliest such instruments date from the first decades of the eighteenth century. The invention of a viable hammer action and the construction of keyboard instruments based on this principle are credited to the Italian harpsichord builder Bartolomeo Cristofori (1655–1731) around 1700. His instrument, called *gravicembalo col piano e forte*, was thoroughly described in 1711 by Scipione Maffei.[5] In 1716 the Parisian harpsichord builder Jean Marius (d. 1720)—influenced by Pantaleone Hebenstreit (1669–1750), a well-known dulcimer player—reported on a *clavecin à maillets*. Yet only Cristofori actually produced instruments, three of which survive. In fact, in the eighteenth century the piano was developed and built by firms primarily engaged in the manufacture of harpsichords.

The hammer action was—and is—a complicated mechanism with many components. The proper activation and return of the hammer so that it is instantly ready to go again with a minimum of effort needed in depressing the key and the subsequent damping of the string, to name only some fundamental aspects, both require this. It is paradoxical that the stringed keyboard instrument in which the player's touch has the most control over loudness is at the same time the one in which the mechanism is the most involved, in which the player's finger is the farthest removed from the vibrating string.

A most important element in the hammer action is the escapement, a means of allowing the hammer to fall back into its normal rest position, ready for operation, even though the release of the key by the finger may not have been completed: this feature is necessary to permit the rapid repetition of the same note. Cristofori had surmounted this difficulty in a clever fashion. Instead of having but one hammer between the key and the string, he had two, one of which was hit by the key lever and which in turn impelled the other against the string; but upon striking the second hammer, the first (called the hopper, or, in Cristofori's terminology *linguetta mobile*) immediately fell back to its normal rest position; in other words, it "escaped," so that the second hammer was also free to fall back regardless of whether the key was still depressed. But this mechanism had the drawback of being excessively bulky, so that other builders of instruments at the time did not avail themselves of it. Cristofori also employed a check, a means of securing the hammer once it fell back to rest position to keep it from rebounding and hitting the string an unwanted second time (see Ex. 2-1). Cristofori's instruments were not immediately influential, and only later did other builders take up their features and develop them.

Much of the eighteenth-century development of the piano took place in Germany, where two important builders were Gottfried Silbermann (1683–1753) and Johann Andreas Stein (1728–1792). After considerable experimentation Silbermann adopted something much like Cristofori's action. These German instruments, which, in the tradition of the clavichord, were small and square, followed one or the other of two main principles. In one the hammer was mounted on the key (the so-called *Prellmechanik, Prell* meaning "bounce or rebound"). In the other, the hammer was detached from the key, the two being connected by a hopper (the so-called *Stossmechanik, Stoss* meaning "push"). The latter, as we have seen, had been employed by Cristofori. In the *Prellmechanik*, each hammer is mounted on a pivot or fork on the key itself, its rear end under an overhanging edge at the back of the interior of the instrument; when the key is depressed, this overhanging edge trips the back of the hammer, causing its front to rise quickly and strike the string forcibly. In the *Stossmechanik*, each hammer is attached to a pivot mounted on a rail that runs along the back of the instrument, and the back part of the key strikes either the bass of the rear of the hammer or a rod or pusher (the jack or hopper) which in turn causes the hammer to rise quickly and strike the string. Both types were eventually provided with escapements. In the case of

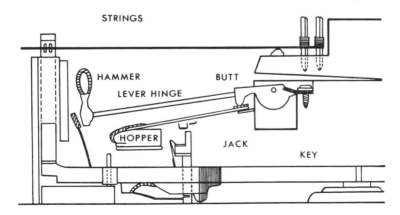

Example 2-1. Cristofori's Piano Action
Reproduced with permission from *Encyclopaedia Britannica*, 14th edition, copyright 1962 by Encyclopaedia Britannica, Inc.

the former (*Prellmechanik*) this was effected by a jointed bar at the back end of the hammer, while in the latter (*Stossmechanik*) it was accomplished by a notch on the underside of the hammer into which the hopper or jack slid when the hammer rebounded from the strings, and a spring forced the hopper or jack back into its original position once the action had been completed. Escapements were a particular feature of pianos built by Stein, whose instruments were highly praised by Mozart on this account.

In 1794 the Stein firm moved to Vienna, Stein's daughter having married Johann Andreas Streicher (1761–1833) in 1793; their pianos became renowned for the lightness, delicacy, and transparency of their tone. Since their instruments usually employed a *Prellmechanik* with escapement, this combination came to be known as the German or Viennese action (see Ex. 2-2). Following the practice in harpsichords, these pianos were often provided with characteristic stops, controlled not by pedals but by levers, some of them operated by the knee: a harp stop (like the buff stop on harpsichords), a swell (louvers over the strings that open and close, making the sound louder or softer), a stop to lift the dampers (the so-called *forte*, or loud, stop), a bassoon stop (heavy paper laid over the string to produce a rustling sound), the moderator (a thin strip of cloth placed between the hammers and the strings), and Turkish music (tambourine and cymbals that beat against the sound board).

Besides Germany, the most important center for the building of pianos in the eighteenth century was London, especially after 1760 when a number of German instrument makers moved there. Johann Christian Bach gave the first public performance on the new instrument in London on 2 June 1768. The Shudi-Broadwood firm, founded in 1728 by the Swiss émigré Burkat Shudi (originally Tschudi, 1702–1803) and continued in association with John Broadwood (1732–1812), was the main manufacturer; they produced pianos from 1773. The early Shudi-Broadwood instruments followed the designs of Johann Christoph Zumpe (fl. 1735–1783), who popularized the square piano employing a single action (i.e., without escapement). But in the 1880s several English firms came out with a different type of piano that was to prove most influential. Its characteristic was a double-action *Stossmechanik* (with escapement), the so-called English action, which made possible a heavier instrument that produced a much stronger tone. Unlike the Stein-Streicher pianos, the Broadwood instruments employed pedals instead of levers. Of the several coloristic stops, they used only the two that were to become standard—the pedal raising the dampers and the *una corda* pedal.

Now we will turn to the last representatives of the old way, in whose work are traces of what was to come. Next we will consider the rise and early development of the new, commencing with Italy and culminating in the work of German composers. Germany through the century gradually assumed stylistic leadership of the new music and continued to exercise that leadership until the end of the nineteenth century. We will also touch on developments in France, England, and Iberia. Although with few exceptions this music was

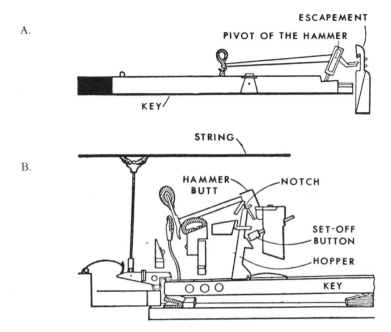

Example 2-2. Eighteenth-century Piano Actions
    A. Stein's Viennese Action
    B. Broadwood's English Action

Reproduced with permission from *Encyclopaedia Britannica*, 14th edition, copyright 1962 by Encyclopaedia Britannica, Inc.

composed for the harpsichord, or occasionally for the clavichord, it can be and is played on the piano, of whose repertory it constitutes an important part.

THE END OF THE BAROQUE IN GERMANY AND FRANCE

The most important German contemporaries of Bach were Johann Mattheson (1681–1764), Georg Philipp Telemann (1681–1767), Johann Christoph Graupner (1683–1760), and George Frideric Handel (originally Georg Friedrich Händel, 1685–1759). Mattheson, a prominent theorist, critic, and writer on music, issued two sets of keyboard works in the old style: the *Harmonisches Denckmahl* or *Pièces de clavecin* (Harmonic Monument or Pieces for Harpsichord, 2 vols., 1714), a set of twelve suites, and *Die wol-klingende Fingersprache* (The Euphonious Language of the Fingers, 2 vols., 1735 and 1737), containing twelve preludes with fugues on two and three subjects. Besides these he produced a sonata (1713) and earlier a sonata and suite for two keyboards (both 1705).

The others are among the foremost composers of their time. Although all composed keyboard music, their contributions do not loom particularly large, neither with respect to the total output of each nor with respect to keyboard literature as a whole. Telemann's work in this field is little known. It is generally oriented to dances of light character, referred to as *Galanteriestücke*. In particular there are the two large collections of minuets (TWV 34 and 35, published 1728 and 1730 respectively)[6] and two of suites, the *Esercizii musicali* (1739–1740), which contains two (TWV 32: 3 and 4), and the later Overtures (TWV 32: 5–10, published 1749), which contains six. The set *Fantasies* (36, TWV 33: 1–36, published 1732–1733) exhibits aspects of the new style. Instead of the grandeur of the toccata-like fantasies of Bach, they are smaller pieces, Italianate in their thematic types and figuration, each cast in two distinct parts with the da capo instruction at the end. In several cases two separate fantasies are connected, the second intended as a midsection between presentations of the first. There are also two sets of easy fugues (TWV 30: 1–20 and 21–26, published 1731 and 1738–1739 respectively) that he obviously intended for teaching, and other miscellaneous pieces.

The keyboard work of Handel, if better known than that of Telemann, also occupies a secondary position in that great composer's work. All of it was composed in England. Handel worked in most of the principal genres of keyboard music.[7] The first set of suites (HWV 426–433) was published in London by J. Cluer (1720), the second (HWV 434–442) published by Walsh also in London in two editions (1727 and 1733); of these only the set published by Cluer was prepared by Handel himself and is considered his best work in the genre. Then there are miscellaneous pieces, among them suites, dances, fantasias, and the set *Fugues or Voluntaries* for harpsichord or organ (6, HWV 605–610/op. 3), published by Walsh (1735).

As indicated, the suites represent his most important contribution. The old "normal" dance forms are treated conventionally. The allemande is the most stylized, working mostly with figural melody in long phrases; the Italian type, the corrente, is used rather than the French; the sarabande appears as the slow movement. Especially well-known are the sarabandes of the Suite in G minor (HWV 432) and the Suite in D minor (HWV 437), which has two doubles. The gigue appears mostly as the Italian *giga*, although we find instances of the imitative French version both with and without inversion of the subject in the second part. Handel likewise treated the preludes in full accordance with the traditions of the genre; they are short and work with figuration. That to the Suite in G minor (HWV 432) is a French overture (he orchestrated this piece for use as an operatic overture).

Dances employing variation form play an important role here. Not only do we find the standard types—the passacaille (Suite in G minor, HWV 432) and the chaconne (see below)—but others as well. There is a minuet with three variations (Suite in D minor, HWV 436), a sarabande with two variations (Suite in D minor, HWV 437), already mentioned, and three airs, each with five variations, here called doubles (Suite in D minor, HWV 428; Suite in E major, HWV 430, known as "The Harmonious Blacksmith"; and the Suite in

B-flat major, HWV 434), which Brahms used. The largest of the variations are two chaconnes, both in G major, both independent works, both on eight-bar themes—the first with twenty-one variations (HWV 435), the other with sixty-two (HWV 442), the latter representing one of the more impressive accomplishments in Baroque keyboard music.

As it happens, however, we find the "normal" arrangement of the movements, as we have it from Froberger, Bach, and others, only in the second set of Handel's suites (1733); yet even here this order appears in but few of them. In the first set of suites (1720)—the only one Handel himself prepared for publication—none has this "normal" order. The departures occur by way of substitutions; not only do we find minuets, airs, gavottes, the passacaille, and chaconnes in place of the traditional dances, but we also find movements that are not dances at all, such as fugues, largos, and prestos. Thus the relationship to the traditional suite has become loose.

The influence of the Italian instrumental ensemble music of the time is pervasive. We see this in the fugues, which are prominent only in the first set of suites. They reveal the driving rhythms, the violinistic type of figuration, and the free treatment of fugal technique. More interesting from the historical point of view, however, are those movements designated simply by tempo markings, since they are new to the keyboard suite; yet they appear only in Handel's first set of suites (see Ex. 2-3). This is symptomatic of the new rapprochement between the suite and the sonata.

Keyboard music again takes a secondary position in the work of Graupner. As cantor in Darmstadt, he was the man who saw fit to reject the offer

Example 2-3. HANDEL: Allegro from Suite in G minor (Book I, No. 7)—Beginning (mm. 1–8)

extended him by the authorities at the Leipzig Thomasschule in 1722, thus opening the way for the offer to be given to Bach. Among Graupner's works, the suite is most important: there are two sets entitled *Partien* (1718 and 1733), the latter with the subtitle *Vier Jahreszeiten* (Four Seasons), of which only the first part ("Winter") has survived. Two other sets, both reminiscent of Graupner's teacher Kuhnau, are the *Monatliche Klavier-Früchte* (1722) and the *Leichte Clavier-Übungen* (manuscript, ca. 1730). Other scattered suites and individual pieces in manuscript bring the total to approximately sixty, of which forty-three are extant, along with some other pieces. Graupner's keyboard suites, in contrast to those of Handel, employ the "normal" dances in the usual order but often substitute other dances (the rigaudon or chaconne) for the final gigue; the standard dances may appear more than once in the same suite and optional dances are inserted as well. Twelve of his suites contain preludes that follow the conventions of the genre. In general Graupner's suites are simpler and smaller than those of Handel's first set.

In France a large body of keyboard compositions generally reflect the old style. The publications of such works usually bear the title *Pièces de clavecin*, and were produced by Nicolas Siret (dates unknown, but two sets published 1716 and 1719), Louis-Nicolas Clérambault (1676–1749), Joseph Bodin de Boismortier (ca. 1689–1765), Francis Dagincourt (1684–1758), Louis-Antoine Dornel (ca. 1680–1765), Louis-Claude Daquin (1694–1772), and Jacques Duphly (1715–1789), among others. But the art of the French keyboard suite culminates in the work of two composers: François Couperin (1683–1733) and Jean-Philippe Rameau (1683–1764), the latter well-known as a composer of operas and ballets and as a theorist of music.

Couperin (known as *Le grand*), a member of a large musical family, was active as an organist in Paris. Unlike the work of his German contemporaries, keyboard music dominates his output, with the emphasis going to the suite. Couperin published twenty-seven suites, which he entitled *ordres* instead of suites, in four volumes, each bearing the title *Pièces de clavecin*, in 1713, 1717, 1722, and 1730. In addition he composed a number of independent dances. He was also the author of a treatise on keyboard playing, *L'art de toucher le clavecin* (1717).[8]

As expected, dances form the basis of Couperin's suites. Dominant is binary form with the double-bar, each half to be repeated. The general style is much as we have seen: the melody is in the uppermost voice and it has a simple accompaniment, such that the texture is light and transparent. Improvised embellishments are important; in a number of cases Couperin presented dances in two versions, one plain, the other ornamented. Of the slower dances, the allemande and sarabande, Couperin recognized two kinds—for the allemande, *legère* and *grave*; for the sarabande, *tendre* and *grave*, corresponding to light and serious characters. The courante and gigue are represented by their French versions. Other dances that appear are the rigaudon, the passepied, and the gavotte. Although a French overture begins the Suite in E-flat major (No. 25), Couperin generally omitted the traditional preludes. Variations (doubles) are common.

Prominent here are the rondeau and passacaille, usually with three or four episodes (or couplets). Further, the rondeau may also appear without variation in the refrain sections, as in the Suite in C major (No. 3, "La favorite"), or the large "Passacaille en rondeau" of the Suite in B minor (No. 8), one of Couperin's largest and most difficult works, in eight couplets. Another large piece in this form is "Les folies françoises ou les dominos" of the Suite in B minor (No. 13).

Along with the usual dances we find others that bear characteristic or descriptive titles. The early suites include such examples as the allemande "L'auguste" of the Suite in G minor (No. 1); the sarabande "La prude" of the Suite in D minor (No. 2); or the allemandes "La fleurie" and "La ténébreuse" of the suites in G minor and C minor (Nos. 1 and 3), and so on. But in the later suites such characteristic titles replace the names of the dances, and the pieces themselves may be virtually independent of dance types, as, for instance, the well-known "Soeur Monique" (in No. 18) and the rondeau "Le rossignol en amour" (in No. 14). Couperin usually gave descriptive titles to rondeaus: "Les barricades mistérieuses," "Les moissoneurs," and "Le gazouillement" (all in No. 6), and "La distraite" (in No. 16). An attractive piece is "La harpée" of the Suite in E minor (No. 21), qualified by Couperin as a *pièce dans le goût de la harpe* (Ex. 2-4). In the rondeau "La bandoline" of the Suite in A major (No. 5), Couperin provided the performance instruction "the right hand legato and the left marcato," to emphasize the character of the mandoline. Several pieces emphasize crossing of hands (*pièces croisées*), an important aspect of keyboard virtuosity, and among many examples are the two musettes of the Suite in A minor (No. 15), the rondeau "Le tic-toc-choc, ou les maillotins" of the Suite in F minor–F major (No. 18), and the *minuets croisées* of the Suite in D major (No. 22).

While Couperin maintained that old attribute of the suite, unity of key, in the arrangement of these dances and other pieces in the suites he largely followed the French rather than the German tradition. Of the four books he published, the first may be viewed as the most Germanic in form: most of its *ordres* preserve the "normal" sequence of the four fundamental dances, the arrangement being varied by the occasional use of more than one courante

Example 2-4. F. Couperin: "La harpée" from Suite in E minor (No. 21)—Beginning (mm. 1–4)

and a varying number of dances added after the gigue. In the subsequent volumes of the *Pièces de clavecin*, Couperin took greater liberties with the traditional members of the suite, at times eliminating them altogether.

Frequently he made little groups of such characteristic pieces to form small entities, little cycles in themselves, within the larger frame of an *ordre*; in a few cases such a group constitutes the entire *ordre*. As examples, consider, in the Suite in C minor (No. 3), the group entitled "Les pèlcrins," which consists of "La marche," "La caristade," and "Le remerciement." Another is in the Suite in F major (No. 4), entitled "Les bacchanales," consisting of "Enjoumens bachiques," "Tendresses bachiques," and "Fureurs bachiques"; or the miniature drama in five acts in Suite in C major–C minor (No. 11), "Les fastes de la grande et ancienne Mxnxstrxndxsx" (standing for "Menestrandise," the title disguised by replacing all the vowels with the letter *x*), a satirical piece depicting a banquet of the musicians' guild. The Suite in D major (No. 10) depicts war: "La triomphante," "Rondeau, bruit de guerre," "Rondeau, allegresse des vainceurs," and "Fanfare," all in the tradition of the *battaglia* as seen in Kerll, Kuhnau, and others. It is clear, then, that we cannot speak of a "normal form" of the suite in Couperin.

The suites by Couperin, as we have seen, contain no preludes. But that he regarded preludes as proper is evident from his treatise *L'art de toucher le clavecin*, which contains eight of them in keys corresponding to those of the *ordres* of the first volume of his *Pièces de clavecin,* presumably for interpolation into performances of these suites. The preludes are short, each of them based on a short thematic motive or type of figuration and embodying the rhythmic freedom characteristic of the genre. In the treatise itself Couperin stresses this aspect, referring to the prelude as a "free" form especially in regard to rhythm and emphasizing the role of the imagination. On the basis of rhythmic freedom, Couperin refers to the preludes as "prose," while equating other "measured" music with "poetry."

The keyboard music of Rameau is devoted to the suite, and again the various volumes all bear the title *Pièces de clavecin*: Book I (1706); Book II (1724, reissued 1731); and *Nouvelles suites de clavecin* (ca. 1728). In addition he arranged five pieces from his *Pièces de clavecin en concert* (1741), as well as *La dauphine* (1747). The set of 1706 contains the single Suite in A minor–A major, that of 1724/1731 has two, in E minor–E major and D minor–D major, and the set of ca. 1736 also contains two, in A minor–A major and G minor–G major, so that in all Rameau produced five suites.

In three of them we find elements of the "normal" disposition of the suite along with a number of modifications. As in Couperin's earlier suites, these involve adding dances after the concluding gigue, except the second Suite in A minor–A major, which ends with a long gavotte preceded by three "optional" dances. All three have the allemande followed by the courante, while the first in A minor–A major and the one in E minor–E major also contain gigues. The sarabande appears in its proper position in the second Suite in A minor–A major, while the first of the suites in A minor–A major, has the sarabande and its double included among the dances following the gigue.

The courantes and gigues are of the French variety. The first Suite in A minor–A major is the only one of Rameau's suites to have a prelude.

The two remaining suites depart from the basic scheme. The first, in D minor–D major from the set of 1724/1731, consists of ten numbers, each with a title *à la* Couperin; the Suite in G minor–G major, the second of the *Nouvelles suites*, has nine numbers that also bear descriptive titles. While some individual numbers in these suites can clearly be related to dances, others clearly cannot, such as "La poule" (The Hen) and the well-known "L'enharmonique" (The Enharmonic [Piece]) of the Suite in G minor–G major. "La poule" is noteworthy for its use of dynamic markings (*forte* and *doux*), that, along with the themes of rapidly repeated notes, aid in the musical depiction of the barnyard, thus maintaining the old genre. Several dances in Rameau's suites have become established in their own right as repertory pieces. Apart from the two just mentioned, there are "Le rappel des oiseaux" (The Return of the Birds) of the Suite in E minor–E major; from the Suite in D minor–D major, which has none of the usual members of the suite, there is "L'entretien des muses" (The Muses' Conversation) and the rondeau "Les cyclopes." From the *Nouvelles suites* the one in A major–minor has "Les trois mains," a virtuoso example of hand crossing, and the Suite in G minor–G major has "Les sauvages" which Rameau also employed in his opera *Les Indes galantes*.

Like Couperin, Rameau sought a larger form for use in his suites and to this end gave prominence to the refrain principle of the rondeau, which not only appears in those pieces with descriptive titles that are rather distant from actual dances, but also usurps the normal form of individual dances themselves. In the first Suite in A minor–A major (1706) Rameau employed it in the courante, the "Venitiènne," and the gavotte; in the set of 1724/1731 he used it in the courante, the two gigues, the musette, and "La villageoise." A peculiarity of Rameau's terminology is that the episodes or couplets are called "reprises" as are also the second parts of dances in the usual binary form. The other effort in the direction of a larger form for use in suites lies in the doubles or variations. Examples of variations are in the rigaudon of the Suite in E minor–E major (1724/1731), "Les niais de Sologne" (The Nestlings of Sologne) of the Suite in D minor–D major from the same collection, and, particularly, the concluding gavotte of the second Suite in A minor–A major (ca. 1728) with six doubles, Rameau's largest venture into variation form.

In comparison with Couperin, Rameau generally was more Baroque, more conservative. The delicacy and refinement of Couperin are not prominent in Rameau: Rameau's rhythms and phrase structures are more regular, the driving rhythms characteristic of the Baroque are common, the accents more pronounced, and the part-writing denser. Couperin was more "modern" in his adaptation to the galant, but in his hands the galant bore little relation to what we will see in the Italian composers of the time.

Another group of composers who emphasized the suite lived and worked in Belgium: Gerhardus Havingha (1696–1753), Josse Boutmy (1697–1779), Dieudonné Raick (1703–1764), and Joseph Hector Fiocco (1703–1741);

but the outstanding figure was Jean-Baptiste Loeillet (1680–1730). A native of Ghent, he was also active in London where he came under the influence of Handel. His published keyboard works comprise two volumes of suites, both printed in London: *Lessons* (ca. 1709–1715) and *Suits of Lessons* (6, 1722–1725, reissued ca. 1730).[9] Here the "German" form with its "normal" succession of dances is to be found. The Italian forms of courante and gigue appear (Loeillet used the English term jigg), along with the English minuet "Round-O" in the Suite in G minor, while the suites in D major and E-flat major contain imitative gigues in the French fashion; the Suite in G minor is noteworthy for its highly figured sarabande with extensive dynamic markings.

OLD AND NEW IN ITALY

Of greater moment for the "progressive" music of the time were developments that took place in Italy. Here as elsewhere we find the same intermingling between old and new, but here the sonata became established as an important genre of keyboard composition. In the work of the more conservative musicians, the keyboard fugue continued in the work of Giuseppe Bencini, Gaetano Greco (ca. 1657–ca. 1728), Antonio Caldara (1670–1736) who was active in Venice and Vienna, and Andrea Basili (1705–1777). We can see the genre's decline in rigor by the end of the century from the work of Nicolo Antonio Porpora (1686–1768), an eminent Neapolitan composer resident in Vienna, for a time the teacher of Haydn; his fugues emphasize free episodes and virtuoso showmanship rather than strict contrapuntal working out. The toccata appears in the work of Francesco Durante (1684–1755) in its smaller one-movement version, and also in that of Leonardo Leo (1694–1744) and Domenico Zipoli (1688–1726), who also composed suites. (The important toccatas of Alessandro Scarlatti have already been considered.) All these composers, in fact, directed their main efforts toward the composition of opera, giving only secondary attention to music for keyboard.

The term *sonata* had been used for many things in the seventeenth century, in accordance with its literal meaning of something to be played, that is, simply an instrumental piece. The term ultimately came to refer more to a work of several movements, two to four being the most usual, either in the same key or in related keys. We can, however, frequently observe a connection to other genres of musical composition. There are sonatas in the work of the conservative composers Azzolino Bernardino della Ciaja (1671–1755) and Zipoli that are virtually identical with toccatas, while fugal pieces for organ in one movement, called sonatas, were composed by Giovanni Battista Martini (1706–1784). Because this use of the term *sonata* represents the older viewpoint, and certainly one not characteristic of the latter part of the eighteenth century, we will deal with such works first before tracing the growth of what leads to the "classical" sonata in the work of Haydn, Mozart, Beethoven, and their contemporaries.

Italy's leading and most celebrated composer of keyboard music in the early eighteenth century was Domenico Scarlatti (1685–1757), the son of Alessandro. He was trained and worked in several Italian cities (Naples, Venice, and Rome) before he moved to Portugal around 1719, where he spent the rest of his career.

Apart from a few isolated fugues and dances, Scarlatti's important output in keyboard music consists wholly of sonatas. Authorities differ as to the exact number, but the consensus estimate is around 560. The earliest of them (thirty pieces) were published, apparently in London, in 1738 or 1739 under the title *Essercizi per gravicembalo*. They were followed in 1739 by Roseingrave's publication of thirty-two more under the title *Suite de pièces pour le clavecin*, in which the works were arranged as suites (such attempts are always the work of editors and publishers, never of Scarlatti himself). But the vast majority of Scarlatti's works are preserved in manuscript: two sets of fifteen volumes, copied for the use of Princess Maria Barbara of Portugal between 1752 and 1757, one set now in Parma, the other in Venice; later Italian copies are

Title page from Domenico Scarlatti's *Essercizi per gravicembalo*, London, 1738–1739. British Museum, London. In 1738 Scarlatti lived in Madrid, where an ambassador of John V made him a knight of the Portuguese Order of Santiago; thus the Cavaliero di S. Giacomo in the title.

From *Decorative Music Title Pages*, G. S. Fraenkel, ed., Dover Publications, Inc., 1968.

in Münster and Vienna. Because no autograph manuscripts exist, it is essentially impossible to assign dates to individual works.

Scarlatti employed the term *sonata* for these works with great consistency. The chief exception is the *Essercizi* (Exercises, 1738 or 1739), but even here individual pieces are called sonatas. Occasionally in the various manuscripts other designations appear: *toccata* in the first of the volumes at Parma, and here and there such names as *fugue, pastorale, aria, capriccio, minuet, gavotte*, and *gigue* appear. Generally, *sonata* is the proper term for these compositions.

Scarlatti's sonatas are one-movement compositions (a few of his early works are sonatas in several movements), and most are cast in the same fundamental scheme—the binary form, *forma bipartita*, with the double-bar near the midpoint, each part to be repeated. Within this simple but fundamental plan Scarlatti was able to produce endless variety. Kirkpatrick believed that 388 of Scarlatti's sonatas were grouped in pairs, each pair the same tonality, and that twelve more appear as little groups of three sonatas, also each in the same tonality, but this view has been disputed.[10]

Most attempts to classify the varieties of the binary form found in Scarlatti's sonatas take as their point of departure the relationship to the fully developed sonata form of the late eighteenth century.[11] Gerstenberg, for one, distinguished three main types. In the first both parts are roughly equivalent in length and the work as a whole is monothematic. In the second several themes are presented in the first part and then somewhat developed but without a full-scale recapitulation. The third comprises the mature sonata form. Benton has provided a similar classification. Kirkpatrick's system, in contrast, avoids any reference to the later sonata form and operates with different terminology. In his parlance,[12] a sonata is symmetrical if both parts are of about the same length and asymmetrical if the second is longer, whereby the passage making the second part longer stands at its beginning and is called excursion; a sonata is closed if both parts commence with the same thematic material and open if the second begins with something different (the closed type, then, has little or no excursion). An open sonata is free if its excursion employs a good deal of new material and concentrated if its excursion operates entirely with themes stated in the first part. These are different ways of describing the same thing, but we can sympathize with Kirkpatrick for his efforts to make clear that there is no direct relation between these sonatas (whether in groups of three or not) and the later form of the piano sonata.

The lack of correspondence between these works and the mature sonata form becomes even clearer when we examine individual works. In the multiplicity of themes introduced by Scarlatti during the course of a sonata the would-be interpreter often cannot decide which is principal and which subordinate, whether the criterion is key relationships or the importance of themes in the unfolding of the work. Accordingly, Kirkpatrick developed his own system based on the view that the complementary relation between the two parts of the *forma bipartita* is the most important formal factor in these works. Thus the reestablishment of the tonic in the restatement of thematic material that originally appeared in a different key constitutes the crux. As he put it, "the real life of a Scarlatti sonata resides in the central section of the first half and in the parallel section of the second."[13] Therefore, "the meeting point in each half of the thematic material which is stated in parallel fashion at the ends of both halves with the establishment of the closing tonality" becomes the central point of a Scarlatti sonata. Kirkpatrick also employed pre-crux and post-crux, along with more the usual terms—opening, continuation, transition, closing, restatement, and the like.

That Scarlatti's sonatas have but the most superficial similarity to the later so-called Classical sonata is evident from the types of themes that are used in them. Their variety is difficult to survey. Hoffmann-Erbrecht has offered four large groups as the basis for an attempt at classification, restricted to themes that appear at the beginnings of sonatas:[14]

- first, themes in which the component motives are grouped in pairs, of which he counts 130 instances
- second, a larger and rather loosely defined group in which there is some variety, embracing echo-like repetitions, repetitions of phrases or bars, and variations of all sorts
- third, the use of themes with contrasting motives, of which he counts ten examples
- fourth, the continuously unfolding type using similar figurational or rhythmic patterns, often with much use of sequences (the German *Fortspinnung* type), of which he counts 275 instances.

Scarlatti's themes are likely to be arresting. Recurring rhythmic patterns are common.

The accompaniment to a theme is important. Indeed, Scarlatti often has made it literally inseparable from the theme itself: the accompaniment is not simply neutral, providing harmonic support for the main voice, but rather the theme is conceived polyphonically so that we can make no distinction between the "theme" and its "accompaniment." We may see this, for instance, in the Sonata in G major (K. 105/L. 204)[15] in fast triple time. Its first theme is dancelike; here the accompaniment enters in the left hand one bar later with an imitation of the first bar of the theme but then goes on to present an important counterfigure that must be regarded as part and parcel of the theme. Another example is the opening of the cantabile sonata in B-flat major (K. 544/L. 497). Furthermore, within a section Scarlatti presents contrasting themes, as, for instance, in the sonatas in D major (K. 29/L. 461, K. 119/L. 415, K. 140/L. 107, K. 490/L. 206). In the Sonata in G major (K. 253/L. 154) and two in B-flat major (K. 202/L. 498, K. 272/L. 145), the excursion takes the form of a pastorale, while in the Sonata in E minor (K. 394/L. 275), the excursion commences with an unexpected cadenza-like passage.

One factor that has made Scarlatti's sonatas so attractive is his highly idiomatic treatment of the keyboard medium. While scholars have long assumed the preferred instrument to have been the harpsichord, Sheveloff has made a case that Scarlatti would have used Cristofori's new piano. In any event, figuration patterns remain fundamental. Wide leaps, rapidly repeated notes (in which the performer is to change fingers on the same note, *mutandi i detti*—as in the Sonata in D major (K. 96/L. 465)—arpeggios, brilliant figuration patterns, and so on, all contribute. Scarlatti often employed rapid trills (tremolos), as in two sonatas in D major (the one just mentioned and K. 119/L. 415), the latter containing a long trill in an inner part. Glissandos also appear: the minuet-like Sonata in F major (K. 379/L. 73) has an ascending scale-run marked *con dedo solo*, with one finger. Many of these features appear in the Sonata in A minor (K. 175/L. 429). Prominent is hand crossing, which we have seen in French keyboard music; it is particularly emphasized in the sonatas in B-flat major (K. 57/L.S. 38), D major (K. 96/L. 465), and especially D minor (K. 120/L. 215).

An important aspect involves color. Especially noteworthy are the many passages where Scarlatti evidently wished to suggest the violent and passionate strumming of the Spanish guitar. This he accomplished either by insistent rapidly repeated chords, often with dissonant appoggiaturas played on the beat (*acciaccature*) which imply a percussive touch, or by a rapidly repeated figuration pattern in the bass. *Acciaccature* appear in the sonatas in D major (K. 119/L. 415, see Ex. 2-5), C major (K. 309/L. 454), and E minor (K. 394/L. 275), which have unusual harmonic progressions; those in E minor (K. 402/L. 427) and D major (K. 490/L. 206), which emphasize dotted rhythms; and one in F major (K. 518/L. 116). Repeated patterns in the bass appear in the Sonata in C major (K. 513/L.S. 3), a pastorale with guitar effects in the contrasting sections, in what seems like an Alberti bass (rare in Scarlatti) in the Sonata in D minor (K. 517/L. 266), or the Sonata in B-flat major (K. 545/L. 500). Examples of mimetic effects could be multiplied. Trumpet or horn themes, which are triadic, dotted, and fanfare-like, exist in abundance, and, not surprisingly, the key of D major is prominent here (K. 96/L. 465; K. 119/L. 415). Among other sonatas with mimetic aspects are two in C major (K. 406/L. 5; K. 420/L.S. 2). A timpani-like figure in the bass characterizes the sonatas in E major (K. 46/L. 25), D minor (K. 120/L. 215), and G major (K. 470/L. 304), while other aspects of orchestral music characterize the Sonata in C minor (K. 37/L. 406)—its unison opening—and two sonatas in G major (K. 260/L. 124; K. 325/L. 37), especially in their violinistic figuration.

Many of Scarlatti's sonatas are related to other genres of composition. One of the most famous among them is a fugue, the Sonata in G minor (K. 30/L. 499, the "Cat's Fugue," named for its irrationally leaping principal theme; this appeared as the last of the *Essercizi* and is a free fugue indeed. Many other sonatas, as suggested, contain themes involved to some extent with fugal imitation. The minuet is explicit in the sonatas in D major (K. 282/L. 484) and G major (K. 471/L. 82), while the gigue lies back of the Sonata in A minor (K. 54/L. 241). Another large group are cantabile, thus partaking of an important aesthetic requirement of the period. In a number of the sonatas, Scarlatti heightens expressiveness by suddenly inserting free passages in cadenza-like style; examples are in the sonatas in C minor (K. 116/L. 452), D major (K. 119/L. 415), and E minor (K. 394/L. 275), and the cantabile Sonata in B-flat

Example 2-5. D. SCARLATTI: Sonata in D major (K. 119/L. 415)—Excerpt (mm. 54–72)

major (K. 544/L. 497), in which these passages are marked *arbitre* (free). Theme-and-variations form appears but once, in the Sonata in A minor (K. 61/L. 136).

In the preface to the *Essercizi* Scarlatti wrote: "Do not expect any profound learning, but rather an ingenious jesting with art, to accommodate you to the mastery of the harpsichord." Indeed, we find something characteristic of the new galant taste—the emphasis on entertainment and diversion coupled with a didactic aim—so that in Scarlatti the sonata became, in its earliest appearance at least, associated with the etude or teaching piece (*Handstück* in the German parlance of the later eighteenth century). But more striking is the "ingenious jesting with art," an aim fulfilled by all the capricious elements that have been noted—"the original and happy freaks," as Burney called them[16]—that come about from the unusual themes, harmonies, and textures, all bound up with an unconventional approach to the medium itself. The combination makes Scarlatti's sonatas unique not only for the eighteenth century but for the general keyboard repertory as well.

The one-movement form was not to become characteristic of the key-board sonata; in fact Scarlatti provided no general model in this regard. Instead, the multimovement sonata became the rule, but it was a rather general rule, for the varieties are many. We find sonatas in four or five movements, others in three, still others in two; and, toward the end of the century, we even find the one-movement scheme in the work of Domenico Cimarosa (1749–1801), best known for his comic operas.

The period beginning in the late 1730s confounds most efforts to create a true picture of the course of events. Scholars lack the ability to date many of the works, adequate bibliographical material, and, more especially, comprehensive and reliable editions of the music. While things have improved in the last several decades, many important gaps remain. But the attempt must be made: what is offered here should be regarded as no more than that.

Typical of the unusual forms that can be found in keyboard sonatas are those of the Neapolitan Francesco Durante, his *Sonates per cembalo divise in studii et divertimenti* (composed ca. 1732), in which old and new are combined. These are two-movement works, each consisting of a studio and a divertimento; the former are conservative pieces in imitative counterpoint while the latter are short and fast virtuoso pieces in binary form with double-bar. Here it is not the form that is characteristic of what the genre is to become, but rather the title *sonate per cembalo* which was used many times as the century progressed. Durante, as already noted, also composed toccatas in the one-movement form.

We have observed that the keyboard sonata was related to Italian chamber music of the time, particularly to its two principal genres, the *sonata da chiesa* and the *sonata da camera*. The former, literally "church sonata," corresponds to the sonata, and the latter, literally "chamber sonata," to the suite or partita. This relationship holds true in the work of Handel, and it can be seen from time to time in the work of Italian composers of keyboard music throughout the century. It is especially clear in the few sonatas by Lodovico Giustini (1685–1743), about whom little is known. Nonetheless Giustini has the distinction of having composed the earliest known music for Cristofori's new instrument, the piano: *Sonate da cimbalo di piano e forte detto volgarmente di martelletti* (12, op. 1, published 1732). Despite its historical prominence, this is modest music of no great merit by an evident amateur. While the suite element is strong here, these works do not respect the norms of the day. Of the twelve pieces, eight are in four movements and four are in five movements, some with names of dances as titles and others with tempo designations. From the *sonata da chiesa* comes the fast fugal second movement, but the fugue writing lapses into homophony as the movement progresses. Dynamic markings abound, as would be expected in music intended for the piano; but such dynamic indications involve simple changes between *forte* and *piano* (a few places require three degrees, *forte*, *piano* and *pianissimo*), and, with crescendo absent, these sonatas for the most part could have been adequately rendered on a larger harpsichord of the time.[17]

The *sonata da chiesa* provided the basis for the sonatas of Benedetto Marcello (1686–1739) who was also a poet, a lawyer, and the author of a satirical critique of opera, the *Teatro alla moda* (1720). Marcello's sonatas for keyboard number something over thirty and during his lifetime existed only in manuscript. Of the twelve in a Paris manuscript, eight show the four-movement scheme of the church sonata, three have three movements, and one has five. There is but one movement specifically connected with the *camera* sonata, a minuet. Binary form, with the double-bar, appears in most of the movements. An unusual feature is cyclic form, an obvious and explicit use of the same thematic material at the beginnings of the movements of a sonata.

Particularly varied are the sonatas of Giovanni Battista Martini of Bologna, the famous composer, theorist, and historian of music known as Padre Martini. He published two collections of keyboard sonatas: the *Sonate d'intavolatura per l'organo e'l cembalo* (1742) and the *Sonate per l'organo e il cembalo* (1747). The earlier set contains works closely related to the chamber and church sonatas; the key remains the same for each movement, and a sequence of five movements is used—prelude, fugue, slow movement, dance movement, and a set of variations (called aria). The preludes appear both in the simple form, using a single thematic motive all the way through, and in the more elaborate sectional form of the French overture; the fugues, which use themes that emphasize figurational elements, display contrapuntal elaboration. Indeed, contrapuntal elements appear in all movements. The later collection, on the other hand, shows the more modern type: the three-movement scheme (Fast–Slow–Fast), which we evidently should associate with the Italian operatic overture, the sinfonia. A similar mixture of the two types of sonata may be seen in the nine sonatas of Giovanni Battista Pescetti (ca. 1704–1766).

Another combination of the two appears in the work of Giovanni Benedetto Platti (ca. 1700–1763), who produced eighteen keyboard sonatas, twelve published in two publications: the *Sonates pour le clavessin sur le goût italien* (6, op. 1, 1742) and the sonatas (6, op. 4, ca. 1746). While these clearly show the influence of the old *sonata da chiesa*, one of them plainly is a *sonata da camera* in four movements—prelude, sarabande, minuet, gigue. Typical is the opening Allegro of the galant Sonata in C major (op. 1 ii), with its opening theme descending scalewise in unison and the following short triadic theme, both related to the *opera buffa* (see Ex. 2-6). Representative of the conservative type is the Sonata in D major (op. 1 i) in four movements—Adagio, Allegro, Largo, and Presto. On the other hand the later set (ca. 1746) shows a mixture: a few have the three-movement scheme, while others reflect the older tradition. Stylized dances are important, the sarabande and siciliano appearing as slow movements, the gigue serving as finale. In the first movements we find something like the later sonata form—the recapitulation is clearly articulated, while the development is both short and free. These sonatas, finally, show a greater range in modulation than was common at this time in this repertory.

Example 2-6. PLATTI: Sonata in C major (op. 1 ii)—Beginning (mm. 1–11)

Sonatas in two movements appear, apart from Martini, in the work of Domenico Paradisi (1707–1791, often known under the Germanized form Paradies) and Domenico Alberti (ca. 1710–ca. 1740), both of whom were famous as virtuoso performers and were active in London. Alberti, for whom the Alberti bass is named, had a particular reputation in England as an innovator in keyboard music. His sonatas existed only in manuscript during his lifetime; the first published collection, containing eight of them, appeared in 1748. The exact number of his sonatas is uncertain, but it is estimated that he produced at least fourteen. Here the two-movement scheme is standard, the first movement in duple time, the second in triple (usually a dance, minuet or gigue), but a few sonatas show the reverse arrangement. Binary form and uniformity of expressive character throughout a movement are the rule. Alberti is generally regarded today as an amateur whose importance has been exaggerated by the bass accompaniment pattern that bears his name.

Paradisi is known for the collection of sonatas that appeared in London in 1754 containing twelve works (there are several later editions as well as manuscript copies). Like Alberti, Paradisi usually cast his sonatas in two movements, but the sequence varies: some have two fast movements, others a slow movement followed by a fast one, and still others the reverse. In the fast movements the relation to the old binary form of the dance suite is clear enough, but in the opening fast movements Paradisi has elaborated the structure to resemble the later sonata form. The idea of thematic contrast in a keyboard sonata was taken over either from the Italian operatic sinfonia, where it had been a long-standing practice, or from the concerto grosso, in which the theme assigned to the solo group contrasts with that assigned to the orchestra. From later in the century we find two-movement sonatas by Abbot Lorenzo de Rossi (1720–1794), Antonio Sacchini (1730–1786), Giovanni Paisiello (1740–1816), and Luigi Cherubini (1760–1842).

Sonatas in two and three movements dominate the large output of Baldassare Galuppi (1706–1785), called *Il Buranello*, who spent his last years in St. Petersburg. The total number of his sonatas is estimated at ninety, most of them in his lifetime circulating in manuscript; one set of six was printed by Walsh in London around the middle of the century. There are about as many in two movements as there are in three, and others are in one, four, and five movements, but all the sonatas printed by Walsh show the three-movement scheme. Essentially galant, Galuppi's sonatas show a certain economy in the number of themes used, along with an emphasis on thematic development and a tendency to virtuoso treatment of the instrument. Both qualities set them off from those of most of his contemporaries. A similar situation exists in the sonatas of Ferdinando Turini (ca. 1749–ca. 1817).

Finally, there is a group of composers whose sonatas are cast in the three-movement scheme. Among these are the famous Milanese composer Giovanni Battista Sammartini (ca. 1701–1775) and the much-traveled Giovanni Marco (or Maria) Placido Rutini (1723–1797). In Sammartini we find the galant style in all its elegant simplicity, its sweet and singing melodies, and prevailing homophonic texture. A minuet usually serves as finale. Much the same goes for Rutini, the total number of whose sonatas has been set at almost ninety, many published in the period 1746–1797. To these we may add Giuseppe Paganelli (1710–ca. 1762) of Padua who was active mostly in Germany and who composed slight but pleasing little sonatas in two and three movements.

Among other Italian composers of keyboard music of the time whose work, as it is presently known, seems of minor importance, are Antonio Ferradini (ca. 1718–1779), Ferdinando Gioseffe Bertoni (1725–1813), Giuseppe Sarti (1729–1802), and Giambattista Grazioli (1746–ca. 1820).

IBERIA AND ENGLAND

In the keyboard music of Spain and Portugal, the influence of Domenico Scarlatti was dominant. This is clear from the work of the Lisbon organist José Antonio Carlos de Seixas (1704–1742), Padre Antonio Soler (1729–1783), who worked at the Escorial, and Manuel Blasco de Nebra (1750–1784). Seixas' varied output comprises sonatas, minuets, fugues, and even works specifically intended for the clavichord. His toccatas are similar to those of Alessandro Scarlatti; his sonatas are varied, some in one movement, others multipartite pieces consisting of up to five movements. In recent years well over a hundred sonatas of Soler have become known. Here the Scarlatti type was the model: they are single movement sonatas, but sometimes in groups of from two to four, all in the *forma bipartita*, usually in fast tempo and with exploitation of the coloristic possibilities of the medium. The sonatas of

Blasco de Nebra, on the other hand, adopt the conventional galant idiom that dominated Italian keyboard music at the time—the two-movement scheme, with simple melodies and stereotyped patterns of accompaniment. Composers of lesser significance include Rafael Anglès (1731–1816), Vincente Rodríguez (ca. 1685–1760), Sebastiàn de Albero (1722–1756), Félix Máximo López (1742–1821), Juan Sessé (1736–1827), Narciso Casanovas (1747–1799), Felipe Rodríguez (1759–1814), and Joaquín Montero (fl. 1764–1815).

In England the modern genres led the way. Here foreign-born composers dominated the scene, as we have seen with instrument building at the time. The work of Scarlatti and Alberti, for instance, was very popular. An important Italian active in London was Felice de Giardini (1716–1796); another was Muzio Clementi, who will be discussed below. In addition to the Italians were the Germans, including Johann Christian Bach (see below), Ignaz Pleyel (1757–1831), and the virtuoso Daniel Steibelt (see below). Then there was the Dutchman Pieter Hellendaal (1721–1799). Among the native English composers were Charles Avison (1709–1770), Thomas Augustine Arne (1710–1778), John Christopher Smith (1712–1795), James Nares (1715–1783), Charles Burney (1726–1814), author of the famous history of music, and James Hook (1746–1827). While Smith composed suites and sonatas in which elements of the one type appear in the other, Arne's set, *Sonatas or Lessons* (8, 1756), may be the first pieces explicitly called sonatas published in England; as in those of Smith, they combine elements from both suite and sonata, as their title suggests. These are mostly two-movement works, but there are some in one (variation form) and in four. Their style is italianate. The two types appear in the sonatas of Burney (6, 1761), who also produced pieces for piano duet.

NEW DEVELOPMENTS IN GERMANY

There seems little doubt about the decisive role of the Italian composers in the development of the sonata as the principal new genre of keyboard music, particularly in the galant style. The influence of Italian musicians generally was felt all over Europe and was usually accepted with enthusiasm, although at some places rejected. Occasionally it provoked spirited controversy, especially in France, where the relative merits of French and Italian music were the subject of heated debate. This situation is reflected in Couperin's conciliatory work, *Les goûts réunis* (1724). But in 1739 Jean Guilain published his *Pièces de clavecin d'un goût nouveau* in which the new taste is plainly the Italian galant. Nevertheless, it was not in France that the new Italian style had its most far-reaching effects: that took place in Germany. Here elements of the new were taken, altered, and combined with older conceptions, leading to the establishment of the genres of instrumental music so familiar today. This development, once again, is difficult to survey. While the starting and ending points are reasonably certain, the steps in between remain far from clear. We can best proceed by distinguishing the older and more conservative works from those that involve the progressive elements from Italy.

The old tradition of the keyboard toccata—and its association with fugue—was continued by Ferdinand Tobias Richter (1651–1711), Wilhelm Hieronymus Pachelbel (1686–1764), Gottlieb (or Theophilus) Muffat (1690–1770), and Johann Ernst Eberlin (1702–1762). Muffat not only continued to write fugues but even perpetuated its older versions, the ricercar and canzona. The fugue also was continued by two pupils of J. S. Bach, Johann Ludwig Krebs (1713–1780) and Johann Philipp Kirnberger (1721–1783); it ultimately became an essentially didactic genre, as reflected in the work of the Viennese theorist Johann Georg Albrechtsberger (1736–1809), although there are some important exceptions to this characterization, as we will see.

More important is the suite. We have already considered the contributions of Handel, Graupner, and Mattheson. Among others who continued the genre are Ferdinand Tobias Richter, Heinrich Nicolaus Gerber (1702–1775), and particularly Gottlieb Muffat, whose set is *Componimenti musicali* (published ca. 1739). Here we find a mixture of the old and the new. Both unity of tonality and the four basic dances appear; four of the suites have eight movements while two have ten. But the new cantabile style, with its bent toward simplicity, came to the fore, particularly in the slower of the older dances, the allemande and sarabande. These always have a clear reprise in the section following the double-bar, thus "rounded" binary form. French and Italian elements appear side by side in the courantes and gigues; in both, but particularly in the gigues, homophony is the rule. Muffat introduced his suites by preludes in sectional form in which imitation is prominent; the prelude of the Suite in C major is a French overture. Movements independent of dances and identified by their tempo markings, and thus more associated with the sonata, also appear.

The suite is also important in the work of Johann Peter Kellner (1705–1772). There are two publications: *Certamen musicum* (Musical Contest, published in succession 1739–1749) and *Manipulus Musices, oder eine Handvoll kurzweiliger Zeitvertreib vors Klavier* (A Small Bundle of Music, or a Handful of Diverting Amusements for the Keyboard, 1753–1756). Here again we can observe elements from the Italian sonata in the suite. In the *Certamen musicum* we find suites that in fact bear little relation to the established form of the genre, so completely has the idea of the sonata taken hold. The preludes and fugues and the allemandes are the only conventional elements that Kellner has retained. The sarabande has been transformed into a simple lyric slow movement in triple time, and in all but one instance a fast Allegro in binary form serves as finale, replacing the gigue. In his *Manipulus Musices*, on the other hand, Kellner has carried the process to the point that none of the dances characteristic of the suite appear at all. Other composers who wrote music in which elements of the suite and the sonata are mixed are the Swede Johan Helmich Roman (1694–1758), Anton Franz Maichelbeck (1702–1750), and Jacob Wilhelm Lustig (1706–1796).

Much the same situation obtains in the work of Conrad Friedrich Hurlebusch (ca. 1696–1765), a German who worked in Amsterdam and who published three collections containing suites and sonatas: *Composizioni musi-*

cali (ca. 1733) and two sets each with the title *Sonate di cembalo* (op. 5 and 6, presumably 1746). While in the first set we find suites in the old tradition, in the latter ones Hurlebusch introduced elements of the sonata.

Symbolic of this change is a new term that came into use at the time—divertimento, which suggests the aim of the music as entertainment and diversion. But the term was used often and rather freely at the time and in different contexts, so that we need to determine the meaning in each case. Generally in the earlier phase the divertimento may be associated with the suite and indeed we have already encountered it in the work of Durante. Most prominent here was the Viennese Johann Christoph Wagenseil (1715–1777). Between 1753 and 1770[18] in Vienna Wagenseil published six sets called divertimenti or sonatas in which once again elements from the sonata have replaced those related to the suite. These pieces are mostly in three movements, two fast ones separated by a minuet. Binary form is used in the fast movements, with thematic material consisting of short motives. Yet Wagenseil retained but few of the traditional types: the gigue, polacca, minuet, and in one case, a prelude (identified as *ricercata*). Besides these divertimenti Wagenseil published an earlier set of suites (*Suavis artificiose elaboratus concentus musicus*, 1740), while various others, including a few sonatas, are preserved in manuscript: all reveal the same traits.

Thus, in Wagenseil as in Kellner, and in several others, the suite was giving way to the sonata. On the other hand, an isolated but in many ways interesting sonata by Gottfried Heinrich Stöltzel (1690–1749), entitled *Enharmonische Klavier-Sonate* (published posthumously 1761), shows a conservative formal orientation. It consists of a prelude in the small form, a rather free fugue, and a fast finale, but it is noteworthy for its enharmonic modulations that necessitate the use of equal temperament. Stöltzel also produced a suite in G minor. Other conservative sonatas that show some influence from the suite can be found in Johann Michael Breunich (1699–1755); Johann Agrell (1701–1765), a Swedish musician active in Germany; Mathias Georg Monn (1717–1750); Friedrich Wilhelm Marpurg (1718–1795); Johann Friedrich Agricola (1720–1774); Johann Philip Kirnberger; Johann Nikolaus Tischer (1707–1774); Johann Ernst Bach (1722–1777); Franz Vollrath Buttstett (1735–1814); and Johann Gottfried Krebs (1741–1814).

Among the composers who gave the new genre a more important place in their work were Johann Joseph Fux (1660–1741) and Johann Adolf Hasse (1699–1783). Fux, the Viennese theorist, composed four suites and seven sonatas. While most of the sonatas are in the modern three-movement scheme, one has two movements and another has three but in the sequence Adagio–Allegro–Adagio. The style is conservative, with themes of the Baroque *Fortspinnung*-type and counterpoint dominating.

Hasse, one of the last great masters of the Italian *opera seria*, on the other hand, included seventeen sonatas among his keyboard compositions; of these six were published by Walsh in London (op. 7, 1758). Although he cast his sonatas in two, three, and four movements, for eight of them he used the three-movement scheme with minuets as finales. The part-writing is largely homophonic, in all respects that of the Italian galant. The only noteworthy feature is their greater length, compared with other sonatas of the time. Thus once again we have Italianate music in a German context. We have seen essentially the same thing in Platti, for instance, an Italian working in Germany, who in his title described his work as being "sur le goût italien" (in the Italian taste).

Among the lesser composers of the latter half of the eighteenth century who worked with the sonata in this way are Georg Andreas Sorge (1703–1778), Christoph Schaffrath (1709–1763), Christoph Nichelmann (1717–1762), Leopold Mozart (1719–1787), Friedrich Gottlob Fleischer (1722–1806), Georg (or Jiri) Benda (1722–1795), Johann Georg Lang (1722–1798), Georg Simon Löhlein (1725–1781), Johann Christoph Monn (1726–1782), Josef Anton Stěpán (1726–1797), Johann Friedrich Daube (ca. 1730–1797), Ignaz von Beecke (1733–1803), Ernst Wilhelm Wolf (1735–1792), Karl Friedrich Fasch (1736–1800), Christian Gottlob Neefe (1748–1798), Friedrich Wilhelm Rust (1739–1796), and Johann Gottlieb Naumann (1741–1801).

More important is the work of the sons of Bach: Wilhelm Friedemann (1710–1784), Carl Philipp Emanuel (1714–1788), Johann Christoph Friedrich Ernst (1732–1795), and Johann Christian (1735–1782). Of these Johann Christoph Friedrich Ernst (the "Bückeburg Bach") is the least known. His sonatas, which he qualified as "leicht" (easy), appeared in two sets, 1785 and 1789, are in three movements, and exemplify the galant character. The most important among Bach's sons was Carl Philipp Emanuel, who held prestigious positions in Berlin and Hamburg, associated himself with leading musicians and writers, and was accounted among the foremost composers of his time. He was the author of a celebrated treatise on keyboard playing, *Versuch über die wahre Art das Klavier zu spielen* (Essay on the True Art of Playing the Keyboard, 1753 and 1762). His most important contribution to keyboard music involves sets that consist mostly of sonatas.

C. P. E. BACH'S PUBLISHED SETS CONTAINING SONATAS

NOTE: Works that are not sonatas are designated [f] for fantasia and [r] for rondo.[19]

A SET DEDICATED TO FREDERICK THE GREAT ("PRUSSIAN SONATAS," COMPOSED 1740–1742, PUBLISHED 1742 OR 1743)

F major (H. 24/Wq. 48 i)	C minor (H. 27/Wq. 48 iv)
B-flat major (H. 25/Wq. 48 ii)	C major (H. 28/Wq. 48 v)
E major (H. 26/Wq. 48 iii)	A major (H. 29/Wq. 48 vi)

A SET DEDICATED TO THE DUKE OF WÜRTTEMBERG ("WÜRTTEMBERG
SONATAS," COMPOSED 1742–1743, PUBLISHED 1744)

A minor (H. 30/Wq. 49 i)   B-flat major (H. 32/Wq. 49 iv)
A-flat major (H. 31/Wq. 49 ii)   E-flat major (H. 34/Wq. 49 v)
E minor (H. 33/Wq. 49 iii)   B minor (H. 36/Wq. 49 vi)

PROBESTÜCKE (EXERCISE PIECES, 18 IN SIX SONATAS, PUBLISHED AS A
SUPPLEMENT TO HIS TREATISE, 1753)

C major (H. 70/Wq. 63 i)   B minor (H. 73/Wq. 63 iv)
D minor (H. 71/Wq. 63 ii)   E-flat major (H. 74/Wq. 63 v)
A major (H. 72/Wq. 63 iii)   F minor (H. 75/Wq. 63 vi)

A SET OF SIX *SONATEN MIT VERÄNDERTEN REPRISEN* (SONATAS WITH
VARIED REPRISES, "AMALIEN" SONATAS, COMPOSED 1758–1759,
PUBLISHED 1760)

F major (H. 136/Wq. 50 i)   D minor (H. 139/Wq. 50 iv)
G major (H. 137/Wq. 50 ii)   B-flat major (H. 126/Wq. 50 v)
A minor (H. 138/Wq. 50 iii)   C minor (H. 140/Wq. 50 vi)

A SET OF SIX (COMPOSED 1750–1760, PUBLISHED 1761)

C major (H. 150/Wq. 51 i)   D minor (H. 128/Wq. 51 iv)
B-flat major (H. 151/Wq. 51 ii) F major (H. 141/Wq. 51 v)
C minor (H. 127/Wq. 51 iii)   G major (H. 62/Wq. 51 vi)

A SET OF SIX (COMPOSED 1744–1762, PUBLISHED 1763)

E-flat major (H. 50/Wq. 52 i)   F-sharp minor (H. 37/Wq. 52 iv)
D minor (H. 142/Wq. 52 ii)   E major (H. 163/Wq. 52 v)
G minor (H. 158/Wq. 52 iii)   E minor (H. 129/Wq. 52 vi)

SIX VOLUMES OF SONATAS, RONDOS, AND FANTASIAS *FÜR KENNER UND
LIEBHABER* ("FOR CONNOISSEURS AND AMATEURS," PUBLISHED 1779–
1787)

SET I (COMPOSED 1758–1773, PUBLISHED 1779)

C major (H. 244/Wq. 55 i)   A major (H. 186/Wq. 55 iv)
F major (H. 130/Wq. 55 ii)   F major (H. 243/Wq. 55 v)
D major (H. 245/Wq. 55 iii)   G major (H. 187/Wq. 55 vi)

SET II (COMPOSED 1774–1780, PUBLISHED 1780)

[r] C major (H. 260/Wq. 56 i)   F major (H. 269/Wq. 56 iv)
G major (H. 246/Wq. 56 ii)   [r] A minor (H. 262/Wq. 56 v)
[r] D major (H. 261/Wq. 56 iii) A major (H. 270/Wq. 56 vi)

SET III (COMPOSED 1763–1781, PUBLISHED 1781)

[r] E major (H. 265/Wq. 57 i)   D minor (H. 208/Wq. 57 iv)
A minor (H. 247/Wq. 57 ii)   [r] F major (H. 266/Wq. 57 v)
G major (H. 271/Wq. 57 iii)   F minor (H. 173/Wq. 57 vi)

SET IV (COMPOSED 1765–1782, PUBLISHED 1783)

[r] A major (H. 276/Wq. 58 i)   [r] B-flat major (H. 267/Wq. 58 v)
G major (H. 273/Wq. 58 ii)   [f] E-flat major (H. 277/Wq. 58 vi)
[r] E major (H. 274/Wq. 58 iii)   [f] A major (H. 278/Wq. 58 vii)
E minor (H. 188/Wq. 58 iv)

SET V (COMPOSED 1779–1784, PUBLISHED 1785)

E minor–major (H. 281/   [r] C minor (H. 283/Wq. 59 iv)
   Wq. 59 i)   [f] F major (H. 279/Wq. 59 v)
[r] G major (H. 268/Wq. 59 ii)   [f] C major (H. 284/Wq. 59 vi)
B-flat major (H. 282/Wq. 59 iii)

SET VI (COMPOSED 1785–1786, PUBLISHED 1787)

[r] E-flat major (H. 288/   [r] D minor (H. 290/Wq. 61 iv)
   Wq. 61 i)   G major (H. 287/Wq. 61 v)
D major (H. 286/Wq. 61 ii)   [f] C major (H. 291/Wq. 61 vi)
[f] B-flat major (H. 289/
   Wq. 61 iii)

Numerous individual works appeared in anthologies. Estimates as to the total number of his sonatas have varied; current listings show around 150. While many remained in manuscript, many were published, usually shortly after composition. Most of them were composed during his years with Frederick the Great (1740–1768): he composed only around thirty in the twenty-odd years in Hamburg, among them such sets as the out-and-out galant sonatas *à l'usage des dames* (H. 184, 185, 204–207/Wq. 54, composed 1765–1766, published 1770) along with the important sets *für Kenner und Liebhaber*. In addition Bach composed a number of minuets, polonaises, sets of variations (one on the "Folies d'Espagne"), and independent rondos; of the latter his "Abschied von meinem Silbermannschen Klavier" (Parting from My Silbermann Clavier [H. 272/Wq. 66], composed 1781) in E minor has become well-known.

Most arresting historically is that C. P. E. Bach ignored the suite and worked instead with the modern form, the sonata. If in Hasse we noted an effort to make the sonata a bigger and more important genre by casting individual movements on a larger scale, we also find this intent in C. P. E. Bach, but in a different way: he increased the range and power of expression. This is immediately evident in the first "Prussian" Sonata in F major. In its slow movement we find passages reminiscent of the operatic recitative and elaborate indications of dynamics, in some cases with provision for a cadenza. In the first movement of the second sonata, after the double-bar comes a long passage in the style of a toccata. In its second movement we find expressive chromaticism and dissonance (see Ex. 2-7). Much the same may be seen in the "Württemberg" Sonatas where the interest in expression appears in the

Example 2-7. C. P. E. Bach: Adagio from Sonata in B-flat major (Prussian Sonatas 2 [H. 25/Wq. 48 ii])—Beginning (mm. 1–6)

first movements, here related to explicit changes in tempo. Dynamic markings abound throughout the set.

The sonata with varied reprise represents a special type that appeared first in 1760 but that recurs only here and there. The variation of the reprise, moreover, is not quite what one might expect: in the first place, it appears only in the outside Allegro movements; in the second, it involves not the recapitulation but rather all the repetitions in the movement. Such a movement is always in binary form, each part to be repeated, but where normally the double-bar with repeat marks would appear, in the movements with varied reprises Bach has eliminated the double-bar and written everything out in full to allow the variations to be made. In earlier examples the types of variation are simple enough—application of figuration, triplets and scale-runs to the melody—but later the process of variation becomes more elaborate and subtle. Again, cadenza-like passages appear.

The sonatas found in the six collections *für Kenner und Liebhaber* represent Bach's most ambitious work. Clearly the audience for these works did not consist of unskilled amateurs who sought entertainment and diversion; rather he aimed at those who had a certain amount of knowledge of music and some sophistication, that is, not merely amateurs but dilettantes and connoisseurs, as is suggested by the term *Kenner.*

To consider, first, the sonatas contained here, the three-movement scheme remains standard, with the slow movement in a contrasting but related key. Among the departures we can note the linking of movements to emphasize continuity in the sonata as a whole (from Set I, sonatas in F major and B minor; Set II, sonatas in G major and F major; Set III, A minor; Set IV, G major; Set V, E minor; Set VI, D major). There is an increase in the degree of elaboration in the first movements, involving particularly the use of themes compounded of short motives. These are exploited in the continuation and the recapitulations. The slow movements continue to be serious and expressive, again with recitative-like passages as well as passages that imply *senza misura* (no strict beating of time), something common in the fantasia (see below). Particularly large are the sonatas in A major and C major, of Set I, which deserve greater recognition than has up to now been accorded them.

Two other genres are represented in this large collection, the fantasia and the rondo. The fantasia represents one of Bach's most individual contributions to the repertory of keyboard music. In the last chapter of his treatise, Bach clearly explained the aim of this sort of piece. The discussion suggests that the background of the fantasia lies in improvisation. As Bach puts it, "a fantasia is said to be free when it is unmeasured and moves through more keys than is customary in other pieces which are composed or improvised in meter." Further, "a free fantasia consists of varied harmonic progressions which can be expressed in all manner of figuration and motives." Such a work is obviously related to the improvised prelude, except that a prelude "prepares the listener for the content of the piece that follows . . . [and] is more restricted than the fantasia,"[20] the latter being completely independent. In the rest of the account Bach offers suggestions for suitable modulations in the improvising of a free fantasia, but emphasizes that the piece must be oriented to a particular tonality.

The fantasias in sets IV, V, and VI of the collection *für Kenner und Liebhaber* obviously are related to this improvised free fantasia. They are sectional works that incorporate much variety, with figuration dominant in the thematic material, passages in free rhythm (unmeasured, *senza misura*) that often involve solo lines, cadenza-like passages ending in fermatas, and sudden changes in harmony (usually chromatic), style, and texture. The Fantasia in E-flat major, from Set IV (H. 277/Wq. 58 vi), for instance, is in three large sections, the first consisting solely of figuration, arpeggios being prominent, with a recitative passage in the middle (see Ex. 2-8); then comes the Poco Adagio, a primarily chordal passage barred in the regular way but with unusual harmonies; finally an Allegro brings back much of the material of the first part.

Two other compositions of this type are not part of the series *für Kenner und Liebhaber*. First, the celebrated Fantasia in C minor (H. 868/Wq. 254, published 1753), included among the illustrative examples in the treatise on keyboard playing, is a work whose expressive power moved the poet Heinrich von Gerstenberg to fit words to it. This he did in two versions, one adapting a soliloquy of Hamlet, the other one of Socrates. The second is the Fantasia in F-sharp minor (H. 300/Wq. 67, composed and published 1787), known as "C. P. E. Bach's Empfindungen" (C. P. E. Bach's Feelings).

The remaining genre in the sets *für Kenner und Liebhaber* is the rondo, which appears in all but Set I. Here the basic scheme is that of the French rondeau, which originally was a dance with the opening section repeated, but

Example 2-8. C. P. E. Bach: Fantasia in E-flat major (*für Kenner und Liebhaber*, Set 4 [H. 277/Wq. 58 vi])—Beginning (m. 1)

contrasting sections, any number of episodes or couplets, appeared between the repetitions. Bach's rondo, however, is more elaborate than the French examples, in keeping with the general trend of his work; the dance aspect is largely eliminated, thematic variation is employed in the rondo section, and occasional passages in free style suggest the fantasia.

In addition, during the period 1754–1757 Bach produced a number of what we call character pieces—short pieces with titles indicative of expressive character or affect, as in "Les langueurs tendres" (H. 110/Wq. 117, 30) and "La capricieuse" (H. 113/Wq. 117, 33). Others are musical portraits of people he knew, as in "La Gleim" (H. 89/Wq. 117, 19). The forms he used are simple: rondo or rounded binary schemes predominate, and many of them are in fact stylized dances.[21]

C. P. E. Bach's work generally has been associated with a peculiarly Germanic trend in the late eighteenth century known as *Empfindsamkeit*, a term difficult to translate but meaning roughly "sensibility" or "sensitivity." This is central in Bach's work, particularly evident in the fantasias and the slow movements of sonatas. Here we clearly see a central issue of the period—the expression of affects by means of purely instrumental music, such music regarded as the "language of emotion (Sprache der Empfindung)."[22] To render the emotional style, Bach preferred that most emotional among the keyboard instruments, the clavichord, which by virtue of this typically Germanic aesthetic held its own in his work in spite of the general ascendance of the piano. The role of emotional expression in Bach's music—and in his playing, in which the large role given to improvisation is difficult to assess today—is well supported both in his own writings, as already suggested, and in those of his contemporaries. Carl Friedrich Cramer referred to "the endless nuances of shade and light" that were heard in Bach's playing, while Reichardt emphasized the range of dynamics that Bach could elicit from his instrument. Reichardt added elsewhere that when Bach plays "his whole soul is involved" and that Bach was the first to bring such complete expressive power to keyboard music. Schubart stated, "when I wish to play a sonata by Bach I must allow myself wholly to sink into the spirit of this great man, so that my own identity becomes Bach's own idiom." All this, then, lifts Bach into a critical position in the development of the new instrumental music in general and keyboard music in particular. In his time he was regarded as an original, even an original genius (*Originalgenie*), and his influence is difficult to overestimate.

Wilhelm Friedemann Bach, the oldest of Bach's sons, has been called the most gifted among them. But in temperament he was restless, a wanderer, unable or unwilling to hold a position for any length of time. Yet he had an enormous reputation as a performer, especially for the originality and brilliance of his improvisations. We can assume that much of his keyboard music was never committed to paper so that what we have represents but a fraction of his actual work. There are sonatas (9, F. 1–9,[23] two of which were published, D major, ca. 1745, and E-flat major, 1748); fantasias (10, F. 14–23, 1778); a set of fugues (8, F. 31, published 1778); a set of polonaises arranged by key (12, F. 12, published ca. 1765); and a concerto for two claviers in F major (F. 10, composed ca. 1773). His fugues, while strictly contrapuntal and employing expressive chromatic harmonies, would tend to connect him with the older generation, but they are on a smaller scale than those of his father; the polonaises are also conservative. The sonatas and fantasias, on the other hand, place him well in the forefront among his contemporaries. The sonatas in particular clearly show his essentially progressive approach: the three-movement scheme is used in conjunction with the Italianate cantabile melody and the expressive traits characteristic of the work of his brother.

If the compositions of C. P. E. Bach and Wilhelm Friedemann Bach represent the more Germanic type of sonata in which serious expression is important, those of the younger brother, Johann Christian Bach, represent the ingratiating and diverting type from the Italian galant at its finest. Johann Christian learned the style in Milan, where he studied with Padre Martini, and he practiced it in London, where he arrived in 1762. The bulk of his keyboard music is in fact given over to sonatas, of which the main collections are two sets (6, op. 5, published 1766, and 6, op. 17, published ca. 1779); other sets were issued later, so that the total number is twenty-two, including three for piano duet.[24] All bear the qualification "for harpsichord or piano," an option that remained common until the early nineteenth century. Most are three-movement works, but a significant minority have two movements. Especially Italianate are the first movements, which feature the cantabile ("singing Allegro") type of theme over a stereotyped accompaniment: among many examples are the sonatas in E-flat major, G major, and A major of op. 17. The first movement of the Sonata in G major (op. 17 iv), for instance, shows all these features: a singing Allegro theme over a simple stereotyped accompaniment, simple harmonies, several themes in the first section, a short

Title page for Johann Christian Bach's *Six sonates pour le clavecin ou le piano forte*, op. 5. London, 1766.
From *Decorative Music Title Pages*, G. S. Fraenkel, ed., Dover Publications, Inc., 1968.

development (more like a transition), and an abbreviated recapitulation. Unusually large is the Sonata in D major (op. 5 ii), that through the use of full chords, dynamic contrasts, and tremolos creates an orchestra-like effect (Ex. 2-9). This is not uncommon in the latter part of the eighteenth century, and such pieces are often in D major. A different work in which Johann Christian Bach approaches the pathétique character is the Sonata in C minor (op. 17 iv), yet the galant also plays an important role in the work, particularly in the sections in E-flat major. Unlike C. P. E. Bach, who used binary form in his finales, J. C. Bach shows greater variety—minuet, variations, rondeau—so that his repertory of forms for the finales resembles that of the Classic period.

For the rest, Johann Christian's output contains sonatas and pieces for four hands and two keyboard instruments. In addition we find two genres that became characteristic of keyboard music—the set of variations on popular melodies and the arrangement of popular orchestral pieces for keyboard. J. C. Bach also produced collections of operatic overtures arranged for keyboard. These last two genres particularly have the dilettante musician in mind, and both became numerous in the late-eighteenth and nineteenth centuries.

Example 2-9. J. C.. BACH: Allegro from Sonata in D major (op. 5 ii)—Beginning (mm. 1–10)

A composer who since the 1960s has emerged as a figure of some significance is Johann Gottfried Müthel (1728–1788), a pupil of J. S. Bach who also had contacts with Telemann and C. P. E. Bach. Again the number of works to come down is small, mostly published in 1756. In all there seem to be nine sonatas, a set of forty-two minuets, two sets of variations (called *Ariosi*), and a keyboard duet. Again the sonatas draw the most attention: Müthel adopted the three-movement scheme but expanded the dimensions of the individual works so that each sonata is roughly twice as long as what was normal at the time. The tendency toward seriousness of expression noted in C. P. E. Bach is also present here: the characteristically varied and elaborately conceived themes full of dynamic contrasts, short rests, and sudden changes of style and register. The same features occur in the variations. Burney noted Müthel's unusual qualities, associating him with C. P. E. Bach but attributing many innovations to him: "I should not hesitate to rank them [Müthel's compositions] among the greatest productions of the present age."[25] Müthel's individual and extreme form of expression set him apart from most of his contemporaries.

FRANCE AT THE END OF THE CENTURY

The influence of the new Italian galant instrumental music was less in France than in Germany. The sonata, for instance, was generally neglected in France. Around 1742, however, a set of six for keyboard was published by Jean Barrière (ca. 1705–1747): these are clearly related to the *sonata da chiesa*. On the other hand, German composers active in Paris from around the middle of the century, such as Johann Schobert (ca. 1735–1767) and Johann Gottfried Eckard (1735–1809), both celebrated keyboardists, published a number of sonatas in the three-movement scheme. While Schobert's were primarily intended for harpsichord, those of Eckard, especially the set published in 1764, were specifically intended for the Stein piano and drew on the special qualities of that instrument (see the discussion earlier in this chapter). This is obvious from the many markings conditioned by the piano: *rinforzando, mezza voce, tenuto, legato*, and so on. Other German musicians active in Paris were Nicolas Joseph Hüllmandel (1756–1823) and Jean-Frédéric Edelmann (originally Johann Friedrich, 1749–1794), the latter advancing the cause of the piano in France.

One French composer of the time whose work merits revival is Claude Balbastre (1729–1799), a pupil of Rameau well known for his virtuoso performances. His keyboard works reveal him to have been associated with the progressive tendencies represented by the German composers just surveyed. His *Pièces de clavecin* (published 1759) show the three-movement scheme of the modern sonata. In these works Balbastre distinguished between the two styles to which we have been referring: the *style intrigué*, the "learned" style of contrapuntal imitation, and the *style galant*, the new pleasing Italianate manner. He also composed sets of variations, one on the "Marseillaise," others on Christmas melodies (*Noëls*, published 1770), along with arrangements of operatic arias. In his publications Balbastre made it clear that the piano could be used in the performance of his works, but the "Marseillaise" variations he intended expressly for piano. Among other native-born French composers we can list Étienne Nicolas Méhul (1763–1817), Jean-Louis Adam (1758–1848), and two composers better known for their operas, Adrien Boieldieu (1775–1834) and Ferdinand Hérold (1791–1833).

Finally, an important genre of the latter part of the eighteenth century that figures prominently in the work of composers in Paris is the accompanied keyboard sonata. This genre occupies an equivocal position in the repertory, part keyboard music, part ensemble chamber music. Basically it is a keyboard sonata with the accompaniment of other instruments, usually violin or flute, sometimes with violoncello, or even others, such as a pair of horns, added as well. The keyboard part has the greatest importance, the accompanying instruments often merely doubling the upper and/or lower voice or voices of the keyboard part, so that in most cases they could be omitted without deforming the work. The genre experienced a rush of popularity in the late eighteenth century.

Its optional instrumentation and the possibility of performance on the keyboard instrument alone (but not in all cases) made the genre appealing to the class of amateur musicians to which it obviously was directed. Along with Schobert and Eckard, Louis-Gabriel Guillemain (1705–1770), Michel Corrette (1709–1795), Jean-Joseph Cassanéa de Mondonville (1711–1772), Jean-Jacques Beauvarlet-Charpentier (1734–1794), Jean-François Tapray (1738–ca. 1819), and Nicolas Séjan (1745–1819), among many others, composed such sonatas. Composers elsewhere also worked with the genre, including Cramer, Clementi, even Haydn and Mozart, and later Dussek, Hummel, and Czerny (more on these later). Generally, though, it had passed its heyday by the 1790s and was superseded by the true sonata for violin and piano in which the parts for each instrument have equal importance (early instances of which were often identified by the qualification *en duo, concertante,* or *obligé*) or, on the other hand, the piano trio.

Fundamental changes took place in the keyboard music of the eighteenth century. The older forms—toccata, fugue, suite—declined while the sonata emerged as the principal new genre. Early in the century the sonata took many forms; by the end of the century much standardization had taken place. This development was carried out primarily by Italian composers, but the lead then passed to Germans. The sons of J. S. Bach were important; C. P. E. Bach and W. F. Bach particularly imparted a new seriousness of expression to the sonata, and their example was followed, for instance, by Müthel. While most keyboard works of the latter half of the eighteenth century were marked *per il cembalo o forte piano* or *pour le clavecin ou fortepiano,* here and there we find music specifically intended for the piano, commencing as early as 1732 with Giustini (an isolated instance) and including Müthel, Eckardt, Balbastre, and Johann Christian Bach, among others. The new style of expressive music had found its proper instrumental medium by the end of the century.

NOTES FOR CHAPTER TWO

1. See, for instance, R. Marshall, "Bach the Progressive: Observations on His Later Works," *Musical Quarterly* 62 (1976): 313–357.

2. Quoted by R. Steglich, "Karl Philipp Emanuel Bach und der Dresdner Kreuzkantor Gottfried August Homilius im Musikleben ihrer Zeit," *Bach Jahrbuch* 12 (1915): 136 n. 33.

3. J. Scheibe, *Critischer Musikus,* Stück 13, quoted in E. Bücken, "Der galante Stil," *Zeitschrift für Musikwissenschaft* 6 (1924): 419.

4. Friedrich Marpurg, *Der critische Musicus an der Spree*, Stück 27 (2 September 1749): 215.

5. See E. Good, *Giraffes, Black Dragons and Other Pianos* (Stanford: Stanford University Press, 1987), 28–39.

6. TWV numbers from M. Ruhnke, *Georg Philipp Telemann: Thematisch-systematisches Verzeichnis seiner Werke*, vol. 1 (Kassel: Bärenreiter, 1984).

7. HWV numbers from B. Baselt, *[Handel:] Thematisch-systematisches Verzeichnis: Instrumentalmusik*. Händel-Handbuch 3. Kassel: Bärenreiter, 1986; keyboard music, 212–337.

8. See M. Cauchie, *Thematic Index of the Works of François Couperin* (Monaco: Lyrebird, 1949).

9. B. Priestman, "Catalogue thématique des oeuvres de Jean-Baptiste, John et Jacques Loeillet," *Revue belge de musicologie* 6 (1952): 226–227.

10. See R. Kirkpatrick, *Domenico Scarlatti* (1953; reprint, Princeton: Princeton University Press, 1983), 251–270 (Ch. 11). Kirkpatrick's principal critic is J. Sheveloff, "Domenico Scarlatti: Tercentenary Frustrations," *Musical Quarterly* 71 (1985): 399–436 and 72 (1986): 90–118.

11. W. Gerstenberg, *Die Klavierkompositionen Domenico Scarlattis*, Forschungsarbeiten des musikwissenschaftlichen Instituts der Universität Leipzig (1933; reprint, Regensburg: Bosse, 1969); R. Benton, "Form in the Sonatas of Domenico Scarlatti," *Music Review* 13 (1952): 264–273.

12. Kirkpatrick, *Domenico Scarlatti*, 265–271.

13. This and the following from Kirkpatrick, *Domenico Scarlatti*, 254–255. This book also contains his attempt at a chronology of Scarlatti's sonatas.

14. L. Hoffmann-Erbrecht, *Deutsche und italienische Klaviermusik zur Bachzeit*, Jenaer Beiträge zur Musikforschung 1 (Leipzig: VEB Breitkopf & Härtel, 1954), 69–71.

15. The L numbers are those assigned to Scarlatti's sonatas in A. Longo, *Scarlatti: Indice tematico delle sonate per clavicembalo* (Milan: Ricordi, 1912); L.S. refers to the supplement; the K numbers, which represent the attempt to classify the sonatas chronologically, have been assigned by Kirkpatrick.

16. C. Burney, *A General History of Music*, vol. 2, ed. P. Scholes (London: Oxford, 1958), 706.

17. Hoffmann-Erbrecht, *Deutsche und italienische Klaviermusik zur Bachzeit*, 81.

18. H. Scholz-Michelitsch, *Das Klavierwerk von Georg Joseph Wagenseil: ein thematischer Katalog*, Tabulae musicae austriacae 3 (Vienna: Böhlau, 1966).

19. The H numbers refer to E. Helm, *Thematic Catalogue of the Works of Carl Philipp Emanuel Bach* (New Haven: Yale, 1989), used in Helm's article on the composer in *The New Grove Dictionary of Music and Musicians* (1980), 1: 855–857, based on the chronology of composition; the Wq numbers refer to the older thematic catalog, A. Wotquenne, *Thematisches Verzeichnis der Werke Carl Philipp Emanuel Bachs* (Leipzig: Breitkopf & Härtel, 1905), mostly based on the chronology of publication; see also R. Wade, *The Catalog of Carl Philipp Emanuel Bach's Estate* (New York: Garland, 1981).

20. These quotations are from C. P. E. Bach, *Essay on the True Art of Playing Keyboard Instruments*, trans. W. Mitchell (New York: Norton, 1949), 430.

21. D. Berg, "C. P. E. Bach's Character Pieces and His Friendship Circle," *C. P. E. Bach Studies*, ed. S. Clark (Oxford: Clarendon Press, 1988), 1–32.

22. This and the following quotations compiled by Steglich, *Bach-Jahrbuch* 12 (1915): 81, 83.

23. F numbers assigned in M. Falck, *W. F. Bach* (Leipzig: Kahnt, 1913).

24. I. Baierle, *Die Klavierwerke von Johann Christian Bach*, Dissertationen der Universität Graz 24 (Vienna: Verlag der wissenschaftlichen Gesellschaften Österreichs, 1974).

25. C. Burney, *The Present State of Music in Germany*, ed. P. Scholes, 2: 240.

CHAPTER THREE

Haydn, Mozart, Beethoven, and Their Contemporaries

It has been said that to be a genius is to be the right person in the right place at the right time. In the world of late eighteenth-century music, such criteria required someone who could take the diverse traditions, forms, types, and genres, and, by judiciously combining them, provide the foundation for the new instrumental music. Fate indeed put such a person on the scene at a critical time: Haydn. Yet his work was both continued and carried into different directions by the two other great figures of the Classic period, Mozart and Beethoven; and Mozart as his younger contemporary in fact influenced the old master in some respects. Our survey will also include other composers.

HAYDN

Joseph Haydn (1732–1809) was able to exploit both the old and the new. On the one hand he was for most of his career in the service of aristocratic families in and around Vienna, particularly the Esterházys, whom he served from 1761 to the end of his life; on the other hand, he was able to get much of his important music published, reaching a much larger audience than was possible for most composers. As the chart of his sonatas shows (see below), from 1774 on he was able to publish all of them not long after their composition. Another factor had to do with the decision of the Esterházy family to spend more and more time at their relatively isolated new summer palace, Esterháza. Thus, although Haydn began to feel cut off from what was going on in Vienna, he was also able to experiment, with the entire musical establishment at the court under his supervision. As he later put it, "I was forced to become original."[1]

Keyboard works do not actually occupy the most prominent position in Haydn's total output—he concentrated on the string quartet and symphony and some of the vocal genres. Among the keyboard works, the fifty-two solo piano sonatas constitute the most important group; our discussion will center around them. They can best be treated chronologically.

HAYDN'S PIANO SONATAS[2]

VIENNA AND LUKAVEC (1750s TO 1760)
    Earliest group (1750s)
        C major (No. 1)
        A major (No. 5, published ca. 1790)
        C major (No. 7)
        F major (No. 9)
        C major (No. 10, published ca. 1790)
        A major (No. 12)
        D major (No. 16)
        E-flat major (No. Es2)
        E-flat major (No. Es3)
        G major (No. G1)

    Four separate sonatas (ca. 1760)
        B-flat major (No. 2)
        G major (No. 6)
        G major (No. 8, published ca. 1790)
        E major (No. 13, published 1805)

ESTERHÁZY
    Nine separate sonatas (composed 1761–1771)
        C major (No. 3)
        D major (No. 4)
        D major (No. 14, published 1806)
        F major (No. 47, published ca. 1788)
        E-flat major (No. 45, published ca. 1788)
        D major (No. 19, published 1788)
        A-flat major (No. 46, published 1788)
        B-flat major (No. 18, published ca. 1788)
        G minor (No. 44, ca. 1788)

    Set of six sonatas (composed 1773, published 1774)
        C major (No. 21)   D major (No. 24)
        E-flat major (No. 22)   E-flat (No. 25)
        F major (No. 23)   A major (No. 26)

Set of six circulated in professionally made copies (composed ca. 1774–1776, distributed 1776, published 1781)

G major (No. 27)	A major (No. 30)
E-flat major (No. 28)	E major (No. 31)
F major (No. 29)	B minor (No. 32)

Set of six *Auenbrugger* sonatas (composed 1771–1780, published 1780)

C major (No. 35)	E-flat major (No. 38)
C-sharp minor (No. 36)	G major (No. 39)
D major (No. 37)	C minor (No. 20)[3]

Three sonatas (published individually 1783–1784)
    A-flat major (No. 43, composed mid 1770s)
    D major (No. 33, composed mid 1770s)
    E minor (No. 34, composed early 1780s)

THE LATE PERIOD (CA. 1784–CA. 1794)
Set of three for Maria Esterházy (composed and published 1784)
    G major (No. 40)
    B-flat major (No. 41)
    D major (No. 42)

Two sonatas published separately (both composed 1789–1790, published 1792)
    C major (No. 48)
    E-flat major (No. 49, for Maria Anna von Genzinger)

Three London sonatas
    D major (No. 51, composed 1789–1790, published ca. 1800)
    E-flat major (No. 52, composed 1794, published 1798)
    C major (No. 50, composed 1794–1795, published ca. 1800)

Fourteen sonatas fall into the first group, those composed during Haydn's time in Vienna following his dismissal from St. Stephen's and including the short period of employment at Lukavec. For the most part these works present a uniform character; they are closely related to the Viennese suite, the first two even bearing the alternative designation *partita*. Most of these early sonatas consist of three movements (No. 6 and 8 have four), all in the same key; one of these movements, usually the second or last, is a minuet and trio. The first and last movements often suggest the sonata principle: they are cast in the rounded binary form that derived from the dances of the suite, with a

Title page for Haydn's set of six sonatas for Caterina and Marianna d'Auenbrugger, composed 1771–1780, published 1780 by Artaria in Vienna.
From *Decorative Music Title Pages*, G. S. Fraenkel, ed., Dover Publications, Inc., 1968.

modulation to the dominant at the end of the first part and, after some excursion in the B part, a return to the tonic. Although themes vary in number, they lack contrast among themselves. Yet the overall scheme is the same as that of the sonata form that later was to take on such importance. The slow movements show the cantabile style—accompanied melody. The aura of simplicity is clear from the simple figuration patterns frequently employed in the accompaniments, especially the Alberti bass. The light, galant character is evident; these are small, unpretentious compositions, *Hausmusik* (domestic music) for keyboard.

Haydn composed some thirty sonatas from the time of his appointment by the Esterházys up to the middle of the 1780s—first nine individual works, then three clearly defined sets of six each, and finally three individual works. While many of these continue to reflect the galant tradition, in others we can note the effects of his isolation. We find him stimulated in part by the new expressive style of C. P. E. Bach, whose influence Haydn readily acknowledged, as well as by Müthel and others. Indeed, Haydn may have taken specific passages in Bach's sonatas as models: Haydn's sonatas in E-flat major

(No. 18), G minor (No. 44), A major (No. 32), C major (No. 48), among others, have been cited.[4] Yet Haydn's efforts were directed equally toward the establishment of a serious style for the new forms of instrumental music that hitherto had mostly galant connotations. Here we may see a broader aspect of C. P. E. Bach's influence. One indication of this new intensity is the use of the minor mode.

Among the sonatas that reveal this new aesthetic are those in G minor (No. 44, ca. 1770), just mentioned, C minor (No. 20, 1771–1780 [?]), B minor (No. 32, ca. 1775), E minor (No. 34, early 1780s), and C-sharp minor (No. 36, 1771–1780). Here Haydn exploited the passionate quality of the minor, striving for something more ambitious that encompasses a greater degree of intensity, yet he also maintained the traditional external form.

Still, most of the sonatas lack this extreme and powerful expression. While representing essentially the continuation of Haydn's earlier—galant—type of sonata, they show some unusual features. Haydn became preoccupied with the overall form of the work: in the Sonata in D major (No. 24, 1773), there is no break between the Adagio and the finale, while in the Sonata in A major (No. 30, ca. 1775), there are no breaks between any of the movements. He also put an unusual emphasis on counterpoint in some of the minuets: in the Sonata in E-flat major (No. 25, 1773), the minuet is canonic, and in the Sonata in A major (No. 26, 1773), it is *al rovescio*, the second half being the retrograde of the first. The Sonata in F major (No. 23, 1773), has an unusually expressive slow movement.

As an example of the unusual combinations and varieties that appear in this group of sonatas, let us consider one of them, the Sonata in C minor (No. 20, 1771 and later), a work that, as already indicated, shows the seriousness associated with the minor. It is in three movements—as indeed are the majority of Haydn's sonatas—a Moderato in 4/4 time, an Andante con moto, A-flat major in 3/4 time, and a final Allegro, again in 3/4 time. The first and last movements Haydn has cast according to the sonata principle, while the Andante is an aria-like piece in rounded binary form. From the standpoint of intensity of expression, the first movement draws the most attention, for it is here that the characteristic seriousness and intensity associated with the minor are most evident. The principal theme, although organized by two regular periods, comprises short motives and is elaborate rhythmically, with syncopations and unusual accentuations. Moreover the theme itself, in thirds, on its restatement is shifted from the right hand to the left, thus providing a measure of contrapuntal interest (see Ex. 3-1). The transition brings dynamic contrasts. A short cadenza-like passage comes before the secondary theme. Yet the closing theme, with its scale patterns and rapid broken-chord accompaniment, is wholly galant. Thus we can already see the balance and contrast among the various thematic elements, each with its own affect, which are so characteristic of late eighteenth-century instrumental music. The development section concentrates on the principal and closing themes, and accumulates figuration in a crescendo before ending with a reference to the transition.

Example 3-1. HAYDN: Moderato from Sonata in C minor (No. 20)—Beginning
(mm. 1–4)

Except for its shortening of the principal theme, the transition, and the key of
the secondary theme, the recapitulation presents the exposition unchanged.
The remaining movements are less problematical. The Andante consists of a
cantabile melody over a slow evenly moving bass and in the contrasting section an extended passage with expressive syncopations. The finale, again
using the sonata principle, is a *perpetuum mobile*, the whole pervaded by a
single rhythmic pattern.

The third group among Haydn's piano sonatas embraces those composed
in the period 1784–1794. The mature Classical style had been firmly established by Haydn in the string quartets of op. 33 (1783) and thereafter was
extended to other genres of musical composition, notably the symphony but
also the piano sonata. The seriousness and intensity of the sonatas composed
in the period 1770–1780 or so have given way to something more moderate
in which Haydn struck a judicious balance between affects (seriousness and
intensity versus galant), formal types (sonata form, song, variations, rondo),
and textures (homophonic versus contrapuntal) in keeping with the Classical
notion of the reconciliation of opposites.

Yet relatively few of Haydn's sonatas reflect this aesthetic, in part because
he composed none after 1794. Nevertheless there are some outstanding
works here: the Sonata in E-flat major (No. 49, ca. 1789, composed for Maria
Anna von Genzinger), with its strict thematic development in the first movement, and the sonatas in D major (No. 51), E-flat major (No. 52, both mid
1790s), and the last one, in C major (No. 50, ca. 1794–1795), all the equal of
the best quartets and symphonies. On the other hand, the set of three dedicated to Marie Esterházy, in G major (No. 40), B-flat major (No. 41), and D
major (No. 42, all 1784) are galant pieces in the two-movement form—each
has a fast movement (in nos. 40 and 42 sets of variations) followed by a
rondo.

Especially impressive and well-known is the last Sonata in E-flat major
(No. 52), a big work in three movements which emphasizes virtuoso elements much in the spirit that Beethoven was later to bring to the genre.[5] The
first movement is an Allegro in sonata form, the second an Adagio in E major
(both tempo designation and relation to main key of the work are unusual),

and the third a Presto, again in sonata form. Haydn establishes the general
tone of the work in the first movement: the principal theme is chordal and in
dotted rhythm (see Ex. 3-2), the figuration is rhythmically propelled, with
rapid scale passages in thirds and broken-chord figuration, and rich sound is
attained by using the extremes of the keyboard range. We may relate this
last to the fuller sound produced by the English action of the Broadwood
pianos described in Chapter Two (Haydn composed the sonata and its two
companions in London). The principal theme also appears as part of the transition and the close. Worthy of attention is the passage immediately before the
closing theme—a diminuendo in descending octaves in the bass accompanied in the right hand by thirty-second note figuration in *pianissimo* dynamic,
which gives way to a brilliant ascending scale-run that leads to the closing
theme (which, as stated, is the principal theme). Figuration, then, is important.
As is customary in big sonatas, the movement ends with a coda.

The Adagio, in three-part form and in E major (unusually distant relation
to the main key of the sonata), presents a simple theme cast in rounded
binary form that is greatly embellished in the galant fashion by scale-runs,
grace-notes, and rapidly repeated notes. The movement modulates far afield;
the second part of the main section gets to G major and C major. The midsection, in E minor, has the air of a development, since it seizes on the dotted rhythm of the principal theme. It also emphasizes figuration.

The finale has elements of virtuosity. The theme itself outlines the tonic
and dominant triads over a pedal-point, a combination that suggests folk

Example 3-2. HAYDN: Allegro from Sonata in E-flat major (No. 52)—Beginning
(mm. 1–5)

dances. Then come fast sixteenth-notes over a triadic leaping bass. The pace slows in the transition, with its syncopations and chromatic elements. Sudden full chords and rhythmic drive characterize the movement generally, which includes an impressive full stop on a dominant seventh-chord and a brief Adagio in the style of a cadenza, after which comes the recapitulation.

This important composition clearly manifests the essential elements of the Classic style. A serious work that emphasizes thematic development, is full of contrast, and exploits the potentialities of its medium—the piano—it fully deserves a place beside Haydn's late symphonies and quartets. In short, Haydn has brought the piano sonata as a genre to a level that enabled it to rival those other genres in artistic stature: he overcame the light, galant character long associated with the genre.

Haydn's keyboard music includes a number of pieces in other genres. The only other large form in which he worked—except the piano trios,[6] many of which are in the tradition of the accompanied sonata described above—is the theme and variations. This form is represented by several works, among which the most important are the two ariettes with variations, in A major (Hob. XVII, 2, composed ca. 1765) and E-flat major (Hob. XVII, 3, composed before 1774, both sets published 1788–1789), and Theme and Variations in C major (Hob. XVII, 5, composed 1790, published 1792). But the outstanding work in this genre is the expressive late set of variations in F minor (Hob. XVII, 6, composed 1793, published 1799), in which a marchlike theme is followed by a trio; thereafter come two variations (one on the march and the other on the trio) and then a coda. Apart from some dances and smaller pieces, the only other significant piano works of Haydn are the early Capriccio in G major (Hob. XVII, 1, composed 1765, published 1788), based on a popular German song, and the Fantasia in C major (Hob. XVII, 4, composed and published 1789), with its tenuto effects in the bass. For piano duet, there are but three works, two partitas or divertimenti, and a sonata.

MOZART

In many respects Wolfgang Amadeus Mozart (1756–1791) differed dramatically from Haydn. While Haydn developed late, Mozart developed early; while Haydn's international reputation developed steadily over the years, Mozart became a celebrity as a child prodigy; and while Haydn's long tenure with the Esterházy family brought him security, Mozart never held a satisfactory position, and his attempt to survive as a free artist, while successful for a time, ultimately failed.

Unlike Haydn and many of his German and Austrian contemporaries, Mozart traveled extensively as a young man. In the company of his father Leopold, a respected and well-known musician, he came to know the various musical genres and styles at first hand. The contact with Italy, of course, was decisive.

Although Mozart was an eminent pianist, for the most part his works for piano solo do not occupy a central position in his work as a composer. As concert pieces for piano, the concertos take the foremost position. The piano sonata was regarded at the time primarily as a piece for teaching or for domestic entertainment, and the same goes for the sets of variations and other, shorter, pieces. Some of the sonatas were used on the tours Mozart undertook as a child. Even so, he cast a few sonatas on a larger scale, imbuing them with serious and intense expression, thus making them rival the concertos and other large-scale compositions, but these remain exceptions.

The nineteen sonatas that form the bulk of his contribution to solo piano literature may be considered in three chronological groups.

MOZART'S PIANO SONATAS[7]

MUNICH (COMPOSED 1775)
   C major (K. 189d/279)
   F major (K. 189e/280)
   B-flat major (K. 189f/281)
   E-flat major (K. 189g/282)
   G major (K. 189h/283)
   D major (K. 205b/284, "Dürnitz," published 1784)

MANNHEIM AND PARIS (COMPOSED 1777–1778)
   C major (K. 284b/309, published 1782)
   D major (K. 284c/311, published 1782)
   A minor (K. 300d/310, published 1782)

VIENNA (COMPOSED 1783–1789)
   Early Phase (composed 1783–1785, published 1784 and 1785)
      C major (K. 300h/330)
      A major (K. 300i/331)
      F major (K. 300k/332)
      B-flat major (K. 315c/333)
      C minor (K. 457, composed 1784, published with the
         Fantasia in C minor, K. 475 [composed 1785], 1785)
   Late Phase (composed 1788–1789)
      F major (K. 533, 494, composed and published 1788)
      C major (K. 545, composed 1788)
      F major (K. 547a/Anh. 135, composed 1788)
      B-flat major (K. 570, composed 1789)
      D major (K. 576, composed 1789)

Here we can observe that during Mozart's lifetime, while his earlier sonatas remained unpublished, many of the others did in fact come out; others appeared after his death. Three notable publications were the set of two in 1782 (D major [K. 284c/311] and A minor [K.300d/310]), published in Paris by Heina as op. 4; and two sets of three published in Vienna in 1784, the first by Artaria as op. 6 (C major [K. 300h/330], A major [K. 300i/331], and F major [K. 300k/332]) and the second by Torricella as op. 7 (D major [K. 205b/284], B-flat major [K. 315c/333], and B-flat major [K. 454, for violin and piano]). The only other publications of his sonatas that he lived to see were of the Fantasia and Sonata in C minor (K. 475, 457) in 1785 and the Sonata in F major (K. 533, 494) in 1788.

Surveying Mozart's sonatas as a group, we observe less of an evolution than in those Haydn. With few exceptions the "small" concept of the genre is maintained throughout: the character, in general, remains that of Haydn's early sonatas, except that Mozart was more Italianate and adopted the "singing allegro" as well as the *buffo* character to a greater extent than Haydn did. Both made few excursions into the larger type of sonata. In Mozart, as in Haydn, the three-movement scheme remains the norm, with either the middle movement or the finale being a minuet; the first movement shows the sonata principle. But in Mozart we can note that character, affect, style, and/or technique change constantly in a way that can only be described as mercurial, and lyrical themes prevail.

In the first group of sonatas, evidently planned as a set of six, the three-movement scheme is dominant. Typical is the Sonata in G major (K. 189h/283), with its initial Allegro in sonata form and a typically cantabile principal theme, a simple Andante in G major and a *buffo* finale; both the fast movements are in the sonata form with short and free developments. The Sonata in B-flat major (K. 189f/281) has a finale of surprising elaboration, incorporating unusual dynamic markings and quasi-improvisational cadenza-like passages. The Sonata in E-flat major (K. 189g/282) reveals an unusual succession of movements: an Adagio, then two minuets (the second being the trio), and a concluding Allegro in sonata form. Finally, the Sonata in D major (K. 205b/284), the "Dürnitz" sonata—the only one of the six that he had published—is on a larger scale. The point of departure here is orchestra music, particularly French, as is evident from the initial powerful chord, then the forceful unison passage followed by a passage featuring dynamic contrasts (see Ex. 3-3); the slow movement is, exceptionally, a *rondeau en polonaise* (polonaise as refrain in a rondo structure), while the finale is a very long set of variations.

The three sonatas composed in Mannheim and Paris represent the continuation of what he had achieved but on a larger scale and with more intense expression. Yet Mozart maintained the traditional external form and, generally, the galant character. We see this in the Sonata in C major (K. 284b/309) and even more so in the very large one in D major (K. 284c/311), which features extensive thematic development in its first movement. The work as a whole has a bigness of conception that relates it to the serious symphonic

Example 3-3. MOZART: Allegro from Sonata in D major (K. 205b/284—Beginning (mm. 1–9)

compositions of the time, as does the key, D major, which was favored in orchestra music; the piece is thus a step beyond the earlier one in D major (K. 205b/311). The Sonata in A minor (K. 300d/310), the first of his two sonatas in the minor, is surprisingly powerful, especially in its first movement by virtue of its tragic principal theme and consistent expressive use of dissonance.

The third and last group of Mozart's sonatas—the ten composed in Vienna—likewise continues generally the same concept of the genre, clearly evident in the sonatas in F major (K. 300k/332) and B-flat major (K. 315c/333). In the latter, Mozart cast the finale in the hybrid sonata-rondo form used so much by Haydn in his later works, in which Haydn transformed the second episode of the rondo into a development section. Typical in all respects is the famous Sonata in C major (K. 545); Mozart himself indicated its didactic intent in his designation of the work as a "little sonata for beginners." There is a "singing Allegro" over an Alberti bass as the principal theme of the first movement, a cantabile slow movement, and a galant rondo. The larger symphonic type of sonata reappears in the Sonata in D major (K. 576). The Sonata in A major (K. 300i/331), on the other hand, smaller in scale, departs from the usual by having a set of variations as its first movement and a minuet as its second, but still attains a literally smashing close with the celebrated *Alla turca*, a rondo involving the percussive effects of "Turkish" music,[8] as its finale. The first movement—all that exists—of a Sonata in G minor (K. 590d/189i/312) has a strong principal theme that associates the work with Mozart's more famous compositions in this key.

In this last group two sonatas require more detailed discussion: the Fantasia and Sonata in C minor (K. 475 and 457) and the Sonata in B-flat major

(K. 570). Originally conceiving them as two independent works, Mozart combined the Fantasia and Sonata for publication in 1785, thus producing his largest composition for piano solo. The fantasia, which precedes the sonata, represents the continuation of the old form that has its roots in the Baroque but which had been emphasized in Mozart's time by C. P. E. Bach. Appearing here are all the aspects associated with that form. Moreover, Mozart fully exploits the pathétique affect associated with the key of C minor. Six large sections contrast with one another. The first phrase, triadic and in octaves, is followed by one consisting of two simple cadences; in the next section a cantabile triadic phrase is stated over an Alberti bass; later there come passages involving considerable virtuosity—motivic work and figuration in fast tempo; a final section recalls the beginning.

The sonata itself is in three movements—an Allegro, an Adagio, and a concluding Allegro. The extreme expression of the fantasia is carried over into the sonata. There is a triadic principal theme in the first movement in octaves and *fortissimo* with a bit of figuration as the agitated response (see Ex. 3-4), a chromatic transition, a cantabile secondary theme, and a climactic closing theme which emphasizes figuration. The Adagio is cantabile but contains sections featuring cadenza-like fantasia passages, abounding in scale-runs and arpeggios. In the finale the pathétique character of the first movement returns; the movement is an irregular rondo with a fantasia passage near the end. This remarkable work doubtless made a profound impression on Beethoven.

Outstanding in a different way is the late Sonata in B-flat major (K. 570, composed in 1789, sometimes regarded as for violin and piano, but the violin part is not by Mozart). This work may be viewed as the refinement, if not the culmination, of the more typical galant type of sonata usually associated with Mozart. It is cast in three movements: an Allegro in sonata form, an Adagio in E-flat major, and a concluding Allegretto in an unusual variant of rondo form. The first movement begins with a placid lyric principal theme, then brings driving figuration in the transition, while the secondary theme is first stated in contrapuntal combination with the principal theme. The development, which works strictly with themes stated in the exposition, makes sudden excursions into the minor and employs a remarkable succession of keys leading from D-flat major to G major. The Adagio has two alternating sections contrasting in character, both in rounded binary form: the first is a solemn melody presented over chords, while the second is agitated, has a short, dotted figure in thirds over sixteenth-notes and octave leaps in the bass. The third movement, as indicated, is an unusual sort of rondo; the repetition of the first episode has been suppressed, while themes from both episodes dominate the long coda. The principal theme in particular draws attention—it is a chromatic melody with syncopations that give it a breathless quality, presented over broken chords. Unlike the Fantasia and Sonata in C minor (K. 475, 457) with their passionate intensity, here is a work still primarily oriented to the galant but that brings a number of elaborations, contrapuntal, harmonic,

Title page for first edition of Mozart's *Fantaisie et Sonate Pour le Forte-Piano*, Artaria, Vienna, 1785. British Museum, London. The dedicatee, Therese von Trattner, was a pupil of Mozart.
From *Decorative Music Title Pages*, G. S. Fraenkel, ed., Dover Publications, Inc., 1968.

and formal. It features those mercurial changes of affect that are common in Mozart, particularly the sudden turns to the minor. This work, then, can take its place beside other great compositions of Mozart's last phase, the last concertos (one for piano, the other for clarinet) and the Clarinet Quintet.

Another category of piano compositions Mozart cultivated throughout his career was the theme and variations, of which he composed sixteen sets. The earliest date from the first tour of the child prodigy (1766), the last from 1791. He composed four on French songs in rapid succession during his sojourn in Paris (1778): the variations on "Je suis Lindor" (K. 299a/354), "Ah! vous dirai-je maman" (K. 300e/265), "La belle françoise" (K. 300f/353), and "Lison dormait" (K. 315d/264), the latter regarded as one of his most successful.

For his variations Mozart with few exceptions used popular tunes of the time. Most come from arias, songs, choruses, and other numbers from operas

Example 3-4. MOZART: Allegro from Sonata in C minor (K. 457)—Beginning (mm. 1–13)

or plays with music by well-known composers: Salieri, Grétry, Sarti, Gluck, and others. One is based on a song by Antoine-Laurent Baudron from Beaumarchais' play *Le barbier de Seville*, while others come from less distinguished but perhaps even more popular works, such as Dezède's vaudeville *Julie* and the farce put on by Emanuel Schikaneder, *Der dumme Gärtner aus dem Gebirg, oder die zween Anton*, with music by Benedikt Schack and Franz Gerl. Still others come from songs, such as the famous "Ah! vous dirai-je maman," or from dances (minuets by Fischer and Duport).

Mozart often included variations on the programs of his public concerts. One of his sets of variations in fact seems to go back to an improvisation he did at his concert of 23 March 1783: the set of ten on "Unser dummer Pöbel meint" (K. 455, composed 1784, published 1785), from Gluck's *Le rencontre imprévue* (later known as *Die Pilger von Mekka*). Moreover, Mozart had some success with the genre; it was important in his concerts, where he reached a large audience, and he was able to publish many of the variations during his lifetime, a distinction not accorded many of his other more ambitious and important compositions.

Mozart made these compositions for the most part rather simple, affecting a popular character. The theme is stated at the outset, followed by a series of variations that contrast from one another, that embellish and/or alter the theme but in such a way that its identity is preserved. We find several standard types here: those that break the theme down into patterns of figuration, either sixteenth-notes, triplets, or broken octaves of the sort that may involve considerable difficulties in execution; those that treat the theme in dotted rhythms; those in the tradition of the French *pièces croisées* that keep a pattern of figuration going by the right hand in the middle register while the left leaps back and forth, crossing over it, playing individual notes or short figurative elements; and those that accompany the theme by a long trill. Most sets contain an innocent and highly embellished Adagio along with a serious, expressive *minore* variation, chromatic and often with syncopations. In the set on "Je suis Lindor" (K. 299a/354, composed and published 1778), the final variation presents the theme as a minuet. Several of the sets have codas that recapitulate, at least in part, the theme in its original form: the variations on "Je suis Lindor," "La belle françoise" (K. 300f/353), "Lison dormait" (K. 315d/264), "Unser dummer Pöbel meint," the Allegretto in B-flat major (K. 500), and Duport's minuet (K. 573). The very last set, on "Ein Weiß ist das herrlichste Ding" (K. 613), is unusual. Here the original song had an instrumental introduction that Mozart kept intact, presenting it with some alteration before each variation; in the last variation Mozart reversed the order, and in the coda he combined the themes of the song and of the introduction contrapuntally.

Throughout Mozart made the last variation provide a suitable finale, fast and brilliant, set off by an immediately preceding Adagio. In many of the later sets, however, he also distinguished the last variation by incorporating elements taken over from the fantasia—arpeggios, solo lines imitative of operatic recitative, and sudden changes of style, texture, and harmony. Such elements appear, for instance, at the end of the sets on "Je suis Lindor," the minuet by Duport, and "Ein Weib ist das herrlichste Ding." Still others go even further, to the extent of having passages marked *cadenza*: the sets on "Lison dormait," Paisiello's "Salve tu Domine," and Gluck's "Unser dummer Pöbel meint." Often this last part is divided into sections that contrast with one another.

A remarkable group of Mozart's piano works, one that is generally neglected, consists of those compositions conceived under the influence of Baroque music, particularly Bach and Handel. During the early years of his time in Vienna, Mozart frequented the salons held by Baron Gottfried van Swieten who was interested in such music and had a large collection of it. Mozart completed two large fantasias, in C major (K. 383a/394) and C minor

(K. 475), the C minor put together later with the sonata in the same key, as described earlier. Two others, in C minor (K. 385f/396) and D minor (K. 385g/397), the former originally with a violin part, were completed by Stadler and presumably Müller respectively. These works date from 1782. Mozart conceived them in the tradition of German Baroque organ music: they are sectional and encompass much contrast of texture, style, key, thematic material, and affect. That is to say, they show features typical of the toccata style—arpeggios, full chords rapidly alternating with one another, and sudden changes of harmony. The large Fantasia in C major concludes with an impressive three-voice fugue. In the same vein are pieces composed for mechanical organ. A fugue for two pianos in C minor (K. 426) in the same idiom was composed in 1783.

Also of interest is Mozart's interpretation of the Baroque keyboard suite (K. 385i/399) which dates from 1782 as well. Although it lacks a general title, this composition apparently was intended to be a full suite, but Mozart failed to complete the work. Extant are an overture, an allemande, a courante, and the beginning of a sarabande. Mozart did not maintain the Baroque unity of key; the overture moves from C major to G major, the allemande is in C minor, the courante in E-flat major, and the sarabande in G major. The overture is a French overture: in the slow first section full chords alternate with a vigorous rhythmic figure, and there are sudden affective changes of harmony; a fast, fugal Allegro, with a subject emphasizing repeated notes and figuration, follows the overture; there is a countersubject and even stretto, and the section throughout is propelled by driving rhythms. Baroque traits are also present in the two dance movements. Missing, however, is the element of variation—cyclic form—that characterized many Baroque suites.

For the rest, Mozart's output of piano music contains individual dances of various kinds and other miscellaneous pieces. His earliest works were minuets composed on the same bass, presumably under the guidance of his father. Outstanding among the later miscellaneous works is the Rondo in A minor (K. 511, 1787). Here Mozart maintained the rondo form, introducing but one departure, not repeating the first episode. But this is no usual rondo; it is, rather, a melancholy Andante featuring an expressive cantabile melody incorporating subtle alternation between minor and major, with episodes that provide contrast, but such that the basic affect is maintained. Two other expressive works are the Capriccio in G major (K. 300g/395, composed 1777), and the Adagio in B minor (K. 540, composed 1788).

For piano duet, there are chiefly sonatas in which the influence of orchestra music is evident. The orchestral influence is clear not only from the three-movement form, that of the operatic sinfonia, but more especially from the character of the themes, the emphatic use of dynamic contrasts, tremolo figuration, octave doubling, and so forth. Moreover, alternation of thematic material between the two parts often reveals the influence of the concerto. While some of these traits may be seen in the early Sonata in C major (K. 19d,

1765), which owes much to J. C. Bach (and which at the same time may be spurious), they are very clear in two works composed in Salzburg, the sonatas in D major (K. 123a/381, 1772) and B-flat major (K. 186c/358, 1773–1774), both played by Mozart with his sister Nannerl. The first of these commences with a strong D major chord much like the *premier coup d'archet* of French symphonies of the time and continues with a Mannheim crescendo, while the Sonata in B-flat major has a quasi-orchestral octave-unison passage at its beginning. Of the other two completed sonatas for piano duet, both composed in Vienna, the Sonata in F major (K. 497, 1786), the largest of all Mozart's works in this genre, is a serious piece pervaded with chromaticism; its first movement is preceded by a slow introduction. The other, in C major (K. 521, 1787), is wholly galant and particularly shows the influence of the concerto. Mozart also composed a theme and variations for piano duet in G major (K. 501, 1786) that resembles the variations for piano solo discussed above. Finally, for two pianos, we have the large Sonata in D major (K. 375a/ 448, 1781), another quasi-orchestral work in the spirit of an Italian *buffa* sinfonia, and the Fugue in C minor (K. 426, 1783), one of Mozart's Baroque-like compositions, complete with a chromatic subject featuring the descending leap of a seventh, a countersubject, inversion, stretto, and motivic breaking down of the subject.

CLEMENTI, DUSSEK, HUMMEL, AND OTHERS

We have seen that, in the latter half of the eighteenth century, solo piano music took up a relatively small portion of composers' compositional work, comprising for the most part minor compositions, frequently in the conventional galant taste. Mozart himself is a case in point: celebrated as a virtuoso pianist in his day, he in fact composed relatively few large-scale works for solo piano, because, as has been mentioned, the concerto provided the main vehicle for approaching the concert-going public. For this reason the varied career of Muzio Clementi (1752–1832) has particular importance. Clementi was active not only as pianist and composer but also as theorist, impresario, conductor, publisher, and instrument builder. He lived and worked mostly in London.

The main difficulty in studying Clementi is that his compositions have come down in numerous editions, the same pieces often having been assigned different opus numbers by different publishers; at times the different editions incorporate significant revisions, even recomposition. Moreover, some earlier works were published much later than they were composed, while still others prove to be arrangements of symphonies and concertos. Tyson's investigations suggest that to use the opus numbers assigned in the original editions is best.[9] Clementi is clearly a major figure in the history of piano music; most important are the piano sonatas, of which there are seventy-one, along with some popular sonatinas, but he also composed other works, mostly didactic, of which the most famous is the *Gradus ad Parnassum* (see below). Of lesser significance generally are the numerous small compositions of all sorts—dances, sets of variations on popular melodies, and so on. Among the dances is the set *Monferrinas* (12, op. 49, 1821, all dates here being of publication), Italian country dances named for a region in Piedmont that enjoyed popularity in early nineteenth-century England. Clementi also composed an outstanding Toccata in B-flat major (op. 11, 1784). As a curiosity, there is the set *Musical Characteristics* (op. 19, 1787) in which Clementi imitates Haydn, Kozeluch, Mozart, Sterkel, and Vanhal.

While Clementi composed sonatas beginning in the early 1770s and continued to do so throughout his career as a composer, except for the fifteen-year period from 1804 to 1820, his most productive period was 1779–1790, especially 1780–1785. Although two different formal schemes appear in these works—the old two-movement scheme along with the newer three-movement one, the latter being more numerous—in his later years Clementi evidently came to regard the latter as standard, since in the 1790s he added third movements to two of the two-movement sonatas of his op. 2 (ii and iv, the new versions published as op. 30 and 31); the four-movement plan appears only in a handful of late sonatas. We find little of the conventional galant sonata here. Like Müthel, C. P. E. Bach, Haydn, and Mozart in some of their later works, Clementi, at least from the 1780s on, regarded the sonata as a large form capable of the most serious expression. He regularly employed formal types common to late eighteenth-century instrumental music. The strong opening Allegro is in sonata form and uses motivic themes; an element of consistency lies in deriving the secondary theme from the principal theme, as indeed Haydn often did. The slow movements are lyrical, and the brilliant finales are in sonata or rondo form. What distinguishes Clementi's sonatas, however, is the virtuoso employment of the piano coupled with the intense quality of the expression, qualities associated particularly, as we will see, with Beethoven. Clementi's writing for the instrument, in short, is big, thick-textured, sonorous, rich in dynamic contrast, exploiting the full range of the keyboard; all this makes his music sound different from that of C. P. E. Bach, Haydn, or Mozart. Moreover, Clementi incorporated a good deal of contrapuntal writing into his sonatas, following what he referred to as "the German manner," by which he meant J. S. Bach.

Several sonatas stand out. The Sonata in G minor (op. 34 ii, 1795), is a large composition, showing in its first movement a slow introduction (not common in sonatas at the time), the characteristically motivic principal theme, the derivation of the secondary theme from it, and considerable dynamic contrast in the development. There is a cantabile slow movement and a finale in sonata form distinguished by counterpoint. Another is the Sonata in B-flat major (op. 24 ii, 1788, revised 1804, known as the "Magic Flute" sonata because the theme of its first movement resembles that of the overture to Mozart's opera), the work Clementi played during the famous competition with Mozart in Vienna, 24 December 1781. The dramatic Sonata in F minor (op. 13 vi, 1785) suggests, in its finale, Beethoven's *Eroica-Prometheus* theme, with slow introduction to the first movement and a canonic second episode in the rondo. Others include the lyrical Sonata in F-sharp minor (op. 25 v, 1790), and the programmatic sonata *Didone abbandonata* in G minor (op. 50 iii, 1821), described as *scena tragica*, in which Clementi moderated his usual impulse toward virtuosity in favor of expressive character. Finally, of the two sonatas in C major (op. 20, 1787, and op. 33 iii, 1794), the latter is particularly brilliant, for Clementi derived it from a concerto.

Clementi produced two didactic works, the first entitled *An Introduction to the Art of Playing the Piano Forte* (op. 42, 1801, revised 1826; this includes an Appendix, op. 43, 1811, revised presumably 1820–1821); the second is the more important *Gradus ad parnassum* (3 vols., op. 44, 1817–1826), a complete course of piano study. While many of its one hundred numbers are etudes, we can find many preludes and fugues and character pieces. Moreover, Clementi grouped about half the pieces into sets ranging from pairs to suites of six.

Another important composer to be considered here is the Czech Jan Ladislaus Dussek (1760–1812), renowned in his time as a pianist. He spent much of his life traveling to give concerts, one of the first pianists to do so, and had extended sojourns in Paris (1786–1789 and 1806–1812), London (1789–1799), and Berlin (1803–1806). His extensive output of piano sonatas is currently set at forty-two, but, as was true in the case of Clementi, different publishers assigned different opus numbers to his works (dates here are of publication).[10] These sonatas are mostly in two movements, with a goodly number in three but only a handful of later ones in four. Dussek retained the conventional formal structures, giving prominence to the rondo in his finales. Apart from the technical difficulties, these works abound in lyrical themes, harmonic color, and cyclic form to the extent that they have come to be regarded as proto-Romantic. Among the more notable sonatas are the three of op. 9 (C. 57–59, ca. 1789), the large Sonata in B-flat major (C. 96/op. 24, 1793); the *Farewell* Sonata in E-flat minor–major (C. 178/op. 44, 1800); the affecting *Élégie harmonique . . . en forme de sonata* in F-sharp minor (C. 211/op. 61, 1806–1807) in honor of his patron Prince Louis Ferdinand of Prussia; *Le retour à Paris* (Sonata in A-flat major [C. 221/op. 64, 1807]), and his last, *L'invocation* (Sonata in F minor [C. 259/op. 77, 1812]). Dussek subsequently changed the title of the sonata *Le retour à Paris* (his titles at times seem purely nominal) to *Plus ultra* in competition with Wölfl (see below), then in London, who had just published a sonata entitled *Non plus ultra*. Among other works of Dussek are two programmatic pieces, *Sufferings of the Queen of France* (C. 98/op. 23, 1793) in ten movements and *The Naval Battle and Total Defeat of the Dutch Fleet by Admiral Duncan* (C. 152, 1797). His works also include two extended fantasias, in F minor (C. 199/op. 55, 1804) and F major (C. 248/op. 76, 1811), both sectional, the former with a fugue, the latter approaching the length and scope of a sonata; the characteristic rondo *La chasse* (C. 146,

1796); and the expressive *La consolation* in B-flat major (C. 212/op. 62, 1807). Dussek also composed sonatas for piano duet.

Another prolific composer of the time was the great Czech virtuoso Johann Nepomuk Hummel (1778–1837), who worked for the Esterházy family in Eisenstadt (1804–1811) and later at the court of Weimar (1819 and after) and had an enormous reputation as a pianist. His piano music includes sonatas, sonatinas, sets of variations, fantasias, fugues, preludes, bagatelles, rondos, and dances, along with music for piano duet.[11] Six large sonatas (published between 1792 and 1825) stand in the foreground; like those of Dussek they are in two and three movements and follow structural principles common at the time. Moreover, they make good use of the sound capacities of the piano. Those that have attracted the most attention are the E-flat major (op. 13, ca. 1805); the irregular and lyrical F minor (op. 20, ca. 1807); and the big one in F-sharp minor (op. 81, 1819).

Remaining generally true to the galant conception of the sonata were:

- Carl Ditters von Dittersdorf (1739–1799), who produced but two sonatas
- Jan Baptist Vanhal (1739–1813)
- Marianne Martínez (1744–1812), a pupil of Haydn who composed three sonatas
- Leopold Kozeluch (1747–1818)
- Franz Xaver Sterkel (1750–1817)
- Johann Friedrich Reichardt (1752–1814), who adhered to the old principle of unity of affect within a movement, but whose sonatas composed after 1809 reveal both a preoccupation with thematic development and a more intense, almost personal, kind of expression
- Joseph Gelinek (1758–1825)
- Maria Auenbrugger (1759–1782)
- Daniel Steibelt (1765–1823)
- Anton Eberl (1765–1807)
- August Eberhard Müller (1767–1817)
- Johann (or John) Baptist Cramer (1771–1858), the composer of some 150 sonatas
- Joseph Wölfl (1773–1812), a virtuoso celebrated for his rivalry with Beethoven, who composed some sixty sonatas, including a big one in C minor that is preceded by an Introduction and Fugue (op. 25 i), a work that doubtless owes much to Mozart
- E. T. A. Hoffmann (1776–1822), mostly known as a writer, all but one of whose six essentially galant sonatas remained unpublished until 1922
- Ludwig Berger (1777–1839).

Mozart's grand piano, built by Anton Walter c. 1780, located in the Mozart House in Salzburg. Modern copies of this model are built to produce a sound close to that of Mozart's period.

Beethoven's grand piano, built by Érard Frères, Paris, 1803, an instrument with the light, graceful structure of the early grand pianos. Beethoven's later instruments, by Broadwood, were of sturdier build.

BEETHOVEN

Ludwig van Beethoven (1770–1827) may provide our best instance of the new status attained by musicians by the early nineteenth century. Unlike Haydn, Beethoven was attached to no court except in his early days at Bonn; like Mozart in his years in Vienna, Beethoven was a free artist making his living from fees from lessons, the proceeds of concerts, royalties from publishers, commissions, and honoraria from members of the nobility. He was able to succeed in Vienna where a few years earlier Mozart had failed.

Most characteristically, Beethoven manifested in his compositions certain ideals that he held and according to which he strove to live and work (not always entirely successfully). In short, he considered wordless instrumental music a viable medium for the expression and communication of ideas, including those associated with the French Revolution, *liberté*, *égalité*, and *fraternité*. He also held to an idea common in eighteenth-century aesthetic thought: the moral value of the artwork, the necessity that it purify and ennoble the audience, an idea that has been linked with Aristotle's notion of catharsis as the true function of tragedy. Beethoven forcibly expressed his view in the *Heiligenstadt Testament* (1802) which he wrote when he realized his increasing deafness was incurable. In his despair he contemplated suicide: "but little more and I would have put an end to my life—only art is what held me back: ah! it seemed impossible to leave the world until I had produced all that I felt called upon to produce."[12] It is as if Beethoven realized that he had been granted powers greater than those accorded to others, that his duty was to exercise these powers, to compose, for the betterment of mankind, and that not even the infirmity of deafness should cause him to waiver or desist.

For a long time it has been known that Beethoven made many sketches, early drafts of various kinds, before putting his compositions into their final form. Since the late 1960s his way of composing has been subjected to intensive study with the aid of new methods of analysis involving identification of the kinds of paper he used, the inks, characteristic features of his handwriting and its changes over the years, and so on. In some cases new insights have been gained, especially in regard to chronology.[13] We will draw upon this new work here as necessary.

Like Mozart, Beethoven was a pianist. But unlike Mozart—and Haydn, too, for that matter—Beethoven emphasized music for solo piano, the sonata in particular, which became in his work as important as any other genre of composition. Here he for the first time worked out new methods of organization, styles, techniques, and even aesthetic orientations, before extending them to other categories of composition. This role for the piano will become apparent as we take up his sonatas chronologically.

Beethoven's work conventionally is divided into three periods: the early phase, up to 1802; the middle phase, 1802–1815; and the late phase, 1815–1827. The piano sonatas may then be grouped into this framework (after 1796 he composed all his sonatas in and around Vienna):

BEETHOVEN'S LARGE PIANO SONATAS[14]

NOTE: WoO designates works without opus number
(Werke ohne Opuszahl).

THE EARLY PHASE
Bonn (WoO 47, "Kurfürsten," composed and published
1782–1783)
E-flat major
F minor
D major

Vienna (1796–1802)
F minor, A major, and C major (No. 1–3, op. 2 i–iii,
composed 1793–1795, published 1796)
E-flat major (No. 4, op. 7, composed 1796–1797,
published 1797)
C minor, F major, and D major (No. 5–7, op. 10 i–iii,
composed 1796–1798, published 1798)
Sonate pathétique, C minor (No. 8, op. 13, composed
1797–1798, published 1799)
E major and G major (No. 9–10, op. 14 i–ii, composed
1798–1799, published 1799)
B-flat major (No. 11, op. 22, composed 1800, published
1802)
A-flat major (No. 12, op. 26, composed 1800–1801,
published 1802)
E-flat major and C-sharp minor (No. 13–14, op. 27 i–ii,
composed 1800–1801, published 1802)
D major (No. 15, op. 28, "Pastoral," composed 1801,
published 1802)

THE MIDDLE PHASE (1802–1815)
1802–1809
G major, D minor, and E-flat major (No. 16–18, op. 31
i–iii, composed 1802, published 1803–1804)
C major (No. 21, op. 53, "Waldstein," composed
1803–1804, published 1805)
F major (No. 22, op. 54, composed 1804, published 1806)
F minor (No. 23, op. 57, "Appassionata," composed
1804–1805, published 1807)

1809–1815
F-sharp major (No. 24, op. 78, composed 1809, published
1810)

G major (No. 25, op. 79, composed 1809, published 1810)
E-flat major (No. 26, op. 81a, "Les Adieux," composed
    1809–1810, published 1811)
E minor (No. 27, op. 90, composed 1814, published 1815)

THE LATE PHASE
A major (No. 28, op. 101, composed 1816, published
    1817)
B-flat major (No. 29, op. 106, "Hammerklavier,"
    composed 1817–1818, published 1819)
E major (No. 30, op. 109, composed 1820, published
    1821)
A-flat major (No. 31, op. 110, composed 1821–1822,
    published 1822)
C minor (No. 32, op. 111, composed 1821–1822,
    published 1823)

There are also four easy sonatas, two from the late Bonn period (in F major [WoO 50] and C major [WoO 51], both incomplete), and two in op. 49 (in G minor and G major, No. 19–20, composed 1795–1797, published 1805).

Beethoven wrote piano sonatas more or less continually throughout his composing career. If we consider only the larger works (excluding the easy sonatas), Beethoven composed eighteen sonatas up to 1802, five of them in a single year, 1801–1802 (these belonging to his "first period"), then ten more between 1802 and 1814 (in his "second period"), and, finally, five more between 1817 and 1823 (his "third period"), and none thereafter. This distribution doubtless has something to do with Beethoven's employment of the piano sonata as a sort of proving ground, as we already suggested and will continue to see.

The Early Sonatas

The three sonatas Beethoven composed in Bonn at age eleven promise much. He cast them all in the three-movement scheme that was standard for the genre in the eighteenth century. The Sonata in E-flat major, while essentially a small composition, exhibits in its first movement real motivic development of themes. More impressive overall, however, is the Sonata in F minor, a true forerunner of the later "Appassionata": there is a slow introduction to the first movement, full of sudden changes in dynamics and chromaticism, followed by an Allegro in sonata form with a theme based on the F minor scale in driving sixteenth-note rhythm (see Ex. 3-5); the secondary theme, as was often true in sonatas of Haydn and Mozart, is in the galant vein, but the closing theme returns to the passionate style of the principal

Example 3-5. Beethoven: First Movement from Sonata in F minor (WoO 47)—
Excerpts
   A. Larghetto maestoso (mm. 1–3)
   B. Allegro assai (mm. 1–3)

theme. The development works with the principal theme but is dramatically
interrupted in midcourse by the reappearance of a passage from the slow
introduction. While the Andante is lighter, greatly embellished after the manner of the time, the dramatic-passionate character comes back in the Presto.
In employing the minor mode here Beethoven followed the example of
Haydn and of the eighteenth century generally. The Sonata in D major, from
this group is even larger, full of brilliance and virtuosity, in much the same
spirit as Mozart's sonatas in this key. Thus these early works show Beethoven
pursuing not the traditional galant variety of sonata, but the more ambitious
and serious conception of the genre as we have seen it in C. P. E. Bach,
Müthel, and certain works of Haydn and Mozart.

   The group of ten sonatas published 1796–1799 forms the bulk of Beethoven's early engagement with the genre and indeed constitutes close to a
third of his total work with it, an unusual degree of concentration. Beethoven
continued the direction he announced in the Bonn sonatas. In fact, he went
a step further—he abandoned the three-movement scheme. Instead he cast
five of the ten sonatas in the four-movement scheme, which we find in relatively few eighteenth-century sonatas but rather in symphonies and the more
serious types of chamber music for strings alone—string quartets and string
quintets. Perhaps Beethoven decided to convert the sonata's traditional didactic aspect that ordinarily involved teaching and learning how to play into one
that involved his own development in composition—to use the genre for his
own preparation for these larger categories. The symphonic character, for
instance, is clear in the Sonata in D major (op. 10 iii). After 1802 Beethoven
generally turned away from the four-movement scheme in his piano sonatas.

The first movements of these sonatas show the use of the sonata form throughout. These are big movements operating with motivic themes of the type we have come to associate with Beethoven. The slow movements are cantabile, generally in simple three-part form or its extension, the five-part form. While most of these movements are on the light side, there are some notable exceptions—the three deeply expressive Largo movements in the sonatas in A major (op. 2 ii), E-flat major (op. 7), and D major (op. 10 iii). The dance movements are either minuets or scherzos, the latter in the sonatas in C major (op. 2 iii) and G major (op. 14 ii) with trios. These remain formally much like those found in Haydn, Mozart, and others, except that the customary galant and often grazioso character is mostly lacking and motivic themes are frequent. The Sonata in E-flat (op. 7) has a *minore* trio that employs broken-chord figuration and dynamic changes.

Two of these works may be singled out for more detailed consideration: the Sonata in C major (op. 2 iii) and the *Sonata pathétique* in C minor. The first of these has the large four-movement scheme so prominent in this group of sonatas. There is an Allegro con brio in sonata form, an Adagio in five-part form, a scherzo with trio, and a concluding Assai allegro in rondo form. The first movement shows Beethoven's characteristic type of thematic materials in abundance—terse motives that involve figurative elements and that are sharply delineated rhythmically, readily identifiable, and susceptible to repetition, development, variation, and combinations of different sorts (see Ex. 3-6). Moreover these motives frequently contrast with one another. Here the secondary theme (G minor) is cantabile, while the closing theme features brilliant figuration. Beethoven has varied the recapitulation by inserting a fantasia-like passage in the style of a cadenza into the closing section, after which the closing section resumes, bringing the movement to a brilliant con-

Example 3-6. BEETHOVEN: Allegro con brio from Sonata in C major (op. 2 iii)—Beginning (mm. 1–9)

clusion. The Adagio, most exceptionally in E major (third relation to the main key of the sonata), shows the five-part structure. The principal theme, with its clearly organized arrangement of phrases, alternates with the secondary theme, which is primarily harmonic in effect, with arpeggiated chords, octaves in the bass, and cantabile scale fragments above. Shortly before the secondary theme's reappearance there is a sudden turn to C major in the principal theme, thus reasserting the main key of the work. The scherzo emphasizes a strongly rhythmical motivic theme that is insistently accompanied by touches of counterpoint, all far removed from the traditional character of the minuet. The trio contrasts sharply, its rapid arpeggios accompanied by accented octaves in the bass. The concluding Assai allegro is a straightforward rondo: the principal theme uses rapidly moving staccato sixth-chords while the first episode consists of a cantabile line over a stereotyped broken-chord bass. Figuration added to the rondo theme in its final appearance produces a brilliant conclusion.

The well-known *Sonata pathétique*, C minor (op. 13, 1799), differs in that it expresses a particular affect, albeit one regarded at the time in a general way—that is, not specifically "pathetic" but rather serious and intense. This is one of but two sonatas to which Beethoven himself gave a descriptive title (the other is the Sonata in E-flat [op. 81a], *Das Lebewohl* or *Les Adieux* (discussed below). The key, C minor, had throughout the eighteenth century been associated with the seriousness of the pathétique, an association it retained in the nineteenth century as well. Beethoven cast the *Sonata pathétique* in three movements: a Grave-Allegro, an Andante cantabile in A-flat, and a concluding rondo, Allegro.

He establishes the pathétique character at the beginning; the Grave introduction proceeds with heavy, solemn chords in dotted rhythm and a cantabile line over ponderous chordal accompaniment. The Allegro part of the movement, in sonata form, commences with an agitated principal theme—rapidly ascending chords, off-beat accentuations, and broken-chord accompaniment—to which the secondary theme, staccato and with grace-notes in a *grazioso* character, provides relief; but rhythmically driven figuration returns with the closing theme. Then, before the development gets underway, Beethoven suddenly reintroduces the grave from the introduction. In other respects the development is regular. In the coda both the principal theme and the theme from the introduction appear once again. The incorporation of the theme from the introduction into the main body of the movement, as we already noted, occurred in the Bonn Sonata in F minor (WoO 47 ii).

The Adagio cantabile offers an example of the large-scale serious slow movement. The form involves alternating sections which contrast with one another after the fashion of a rondo. The principal section moves slowly, a cantabile line given out in mostly even notes over an accompaniment of broken chords, while the first episode is similarly constituted but has different thematic materials. The second episode brings contrast with its agitated triple accompaniment, the crescendo that culminates in a *forte-piano*, staccato chords, and sudden harmonic changes. Strictly speaking, in the slow movement this episode alone expresses the pathétique.

The finale, as stated, is a rondo. Here Beethoven brings the pathétique character back. Along with the principal theme, disconsolate despite the grace-notes, are two secondary themes, both longer than the principal theme itself. The first has figuration themes of eighth-notes and triplets that accompany a chordal theme, while the second features an extended passage in two-voice writing and figuration.

The last five sonatas of Beethoven's early group, those that appeared in 1802, show the innovation characteristic of his treatment of the genre. This involves the overall organization of the sonata—the relationships between the different movements and the forms employed within them.

Most innovative are the two, E-flat major and C-sharp minor (op. 27), each of which Beethoven specifically designated *sonata quasi una fantasia*. The fantasia character was by no means entirely new to the piano sonata, as is clear from Haydn's, Mozart's, and even some of Beethoven's earlier essays in the genre. In these earlier sonatas, however, the fantasia character took the form either of passages in fantasia style inserted during the course of a movement, or of a fantasia movement that precedes the work as a whole; in the sonatas of op. 27, on the other hand, the fantasia aspect affects the disposition of each work as a whole.

Both sonatas are cast in three movements. In the Sonata in E-flat, we clearly see the fantasia character in the first movement, which is divided into three parts: Andante–Allegro–Andante; note here that there is nothing of the usual Allegro movement in sonata form. The first movement of the companion Sonata in C-sharp minor (this movement being the one that gave rise to the work's designation "Moonlight," which did not come from Beethoven) is also in three-part form. This change in the form and character of the first movement reorients the overall structure of these works away from the traditional conception of the genre. In both the biggest movement is the finale, to which the preceding movements lead—a sonata-rondo in the E-flat major sonata and a dramatic movement in sonata form in the other. The Sonata in E-flat major is noteworthy for two other features, both related to the fantasia character: the movements are to be played without pause, and the theme of the slow movement, an Adagio, reappears briefly near the end of the finale, thus manifesting the principle of cyclic form.

For the three other sonatas of the group, in B-flat major (op. 22), A-flat major (op. 26), and D major (op. 28), Beethoven returned to the four-movement scheme characteristic of his early involvement with the genre. The sonatas in B-flat major and D major are conservative, although the D major, which has become known as the "Pastoral" (probably on account of the pedal-points that accompany the principal themes of the first and last movements—drone basses are a hallmark of the pastoral), is one of the few in which it has been shown that all movements are thematically related.[15] In the Sonata in A-flat, however, a set of variations has usurped the place of the big first movement in sonata form. Moreover, the sonata has a slow movement with the title "Marcia funebre sulla morte d'un eroe" (Funeral March on the Death of a Hero), marked Maestoso andante, which clearly foreshadows the slow movement of the *Sinfonia eroica*. The A-flat sonata then clearly points to the pair of fantasy sonatas (op. 27) that Beethoven composed immediately afterward.

Sonatas of the Middle Period

Here we note some falling off in the production of piano sonatas: Beethoven composed the three of op. 31 in 1802, but the next three come at the rate of one a year over the period 1803–1805. As in the groups just discussed, nowhere did he follow a fixed formal scheme. While the old four-movement plan appears once, in the Sonata in E-flat major (op. 31 iii), the three-movement scheme is much in evidence, as in the sonatas in G major (op. 31 i) and in D minor (op. 31 ii). But Beethoven varies the three-movement plan too; in the sonatas in C major (op. 53) and F minor (op. 57), the slow movement is linked to the finale; in op. 53 it is called *introduzione*. The Sonata in F major (op. 54) is unusual in that it consists of two movements, a slow one followed by a fast one. Thus, Beethoven has cut out the minuet or scherzo movement as a consequence of his turn away from the four-movement arrangement, although elements of the minuet appear in the first movement of the Sonata in F major (op. 54). In the face of all these two- and three-movement sonatas, the organization of the only four-movement work in the group, in E-flat major (op. 31 iii), arouses interest because it is by no means what we expect—the scherzo, in 2/4 time, stands in second place (not in third), and for the slow movement we find a cantabile minuet.

In the first movements of these sonatas we find the sonata form and all the dramatic and virtuoso features generally associated with Beethoven's piano music. Noteworthy is the Sonata in F minor (op. 57), the first movement of which dispenses with the double-bar and thus with the repetition of the exposition. The themes employed in these movements are motivic, brief, highly characteristic, and full of potential for development; see particularly the often-quoted theme in the Sonata in E-flat major (op. 31 iii). These themes frequently consist of triads, as in the Sonata in F minor (op. 57), or of elements derived from figuration as in the Sonata in C major (op. 53). The Sonata in D minor (op. 31 ii) presents an early instance of the evolving theme. Here Beethoven has conceived the principal theme not as something fixed but as representing a process, an evolution; moreover, in the beginning of the recapitulation he introduces passages in recitative style. In the lyrical Sonata in F major (op. 54), on the other hand, the opening movement is a minuet into which elements of the sonata form have been incorporated.

Of the remaining movements, the slow movements present little that is unusual: the Adagio in the Sonata in D minor (op. 31 ii), variations in the Sonata in F minor (op. 57), and the Andante grazioso in the Sonata in G major (op. 31 i), so that the short, transitional slow movement in the Sonata in C major (op. 53) offers but a moderate exception to this conventionality. For the finales Beethoven has used either sonata or rondo form, the former predominating. Three are in sonata form—the sonatas in E-flat major (op. 31 iii), D minor (op. 31 ii), and F minor (op. 57); two employ the rondo—the sonatas in G major (op. 31 i) and C major (op. 53). The unusual Allegretto of the two-movement Sonata in F major (op. 54) attests to the work's lyrical, perhaps more intimate, character.

These sonatas, along with a few others such as the *Sonata pathétique* and the Sonata in C-sharp minor (op. 27 ii), are among the most popular and successful compositions in this genre composed by Beethoven or anyone else, for that matter. They share a fortunate combination of qualities: they are large concert pieces in which Beethoven's particular motivic type of theme and consequent thematic development appear in association with virtuoso exploitation of the piano. This combination has proven to be potent. It appears to have had but one real forerunner—Clementi.

The dramatic qualities make an impressive appearance in the Sonata in C major ("Waldstein," op. 53). This work is remarkable for its consistent use of figurative elements. The principal theme of the first movement—the longest movement in Beethoven's sonatas up to this time—is little more than a rapidly repeated chord in subdued dynamics (see Ex. 3-7A), and upon repetition the chord is simply broken up. In this theme, therefore, the rhythmic motion is great while the speed of harmonic change is slow. The secondary theme, in the unusual key of E major (third relation to the tonic), is chordal and thus presents an effective contrast, but figuration returns in the closing theme, which consists of arpeggios. A remarkable passage occurs toward the end of the development in the retransition to the recapitulation. Here a large crescendo exploits thematic material consisting exclusively of figuration, the rhythmic motion very fast (sixteenth-notes for the most part). Again we note the static quality in the harmonic rhythm, with the entire passage restricted to the dominant triad. An ostinato-like figure that descends through a fourth in the bass accompanies ascending scale fragments in a gradual crescendo, culminating in an abrupt descending scale-run to usher in the recapitulation (see Ex. 3-7B). The principal theme of the finale involves another crescendo—a triadic cantabile line over figured accompaniment that is repeated twice, each time louder and with greater amounts of figuration (see Ex. 3-7C). As before we note the combination of slow harmonic rhythm and fast figuration. In its clearly virtuoso character this sonata has much in common with the concerto. The short slow movement serves as an introduction to the finale; originally Beethoven intended a complete piece here, which he withdrew from the sonata and published separately as the Andante Favori in F major (WoO 57, published 1805).

The dramatic-passionate or pathétique character also appears in the "Appassionata" sonata (again the name does not come from Beethoven). The pathétique is evident at once from the principal theme of the first movement. Triadic, characterized by dotted rhythm, in subdued dynamic, it comes to rest with a trill in the cadence (Ex. 3-8A); its repetition leads to a sudden,

Example 3-7. BEETHOVEN: Sonata in C major (op. 53)—Excerpts
   A. Allegro con brio: Principal theme—Beginning (mm. 1–4)
   B. Allegro con brio: Retransition—Beginning (mm. 141–148)
   C. Rondo—Beginning (mm. 1–8)

loud, arpeggiated diminished-seventh chord, after which the theme is restated but punctuated by sudden interjections of chords. While the secondary theme—which study of the sketches reveals that Beethoven added late in the process of composition—appears to stand in great contrast, it actually shares two features with the principal theme—the dotted rhythms and the triadic nature of the melody (Ex. 3-8B). We can also note the impressive motivic

Example 3-8. BEETHOVEN: Allegro assai from Sonata in F minor (op. 57)—Excerpts
    A. Principal theme (mm. 1–4)
    B. Secondary theme (mm. 35–37)

development of the materials and, in the recapitulation, the transformation of the principal theme so that it appears *piano* with rapidly repeated sixteenth-notes in the accompaniment. The slow movement, a set of variations in D-flat major, provides respite. But the dramatic pathétique returns with a vengeance in the finale with its "whirlwind" principal theme consisting of fast scale-runs that then become the accompaniment for a chordal theme again characterized by dotted rhythm. In this movement Beethoven has disturbed the usual proportions by enclosing the second part of the movement (development and recapitulation) within the double-bars, thus repeating it rather than the first part (exposition).

In the period between 1809 and 1814, Beethoven composed but four piano sonatas. Again he conformed to no overall basic formal plan, to no fixed conception about what the large form of a piano sonata is or should be. The two-movement form appears twice—in the sonatas in F-sharp major (op. 78) and E minor (op. 90); the others employ the three-movement scheme— sonatas in G major (op. 79) and E-flat major (op. 81a), except that in this last, as in the earlier Sonata in C major (op. 53), the second movement serves as introduction to the finale. In general these sonatas, with the exception of the Sonata in E-flat major (op. 81a), are smaller than those in the group that immediately precedes them.

Sonata form again is dominant in the first movements, but, again, except for the Sonata in E-flat major, it is not the large dramatic kind, full of extreme contrasts and requiring a high degree of virtuosity. Rather the character of these movements is lyrical, as in the broad cantabile themes of the first movements of the sonatas in F-sharp major (op. 78) and E minor (op. 90). The first movement of this last work is a free sonata form from which the usual double-bar is absent, while that of the Sonata in G major (op. 79), marked *Presto alla tedesca*, is short and simple, in lilting triple time, much in the character of a dance (a *Teutsche* or ländler, simple forms of the waltz popular at the time). Two sonatas of this group have slow introductions to the first movements—the sonatas in F-sharp major (op. 78), where it is short, and E-flat major (op. 81a). These sonatas, moreover, lack the minuet/scherzo movement altogether.

For the finales of these sonatas Beethoven chose traditional forms. The rondo scheme appears in the sonatas in G major (op. 79) and E minor (op. 90); sonata form is used in the Sonata in E-flat major (op. 81a), while the sonata-rondo appears in the Sonata in F-sharp major (op. 78). Most unusual is the slow *sangbar* (singable) rondo with contrasting episodes in the Sonata in E minor (op. 90), marked *teneramente*—the finale of a two-movement sonata.

In this group, the sonata with the most conventional form is also in other ways the most unusual—the Sonata in E-flat (op. 81a). Beethoven has given titles to each of its three movements: for the first "Das Lebewohl," "Les Adieux" (The Farewell), and, for the others, "Die Abwesenheit" (The Absence) and "Das Wiedersehen" (The Reunion)—hence, a program sonata. The work is generally known by its French translation; Beethoven, insisting on the German, claimed that one says "lebe wohl" to a single person but "adieu" to assemblies and whole towns.[16] In character, he intended something more intimate. The subject matter and other details point to Dussek's "Farewell" Sonata in E-flat major (published 1800, see above).

Sonatas of the Late Period

The last five sonatas, composed by Beethoven between 1816 and 1822, again present much variety. New elements appear, and Beethoven himself was conscious of taking a new direction in his music, such that he declared it had nothing at all to do with what he had previously composed: "It is somewhat better." The three-movement plan remains dominant, as in the sonatas in A major (op. 101), E major (op. 109), and A-flat major (op. 110), while the two-movement plan appears in the Sonata in C minor (op. 111), and the four-movement scheme in the Sonata in B-flat major (op. 106), a scheme he had not employed since 1803 (Sonata in E-flat major [op. 31 iii]).

The term *Hammerklavier* associated with op. 106 has no programmatic or expressive significance; it is simply the German word for pianoforte and was used by Beethoven in his later years instead of the Italian terms *pianoforte* or *fortepiano*. It is noteworthy, however, that Beethoven has here modified–and the correspondence shows that he did this with some vehemence–the earlier designation of sonatas as playable on either harpsichord or piano ("pour le clavecin ou fortepiano") to exclude the harpsichord.

Two musical types not hitherto characteristic of Beethoven's piano sonatas receive emphasis in the late sonatas and in his late work generally— fugue on the one hand and variations on the other. He treated both in an individual manner. Fugue appears in three contexts: as a separate movement or an extended passage in a movement, as in the sonatas in B-flat major (op. 106) and A-flat major (op. 110); as a development section, as in the sonatas in A major (op. 101) and B-flat major (op. 106); and as part of a set of variations (see below). The most grandiose example of fugue in these piano sonatas is the finale of the Sonata in B-flat major (op. 106), marked *Fuga a tre voci con alcune licenze* (fugue in three voices with a few licenses). In this extended sectional composition, which poses formidable challenges to the interpreter, Beethoven employs inversion and cancrizans, devices long associated with learned counterpoint. Inversion is also featured in the finale of the Sonata in A-flat major (op. 110). Variation form appears twice, both times in the finale, in the sonatas in E major (op. 109), with six variations, and C minor (op. 111), with four variations and an elaborate coda. In both the themes are short and simple, cast in the usual binary form. Both commence quietly, the variations in turn bringing in changes, progressing to a climactic point, and then subsiding and ending with a reprise of the theme in something approaching its original form. For the climactic points, which are noteworthy for their lyrical power, Beethoven developed an original way of writing for the piano. This involves small note-values (32nd-notes), intense figuration in the accompaniment, and use of the extremes of the keyboard range (Ex. 3-9).

As elsewhere in Beethoven's sonatas, we find elements of the fantasia. First, Beethoven has associated the fantasia element with cyclic form. In the Sonata in A major (op. 101), the theme of the first movement recurs immediately before the finale, while in the Sonata in A-flat major, it is the theme of the Adagio that recurs, this time between two sections of the fugue. Other the-

Example 3-9. Beethoven: Third Movement (Variations) from Sonata in E major (op. 109)—Excerpt (mm. 166–172)

matic correspondences have also been found.[17] We noted a similar principle of repetition in the fantasia-sonata in E-flat major (op. 27 i). Second, Beethoven has incorporated the quasi-improvisational style associated with the fantasia into the sonata. We find this, first and foremost, in the introduction to the finale of the Sonata in B-flat major (op. 106), which contains *senza misura* (Ex. 3-10); other examples appear in the adagio sections of the first movement of the Sonata in E major (op. 109), and the Adagio movement of the Sonata

in A-flat major (op. 110), with a recitative, and, finally, the coda of the second
movement of the Sonata in C minor (op. 111).

The old minuet/scherzo movement with trio disappears almost completely; we find it only in the Sonata in B-flat (op. 106). In its place the other
sonatas bring different things: a march in the Sonata in A major (op. 101) and
violent fast movements in the sonatas in E major (op 109) and A-flat major
(op. 110). Likewise, Beethoven has modified the slow movement in these
late sonatas. Apart from the long sets of variations (see above), we find recitative, arioso, and fugue in the Sonata in A-flat major (op. 110) and in the short
Adagio of the Sonata in A major (op. 101). The only "set" slow movement in
the old sense appears in the Sonata in B-flat major (op. 106).

This shifting around of the various movements and forms in the piano
sonata had an effect on the structural type that had long been the mainstay of
the genre: the sonata form. Beethoven maintained the traditional big opening
movement in the sonatas in B-flat major (op. 106) and C minor (op. 111), but
others are different. The Sonata in A-flat major (op. 110) shows sonata form
appears in the first movement, but Beethoven has given it a lyrical interpretation, emphasizing cantabile themes and reducing the significance of the
development; in the Sonata in A major (op. 101), he replaced the development with a lyrical Allegretto, and in the Sonata in E major (op. 109), he eliminated the sonata form altogether. We have already noted that in two of the
movements in sonata form Beethoven has used fugue in the development—
in the sonatas in A major (op. 101), the finale, and B-flat major (op. 106), the
first movement.

Example 3-10. BEETHOVEN: Largo (Introduction to Finale) from Sonata in B-flat
major (op. 106)—Beginning (mm. 1–2)

As we have seen, the piano sonata occupied a central position in Beethoven's work. In this genre he consistently forged new interpretations and
procedures that he then incorporated into other genres. The big four-movement early sonatas paved the way for the string quartets (op. 18) and the first
two symphonies; similarly the sonatas (op. 31, 53, and 57) are predecessors
of the large string quartets (op. 59 and 74), the great symphonies, and other
works of the middle phase, while the last five piano sonatas take us directly
into the world of the late string quartets.

Variations .

The other large form of piano music that Beethoven cultivated was theme
and variations. There are twenty-one sets of variations, in which we can distinguish two types. First we have the "popular" type, works related to Beethoven's public concerts, in which melodies of songs and arias popular at
the time are taken as the basis of variations (pieces by Dittersdorf, Salieri,
Paisiello, Righini, and Süssmayr, as well as "Rule Britannia," "God Save the
King," and a theme from his own *Ruins of Athens*). These sets are the result
of Beethoven's improvisations at concerts and in general resemble the variations of Mozart in character and intent.

Then we have the more ambitious and serious essays in the genre, works
composed in the same spirit as the piano sonatas and thus lacking this popular orientation.

BEETHOVEN'S PRINCIPAL SETS OF VARIATIONS

Variations (6) on an Original Theme, F major (op. 34, composed
    1802, published 1803)
Variations (15) with Fugue on a Theme from *Prometheus*, E-flat
    major (op. 35, composed 1802, published 1803)
Variations (32) on an Original Theme, C minor (WoO 80,
    composed 1806, published 1807)
Variations (33) on a Waltz of Diabelli, C major (op. 120,
    composed 1819–1823, published 1823)

Two of these are based on themes original with Beethoven, one being a
theme used in other works (the earlier ballet *The Creatures of Prometheus*
and the later *Sinfonia eroica*), so that only one is based on a theme from
outside—the Diabelli variations.

Concerning the variations in F major and E-flat major (op. 34 and 35),
Beethoven wrote his publishers that these works "have been worked out in
an entirely new manner," something totally different from previous sets of

variations, and thus that they constitute a "new idea," a "complete innovation," on his part.[18] The works certainly present unusual features. In the set in F major we find constant changing of key throughout: the theme is in F major, the first variation is in D major, the variations successively are in B-flat major, G major, E-flat major, and C minor, and F major returns near the end, so that the progression of keys mostly descends in thirds. The theme itself is a simple cantabile Adagio in three-part form, and the variations present the expected changes in character which here are pronounced: a minuet (iv), a march (v), and a bright Allegretto with the theme staccato in octaves over broken-chord accompaniment (vi). At the end stands a long and elaborate coda incorporating fantasia elements, a reprise of the theme, and finally motives from the theme, accompanied by brilliant figuration.

In the so-called *Prometheus* variations we can also note several original elements. First there is the relation to the old Baroque variations on an ostinato or ground: in an *Introduzione* the bass part of the theme is stated first and three variations on it follow; then the melody appears with its bass part as the accompaniment (Ex. 3-11). Beethoven followed this procedure in the *Sinfonia eroica* but not in the earlier ballet. Of the succeeding variations, some employ the melody while others only its bass. Second, we can note that after an impressive *minore* variation and a Largo with fantasia passages, there is a free fugue on the bass part, after which the theme is reprised in the long coda. An association with C. P. E. Bach has recently been disclosed.[19]

If the Variations in E-flat major (op. 35) represent a rapprochement between the usual practice of variation and the old practice of variations on an ostinato, then the Variations in C minor (WoO 80) impressively revive the earlier practice in its original force and magnitude. Here the theme, a real ostinato, eight bars in length and in triple time, is closely related to the eighteenth-century chaconne (Ex. 3-12).

The last work in variation form to be considered here is the celebrated Variations on a Waltz by Diabelli.[20] The theme was composed by the Viennese music publisher Anton Diabelli who submitted it to fifty composers in the hope that each would compose a variation on it, all fifty then to be published together. Beethoven delayed, so his contribution could not be included in the collection but his effort resulted ultimately in one of the largest sets of variations ever composed for keyboard. Again, this is Beethoven's only large set of variations to be based on a theme by another composer—in fact, a simple waltz, very much in the popular character generally associated with the genre, but containing elements that Beethoven found readily exploitable.

In accordance with the usual interpretation of this genre, we find contrast among the individual variations, each of which has its own character, often associated with some well-known type. We find marches (i, xvi, and xvii); a *serioso* (vi); a French overture (xiv); a lyrical Fughetta (xxiv) that recalls the finale of the Sonata in A-flat major (op. 110); four in the minor (ix and xxix–xxxi), the last three of them very slow and serious, particularly the very last which can be related to Bach's Goldberg variations; the brilliant triple fugue in E-flat major that follows these slow variations suggests both Bach

Example 3-11. BEETHOVEN: Variations in E-flat major (op. 35)—Excerpts
  A. Introduction—Beginning (mm. 1–9)
  B. Theme—Beginning (mm. 67–74)

and Handel. Two variations parody other composers—Leporello's "Notte e giorno faticar" from Mozart's *Don Giovanni* (xxii) and an etude by Johann Baptist Cramer (xxiii). At the very end, as if to recall the dance character of Diabelli's waltz and the old galant associations of the genre, Beethoven presents the theme as a stylized and elaborate minuet and in the coda suggests the end of his Sonata in C minor (op. 111).

It is the interpretation of the theme and variations as a genre that constitutes the originality to which Beethoven referred in the letter (in reference to op. 34 and 35) quoted above. In the hands of his contemporaries and immediate predecessors (Mozart, for one), the genre was regarded as popular, galant, and brilliant. While Beethoven has preserved this character in many of his sets, we have seen that he departed from it in these large sets, which became major compositions. In fact, in two cases he associated this innovating with the revival of the Baroque variations on an ostinato.

Example 3-12. BEETHOVEN: Variations in C minor (WoO 80)—Theme and First
Variation (mm. 1–16)

Other Works

Then there are numerous miscellaneous pieces—dances (minuets, Austrian ländler, waltzes) and a few others. Notable here are the three sets known as Bagatelles, or, as Beethoven called them, "Kleinigkeiten" (Little Things). The three sets of these short and simple pieces, mostly in three-part form, are op. 33, 119, and 126 (composed 1801–1802, 1820–1822, 1823–1824; published 1803, 1823, and 1825 respectively). Beethoven clearly planned the last set as a cycle, but the same claim has also been made for op. 119. Then we can note other little pieces of different kinds, including the famous "Für Elise" in A minor (should actually be "Für Therese," WoO 59, composed 1808 or 1810, not published until 1867), and the "Lustig–Traurig" (Happy–Sad, WoO 54, composed presumably in the 1790s, published 1888) in C major–C minor. Other works he seems to have intended for use in his public appearances. Among these are the three rondos also composed in the 1790s: two in C major and G major (op. 51, composed 1796–1798, published 1797 and 1802 respectively) and the well-known rondo, *Wut über den verlorenen Groschen* in G major (Rage Over the Lost Penny, op. 129, composed 1795, published 1828). In the same popular and brilliant vein is the Polonaise in C major (op. 89, composed 1814, published 1815). Of a different order are the few works that suggest the Baroque tradition, evident in the variations. Each of two early preludes (op. 39, composed presumably 1789, published 1803) modulates successively through all the keys in accordance with the circle of fifths; and the earlier independent Prelude in F minor (WoO 55) was composed around 1803, published 1805. Larger is the Fantasia in B major (op. 77, composed 1809, published 1810). This piece, which commences in G minor, begins in the fashion of a late eighteenth-century fantasia, but at the Allegretto it goes over into variation form and ends with a coda. For piano duet Beethoven composed little: an early galant Sonata in D major (op. 6, composed 1796–1797, published 1797), a set of three marches (op. 45, composed 1803, published 1804), and two sets of variations (WoO 67 and 74, composed 1792 and 1796–1797, published 1794 and 1805 respectively). Finally, he made an arrangement of the Grand Fugue (op. 133, the original finale of the Quartet in B-flat major, op. 130) for piano duet (op. 134, composed 1826, published 1827).

In conclusion we can make several general observations about Beethoven's piano music. We have noted the emphasis placed on the piano sonata: formerly this genre had not been regarded as belonging to the important large forms of musical composition, but as something small, in the galant idiom and intended chiefly for use in teaching. With Beethoven the genre may be related to teaching, but in a different sense. For here it is himself he is teaching, using the genre as a proving ground. The choice was determined by his involvement with the large forms of instrumental music and the fact that the piano was his instrument. Thus it is with his work that the genre came into its own as a large form of piano music. Much the same applies to the variations. Finally, in his shorter pieces and in the emphasis on lyricism in the late sonatas, Beethoven anticipated the Romantics.

NOTES FOR CHAPTER THREE

1. See the roughly contemporary biographical account of Griesinger, available in V. Gotwals, *Joseph Haydn: Eighteenth-Century Gentleman and Genius* (Madison: University of Wisconsin Press, 1963), 17.

2. The enumeration of Haydn's piano music follows that of A. von Hoboken, *Joseph Haydn: Thematisch-bibliographisches Werkverzeichnis*, 3 vols. (Mainz: Schott, 1957–1978). Hoboken's numbers (usually shown as "Hob.") do not reflect chronology. This discussion uses the chronology developed by A. Brown, *Joseph Haydn's Keyboard Music* (Bloomington: Indiana University Press, 1986), 117–123. Es2 and Es3 were assigned to sonatas discovered after the older enumeration had been completed (Es is German for E-flat). Since most of Haydn's piano sonatas are in Hoboken's group XVI, we have omitted the customary Hob. and the Roman numbers. Among several concordances of the various enumerations of Haydn's sonatas is M. Hinson, *Guide to the Pianist's Repertoire*, 2nd ed. (Bloomington: Indiana, 1987), 358–359. Piano trios are not included; thus, the Sonata/Divertimento in D major (Hob. XIV: 5) does not appear here because it may originally have had parts for violin and cello. Unless otherwise indicated, dates refer to composition.

3. The Sonata in C minor (No. 20), included in this publication, was begun in 1771.

4. U. Leisinger, "New Light on C. P. E. Bach and Joseph Haydn," unpub. paper read before the American Musicological Society, Chicago (1991).

5. See the discussion in L. Ratner, *Classic Music: Expression, Form, and Style* (New York: Schirmer, 1980), 412–421. His interpretation differs in some respects from that presented here.

6. See C. Rosen, *The Classical Style* (New York: Viking, 1971; New York: Norton, 1972), 351–365, and Brown, *Joseph Haydn's Keyboard Music*, 73–83 and passim.

7. The K numbers, assigned to Mozart's works in chronological order, are the work of L. Koechel, *Chronologisch-thematisches Verzeichnis sämmtlicher Tonwerke Wolfgang Amadé Mozarts* (Leipzig: Breitkopf & Härtel, 1862), as revised, first by A. Einstein (3rd ed., 1937) and then by E. Reichert, F. Giegling, A. Weinmann, and G. Sievers (6th ed., Wiesbaden: Breitkopf & Härtel, 1963). In the revisions mentioned, some of Koechel's original numbers have been changed; in this book the new number appears first and the original one after the slash. Publication dates are given only for those sonatas that appeared during Mozart's lifetime. Incomplete works are not included. The dating of the sonatas K. 189d–K. 205b and of the sonatas K. 300d–300k has been established by W. Plath, "Zur Datierung der Klaviersonaten KV 279–284," *Acta Mozartiana* 21 (1974): 26–30, and "Beiträge zur Mozartautographie II: Schriftchronologie 1770–1780," *Mozart-Jahrbuch 1976–1977* (Kassel: Bärenreiter, 1978), 131–173; that of the Sonata K. 315c/333 by A. Tyson, *Mozart: Studies of the Autograph Scores* Cambridge: Harvard, 1978), 73–81; see also pp. 20 and 29. The Sonata in F major (K. 547a/Anh. 135) contains Mozart's own adaptations of the second movement of the Sonata in F major for violin and piano (K. 547) and the third movement of the Sonata in C major (K. 545); Anh. = Anhang (Appendix). Conventional numbering of the sonatas does not appear here because it is no longer relevant.

8. Bass drums, cymbals, and tambourines used by Turkish mercenaries in the employ of the nobility in Austria and southern Germany at the time, also known as Janissaries; some pianos of the time had a stop that produced the effect of these instruments.

9. A. Tyson, *Thematic Catalogue of the Works of Muzio Clementi* (Tutzing: Schneider, 1967), 11–12 and passim. Among several concordances of the various editions of Clementi's sonatas, see, for example, M. Hinson, *Guide to the Pianist's Repertoire*, 2nd ed., 202–204.

10. See H. Craw, who has assigned C numbers to Dussek's compositions in his *A Biography and Thematic Catalog of the Works of Dussek* (unpub. diss., Southern California, 1964). W. Newman, *The Sonata Since Beethoven* (Chapel Hill: University of North Carolina Press, 1969), 664–665, provides a concordance of the opus numbers under which Dussek's sonatas were published.

11. Dates of publication according to J. Sachs, "A Checklist of the Works of Johann Nepomuk Hummel," *Notes* 30 (1975–1976): 732–739.

12. Often reproduced, in different translations; readily available in *The Beethoven Compendium*, ed. B. Cooper (London: Thames & Hudson, 1991), 170–171.

13. These have been summarized in D. Johnson, J. Kerman and A. Tyson, *The Beethoven Sketches* (London: Oxford, 1989), with full bibliography. More interpretative and analytical is B. Cooper, *Beethoven and the Compositional Process* (Oxford: Clarendon, 1990), which contains studies of the sonatas in D minor (op. 31 ii) and C major (op. 53).

14. See G. Kinsky and H. Halm, *Das Werk Beethovens: Verzeichnis seiner sämtlichen vollendeten Kompositionen* (Munich: Henle, 1955).

15. L. Misch, *Die Faktoren der Einheit in der Mehrsätzigkeit der Werke Beethovens: Versuch einer Theorie des Werkstils*, Veröffentlichungen des Beethovenhauses in Bonn, ser. 4, vol. 3 (Munich-Duisburg: Henle, 1958).

16. Letter to Breitkopf & Härtel, 9 October 1811; see *The Letters of Beethoven*, vol. 1, ed. and trans. E. Anderson (New York: St. Martin's Press, 1961), 337–338.

17. A. Knab, "Die Einheit der Beethovenschen Klaviersonate As-Dur op. 110," *Zeitschrift für Musikwissenschaft* 1 (1918–1919): 388–399; more recently, W. Kinderman, "Integration and Narrative Design in Beethoven's Piano Sonata in A-flat Major, Opus 110," *Beethoven Forum*, vol. 1, ed. C. Reynolds (Lincoln: University of Nebraska Press, 1992), 111–145.

18. Letter to Breitkopf & Härtel, October 1802; see *The Letters of Beethoven*, ed. and trans. E. Anderson, 1: 76–77.

19. E. Derr, "Beethoven's Long Term Memory of C. P. E. Bach's Rondo in E♭, W. 61, No. 1," *Musical Quarterly* 70 (1984): 45–76.

20. See W. Kinderman, *Beethoven's Diabelli Variations* (Oxford: Clarendon, 1987), to which the following account is indebted.

CHAPTER FOUR

The Early Nineteenth Century

The nature of the change that Romanticism brought to music in the early nineteenth century has often been misunderstood. For the most part the misconceptions rest on an imperfect appreciation of the intents and accomplishments of Haydn and Mozart, so that the relation between the work of these musicians and that of Beethoven and Schubert has at times been misconstrued.

The great change in musical style—among the most far reaching and thoroughgoing in the whole history of music—took place somewhat before 1750 (see Chapter Two). This change brought instrumental music to the forefront; from the modest genres of the galant emerged the string quartet, the symphony, the sonata, and the rest, all genres that were based on the newly worked out technique of thematic development. But a composer's intent often went beyond this. He or she conceived each large musical work as an entity, a totality that was at the same time a wholly individual creation. Hence, the idea that the musical artwork, in these large forms at all events, was the unique expression of the composer had been clearly established in the mature works of Haydn and Mozart, if not earlier, and therefore does not represent anything new when we encounter it in the work of subsequent composers.

A leading preoccupation of the Romantic literary movement, particularly in Germany—where it went back to the 1790s—had to do with music. Music figures prominently in essays and stories by, for instance, Wackenroder, Tieck, Novalis, and, particularly, E. T. A. Hoffmann, himself a composer. Part of this interest in music among literary people had to do with the power that came to be attributed to the art at the time, that of being able to express the subtlest and most powerful human emotions more directly and accurately than any other artistic medium—to speak the unspeakable. Music, then, became the vehicle for the expression or characterization of explicit extramusical ideas.

This lies back of a fundamental change that took place in the early nineteenth century, and here piano music is important. This change involved repertory. While composers continued to cultivate the large Classical sonata, particularly as it appears in the work of Beethoven, that genre lost its leading position. In its place came something new, a small form that was eagerly seized upon and made a typical Romantic genre of musical composition: the character piece. This is a small composition, usually in a simple form (the ternary scheme, A–B–A, in which the midsection contrasts with the other, is the most common). To such pieces, which were primarily lyrical, composers often gave descriptive, expressive, or programmatic titles that indicate what they are intended to express or what the proper associations are.

Such descriptive compositions, as we have observed, are not new. We can refer to pieces of this kind in the English virginal music of the Elizabethan era or in the Biblical Sonatas of Kuhnau, as well as in the extensive French keyboard repertory of the Baroque, particularly the work of François Couperin. Toward the end of the eighteenth century we begin to see keyboard pieces (a common designation was *charakteristisches Klavierstück*) that represent a particular affect, in collections and individual pieces, for example, by C. P. E. Bach, C. G. Füger, Johann Abraham Peter Schulz (1747–1800), Carl Friedrich Zelter (1758–1832), and Friedrich Rellstab (1759–1813). Even earlier is the poet Sperontes' *Singende Muse an der Pleisse* (first published 1736; his real name was Johann Sigismund Scholze, 1705–1750), which consists of songs with keyboard accompaniment but which may be performed without the singing, thus becoming, to anticipate Mendelssohn, "songs without words." Another small form in the keyboard music of the time was the *Handstück*, a teaching piece or study frequently emphasizing virtuosity, in which a particular character or affect was expressed. Such pieces are prominent in the work of Daniel Gottlob Türk (1750–1813), who published many collections of these small pieces, as well as eight sets of sonatas. He also included twelve *Handstücke* as examples in his treatise, the *Clavierschule* (1789).

But this new genre did not seize the attention of leading composers until the early years of the nineteenth century. Beethoven, for one, produced a few works of this kind, as we have noted, calling them bagatelles, or trifles, modest works, intended and recognized as such. It is not until the 1820s, in the work of Schubert, that we see a leading composer emphasizing the new genre; Beethoven's late bagatelles also date from this time.

The change in attitude seems to have stemmed in part from the work of two Bohemian composers, Václav Jan Tomášek (1774–1850) and Jan Václav Voříšek (1791–1825). Tomášek composed such small pieces beginning around 1810, calling them eclogues, rhapsodies, and dithyrambs, of which the last was given to pieces somewhat longer than the others. His pupil Voříšek, who was active in Vienna, used the designation *impromptu*. Here music acquired a poetic meaning in which reflection became a leading principle, aiming at spontaneity of expression, or at least the appearance of such spontaneity. Another composer important here was Heinrich Marschner (1795–1861), known mostly for opera, but who published two sets of impromptus (op. 22 and 23) and two sets entitled simply *Charakterstücke* (op. 18 and 181), along with many other works for piano, including seven sonatas. Other descriptive titles used for such pieces in the early nineteenth century include: *Albumblatt* (Album Leaf, a short and intimate piece in the spirit of something written on a page of the autograph album of a close friend), Fantasy or *Fantasiestück*, Nocturne or *Nachtstück*, Humoresque, Song without Words, Intermezzo, Prelude, Scherzo, Caprice, or, simply, Lyric Piece.

All these character pieces show simplicity of form, the ternary plan, as already indicated, being found in most. Lyricism came to the fore along with the coloristic aspect of harmonic changes. At the same time, many such pieces resemble individual movements of a sonata and, as will be seen, some larger character pieces even employ the sonata form itself, or some variant of it. Nocturnes, intermezzi, and impromptus often resemble slow movements; scherzos and rondos are like their counterparts in sonatas. This seems an indication that the small form was coming to the fore while the old form of the sonata was receding into the background. On the other hand, the descriptive titles of the character piece appear in sonatas. By way of example we can refer to two *sonates caractéristiques*, one by Eberl in F minor (op. 12), the other by Moscheles (op. 27); Moscheles' *Sonate mélancolique* in F-sharp minor (op. 49); and large compositions by Carl Loewe (1796–1869), which include the *Grande sonate élegique* in F minor (op. 32), *Zigeuner* (gypsy) sonata (op. 107b), and two works he identified as symphonic poems for piano. Pathétique sonatas belong here as well and are by no means new; along with Beethoven's famous example goes one by Ludwig Berger also in C minor (revised version, op. 7, published 1815). The Sonata in F minor by E. T. A. Hoffmann (op. 30, composed 1807–1808, in four movements that follow one another without pause) is also related to these characteristic sonatas.

An important secondary figure is Johann Wilhelm Hässler (1747–1822). His voluminous output includes a great many sonatas (several of which are associated with fantasias, caprices, and preludes), fantasias, a set of preludes in all the major and minor keys (op. 47, 1817, 360 strong), *Études en quatre-vingt valces* ([*valses*], op. 29), and sets of variations. Some of his sonatas are large (the *grandes sonates*, particularly op. 26), but others are small (*leichte Sonaten*) and even didactic (*sonates instructives*); still others are known as *Sonates expressives* (6 in all, 3 each in op. 16 and 32). Some of the sonatas are preceded by caprices or fantasias. More to our point is the set *Pièces caractéristiques* (5, op. 27), all of which are based on the same theme. One of Hässler's most popular works is the Grande Gigue, D minor (op. 31).

An important composer in whose work piano music does not assume a prominent position is Carl Maria von Weber (1786–1826). In his earlier years, before he established himself as a conductor and composer of opera, concertizing was his main activity, clearly suggested in the genres that he emphasized in his music for piano. In the numerous sets of themes and variations, many of the themes are taken from theatrical works of the time or from popular songs and dances. Among them are early sets of allemandes and ecossaises, the *Favorit-Walzer* for the Empress Marie-Louise of France (6, J. 143–148, composed and published 1812),[1] and then the larger works—among them the *Grande Polonaise* in E-flat major (J. 59/op. 21, composed 1808, published 1810) and the *Polacca brilliante* in E major (J. 268/op. 72, composed 1819, published 1821, also known as *L'hilarité*). Among Weber's most important compositions is the celebrated *Aufforderung zum Tanz* (Invitation to the Dance) in D-flat major (J. 260/op. 65, composed 1819, published 1821). This is based on the waltz, cast in rondo form with an introduction and epilogue. Weber's own annotations make it clear that the piece is programmatic: the introduction, the tentative approach to the lady, the invitation to dance, the acceptance, and so on. This piece represents the first among the large-scale concert waltzes and the first programmatic piece based on the waltz.

Weber also produced two works that we can relate to the character piece: the *Momento capriccioso* in B-flat major (J. 56/op. 12, composed 1808, published 1811) and the *Rondo brilliante* in E-flat major (J. 252/op. 62, composed and published 1819), also known as *La gaité*. In these virtuosity is paramount, as is clear from the constant employment of figuration to decorate the light and elegant "salon" melodies.

But Weber also cultivated the piano sonata. There are four.

WEBER'S PIANO SONATAS

C major (No. 1, J. 138/op. 24, composed and published 1812)
A-flat major (No. 2, J. 199/op. 39, composed and published 1816)
D minor (No. 3, J. 206/op. 49, composed 1816, published 1817)
E minor (No. 4, J. 287/op. 70, composed 1819–1822, published
    1823)

These have little in common with the sonatas Beethoven composed during these years: rather Weber maintained the old forms and connotations of the sonata. Three of them are in four movements (the Sonata in D minor, lacks the minuet). We find sonata form in the first movements and rondo form in the finales. In the slow movements and minuets we find the three-part scheme. Thus Weber's sonatas are conventional in form. What attracts attention is the variety in the individual movements, especially the style contrasts among the various themes, the sudden changes, and the prominence of virtuoso elements. Weber intended the Sonata in E minor as programmatic. Its key had conventionally been associated with sadness but Weber has gone further and made a link with mental disturbance and depression, capping the whole off with a tarantella finale, a dance of death.

We will now review the piano music of the principal composers from the first half of the nineteenth century—Schubert, Mendelssohn, Schumann, and Chopin—and then take a quick look at the situation in the United States.

SCHUBERT

Franz Peter Schubert (1797–1828) stands at the crossroads. In his works we find not only the old Classic large form, the sonata, but also the new Romantic genre, the character piece. This situation has made Schubert difficult to classify. It is ironic that of all the composers who may be associated with Viennese Classicism, Schubert is the only one who actually was a native-born Viennese, yet his essential similarity to these composers has often been questioned. There is one significant difference, however; since, unlike Haydn, Mozart, Beethoven, and most other composers of the time, Schubert was neither a virtuoso pianist nor a conductor, he remained in effect shut out of the main avenues by which a composer cultivated an audience. Moreover, relatively few of his compositions were published during his lifetime, so that he made no great impact on European musical life.

His fame in large measure rests on his songs, of which there are more than six hundred. Yet in the later years of his life, the output of songs fell off as he devoted himself more and more to instrumental music, particularly the large forms. In a letter of 31 March 1824 he makes his attitude clear, stating that, while he has been engaged in the composition of some songs, he has concentrated on string quartets and the octet: "in fact," he continues, "I intend to pave my way to grand symphony in this manner."[2] Along with chamber music, however, there is an abundance of piano music of all kinds. We will commence our survey with the piano sonata, a genre that also played an important part in his aim, as he put it, to "pave the way to grand symphony." Moreover, he cultivated the sonata throughout his career as a composer, producing some twenty-two in all, shown here in chronological order by dates of composition.

SCHUBERT'S PIANO SONATAS

NOTE: Asterisks denote incomplete compositions.

THE EARLY SONATAS
First group (composed 1815–1816)
*E major (D. 157, composed 1815, published 1888)
*C major (D. 279, composed 1815, published 1888)
E major (D. 459 and 459A, composed 1816, published 1843 as *Fünf Klavierstücke*)

Second group (composed 1817)
A minor (D. 537/op. 164, published ca. 1852)
A-flat major (D. 557, published 1888)
E minor (D. 566, published 1888)
D-flat major (D. 567, published 1897); second version, E-
flat major (D. 568/op. 122, composed 1826, published
1829)
*F-sharp minor (D. 570–571: two Allegro fragments and a
scherzo, published 1897)
B major (D. 575/op. 147, published 1846)

THE TIME OF CHANGE (1818–1819)
*C major (D. 613: second movement only completed,
composed 1818, published 1897)
*F minor (D. 625: three movements completed, composed
1818, published 1897)
*C-sharp minor (D. 655: sketch of first movement,
composed 1819, published 1897)
A major (D. 664/op. 120, composed ca. 1819, published
1829)

MATURITY
First group (composed 1823–1826)
*E minor (D. 769A: fragment of first movement,
composed 1823, published 1958)
A minor (D. 784/op. 143, composed 1823, published
1839)
*C major (D. 840, "Reliquie," last two movements
incomplete, composed 1825, published 1861)
A minor (D. 845/op. 42, composed 1825, published 1826)
D major (D. 850/op. 53, composed 1825, published 1826)
G major (D. 894/op. 78, "Fantasy," composed 1826,
published 1827)

The late sonatas (composed 1828, published 1839)
C minor (D. 958/op. posth.)
A major (D. 959/op. posth.)
B-flat major (D. 960/op. posth.)

Schubert composed two sonatas in 1815 and one in 1816, six in 1817, three in 1818, one in 1819, two in 1823, three in 1825, and three in 1828, nine of these incomplete. Quantitatively, therefore, there are three high points: 1817, 1825, and 1828. It was around 1825 that Schubert expressed his determination to devote himself more and more to the large forms of instrumental music.

We should also note that only three—those in A minor (D. 845), D major (D. 850), and G major (D. 894)—were published during his lifetime.

Although two remained incomplete, the early sonatas of 1815–1816 provide an accurate indication of the type of sonata to be favored by Schubert. He accepted the four-movement scheme as standard (the Sonata in E major [D. 459] is an exception in five movements), and it remained so in his work. In Schubert's sonatas, that is, we do not find the varieties in the arrangement, forms, and compositional procedures that we encountered in the sonatas of Beethoven. Instead, as is evident in these early works, Schubert worked mostly with new types of themes and a new treatment of the sonata form. The themes are lyrical, often balanced in antecedent and consequent phrases; all the interest goes to the theme itself as a melody rather than to its inherent susceptibility to thematic development. Indeed, he kept the development sections short. Instead of working with short motives, as was characteristic of Beethoven, he selected one phrase of his theme and used it as the basis for a sequential passage with modulations.[3] This approach provides the basis for a fundamental aspect of Schubert's art: the prominence he gave to modulation, the free use of keys, slipping from one to another in an unexpected, often surprising fashion, emphasizing sonority instead of formal aspects of music.

Schubert cast his slow movements in what is usually called song form: alternating sections, usually three (A–B–A), but sometimes five (A–B–A–B–A, or some other variant), in some cases embodying considerable contrast. (See the Sonata in E major [D. 157], in which harmonic surprise is important.) The minuets, scherzos, and trios present much that is expected, except, again, the astonishing freedom of modulation (see, again, the sonata in E major [D. 157]). The scherzo of the Sonata in E major (D. 459), is fast, exploits motivic themes, and abounds in sudden dynamic changes.

An important aspect is the small scale and generally moderate character of these early sonatas. This is clear from the tempo and character designated by Schubert: Allegro moderato, Allegro ma non troppo, or Andante (Adagio is unusual). The moderate first movements require neither long, weighty codas nor brilliant finales. From this aspect we would associate the early sonatas of Schubert more with the ideals of Mozart and the galant tradition of the eighteenth century than with Beethoven.

The six sonatas of 1817 present Schubert's first group of complete works in this genre (only the Sonata in F-sharp minor [D. 570–571], is incomplete here). Generally they present the features observed in the early group but on a larger scale. Greater length and elaboration characterize the sonatas in A minor (D. 537/op. 164), E-flat major (D. 568/op. 122), and B major (D. 575/op. 147). Varied thematic material abounds in the first movements of these sonatas: the Sonata in A minor, with its lyrical principal theme, the succeeding dancelike melodies and their appropriate accompanimental figures, and the unexpected change of key, is typical. Moreover, this sonata—Schubert's first large work in the minor—is also interesting for its exploitation of the sonorous possibilities of the piano. These include, in the first movement, the full and widely spaced chords of the principal theme, the crescendo in the transition with its syncopated accentuations and incessantly driven rhythmic motives, the dramatic pause preceding the entrance of the secondary theme, and the soft pedal-point that accompanies the closing theme. Yet the development sections of these sonatas continue to remain short. In the sonatas in A minor and E-flat major, the development does not work with themes from the exposition, but with new material, making only some reference to themes already introduced, again with great freedom in modulation. The large Sonata in B major, although it employs the principal theme as the basis for a modulating sequence, displays Schubert's preoccupation with sonority: sudden modulations, enharmony, changes in key signature, and dynamic effects. In the slow movement we again find song forms in three and five parts, minuets and trios as third movements (the sonata in B major has a scherzo), and easygoing finales, generally in sonata form (that of the sonata in A minor has a simple rondo, the same episode appearing twice).

The next group of sonatas reveals uncertainty. The set form of the 1817 group does not appear; instead we find evidence of experimentation. Although the Sonata in C major (D. 613), of which Schubert completed but one movement, was apparently to be in the same style as the works of 1817, we notice unusual aspects in the others. Two of the four works are in the minor, and both are incomplete. In the sonatas in the minor the first movements emphasize motivic themes and intense expression. This is particularly true of the Sonata in F minor (D. 625)—the key of Beethoven's "Appassionata"—with its wide leaps and virtuoso figuration. In all this we see Schubert attempting to make his sonatas more in the spirit of Beethoven's middle-period sonatas. But the similarity could be somewhat misleading, since in spite of the preoccupation with motivic themes and their working-out, Schubert continued to exploit the resources of harmony in a coloristic way. Consider the Sonata in F minor, the first movement of which contains sudden enharmonic shifts, the first to E major in the exposition (whereby A-flat = G-sharp) and the second to C-sharp minor in the development (whereby D-flat and A-flat = C-sharp and G-sharp), ultimately returning to F minor; this is foreign to Beethoven.

In view of this effort at heightening the expressive capacities of the piano sonata, Schubert's next work in the genre comes as a surprise. The popular Sonata in A major (D. 664/op. 120, 1819) suggests a return to the 1817 type of sonata. It is small and intimate, in three movements. The lyrical impulse is dominant, the development of the first movement short and modest despite the octave runs and with but little thematic connection to the exposition. There is a slow movement in simple three-part form and the light finale in sonata form (recapitulation in the subdominant), interrupted by a secondary theme consisting of scale figuration.

Yet this work is symptomatic of what was to come in the next group of sonatas, those composed in 1825 and 1826. These compositions take on particular importance in the work of Schubert as a whole, since they were composed at the time when he expressed his desire to emphasize the composition of large instrumental works. Moreover, these sonatas count among his first successes in this area, since three of them were published shortly after their completion and received favorable notices in the press: A minor (D. 845/op. 42), D major (D. 850/op. 53), and G major (D. 894/op. 78). Here not much is different from the sonatas of 1817 except that he cast most of these sonatas on a much larger scale and major keys predominate. Moreover, he established the four-movement scheme as the rule (except for the three-movement Sonata in A minor [D. 784/op. 143]). Possibly drawing on his motivic work in the sonatas of 1818–1819, Schubert here systematically used thematic material from the expositions in the developments. He also gave a new importance to the codas in movements in sonata form. As before, the slow movements reveal the song form with its alternating sections (except for the theme and variations in the Sonata in A minor [D. 845/op. 42]). Among the four-movement sonatas, a minuet appears in the Sonata in G major (D. 894/op. 78), scherzos in the others. Finally, as something of a departure, for the finales Schubert established as his standard the rondo form with one episode, usually treated with some freedom and with contrast between the different thematic components.

Again the lyric impulse coupled with an even-more-grandiose exploitation of the sonorous capabilities of the piano are the most important aspects. Good examples are in the first movements of the sonatas in A minor (D. 845/op. 42) and G major (D. 894/op. 78): in the former, at the close of the exposition, the principal theme is stated in a resounding *fortissimo*, while near the beginning of the development the same theme is stated successively in different registers, and in the coda there is an impressive accumulation such that the piano seems to have been conceived orchestrally. Similar features abound in the Sonata in G major (D. 894/op. 78); one should note especially the development of the first movement with its large-scale crescendo and the harpsichord-like *pianissimo* effect in the trio. In the second movement of the Sonata in A minor (D. 845/op. 42) the third variation is characterized by dotted rhythms, wide octave leaps, changes in registration, chromaticism, and sudden changes of dynamics.

Of a different order is the ambitious Sonata in D major (D. 850/op. 53), which gives prominence to something not at all usual in Schubert—virtuosity. This quality appears at once in the first movement: the abrupt *fortissimo* opening, the loud repeated chords in fast tempo, and the triplet figuration (see Ex. 4-1). The impulse is largely rhythmic, and this aspect, while never really lacking in the movement even in the lyrical secondary theme, culminates in the development. Such a large-scale first movement needs and gets a long and serious slow movement, a Con moto, A major, in five-part form. A particularly Romantic sonority is achieved toward the end of the episode with the gentle dissonance between the thirds of the right hand and the static minor seventh in the bass. The scherzo too is suitably vigorous, with full chords in dotted rhythms and a *pianissimo* trio consisting entirely of repeated chords and unexpected changes in harmony. The finale presents, as is typical of Schubert, great variety. A naive, innocent, harmonically simple rondo theme is varied each time it appears, the figuration becoming more excited

Example 4-1. SCHUBERT: Allegro vivace from Sonata in D major (D. 850/op. 53)—
Beginning (mm. 1–12)

and brilliant in the episodes, the second of which is a closed three-part form
with a vigorous midsection of full chords, and octave passages that make a
strong contrast to the lyrical rondo theme. The bigness of conception and
the virtuoso treatment are doubtless related to the fact that Schubert composed the work for his friend Karl Maria Bocklet, a pianist of great skill.
    Schubert composed his last three sonatas in the late summer of 1828.
The basic aspects again are familiar: the four-movement scheme is found in
all the large first movements which are in sonata form; the Andantes are in
song form (five-part in the Sonata in C minor [D. 958], three-part in the others); and there are two scherzos and one minuet (in the Sonata in C minor [D.
958]), with rondos as finales. While these works may represent the culmination of Schubert's sonata composition, they also represent a combination of

Schubert's two previous ways of dealing with the big first movement in sonata form. In the expositions of the sonatas in C minor (D. 958) and A major (D. 959), we find the characteristic wealth of varied thematic material: the full chords, dotted rhythms, and figuration of the Sonata in C minor (D. 958) and the sonorous opening of the Sonata in A major (D. 959), with its sustained chords against descending octave leaps in the bass along with the more lyrical secondary themes. In the Sonata in B-flat major (D. 960), however, all is lyricism, both in the broad, cantabile principal theme given out over rich harmonic accompaniment and the lighter secondary theme which in turn dissolves into ländler-like triplets at the close. But in the development sections Schubert generally has not exploited themes from the exposition; instead he introduces new themes. This is most evident in the sonatas in C minor (D. 958) and A major (D. 959), where the principal themes certainly appear to possess the possibility of being broken down into component motives for development, but Schubert does not do this, preferring to retain characteristic rhythmic and accompanimental figures which lead to the presentation of new thematic material. The Sonata in B-flat major (D. 960), on the other hand, employs its lyric principal theme in the development as the basis for a long modulating sequence but eventually introduces a totally new theme that is worked to a grandiose climax, after which the principal theme returns. In all these sonatas, modulation plays an important role.

The slow movements present simple, at times innocent, melodies that could easily have been used in songs, with clear, balanced phrases over unobtrusive accompaniments. But in the contrasting sections Schubert brings variety, attaining big climaxes in the sonatas in C minor (D. 958) and A major (D. 959). In the Andante, in C-sharp minor, of the lyrical Sonata in B-flat major (D. 960), Schubert contrasts the slow melancholy melody in thirds over the broken-chord figure in the accompaniment with the broad chordal lyricism (in A major) of the midsection, also making a gentle change to the major near the end.

The third movements are light and dancelike, while the finales, in rondo form, employ schemes that are less regular than what Schubert had used before, particularly the sonatas in A major (D. 959) and B-flat major (D. 960). All have variety, abundant opportunities for display, and effective finishes.

Schubert, therefore, reached his own individual interpretation of the piano sonata, in which he placed less emphasis on the motivic development so prominent in Haydn and Beethoven. We find instead an essentially lyrical interpretation of the genre, with emphasis going to the themes themselves and not to what can be constructed from their component elements. If the influence of Beethoven can be found at all, it lies in the large dimensions and profound character of these works. While we can readily perceive the large dimensions, it is different with profound character. For Schubert has achieved this profundity not by the employment of learned or difficult musical procedures, as composers often had done in the past, but by the melodies themselves. Again we can find some examples in the work of Beethoven, especially in the late works. Schubert took this conception and made it the *sine qua non* of his art.

Much has been made of the songlike qualities in Schubert. This involves not just the melodies but also that great accomplishment of Schubert's work with songs—the characteristic accompaniment that makes possible the musical interpretation of the poem being set. Einstein, for one, has identified several movements from piano sonatas as related to or having "affinities" with individual songs:[4] for instance, between the slow movements of the Sonata in A major (D. 664) and "Der Unglückliche" (D. 713), of the Sonata in D major (D. 850/op. 53) to "Fülle der Liebe" (D. 854), and of the Sonata in A major (D. 959) to "Pilgerweise" (D. 789), while the finale of the same sonata is associated with "Im Frühling" (D. 882) and the first movement of the Sonata in B-flat major (D. 960) is related to Mignon's song "So lasst mich scheinen" (D. 727 or 877 iii). While some of these "affinities" may be speculative, they are inspired by the fact that song melodies are featured in several of Schubert's large instrumental works, of which "Die Forelle" (The Trout, piano quintet) and "Der Tod und das Mädchen" (Death and the Maiden, string quartet) are only the most familiar.

Schubert also essayed the fantasia. There are two early efforts—the Largo in C minor (D. 993, composed 1812) and the Fantasia in C major (D. 605, known as the "Grazer," presumably composed 1821–1823). But the most arresting example and one of his most grandiose compositions is the Fantasia in C major, called the *Wanderer* (D. 760/op. 15, composed 1822, published 1823) (see Ex. 4-2). A quatrain from the song of the same title (D. 489/op. 4 i, composed 1816) supplies the theme; its text is:

> *Die Sonne dünkt mich hier so kalt,*
> *Die Blüte welk, das Leben alt,*
> *Und was sie reden, leerer Schall,*
> *Ich bin ein Fremdling überall.*

> The sun seems so cold to me here,
> The blossom decayed, life old,
> And what they speak, empty noise;
> I am a stranger everywhere.

This clearly represents Romantic melancholy. From these four lines Schubert has generated a large work of four closely connected movements to be played without pause: a brilliant opening Allegro, an Adagio (E major), a Presto (actually a scherzo with two different trios), and a concluding Allegro with a triumphant fugal beginning. The slow movement, in variation form, is closest to the song, at least at the beginning, and elements of this theme dominate the entire work. Thus we have the first large piano work by a major composer to be cast completely in cyclic form.[5] Whether or not the poem provides a program for the work is open to question. Noteworthy is the absence here of sonata form and of thematic development—Schubert has replaced development by variation. Conceived on an orchestral scale, with many tremolos, crescendos, broken octaves, full chords, and scale-runs, this work has no real predecessor and few successors. Significantly, it was later arranged for piano and orchestra by a composer who appreciated the presumed poetic basis, cyclic form, and virtuosity: Liszt.

Let us now turn to the lyrical character pieces for which Schubert took as his model the work of Tomášek and Vořišek. He produced four sets.

SCHUBERT'S CHARACTER PIECES

Moments musicals [sic] (4, D. 780/op. 94, composed 1823–1828, published 1828)
Impromptus (4, D. 899/op. 90, composed 1827, i and ii published 1827, iii and iv published 1857)
Impromptus (4, D. 935/op. 142, composed 1827, published 1839)
Klavierstücke (3, D. 946, composed 1828, published 1868)

The smallest of these are the six *Moments musicals* (following Einstein this retains Schubert's incorrect French), originally published in two volumes of three pieces each, except that two of them had already appeared under different titles: the Allegro moderato in F minor (iii) as "Air russe" (1823) and the Allegretto in A-flat major (vi) as "Plaintes d'un troubadour" (1824). Schubert's concept of the character piece is clear; simple repetitive formal schemes, mostly three part form, as in the Moderato in C major (i); with a transitional passage back to the reprise of the first section, as in the Allegretto in A-flat major (vi) where the midsection is labeled "trio"; and with a coda, as in the Moderato in C-sharp minor (iv). Schubert extended this to the five-part plan with the secondary passage appearing twice (varied the second time) in the popular Andantino in A-flat major (ii). Somewhat more elaborate, the well-known Allegro moderato in F minor (iii) has two subordinate passages with the principal theme appearing at the beginning and the end. Thus the only exception is the vigorous Allegro vivace in F minor (v), which is in binary form with each part to be repeated.

Throughout we can note Schubert's preoccupation with harmonic changes and modulation, particularly in the Moderato in C-sharp minor, where the midsection stands in enharmonic relation to the principal part. Enharmonic changes are also prominent in the Allegro vivace, F minor (v), which is also distinguished by the insistent "square" rhythms characteristic of the *all'ongarese* (Hungarian idiom). Then there is the rhythmically elaborate theme of the Moderato in C major (i), with its triplet eighth-notes alternating with dotted quarters and eighths. Or, finally, in the lyrical Andantino in A-flat major (iii) Schubert has contrasted the placid, slow-moving chordal melody

Example 4-2. SCHUBERT: Fantasia in C major (*Wanderer*, D. 760/op. 15): Excerpts
   A. Allegro con fuoco ma non troppo—Beginning (mm. 1–6)
   B. Adagio—Beginning (mm. 189–193)
   C. Presto—Beginning (mm. 245–251)
   D. Allegro [Fugato]—Beginning (mm. 598–607)

with the gentle cantabile of the episodic section (F-sharp minor), which in turn he has made impassioned by the *fortissimo* dynamic level upon its restatement.

The impromptus present much the same thing, but on a somewhat larger scale. The first set of four comprises an Allegro molto moderato in C minor, an Allegro in E-flat major, an Andante in G-flat major, and an Allegretto in A-flat major. Again we find simple formal schemes. Schubert uses three-part form in the Allegretto, to which he added codas in the Allegro and Andante in and which he extended into the five-part scheme with coda in the Allegro molto moderato. In the Allegro and the Allegretto he has contrast among the sections: the opening Allegro molto moderato features the lyric theme stated first as unaccompanied melody and then harmonized in block chords; in the

episode it appears in varied form and has been provided with an arpeggiated triplet accompaniment. In the Allegretto the principal section is divided into distinct parts—first, a theme consisting of descending scale figuration; this figuration then provides the accompanying figure to a lilting dancelike melody in the left hand; finally, the music moves into an easy cantabile line with light arpeggiated triplet accompaniment; to all this, the agitated and passionate trio in C-sharp minor comes as a strong contrast.

Typically Schubertian, however, is the lyrical Andante in G-flat major (the original publisher had it transposed to G major). It is uniform in character throughout, with a long cantabile line over a flowing arpeggio accompaniment and coloristic changes in harmony. Here Schubert has attained a new and characteristic sound quality or sonority that in fact is a fundamental aspect in the conception of the piece (Ex. 4-3). This preoccupation with sonority is revealed elsewhere in the impromptus. For example, in the first one, Allegro molto moderato in C major, at the first return of the principal section, the dynamic suddenly becomes *pianissimo*, and the melody is given out in the bass to the accompaniment of rapidly repeated octaves in the right hand; in this context, the shift from minor to major seems almost magical. Such an exploitation of sonority, of color produced by harmonic change and texture, is something new, something typically Romantic.

The situation is more complex in the next set of impromptus (D. 935). Ostensibly these four works were planned as a sequel to the previous set, as is born out by Schubert's manuscript. But Schumann, who reviewed them upon their publication, took them as forming a Sonata in F minor, a view shared by Einstein.[6] Aspects supporting this interpretation include the formal organization of the individual pieces, the key relations between them, and the formal types Schubert has used. There is, first, an Allegro moderato in F minor, then an Allegretto in A-flat, an Andante in B-flat major, and, concluding, an Allegro scherzando in F minor. Such a plan is certainly not to be found in the earlier set of impromptus. But the musical forms themselves are unusual: the third piece is a theme and variations, a form not particularly associated with the impromptu nor even with the character piece; the second piece is in three-part form with rounded binary form in each part and the midsection called "trio," so that it can easily be viewed as a sort of minuet (Einstein describes it as being in sarabande rhythm); and the last piece resembles the irregular rondo structure that often appears in Schubert's sonatas. The main difficulty, then, with the interpretation of these four impromptus as a sonata lies with the first movement which clearly does not resemble anything evident in Schubert's sonatas. The opening section, with its abundance of themes and its modulation from F minor to A-flat major, would certainly qualify as an exposition of sorts, but it lacks both the double-bar and a development. The development, as Einstein says, has been "replaced" by an episode that contrasts completely in style and has no thematic connection with the exposition; moreover, this episodic section returns in full near the end, after which the principal theme is heard in abbreviated form. This first piece, then, differs radically from what Schubert was wont to employ in his piano sonatas, and, whatever original features Schubert brought to the sonata, this sort of formal innovation is not among them. All in all, the case for calling these four impromptus a sonata, while it has something to recommend it, is by no means conclusive.

In other respects these pieces show features similar to what we noticed in the previous set of impromptus. Again the emphasis on sonority attracts attention, mostly through the freedom of modulation and the frequent har-

Example 4-3. SCHUBERT: Impromptu in G-flat major (op. 90/D. 899 iii)—Beginning (mm. 1–4)

monic surprises. An example may be found in the first piece, in Einstein's "replaced" development: it is *pianissimo* but *appassionato* with triadic six-teenth-note figuration in the middle register, while above and below come short, fragmentary phrases that often outline chords. Another characteristic passage appears in the Allegretto (ii), in the transition before the reprise of the principal section, where the fragmentary arpeggio figures are used in a diminuendo to the accompaniment of a softly sustained diminished triad as the harmonic motion goes from G-flat major to the dominant, C major.

The Andante and the concluding Allegro scherzando deserve special comment. The Andante brings five variations and coda on a theme Schubert used on other occasions, best known as the *Rosamunde* theme (it is the second entr'acte of that ballet). In modified rounded binary form (the reprise is varied), simple in the regularity of its phrase structure, the melody is given out over an easy regular accompaniment. While the variations all adhere to rounded binary form, in character they contrast: the figural first variation, the dancelike second and fifth (the fifth seems in fact like an elaboration of the second), the third in B-flat minor, with its lilting accompaniment, the rich harmonies of the fourth in G-flat major, and the short coda at the end. The concluding Allegro scherzando is a typical example of the *all'ongarese* in its principal section, which is in the minor. It is in fast triple meter with grace-notes and has a leaping accompaniment and accents on weak beats, both of which at times suggest a switch to duple meter. In addition we find parallel thirds, grace-notes in the melody, and ornate scale figuration and trills that bring the passage to a close.

Schubert's other set of impromptus are the Klavierstücke (D. 946). Composed in 1828, Schubert left them unpublished and they appeared, under the anonymous editorship of Brahms, only in 1868. Apparently he had planned another set of four impromptus but only completed these three: an Allegro assai in E-flat minor (ending in E-flat major); an Allegretto in E-flat major; and an Allegro in C major. Again the formal plans are simple and regular: simple three-part form (with retransition) in the Allegro in C major, and simple five-part form with contrasting episodes in the two others, except that in the Allegro assai in E-flat minor, the first episode returns at the end. In two of them Schubert has used rounded binary form: in the second episode of the Allegro assai in E-flat major and in all of the Allegretto in E-flat major. Einstein[7] regarded these as typical and conventional examples of standard types. The first is *alla francese*, as is mostly clearly seen from its second episode, a romance with the melody given out in parallel sixth-chords decorated by grace-notes; the Allegretto in E-flat major is *all'italiana* with its lilting melody in parallel thirds (6/8 meter); the last is *all'ongarese* once more, fast and with sharply accentuated syncopations. We find harmonic effects here, but in less profusion than elsewhere in Schubert's character pieces; there are enharmonic changes in the first Allegretto in the passage leading to the second episode, as well as in an episode in the Allegro in C major (iii), featuring chords in a rhythmic pattern. With these pieces Schubert may have wanted to try for a simpler and more popular style in his impromptus, but he was dissatisfied with this particular result. Many critics have agreed with him.

Along with these come other pieces of lesser stature: the *Albumblatt* (D. 844, composed 1825), actually a waltz, and a number of separate allegros, adagios, andantes, allegrettos, and scherzos.

In the tradition of Mozart but not of Beethoven, Schubert produced a large number of pieces for piano duet, which reflect an important Viennese tradition. Most of these are clearly domestic, small, easy, pleasing works for entertainment at home. Among them are various dances, ländler and *Deutsche Tänze*, as well as marches (among them the two sets of *Marches*

Militaires, 3, D. 733/op. 51, composed 1818, published 1826; and 6, D. 819/ op. 40, composed 1818 or 1824, published 1825), and two three-movement *Divertissements*, one Hungarian in G minor (D. 818/op. 54, composed presumably 1824, published 1826), the other French in E minor (D. 823/op. 63 i and 84, composed ca. 1825, published 1826 and 1827), as well as several overtures, some of which are arrangements of his own orchestral works. But he also produced large compositions for the duet medium: variations, sonatas, and fantasias. Of the three sets of variations by Schubert, two are small and conventional (both on French melodies), but the other is larger— this is the variations on an original theme in A-flat major (8, D. 813/op. 35, composed 1824, published 1825). The duet sonata, also cultivated by Mozart, appears twice: the early galant and virtuosic Sonata in B-flat major (D. 617/op. 30, composed 1818, published 1823) and the large one in C major (D. 812/op. 140, composed 1824, published 1837), in four movements, known as the Grand Duo. It had been thought that this was an arrangement by Schubert for piano duet of a lost symphony (the so-called Gmunden-Gastein symphony), and the piece has even been orchestrated, but we now know that there is no lost Gmunden-Gastein symphony and that references interpreted as referring to that nonexistent work actually refer to Schubert's last Symphony in C major (D. 849/944, the "Great"). The claim, nonetheless, serves as an indication of the scope of the work. As for the fantasia, which we have already encountered in Schubert's piano solo music, we find it for piano duet among his earliest compositions: the three-movement Fantasia in G major (D. 1, composed 1810, published 1888), his first known composition, and the four-movement Fantasia in G minor (D. 9, composed 1811, published 1888). Both works seem much like sonatas. But the next, the Fantasia in C minor (D. 48, composed 1813, published 1871), also known as *Grande Sonate*, reveals a relationship to Mozart's large quasi-baroque piano fantasias, with its toccata-like passages and concluding fugue. The third and last of Schubert's fantasias for piano duet is again one of his largest and most characteristic works—the Fantasia in F minor (D. 940/op. 103, composed 1828, published 1829), its movements played without pause and with the cantabile principal theme of the first movement reappearing just before the finale. One other work to be mentioned is the long, passionate Allegro in A minor (D. 947/op. 144, composed 1828, published 1840), to which the publisher gave the name *Lebensstürme* (Storms of Life).

In the piano music of Schubert, then, we find a broad division into two main classes, the old large form of piano music, represented principally by the sonata handed down from Haydn, Mozart, and Beethoven, and the new small, essentially lyrical character piece that was to become of prime significance for Romantic music. There are, as has been noted, innumerable instances of the capability of a new tradition to influence an older one, in some respects even to cause important changes in the older. The *Wanderer* Fantasia offers an example of the two traditions being drawn together in one large-scale work—the older fantasia coupled with a literary connection and pianistic virtuosity. But the two bodies of music, generally speaking, existed side by side throughout the nineteenth century, and a composer's relation to and treatment of them often suggests his or her basic orientation.

MENDELSSOHN

Unlike Schubert, Felix Mendelssohn-Bartholdy (1809–1847) spent his career in the forefront of European musical life, universally known and admired as composer, conductor, pianist, and even administrator. Immensely gifted (a true prodigy), born into a wealthy family and living in Berlin—long a seat of musical conservatism but by this time an important political and cultural center—Mendelssohn received a broad, humanistic education. His musical training was in the hands of Carl Friedrich Zelter, a proponent of eighteenth-century rationalism and an admirer of Bach. Zelter's traditionalist approach involved not only an emphasis on clarity and regularity, both important in the galant style of the eighteenth century, but also an interest in J. S. Bach. Zelter's legacy also included a belief that music was capable of expressing affects, states of mind—the old doctrine of the affections.

While piano music may not have occupied a dominant position in Mendelssohn's work, his compositions parallel those of Schubert to the extent that they share both traditions of solo music for the instrument, the older one involved with the large forms and the newer one emphasizing the character piece.

Of the large forms, Mendelssohn composed three piano sonatas. These sonatas are early works—when he composed the last Mendelssohn was eighteen. He did not continue working with the genre, but turned elsewhere, thus providing an early example of the decline in the position of the piano sonata in the nineteenth-century repertory generally. He published but one of them: the E major (op. 6).

MENDELSSOHN'S PIANO SONATAS

G minor (op. 105, composed 1821, not published until 1868)
E major (op. 6, composed and published 1826)
B-flat major (op. 106, composed 1827, not published until 1868)

The earliest, the Sonata in G minor, is a little piece in all respects. It is in three-movement form, the outer movements in sonata form with double-bar, the middle movement an Adagio cantabile in the five-part scheme with the episode appearing twice. The two remaining sonatas, on the other hand, are more ambitious. The Sonata in E major (op. 6) consists of four movements to be played without pause. It also displays cyclic form, the recalling of the principal theme of the first movement near the end of the finale. Moreover the sonata is unusual in that Mendelssohn cast none of the movements in sonata form; the first and last are in a sort of rondo, the second (slow) movement is a minuet, and the third movement is an Adagio in the style of a fantasia, using the recitative style marked *senza misura*, with contrasting passages. It seems evident that this work was influenced by the late sonatas of Beethoven: cyclic form, the unusual disposition of the movements, and in particular the nature of the thematic material of the first movement suggest that Mendelssohn modeled the work on Beethoven's Sonata in A major (op. 101),[8] even though he replaced Beethoven's march by a minuet and dropped the fugal passage in the finale.

The Sonata in B-flat major (op. 106) is also a large work in four movements with cyclic form. But here in the first movement we find sonata form as well, complete with double-bar, a light scherzo as the second movement, a simple Andante quasi Allegro in E major (tritone key relation) as the slow movement, and a dramatic Allegro molto that leads to the finale, an Allegro moderato in rondo form. Only the interlude between the third and fourth movements makes the formal plan of the work somewhat unusual.

Mendelssohn composed three sets of variations, but only one set, the *Variations sérieuses*, have found their way into the piano repertory. Here we encounter nothing of the galant character so often associated with this genre; rather, seriousness makes itself evident at once in the theme itself, in the minor, sixteen bars long but in an irregular form and incorporating chromaticism. The seventeen variations that follow display different characters: staccato chords alternating between the hands (iii), a long crescendo with changes in register (vi), a chromatic fughetta (x), cantabile (xi), an Adagio in the parallel major (xiv) which is followed by an unusual variation that goes from *pianissimo* to *forte* and then diminuendo with tied chords in the right hand (xv), and at the end a brilliant coda.

MENDELSSOHN'S SETS OF VARIATIONS

Variations sérieuses, D minor (17, op. 54, composed 1841, published 1842)

Variations, E-flat major (5, op. 82, composed 1841, published 1849)

Variations, B-flat major (5, op. 83, composed presumably 1841, published 1850, also arranged for piano duet, op. 83a)

One more group of works by Mendelssohn related to the traditional large forms comprises the fantasias. There are two large works to be considered:

the *Fantasia on an Irish Song* in E major ("The Last Rose of Summer," op. 15, composed 1827, published 1833) and the Fantasia in F-sharp minor (op. 28, composed 1833, published 1834). Apart from these is a set of shorter pieces called Fantasias or Capriccios (3, op. 16, composed and published 1829), but these belong rather among the character pieces. The first of the large fantasias resembles other fantasias we have discussed: it is based on a song (in common with Schubert's *Wanderer* Fantasia) and it exhibits sudden changes in affect and style. After a cadenza-like opening, it presents the simple song melody (Adagio in E major), then moves to Presto agitato in E minor, followed by sections with melodies in recitative style. All this was common in the fantasia in the late eighteenth and early nineteenth centuries.

The Fantasia in F-sharp minor (op. 28), on the other hand, is a much larger work, cast in three movements to be played without pause: its size renders it equivalent to a large sonata. The relationship to that genre seems evident too from the fact that this work was also known as *Sonata écossaise* (Scotch Sonata). It has similarities with Beethoven's *Sonata quasi una fantasia* in C-sharp minor (op. 27 ii): first an Allegro in F-sharp minor in simple ternary form, then an Allegro con moto in A major (actually a scherzo and trio, but in duple, not triple, time), and third, a typically brilliant finale in F-sharp minor, in sonata form with double-bar. A brief agitato passage serves as transition between the first and second movements.

Some of Mendelssohn's other works that aspire to the large form are doubtless individual movements from projected piano sonatas. One is the Andante cantabile e presto agitato in B major–minor (composed 1838, published 1839), a lyric slow movement followed by a brilliant rondo. Similarly organized are the two Clavierstücke. For piano duet there is an Allegro brilliant in A major (op. 92). But it is evident that Mendelssohn's main interest in piano music involved the character piece.

MENDELSSOHN'S PRINCIPAL CHARACTER PIECES

NOTE: *Songs Without Words* are listed separately.

Capriccio, F-sharp minor (op. 5, composed and published 1825)
Characteristische Stücke (7, op. 7, published 1827): Sanft und mit
    Empfindung, Andante, E minor; Mit heftiger Bewegung,
    Allegro vivace, B minor; Kräftig und feurig, Allegro vivace, D
    major; Schnell und beweglich, Con moto, A major; Ernst und
    mit steigender Lebhaftigkeit or Fuga, Sempre legato, A major;
    Sehnsüchtig, Andante, E minor; Leicht und luftig, Presto, E
    major
Rondo capriccioso, E major (op. 14, composed 1824, published
    1827)
Fantasias or Caprices (3, op. 16, composed and published 1829)

Caprices (3, op. 33, composed 1833–1835, published 1836)
Capriccio, E major–minor (op. 118, composed 1837, published 1872)
Scherzo à capriccio or Presto scherzando, F-sharp minor (composed 1835–1836, date of publication uncertain)

The capriccio, which is so important here, is a genre of keyboard music that over time has taken on different styles and techniques of composition: in the Renaissance and Baroque it was an imitative contrapuntal form of capricious character; later it resembled the fantasia of the late-eighteenth century, as in Clementi; it has also been associated with the etude, as in Müller, and with the potpourri, a medley of numbers from operas and musical shows popular at the time, often with variations and virtuoso cadenzas. To the extent that the capriccio or caprice was associated with virtuosity, there would also be a connection to Paganini as well in his famous Caprices (24) for solo violin.

Mendelssohn's capriccios reflect this varied background. The earliest among them, in F-sharp minor (op. 5), is a large work in three-part form with coda. Each of the sections in turn displays a smaller three-part form in which the midsection is a little development, and the coda employs thematic material from the second large section. The piece is intended for brilliant display as the figuration clearly signifies. The Capriccios (op. 33) are similar: while Mendelssohn cast all of them in three-part form, the first, in A minor, and the last, in B-flat minor, have slow introductions that resemble the fantasy of the eighteenth century, while the main sections, both Presto, are like the first movements of sonatas. A similar range may be seen in the independent Capriccio in E major–minor (op. 118), in rondo form.

These are large works that have relations not only with the eighteenth-century fantasia but also with the larger movements of the sonata. The Fantasias or Caprices (op. 16), on the other hand, are smaller; all are in three-part form and avoid the contrasts found in the works just discussed. Particularly characteristic is the second, Presto scherzando in E minor, a typically light, airy scherzo, with evenly moving staccato chords embellished with grace-notes in the high register.

Then there are the *Charakteristische Stücke* (Characteristic Pieces, op. 7), the first set by a major composer to have been given this title. Although in many cases the external formal schemes are what would be expected—simple repetitive plans and rounded binary, ternary, or rondo forms—the pieces surprise for the prominent role they give to archaic features. The first, despite its regular formal plan, is a cantabile, much like a prelude by Bach, with incessant use of a single pattern of figuration; the scherzo-like "Leicht und luftig" is similar. But we note the emphasis on counterpoint: the "Kräftig und feurig" is a fugue with an extended subject in driving sixteenth-note figuration, not unlike the violinistic subjects in Bach; in the working-out stretto is prominent. Most impressive, however, is "Ernst und mit steigender Bewegung" or "Fuga," with its slow, triadic, ricercar-like subject and fully developed countersubject, the theme itself divided into component motives that are separately exploited in the working-out. Moreover, Mendelssohn employs the standard fugal learned devices—diminution and augmentation—and only at the very end does he relax the fugal procedure. This piece reveals specific indebtedness to the Fugue in E major in Part II of Bach's *Well-Tempered Clavier.*

These character pieces, then, present features that are totally unexpected in this context. But Mendelssohn's main contribution to the genre, to be found in the eight sets of his *Lieder ohne Worte* (Songs Without Words), each containing six pieces, is more in the mainstream.

MENDELSSOHN'S SONGS WITHOUT WORDS

Set I (op. 19b, composed 1829–1830, published 1830): Andante con moto, E major; Andante espressivo, A minor; Molto allegro e vivace, A major; Moderato, A major; Poco agitato, F-sharp minor; "Venetianisches Gondellied," Andante sostenuto, G minor

Set II (op. 30, composed 1833–1834, published 1835): Andante espressivo, E-flat major; Allegro di molto, B-flat minor; Adagio non troppo, E major; Agitato e con fuoco, B minor; Andante grazioso, D major; "Venetianisches Gondellied," Andante tranquillo, F-sharp minor

Set III (op. 38, composed 1836–1837, published 1837): Con moto, E-flat major; Allegro non troppo, C minor; Presto e molto vivace, E major; Andante, A major; Agitato, A minor; Duetto, A-flat major

Set IV (op. 53, composed 1839–1841, published 1841): Andante con moto, A-flat major; Allegro non troppo, E-flat major; Presto agitato, G minor; Adagio, F major; "Volkslied," Allegro con fuoco, A minor; Molto allegro vivace, A major

Set V (op. 62, composed 1842–1844, published 1844): Andante espressivo, G major; Allegro con fuoco, B-flat major; Andante maestoso, E minor; Allegro con anima, G major; "Venetianisches Gondellied," Andante con moto, A minor; Allegretto grazioso, A major

Set VI (op. 67, composed 1843–1845, published 1845): Andante, E-flat major; Allegro leggiero, F-sharp minor; Andante tranquillo, B-flat major; Presto, C major; Moderato, B minor; Allegro non troppo, E major

Set VII (op. 85, 1834–1845, published 1850): Andante espressivo, F major; Allegro agitato, A minor; Presto, E-flat major; Andante sostenuto, D major; Allegretto, A major; Allegretto con moto sempre cantabile, B-flat major

Set VIII (op. 102, composed 1842–1845, publication date
uncertain): Andante un poco agitato, E minor; Adagio, D
major; Presto, C major; Un poco agitato ma andante, G minor;
Allegro vivace, A major; Andante, C major

The designation *songs without words* is apparently Mendelssohn's own.
It appears in the correspondence with his sister Fanny, and an early manuscript sketch of one of the pieces uses the term. The title of the original edition of the first set, published in London, was *Six Songs for the Pianoforte
Alone* but the title given the same pieces in the French edition was simply
Romances. Yet the idea is clear. A song without words is a short piano piece
in the manner of a song, hence a simple lyric piece. The melody is typically
in balanced phrases over an accompaniment that operates with the same figuration pattern throughout. In most cases the same thematic material is used
throughout a piece, but in some contrast is introduced.

Generally, Mendelssohn avoided descriptive titles here. Three pieces he
called "Venetianisches Gondellied" (Venetian Gondola Song), the equivalent
of a barcarole, and another piece is called "Volkslied" (Folk Song, op. 53 v).
Three other pieces have acquired titles: the "Jägerlied" (Hunter's Song, op.
19b iii), the "Funeral March" (op. 62 iii), and the "Spinnerlied" (Spinning Song,
op. 67 iv). A connection between the *Lieder ohne Worte* and Mendelssohn's
own songs has been noticed: the Adagio in F major (op. 53 iv) is similar to
"Auf den Flügeln des Gesangs" (On the Wings of Song, op. 34 ii). The song
"Herbstlied" (op. 63) originally had been intended as a song without words.
For the others, no specific expressive character is explicit—we must glean it
from the music itself.

Some similarity between these pieces and a set by one of Mendelssohn's
teachers, Wilhelm Taubert's *An die Geliebte, Acht Minnelieder* (op. 16, 1831),
has also been noticed. Here Taubert took lines from poems of Goethe, Hauff,
and others to serve as titles and thus to convey not only the intended affect but
also the concept of their being songs for piano. Another possible influence
may come from the small etudes of Ludwig Berger (op. 12, 1820, or op. 22, ca.
1830). But the greatest influence appears to stem from the polyphonic social
song (the *geselliges Lied*) which had been cultivated by Zelter, one of Mendelssohn's principal teachers and the director of the Singakademie in Berlin.
We can distinguish three basic types in the *Lieder ohne Worte*, all associated
with the repertory of the polyphonic song:[9] the solo song with piano accompaniment, the duet with piano accompaniment, and the more elaborate choral
song for four voices without accompaniment. The first type, the solo song, is
most common: a simple lyric melody in balanced phrases over an accompaniment, standard for a song (see Ex. 4-4). Examples of the next type, the duet
with accompaniment, are the one piece called "Duetto" (op. 38 vi), in lilting
6/8 with supporting bass and light arpeggiated accompaniment and two of the
"Venetian Gondola Songs" which present their melodies in parallel thirds

Example 4-4. MENDELSSOHN: "Venetianisches Gondellied" in F-sharp minor from *Lieder ohne Worte* (op. 30 vi)—Beginning (mm. 1–15)

using embellishment, all over simple accompaniments. Other duets include the Moderato (op. 67 v) and the Allegro agitato (op. 85 ii). In the third type, the four-part choral song, the melodies are presented chordally with accompaniment. Among these pieces are the Allegretto (op. 85 v), the Adagio (op. 102 ii), and the Andante (op. 102 vi). For the few of the *Lieder ohne Worte* that have rapid tempos and employ varieties of figuration as thematic material, we can assume a background in instrumental music. Among many examples are the Molto allegro e vivace (op. 19b iii), the Agitato e con fuoco (op. 30 iv), and the long Agitato (op. 38 v). Needless to say, there are instances in which elements from two or more of these types appear in one piece.

Mendelssohn also produced independent character pieces: the Scherzo in B minor (composed and published 1829); the *Gondellied,* Allegretto non troppo in A major (composed 1837, published 1838); and the *Albumblatt* in E major (op. 117, composed 1837, published 1872), all of which we can readily associate with the song without words. There is also a *perpetuum mobile,* Prestissimo in C major (op. 119). The teaching piece is represented by the set *Kinderstücke* (op. 72, composed 1842, published 1847).

We have already noted the impact of Baroque music on Mendelssohn in the *Charakteristische Stücke* (op. 7). He was involved with this music through his work with Zelter which led to, among other things, the famous revival of Bach's *St. Matthew Passion* in 1829. Among the most important aspects of the Baroque spirit in his composition is the emphasis on the prelude and fugue, or the prelude by itself, which testifies to the example of *The Well-Tempered Clavier.*

MENDELSSOHN'S PRELUDES AND FUGUES

Preludes and Fugues (op. 35, composed 1834–1836, published 1837): Prelude, Allegro con fuoco, and Fugue, E minor–major; Prelude, Allegretto, and Fugue, Tranquillo e sempre legato, D major; Prelude, Prestissimo staccato, and Fugue, Allegro con brio, B minor; Prelude, Con moto, and Fugue, Con moto ma sostenuto, A-flat major; Prelude, Andante lento, and Fugue, Allegro con fuoco, F minor; Prelude, Maestoso andante, and Fugue, Allegro con brio, B-flat major
Prelude, Allegro molto, and Fugue, Allegro energico, E minor (for the album *Notre temps*, an anthology of Christmas pieces by leading composers [composed 1827–1841, published 1842])

Their uniform character makes it clear that Mendelssohn modeled these preludes on those of Bach. While some of them operate with figuration, others are cantabile as well as being based on a single melodic pattern. Examples are the well-known Prelude in E minor, with its marcato melody in the midrange accompanied above and below by arpeggios; the Prelude in A-flat major, a duet over arpeggiated accompaniment; and the Prelude in F minor, a cantabile line accompanied by rich chords. The fugues likewise reveal indebtedness to Bach. There is the canzona-like subject of the Fugue in F minor, while a subject resembling the ricercar appears in the Fugue in A-flat major; Mendelssohn also used subjects consisting of driving figuration, as in the fugues in B minor and B-flat major. The subject of the Fugue in E minor (for *Notre temps*) is especially noteworthy, beginning with a downward leap of a seventh and then ascending scalewise in dotted rhythm. Here Mendelssohn breaks the subject down into its component motives and treats them separately, combined, and in stretto, among other devices. Free, nonfugal episodes appear frequently; for example, the Fugue in A-flat major, with its ricercar subject, is a double fugue that presents both subjects in contrapuntal combination and includes nonfugal episodes. The first of the two in E minor is a long and elaborate piece. In it an extended, gradual accumulation employs the subject in inversion, culminating in a chorale-type melody of Mendelssohn's composition despite similarities to the hymn "Ein' feste Burg," and at the end returns to the Andante of the beginning. Here the fugue has approached the character piece. In the same spirit Mendelssohn also produced a set of Preludes (3, composed 1836, published 1868).

There remain the didactic works, the etudes, of which Mendelssohn composed four, all in 1836: the Etude in F minor (composed 1836 for the Moscheles-Fétis *Méthode des méthodes*, published 1840); and the set (3, op. 104b, composed 1834–1836, published presumably 1838), consisting of Presto in B-flat minor; Allegro con moto in F major; and Allegro vivace in A minor. As is typical of the genre, each concentrates on a particular problem of pianistic execution; for instance, the accompanying of a marcato melody with arpeggiated figuration (Etude in F minor), a study in arpeggios and chords (Allegro vivace in A minor), and cantabile playing in the middle range with octaves in the bass and arpeggios above, all *pianissimo* (Presto in B-flat minor). This focus on a particular problem of execution produces a certain thematic coherence and uniformity of character, so that these etudes are close in spirit to the preludes. A close relation between the two persists in nineteenth-century piano music.

Mendelssohn's sister Fanny (1805–1847), who married the painter Wilhelm Hensel, was an accomplished pianist who composed extensively, but because of her family's views on the proper role of women, she published little—in fact six of her songs appeared among those of Felix's op. 8 and op. 9. Yet five sets of lyrical character pieces in the same vein as much of her brother's *Lieder ohne Worte* were in fact published: the *Lieder* (4, op. 2, published 1846), two sets of *Melodien* (op. 4 and 5, both published 1847), and two sets of *Lieder ohne Worte* (4, op. 6, published 1847, and 4, op. 8, composed 1840, published 1850). Most of her work, which includes sonatas, remains unpublished.

SCHUMANN

Perhaps the most Romantic composer of piano music of the first half of the nineteenth century was Robert Alexander Schumann (1810–1856), in whose hands the character piece came into its own, replete with literary and other references and associations. Like Mendelssohn, Schumann received a broad humanistic education. His interest in literature was intense—he even worked on a novel. The uncertainties of a career in music prompted him to begin the study of law, but he soon abandoned these studies. We know of the relationship to the conservative piano teacher Friedrich Wieck (1785–1875), the difficult courtship of Wieck's daughter Clara, the apparent mercury poisoning that cut short his career as a pianist, and his subsequent work as editor-critic, composer, and later conductor. Hanging over it all was the mental illness that in the end overcame him.

The dual preoccupation with literature and music is one of Schumann's most important characteristics; a fundamental aspect involves both his composing and his critical writing. In the pages of his reviews Schumann emerges as an ardent supporter of the new and serious forms of Romantic music and thus as the opponent of virtuoso display for its own sake. In his writing he often made this case in dialogue form, calling the fictitious participants the *Davidsbündler* (Companions of David); their goal was to defeat the musical Philistines of the time and to raise art music to new heights.[10] E. T. A. Hoffmann and Jean Paul, both of whom influenced Schumann, used dialogue form in their critical writing. Among the members of this imaginary organization are Florestan (bold, impetuous, passionate, somewhat nervous); Eusebius (reflective and dreamy); and Raro (wise and rational, capable of drawing the best from opposing points of view). While these characters correspond to aspects of Schumann himself (in its first edition his first piano sonata was attributed to Florestan and Eusebius and the same goes for other compositions), others represent actual people: F. Meritis stands for Mendelssohn; Jeanquirit for Stephen Heller; Knif for Fink (the conservative rival editor and critic, whose name Schumann has spelled backwards); and Chiara, Chiarina, and Zilia, all three of which refer to Clara. We will see how these figure in his compositions.

Generally, Schumann's way of writing music is more complex than that of Schubert and Mendelssohn; in place of regularity, periodicity, and clarity, we find ambiguity in Schumann. This emerges from his rhythm: tied notes and syncopations obscure the beat, which often alternates between subdivisions by two, three, or more (see Ex. 4-5A, below). The harmony follows suit; the tonic is often stated in a weak position, while chromaticism, suspensions, and unresolved dissonances give rise to a feeling of instability. In Schumann's part-writing, the melodic line, often fragmentary, wanders from part to part, and the types of accompaniment vary. In other pieces he fixes on a single pattern which he reiterates throughout. Thus, Schumann's music often creates anything but a sense of strength and stability.

The character piece stands out clearly as the most important single genre in Schumann's piano music. Although there are three sonatas, a few sets of etudes, and sets of variations, he gave the character piece by far the most attention; it served as the locus of his most representative works. The urge to compose in the large forms, while not absent in Schumann, appears in a new guise—that of composing cycles of character pieces conceived as entities, generally called suites, so that the character piece became the basis for a new large form. (Until around 1840 Schumann composed almost exclusively for the piano.)

SCHUMANN'S CHARACTER PIECES[11]

Papillons (12, op. 2, composed 1829–1831, published 1831)

Intermezzos (6, op. 4, composed 1832, published 1833)

Impromptus on a Theme of Clara Wieck (10, op. 5, composed
    and published 1833; revision published 1850)

Davidsbündlertänze (18 in 2 vols., op. 6, composed and
    published 1837; in the second edition, 1850–1851, Schumann
    changed the title to *Die Davidsbündler*)

Carnaval—Scènes mignonnes sur quatre notes (21, op. 9,
    composed 1833–1835, published 1837): Préambule, "Pierrot,"
    "Arlequin," "Valse noble," "Eusebius," "Florestan," "Coquette,"
    "Relique," "Papillons," "ASCH-SCHA–Lettres dansantes,"
    "Chiarina," "Chopin," "Estrella," "Reconnaissance," "Pantalon
    et Columbine," "Valse allemande," "Intermezzo. Paganini,"
    "Aveu," "Promenade," "Pause," "Marche des 'Davidsbündler'
    contre les Philistins"

Phantasiestücke (8, op. 12, composed 1837, published 1838):
    "Des Abends," D-flat major; "Aufschwung," F minor; "Warum,"
    D-flat major; "Grillen," D-flat major; "In der Nacht," F minor;
    "Fabel," C major; "Traumes-Wirren," F major; "Ende vom
    Lied," F major

Kinderscenen (13, op. 15, composed 1838, published 1839): "Von
    fremden Ländern und Menschen," G major; "Kuriose
    Geschichte," D major; "Hasche-Mann," B minor; "Bittendes
    Kind," D major; "Glückes genug," D major; "Wichtige
    Begebenheit," A major; "Träumerei," F major; "Am Camin," F
    major; "Ritter vom Steckenpferd," C major; "Fast zu ernst," G-
    sharp minor; "Fürchtenmachen," G major; "Kind im
    Einschlummern," E minor; "Der Dichter spricht," G major

Kreisleriana (8, op. 16, composed and published 1838): Äusserst
    bewegt, D minor; Sehr innig und nicht zu rasch, B-flat major;
    Sehr aufgeregt, G minor; Sehr langsam, B-flat major, Sehr
    lebhaft, G minor; Sehr langsam, B-flat major; Sehr rasch, C
    minor; Schnell und spielend, G minor

Arabeske, C major (op. 18, composed 1838–1839, published 1839)

Blumenstück, D-flat major (op. 19, composed and published
    1839)

Humoreske, B-flat major (op. 20, composed and published 1839)

Novelletten (8, op. 21, composed 1838, published 1839): Markirt
    und kräftig, D minor; Äusserst rasch und mit Bravour, D
    minor; Leicht und mit Humor, D major; Ballmässig, D major;
    Rauschend und festlich, D major; Sehr lebhaft, mit vielem
    Humor, A major; Äusserst rasch, E major; Sehr lebhaft, C-
    sharp minor

Nachtstücke (4, op. 23, composed 1839, published 1840): Mehr langsam, oft zurückhaltend, C major; Markirt und lebhaft, F major; Mit grosser Lebhaftigkeit, D-flat major; Einfach, F major

Faschingsschwank aus Wien (5, op. 26, composed 1839–1840, published 1841)

Romanzen (3, op. 28, composed 1839, published 1840): Sehr markirt, B-flat minor; Einfach, F-sharp major; Sehr markirt, B major

Charakterstücke (or *Album*) *für die Jugend* (43, op. 68, composed and published 1848)

Marches (4, op. 76, composed and published 1849): Mit grösster Energie, E-flat major; Kräftig, G major; "Lager-Scene," B-flat major; Mit Kraft und Feuer, E-flat major

Waldscenen (9, op. 82, composed 1848–1849, published 1850): "Eintritt im Walde," B-flat major; "Jäger auf der Lauer," D minor; "Einsame Blumen," B-flat major; "Verrufene Stelle," D minor; "Freundliche Landschaft," B-flat major; "Herberge," E-flat major; "Vogel als Prophet," G minor; "Jagdlied," E-flat major; "Abschied," B-flat major

Bunte Blätter (14, op. 99, composed 1836–1849, published 1852): Stücklein (3), A major, E minor, E major; "Albumblätter" (5), F-sharp minor, B minor, A-flat major, E-flat minor, E-flat major; "Novellette," B minor; Präludium, B-flat minor; March, D minor; "Abendmusik," B-flat major; Scherzo, G minor; "Geschwindmarsch," G minor

Phantasiestücke (3, op. 111, composed 1851, published 1852): Sehr rasch, mit leidenschaftlichem Vortrag, C minor; Ziemlich langsam, A-flat major; Kräftig und sehr markirt, F minor

Albumblätter (20, op. 124, composed 1832–1845, published 1854)

Gesänge der Frühe (5, op. 133, composed 1853, published 1855)

The titles for most of these pieces reflect their Romantic nature: intermezzos, impromptus (which here Schumann has interpreted as variations), romances, fantasias (*Phantasiestücke*), nocturnes, arabesques, album leaves, and even marches. Others are more individualistic, descriptive, and characteristic or programmatic, and here the extramusical associations are more significant: *Papillons, Carnaval, Davidsbündler,* and so forth. The term *Blumenstück* is used to describe a type of painting (Flower-piece), but also was associated with Jean Paul's novel *Siebenkäs,* while *Papillons* and *Carnaval* appear to be connected with the masked ball scene near the end of the same writer's novel *Flegeljahre.* Associations with writings of E. T. A. Hoffmann appear in Schumann's *Kreisleriana,* the *Phantasiestücke,* and the *Nachtstücke.* A motto from Friedrich Hebbel prefaces "Verrufene Stelle" in *Waldscenen,* while the set as a whole is thought to have been inspired by Heinrich

Laube's *Jagdbrevier*, a set of poems about the forest and hunting. The *Bilder aus Osten* (op. 66), for piano duet, is expressly referred by Schumann himself to Friedrich Rückert's *Makamen*, German versions of epic Persian poetry. The second of the *Novelletten* he entitled "Sarazene and Suleika" in his original draft, thus associating it with Goethe's *West-östlicher Divan*, a collection of poems on Persian models. Finally, there are the *Davidsbündler*, already mentioned, who are celebrated not only in op. 6 but also in *Carnaval*, as will be shown. Thus, a large and important number of Schumann's character pieces are connected with German literature, an emphasis not found in the work of his predecessors but which becomes fundamental for Romantic music.

We may group Schumann's character pieces roughly under three headings: first, the suites or cycles of pieces (often miniatures) that are related to each other in subject matter and the musical themes used; second, the sets of pieces that individually are not related to one another; and, third, the larger independent pieces. Belonging to the first, and most numerous group, are *Papillons*, the Impromptus, the *Davidsbündlertänze*, *Carnaval*, the *Phantasiestücke* (op. 12), the *Kinderscenen*, *Kreisleriana*, the *Nachtstücke*, the *Faschingschwank aus Wien*, the *Waldscenen*, and the late *Gesänge der Frühe*. The other two groups are smaller: in the second are the Intermezzos, the *Novelletten*, the *Romanzen*, the Marches, the *Charakterstücke für die Jugend*, *Bunte Blätter*, the *Phantasiestücke* (op. 111), and the *Albumblätter*, while in the last are the *Arabeske*, the *Blumenstück*, and the *Humoreske*.

To begin with the first, the *Papillons* (Butterflies) consist of dances, mostly related to the waltz. Thus right at the outset we note Schumann's preoccupation with the literary, represented here by the masked-ball scene in Jean Paul's novel *Flegeljahre* (the significance of butterflies is not entirely clear). While the forms used are simple, Schumann has avoided the traditional patterns. Usually we find three or four short sections, each generally to be repeated, with some reprising of earlier material, often with introductions and codas. The piece in F-sharp minor (iii) has a canon at the octave reminiscent of Haydn's *Hexen-Minuet* (Witches' Minuet) in the third movement of his String Quartet, D minor (op. 76 ii). In the finale of the set Schumann has introduced the "Grossvater-lied," a German song popular in the seventeenth and eighteenth centuries; the tune reappears in *Carnaval*. The Impromptus (12, op. 5) are also very short; they are variations on a theme that resembles one by Clara Wieck, from her *Romance varié* (op. 3) for piano, but they incorporate a motto theme (involving the notes C–F–G–C), and material from his unfinished Symphony in G minor. Here the principle of thematic variation has been influenced by Beethoven's *Prometheus/Eroica* variations, since Schumann has used the theme's melody and bass both separately and in combination.[12]

In the *Davidsbündlertänze* Schumann brings aspects of his imaginary organization to artistic expression. In the first edition individual pieces were signed with an *F* or an *E*, designating either "Florestan" or "Eusebius" as the alleged composer (in some cases both). Again we note a connection with dance types along with simplicity of formal organization. Florestan's restlessness appears in "Ungeduldig" (Impatient, iv), ostensibly a ländler but with a syncopated upper part using tied notes so that the accent constantly falls half a beat too late, while Eusebius' reflective nature is exhibited in "Einfach" (Simple, v) and the cantabile "Zart und singend" (Delicate and Singing, xiv).

Schumann's best-known and most comprehensive work of this kind is *Carnaval* (op. 9, 1834–1835), which resembles a suite in the usual understanding of the term. Schumann provided it with a subtitle, *Scènes mignonnes sur quatre notes* (Small scenes on four notes), with the term scenes suggesting theater or painting.[13] We can understand the principal associations in *Carnaval* from the titles Schumann gave to individual numbers: references to the Italian *commedia dell'arte*, to Schumann's own *Davidsbündler*, and to actual people. The whole creates the impression of a festive masked ball in which all these characters are taking part.

Several factors combine to produce overall consistency and unity. One of these is an extramusical association in which letters of the alphabet stand for musical notes: ASCH and SCHA, the former being the name of the city where Ernestine von Fricken, with whom Schumann had been in love, lived, the latter being those letters in his own last name that lent themselves to this sort of thing. The musical equivalents of ASCH are A-flat, E-flat, C, B (since in German A-flat is As, E-flat is Es, pronounced "s," and B is H), and A-flat, C, B; and for SCHA, E-flat, C, B, A. Schumann gives these without explanation as "Sphinxes" between viii and ix. He employed these notes prominently in most of the numbers in *Carnaval*, especially at their beginnings, so that this letter–note correspondence constitutes an important element in the overall conception.

The opening "Préambule" and the concluding March share thematic material, the latter also employing the "Grossvaterlied" previously used in the finale of *Papillons*. Numbers often are run together, as "Florestan" (vi) and "Coquette" (vii), or, more extended, between "Reconnaissance" (xiv), "Pantalon et Columbine" (xv), and "Valse allemande" (xvi). An attacca indication appears between "Pause" (xx) and "Marche" (xxi); the "Valse allemande" is followed by "Paganini" (called Intermezzo) after which the waltz is repeated *senza replica*. "Replique" (viii) is a short variation and development of part of the number that precedes it, "Coquette" (vii). The principal key is A-flat major to which the other keys used are closely related—E-flat major, B-flat major, G minor, C minor, F minor, D-flat major—so that overall tonal coherence results. Thus Schumann has organized the work as a complex whole.

The individual numbers of *Carnaval* are short and are cast in binary form or forms that usually seem related to the dance. All embody a specific affect or character. Particularly noteworthy is the musical expression of "Eusebius" (v), an Adagio with a melody that meanders in sextuplets, quintuplets, and triplets over a slow chromatic accompaniment employing suspensions and not using the triad in root position, thus creating an aura of dreaminess (see Ex. 4-5A). This is immediately followed by "Florestan" (vi), a Passionato in which the melody rises impetuously over an assertive accompaniment of repeated chords and in which there are sudden and nervous changes (see Ex.

4-5B), the piece running on into the next one, "Coquette." Other members of the *Davidsbündler*, not all of them imaginary, represented here are "Chiarina" (xi), Clara, portrayed by a passionate waltz; "Estrella" (xiii), Ernestine von Fricken, characterized by a lyrical but irregular waltz; and, of course, at the end, the "March of the 'Davidsbündler' Against the Philistines." The historical figures are Chopin, represented by a short piece in typical nocturne style (xii), and Paganini, by a virtuoso intermezzo to the "Valse allemande"; in the waltz section he quotes in part a theme of Clara's.[14]

In *Carnaval*, then, Schumann has brought together in a single variegated work features we have previously seen in separate compositions: the use of short dance types, as in *Papillons*; the employment of cyclic form with variations, as had been done in a somewhat different way in the Intermezzos (op. 4); and the extensive extramusical associations, the letter–note relationships, used in the early *Abegg* variations (see below) and perhaps suggested by the custom of composing pieces on the name "Bach."

The *Phantasiestücke* (op. 12) and the *Kreisleriana* differ in important respects from the pieces just considered. Both sets have associations with E. T. A. Hoffmann, as already noted. Although they are often played in full, Schumann seems to have thought of these as sets of independent pieces, as may be adduced from the key relationships among the pieces (less close than those, for example, in *Carnaval*), and the fact that each piece is separate, without attacca indications. The most usual formal plan here is the ternary scheme, the midsection providing at least some contrast in key, character, and thematic material; but since this midsection, apart from its key, often retains some element of the opening part, the espressive character is mostly uniform throughout.

In the *Phantasiestücke* (op. 12) Schumann has given each piece a characteristic title. "Des Abends" (Of the Evening, i) is a quiet lyrical nocturne, the melody moving in slow even notes over a gentle arpeggio accompaniment, uniform in character throughout. But "In der Nacht" (In the Night, v) is a strong, passionate piece (the key is F minor, long associated with the passionato), in which an irregular melody of fragmentary phrases is given out over a furiously agitated accompaniment of broken chords, an altogether different kind of nocturne. "Aufschwung" (Soaring, ii) has a rondo-like structure in which the brilliant alternates with the lyrical; in "Fabel" (Fable, vi) the lyrical alternates with the capricious, while "Traumes-Wirren" (Confusion of Dreams, vii) is only capricious, and the concluding piece, "Ende vom Lied" (End of the Song, viii) is sturdy. Thus, the set encompasses great variety. For the later set of *Phantasiestücke* (op. 111), Schumann did not provide characteristic titles.

In *Kreisleriana*, however, Schumann on the whole made the individual pieces longer than those in the *Phantasiestücke*. Again we find slow lyric pieces (ii, iv, vi) alternating with brilliant pieces that abound in figuration and dramatic effects (i and v).

Among the other sets of short pieces the *Kinderscenen* and the later *Waldscenen* have become well known, both widely used as children's pieces,

Example 4-5. SCHUMANN: *Carnaval* (op. 9)—Excerpts
    A. Eusebius—Beginning (mm. 1–4)
    B. Florestan—Beginning (mm. 1–12)

although Schumann did not intend them as such; rather the qualification "for small and large children" (für kleine und grosse Kinder) that Schumann used for his later pieces for piano duet (op. 85) seems appropriate. The key relationships are such that each set can be performed as a whole, thus constituting a suite, although there is no indication that this was Schumann's intent. Most of the pieces show the simple three-part scheme, and programmatic titles elucidate the character of each piece. The famous "Träumerei" (Dreaming, vii) provides a prototypical example of Schumann's lyrical ambiguity. In the *Waldscenen* we find some unusual examples of this. First, "Verrufene Stelle" (Accursed Place, iv) takes its motto from Hebbel, referring to decaying flowers in the shade that surround the one that survives, living not from the sun but from human blood. This vision is depicted by phrases marked staccato and soft chords in dotted rhythms. Second, the well-known "Vogel als Prophet" (Prophet Bird, vii), *pianissimo* with piquant dissonances, involves cross-relations, along with the rising and falling of fragmentary phrases.

Other cycles that belong here include the *Nachtstücke*, and the late *Gesänge der Frühe*. The *Nachtstücke* are not nocturnes in the sense of those by Chopin (see below); rather Schumann has made them complex and darkly expressive, often with funereal allusions. He had originally planned to give titles to the individual numbers. In common with *Kreisleriana*, the *Nachtstücke* show the enlarged form with two more-or-less contrasting sections. He provided a counterpart to the *Nachtstücke* in the late *Gesänge der Frühe*, which portray the sunrise.

The *Faschingsschwank aus Wien* (Vienna Carnival Prank) presents an altogether different situation. Here we encounter five sections, but since they are considerably longer than the individual numbers of the sets we have been considering, we can refer to them as movements: an Allegro in B-flat major; Romanze in G minor; Scherzino in B-flat major; Intermezzo in E-flat minor; and a finale, Höchst lebhaft, again in B-flat major. There are no descriptive titles. The first piece is in large sectional form that does not correspond to any conventional plan: rondo-like, it has five contrasting episodes in which some parody is found. The fourth episode contains a quotation from the *Marseillaise* (herein may lie the prank referred to in the work's title, since that song was forbidden at the time in conservative Vienna), while the fifth is related to the slow movement of Beethoven's Sonata in E-flat major (op. 31 iii). The finale, on the other hand, is in sonata form with coda. Of the internal movements, the second is lyrical with a florid melodic line, the fourth is impassioned, in ternary form but without much contrast, and in the middle is a short scherzo without trio. In its key relationships and the formal features displayed in its movements, the *Faschingsschwank aus Wien* seems like a sonata, despite the layout of the first movement; in an early version Schumann in fact had called it *Grande sonate romantique*.

In the second group, those in which there is no overriding idea connecting the individual pieces, we have the early Intermezzos, the *Novelletten*, the *Romanzen*, the set of stylized Marches, the set of children's pieces entitled *Charakterstücke für die Jugend*, the *Bunte Blätter*, and the late *Albumblätter*.

Although Schumann referred to the Intermezzos as "longer *Papillons*," they are a set of independent pieces, not a cycle; all six are in the three-part form so common in the character piece. The *Novelletten* likewise display great variety. Two of them involve dance: "Ballmässig" (Like a Ball, iv) is a waltz and "Rauschend und festlich" (Rushing and Festive, v) a polonaise; another is a march (i), while another offers bravura playing (ii). Throughout Schumann employs simple three- and five-part schemes, often organized in rounded-binary form, the episodes called either trio or intermezzo. He provides a typically Romantic touch at the end with the muted "Stimme aus der Ferne" (Voice from the Distance, viii). In the *Romanzen* Schumann continued to favor the three-part form, but in the third there are three contrasting sections which he again calls intermezzos. The marches he himself related to the confrontations during the revolutionary year, 1848.

The *Charakterstücke* (or *Album*) *für die Jugend* (op. 68, 1848), intended for children, contains many well-known short pieces, among them "Wilder Reiter" (Wild Horseman), and "Fröhlicher Landmann" (The Happy Farmer), along with more unusual pieces that are elaborations of chorale melodies, a little prelude and fugue, a folk-song setting ("Mai, lieber Mai"), and the more difficult "Knecht Ruppert" (Knight Ruppert). The set provides a remarkable instance of a composer's preserving his artistic individuality while working in a simple vein; Schumann suppressed a number of pieces intended for this set which have subsequently been published.

Two other sets belong to the category of the album leaf: the fourteen *Bunte Blätter*, variously translated as "variegated leaves" and "promiscuous leaves," the latter indeed leaving something to be desired, and the twenty of op. 124. Unlike *Kinderscenen* and *Waldscenen*, these are far from presenting uniform and consistent impressions, since both comprise pieces written over a period of many years, some of the *Albumblätter* going back as far as 1832.

Let us now turn to the third and last of the groups we distinguished at the outset of this discussion of Schumann's character pieces, the larger, more extended pieces. Here Schumann achieved a larger structure, not by creating a succession of short pieces, but by casting the piece itself on a larger scale. He did this in three lesser-known works composed in 1838–1839: *Arabeske* in C major (op. 18); *Blumenstück* in D-flat major (op. 19); and *Humoreske* in B-flat major (op. 20). The plan common to all is that of the rondo, simple in the *Arabeske*, but with variations and elaborations in the other two. The elaborations in *Blumenstück* involve an introductory passage before the rondo (refrain) and casting the various episodes themselves in three-part form. Schumann carried this further in the *Humoreske*, a long sectional work encompassing great variety and with some sections reprised. Such an unusual arrangement may reflect an origin in improvisation and perhaps the inspired expression of Schumann's own personal emotions, as seems clear in his letter to Clara of 11 March 1839: "I have been sitting the whole week at the pianoforte, composing and laughing and crying all at once; you will find all this beautifully depicted in my op. 20, the 'great *Humoreske*'. . . ."[15]

Although character pieces take the first position among Schumann's compositions for piano, the old forms—the sonata, the fantasia, the toccata, the theme and variations—are also represented in his work. As the largest of these, the sonata draws our attention first. Schumann completed three.

SCHUMANN'S PIANO SONATAS

F-sharp minor (No. 1, op. 11, composed 1832–1835, published
      1836; 3rd ed. published 1844)
G minor (known as No. 2, op. 22, composed 1833–1838,
      published 1839)
F minor (known as No. 3, op. 14, originally entitled *Concert sans
      orchestre*, composed 1835–1836, published 1836; revision
      published 1853)

These are early works; after 1838 Schumann did not work in the genre at all except for the children's sonatas (op. 118) and the revisions of earlier works in 1853. Yet despite his early concentration on the sonata, his approach was hesitant, as the relatively long periods of composition and revision testify; this reluctance may be related to the preference for the small form at the time and the general decline of the large form that we have already noted. This hesitancy reveals itself in several ways. First, there are early sketches of sonatas or sonata movements: the first and last movements of a Sonata in A-flat major (1831–1832), other movements belonging to an unfinished Sonata in B-flat major (1832, on which he also worked in 1836), and an unfinished Sonata in F minor (1833–1837), which he went so far as to refer to as Sonata No. 4. Second, there are works planned or probably planned as sonatas that appeared under different designations: the Sonata in F minor (op. 14), originally a five-movement work, had its two scherzo movements eliminated at the publisher's insistence, so that it could appear as Concerto Without Orchestra; in his revision of 1853, however, Schumann restored the title Sonata and with it one of the two scherzos. As we have seen, the *Faschingsschwank aus Wien* had been planned as a sonata. Finally, the large Allegro in B minor (op. 8, composed 1831, published 1835) seems to have been conceived as the first movement of an intended sonata, while the Scherzo and Presto passionato in F minor and B-flat major, respectively (WoO 5,[16] composed 1835–1836, not published until 1866), were originally intended for the sonatas in F minor (op. 14) and G minor (op. 22).

In any event, the three completed works called sonata are large works, in four movements (first published version of op. 14 in three), fully in accordance with the conception of the genre as it had come down from Beethoven and Schubert: the large opening movements in sonata form, the equally large finales in sonata or rondo form, and the scherzos and slow movements in three-part form (sonatas in F-sharp minor and G minor) or variations (Sonata in F minor). In the Sonata in F minor, the scherzo is second while the slow movement is third. Throughout Schumann has retained the conventional key relations among the movements; all except one are in the same key—the slow movements of the sonatas in F-sharp minor and G minor, in the relative minor and subdominant respectively, and the scherzo of the Sonata in F minor in a more remote key, D-flat major. In the first movements we find sonata form with the double-bar and repeat of the exposition. An unusual feature is presented by the Sonata in F minor—the theme of its slow movement appears in the other movements as well, making the work yet another example of cyclic form.

The Sonata in F-sharp minor is noteworthy in several ways. It features a rhetorical slow introduction, a broad melody with sharply accentuated dotted rhythms over an arpeggiated accompaniment of fast triplets (recalled in the development), then the dominance of the motivic principal theme, related to the *fandango*, throughout the Allegro part of the movement. We also find the enharmonic modulations and the apparent striving for an orchestral type of sound as evidenced by the timpani-like figure in the bass that precedes the statement of the principal theme. And thick chordal writing prevails. Thematic contrast is more the rule in the other two sonatas. As finales we find the rondo, something Schumann may have taken over from Schubert, and the sonata-rondo in the sonatas in F minor and G minor. These finales are large and difficult, designed to provide brilliant and effective conclusions.

In between are the scherzos and slow movements. Schumann has maintained the chief attributes of the type in the scherzos: the fast triple time, the capricious character, the overall three-part form with trio as midsection. The scherzo in the Sonata in F-sharp minor has two different trios. The second stands in great contrast with the rest of the movement, with its pomposity, the polonaise rhythm, and near the end the fantasia-like passage (marked *quasi oboe.*) Following the practice in the *Novelletten* and the *Romanzen*, this episode is called Intermezzo. In the Sonata in F minor we find the three-part form, the trio, not so called by Schumann, employing thematic material from the scherzo part of the movement.

Two of the slow movements are in no way different from character pieces, as indeed could also be said of Schubert's slow movements. The sonatas in F-sharp minor and G minor have slow movements in simple three-part form, the latter including a coda. The marking in the slow movement of the Sonata in F-sharp minor draws interest. It is called Aria and bears the marking *senza passione, ma espressivo*, surely a fine distinction, Romantic in its ambiguity. In the Sonata in F minor, the Andantino is *quasi variazioni*, four variations on a theme by Clara Wieck.

As in Schubert we can again find relationships between the sonatas and songs. For the Sonata in F-sharp minor Schumann took the theme of the second movement from his song "An Anna" (WoO 10 ii, composed 1828), part of which he also used as the basis for the slow introduction to the first movement; that of the slow movement of the Sonata in G minor, he freely adapted from another song, "Im Herbste" (WoO 10 iii, composed 1828).

Along with the sonata Schumann cultivated the fantasia. We have seen that the fantasy piece (*Phantasiestück*) holds an important position among the character pieces. But the fantasia is something altogether different, as we have seen from Schubert—a large multi-movement work of the same weight as a sonata. Yet Schumann did not always recognize much difference between the two. In his review of sonatas of Schubert he wrote, "So let them [composers] write sonatas or fantasias (what's in a name?)."[17] This large Fantasia in C major (op. 17, composed 1836, published 1839), dedicated to Liszt, is perhaps Schumann's most important work for piano solo. It bears a caption from the great Romantic writer and critic Friedrich Schlegel:

> *Durch alle Töne tönet*
> *Im bunten Erdentraum*
> *Ein leiser Ton gezogen*
> *Für den, der heimlich*
>   *lauschet.*

> Among all the sounds
> In the bright dream of earthly life
> There is emitted a soft tone
> For him who listens in
>   secret.

There are three large movements: Durchaus fantastisch und leidenschaftlich vorzutragen in C major; Mässig, durchaus energisch, in E-flat major, a scherzo; and as finale, a slow movement, Langsam getragen, durchweg leise zu halten, again in C major. Originally each movement bore a title: "Ruinen" (Ruins), "Triumphbogen" (Triumphal Arch), and "Sternenkranz" (Starry Ring). Having composed it for performance at the dedication of a monument to Beethoven in Bonn, in the first movement Schumann quotes a song from Beethoven's cycle *An die ferne Geliebte* (To the Distant Beloved, op. 96); yet he could equally have had in mind the state of his own relations with Clara Schumann at the time.

The first movement we can best regard as a variant of sonata form: a large binary structure (exposition and recapitulation), the development consisting of episodes within the recapitulation.[18] The opening is arresting—the declamatory melody stated in octaves over an accompaniment of figuration that is maintained for most of the exposition. Variation replaces development here: the principal theme is repeated in lyric guise, the transition theme reappears in varied form in the section "Im Legenden-Ton" (In the Style of a Legend), which is an interlude in the recapitulation, and there are different accompaniments to the secondary theme. The second movement constitutes the largest scherzo-like piece in Schumann's work. It is rondo-like with two episodes, and the scherzo theme is varied upon each appearance. Moreover, this theme possesses an orchestral quality—full chords ranging over the extent of the keyboard, intensified each time the theme appears. The last movement resembles the first in a general way: after a quiet introduction, an extended section is stated twice (quasi exposition and development) followed by a coda that recalls the opening; as a whole, the movement exhibits great variety. The climax, developed out of a lyrical line, takes place in the second section.

The Toccata in C major (op. 7, composed 1829–1833, published 1834) represents another traditional type. Apart from its emphasis on virtuosity, this piece shows little relation to earlier forms of the toccata. Schumann has rather cast it as a large and strict sonata form complete with double-bar. The principal theme consists of figuration in chords that moves in rapid sixteenth-notes; while the secondary theme presents a short, cantabile phrase, the sixteenth-note accompaniment is retained. In the development Schumann introduces a new theme featuring rapid octaves.

The last of the works in the large forms to be considered are the sets of themes and variations. Yet we must recognize that the usual distinctions are not adequate, since Schumann incorporated the variation principle in sets of character pieces (particularly the Impromptus and *Carnaval*) and in his etudes (one on a theme of the Beethoven and the famous *Symphonic Etudes*). Schumann's variations cast in the traditional mold are listed below.

SCHUMANN'S SETS OF VARIATIONS

Theme on the Name *Abegg* with Variations (op. 1, composed
    1829–1830, published 1831)
Sehnsuchtswalzervariationen (originally op. 10, composed 1832–
    1833; also called *Scènes mignonnes, Scènes musicales sur un
    thème connu* and *sur un thème connu de Fr. Schubert*)

Schumann based the *Abegg* variations on a theme of his own, one perhaps influenced by a march of Moscheles. As in *Carnaval* he drew on correspondence between letters of the alphabet and musical pitches: Abegg, the name of a family Schumann knew, yields the musical theme A–B-flat–E–G–G. The *Sehnsuchtswalzer* Variations, on the other hand, he based on a well-known waltz, a piece with a varied history that had been attributed to Beethoven but actually is Schubert's "Trauer-Walzer" (D. 365/op. 9). Of the two, the *Abegg* variations are the more important (the *Symphonic Etudes* are discussed below).

We have seen the influence of Baroque music in Mozart, Beethoven, and, particularly, Mendelssohn. The Baroque influenced Schumann as well. We find a prelude in the *Bunte Blätter* (op. 99 x), a canon as the last of the *Albumblätter* (op. 124), and a fughetta in the *Clavierstücke* (op. 32 iv). In addition Schumann composed a Prelude and Fugue in 1832, made sketches for other fugal and canonic pieces, one of which seems to have been intended as a finale for the Impromptus (op. 5), and composed two sets of fugues, the set of four (op. 72, composed 1845, published 1850) and the Pieces in Fughetta Form (7, op. 126, composed 1853, published 1854). Then there are works for pedal piano, an instrument in which a separate piano action was played by the feet, in principle like the organ or the large form of harpsichord: the *Studien* (op. 56) and *Skizzen* (Sketches, op. 58, both composed 1845, published 1845 and 1846 respectively). Thus the fugue writing of Bach had the greatest impact, here and elsewhere.

Schumann's largest work of this type, however, is the set entitled Fugues on the Name *Bach* (6, op. 60, composed 1845, published 1846) for pedal piano or organ. Much besides the fugue subject has been inspired by Bach. These are large works for the most part in strict counterpoint. The subjects resemble types current in Bach: the old ricercar (i, iv, and vi), a gigue (v), cantabile (iii), and a long subject in two parts, a terse statement of the B-A-C-H theme in dotted rhythm followed by driving figuration (ii). Schumann includes the old learned devices: augmentation, diminution, even retrograde, the last specifically identified in the score (iv). The last of these, a true double fugue, is the largest piece in the set.

The last important group of Schumann's works for solo piano music to be discussed—the etudes—reminds us of the composer's early ambition to be a virtuoso pianist.

SCHUMANN'S ETUDES

Etudes after Caprices of Paganini (6, op. 3, composed and
    published 1832)
Études de concert after Caprices of Paganini, Set II (6, op. 10,
    composed 1833, published 1835)
Etudes in the Form of Variations on a Theme of Beethoven
    (WoO 31, composed 1831–1835, published 1976)[19]
Symphonische Etüden (12, op. 13, composed 1834–1837,
    published 1837; revised as *Études en forme de variations*,
    9 and finale, and published 1852; 3rd ed., 1861)[20]

An important influence on the etude in the nineteenth century was Paganini, legendary master of the violin. Since the etude is intended primarily as a means of improving playing technique or developing and displaying mastery over the instrument, we can well expect that the foremost virtuoso performer of the day should become associated with it. Paganini's famous Caprices for unaccompanied violin (1820) formed the basis for countless sets of etudes for piano, not only by Schumann, but also by two such opposite artistic temperaments as Liszt and Brahms.

The most important work in this genre, however, is the famous Symphonic Etudes in C-sharp minor and D-flat major (op. 13). In its final form this consists of twelve etudes of which nine are variations on the theme (i, ii, iv, v, vi, vii, viii, x, xi) and three are not (iii, ix, and xii). Five other variations that Schumann originally intended for the set but then rejected are sometimes included. The theme, in binary form, is solemn, a slowly moving line accompanied by full chords. The etudes themselves vary in character: staccato and quasi-contrapuntal (i), an impassioned lyrical line supported by a slow-moving bass with rapid chords in the middle (ii), a light and airy piece with a cantabile line in the middle and rapid staccato passages above (iii, not a variation), a study in sforzando chord playing (iv), a scherzando (v), a bravura study with wide leaps for the left hand (vi), a perpetual motion (vii), a marcato (viii), another light piece (ix, not a variation), dense chords in the right hand against scale figuration in the left (x), and a final lyrical piece (xi). The finale (xii) employs part of the theme only, using it to develop a crescendo that culminates in a grand climax. Here again Schumann's full chords produce a quasi-orchestral effect, thus justifying the word *symphonic* in his title. Near the end a surprising turn to the major affords an dramatic high point that prepares the conclusion. In every way this is one of Schumann's most effective and representative works.

Schumann also produced a small body of works for piano duet and two pianos. For the former, there are the early polonaises of 1828 (8, WoO 20) and the *Bilder aus Osten* (6, op. 66, composed 1848, published 1849), the *Clavierstücke für kleine und grosse Kinder* (12, op. 85, composed 1849, published 1850), and two sets of dances, *Ballscenen* (9, op. 109, composed 1851, published 1853) and *Kinderball* (6, op. 130, composed 1853, published 1854). For two pianos there is a major work, the Andante and Variations in B-flat major (op. 46, composed 1843, published 1844), originally scored for two pianos, two violoncellos, and horn.

Clara Wieck Schumann (1819–1896), Robert's wife, was also a noted pianist in her own right who composed extensively. That she is among the most outstanding musical prodigies is clear from the fact that around the age of ten she produced her first published pieces, a set of polonaises (4, op. 1, composed around 1828, published 1830). At this time she began concertizing under the guidance of her father (1830–1831), later making tours to Copenhagen (1842), Russia (1844), and, repeatedly, England (1856 and after). Since most of her compositions date from the 1830s, before her marriage, it is evident that she set her ambitions aside to meet the needs of her family. In her compositions for piano she emphasized the character piece; for example, she wrote two sets of Romances (3, op. 11, composed 1838–1839, published 1839; and 3, op. 21, composed 1853, published 1855 or 1856 with a dedication to Brahms), the *Pièces caractéristiques* (4, op. 5, composed 1835–1836, published 1839), and *Soirées musicales* (6, op. 6, composed ca 1835–1836, published 1836). Yet she also essayed the traditional genres, with Variations (op. 20, composed 1853, published 1854), based on the "Albumblatt" of Robert's *Bunte Blätter* (op. 99 iv), a theme later used by Brahms; two scherzos (op. 10 and op. 14); and a set entitled Preludes and Fugues (3, op. 16, composed 1845, published 1846). As in the case of Fanny Hensel, much of her music has remained unpublished.

Two others were Louis Spohr (1784–1859) and Norbert Burgmüller (1810–1836). Spohr, a famous violinist and composer, produced a single sonata, in A-flat major (op. 125, composed and published 1843), emphasizing lyricism, and Rondoletto in G major (op. 149, composed 1848). Burgmüller, praised by Schumann, showed great promise that his early demise did not permit him to fulfill. He composed a Sonata in F minor (op. 8), a Rhapsody in B minor (op. 13), and a Polonaise in F major (op. 16), all full of lyricism and color. His early emphasis on the large form follows the pattern of Mendelssohn, Schumann, and, as we will see in the next chapter, Brahms.

CHOPIN

The last great composer of piano music to be considered here is Frédéric Chopin (1810–1849). Born in Poland of French parents, Chopin early decided on a musical career and upon graduation from the Warsaw Conservatory began concertizing. Yet he settled in Paris in 1831, where he devoted himself to playing locally, composing, and teaching. He belonged to the leading intellectual and artistic circles in Paris, and knew Liszt, Mendelssohn (who was in Paris in 1831–1832), Hiller, Berlioz, Paganini, Rossini, and Bellini, as well as de Musset, Balzac, Delacroix, Heine, the Polish poet Adam Mickiewicz, and the novelist George Sand (Aurore Dudevant) with whom he had a liaison that lasted some ten years, 1837–1847. He was also acquainted with Schumann. But, as we will see, he was by no means a literary musician after the fashion of Schumann.

More than any other leading composer, Chopin devoted himself to the piano, to the virtual exclusion of all other media; of symphonies, operas, and oratorios he composed none. Chamber music is represented by a sonata for cello and piano and a piano trio; it was piano music and chiefly genres associated with the character piece to which he directed his attention. Thus, along with character pieces (including nocturnes, impromptus, intermezzos, and ballades), he composed etudes, preludes, and dances (mazurkas, polonaises, waltzes). Yet he also essayed the larger forms of the older tradition—three sonatas and two sets of variations. Then there is a group of smaller works.[21]

Among his earliest works are polonaises, rondos, and other concert pieces, especially for piano and orchestra, works directed particularly to the concert platform (composed 1827–1829). But even during these early years Chopin showed signs of turning in a different direction with the etudes (op. 10) and the nocturnes (op. 9 and op. 15), and during the disappointing stay in Vienna in 1830–1831 he commenced the Scherzo in B minor (op. 20) and the Ballade in G minor (op. 23). This was the direction he was to follow; thereafter works he specifically intended for concert-giving are relatively scarce.

We have considered the character piece primarily as a small form that Romantic musicians developed as they turned away from the chief large form of piano music, the sonata. Schumann, as we have seen, extended the range and scope of the character piece both by producing larger and more complex works and by linking shorter pieces to comprise what we call suites. In his efforts to create character pieces on a larger scale, Chopin chose the former possibility, creating bigger and more elaborate compositions. Yet he continued to work with the older, smaller type of character piece, as is evinced by the impromptus, nocturnes, preludes, and the many stylized dances, as well as individual pieces like the *Berceuse*; the larger character piece is represented by the scherzos, the ballades, and the polonaises.

The establishment of the scherzo as an independent genre is associated with the practice of separately putting out movements that together could form a sonata. Chopin produced four scherzos.

CHOPIN'S SCHERZOS

B minor (No. 1, op. 20, composed 1831–1832, published 1835)
B-flat minor (No. 2, op. 31, composed and published 1837)
C-sharp minor (No. 3, op. 39, composed 1838–1839, published 1840)
E major (No. 4, op. 54, composed 1841–1842, published 1843)

All have the same formal plan: the scherzo proper, a midsection called trio, and the repeat of the scherzo. The Scherzo in C-sharp minor is in a five-part form that includes two statements of the trio, a procedure with ample precedence. Two of the scherzos commence with impressive flourishes (the B minor and C-sharp minor), and two have codas (the C-sharp minor and E major). As we have seen, the scherzo originally was no more than a fast minuet and hence could be expected to show the rounded binary form typical of the minuet. Chopin in fact follows this model, but he obscures the divisions by introducing variations that with the exception of the Scherzo in B minor, the earliest, make the use of double-bars and repeat marks impossible. The trios also show repetitive plans that ally them with rounded binary form. Thus the traditional formal scheme underlies Chopin's scherzos.

These pieces are on a larger scale than what had been normal in the scherzo movements of sonatas up to the 1830s. Chopin brought this change about by introducing several themes contrasting in character, as evident from the well-known Scherzo in B-flat minor. First there is the upbeat triplet run in the bass that is repeated three times and followed by full chords in dotted rhythm; then there is the brilliant figure accompanied by chords; finally a lyrical phrase accompanied by rapid broken-chord figuration, which rises, attains a climax, and passes to a section in the manner of a closing theme, with figuration and chords. Thereafter the whole is repeated with variations. Thus we may regard the piece as an elaboration of the traditional form of the scherzo. In the Scherzo in B minor, the second part of the scherzo section presents a development of themes stated in the first, so that we find a rapprochement to sonata form.

The trios contrast with the scherzos, as was indeed customary; they are subdued, slower, lyrical, and more uniform in character. The trio of the Scherzo in B minor is the simple setting of the popular Polish Christmas song "Lulajze Jezuniu," accompanied by chords. That of the Scherzo in C-sharp minor is chorale-like, with a filigree of broken-chord figuration between the different phrases. In the Scherzo in E major, the trio takes the form of a cantabile melody accompanied sparsely by broken-chord patterns. The trio of the Scherzo in B-flat minor is more elaborate: first, a simple melody using repeated notes and accompanied by chords, and then a more motivic part using figuration. But as the trio proceeds, its character changes and it draws thematic material from the scherzo proper, thus coming to resemble a development.

The ballades are Romantic in the more specific sense that they suggest a connection with works of literature. There are four.

CHOPIN'S BALLADES

G minor (No. 1, op. 23, composed 1831–1835, published 1836)
F major (No. 2, op. 38, composed 1836–1839, published 1840)
A-flat major (No. 3, op. 47, composed 1840–1841, published 1841)
F minor (No. 4, op. 52, composed 1841–1842, published 1843)

With these Chopin brought to piano music something largely of his own devising. As a genre of verse the ballad can briefly be described as an anonymous narrative involving legendary or historical events, generally with a tragic outcome, frequently associated with violence and the supernatural. Thus, the ballad contained elements with which the Romantics could readily identify. It enjoyed favor in the late eighteenth and early nineteenth centuries: associated with the distant past, as the vestige of ancient poetry, it came to be the northern counterpart of the chivalric epics of France. Leading poets of the time, particularly in Germany, felt stimulated to write new ballads that corresponded to those older ones of folk origin; many composers set ballads, old as well as new, to music.

In the early stages of the character piece we have noted the role played by the Bohemian composer Tomášek. Along with smaller works called eclogues, Tomášek composed larger ones which he called rhapsodies. He stated in his autobiography: "I wanted to attempt to write pieces in which seriousness along with strength and energy are predominant. In this I approached primitive times with their rhapsodies, which struck through my soul like a magic blow: I saw and heard them declaiming long passages from Homer's *Iliad* and sending everyone into a state of enthusiasm."[22] Here, then, is an attempt to compose music that would correspond to epic poetry, a rhapsody, or by extension, a ballad. Apart from Tomášek there are intimations of the idea in Schumann: the *Davidsbündlertänze* (op. 6 v) is entitled "Balladenmässig" and in the first movement of the Fantasia in C major (op. 17), a passage is marked "Im Legenden-Ton" (in the tone of a legend), hence epic narrative. Chopin was acquainted with the ballads of Adam Mickiewicz, a Polish poet who lived in Paris at the time. But it is not clear that Chopin modeled any of his ballades on specific poems of Mickiewicz or anyone else, even though various opinions have been expressed on the matter. It seems, rather, that he envisioned a musical genre that corresponded to the poetic ballad.[23]

In any case, Chopin had no real predecessor here. Tomášek's rhapsodies were all in simple three-part form. Chopin, however, conceived his ballades as large, elaborate compositions which often prove to be outgrowths of this basic scheme. The Ballade in F major is straightforward: the contrasting episode appears twice and there are transitional passages and a coda. The Ballade in A-flat major has one contrasting episode but includes a long transitional passage leading up to the climactic restatement of the principal part. It has also been interpreted as a free sonata form, although its development consists largely of free figuration unrelated to the thematic material of the exposition. Less regular is the Ballade in F minor, which contains three separate episodes, the second restated near the end, and the third like a development. Finally, the Ballade in G minor, the first of the series, may in fact be viewed as a sort of sonata form, with introduction and coda, and with the secondary theme appearing first in the recapitulation.

An important element in the ballades is the use throughout of the same theme in varied form. This principle is important in Romantic music, particularly since Schubert's *Wanderer* Fantasia. All of Chopin's ballades show it to some extent. In the Ballade in G minor, Chopin transforms the lyrical secondary theme into something heroic in the development; in the Ballade in F major, he varies the principal theme by using different accompaniments; in the Ballade in F minor, he varies the principal theme itself each time it appears. But he carries the principle furthest in the Ballade in A-flat major, where not only does he transform the principal theme itself from lyrical to heroic, but also uses it to provide the material for the secondary theme. This close relation between the two is evident in the virtuoso transition leading to the climactic re-entrance of the principal theme, in which the secondary theme is changed to the principal theme right before one's ears (Ex. 4-6).

We can relate the use of thematic variation in the ballades to the strophic form of the poetic ballad: strophic settings of ballads—by definition—use the same music for each strophe. Moreover, the compound meters Chopin consistently employs in these pieces may relate to the poetic meters used in ballads. Consider the ballad tone or rhapsodic opening of the Ballade in G minor, which seems to set the stage for a narrative of some moment. Sudden and effective contrasts abound: for instance, the crashing entrance of the secondary theme of the Ballade in F major, after the gentle lilt of the siciliano-type principal theme, or the dramatic transformation of the secondary theme in the Ballade in G minor. Impressive virtuoso display comes at the end of the Ballade in F minor. Passages involving virtuoso figuration appear in each of the ballades.

Chopin's intent seems clear—the establishment of a new, large, and difficult genre of the character piece inspired by the poetic ballad, a kind of character piece somehow the equivalent of the sonata, that could also serve as the mainstay of a serious concert. Quantitatively, however, Chopin's work consists mostly of shorter character pieces, and we now turn to these. Among his most typical works are the nocturnes.

CHOPIN'S NOCTURNES

PUBLISHED DURING HIS LIFETIME

Larghetto, B-flat minor; Andante, E-flat major; Allegretto, B major (No. 1–3, op. 9, composed 1830–1831, published 1832)

Andante cantabile, F major; Larghetto, F-sharp major; Lento, G minor (No. 4–6, op. 15, composed 1830–1833, published 1833)

Larghetto, C-sharp minor; Lento sostenuto, D-flat major (No. 7–8, op. 27, composed 1834–1835, published 1836)

Andante sostenuto, B major; Lento, A-flat major (No. 9–10, op. 32, composed 1836–1837, published 1837)

Lento (or Andante sostenuto), G minor; Andante (or Andantino), G major (No. 11–12, op. 37, composed 1838–1839, published 1840)

Lento, C minor; Andantino, F-sharp minor (No. 13–14, op. 48, composed and published 1841)

Andante, F minor; Lento sostenuto, E-flat major (No. 15–16,
  op. 55, composed 1843, published 1844)
Andante, B major; Lento, E major (No. 17–18, op. 62,
  composed and published 1846)

PUBLISHED POSTHUMOUSLY
  Andante, E minor (No. 19, op. 72 i, composed 1827,
    published 1855)
  Lento con gran espressione, C-sharp minor (No. 20, KKp
    1215–1222 and 1306, composed ca. 1830, published 1875)
  Andante sostenuto, C minor (No. 21, KKp 1233–1235,
    composed ca. 1825 or later, published 1938)

In the eighteenth century the *notturno* (night piece) was a serenade for a small ensemble, often of wind instruments, to be played out-of-doors and normally comprising three to five or more movements. Chopin's conception was totally different, representing a new genre. Yet here again he had predecessors: the Irish pianist and composer John Field (1782–1837) for one; the Polish pianist and composer Maria Szymanowska (1789–1831), for another. Field published some twenty pieces bearing this title between 1815 and 1834. These are in three-part form with lyrical melodies, often embellished, and accompanied by standard patterns of broken-chord figuration in the bass; generally a uniform character is maintained. Much depended on the performer's ability in cantabile playing and in effective use of the pedal.

Chopin adopted this concept but changed it into something of greater artistic moment. The basic type remained the same: a simple lyrical melody over an accompaniment based on a stereotypical pattern, the melody usually ornamented by grace-notes, coloratura runs, and elaborate ornamental figures (*fioriture*). He presents the melody often in parallel thirds, sixths, and, at the climaxes, octaves, constructing it in regular periods of balanced phrases organized by a simple repetitive scheme (see Ex. 4-7). The small scale of the nocturne is confirmed by the tempo designations indicated by Chopin, modified by expressions such as *espressivo, dolce,* or *languido e rubato*. While some of Chopin's nocturnes preserve the same character all the way through, thus following Field's model, the majority depart by introducing a contrasting midsection in a new key that uses different thematic material and a different style of writing, often including a transitional passage and coda; for example, the Allegretto in B major (op. 9 iii), the Larghetto in C-sharp minor (op. 27 i), the Lento in C minor (op. 48 i), and the Lento in E major (op. 62 ii). All of these are agitato in their midsections, but the Lento in C minor (op. 48 i) uses the arpeggiated figure of the midsection as accompaniment for the restatement of the principal section. The Andantino in C-sharp minor (op. 48 ii) displays a principal melody with an unusual organization of long and irregular phrases.

Example 4-6. CHOPIN: Ballade in A-flat major (op. 47)—Excerpts
    A. Principal theme—Beginning (mm. 1–8)
    B. Secondary theme—Beginning (mm. 52–58)
    C. Transition to Reprise—Excerpt (mm. 185–192)

Because of the nocturnes' simplicity and obvious exploitation of melodic lyricism, the claim has been made that Chopin deliberately adopted a vocal idiom, particularly the melodic style of the arias of Bellini. The ornamentation seems to confirm this. Objections to this idea involve, first, the model set by Field that had nothing to do with Bellini and, second, that Chopin began composing nocturnes while still in Warsaw before he became acquainted with Bellini's music. At the same time, the similarities are clear enough: Chopin could well have been influenced by the Italian opera of the time, if not specifically by Bellini. Simple lyricism is what has made Chopin's nocturnes so characteristic and popular; instances of "nocturne style" can be found in others of his works.

Another group of Chopin's smaller character pieces is formed by the impromptus, shown in order of composition.

CHOPIN'S IMPROMPTUS

Fantaisie-Impromptu, Allegro agitato, C-sharp minor (No. 4, op. 66, composed ca. 1834, published 1855)
Allegro assai, quasi presto, A-flat major (No. 1, op. 29, composed and published 1837)
Andantino (or Allegretto), F-sharp major (No. 2, op. 36, composed ca. 1839, published 1840)
Allegro vivace (or Tempo giusto), G-flat major (No. 3, in two versions of which the second is op. 51, composed 1841–1842, published 1843)

Here we are dealing with a genre that, as we have seen, had been cultivated before Chopin. By and large he maintained the features traditionally associated with it—the three-part formal plan with the midsection forming a contrast with the principal section. In turn he conceived the individual sections in accordance with simple repetitive schemes, as the A A′ B A C scheme in the principal section of the impromptus in A-flat major and G-flat major and the A B A′ C scheme of the Impromptu in F-sharp major; similar structures occur in the midsections too. The principal thematic material is less cantabile than that found in the nocturnes and, instead, is based on figuration, triplets in the impromptus in A-flat major and G-flat major, a complex two against three in the *Fantaisie-Impromptu*, actually four groups of sixteenths against two sextuplets of eighths. The exception is provided by the Impromptu in F-sharp major, where the "black-key" melody is irregular in structure and ornamented. Contrast is brought by the midsections, of which the best example is in the famous *Fantaisie-Impromptu*. There is also the cantabile melody in the left hand in the Impromptu in G-flat major, and the impressive martial passage in the Impromptu in F-sharp major. The impromptus, therefore, are larger and more elaborate than the nocturnes, show more complex musical procedures, and are technically more demanding.

Among the other character pieces are several that Chopin published individually, the best known of which are the Berceuse in D-flat major (op. 57, composed 1843–1844, published 1846) and the Barcarolle in F-sharp minor (op. 60, composed 1845–1846, published 1846). The former is unusual in that it is based on an ostinato harmonic progression one bar in length that is repeated throughout, over which a lilting melody is spun out continuously with constant variations and embellishments. The Barcarolle is more conventional. In three-part form with introduction and coda, its principal theme, a simple melody, is stated in parallel thirds (with some embellishments) over a patterned accompaniment, while in the midsection the same thematic material is given an entirely different accompaniment of chords that leads to the *fortissimo* restatement of the theme in its original form. In principle the piece is related to Mendelssohn's gondola songs, but on a larger scale.

Example 4-7. CHOPIN: Nocturne in D-flat major (op. 27 ii)—Beginning (mm. 1–11)

Chopin's lesser-known character pieces include the Bolero in A minor (op. 19, composed 1833, published 1834), the Tarantella in A-flat major (op. 43, composed and published 1841), both bravura pieces, a short Moderato in E major (composed 1843, published 1910), a *Marche funèbre* in C minor (op. 72 ii, composed ca. 1827, published 1855) that reappeared in modified form in the Sonata in B-flat minor; and several other short pieces.

An important group among Chopin's piano works is formed by the etudes (or studies) and the preludes.

CHOPIN'S ETUDES AND PRELUDES

ETUDES
  Set of 12 (op. 10, composed 1829–1832, published 1833)
  Set of 12 (op. 25, composed ca. 1835, published 1837)
  Nouvelles études (3, KKp 905–917, composed 1839 for
      Moscheles' and Fétis' *Méthode des méthodes*, published
      1840)

PRELUDES
  A-flat major (KKp 1231–1232, composed 1834 for Pierre Wolf,
      published 1918)
  Set of 24 (op. 28, composed ca. 1836–1839, published 1839)
  C-sharp minor (op. 45, composed and published 1841)

The etude, of course, is primarily a teaching piece—study or exercise—designed as a vehicle for the pianist to improve his or her technical ability, except that such pieces at the same time offer the opportunity to display the pianist's skill. Typically an etude will concentrate on one technical problem of execution, so that a certain consistency results since the same kind of thematic material for the most part is maintained throughout. But, on account of their expressive qualities, Chopin's etudes resemble virtuoso character pieces. Characteristic etudes were by no means unknown (there were examples by Moscheles [op. 95] and Cramer), but Chopin's are remarkable for their harmonic richness and exploitation of the sound capabilities of the piano.

The prelude, on the other hand, achieves much the same result in a different way and from a different point of departure. The model, here as elsewhere, was provided by the preludes of Bach's *Well-Tempered Clavier*, each of which, as we have seen, in principle employs the same thematic material throughout, usually based on patterns of figuration. The principal distinction between preludes and etudes, in Chopin at least, is that the etudes are larger and the preludes smaller.

The preludes (op. 28) represent his principal contribution to the genre. Each is in a different key. Following Bach's example, they have been arranged according to a simple tonal plan, in pairs beginning with C major, each prelude in the major followed by one in the relative minor, then ascending a fifth and repeating the pattern, for example, C major–A minor, G major–E minor, D major–B minor. Chopin followed a similar plan in the etudes (op. 10), but did not carry it out strictly: again the grouping is in pairs, an etude in the major followed by one in the relative minor and then ascending a third and repeating the pattern (C major–A minor, E major–C-sharp minor, G-flat major–E-flat minor), but Chopin broke the arrangement after the third pair, although the last two pairs consist of one in the major and one in the relative minor. No such arrangement occurs in the etudes (op. 25).

In most of the etudes, Chopin employed the ubiquitous three-part form, often with coda. As has been suggested, he often does not introduce contrast, echoing in the midsection the same thematic material as in the principal section but modulating into distant keys, so that when the theme is restated in its original form and key, one has the feeling of a recapitulation. Important exceptions to this are the Lento in E major (op. 10 iii), which resembles a nocturne and bears comparison specifically with one in the same key (op. 62 ii); the Vivace in E minor (op. 25 v); and the Allegro con fuoco in B minor (op. 25 x).

The character of each etude, as already indicated, is bound up with the technical problem to which it is addressed. A few of these are indicated (some etudes appear under more than one heading).

CHOPIN'S ETUDES: TECHNICAL PROBLEMS ADDRESSED

ARPEGGIO STUDIES Allegro, C major (op. 10 i); Allegretto, E-flat major (op. 10 xi); Molto allegro con fuoco, C minor (op. 25 xii)

SCALE PASSAGES Presto, C-sharp minor (op. 10 iv); Allegro, F major (op. 10 viii); Presto, F minor (op. 25 ii)

CHROMATIC SCALE PASSAGES Allegro, A minor (op. 10 ii); Lento, C-sharp minor (op. 25 vii)

DOUBLE NOTES Vivace, C major (op. 10 vii)

SCALES IN THIRDS AND SIXTHS Vivace, D-flat major (op. 25 viii)

LEGGIERO CHORD PLAYING Vivace assai, A-flat major (op. 10 x); Vivace, D-flat major (op. 25 viii)

CHORDS ACCOMPANIED BY RAPID FIGURATION Allegro con fuoco, C minor (op. 10 xii, "Revolutionary"); Lento-Allegro, A minor (op. 25 xi, the "Winter Wind")

SYNCOPATIONS AND OTHER RHYTHMIC PROBLEMS Andantino, F minor, and Allegretto, A-flat major (*Nouvelles études* i and iii)

OCTAVES Allegro con fuoco, B minor (op. 10 x)

LEFT-HAND MELODY Vivace, C major (op. 10 vii); Vivace, E minor (op. 25 v, midsection); Lento, C-sharp minor (op. 25 vii)

CANTABILE Lento, E major (op. 10 iii); Andante, E-flat minor (op. 10 vi); Allegretto, E-flat major (op. 10 xi, combined with legato arpeggios); Allegro sostenuto, A-flat major (op. 25 i, "Harp"); Vivace, E minor (op. 25 v, in the midsection); Lento, C-sharp minor (op. 25 vii)

The preludes differ from the etudes only in their smaller size. Some are small indeed, several being less than twenty bars long: the Largo in C minor (op. 28 xx), the shortest, has but twelve bars, while the Andante in A major (op. 28 vii), has fifteen. The longest of them, on the other hand, the Andantino in A-flat major (op. 28 xvii), comprises ninety bars. Like the etudes, most of the preludes are dominated thematically by a single motive. Often this consists of rapid figuration, as in the Agitato in C major (op. 28 i); the Molto agitato in F-sharp minor (op. 28 xiv); and the Allegro in E-flat minor (op. 28 xiv), to name only three. But the thematic material can also be lyrical, usually employing a short rhythmic pattern: the Largo in C minor (op. 28 xx); the Andantino in A major (op. 28 vii); the Cantabile in B-flat major (op. 28 xxi); and the Lento in F-sharp minor (op. 28 xiii). The single Prelude in C-sharp minor (op. 45) is also of this type. The contrasting midsections in a few of these lyrical preludes cause them to resemble nocturnes, as in the famous Sostenuto in D-flat major (op. 28 xi, known as the "Raindrop" Prelude). In its midsection, the emphatic chordal melody in the bass, associated with a crescendo, provides contrast to the lyrical melody of the principal part; only the eighth-note motion of the first section remains constant. Two notable instances in which Chopin pits a lyrical melody against rapid figuration are provided by the Vivace in G major (op. 28 iii), where the grazioso melody in chords is accompanied by rapid scale figuration, and, more dramatically, in the Allegro appassionato in D minor (op. 28 xxiv), where a declamatory melody of wide leaps in dotted rhythm is punctuated by sudden furious scale-runs, all over an agitated accompaniment. Consider also the curious and much-analyzed Prelude in A minor (op. 28 ii), in which a short melodic phrase is stated four times over a grinding, dissonant accompaniment fraught with tonal ambiguity.

The character pieces of Chopin, unlike many of those by Schumann and Liszt, tend to lack literary associations. There is no trace of this sort of connection in the impromptus, scherzos, nocturnes, and etudes, and it exists only in a general way in the ballades. Nor does there seem to be any link between the preludes and literature, unless one views them as fragments and interprets them as a musical equivalent of the literary fragment, a genre cultivated by Romantic writers.

In the large forms, there are three sonatas and one fantasia.

CHOPIN'S LARGER PIANO WORKS

Sonata, C minor (No. 1, op. 4, composed ca. 1827–1828,
     published 1851)
Sonata, B-flat minor (No. 2, op. 35, composed ca. 1837–1839,
     published 1840)
Sonata, B minor (No. 3, op. 58, composed 1844, published 1845)
Fantasia, F minor (op. 49, composed 1840–1841, published 1841)

The piano sonatas represent Chopin's principal accomplishment in the older tradition of the large forms. He maintained that tradition in all its essentials: there is the big Allegro first movement in sonata form, the scherzo second (a Minuetto in the Sonata in C minor), the slow movement, and the brilliant Allegro as finale. In two cases Chopin used rondo form (sonatas in C minor and B minor); we will consider the third, a very special case, below. Key relations among movements also remain largely traditional. In the Sonata in C minor, only the first and middle movements are in the tonic, while in the other two, the slow movement also is in the main tonality. The scherzo (or minuet) regularly is in a related key, except for the Sonata in B minor, where the relation, unusually, is a tritone.

In his treatment of sonata form, Chopin adhered to the old scheme complete with double-bar and repeat marks at the close of the exposition. In the exposition contrasting themes are presented, the first forceful and motivic (especially in the Sonata in B-flat minor), the secondary in the dominant or relative minor and lyrical in nature (in the early Sonata in C minor, it clearly has been derived from the principal theme). In all three Chopin exploits the motivic principal theme in the developments (in the Sonata in B minor, important use is also made of the secondary theme, which forms an impressive climax). Peculiar to Chopin is the individual treatment of the recapitulations. They commence not with the principal theme but with the secondary theme, with the principal theme reserved for the end. In the early Sonata in C minor, the recapitulation commences in the "wrong" key, B-flat minor. In general, however, Chopin accepted the traditional concept of the form.

The scherzos also employ the traditional scheme: the scherzos proper are in expanded rounded binary form and their trios in simple repetitive schemes. While the minuet of the early Sonata in C minor is in all respects a small piece, the scherzos in the other two are large. That of the Sonata in B-flat minor features elaborate and virtuoso material, a fast motivic theme using staccato repeated chords offset by soft, chromatic octave passages in the bass; its trio is like a nocturne. The scherzo of the Sonata in B minor presents a theme in *leggiero* figuration, while in the trio a lyrical melodic line appears in the middle register accompanied by chords involving dissonant suspensions.

Again in the slow movements we find conventional elements. Three-part form appears in all. The Larghetto of the Sonata in C minor is unusual for the quintuple meter, while the Largo of the Sonata in B minor suggests a nocturne. By far the most celebrated of these movements is the Marche funèbre of the Sonata in B-flat minor. Here the ponderous march, its melody full of repeated notes in dotted rhythm accompanied by dense chords in the bass and highlighted by a sudden turn to the relative major, is set off by the cantabile trio in D-flat major. We can note that both sections of this movement are cast in rounded binary form, a form standard in marches.

In the finales we meet with rondos in the sonatas in C minor and B minor, the second a sonata-rondo. Against these stands the unconventional finale of the Sonata in B-flat minor, a movement that has caused much comment. For here, instead of a large-scale and impressive fast movement, we have a short piece (seventy-five bars) in uniform character, consisting of rapid scale passages, the two hands an octave apart throughout, played at whirlwind speed but *sotto voce* up to the end. This movement is related to the prelude or etude, and Chopin's use of such a piece as finale to a sonata represents a departure.

All in all, then, Chopin's sonatas stand reasonably well in the tradition of the genre as it had come down from the late eighteenth century and developed through the work of Beethoven, Schubert, and their contemporaries.

Much the same situation obtains in the other large work that exemplifies a standard category, the Fantasia in F minor (op. 49), which ends in A-flat major. We have seen instances of the fantasia being treated as a large form in three or four movements, in sum roughly equivalent to a sonata; and Schumann gave his view that there was little difference between the two. Yet this claim can certainly not be made for Chopin's Fantasia—at least it is smaller than his sonatas—even though it clearly is a major work. He cast it in one long movement in loose sonata form, using a short march as an introduction; there is a coda. The looseness has to do with the fact that the development does not "develop" themes from the exposition, but rather restates them in various keys and dispositions; yet a dramatic climax is nevertheless attained. The recapitulation is prepared by a Lento sostenuto in B major. Unlike some other fantasias we have discussed, this one does not make use of thematic variation.

The last group of Chopin's piano works brings us back to a genre that has a long tradition in keyboard music—the elaboration of dances. Like his predecessors, Chopin worked with popular dances, in his case waltzes, mazurkas, and polonaises. We turn first to the waltz, the great international dance of the time. The earliest waltzes by Chopin are individual dances published long after his death (in A-flat major, E major, E-flat major, and E minor); these are not shown here. Sets that he composed somewhat later were published posthumously in 1855; the main corpus of waltzes were published by Chopin himself.

CHOPIN'S WALTZ SETS

PUBLISHED POSTHUMOUSLY, 1855
> Lento, A-flat major; Moderato, B minor (op. 69, composed
> 1829–1835)
> Waltz, G-flat major; Waltz, F minor; Moderato, D-flat major
> (op. 70, composed ca. 1833)

PUBLISHED BY CHOPIN
> Grande valse brillante, Vivo, E-flat major (op. 18, composed
> ca. 1831, published 1834)

Grandes valses brilliantes: Vivace, A-flat major; Lento, A
minor; Vivace, F major (op. 34, composed respectively
1835, 1831, and 1838, published 1838)
Grande valse, A-flat major (op. 42, composed and published
1840)
Valses: Molto vivace, D-flat major ("Minute" Waltz); Tempo
giusto, C-sharp minor; Moderato, A-flat major (op. 64,
composed 1846–1847, published 1847)

Until this time the waltz in piano music was a short, modest piece, often
with rustic overtones as in the German ländler, with trio. Later the waltz
became an elegant dance cultivated in the refined circles of the aristocracy, in
which context it could also appear as a bravura piece, as had been demonstrated by Weber's *Aufforderung zum Tanz* (Invitation to the Dance), mentioned earlier. This type of waltz provided the basis for Chopin's. The earliest
among them, however, are modest in all respects—short and simple with
midsections called trios. But the really representative examples are those he
himself published. In these, as in Weber, the waltz is elegant and brilliant.

Chopin did not adhere to a single formal scheme in these waltzes. Generally speaking, he has cast them in several sections with the first as the waltz
proper; it recurs near the end, while in between come short, contrasting sections that are in effect separate waltzes in themselves. This can be seen in the
Grande Valse Brilliante in E-flat major. Sometimes Chopin introduces a
refrain, as in the Grande Valse in A-flat major (op. 42), which has three such
complete waltzes as episodes; the principal section of this waltz is noteworthy for its cantabile theme in even notes and its smooth broken-chord accompaniment and two-against-three rhythmic conflict. Frequently there will be a
martial introduction, ceremonial and fanfare-like, as well as a brilliant coda:
both may be seen in op. 18 and 34. The Grande Valse Brilliante in A-flat
major even employs rounded binary form in all its sections. But not all
Chopin's waltzes have this elegant brilliance. We can point to the melancholy
Lento in A minor (op. 34 ii) and Moderato in B minor (op. 69 ii), while the
Tempo giusto in C-sharp minor (op. 64 ii) suggests the nocturne in its lyrical
principal section. Much shorter than these and thus resembling the earlier
waltzes is the popular "Minute Waltz" in simple three-part form, the first part
featuring a theme in scale passages, the second lyrical. Chopin's waltzes thus
follow the norms of music actually used for dancing and thus exhibit little of
the stylization that so often characterizes dances adapted to the piano.

More individual than the waltzes are those dances that relate to Chopin's
native Poland—the mazurka and the polonaise. There are some sixty
mazurkas. Chopin began composing them as early as the mid 1820s; a number of these early efforts survive but he did not see fit to publish them. Thus,
in addition to the mazurkas listed, there are a handful of others.

CHOPIN'S PUBLISHED MAZURKAS

MAIN CORPUS, PUBLISHED BY CHOPIN HIMSELF

Mazurka, F-sharp minor; Mazurka, C-sharp minor; Vivace, E major; Presto ma non troppo, E-flat minor (op. 6, composed 1830–1831, published 1832)

Vivace, B-flat major; Vivo ma non troppo, A minor; Presto ma non troppo, A-flat major; Vivo, G major (op. 7, composed 1830–1831, published 1832)

Vivo e risoluto, B-flat major; Lento ma non troppo, E minor; Legato assai, A-flat major; Lento ma non troppo, A minor (op. 17, composed ca. 1832, published 1834)

Lento, G minor; Allegro non troppo, C major; Moderato con anima, A-flat major; Moderato, B-flat minor (op. 24, composed 1834–1835, published 1836)

Allegro non tanto, C minor; Allegretto, B minor; Allegro non troppo, D-flat major; Allegretto, C-sharp minor (op. 30, composed 1836–1837, published 1838)

Lento, G-sharp minor; Vivace, D major; Semplice, C major; Mesto, B minor (op. 33, composed 1837–1838, published 1838)

Andantino, E minor; Animato, B major; Allegretto, A-flat major; Maestoso, C-sharp major (op. 41, composed 1838, published 1840)

Vivace, G major; Allegretto, A-flat major; Moderato, C-sharp minor (op. 50, composed 1841–1842, published 1842)

Allegro non tanto, B major; Vivace, C major; Moderato, C minor (op. 56, composed 1843, published 1844)

Moderato, A minor; Allegretto, A-flat major; Vivace, F-sharp minor (op. 59, composed and published 1845)

Vivace, B major; Lento, F minor; Allegretto, F-sharp minor (op. 63, composed 1846, published 1847)

SETS PUBLISHED POSTHUMOUSLY, 1855, INCLUDING BOTH EARLY AND LATE MAZURKAS

Vivace, G major; Cantabile, G minor; Allegretto, C major; Moderato animato, A minor (op. 67, composed variously 1835–1846, published 1855)

Vivace, C major; Lento, A minor; Allegro ma non troppo, F major; Andantino, F minor (op. 68, composed variously 1829–1830, published 1855)

Published separately, early 1840s
  Mazurka à Emile Gaillard, A minor (KKp 919–924)
  Mazurka, A minor (for the album *Notre temps*, published
    1842)

note: Related to this last group is the early Rondo à la Mazur, F major
  (op. 5, composed 1826, published 1828).

Although mazurkas had been current in the repertory since the early years of the nineteenth century, those of Chopin are on a higher artistic level. He employed many different schemes, no one of which predominates. While some of the earlier mazurkas show the simple three-part scheme, the mazurka proper and its trio, others do not. In any case, a mazurka is sectional, with repetition of sections an important principle; usually three or four sections that contrast in key, thematic material, and character are repeated in various combinations.

To gain a better understanding of these little pieces, we should know something of the underlying original Polish dance types. The mazurka, named for the Mazur people of Mazovia, is but one of several related dances that go under the generic name of *oborek*, which denotes a turning dance for couples. Three kinds of mazurkas have been distinguished: the *kujawiak*, a slow and serious dance, named after the Kujawy region; the *mazur*, in faster tempo; and the *obertas*, sometimes called *oborek* (thus making the terminology unclear), the fastest of all. In the *kujawiak* the minor mode predominates, often with raised fourth and lowered seventh, and the slow tempo permits much embellishment as well as rubato. In the faster *mazur* and *obertas* dotted rhythms and wide leaps replace the embellishments. The main rhythmic features are these dotted rhythms and irregular accentuations, especially at the ends of phrases, where the second or third beat often gets the accent. Grace-notes, ornamental figures, and scale-runs are important. These dances were often sung to the accompaniment of the *dudy*, a form of bagpipe, which produced a drone bass, something Chopin frequently retained in his mazurkas.

While the majority of Chopin's mazurkas are of the moderate *mazur* type, we find examples of the slow *kujawiak*, such as the four Lentos, three in A minor (op. 17 ii, iv, and op. 68 ii, see Ex. 4-8A) and one in G minor (op. 24 i), as well as the fast *obertas*, such as the Presto in E-flat minor (op. 6 iv, see Ex. 4-8B), the Presto in A-flat major (op. 7 iii), and the Allegro ma non troppo in F major (op. 68 iii). Chopin restricts the drone bass to one section of a mazurka, as in those in C-sharp minor and E minor (op. 6 ii and iii), the Vivace in F major (op. 7 i), the popular Vivo e risoluto in B-flat major, and two Lentos ma non troppo in E minor and A minor (op. 17 i, ii, and iv), the Andantino in E minor (op. 41 ii), the Allegro non tanto in B major (op. 56 i), and the Allegro ma non troppo in F major (op. 68 iii), to identify some of the more obvious. Modal inflections also appear here and there. A particularly clear example of the Mixolydian is in the Vivo in G major (op. 7 v), and of the Phrygian in the Maestoso in C-sharp minor (op. 41 i) and in the midsection of the Allegretto in A-flat major (op. 41 iv). Especially common is the Lydian, as in the Allegro non troppo in C major (op. 24 ii); the Allegretto in A-flat major (op. 41 iv, which, as we saw, also uses the Mixolydian); and the Vivace in C major (op. 56 ii), or in the minor, Lento in A minor (op. 68 ii, beginning).

Example 4-8. CHOPIN: Mazurkas—Excerpts
    A. *Kujawiak*: Lento in A minor (op. 68 i)—Beginning (mm. 1–8)
    B. *Obertas*: Presto ma non troppo in E-flat minor (op. 6 iv)—Excerpt
    (mm. 1–8)

Here—in contrast to the waltzes—we are dealing with stylized dances: Chopin has taken the essential features of the dance and used them singly and in combination, while also drawing in other musical procedures. Along with modal scales, the drone bass, and the characteristic rhythmic and melodic patterns associated with the dance, we find occasionally contrapuntal elaboration, as in the Moderato in B-flat minor (op. 24 iv), the Moderato in C-sharp minor (op. 50 iii), the Moderato in C minor (op. 56 iii), and the Vivace in F-sharp minor (op. 59 iii), in the reprises of which the counterpoint approaches imitation. Or we find harmonic elaboration in the extremely chromatic mazurkas, the Lento ma non troppo in A minor (op. 17 iv), with its nocturne-like *fioriture*; the Moderato in B-flat minor (op. 24 iv), with its suspensions; the Moderato in A minor (op. 59 i); and the Andantino in F minor (op. 68 iv). Although most of the mazurkas are short and seemingly rather modest pieces, a few are larger: the Moderato in B-flat minor (op. 24 iv), already noticed for its use of counterpoint, chromaticism, and suspensions; the Mesto in B minor (op. 33 iv), with the unusual amount of contrast between the sections; the Moderato in C-sharp minor (op. 50 iii), in which the use of counterpoint has already been noted; the Allegro non tanto in B major, and the long Moderato in C minor (op. 56 i and iii). When stylized in this way, the originally simple folk dance becomes in effect a character piece.

One characteristic feature of the mazurkas is their lack of bravura, so important elsewhere in Chopin. But he asserted this aspect in his other dances native to Poland, the polonaises. Again there are some early works—some of them as early as 1817—but only one of these was definitely published during Chopin's lifetime; others were not published until after his death. Then there are the five that comprise the main corpus.

CHOPIN'S POLONAISES

EARLY

Allegro ma non troppo, G minor (KKp 889 and 1301, composed and published 1817)

Allegro moderato, B-flat minor (KKp 1188–1189, composed and possibly published 1826)

Allegro maestoso, D minor; Allegro ma non troppo, B-flat major; Allegro moderato, F minor (op. 71, composed 1817–1827, published 1855)

Polonaise, G-flat major (KKp 1197–1200, composed 1828–1829, published 1870)

THE MAIN CORPUS

Allegro appassionato, C-sharp minor; Maestoso, E-flat minor (op. 26, composed 1834–1835, published 1836)

Allegro con brio, A major ("Military"); Allegro maestoso, C minor (op. 40, composed 1838–1839, published 1840)

Polonaise, F-sharp minor (op. 44, composed 1840–1841,
    published 1841)
Maestoso, A-flat major ("Heroic," op. 53, composed
    1842–1843, published 1843)
Polonaise-Fantaisie, A-flat major (op. 61, composed
    1845–1846, published 1846)

NOTE: We should add the Andante spianato and Grande polonaise in
G minor and E-flat major. The polonaise was composed 1830–1831,
originally for piano and orchestra; the Andante spianato, presumably
composed 1834, was added to the polonaise, which Chopin had arranged
for piano solo, and the two published as op. 22 in 1836.

While the mazurkas are small, intimate pieces, the polonaises are the
opposite; they are large-scale, brilliant works intended for the concert hall.
Yet the early polonaises are small pieces showing the simple repetitive
schemes ordinarily found in dances—especially the rounded binary form—
and they have midsections called trios; they even use the da capo to call for
the restatement of the opening section. Noteworthy among the early polonaises is the Allegro moderato in B-flat minor (KKp 1188 and 1189), which
Chopin composed just before his departure from Warsaw in 1826 and possibly published the same year. The polonaise proper, its melody presented
first in thirds and then in chords, is marked *dolente* but the trio uses as its
melody an aria, "Vieni fra questa braccia," from Rossini's comic opera *La
gazza ladra*, which had been introduced to Warsaw in 1826.

In the polonaises composed in Paris, however, the type is expanded,
with the virtuoso elements brought to the fore. In the first two sets (op. 22 and
op. 40), the ternary scheme obtains, with rounded binary form evident in the
polonaises proper and in some of the midsections. But Chopin has increased
the dimensions. Popular in this group is the "Military" polonaise in A major
(op. 40 i).

The next two polonaises, in F-sharp minor (op. 44) and A-flat (op. 53),
are stylized concert pieces. The former is among the most interesting of
Chopin's larger works. After a short introduction of octave figures in the bass
comes the polonaise itself, a vigorous theme with insistent accompaniment,
both in the typical polonaise rhythm; this is followed by several episodes, the
second being a *tempo di mazurka*, after which the introduction reappears to
herald the final statement of the first section, the polonaise proper. The popular Maestoso in A-flat is less elaborate. The brilliant introduction exploits
the full range of the keyboard, with chromatic chordal runs, the bravura
polonaise theme in thirds and with grace-notes, the melody high, and the
accompaniment emphasizing the bass. The main subordinate section is
bravura, with its ostinato figure in octaves in the bass and the theme in dotted rhythm above, everything progressing from *sotto voce* to a resplendent *for-*

tissimo. A meandering chromatic transitional passage leads to the culminating statement of the polonaise theme, and there is a short coda.

A special case is presented by the Polonaise-Fantaisie in A-flat major (op. 61), an unusual and ambitious work. The fantasia, as we have seen, was among the large forms, as evidenced by Chopin's other contribution (see above). Since the polonaise also had been manifested as a large form, it seems reasonable for Chopin to have combined the two, as represented here. Its form is complicated, basically a large ternary plan with introduction, coda, and extended transitional passages before and after the secondary section. But there are many changes of key, short episodes, one in the form of a mazurka, and variations. Themes from one section recur in another (particularly the second transition). Moreover, Chopin has elided the beginnings and endings of sections by short transitional passages. This degree of elaboration is characteristic of his late work.[24]

Of other works there are not many: a few early rondos; the large Allegro de concert in A major (op. 46, composed presumably 1840–1841, published 1841), an out-and-out bravura display piece in the form of a rondo with two episodes, one based on a variant of the rondo; and the simple *Écossaises* (Scotch [dances], composed 1826). There are also sets of variations, all on popular melodies of the time: an operatic aria by Herold (op. 12), the German song "Steh' auf, steh' auf, o du Schweizerbub" (KKp 925–927), the *Souvenir de Paganini* (KKp 1203), and a single variation on a march by Bellini for the collection *Hexameron* (KKp 903–904, composed 1837, published 1839). For two pianos there is a Rondo in C major (KKp 1086–1089/op. 73, composed 1828, published 1855), originally for piano solo.

Chopin's works have become a mainstay of the pianist's repertory. Alone among the great composers of the century, he concentrated on composing for the piano, so that there is a certain justice in the consistent popularity of his music. Further, his exploitation of the instrument's capacities involved him in experimentation, using novel harmonies and devising new ways of handling the instrument. Examples are the quintuple meter in the slow movement of the early Sonata in C minor, or the elaborate counter-rhythms in the *Nouvelles études*. His harmony often exploits strong unresolved dissonances, as in such etudes as the Andante in E-flat minor (op. 12 vi), the Allegro in F major, and Vivace in E minor (op. 25 ii and iii), the last two of which make bold use of the appoggiatura, or, to pick an extreme case, the Prelude in A minor (op. 28 ii). His use of modal scales in the mazurkas has also been mentioned. These novelties aroused attention at the time, not always favorable. In 1834 a prominent critic, Ludwig Rellstab (1799–1860), attacked Chopin; of the mazurkas (op. 7), he noted "ear-splitting discords, forced transitions, harsh modulations, ugly distortions of melody and rhythm," their "odd originality," and the use of "strange keys," "unnatural positions," and "perverse combinations." Of the Nocturnes (op. 9) Rellstab wrote: "Where Field smiles, Chopin makes a grinning grimace; where Field cries, Chopin groans; where Field puts some seasoning into his food, Chopin empties a handful of cayenne pepper."[25] Yet precisely these innovations, among others, have given Chopin's works the position they now enjoy.

THE UNITED STATES

Piano music in the United States[26] at this time resembles that in Europe—most of the composers and performers in fact were emigrants—except that the more serious, elaborate, and complex forms did not achieve prominence until the end of the nineteenth century. The repertory around 1800 consisted mostly of short character pieces, variations, mostly on songs popular at the time, independent rondos and fantasias of the potpourri or medley variety, and a small number of sonatas in the galant style. Among the most important composers were Raynor Taylor (1747–1825), John Christopher Moller (1755–1803), Alexander Reinagle (1756–1809), Benjamin Carr (1768–1831), James Hewitt (1770–1827), Anton Philip Heinrich (1781–1861), Christopher Meineke (1782–1850), and Charles Gilfert (1787–1829).

Of these, Reinagle, Carr, Hewitt, and Heinrich stand out. Reinagle, a native of England who came to New York in 1786 and later settled in Philadelphia, worked as teacher, impresario (he established the New Theater), pianist, and singer and was the most accomplished composer in the group. Among his works for piano are a set of four sonatas in D major, E major, C major, and F major (composed ca. 1780–1790, not published until 1978), all in the galant style current in Europe at the time, and a number of shorter pieces that include a set of variations on Scotch tunes which was published first in London prior to his arrival in the United States and then again in Philadelphia. His sonatas rank among the most outstanding works composed at the time in the United States.

Carr, who came to the United States from Great Britain in 1793, settled in Philadelphia where he established himself as a music publisher. He composed six pieces which he entitled sonatas, published in F. Linley's *A New Assistant for the Pianoforte or Harpsichord* (1796); these are short, unassuming pieces, one of them for piano duet. He also brought out a programmatic piece of the *battaglia* genre, *The Siege of Tripoli* (op. 4, published 1804–1805), in rondo form, a descendant of Frantisek Koczwara's famous *The Battle of Prague* (op. 13/24, published 1788) and of Dussek's *Naval Battle* (see above).[27]

Hewitt also came from Great Britain, but a year earlier than Carr (1792), and lived both in New York and Boston. Hewitt was a more resourceful composer who produced a set of three sonatas in the two-movement scheme (op. 5, published 1795–1796), one of which has as its finale a set of variations on "The Plough Boy," a song from a popular comic opera of the time. He also produced two other sonatas, a "grand military sonata" entitled *The Fourth of July* (published 1801) not in the traditional form, and one dedicated to a Miss Mount (published 1809). But doubtless his best-known effort, mostly adapted from a piece by Natale Corri, is yet another programmatic *battaglia, The Bat-*

tle of Trenton (1797). Such pieces evidently went over well in the aftermath of the Revolution.

Heinrich, an emigrant from Germany who led a wandering life, spending time in Kentucky (1817–1820) and later Boston, but with trips back to Europe, composed a number of unconventional works. These are mostly contained in three publications: *The Dawning of Music in Kentucky* (op. 1, published 1820), *The Western Minstrel* (op. 2, also published 1820), and *The Sylviad* (op. 3, published in two volumes, 1823 and 1825–1826). The bulk of these sets consists of marches, rondos, and dances of various kinds, notably cotillions and waltzes, along with sets of variations and individual character pieces. There are also some larger efforts: the highly irregular sonata "La buona mattina" in three movements, ostensibly in D major but ending in B-flat major; "A Sylvan Scene in Kentucky, or The Barbecue Divertimento" (its movement entitled "The Banjo" is an effective representation of that instrument's sound, composed long before the more famous one of Gottschalk, discussed in Chapter Six); the "Chromatic Ramble," an harmonic labyrinth with an ad libitum solo part; and the brilliant Toccatina capriciosa.

NOTES FOR CHAPTER FOUR

1. J. numbers assigned in F. Jähns, *Carl Maria Weber in seinen Werken: chronologisch-thematisches Verzeichnis seiner sämmtlichen Compositionen* (Berlin: Schlesinger, 1871; Berlin-Lichterfelde: Lienau, 1967).

2. O. Deutsch, *Schubert: A Documentary Biography* (New York: Norton, 1947), 456. The D numbers associated with Schubert's works represent their chronological order as assigned by Deutsch, *Franz Schubert: Thematisches Verzeichnis seiner Werke*, Neue Ausgabe sämtlicher Werke, ser. 8, vol. 4 (Kassel: Bärenreiter, 1978). Many of his works are known by the opus numbers assigned them upon publication, which are shown here as well. Because of their number and importance, incomplete sonatas are included.

3. The exception here is the Sonata in C major (D. 279), in which the principal theme of the first movement is motivic and highly rhythmic, features exploited in the development.

4. A. Einstein, *Schubert: A Musical Portrait* (New York: Oxford, 1951), 157, 267–268, 223, and 287, respectively.

5. On cyclic form see D. Montgomery, "The Myth of Organicism: Science to Great Art," *Musical Quarterly* 76 (1992): 17–66.

6. Schumann's review may be read, among others, in his *On Music and Musicians*, ed. K. Wolff, trans. P. Rosenfeld (New York: Pantheon, 1946), 118–120; see also Einstein, *Schubert: A Musical Portrait*, 284.

7. Einstein, *Schubert: A Musical Portrait*, 288.

8. W. Georgii, *Klaviermusik*, 3rd ed. (Zurich: Atlantis, 1950), 293; more recently, J. Godwin, "Early Mendelssohn and Late Beethoven," *Music and Letters* 55 (1974): 272–285.

9. See H. and L. Tischler, "Mendelssohn's Songs Without Words," *Musical Quarterly* 33 (1947): 1–16.

10. See Schumann's own account in the Preface to his collected essays and reviews, available in his *On Music and Musicians*, ed. K. Wolff, 25–26.

11. Dates in this section from K. Hofmann and S. Keil, *Robert Schumann: Thematisches Verzeichnis seiner im Druck erschienenen musikalischen Werke mit Angabe des Jahres ihres Entstehens und Erscheinens*, 5th ed. (Hamburg: Schuberth, 1982).

12. C. Becker, "A New Look at Schumann's Impromptus," *Musical Quarterly* 67 (1981): 568–586.

13. Note that Schumann also used the term *scenes* in *Kinderscenen* and *Waldscenen* as well as in the early Variations on the "Sehnsuchts-Walzer" (Yearning Waltz) attributed to Schubert.

14. See, generally, W. Boetticher, "Zur Zitatpraxis in R. Schumanns frühen Klavierwerken," *Speculum musicae artis: Festgabe für Heinrich Husmann*, ed. H. Becker and R. Gerlach (Munich: Fink, 1970), 63–73, esp. 71.

15. F. Niecks, *Robert Schumann* (London: Dent [1825]), 200.

16. WoO (= Works without opus number) designations as given in K. Hofmann, *Die Erstdrucke der Werke von Robert Schumann*, Musikbibliographische Arbeiten 6 (Tutzing: Schneider, 1979).

17. Schumann, *On Music and Musicians*, 65.

18. See L. Roesner, "Schumann's Parallel Forms," *Nineteenth Century Music* 14 (1991): 265–278.

19. The theme by Beethoven that Schumann uses here is the Allegretto of the Symphony in A major (op. 92).

20. Originally ascribed to Florestan and Eusebius.

21. The bibliographical situation of Chopin has improved of late, particularly with the thematic catalog: K. Kobylanska, *Frédéric Chopin: Thematisch-bibliographisches Werkverzeichnis*, trans. H. Stolze (Munich: Henle, 1979), which effectively has replaced that of M. Brown; KKp stands for numbers used in her *Rekopisy Utworow Chopina* (Cracow, 1977), a catalog of Chopin's manuscripts. Scholars still differ as to when Chopin composed certain works.

22. Quoted by W. Kahl in his article "Ballade," *Die Musik in Geschichte und Gegenwart*, vol. 1 (Kassel: Bärenreiter, 1949–1951), 1134.

23. See J. Parakilas, *Ballads Without Words: Chopin and the Tradition of the Instrumental Ballade* (Portland OR: Amadeus, 1992).

24. See J. Kallberg, "Chopin's Last Style," *Journal of the American Musicological Society* 38 (1985): 238–261.

25. Quoted by W. Murdoch, *Chopin: His Life* (London, 1933), 155–156.

26. See J. Clark, *The Dawning of American Keyboard Music* (New York: Greenwood, 1988).

27. See L. Pruett, "Napoleonic Battles in Keyboard Music of the Nineteenth Century," *Early Keyboard Journal* 6 (1988–1989): 73–89.

CHAPTER FIVE

Liszt and Brahms and Their Age

Although the large forms—the sonata, the fantasia, and variations—that had dominated the repertory of piano music in the Classic period continued to exist, they experienced a decline in importance in the Romantic. Their place was usurped by new and more typically Romantic genres of compositions, those with extramusical associations, primarily the character piece in its various guises. The two tendencies, however, were by no means mutually exclusive: composers at times mixed elements of both.

Important in the aesthetic view of the time was the conception of the art work as the unique individual expression of its author—in regard to music particularly, as the manifestation of his or her own emotions. This view affected not only the composer but also the performer. Certainly the increase in concert activity since the early eighteenth century added to the significance of the performer. In addition, this concept reflected a view of art that arose in the eighteenth century but that became prominent in the nineteenth: if artistic creation is taken as having its origin in the realm of the supersensible, if not divine, then the artist becomes a person set off from others by insights that they lack, as one in intimate contact with a higher domain of which the others know nothing. We can easily see that such a view would have special consequences when extended to the performer of music along with the composer. Often the musician united both functions: C. P. E. Bach, Mozart, Beethoven, and Clementi, to name only a few, were regarded as among the foremost virtuoso pianists of their day; Weber, Mendelssohn, Schumann, Chopin, and Field were also known as virtuosos of the instrument. Schubert seems to have been one of the very first composers of the first rank to compose a large body of piano music without himself being a prominent performer on the instrument.

Yet it became more common, as the century wore on, to have virtuoso performers who were not particularly identified with or known for their musical compositions, whose reputations and livelihoods depended rather on their skill as performing artists playing chiefly music composed by others. Virtuosity made this possible, a virtuosity that sometimes came to be regarded as awe-inspiring if not supernatural or demonic. To the performing artist, therefore, came the advantages associated with the creative artist, the composer. Among these virtuosos in the early part of the nineteenth century were Ignaz Pleyel; Joseph Gelinek; Daniel Steibelt, a rival of Beethoven; Anton Eberl; August Eberhard Müller; Johann Baptist Cramer; Ludwig Berger, the teacher of Mendelssohn; Johann Nepomuk Hummel; August Alexander Klengel (1783–1853); Ferdinand Ries (1784–1838); Friedrich Kalkbrenner (1785–1849); Johann Peter Pixis (1788–1874); Maria Szymanowska; Carl Czerny (1791–1857); Franz Hünten (1793–1878); Ignaz Moscheles (1794–1870); Henri Bertini (1798–1876); Henri Herz (1803–1888); Louise Farrenc (1804–1875); Sigismond Thalberg (1812–1871); Théodore Döhler (1814–1856); Adolf von Henselt (1814–1889); Edouard Wolff (1816–1880); Alexander Dreyschock (1818–1869); Hans von Bülow (1830–1894); Carl Tausig (1841–1871); and, as we shall see in some detail, Franz Liszt (1811–1886).

Undergirding this emphasis on public concerts and virtuosity were developments in the design of the piano itself, developments that made the instrument far more powerful sounding than it had been. In general the changes involved the use of heavier strings and strengthening the case and frame the better to increase support against the increased tension. Although the Stodardt firm in London had used metal to brace the piano frame in the early 1780s, John Isaac Hawkins of Philadelphia began using iron frames for his upright pianos in 1800, while Alphaeus Babcock of Boston produced a full, single, cast-metal frame in 1825. Still, this type of construction came into general use only in the second half of the century, with builders in the United States leading the way.[1] In 1821 the Parisian firm of Érard also developed a double escapement that afforded much greater ease in repetition, the rapid reiteration of the same key. Another decisive improvement in the quality and power of the instrument's tone was produced by cross-stringing, introduced by Henri Pape in Paris in 1821: instead of having all the strings running parallel to each other, they are arranged in two layers, the treble strings in a fan underneath and the bass strings on top. This not only allowed more strings to be positioned over the highly resonant central portion of the sound board, but also, by bringing the treble and bass strings close together, facilitated the generation of partial tones, thus producing a far richer tone quality. The combination of cross-stringing and the full metal frame along with consistently high standards of workmanship distinguished the products of the Steinway firm, founded by Heinrich Engelhard Steinweg (1797–1871), who came to New York from Braunschweig in 1850. Thus the modern concert grand piano came to be.

Other developments to be noted: the range of the keyboard grew from five-and-a-half to six-and-a-half octaves in Beethoven's time to the modern standard of seven octaves by 1860. The range of variation in quality of tone was increased, first by the moderator (already described), operated by a pedal or knee-lever), and then by three pedals. The damper pedal lifted the

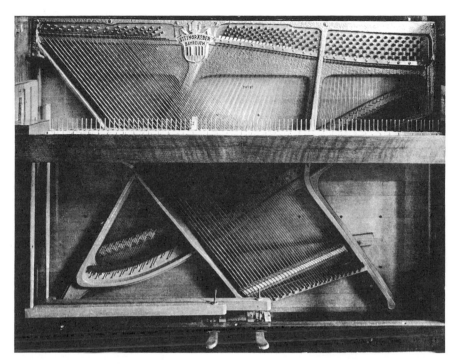

Cross-stringing.

dampers, permitting the strings to vibrate freely; the *una corda* pedal shifted the entire action sideways so that the hammer would strike but one of the strings that produced each note. Most recently, the *sostenuto* pedal was added; when the player depresses this pedal, the strings struck by the hammers are left undamped. All but the moderator have survived in the modern piano.

Hand in hand with the development of the instrument itself went a growing interest in pianistic virtuosity which showed itself in increased attention to piano methods—instruction manuals and courses of study in piano playing, some of which commence at the elementary level and continue up to the most advanced stages. Such teaching methods go back to the sixteenth century, but they became more numerous in the eighteenth century. We mention some of the best known: François Couperin's *L'art de toucher le clavecin* (1717), Jean-Philippe Rameau's statement published with the second book of his *Pièces de clavecin* (1724), Carl Philipp Emanuel Bach's *Versuch über die wahre Art das Klavier zu spielen* (2 vols., 1753–1762), and Dussek's *Instructions on the Art of Playing the Pianoforte* (London, 1796). With the coming of the nineteenth century, the number of such publications, many by prominent virtuosos, increases. Some of the more important are: Johann Baptist

Cramer's *Grosse praktische Pianoforte-Schule* (1815); Hummel's *Ausführliche theoretisch-praktische Anweisung zum Pianofortespiel* (1828); Kalkbrenner's *Méthode pour apprendre le pianoforte à l'aide du guidemains* (1820s); and Czerny's famous *Vollständige theoretisch-praktische Pianoforteschule* (op. 500, 1839). Three important works of this kind from the middle of the century are Moscheles and Fétis' *Méthode des méthodes* (1837), Sigmund Lebert and Ludwig Stark's *Grosse theoretisch-praktische Klavierschule* (1858), and Adolf Kullak's *Ästhetik des Klavierspiels* (1861). Along with such instruction works go countless collections of teaching pieces, etudes, and the like, such as Clementi's well-known *Gradus ad Parnassum* (1817–1826) or the many by Czerny and Cramer.[2]

The increased emphasis on virtuosity had an impact on repertory. A new body of bravura piano music aimed to exploit these new capabilities and in particular to provide the performer with the opportunity to make a profound impression, a "hit." We have already seen this attitude to some extent in the etudes of Chopin, which are as much *bona fide* concert pieces as they are etudes for the development of piano technique. We also find the nineteenth-century equivalent of the old intabulation, transcriptions for piano of popular compositions of the time. Here opera was singled out: on the one hand there are arrangements of individual numbers from a popular opera or variations on the theme of a popular aria or duet (we have noted this in the work of Mozart and Beethoven), and, on the other hand, there are larger pieces that successively present the highlights, themes from the most popular numbers of an opera or other piece of musical theater, under the general title of potpourri, fantasia, reminiscences, paraphrase, or something similar. The emphasis was on virtuosity, the creation of a piece guaranteed to make an impression on the audience. Such works existed in abundance in the nineteenth century. Outstanding examples include Thalberg's fantasias on Rossini's *Moses* and *La donna del lago* and on Mozart's *Don Giovanni*.[3] On the other hand, Schumann directed his polemic, expressed through his *Davidsbündler*, in some measure against this kind of music. Composers also made arrangements for piano of individual excerpts from operas.

Thus, three principal divisions emerged in the repertory of piano music of the nineteenth century: the old genres involving the large forms from the eighteenth century; the new genres associated with the character piece and often involving explicit extramusical associations; and those connected with virtuosity and the newly developed capabilities of the instrument, which placed the performer in the forefront. Naturally we find cases in which elements from one group appear in another or even instances where all three are combined. Generally, however, we can readily distinguish the three. In this realm, two great figures stood above their contemporaries, each involved with the repertory in a different way: Franz Liszt and Johannes Brahms. Liszt, as will emerge, emphasized virtuosity and the new Romantic genres of composition, while Brahms for the most part returned to the ideals of the older Classical tradition.

LISZT

While the piano stands at the center of Liszt's artistic accomplishment, he made important contributions to other branches of musical composition. Although born in Hungary (in an area that is now part of Austria), he settled in Paris, where in 1839 he launched his spectacular virtuoso career which took him all over Europe—Hungary, London, Vienna, Germany, Spain, Portugal, Turkey, Russia, Moldavia, Poland, and Denmark. But in 1847 he dropped concertizing and the next year became musical director of the court of Weimar where he devoted himself to conducting, composition, writing, and teaching. After 1861 he divided his time between Weimar, Budapest, and Italy. Everywhere he was in contact with leading writers and musicians—in Paris with Chopin, Berlioz, Paganini, Rossini, Fétis, Lamartine, and Victor Hugo, as well as George Sand and the Countess Marie d'Agoult (who wrote under the pseudonym Daniel Stern and with whom he formed a liaison that lasted some ten years). Later his circle included Wagner, Bülow, for a time Nietzsche, and many others. Like Weber and Schumann, Liszt was a musician with literary aspirations: he wrote articles and books on important topics in the musical life of the time.[4]

Liszt made his reputation chiefly as a pianist. In so doing, he identified himself with the Romantic cult of virtuosity. Most important here was the development and exploitation of an amazing technique that seemed to border on sorcery. In this he followed the example of Paganini, whose bearing in concerts was such as to excite the suggestion that he was possessed of demonic powers. The use of a black costume fostered this impression, along with haughty posturing, elaborate gesturing, and other mannerisms. Liszt was also the first pianist to appear by himself, unassisted, for a whole concert. The custom had been for a pianist to appear together with other musicians, singers, and players, often with an orchestra, since the mainstay of the repertory of the public concert had been the concerto. But Liszt appeared alone and established the modern sense of the term *recital* which he borrowed from the poetic and dramatic readings popular in the Parisian salons of the time.

He also developed a totally new style of playing and writing for the instrument. Instead of working largely with scale technique, the stock-in-trade of Hummel, Czerny, and their contemporaries, Liszt exploited the capacities of the instrument in an unheard-of fashion. He employed rapid and coloristic changes of register; used dense chords and octave passages in all ranges, frequently associated with wide leaps, arpeggios over the full extent of the keyboard, scales in thirds, sixths, octaves, and even in full chords, diatonic and chromatic; created elaborate cadenzas and recitative-like passages; added vibrato figurations; and often put a melody in the middle register accompanied by difficult figuration ranging over the whole keyboard. Many reports from those who heard him perform, such as Schumann and Berlioz, testify to the enormous effect he produced on an audience.

A survey of Liszt's life reveals four broad periods: a preparatory phrase, the period of concertizing (1839–1847), the years at Weimar (1848–1861), and the period of semi-retirement. In each the activity that principally engaged him determined the kinds of musical compositions he produced. During the 1830s and 1840s his musical composition emphasized those genres most closely connected with concertizing—etudes, operatic potpourris, and other types in which bravura elements were primary; in the 1850s he turned away from this and devoted himself to the character piece and to a few essays in the large forms; in the last phase, the virtuoso impulse died down, replaced by short and simple pieces employing unusual harmonies. In general Liszt neglected the more traditional genres, such as the sonata and variations, although he made important contributions to each.[5] In the discussion of his piano music, we will begin with the etudes and Hungarian Rhapsodies, then take up the character piece, after which we turn to his other works.

PRINCIPAL COLLECTIONS OF LISZT'S ETUDES

Études d'une exécution transcendante (12, S. 139,[6] composed
    1851, published 1852): Preludio, C major; Molto vivace, A
    minor; "Paysage" (Landscape), F major; "Mazeppa," D minor;
    "Feux-follets" (Fireflies), B-flat major; "Vision," G minor;
    "Eroica," E-flat major; "Wilde Jagd" (Wild Hunt), C minor;
    "Ricordanza," A-flat major; Allegro agitato molto, F minor;
    "Harmonies du soir" (Evening Harmonies), D-flat major;
    "Chasse-neige" (Snow Sleigh), B-flat minor
Études d'une exécution transcendante d'après Paganini (6, S. 140,
    first version composed 1838, published 1840; second version
    [S. 141], composed and published 1851)
Ab Irato: Grande étude de perfectionnement (S. 143, composed
    and published 1852)[7]
Études de concert (3, S. 144, composed ca. 1848, published 1849):
    "Il lamento," A-flat major; "La leggierezza," F minor; "Un
    sospiro," D-flat major
Études de concert (2, S. 145, composed 1862–1863, published
    1863): "Waldesrauschen" (Forest Rustling); "Gnomenreigen"
    (Gnomes' Dances)[8]

In these works we encounter Liszt's virtuosity in all its extremes and varieties; the most difficult elements of his piano technique are found here. That this was deliberate on his part is suggested by the appellation "transcendental": the degree of difficulty transcended that of other etudes of the time.

Through the three versions of the *Transcendental Etudes*, the changes made by Liszt always serve to increase the degree of difficulty. We can see this, for example, in "Mazeppa." In the first version this is a study in thirds; in the later revisions the figuration grew ever more elaborate. The piece ultimately evolved into a study that presents a slow-moving melody in octaves at the extremes of the piano's range accompanied by rapid chordal figuration, up and down the whole expanse of the keyboard. (The thematic material used here reappears in Liszt's symphonic poem of the same title.) In their final versions as *Transcendental Etudes*, Liszt gave many of them descriptive titles so that they came to resemble character pieces.

In form these etudes are sectional, generally in a basic ternary plan, often with some variations. But Liszt obscures this basic ternary plan by extensive thematic transformation, so that often the midsection employs the same thematic material as the other sections. Typical is the scheme in "Wilde Jagd": of its three themes the second and third (both containing a figure derived from the first) appear first in lyric and then in heroic-dramatic guise. The large Allegro agitato molto in F minor suggests a loose sonata structure: three themes are stated, developed (a procedure that involves modulating statements of the three themes), and, after a brilliant rhetorical climax, recapitulated.

Among the more brilliant and technically demanding are "Mazeppa"; "Feux-follets," an allegretto in which harmonic color is important; "Eroica," martial with a slow, ponderous melody and dotted figures, suggestive of a funeral march; "Wilde Jagd," featuring cross-rhythms, octave passages, and scale-runs, on the whole resembling a Chopin ballade, and "Chasse-neige," with its lyrical beginning and gradual crescendo and accumulation. Other brilliant etudes that do not have descriptive titles are the Preludio in C major, which resembles Chopin's first prelude in the same key (op. 28 i); the Molto vivace in A minor; and, particularly, the impressive Allegro agitato molto in F minor (the appassionato key), which is related to Chopin's etude in the same key (op. 10 ii). But not all these etudes concentrate on the bravura: there are notable lyrical pieces that require a cantabile style from the performer. Such are "Paysage," with its siciliano-like rhythm expressing the pastoral; "Ricordanza"; and "Harmonies du soir," the latter with a grand climax (Ex. 5-1). Liszt created a ceremonial aura in "Vision" with its crashing chords, unusual harmonic progressions, and magnificent climax near the end.

The *Transcendental Etudes* display two styles typically employed by Liszt. The first, which we have already mentioned, consists of a cantabile melody that moves in slow, even notes and is accompanied by rapid virtuoso figuration. Almost all these etudes have passages of this kind of writing. For instance, "Vision" opens with such a melody in heavy chords in the bass accompanied by light arpeggio figures that begin in the treble but gradually involve the entire range of the keyboard. This cantabile style also appears in the Allegro agitato molto in F minor, especially in the midsection, and in "Harmonies du soir" and "Chasse-neige." The other prominent feature is the cadenza, a long solo line incorporating scale-runs and arpeggios, or involv-

Example 5-1. Liszt: "Harmonies du soir" from *Transcendental Etudes* (S. 139 xi)—
Excerpt (mm. 97–105)

ing parallel chords moving rapidly up and down the keyboard. These occur
in "Paysage," "Feux-follets," and the Allegro agitato molto in F minor. Also
related are simple recitative-like passages, as in "Mazeppa" and "Ricordanza."

It is significant that Liszt based another set of etudes that he characterized
as "transcendental" on compositions of Paganini. As has been pointed out,
Paganini was the foremost virtuoso of his day and served as a model for Liszt
in his early career as a concert artist. Like the first set of *Transcendental
Etudes*, the one based on Paganini's music begins with a Preludio and con-

tinues with a series of etudes. But these etudes are based on Paganini's Caprices for unaccompanied violin (op. 1). "La Campanella" is particularly well known; the tune also served Liszt as the subject for an independent Fantasia for piano (S. 420), also in variation form. Also familiar are "La Chasse" (v) and the sixth etude which is based on Paganini's twenty-fourth Caprice. Here Liszt retains the variation structure of the original (this theme was also employed by Brahms and Rachmaninov).

The association of the etude with the character piece is prominent in the remaining etudes of Liszt. *Ab Irato* represents rage by its insistence on heavy, thick chords in rapid tempo in the extreme bass, while at the same time being a study in the rapid execution of chords. The Concert Etudes (3, S. 144), have descriptive titles only in their French edition. Of this group, "Un sospiro" in D-flat major is a study in cantabile playing, in which a short phrase in even notes is repeated with many ornamental variations. The Concert Etudes (2, S. 145), "Waldesrauschen" and "Gnomenreigen," are likewise pictorial.

Another important group of works that were composed mostly during Liszt's period of concertizing are the famous *Rhapsodies hongroises* (19, Hungarian Rhapsodies, S. 244). The first fifteen of these were published by 1853 (the first had appeared as early as 1847), while the last four are late works dating from 1882 to 1885. Here the impulse toward virtuosity is combined with what Liszt took to be Hungarian gypsy melodies, which he regarded as the authentic voice of the Hungarian people. What he actually heard and used was salon music performed in the cities. But whatever the result, the intent certainly is clear, and Liszt's motivations, here and elsewhere, are commendable.

Liszt reported on the Hungarian Rhapsodies in his book *Des Bohémiens et de leur musique en Hongrie* (The Bohemians and Their Music in Hungary, 1859). From this it emerges that he had assembled a large collection of these "gypsy" melodies which he considered central to Hungarian culture, parts of a larger totality, parts that, in their variety of forms and types, he viewed as corresponding to components in a great gypsy epic. This conception lies behind the term *rhapsody*: the epic quality imputed to the melodies and their texts.[9] The Hungarian Rhapsodies were preceded by earlier versions (S. 242, published in ten installments, 1839–1847) under the title *Magyar dallok* (Hungarian National Melodies). In the last six installments he introduced the term *rhapsody*, calling them *Magyar rhapsodiák* (Hungarian Rhapsodies).

Despite the origin of the materials used by Liszt, he incorporated many features of Hungarian folk music in the Hungarian Rhapsodies. Three of them have descriptive titles: "Héroide-élégiaque" (v), "Le Carneval à Pesth" (ix), and "Marche de Rákóczi" (xv). We frequently find the so-called "gypsy scale," using the augmented fourth, the minor sixth, and the major seventh, thus producing the augmented second between the sixth and seventh steps of the scale. In several of the Hungarian Rhapsodies, for example those in A minor and C-sharp minor (xi and xii), Liszt imitates on the piano the sound of the czimbalom, an Hungarian dulcimer-like instrument. Moreover, he made use of a characteristic type of Hungarian melody: a phrase commences in very long, slow-moving notes; suddenly rapid ornamental figures appear, the effect being both rhapsodic and sad—as Liszt put it, "to be played in the haughty and melancholy manner of the gypsies" (vii). Frequently he used the qualifications "mesto" (sad), "con duolo" (with sadness), or "malinconico" (melancholy). The effect is pronounced in the Rhapsody in C-sharp minor (viii), which dispenses altogether with a time signature at the beginning, thus adding the rhapsodic element of free rhythm (Ex. 5-2). We find this same characteristic type of melody in the Rhapsody in D minor, and in the popular one in C-sharp minor (ii), while traces of it appear in most of them—in the many melodies using slow notes with sudden interjections in dotted rhythm, sharply accentuated chords in the accompaniment, unexpected bursts of figuration, and so on. Added to these are features more typical of Liszt—recitative-like phrases and embellished cadenzas.

Another form that appears in the Hungarian Rhapsodies may also be related to Hungarian folk music: the *czárdás*, a gypsy dance in two parts. The slow first part employs the type of melody described above while the second is rapid. These two parts and their respective styles were called *lassú* and *friss*, designations that appear in these compositions, notably the famous one in C-sharp minor (ii). Yet another trait derived from Hungarian music is the presentation of the melody in parallel thirds, as in the Rhapsody in C-sharp minor (i).

The Hungarian Rhapsodies are also bravura display pieces. Their form is usually loose and involves contrasting sections. The beginning is often slow, melancholy, rhapsodic; contrasting sections follow, possibly a grazioso succeeded by an impassioned recitative, a capriccioso, capped off by a grand and brilliant conclusion. The technical difficulties often are great, the possibilities for showmanship abundant. Thus, in these pieces we can see a curious duality in Liszt's makeup: on the one hand, the high-minded purpose, the lofty objectives, and, on the other, the intrusion of elements aimed at popular acclaim, exploiting the grandiloquent gesture. Yet the aesthetic seems similar to that of Italian opera. For the grand scenes, for instance "mad scenes," as in Donizetti's *Lucia di Lammermoor* or Verdi's *Macbeth*, the composers employ virtuoso elements, particularly florid coloratura—bravura goes hand in hand with significant moments.

Another piece related to the Hungarian Rhapsodies is the *Rhapsodie espagnole: Folies d'Espagne et jota aragonese* (S. 254, composed ca. 1863, published 1867). Here Liszt has given two Spanish melodies a treatment similar to that in the Hungarian Rhapsodies. The first of them is the famous *La Folia* so often used as an ostinato in the seventeenth and eighteenth centuries.

Example 5-2. Liszt: Hungarian Rhapsody in C-sharp minor (S. 244 viii)—Beginning (mm. 1–8)

LISZT'S CHARACTER PIECES

PRINCIPAL COLLECTIONS

Apparitions (3, S. 155, composed and published 1834)

Années de pèlerinage

Première année: Suisse (9, S. 160, composed 1835–1854, published 1855)[10] "La chapelle de Guillaume Tell," "Au lac de Wallenstadt" "Pastorale," "Au bord d'une source," "Orage," "Vallée d'Obermann," "Eclogue," "Le mal du pays," "Les cloches de Genève"

Deuxième année: Italie (7, S. 161, composed 1837–1849, published 1858) "Sposalizio," "Il pensieroso," "Canzonetta del Salvator Rosa," "Sonetto 47 del Petrarca," "Sonetto 104 del Petrarca," "Sonetto 123 del Petrarca," "Après une lecture de Dante: Fantasia quasi sonata." Supplement, *Venezia e Napoli* (3, S. 162, composed 1859, published 1861) "Gondoliera," "Canzone," "Tarantella"[11]

Troisième année: (7, S. 163, composed 1867–1877, published 1883) "Angelus! Prière aux anges gardiens," "Aux cyprès de la villa d'Este: Threnodie" (in two different versions); "Les jeux d'eaux à la villa d'Este," "Sunt lachrymae rerum: En mode hongrois," "Marche funèbre: En mémoire de Maximilien I, Empereur de Mexique † en 19e Juin 1867," "Sursum corda"

Harmonies poétiques et religieuses (10, S. 173, composed 1842-1852, published 1853) "Invocation," "Ave Maria," "Bénédiction de Dieu dans la solitude," "Pensée des morts,"[12] "Pater noster," "Hymne de l'enfant à son réveil," "Funérailles," "Miserere (d'après Palestrina)," Andante lagrimoso; "Cantique d'amour"

Ballades: D-flat major (S. 170, composed 1845–1848, published 1849); B minor (S. 171, composed 1853, published 1854)

Consolations (6, S. 172, composed 1849–1850, published 1850)

Légendes (2, S. 175, composed 1863, published 1866) "St. François d'Assise: La prédication aux oiseaux," "St. François de Paule marchant sur les flots"

Weihnachtsbaum: Arbre de Noël (12, S. 186, composed 1874–1876, published 1882) "Psallite," "O heilige Nacht," "Die Hirten an der Krippe," "Adeste fideles," Scherzoso; "Carillon," "Schlummerlied," "Altes provencalisches Weihnachtslied," "Abendglocken," "Ehemals!," "Ungarisch," "Polnisch"

Elegies: A-flat major (S. 196, composed 1874, published 1875);
A-flat major (S. 197, composed 1877, published 1878)[13]
Historische ungarische Bildnisse (Pictures from Hungarian
History, 7, S. 205, composed 1870–1885, published 1956)

PRINCIPAL INDIVIDUAL COMPOSITIONS

Lyon (S. 156 i, composed 1834, published 1842)[14]

Scherzo and March (S. 177, composed 1851, published 1854)

Berceuse (S. 174, first version composed and published 1854;
second version, composed 1862, published 1865)

"Nuages gris" (S. 199, composed 1881, published 1927)

"La lugubre gondola" (S. 200, first version composed 1882,
published 1916; second version [the arrangement of an
earlier piece for solo string instrument and piano, S. 134],
published 1886)

"R. W.—Venezia" (S. 201, composed 1883, published 1927)

"Am Grabe Richard Wagners" (S. 202, composed 1883,
published 1952)

"Schlaflos! Frage und Antwort" (S. 203, composed 1883,
published 1927)

"Trauervorspiel und Trauermarsch" (S. 206, composed 1885,
published 1887)

"En rêve" (S. 207, composed 1885, published 1888)

"Unstern: sinistre, disastro" (S. 208, composed ca. 1886, date
of publication unknown)

Bagatelle without Tonality (S. 216a, composed 1883,
published 1956)

These works are of great importance for Liszt as a Romantic musician. Here we encounter an aspect of his work that frequently stands in contrast to the musical *grand seigneur*, the towering virtuoso of the piano, the idol of European concert life—his belief in a cardinal aesthetic tenet of Romanticism, the ability of music to suggest or express ideas, emotions, and impressions of different sorts—in short its capability of giving expression to extramusical subject matter. In this it was chiefly the association between music and poetry that drew Liszt's attention; one of his central convictions had to do, as he put it, with "the renewal of music through its inner connection with poetry."[15] Or, as he expressed in the preface to his early collection, the *Album d'un voyageur*, he was working with a rarefied art form, not for the many but for the few, in which he made the attempt to put into music the impressions nature made upon his soul, to express the "intrinsic and poetic meanings of things."

Liszt frequently drew on the work of leading writers and artists for the subject matter of his character pieces: Byron, the arch-Romantic of English poetry, is represented by quotations from *Childe Harold's Pilgrimage*, and indeed the idea of pilgrimage was central in the *Années de pèlerinage*, Liszt's largest set of character pieces. The French Romantic poet Lamartine provided the inspiration for the *Harmonies poétiques et religieuses*; Victor Hugo wrote the poem that gave rise to Liszt's "Dante" Sonata ("Après une lecture de Dante: Fantasia quasi sonata") as well as the epic *Mazeppa*, a subject also essayed by Byron; *Consolations* was a collection of poems by the critic Saint-Beuve; "Vallée d'Obermann" and "Le mal du pays" are prefaced by excerpts from a popular French novel, Senancour's *Obermann*, which was written as early as 1804, but did not become influential until its reprint of 1830. A poem of Schiller inspired "Au bord d'une source." From earlier literature we find Petrarch (sonnets that Liszt had originally composed as songs) and Dante, with whom Liszt became familiar by way of Victor Hugo. From the visual arts we find Raphael ("Sposalizio"), Michelangelo ("Il pensieroso"), and Rosa, a poet as well as a painter. Stories related to two saints, Francis of Assisi and Francis of Padua, provided the background for the *Légendes*. The late nocturne "Schlaflos! Frage und Antwort," less known, comes from a poem by Toni Raabe. An unusual case is presented by the *Années de pèlerinage*, particularly the first two volumes, which relate to Liszt's years in Switzerland and Italy in the company of the Countess Marie d'Agoult, and thus are to an extent autobiographical. The later set, long thought to have been associated with Rome, has been shown to have important associations with his native Hungary.[16] The early *Lyon*, on the other hand, has associations with social issues involving the silk workers of that city in the aftermath of the revolution of 1834.[17]

We can group the character pieces themselves generally into the established formal types even though the titles given them may be different. Chopin's influence is obvious in the ballades and scherzos. Several pieces bear the title "feuille d'album" (album leaf). But such designations are in the minority; instead of such appellations as intermezzo, song without words, impromptu, we meet descriptive or characteristic titles, which Liszt used for typical varieties of character pieces. For example, "Un soir dans les montagnes" from the early *Album d'un voyageur* and the late "Schlaflos! Frage und Antwort" are nocturnes, as is "Harmonies du soir" from the *Transcendental Etudes*. The first of these has in its midsection a thunderstorm that Liszt later developed as a separate piece in *Années de pèlerinage*; he also portrayed a storm in the legend "St. François de Paul marchant sur les flottes." The singing of birds dominates the other legend, "St. François d'Assise: La prédication aux oiseaux." Running water is depicted in "Au bord d'une source" and "Les jeux d'eau à la villa d'Este," both from *Années de pèlerinage*, the latter a brilliant allegretto with light arpeggio figures. Then there are pastoral compositions, such as "Ranz de vaches" from the earlier *Album d'un voyageur* and "Eclogue" from *Années de pèlerinage*. An unusually large number have to do with affects of mourning and lamentation, especially among the later works. From the third book of *Années de pèlerinage* come "Aux cyprès de la villa d'Este: Threnodie" (which appears in two settings), "Sunt lachrymae rerum," and "Marche funèbre," and from *Harmonies poétiques et religieuses* come the elaborate "Pensée des mortes" and "Funérailles," the latter with its military-heroic midsection that is indebted to Chopin's Polonaise in A-flat major (op. 53). "Eroica" from the *Transcendental Etudes* can also be included here. One more important group consists of pieces based on religious subjects; we find these in the early part of *Années de pèlerinage*, as "La chapelle de Guillaume Tell" and "Les cloches de Genève" and in *Harmonies poétiques et religieuses*. Indeed, in this set we find such works as the "Ave Maria" and "Pater noster," in which Liszt underlays the texts of Latin prayers, and the "Bénédiction de Dieu dans la solitude" and the "Miserere (d'après Palestrina)." By means of simple chords, diatonicism, and the absence of time signatures, the latter suggests the archaic but "pure" style of the sixteenth-century composer. In "Pensée des mortes" Liszt employed Psalm 129, "De profundis," and again underlaid the Latin words, the constantly repeated chords suggesting the recitation of *falso bordone*.[18] Religious subjects prevail in the two *Légendes* and in the third part of *Années de pèlerinage* ("Angelus! Prière aux anges gardiens," "Sursum corda," and several others). Christmas songs form the basis for much of the little-known collection *Weihnachtsbaum*.

Virtuosity, so important in the etudes and Hungarian Rhapsodies, is less so in the character pieces. The most demanding among them appear in the earlier sets of *Années de pèlerinage*: "La chapelle de Guillaume Tell," "Orage," and "Vallée d'Obermann" from *Suisse* and the large "Dante" Sonata from *Italie*. The later sets lack virtuoso elements, the *Consolations* being especially simple. Less known are the pieces composed by Liszt in his old age; for example, "Nuages gris," "La lugubre gondola," "Schlaflos!," and "Unstern," which are short and simple in technique, emphasizing sparse textures, but which seem experimental by virtue of the chromatic, dissonant harmony that gives prominence to the tritone; the title "La lugubre gondola," of course, suggests Mendelssohn's *Songs Without Words*.

Each of the first two books of *Années de pèlerinage* features one piece that is significantly larger and of much greater weight than the rest. In *Suisse* this is "Vallée d'Obermann," related to Senancour's novel. The piece is important in Liszt's development as a composer since it is among the first to show basic aspects of his art: the literary background, the use of a single theme that appears in varied forms throughout, and virtuosity. The other, the concluding number in *Italie*, is even bigger: "Après une lecture de Dante: Fantasia quasi sonata," the latter designation precisely the reverse of Beethoven's *sonata quasi una fantasia*. This is a large virtuoso piece in sections that follow one another in uninterrupted succession, all of them related by the consistent use of four themes and their variants. There is the slow introduction, Andante maestoso, in full octaves descending by tritones (the interval known in the Middle Ages as "diabolus in musica" [the devil in music], vividly depicting "Inferno"), followed by a Presto agitato assai (also designated "lamentoso"), with rapidly moving broken octaves in sextuplets and a chromatic stepwise line. Later, at the Andante quasi improvisato, the Presto theme is presented in varied form, as it is again in the Adagio. Toward the end Liszt restates it in

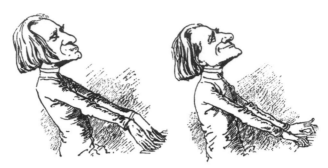

a.

b.

c.

d.

e.

f.

something like its original form. Thus, we have a large sectional work in cyclic form that in size and scope corresponds to a sonata or multimovement fantasia. Further, it contains passages as difficult as those of the *Transcendental Etudes*. Both these large character pieces, in fact, seem like symphonic poems for piano.

The other large-scale works for solo piano are, externally at least, divorced from the character piece.

LISZT'S OTHER LARGE WORKS FOR SOLO PIANO

Grosses Konzert-Solo (S. 176, composed presumably 1849–1851, published 1851)[19]

Sonata, B minor (S. 178, composed 1852–1853, published 1854)

Variationen über das Motiv von Bach: Basso continuo des ersten Satzes seiner Kantate *Weinen, Klagen, Sorgen, Zagen* und des *Crucifixus* der H-moll Messe (S. 180, composed 1862, published 1864)[20]

The Concert-Solo and the Sonata in B minor have much in common with the "Dante" Sonata. Both are sectional, use cyclic form, and afford opportunity for virtuoso display. But the sonata—the only work to which Liszt gave this designation—is far and away the more important. It is cast in a single long, continuous movement with many clearly definable sections. Liszt uses four basic themes that he transforms extensively during the course of the work (see Ex. 5-3): (A) In the opening Lento assai, the theme is made up of staccato and separated chords over a descending bass in dotted rhythm, similar to the motive for Wotan's anger in Wagner's *Ring of the Nibelung*. (B) What we might call the principal theme appears in the next section, Allegro energico, in two motives, one employing wide leaps and dotted rhythms and the other with strongly marked repeated notes preceded by an upbeat triplet figure. Liszt uses these two motives singly and together, subjecting them to

Opposie: Franz Liszt, the Sun King of the Piano, in concert. a. He closes his eyes and seems to be playing only to himself. b. Pianissimo: St. Francis preaches to the birds; his face becomes transfigured. c. Hamlet's broodings; torments of Faust. The keys tremble with sobs. d. Reminiscences: Chopin, Sand, O the joys of youth, perfumes, moonbeams, love. e. Dante: Inferno. The damned and the piano groan. Orcan shakes the gates of Hell. f. He wanted nothing more than to play for us, to express himself in music. Applause, shouts, and bravos.
Drawings by Jankó.

variations. The first of them appears in recitative style over an arpeggiated accompaniment and later as Dolce con grazia, while the second appears in a lyrical version, the upbeat eliminated and the note values augmented, "cantando espressivo" and "dolcissimo." The two remaining themes are of lesser import: (C) the third, the grandioso theme, slow over ponderous, thick, repeated chords and (D) the fourth, the Andante sostenuto, lyrical, used in combination with the cantabile version of the second motive of the principal theme.

In its overall organization this work differs radically from traditional sonatas. It has many sections contrasting in character, some of which recur. There are two principal ways of interpreting the structure of the work. The first views it as a single, long, complex movement in sonata form, with many episodes and other aspects that obscure its relation to the model. According to the other, the sonata is a four-movement work in which the movements are connected and in which the same themes are used throughout.[21] This formal ambiguity is typical of Romanticism; indeed Liszt may have been influenced by Schubert's *Wanderer* Fantasia and Schumann's Symphony in D minor (op. 120). As in the large pieces in the *Années de pèlerinage* discussed earlier, the principles are the same as those Liszt used in his symphonic poems, except for the absence of a program or descriptive title.

The work begins solemnly with the Lento assai, which returns at the end; the forceful Allegro energico, which presents the principal thematic material, comes next, and not only is repeated in similar form near the close but also reappears during the course of the sonata as a three-voice fugue. Toward the end of the first Allegro energico there are rapid changes of tempo and character with much fast octave work, which leads to a culmination that introduces the Grandioso. We encounter passages of great technical difficulty and climaxes of considerable proportions along with rhetorical passages, partic-

Example 5-3. LISZT: Sonata in B minor (S. 178)—Excerpts
    A. Lento assai (mm. 1–3)
    B. Allegro energico (mm. 8–15)
    C. Grandioso (mm. 105–113)
    D. Andante sostenuto (mm. 331–338)

ularly those in recitative style. In short, the Sonata in B minor is Liszt's largest composition for piano solo, one of the few important works in its genre after Beethoven and Schubert.

Another large work by Liszt goes back to Bach. It is based on the chromatic ostinato first used by Bach in the first movement of the cantata *Weinen, Klagen, Sorgen, Zagen* (BWV 12), a movement which with some revisions appears as the "Crucifixus" of the Mass in B minor. Following Bach, Liszt has organized the piece in variation form, each variation corresponding to a statement of Bach's melody. The variations are preceded by an introductory Andante and followed by a recitative-like passage. They end with a coda in which the hymn "Was Gott tut das ist wohlgetan" appears, with text underlaid to make the point explicit. This hymn also figures in Bach's cantata. Thus, Liszt has set the darkness and lamentation of the ostinato against the affirma-

B.

continued

Example 5-3, *continued*

C.

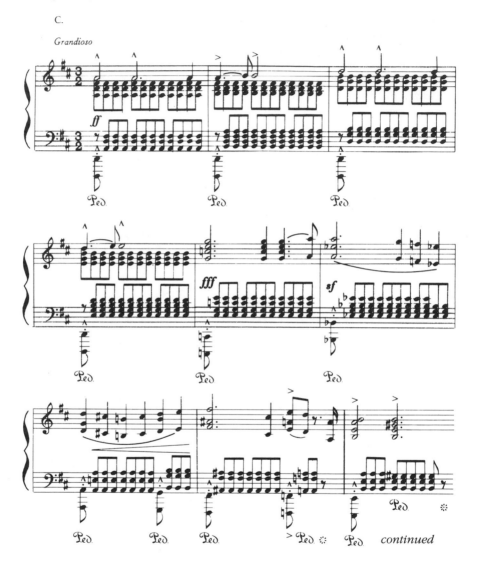

continued

tion of the hymn, so that typically Romantic features characterize a composition that takes its structural procedure from the Baroque.

There is a large body of smaller works of various kinds for solo piano.
Among the original works are numerous dances: waltzes, mazurkas, galops,
polonaises, polkas, and Hungarian *czárdás*; there are also marches. These lit-

D.

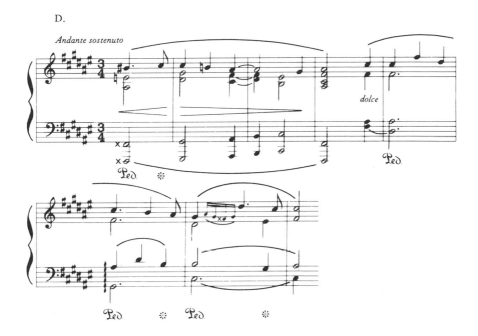

tle pieces frequently come with descriptive titles: *Valse de bravoura, Valse mélancolique, Caprice-Valse, Mazurka brilliant, Grand Galop chromatique,* and so on. Important here are the four *Mephisto Waltzes,* the first two of which (S. 514, composed 1859–1860, published 1862; and S. 515, composed and published 1881) are transcriptions of orchestral pieces, while the last (S. 696, 1885) remained unfinished; the third (S. 216, composed 1883) is especially gripping. The late *Valses oubliées* (4, Forgotten Waltzes, S. 215, composed presumably 1881–1885, the first three published 1881–1884, the fourth 1954) are especially noteworthy: these are stylized waltzes full of unusual harmonic, rhythmic and coloristic effects, and including impassioned episodes in Liszt's grandiloquent manner. Finally, Liszt provided a variation, the introduction, interludes, and a finale, all in bravura style, for the set of variations on Bellini's march in *I puritani,* each by a different composer (Chopin, Thalberg, Pixis, Czerny, and Herz), and published under the title *Hexameron* (1837).

Liszt was also active as a transcriber, arranging popular works of the time in an effective fashion for performance on the piano. These settings—some two hundred in number—make up the largest group among Liszt's work for piano solo. Perhaps most important are those based on pieces from operas and published under various titles (*Reminiscences, Transcription,* or *Fantasia*) that have already been mentioned as important during his years of concertizing. In addition are individual pieces; examples are shown here according to the composer whose music is arranged.

LISZT'S PIANO TRANSCRIPTIONS FROM OPERA— EXAMPLES

MOZART: *Don Giovanni* (S. 418, composed 1841, published 1843); *Le nozze di Figaro* (S. 697, 1842, unfinished, completed by Busoni, published 1912)

MEYERBEER: *Les Huguenots* (S. 412, composed 1836, published 1837); *Robert le diable* (S. 413, composed and published 1841); *Le Prophète* (S. 414, composed and published presumably 1849–1850)

BELLINI: *I puritani* (S. 390, composed 1836, published 1837); *La sonnambula* (S. 393, composed 1839–1841, published 1842); *Norma* (S. 394, composed 1841, published 1844)

VERDI: *Ernani* (S. 432, composed ca. 1849, published 1860); *Rigoletto* (S. 434, composed 1859 and published with the "Miserere" scene from *Il trovatore* [S. 433, also composed 1859] in 1860)

WAGNER (excerpts from the music dramas): "Liebestod" from *Tristan und Isolde* (S. 447, composed 1867, published 1868); various parts of *Die Meistersinger, Rheingold,* and *Parsifal,* among others

---

In addition to transcriptions from operas, there are arrangements of instrumental works and songs. Prominent among the former are the *partitions de piano* of Beethoven's symphonies (S. 464), six of Bach's preludes and fugues for organ (S. 462), and Berlioz' *Symphonie fantastique* (S. 470), as well as Liszt's own *Totentanz* (S. 188). Among the songs arranged by Liszt are some fifty by Schubert, notably sets of twelve each from *Winterreise* (S. 561) and *Schwanengesang* (S. 560), along with songs of Mendelssohn, Franz, and Chopin (*Chants polonaises*). Liszt also arranged a number of his own songs, among them the Petrarch sonnets that found their way into *Italie*, the second book of *Années de pèlerinage*; in the case of the *Liebesträume*, the piano arrangements have become better known than the songs from which they were transcribed, especially the *Liebestraum* in A-flat (S. 541 iii), the arrangement of his setting of Freiligrath's poem "O lieb' so lang du lieben kannst" (S. 298). The late "San Francisco" (S. 499, composed 1881) is also an arrangement. In general these transcriptions, usually overlooked, could form welcome additions to the repertory. Liszt was also active as an editor: he published his own editions of Beethoven's piano works, selected works of Weber and Schubert, organ music of Bach, etudes of Chopin, and exercises of Clementi.

Liszt composed a small body of music for piano duet and two pianos. Here original compositions are in the minority and arrangements in the clear majority. The original pieces are, for piano duet, a polonaise and a set of variations on *Chopsticks* (S. 256); for two pianos, a large Konzertstück on themes from Mendelssohn's *Songs Without Words* (S. 257). Arrangements include Liszt's own symphonic poems (for piano duet as well as for two pianos), Field's nocturnes (piano duet), Beethoven's Ninth Symphony (S. 657), Schubert's *Wanderer* Fantasia (S. 653), and his own two symphonies, *Faust* and *Dante* (both for two pianos, S. 647 and 648 respectively), to name only some.

The piano stood at the center of Liszt's life and work. By his technical mastery of the instrument, he became the most prominent musician in Europe; by the music he wrote for it, aside from the purely bravura pieces, he allied himself with the progressive tendencies in musical composition of the time.

BRAHMS

The principal counterpart to Liszt was Johannes Brahms (1833–1897).[22] The differences are striking. Brahms had little of the international quality of Liszt, at least not until he had become a fully mature musician, and although a pianist and conductor by profession, he was not much in public view. Indeed he characteristically made his Viennese debut as a pianist with chamber music—piano quartets. After 1875 he found it possible to give up regular conducting and to support himself by composing, teaching, and giving occasional concerts.

In spite of his tendency toward withdrawal, Brahms came to be regarded as the head of the group of musicians opposed to the music of Liszt and Wagner, known as the Neo-German school, with its emphasis on the expression of extramusical subject matter and novel musical forms and types. In 1853 Schumann, with whose family Brahms became closely associated, had hailed Brahms as "a new power in music . . . called to give expression to his time in ideal fashion."[23] In 1860 Brahms' name appeared among the signers of a manifesto directed against the Neo-German school, thus making him prominent in the opposition to this kind of music. Other musicians with whom he was closely connected included the critic and aesthetician Eduard Hanslick, the violinist Joseph Joachim, and the pianist, conductor, and editor Hans von Bülow, who had also been allied with Wagner.

We can discern Brahms' essentially conservative attitude in most of his music for piano. He commenced, as had Schumann before him, with the old large forms, the sonata and variations, which he then abandoned for the various types of character pieces. If we take his piano music by types—beginning with the sonatas, moving to the variations, and then coming to the character pieces—we also, generally speaking, follow his emphases chronologically. Afterward we can look briefly at other works, some smaller pieces and music for piano duet and two pianos.

Like Schumann, Brahms composed three piano sonatas.

BRAHMS' PIANO SONATAS

C major (No. 1; op. 1, composed 1852–1853, published 1853)
F-sharp minor (No. 2; op. 2, composed 1852, published 1854)
F minor (No. 3; op. 5, composed 1853, published 1854)

All three were composed virtually at the same time (he completed the F-sharp minor first) and published during the year of his only real tour. On the tour he accompanied the violinist Reményi and met important musicians, among them Joachim, Liszt, Hiller, Reinecke, and, especially, Schumann and his family. As expected the sonatas show similar features; the decisive influences came from Schubert and Schumann. These are large, difficult, and in some ways, rather extreme compositions, clearly intended as major works. Suitably enough, Brahms used the large four-movement scheme also employed by Schubert and Schumann, but, as we have seen, not by Liszt; only the Sonata in F minor departs from this, but by expansion, the addition of a fifth movement. We find the big opening movement in sonata form with coda, the lyrical slow movement, the scherzo with trio, and the finale (sonata form in the Sonata in F-sharp minor, rondo form in the others). In the Sonata in C major, no pause comes between the scherzo and the finale.

Key relationships, for the most part traditional, Brahms has worked out in a consistent fashion. In the Sonata in F-sharp minor, all movements—unusually—are in the minor. The other two show a more elaborate tonal plan that involves the establishment of a second key which serves as contrast to the tonic. In the Sonata in C major, this key is E minor (secondary theme in the first movement, the scherzo and the main theme of the rondo), and in the Sonata in F minor, it is D-flat major (development of the first movement, the Andante, the trio, and the second episode of the rondo). This recurrence of keys plays an important role in the cyclic construction of these works, we will note below.

Turning to the first movements, we observe Brahms' adherence to the Classical tradition. The presence of exposition, development, and recapitulation sections is easily established, and the important codas testify to the significance Brahms attributed to these works. Moreover, he employed the old *forma bipartita* with repeat of the exposition, in the sonatas in C major and F minor; the exposition of the Sonata in F-sharp minor is not repeated. Squarely in the old tradition are the principal themes used by Brahms, which are typically strong, triadic, and motivic: the full chords in dotted rhythm of the Sonata in C major; the brilliant fast staccato octave runs of the Sonata in F-sharp minor that range over much of the keyboard; and the equally wide-ranging chordal theme of the Sonata in F minor, with its characteristic rhythmic figure (see Ex. 5-4A, below). Also present are transition passages based on the principal themes, lyrical secondary themes that provide contrast, and closing sections. The principal themes, which contain possibilities for working out, Brahms has exploited in the developments, which work up to impressive climaxes. He has shortened the recapitulations as compared to the expositions (note the false recapitulation, in the Sonata in F minor), and the codas provide grand culminations, again exploiting the principal themes. All this shows Brahms' traditional orientation.

The slow movements (all andantes) are similar to character pieces. Here the relation to lyric poetry—not a Classical trait—is significant. Two of these andantes are associated with poems and melodies of the German *Minnesinger* of the Middle Ages: the "Winterlied" (Winter Song) of Count Kraft von Toggenburg in the Sonata in F-sharp minor, and an anonymous poem ("Verstohlen geht der Mond auf") in the Sonata in C major; this last, however, is not a real *Minnelied* but an imitation by Zuccalmaglio. (Brahms also used the poem for a choral setting in his *Deutsche Volkslieder.*) The Andante of the Sonata in F minor is based on a love poem by Sternau, three lines of which appear as a caption. Brahms further made the relation to poetry clear in the Sonata in C major, by underlaying words of the text to the notes of the principal theme on its first statement. His associating of these movements with poetry testifies to the Romantic aspect of his orientation: his turn to the Classical tradition, comprehensive though it appears, was not complete.

While we can regard the andantes in the sonatas in C major and F-sharp minor as cast in variation form, we can also associate this procedure with strophic form, characteristic of song settings. Both movements are in four sections, all based on the same melody; in the Sonata in C major, the third strophe, where the most variation takes place, returns to the main key, C major, and provides the climax of the movement, so that this movement corresponds to the varied strophic form. The *Minnesinger* element in both the andantes is evident from the use of the old Bar form into which Brahms has cast their principal themes (a Bar is in the form A A B), less clear in the Sonata in F-sharp minor. Brahms likewise derived the implied alternation between a soloist and a choral refrain that appears in the Andante of the Sonata in C major from the vocal practice of the *Minnesinger.* The Andante of the Sonata in F minor, on the other hand, associated with the poem by Sternau, is more conventional; it is in three-part form with an important coda. Its main theme consists of a line moving in thirds and in even quarter notes, first descending, then ascending, the whole section cast in rounded binary form. The midsection, in D-flat major and consisting entirely of chords, is harmonic in its effect, while the coda, in the same key, presents a simple melody in sonorous chords over a dominant pedal-point. (The melody resembles the end of Hans Sachs' monologue that Wagner was to use in the second act of *Die Meistersinger von Nürnberg.*) It brings the movement to its impressive climax; the principal theme is recalled at the very end. This sonata, as already mentioned, has a second and shorter slow movement (the "Rückblick" [Glance Backward]) that is also in three-part form. It is based on the main theme of the Andante but is in the minor (B-flat minor). The parallel thirds of the earlier movement appear here as well, but now accompanied by a timpani-like figure in the bass.

In the scherzos we find the usual form with trios, rather short in the Sonata in F-sharp minor. The rhythms are vigorous and the chords full, sometimes loud and heavily accented, as in the sonatas in C major and F minor, sometimes soft and staccato, in the Sonata in F-sharp minor. This density of part-writing, the use of chords with doublings, is characteristic of Brahms. The most variety is found in the scherzo of the Sonata in F minor, which has a wide-ranging theme in staccato octaves ornamented by grace-notes, all interspersed with short rests that create syncopations. The trios form a contrast with the scherzos, bringing lyricism again to the fore.

For the finales Brahms employs rondo form in the sonatas in C major and F minor and sonata form with thematically related slow introduction in the Sonata in F-sharp minor, thus generally following the tradition of Schubert and Schumann. These are large compositions with contrast and variety that serve to provide impressive conclusions. Brahms treated the rondo form freely. That of the Sonata in C major has two episodes—the first in three-part form with a codetta and the second with "Scotch" associations, its theme coming from Schumann's song "Hochländers Abschied" (Highlander's Farewell, op. 25 xiii). The rondo of the Sonata in F minor is regular until the second episode has been introduced, but from here on Brahms departs from the normal scheme, concentrating on developing the theme of this episode. He returns only once—and briefly—to the principal theme of the rondo before the coda. Free treatment of the rondo is characteristic of both Schubert and Schumann. In the finale of the Sonata in F-sharp minor, in sonata form, we find a cantabile principal theme in which a written-out ritard is important. It is a capricious ländler with wide leaps, grace-notes, and suspensions, presented with piquant cross-relations in the recapitulation. But this principal theme becomes big and impressive in the development and coda.

An important question has to do with the relationships between the component movements, how they fit together to make a larger artistic entity. While there has been much speculation on this in regard to the Classical composers, with varying results, the sonatas of Brahms furnish the opportunity to reach definite conclusions. Elements of consistency, coherence, and unity are present in the Sonata in C major, especially between the principal themes of the first and last movements on the one hand and the second and third movements on the other; but the work does not appear to be characterized by a thorough-going cyclic organization. With the other two sonatas it is different. The Sonata in F-sharp minor represents an extreme case, since Brahms clearly has made a single theme underlie the whole composition; it appears in different guises in all movements. In the Sonata in F minor, while the thematic relation between the second and fourth movements is made explicit (see above), the cyclical relations go much farther. There is the general correspondence between the passages in D-flat major, the important counter-tonality: the development of the first movement, the coda to the Andante, and the important second episode of the rondo (see Ex. 5-4B–D).[24] This use of cyclic form with emphasis on thematic variation or transformation associates Brahms more with the procedures of Liszt than is commonly believed, as also does his preoccupation with poetry.

We can find characteristic features of Brahms' way of writing for the piano in abundance. Most common, as already suggested, is his well-known density of texture through the use of full chords with doublings. Melodies often appear in parallel thirds or sixths, as in the "Rückblick" of the Sonata in

A.

continued

Example 5-4. Brahms: Sonata in F minor (op. 5)—Excerpts
    A. Allegro maestoso—Beginning (mm. 1–11)
    B. Allegro maestoso: D-flat major section of Development—Beginning
       (mm. 90–96)
    C. Andante molto: Coda—Beginning (mm. 144–150)
    D. Finale: Second Episode—Beginning (mm. 140–147)

Example 5-4, *continued*

continued

F minor, the main theme of the rondo of the Sonata in C major, or the scherzo
and trio of the Sonata in F-sharp minor. Or the melody is stated in full chords,
as at the end of the Andante of the Sonata in F minor, the beginning of the
second episode of the rondo of the same sonata, or the third movement of the
Sonata in C major; such instances can be multiplied. We can also find impressive chordal passages at the beginnings of each sonata, with the themes
encompassing a wide range, in the sonatas in F-sharp minor and F minor. In
the Sonata in F-sharp minor, Brahms resorted to the unusual expedient of
employing three staff lines for the notation of certain passages in the second
and fourth movements to bring out clearly the various elements of which
they are compounded. This density of texture has been associated with an
"orchestral" treatment of the piano: here and there passages suggest orchestral effects—the bass tremolo near the opening of the Sonata in F-sharp
minor, with the rising sequence in the right hand coupled with a crescendo;
or the bass timpani effects in the trio of the same sonata, which also appear
in the "Rückblick" of the sonata; and at the end of the development in the first
movement of the Sonata in C major, the left hand clearly suggests horns.

Another facet of Brahms' style evident in the sonatas has to do with rhythmic complexities and subtleties. The most common of these is hemiola, two
in one part against three in another, as in the Sonata in F minor, in several
places in the first movement and the finale. In its second episode this finale
also contains three against four, this rhythmic subtlety used as a means of thematic variation. Syncopations are common. Moreover, Brahms has subtly
written accelerations and ritards right into the notation itself: we find such an
acceleration in the secondary theme of the first movement of the Sonata in F
minor. In the Sonata in F-sharp minor we find a ritard at the end of the principal theme in the exposition of the first movement; in the passages in thirds,

the sixteenth-notes give way first to eighth-note triplets and then to eighth-notes.

To summarize this discussion of Brahms' piano sonatas, in general they conform to the grand tradition of the genre established by Beethoven and continued by Schubert, Schumann, and Chopin: the tradition of the sonata as a large, difficult, involved, dramatic, virtuoso composition. Much of this goes back specifically to Beethoven, as has been suggested, and the resemblance of thematic material between the openings of Brahms' Sonata in C major and Beethoven's late Sonata in B-flat major (op. 106, "Hammerklavier") is clear. Brahms' choice of keys for the various movements also parallels that of these composers. The slow introduction to the finale of the Sonata in F-sharp minor calls to mind the slow movement of Schumann's Fantasia in C major (op. 17). The more Romantic features include the free treatment of rondo form, the

close connection to song forms, the poetic associations of the slow movements, and the emphasis throughout on lyric themes. For all Brahms' evident
opposition to Liszt, many passages in the Sonata in F-sharp minor seem much
in the manner of Liszt: the furious octaves in the first movement, the *espressivo* unaccompanied lines moving in thirds and pausing on long fermatas in
the Andante, the grand climax marked *grandioso*, and the cadenza-like passages in the finale; finally, of course, there is the emphasis on cyclic form.

The next group of Brahms' piano works are those in variation form.

BRAHMS' SETS OF VARIATIONS

Variations (16) on a Theme of Schumann, F-sharp minor (op. 9,
    composed and published 1854)
Variations (11) on an Original Theme, D major (op. 21 i,
    composed 1857, published 1862)
Variations (13) on an Hungarian Song, D major (op. 21 ii,
    composed ca. 1854, published 1862)
Variations (25) and Fugue on a Theme of Handel, B-flat major
    (op. 24, composed 1861, published 1862)
Studies (Variations) on a Theme of Paganini, A minor: two sets,
    each of fourteen variations (op. 35 i and ii, composed
    1862–1863, published 1866)

Brahms borrowed the themes chiefly from prominent composers: the
"Albumblatt" of Schumann's *Bunte Blätter* (op. 99 iv, on which Clara Schumann also composed a set of variations), the twenty-fourth Caprice of Paganini, and the Suite in B-flat major of Handel (his No. 9). All are characterized
by brevity and simplicity, and all operate with rhythmic patterns. The theme
from Handel is cast in binary form, each part to be repeated, and Brahms
moreover quotes Handel's theme exactly at the beginning of his set. The
theme from Paganini is also in binary form, while that from Schumann is in
three-part form and mostly in four-part harmony, the bass serving as a
counter-voice to the melody. The qualities of brevity and simplicity are also
present in the other themes employed by Brahms in his sets of variations. The
original theme (op. 21 i), chordal but marked espressivo and legato, is again
in two-part form, while the Hungarian Song, only eight bars long, fast, and in
heavily accented chords, uses the unusual time signature 3/4 C, designating
the alternation of bars in 3/4 with bars in 4/4 (Ex. 5-5).
In his variations Brahms normally follows the harmonic basis of the
theme closely, although there are exceptions, and he also exploits motives
contained in the theme. But the difference in character among the variations

Example 5-5. Brahms: Variations on an Hungarian Song in D major (op. 21 i)—
Theme (mm. 1–8)

is more important. Brahms devises new textures and new types of figuration,
moves the melody to an inner voice or the bass, and so on. In the Schumann
variations (op. 9) he often puts the theme in the bass, even emphasizing the
important bass part of Schumann's theme. In the Hungarian variations Brahms
maintains the alternation between 3/4 and 4/4 in most of the variations
(ix–xiii use regular meter, either 2/4 or 6/8).

Brahms usually makes the character of variations clear through the ways
he marks them: for example, scherzo or scherzando, as in the Schumann
variations (xii), grazioso in the Handel variations (xviii), largamente in the
1860 set on a theme of Clara Schumann (i), adagio in the Handel set (xiii).
Each set has either one or a group of variations in the minor. Contrapuntal
elaboration plays an important role in Brahms' art of variation; it is emphasized in the Schumann variations where canon appears (vii, x, xiv, and xv),
in the Variations on an Original Theme (op. 21 i), and of course in the fugue
that ends the Handel variations.

This last large set of variations we can regard as the culmination of
Brahms' efforts in this genre. Brahms took the theme itself—which Handel
had used as the basis for a set of five variations—verbatim from Handel's
suite, even retaining Handel's designation Aria. Then come the variations,
each with its own character that results from the consistent use of a melodic
or rhythmic motive, e.g., the staccato figure of two eighths and a sixteenth-
note (i), chromatic triplets (ii), legato chords (iii), fast octaves and leaps (iv),
and so on. Some of the more unusual variations deserve notice: the two-
voice canon, each voice in octaves (vi), which suggests Bach's two-part
Invention in B-flat major; the heavy chromatic chords, sostenuto and *fortis-*

simo (ix), the ponderous Largamente in B-flat minor (xiii), and the musette with siciliano rhythm and mordents (xix). Finally there comes the fugue whose subject derives from Handel's theme, with driving sixteenth-note figuration emphasizing sequential writing. Although Brahms has used the learned devices—augmentation and inversion, along with motivic breaking down of the subject—he made some departures from strict form. The subject and its contrapuntal accompaniment often appear in parallel thirds or sixths, and broken-chord figuration at times replaces contrapuntal elaboration. (Much of this appears in the fugal finale of Beethoven's Sonata in B-flat major [op. 106]—even the key is the same.)

The Paganini variations present an interesting situation. Brahms gave them the title *Studien* (Studies or Etudes). In extending the etude character, which already belonged to the original context of Paganini's theme, to the genre of theme and variations, Brahms has fallen back on an old Baroque tradition, that of Corelli's *La Folia* (note also the example of Schumann's *Études en form de variations*). Each etude or variation has its own character which in turn is bound up with a specific problem of pianistic execution, such as passages in thirds and sixths, octave leaps and arpeggios, scales, and legato playing involving shifting fingers on the key.

After completing the sonatas and the earlier among the sets of variations, Brahms turned to the smaller forms of piano music which he made into something very much his own—the various types of character piece. While such pieces are present among his early works, he dropped the genre for a time only to emphasize it once again in his late works.

BRAHMS' CHARACTER PIECES

Scherzo, E-flat minor (op. 4, composed 1851, published 1854)
Ballads (4, op. 10, composed 1854, published 1856): D minor, D
    major, B minor, and B major
Klavierstücke (8, op. 76, composed 1878, published 1879)
    Set I: Capriccio, F-sharp minor; Capriccio, B minor;
        Intermezzo, A-flat major; Intermezzo, B-flat major
    Set II: Capriccio, C-sharp minor; Intermezzo, A major;
        Intermezzo, A minor; Capriccio, C major
Rhapsodies (2, op. 79, composed 1879, published 1880): B minor
    and G minor
Fantasias (7, op. 116, composed 1891–1892, published 1892)
    Set I: Capriccio, D minor; Intermezzo, A minor; Capriccio, G
        minor
    Set II: Intermezzo, E major; Intermezzo, E minor; Intermezzo,
        E major; Capriccio, D minor

Intermezzos (3, op. 117, composed and published 1892): E-flat
major, B-flat minor, and C-sharp minor
Klavierstücke (6, op. 118, composed and published 1893):
Intermezzo, A minor; Intermezzo, A major; Ballade, G minor;
Intermezzo, F minor; Romanze, F major; Intermezzo, E-flat
minor
Klavierstücke (4, op. 119, composed and published 1893):
Intermezzo, B minor; Intermezzo, E minor; Intermezzo, C
major; Rhapsody, E-flat major

The early Scherzo in E-flat minor is Brahms' largest character piece and
resembles the corresponding movements in his sonatas. Marked *Rasch und
feurig* (Fast and with fire, presumably Allegro con fuoco), it is cast in the
large form of scherzo with two different trios. The theme itself, based on fragmentary phrases, has a rhythmic propulsiveness that is offset by the lyricism
of the trios. Its size and the varieties it encompasses suggest that the scherzo
originally was part of a projected sonata, although there is the example of
Chopin, who produced four independent scherzos.

The Ballads (op. 10), however, approach the more common type of character piece. There are four pieces, three ballads and one (the third) called Intermezzo. Yet these ballads have nothing in common with the large-scale virtuoso productions of Chopin, even though the ultimate inspiration in ancient
epic and tragic poetry may well be the same. Brahms made this inspiration
explicit in the first by relating it to the Scotch poem "Edward," which had
been published by Herder in his influential collection of folk poetry. In the
grim poem a mother questions her son concerning his blood-stained appearance and eventually discovers that he has murdered his father; it turns out that
she in fact instigated the act. Brahms has used the ternary structure, the opening evidently suggesting dialogue, the midsection the grisly revelation, and
the reprise depicts the son's voluntary exile. Moreover, Brahms suggests the
strophic form of the original ballad by using the same thematic material in all
sections of the piece. The close link to the poem associates this piece with the
slow movements of the piano sonatas. On the other hand, the other three
works of op. 10 do not suggest links to literature; nor do they show the concept of ballad nearly as clearly. The schemes employed in them resemble
those common in the character piece: ternary form (iii), binary form (iv), and
an unusual arrangement involving a principal section, two episodes, and a
coda (ii).

Except for his work with the variations, Brahms abandoned the composition of solo piano music for some twenty years (1854–1878), then resumed
it in the Klavierstücke (op. 76) and the two Rhapsodies (op. 79), only to leave
it again for twelve years (1879–1891), finally concentrating on it in the four
late collections that comprise some thirty pieces. In spite of the gaps in their

composition, these character pieces present so many common features that we can treat them together.

In these sets the titles used by Brahms display his tendency toward generalization. The early set of ballads, as we have seen, contained one intermezzo; then, although there are Rhapsodies (op. 79) and Fantasias (op. 116), the tendency was toward the neutral and general designation Klavierstück (Piano piece) except for the one set of Intermezzos (op. 117). Even the designation Fantasia (op. 116) seems to possess no programmatic or affective connotations. In fact the pieces of op. 118 originally were to have been published under the title Fantasias, which Brahms changed to the neutral designation Klavierstücke. Brahms had originally intended to use the designation Notturno for the Intermezzo in E major (op. 116 iv) and Capriccio for the Rhapsody in E major (op. 79 i). His change of mind confirms the tendency toward a neutral, generalized designation: Intermezzo. In regard to the titles, Intermezzo leads with eighteen instances; next is Capriccio with seven; there are three entitled Rhapsody, one Ballad, and one Romanze. The difference, which involves size and scope, is between larger and smaller pieces: the ballads and rhapsodies are the larger, the intermezzos and romance the smaller, and the capriccio lies in between. Yet this distinction does not hold in all cases, for a few intermezzos are sizeable pieces, such as those in A major and E-flat minor (op. 118 ii and vi).

In general, the ballad and the rhapsodies retain their normal connotations as large dramatic pieces.[25] But, as we have seen, these are much less numerous than the smaller pieces, the general character of which is suggested by the markings Brahms has used. For the intermezzo we find again and again designations indicating moderation, sensitivity, and grace, as *Grazioso, anmutig ausdrucksvoll* (Graceful, charming, expressive) in the Intermezzo in A-flat major (op. 76 iii); *Con grazia ed intimissimo sentimento* (With grace and the most intimate sentiment) in the Intermezzo in E minor (op. 116 v); the simple *Grazioso* in the Intermezzo in B-flat major (op. 76 iv); *Sanft bewegt* (Softly moving) in the Intermezzo in A major (op. 76 vi); *Moderato semplice* in the Intermezzo in A minor (op. 76 vii); *Andante teneramente* in the Intermezzo in E major (op. 116 vi); and so on. In this context the more serious *Largo e mesto* of the Intermezzo in E-flat minor (op. 118 vi) and the *Andante un poco agitato* of the Intermezzo in E minor (op. 119 ii) stand out. The capriccios, on the other hand, are active and vigorous: here we find, along with the *Grazioso* of the Capriccio in C major (op. 76 viii), expressions like *energico* and *agitato*, as in the capriccios in D minor (op. 116 i and vii) and C-sharp minor (op. 76 v). The same holds for the rhapsodies and ballads.

We have noted that the character piece as a genre was often closely bound up with literary works and have further seen that this applies to Brahms' early piano music, not just the Ballads (op. 10) but also the sonatas. While this tendency, however, is not prominent in the late character pieces, there are two notable exceptions: the Rhapsody in B minor (op. 79 i), which has affinities to a Scottish ballad set by Carl Loewe ("Archibald Douglas") and the Intermezzo in E-flat major (op. 117 i), which Brahms explicitly associated with a Scotch lullaby that he found in Herder's collection of folk poetry, the source he had drawn upon earlier in the "Edward" Ballad (op. 10 i). Beyond these we find no overt literary associations in these late character pieces, a circumstance that contributes to the general and neutral tone we have observed. At the same time, since we can find parallels to Brahms' songs, he obviously had expressive intentions in these pieces but decided not to divulge these in the titles.

Formally, these pieces present similar features. By far the most common is the old ternary scheme that had long dominated the character piece. Here we find it many times without elaboration; for instance, the Intermezzo in A major (op. 76 vi), the Capriccio in G major (op. 116 iii), the Intermezzo in E major (op. 116 vi), the large Intermezzo in E-flat minor (op. 118 vi), and the Romanze in F major (op. 118 v), with the reprise varied in the Capriccio in C-sharp minor (op. 76 v). Brahms occasionally expanded this basic formal type to a scheme of five or more sections in a fashion similar to the rondo: a single episode that appears twice in the Capriccio in C-sharp minor (op. 76 v) and the Intermezzo in F minor (op. 118 iv) and two contrasting episodes with a coda that appear in the Capriccio in B minor (op. 76 ii) and the Rhapsody in B minor (op. 79 i). Yet we also can find some unusual formal schemes here. There is a simple binary structure with coda in the short Intermezzo in A minor (op. 118 i). The old rounded binary scheme appears in the Intermezzo in A minor (op. 76 vii), with eight bars of introduction that are repeated at the end, and the Intermezzo in E minor (op. 116 v); and we can note that rounded binary form appears internally in some of these pieces: in the principal section of the Intermezzo in A major (op. 76 vi), in the midsections of the Capriccio in D minor (op. 116 vii) and the Intermezzo in C-sharp minor (op. 117 iii), and, without repeat of the second part, in the Capriccio in G minor (op. 116 iii). A few pieces reveal a freer sectional plan that does not correspond to any recognized scheme: the Capriccio in D minor (op. 116 i), the Intermezzo in E major (op. 116 iv), and the Intermezzo in C major (op. 119 iii). While the capriccio and intermezzo here might be regarded as free treatments of the rondo and ternary principles respectively, the Intermezzo in C major is a single continuous whole that uses the same thematic material throughout. Finally, we can note one instance of sonata form, in the Rhapsody in G minor (op. 79 ii).

If formally these character pieces reveal a general homogeneity, the same holds in regard to musical style. Here as elsewhere the work of Brahms lacks bravura display and ornamentation for its own sake, which seems clear enough in the early sonatas, particularly the F-sharp minor. Brahms' inclination toward density of texture, however, is abundantly evident, so that the relative sparseness of the Intermezzo in E major (op. 116 iv) attracts notice. Again we find melodies that take chordal form, stated in thirds, sixths, and octaves, and with doublings; or melodies that consist of arpeggiated chords that often move in thirds. Both features appear in the Capriccio in G minor (op. 116 iii) and the intermezzos in E major (op. 116 v), E-flat major (op. 117 i), and B minor (op. 119 i). In some places Brahms puts the melody into an inner voice of a dense texture, as in the well-known "Scotch Lullaby," the Intermezzo in E-flat major (op. 117 i), and a number of others.

This brings up the relationship between the main voice and the accompaniment. While in many cases it is the usual simple one, we can find instances in which an important line is presented buried in the accompaniment, as in the Intermezzo in E major (op. 116 vi), where one is not entirely certain which part is to be brought out. The Intermezzo in A major (op. 118 ii) is remarkable, since it displays several procedures taken over from counterpoint (see Ex. 5-6): inversion of the main theme and then canon of a free sort followed by double counterpoint (exchange of parts) in the midsection. Double counterpoint also appears in the Romanze in F major (op. 118 v) and in the Intermezzo in A minor (op. 76 vii).

Brahms also used rhythmic elaboration to articulate separate elements in a particular passage. The playing off of two against three (hemiola) is the most common; out of many instances we can mention the intermezzos in A major (op. 76 vi), A minor (op. 116 ii), and F minor (op. 118 iv). The use of elaborate rhythm in a melodic line may be seen in the Intermezzo in B-flat major (op. 76 iv), with its dotted rhythms and syncopated accompaniment, both over a sustained subdominant pedal-point in an inner part. Another use of syncopation in a melodic line appears in the Intermezzo in A-flat major (op. 76 iii). Such rhythmic elaborations associate Brahms with Schumann.

Several other points can be made about Brahms' character pieces. It is clear, first, that in his hands the character piece has become more generalized, avoiding overt extramusical associations, as indeed is symbolized by the designation Intermezzo. Brahms has also avoided virtuoso-bravura elements, so that the predominant aura is of moderation. The forms used are simple, the scope usually small (excluding the rhapsodies, ballads, some of the capriccios, and a few of the intermezzos). Along with this simplicity goes an emphasis on strict compositional procedures, a high degree of harmonic and rhythmic elaboration, unusual use of counterpoint, and extensive use of thematic variation. The use of strict procedures was not unknown in the character piece—both Mendelssohn and Schumann set examples here. Yet it seems as if Brahms were looking backward, avoiding both the literary connections and the brilliance that had been exploited by Liszt and others and instead returning to something more disciplined and sober.

Brahms also composed "neoclassical" pieces, if we can use this term in regard to the nineteenth century: two gigues and two sarabandes (WoO 3 and 4, composed 1855, published 1917 and 1922), in which the gigues, following eighteenth-century practice, are fugal and employ inversions of their themes in the second section; there is also an arrangement of the gavotte from Gluck's *Paride ed Elena*. Parallels to the eighteenth-century sarabande have been found in the Intermezzo in A minor (op. 116 ii).[26] Then there are etudes or studies in two sets: five large pieces (published variously 1869 and 1879) and the set of fifty-one (WoO 6, published 1893). While the latter are etudes, study pieces, in the usual sense, the former set draws interest because it con-

Example 5-6. BRAHMS: Intermezzo in A major (op. 118 ii)—Excerpts
    A. First section—Beginning (mm. 1–4)
    B. First section—Near end (mm. 35–38)
    C. Midsection—Beginning (mm. 49–52)

sists of reworkings of pieces by other composers; in Chopin's Etude in F minor (op. 25 ii), Brahms has replaced the triple scale-runs with scales in thirds and sixths. He also made use of the sonatas and partitas of Bach, including the famous Chaconne in D minor, which he arranged for piano, left-hand; Weber's Rondo in C major; and Schubert's Impromptu in E-flat major (D. 899/op. 90 ii).

There is also a small body of music for piano duet and for two pianos, most of which exists in other versions. For two pianos Brahms composed the famous Variations on a Theme of Haydn (op. 56b, composed and published 1873), best known in the version for orchestra, and the Sonata in F minor (op. 34b, composed 1864, published 1872), best known as a piano quintet. The former, of course, reveals Brahms' conservative preoccupations: his use of a theme attributed at the time to Haydn and of an ostinato structure in the finale. The variations themselves are of a now-familiar type: character variations, such as the march, scherzo, and siciliano. Among the piano duets are the two sets of *Liebeslieder* Waltzes (op. 52a and 65a, the first set composed and published 1874, the second 1877), both of which in their original versions are scored for vocal quartet with accompaniment for two pianos; these pieces are in the old tradition of German social song. In a lighter vein are the Waltzes (op. 39, composed 1865, published 1867) and the Hungarian Dances (four sets, two published 1869, the others 1880), both of which exist in versions for piano duet and for piano solo. All this leaves a single work of serious nature for piano duet, the Variations on a Theme of Schumann (10, op. 23, composed 1861, published 1863), based on what was known as Schumann's "Letzter Gedanke" (Last Thought), a work that has much in common with Brahms' other sets of variations.

In conclusion we may make a short comparison between Brahms and Liszt, the two composers who best represented the two principal tendencies in nineteenth-century music. The differences, however, are not always as obvious as one might think. While Liszt was universally known as the pre-eminent virtuoso pianist and at the center of international musical life, Brahms made relatively few public appearances, preferring on the whole a retiring life. Liszt concentrated on the new Romantic types of composition, virtually ignoring the traditional ones, changing them radically on the few occasions when he took them up. Brahms did the reverse, deliberately working with the old genres, not only those from the earlier nineteenth century but from the eighteenth as well. This difference—and it is of basic importance—emerges clearly from the sonatas composed by each: where Brahms by and large adhered to the traditional model, Liszt converted the sonata into a large-scale quasi-symphonic poem for piano. While both shared an interest in the music of Bach, Liszt took his inspiration from it and then adapted it to his new aesthetic ends; Brahms conscientiously recreated whole genres in terms of contemporary practice. A final point, an unusual one, concerns the influence of Paganini: where Liszt drew on the example Paganini set for public appearances, Brahms' interest was solely compositional, whereby he took a well-known melody of the composer and used it to fashion a set of variations in the old tradition.

NOTES FOR CHAPTER FIVE

1. See W. Sumner, *The Pianoforte* (New York: St. Martin's, 1966), 66, 71–72.

2. For an extensive bibliography of this little-surveyed area, see H. Haase, "Klavierschule," *Die Musik in Geschichte und Gegenwart* 7 (1958): 1184–1194. More recent: M. Schneider, *Studien zu den Klavierschulen im deutsch-sprachigen Raum vom 1884 bis 1900.* Unpub. diss., Vienna, 1980.

3. See D. Presser, "Die Opernbearbeitung des 19. Jahrhunderts," *Archiv für Musik-wissenschaft* 12 (1955): 227–238.

4. It is now thought that Liszt himself did in fact write the books and articles that appeared under his name: see A. Main, "Franz Liszt, the Author, 1834–1837," *La musique et le rite sacre et profane*, ed. M. Honegger and P. Prévost (Strasbourg: University of Strasbourg, 1986), 637–656. This refutes earlier arguments, particularly those of E. Haraszti, in, for instance, "Franz Liszt, Author Despite Himself," *Musical Quarterly* 33 (1947): 490–516.

5. The bibliographical situation for Liszt leaves much to be desired. The collected edition of his musical works remains incomplete, and as of 1994 there is no thematic catalog. The best listing of his works is in H. Searle's article on Liszt in *The New Grove Dictionary of Music and Musicians*, ed. S. Sadie, vol. 11 (London: Macmillan, 1980), 57–64, 68–70, based on an earlier listing by P. Raabe. The S numbers assigned to Liszt's works stem from Searle, with the R numbers used less frequently. See also W. Dömling, *Liszt* (Laaber, 1985). The situation is complicated by Liszt's habit of reworking a piece and including different versions of it in different collections, sometimes retaining the title and sometimes not.

6. This represents for the most part the third revision of etudes that originally were published in two collections: first, the *Études en douze exercises* (S. 136/op. 1, composed 1826, published 1827) and, second, the *Grandes études* (S. 137, composed 1837–1838, published 1839).

7. This is a revision of the *Morceau de salon* (S. 142), composed for Moscheles and Fétis' *Méthode des méthodes* (1837), although Searle gives the date of composition as 1840.

8. Originally composed for inclusion in Lebert and Stark's *Grosse theoretisch-praktische Klavierschule* (Stuttgart: Cotta, 1838).

9. See D. Altenburg, "Liszt's Idee eines ungarischen Nationalepos in Tönen," *Studia musicologica* [Hungary] 28 (1986): 213–233.

10. Early versions of some of these pieces appeared in *Album d'un voyageur* (3 vols., S. 156, composed 1835–1836, published variously 1836, 1840, and 1942).

11. The Petrarch sonnets originally were songs composed as early as 1838–1839 (S. 270); they were then (1839) arranged by Liszt himself for piano (S. 158, published 1846). *Venezia e Napoli* likewise exists in an earlier version (S. 159).

12. An early version of this piece appeared under the title "Harmonies poétiques et religieuses" (S. 154, 1835).

13. Originally for violin and piano.

14. Originally part of *Années de pèlerinage*, Book I.

15. Letter to Agnes Street-Klindworth, 16 November 1860, in *Franz Liszts Briefe*, ed. La Mara, vol. 3 (Leipzig: Breitkopf & Härtel, 1893–1904), 135; quoted by, among others, S. Sitwell, *Liszt* (London: Cassel, 1934), 210.

16. D. Pesce, "Liszt's 'Années de pèlerinage,' Book Three: A Hungarian Cycle?" *Nineteenth Century Music* 13 (1990): 207–229.

17. A. Main, "Liszt's *Lyon*: Music and Social Conscience," *Nineteenth Century Music* 4 (1981): 209–227.

18. *Falso bordone* is a simple four-voice setting of a liturgical chant. The style was often used in the opera of the time to express the religious character of a scene.

19. This work exists in two other versions: the Grand Solo de concert for piano and orchestra (S. 365, composed ca. 1850 but unpublished) and the Concerto pathétique for two pianos (S. 258, composed 1856 and published 1886).

20. This was subsequently arranged by Liszt for organ (S. 673, composed 1863, published 1865). There is another work on the same theme, a prelude (S. 179, composed 1859, published 1863). For "continuo" Liszt should have had "ostinato."

21. Among others, W. Newman, *The Sonata Since Beethoven*, 3rd ed. (New York: Norton, 1983), 253, shows these options in graphic form.

22. The bibliographical situation has been greatly improved by the recent appearance of a thematic catalog: M. McCorkle, *Johannes Brahms: Thematisches-bibliographisches Werkverzeichnis* (Munich: Henle, 1984).

23. Quoted from *Robert Schumann on Music and Musicians*, ed. K. Wolff, trans. P. Rosenfeld (New York: Pantheon, 1946), 253.

24. See F. Kirby, *A Short History of Keyboard Music* (New York: Free Press/Schirmer, 1966), 324, and later D. Kraus, *Johannes Brahms: Composer for the Piano* (Wilhelmshaven: Noetzel, 1988), 33–34.

25. Of interest here is Chopin's distinction between a rhapsody and ballad, as reported by his pupil Pozniak: in a rhapsody a role is played by swords, in a ballad by poison and daggers—quoted by W. Kahl, "Ballade," *Die Musik in Geschichte und Gegenwart* 1 (1951): 1135.

26. W. Horne, "Brahms' Düsseldorf Suite Study and his Intermezzo, Opus 116, No. 2," *Musical Quarterly* 73 (1989): 249–283.

CHAPTER SIX

The Later Nineteenth Century

THE GERMANIC COUNTRIES

Our discussion of piano music in the nineteenth century has up to now centered around the work of the major composers—Weber, Schubert, Mendelssohn, Schumann, Chopin, Liszt, and Brahms—whose importance is not limited to this repertory. While most major composers up to the end of the 1880s generally devoted considerable attention to piano music, in the second half of the century the situation began to change. Ignoring for the moment Liszt and Brahms, we are struck by the fact that composers of central importance no longer devote much attention to piano music; the contributions of Wagner, Bruckner, Mahler, and Strauss to this repertory are either virtually nonexistent or of little significance in their work as a whole.

Wagner's music for piano consists with one exception of early works.[1] His very first published work was a Sonata in B-flat major (WWV 21/op. 1, composed 1831, published 1832), and there were three early unpublished and now lost sonatas, two for piano solo in F minor and D minor (WWV 2 and 5), and one for piano duet in B-flat major (WWV 16, 1831). He made two further essays in the genre, the Sonata in A major (WWV 26/op. 4, composed 1832, not published until 1960) and a last sonata, also in the same key, for Mathilde Wesendonck (WWV 85, composed 1853, published 1878). His second published work was the Polonaise in D major (WWV 23, 1832) for piano duet, also in a version for piano solo. There is also an early Fantasia in F-sharp minor (WWV 22, composed 1831), which has passages in recitative style. All this suggests that at first Wagner saw himself as a composer of essentially traditional orientation; as we know, it turned out otherwise. Nevertheless, he later produced a handful of character pieces, a song without words, three album leaves, a polka, and a waltz. Possibly of greater significance for Wagner's work as a whole was his arrangement for piano of Beethoven's Ninth Symphony (WWV 9, 1830–1831).

Neglect of piano music also characterizes the work of Bruckner, Mahler, and Strauss. Bruckner, a noted organist, composed but a few character pieces for piano, most of which are early compositions. Mahler composed nothing for piano beyond accompaniments to songs. Early in his career Strauss composed a relatively small number of piano works, a Sonata in B minor (op. 5, composed 1880–1881, published 1883), and two sets of character pieces— Klavierstücke (5, op. 3, composed 1880–1881, published 1881), and *Stimmungsbilder* (5, Mood Pictures, op. 9, composed 1882–1884, published presumably 1884). Other compositions, among them a fantasia, a sonatina, and a set of variations, have remained unpublished.

Here and there we will find exceptions to this state of affairs, usually in countries other than Germany. Franck and Grieg are among the most prominent, while in Germany Reger comes to mind. But these do not alter the general picture: the attention of composers had shifted. Among the major composers orchestral music now held the lead. Those who continued to emphasize the piano in their work were for the most part secondary figures.

Until the last decade of the nineteenth century, the development of piano music—and most other kinds of music as well—continued to be in the hands of composers in the Germanic countries (Germany, Austria, and Switzerland). Generally, they were the creators of the principal genres of piano music and they provided the example for the rest of Europe. Thus our survey first examines German piano music and then explores the effects of this German art of piano music elsewhere.[2]

The character piece occupied a preeminent position in the repertory of the time. Many factors contributed to this prominence. Briefly, new methods of manufacturing in the industrial age made pianos generally available. At the same time, growth in industry and commerce created a large affluent middle class who came to regard ownership of a piano as a necessary symbol of their new social position. For this market the character piece, essentially unpretentious and undemanding, served well.

Schumann doubtless exercised the greatest influence on Germanic composers of the time. We find strong confirmation of this in the work of Theodor Kirchner (1823–1903). His work for piano is dominated by the character piece in its smallest and simplest form, the miniature, a title he used for a set of pieces (op. 62). Others of his titles confirm his dedication to the musical world of Schumann: *Phantasiestücke* (op. 14); *Neue Davidsbündlertänze* (op. 17); *Aquarellen* (Watercolors; op. 21); *Romanzen* (op. 22); *Nachtbilder* (Night Pictures, op. 25); *Florestan und Eusebius, Nachklänge* (Florestan and Eusebius, Echoes, op. 53); *Neue Kinderscenen* (op. 55), and many album leaves. As homage to Mendelssohn, the other leading spirit in Leipzig at the time, he produced a set of Lieder ohne Worte (op. 13). Like Liszt, Kirchner arranged songs for piano solo, selecting those of Schumann and Brahms. He made no attempt at the large forms; preludes and etudes there are, to be sure, but the largest form he essayed was the sonatina. Everything is small, simple, modest, and rather sweet.

A similar situation occurs in the work of Adolf Jensen (1837–1879), except that he was sympathetic to and influenced by Wagner. Again the small form of the character piece dominates: among many others, all published in the 1860s and 1870s, are the *Fantasiestücke* (op. 7); *Lieder und Tänze* (op. 33, see Ex. 6-1); *Nocturnos* (op. 38); *Ländler aus Berchtesgaden* (Ländler from Berchtesgaden, op. 46), and *Scènes carnavalesques* (op. 56) which clearly invoke Schumann's world. His best-known and most representative work is *Erotikon* (7, op. 44), pieces with titles taken from Greek poetry. But Jensen also strove for bigger things, as in his Sonata in F-sharp minor (op. 25), and neobaroque *Deutsche Suite* in B minor (German Suite, op. 36). The latter consists of five movements in the traditional arrangement (Allemande, Courante, Sarabande, and Gigue, with two Gavottes between the Sarabande and Gigue), but Jensen has turned the dances into Romantic character pieces. He also composed a large body of music, mostly character pieces, for piano duet.

Also of this group are Robert Volkmann (1815–1883), Clara Schumann's stepbrother Woldemar Bargiel (1828–1897), and the teacher-theorist Ludwig Thuille (1861–1907). Of the three, Bargiel, a friend of Brahms and editor of the first critical edition of Chopin's works, is the most important. Piano music forms the most significant portion of his musical compositions, emphasizing small character pieces in Schumann's manner, yet often manifesting powerful expression: *Notturnos* (3, op. 3); and *Fantasiestücke* (3, op. 9); and Impromptu in G minor (op. 45). Yet the large forms are also present: four fantasias in B minor (op. 5), D major (op. 12), C minor (op. 19), and, once again,

Example 6-1. Jensen: Romance in E minor (op. 33 vi)—Beginning (mm. 1–9)

one in B minor (op. 27); a Sonata in C major (op. 34); and a Suite in C major (op. 7). The suite consists of movements that Bargiel has named after the eighteenth-century dances, but, like Jensen, he has transformed them into typical nineteenth-century character pieces. Bargiel also composed large works for piano duet: two suites (op. 21 and 31); a Sonata in G major (op. 23); and a gigue. The suites contain character pieces arranged so as to be comparable to a sonata, similar to Schumann's own *Faschingsschwank aus Wien.* Volkmann, like many of his contemporaries, appears at his best in the small character pieces, which he composed mostly 1853–1857 during his stay in Vienna. These include his *Buch der Lieder* (Book of Songs, op. 17) that bears some relation to Mendelssohn; *Deutsche Tanzweisen* (German Dance Tunes, op. 18); and *Wanderskizzen* (Sketches of Wandering, op. 23). But like Jensen and Bargiel, Volkmann also made efforts in the large forms: a Sonata in C minor (op. 12); and, like Brahms, an impressive set, Variations on a Theme of Handel (7, op. 26). Thuille, a professor at the academy in Munich, contented himself with the composition of character pieces, of which his "Threnodie" (op. 37 i) is often heard.

Of somewhat greater standing was the Hungarian-born Stephen Heller (1813–1888) who spent much of his life in Paris. Like Chopin he composed piano music to the virtual exclusion of all else. While he composed in the large forms (four sonatas and several sets of variations), most of his comprehensive output, like that of the composers we have just mentioned, he gave over to the character piece. Especially Schumannesque are the cycle *Spaziergänge eines Einzelnen* (Walks of a Single [Person], 6, op. 78); *Im Walde* (In the Woods, 7, op. 86); *Wanderstunden* (Hours of Wandering, 6, op. 80); *Scènes d'enfants* (op. 124); and a set associated with the novelist Jean Paul, *Blumen-, Frucht- und Dornenstücke, Nuits blanches* (Flower-, Fruit-, and Thorn-Pieces, White Nights, op. 82), whom Schumann also celebrated. Along with these are scherzos, ballades, caprices, dances, songs without words, preludes (op. 81, 117, 119, 150, and posthumous), and, particularly, etudes in which the influence of Cramer and Moscheles is evident.

Other composers of this time are Ferdinand Hiller (1811–1885), the virtuoso Adolf von Henselt, Eduard Franck (1817–1893), Cornelius Gurlitt (1820–1901), Rudolf Niemann (1838–1898), and Hans Huber (1852–1921). Again the small form of the character piece is most prominent. The gifted Hiller produced many attractive character pieces, among them a set entitled *Ghasele* (op. 54), in which the repeating line of the ghasel, a Persian verse form, is suggested by a short refrain; he also composed etudes. In his *Moderne Suite* (op. 114) Hiller justified the title by replacing the traditional dances with contemporary character pieces. Gurlitt is known especially for a novelty piece, a set of variations on "Ach, du lieber Augustin" (op. 115), each variation in the style of a different composer. Henselt, a virtuoso pianist, has become noted for his etudes. Of this group, therefore, only Franck and the Swiss Huber made excursions into the large form, the sonata.

The progressives of the time were members of the Neo-German group, followers of Wagner and Liszt, the latter being the more important here. In this assessment we must distinguish between Liszt's influence as a pianist and his influence as a composer, and it is the latter that claims our attention. The Sonata in B-flat minor (composed 1857) of Julius Reubke (1834–1858) not only parallels the formal plan of Liszt's own sonata but is long, difficult, and intense. Another composer of piano music associated with Liszt was Joseph Joachim Raff (1822–1882), a strong supporter of the Neo-German school who nonetheless cultivated traditional forms of piano music. While Raff emphasized character pieces, like other composers we have been discussing he also made efforts in the large forms: two sonatas (op. 14 and 168) and four suites of which the one in D major (op. 91) consists of a gigue with variations that offer much contrapuntal interest. Raff also wrote music for piano duet and for two pianos. Connected with this group was the Swiss Hermann Goetz (1840–1876) who composed character pieces and other works, many for piano duet; outstanding for the latter medium is his Sonata in G minor (composed 1865, published 1878). We have already taken note of Wagner's influence on the work of Jensen.

A number of composers stood in strong opposition to the Neo-German group and associated themselves with Brahms. These included Carl Reinecke (1824–1910), Heinrich von Herzogenberg (1843–1900), Elisabeth von Herzogenberg (1847–1892), and Robert Fuchs (1847–1927). Reinecke composed a large body of music in which Schumann's and Brahms' influence is clearly perceptible: variations on themes of Bach and Handel (op. 24 and 84 respectively, the former for piano duet); Fantasy in the Form of a Sonata in C major (op. 15); a Ballade in A-flat major (op. 20); some easy sonatinas (op. 47 and 98); and a set of preludes and fugues (op. 65). Among other works we find *Ernstes und Heiteres* (Serious Things and Serene Things, op. 145, 1877); a set of twelve etudes and twelve dances; a Sonata in C minor, for piano left hand (op. 179); and, as a curiosity, *Studien und Metamorphosen* (Studies and Metamorphoses, op. 235) in which Reinecke took themes from Haydn, Mozart, and Beethoven and modified them extensively. He also cultivated the character piece. Fuchs emphasized the character piece as well, but also composed three sonatas, in G-flat major (op. 19), G minor (op. 88), and D-flat major (op. 109). He devoted much attention to pieces for children. In the work of Herzogenberg, we find, apart from character pieces, several sets of variations and etudes as well as works for piano duet (large sets of variations along with smaller pieces); there is in addition the Variations in D-flat major (op. 13) for two pianos. Elisabeth von Herzogenberg published a set of character pieces (8, 1892). Others were Julius Otto Grimm (1827–1903), Albert Dietrich (1829–1908), a close personal friend of Brahms, and Bernard Scholz (1835–1916).

Felix Draeseke (1835–1913) of Dresden is a distinctive figure, initially an adherent of the Neo-German school who later became their strong and articulate opponent. Early he composed a large *Sonata quasi fantasia* in C-sharp minor (op. 6, composed 1862–1863), in cyclic form, in which he gave Beethoven's model a Lisztian interpretation. Particularly noteworthy among his character pieces is the set *Fata Morgana, ein Ghaselenkranz* (op. 13, composed 1876–1877), another cycle (he calls it a "wreath") based on the Persian ghasel. Like Hiller, Draeseke uses a refrain structure; the work also displays contrapuntal writing.

This discussion of composers whose sympathies were close to those of Brahms brings up another subject, the influence of Baroque practices on nineteenth-century piano music. We have seen it in Beethoven, Mendelssohn, Schumann, Liszt, and Brahms, not to mention Mozart before them. If we take the prelude as a manifestation of this influence, then we have to include Chopin and lesser composers as well. Most often this influence stems directly and specifically from Bach, the first critical complete edition of whose works was undertaken in the last half of the century (the Bachgesellschaft [Bach Society] edition), with Brahms, characteristically, among the editors. Herzogenberg, who took part in founding the Bach Society in Leipzig, was a close friend of Philipp Spitta, the great biographer of Bach. We have seen that both Fuchs and Draeseke emphasized counterpoint. Other German composers influenced by Baroque music are the conservative Viennese theorist and teacher Simon Sechter (1788–1867), Franz Lachner (1803–1890) of Munich, Friedrich Kiel (1821–1885) of Berlin, and August Halm (1869–1929). Kiel composed both a set of gigues (op. 36) and a suite (op. 28), along with Variations and Fugue (op. 17), two sets of fantasias (op. 56 and 68), and two sonatas, both in D major (op. 16 and one in a single movement, published as the first movement of the Suite, op. 28 ii). Individual works of this conservative bent appear from time to time in the work of composers not generally associated with the movement; there is Jensen's *Deutsche Suite* (German Suite), already mentioned. Later we will note examples of this Baroque influence in Scandinavia and, particularly, France. Baroque forms, then, continue implicitly throughout the nineteenth century before asserting themselves again in the twentieth. On the other hand, as we have seen, Bargiel retained only the names of eighteenth-century dances in his Suite in C major (op. 7).

Two composers stand out, one older, the other much younger: Joseph Rheinberger (1839–1901) and Max Reger (1873–1916). Rheinberger's music displays a certain learned quality which is particularly clear from his interest in the large forms of the past.[3] Character pieces, to be sure, appear in profusion but are for the most part early works. Among his efforts in the large forms are the *Sinfonische Sonate* in C major (Symphonic Sonata, op. 47), the title clearly revealing his aspirations; and the *Romantische Sonate* in F-sharp minor (Romantic Sonata, op. 184), along with two other sonatas in D-flat major (op. 99) and E-flat major (op. 135). Other works exemplify his conservative stance: toccatas (op. 12 and 104); pieces in fugal form (op. 39 and 68); a Prelude and Fugue (op. 33); an Etude and Fugato (op. 42); and character pieces in canonic form (op. 180). Noteworthy is Rheinberger's set of preludes in the form of etudes (24, op. 14), in which he employs a sequence of keys, one symptomatic of the chromatic tendencies of the time. The tonalities are in groups of four according to the notes of the three possible diminished-seventh chords (C–E-flat–F-sharp–A, F–A-flat–B–D, and B-flat–D-flat–E–G); as in Bach, the pieces are in pairs, first the major, then the minor. Like Brahms, Rheinberger composed sets of variations, one of them called *Klaviervorträge*

(Piano Performance Pieces) on a theme of Handel (op. 45 ii), and "Improvisation" on a theme from Mozart's *Zauberflöte* (op. 51). In line with this conservative orientation is his arrangement for two pianos of selections from Bach's Goldberg variations (completed 1883), the excerpts included having been chosen by Max Reger.

Next to Brahms, Reger stands out as the outstanding German composer of piano music of the late nineteenth century.[4] Sympathetic to the Neo-German group early in his career, Reger later turned away and devoted himself, like Brahms, to the traditions of Mendelssohn, Schumann, and the Baroque, although elements of Chopin, Liszt, and Brahms, particularly the extensive use of chromaticism and harmonic ambiguity, are by no means lacking. Yet, as was typical of the time, the character piece predominates. We can readily associate sets such as the following with Schumann: *Lose Blätter* (Loose Leaves, 14, op. 13, composed and published, 1894); *Aus der Jugendzeit* (From the Time of Youth, 20, op. 17, composed 1895, published 1902); *Humoresken* (5, op. 20, composed 1898, published 1899); *Fantasie-Stücke* (7, op. 26, composed 1898, published 1899); *Bunte Blätter* (9, Multicolored Leaves, op. 36, composed and published 1899); Intermezzos (6, op. 45, composed and published 1900); *Episoden* (Episodes, 8, op. 115, composed and published 1910); and the pieces *für kleine und grosse Leute* (for little and big people, composed and published 1910), an obvious variation of Schumann's phrase. Other smaller pieces of didactic intent are the *Kleine Vortragsstücke* (Little Recital Pieces, op. 44, composed and published 1900) and, particularly, the large set in four parts, *Aus meinem Tagebuch* (From My Diary, op. 82, composed and published 1904–1912). In the style of Brahms are the two sets of waltzes (both in op. 11, composed 1893), and the *Charakterstücke* (7, op. 32, composed and published 1899), while Grieg (see below) seems to have provided the inspiration for *Silhouetten* (7, op. 53, composed 1900, published 1901) and Schumann and Brahms for the twelve *Träume am Kamin* (Dreams by the Hearth, 12, op. 143, composed 1915, published 1916). Chopin, however, provided the model for the twelfth of the set, Reger's last work for the piano. Finally, there is a satirical contribution to the literature of popular salon music, a piece entitled "Ewig dein!" (Eternally Yours!, op. 17523, 1907), marked to be played *Noch schneller als möglich* (Even faster than possible), but with performance rights prohibited.

Reger did not take up the larger forms of piano music until comparatively late in his career, and even then he avoided the standard form, the sonata; in this vein he composed four sonatinas—in E minor, D major, F major, and A minor (op. 89, composed 1905–1908, published 1905 [i and ii] and 1908 [iii and iv]). He chose, instead, the other large form, the theme and variations, including the fugal finale that had become customary since Beethoven. There are two large sets, one on a theme of Bach (14, op. 81, composed and published 1904), the other on a theme of Telemann (24, op. 134, composed and published 1914), a late work. Reger used Baroque sources, as did Brahms, but he avoided the obvious: the theme from Bach is the oboe obbligato part to a duet in the cantata "Auf Christi Himmelfahrt allein" (BWV

128), while that from Telemann is the Minuet of the First Suite for Oboe and Strings in his *Musique de table*, Part III (1733). Both sets are large and elaborate works that take their point of departure from Beethoven's famous Diabelli variations. Moreover, Reger had a broader concept of variations than did other composers: most often he transformed the traditional form into a fantasia based on motives taken from the theme, varying both its rhythm and characteristic melodic intervals.

Reger also composed two large sets of variations for two pianos, and here the example of Brahms' set on Haydn was doubtless decisive: one on a theme of Beethoven (op. 86, composed and published 1904), the other on a theme of Mozart (op. 132a, composed and published 1914), the latter originally scored for orchestra. The theme from Beethoven is the Bagatelle in B-flat minor (op. 119 xi), while that from Mozart is from the Sonata in A minor (K. 300i/331), where it also serves as the theme for a set of variations, so that the situation is analogous to Brahms' set on a theme of Handel. Reger's other large work for two pianos is reminiscent of his organ music: the Introduction, Passacaglia, and Fugue in B minor (op. 96, composed and published 1906), wherein the passacaglia involves variation form. For piano duet there are mainly smaller pieces, chiefly dances, in the spirit of Brahms, such as the early *Waltz-Caprices* (12, op. 9, composed 1892) and the *Deutsche Tänze* (10, op. 10, composed 1893), but several are character pieces, such as the *Pièces pittoresques* (5, op. 34) or the *Burlesken* (6, op. 58).

FRANCE

In the seventeenth and eighteenth centuries French musicians waged heated battles regarding the relative merits of Italian music and musicians as opposed to their own. But in the later eighteenth and nineteenth centuries France's great musical rival became Germany; even though Italian opera remained capable of stimulating controversy, the new Germanic art of instrumental music clearly got the most attention. In the field of piano music additional influences came from Chopin and Liszt.

In the tradition of Liszt was his friend the composer Charles Valentin Morhange, known as Alkan (1813–1888), who was active in Paris. Although a superb piano virtuoso, he did not concertize extensively. But he composed some of the most fabulously difficult works ever conceived for the piano, for which Liszt's term "transcendental execution" would be entirely appropriate. This virtuosity he employed in the conventional types of music: his Grande Sonate, *Les quatre âges* (The Four Ages, op. 33, 1848) that is programmatic and also offers an early example of progressive tonality (each movement in a different key); *Toccatina* (op. 75); Etudes in the major keys (op. 35) and minor keys (op. 39); the Grand Etudes (3, op. 76); and a set of preludes in all the keys (op. 31). A glimpse of twentieth-century preoccupations is given by his etude *Chemin de fer* (Railroad, op. 27), a graphic representation of a steam engine. Yet Alkan in his voluminous output also included miniatures, as in the two sets entitled *Chants* (op. 38, published 1857) and *Motifs (Esquisses)* (Motives [Sketches], 48 in four sets of twelve each, op. 63). And there is his unique *Bambordo Carillon* for pedal piano with two players (four feet).

The two most important French composers of piano music of the time were Charles Camille Saint-Saëns (1835–1921) and Gabriel Urbain Fauré (1845–1924). Both were organists by profession but in their composition neglected that instrument in favor of the piano. Saint-Saëns, a strong opponent of Liszt and Wagner, nevertheless reveals a Germanic orientation, tempered by Chopin. In his large body of piano music he made no attempt at the large form, the sonata. The sole work in anything approaching a large form is his neobaroque Suite in the Old Style (op. 90); there is also a late set of Fugues (op. 161). Otherwise, we find the usual types: Bagatelles (op. 3); Album Leaf (op. 72); three mazurkas, two in G minor (op. 21 and 24) and one in B minor (op. 66); Etudes (op. 52 and 111), as well as a set for the left hand alone (op. 135); and so forth. For two pianos he composed the well-known Variations on a Theme of Beethoven (op. 35), along with the Polonaise (op. 77) and the Scherzo (op. 87), and, for piano duet, several sets of character pieces.

Fauré, less involved with the Germanic tradition, followed the example of Chopin. Along with his early *Romances sans paroles* (op. 17, composed ca. 1863, published 1880)[5] and the *Pièces breves* (op. 84, composed 1869–1902, published 1902), there are barcaroles and nocturnes, thirteen of each, five impromptus, four waltz-caprices, a set of nine preludes, and a single mazurka. The larger form of character piece is represented by the single Ballade in F-sharp major (op. 19, composed 1879, published 1880), which he later arranged for orchestra. For piano duet, he composed a set of six pieces, *Dolly* (op. 56, composed 1893–1896, published 1894–1897). Fauré's music is idiomatic to the piano but, unlike Liszt's, for instance, is often subdued and delicate, on the one hand, and full of novel harmonic touches on the other. Also in sharp contrast to Liszt is the complete absence of programmatic or pictorial associations.

Of lesser importance are Emanuel Chabrier (1841–1894) and Ernest Chausson (1855–1899). Chabrier's most important work for piano is a set, *Pièces pittoresques* (10, 1880), while Chausson composed a character piece, *Paysage* (Landscape, op. 38, 1895), and another set entitled *Quelques danses* (3, op. 26, 1896, including a prologue—the Pavan of this set has become well known). Piano music was also composed by the leading French operatic composers of the time: Ambroise Thomas (1811–1896), Charles Gounod (1818–1893), Georges Bizet (1838–1875), and Jules Massenet (1842–1912). Of these, Gounod and Bizet are the most important. Along with a number of character pieces Bizet composed a big set entitled *Variations chromatiques* (14, op. 3, published 1868) using the ostinato principle and including a coda; in contrast, Gounod produced various small character pieces in a popular vein (waltzes, musettes, marches, pastorales, meditations, melodies, and the like). Thus we come to popular salon music, well represented in Benjamin Godard (1849–1895), Moritz Moszkowski (1854–1925), and Cécile Chaminade (1857–1944).

The outstanding French composer of piano music of the time was César Auguste Franck (1822–1890), a native of Liège in Belgium who became a French citizen in 1873. Like Saint-Saëns and Fauré he was an organist by profession and for some time was professor of organ at the Paris Conservatory. Although he must be counted among the great composers of organ music, he composed more for the piano, but many of these pieces have passed out of the repertory. This is especially true of the early piano pieces, those composed up to 1845, in which the conventional types appear to the exclusion of all else. There are fantasias of the potpourri type, variations on themes from popular operas, an Eclogue (FWV 11/op. 3),[6] a Grand Caprice (FWV 13/op. 5), three fantasias (FWV 16/op. 11, FWV 17/op. 12, and FWV 18/op. 15), but also sonatas, along with similar works for piano duet. D'Indy stated that, despite the various titles given these works by Franck, the same formal plan is found in all of them: simple three-part form, the midsection fast, and the whole often preceded by a slow introduction.[7] All this testifies to Franck's entirely conventional approach to piano music at this stage of his career. Thereupon, as far as keyboard music is concerned, he abandoned the piano in favor of the organ. When he returned to the composition of piano music in the late 1880s, the change could hardly have been more profound. Gone are the conventional and popular types of composition; in their place we find large and serious works. Yet in his later work Franck avoided the customary large forms—sonata, fantasia, variations—finding his model rather in the music he had been composing for organ. There are two of these large works (dates here are of composition): *Prélude, chorale, et fugue* in B minor (FWV 21, 1884) and *Prélude, aria, et finale* in E major (FWV 23, 1886–1887); and a short piece, *Danse lente* (FWV 22, 1885).

Both the large works have proportions approaching those of a sonata, a genre with which in other respects they have little in common. The *Prélude, chorale, et fugue* he originally thought of as a prelude and fugue in the tradition of Bach, but then inserted a chorale-like slow movement. As with his large organ works, he emphasizes cyclic form; the themes of the prelude and of the chorale are varied and brought together in the fugue. The prelude itself consists to a large extent of figuration and thus is an offshoot of the old conception of the form, as in Bach. The *Prélude, aria, et finale* is similar. Following the eighteenth-century precedent, Franck has cast the aria in variation form and again brings all the themes of the work together in the finale, which is in a sort of sonata form. On his own admission, Franck took the unifying device of cyclic form, common in nineteenth-century French music, from the late works of Beethoven. Both works reveal Franck's characteristically rich and sonorous harmonies, with particular emphasis on ninth-chords, and his interest in counterpoint. Finally, in 1873 Franck arranged for piano his *Prélude, fugue, et variation* (FWV 30/op. 18; piano arrangement, FWV 30a), an organ work included in his first set of pieces for that instrument.

Among Franck's younger contemporaries were Vincent d'Indy (1851–1931) and the Belgian Guillaume Lekeu (1870–1894), both of whom were his students, and Paul Dukas (1865–1935). D'Indy, clearly the most important of the three, reveals the German influence. Among the many character pieces are the early *Romances sans paroles* (op. 1, 1870); the Nocturne (op. 26, 1886); Promenade (op. 27, 1887; and *Schumanniana* (3, op. 30, 1887). In the spirit of Liszt he produced pieces associated with travel: the *Poème des montagnes* (op. 15, 1881) and *Tableaux de voyage* (13, op. 33, 1889), while *Helvetia* (3, op. 17, 1882), despite its title, consists of waltzes. For children, there are three volumes of *Pièces pour les enfants de tous les âges* (Pieces for Children of All Ages, 24, op. 74, 1919) in the style of various composers, along with several other sets, and arrangements of French folk dances. Yet d'Indy also composed large works. In the spirit of Franck he conceived the Sonata in E major (op. 63, 1907). Despite its rich harmonies full of unresolved dissonances, we may find its structural model in Haydn, Mozart, and Beethoven. Of its three movements, the first is a theme and variations, the second is a scherzo, and the finale, in sonata form, makes prominent use of the theme of the first movement. Somewhat earlier he had produced a smaller essay in a related form, the *Petite sonate dans la forme classique* (op. 9, 1880). Near the end of his career he composed two large works that involve variation form, *Thème varié, fugue, et chanson* (op. 85, 1925) and *Fantaisie sur un vieil air de ronde française* (op. 99, 1930). Finally, d'Indy composed the neoclassical *Menuet sur le nom de Haydn* (op. 65, 1909) and for piano duet *Petite chanson grégorienne* (op. 60, 1906).

The few piano works of Lekeu, who died at the age of twenty-four, show much promise: there is a *Tempo di Mazurka* (composed 1887), a Sonata in G minor (1891), with an impressive fugue, and a set of Pièces (3, 1892). Dukas, who became known for his dramatic and orchestral works, composed two interesting pieces in large forms for piano: a Sonata in E-flat minor (composed 1901, published 1906), and *Variations, interlude, et finale* (composed 1903, published 1907), the latter based on a theme of Rameau. The small forms are represented by his *Prélude élégiaque sur le nom de Haydn* (composed 1908, published 1910), and a character piece, *La plainte, au loin, du faune* (1920), on the death of Debussy.

OTHER COUNTRIES OF WESTERN EUROPE

The German art of instrumental music never became an important branch of musical composition in Italy, the land of opera, and piano music constituted a small part of what little instrumental composition there was. In the early part of the century, there was Francesco Pollini (1762–1846), a pupil of Mozart, who produced *Esercizi in forma di toccata* (32, op. 42) along with fantasias, variations, rondos, and toccatas, and three sonatas, while the opera composer Gioachino Rossini (1792–1868) produced a number of attractive character pieces. The most important Italian composer of piano music in the nineteenth century, however, was Giovanni Sgambati (1841–1914), a virtuoso who studied with Liszt and taught at the Rome Conservatory. He composed a large number of piano pieces, mostly small character pieces, often with dif-

ferent opus numbers assigned the same piece by different publishers: Nocturnes (op. 3, 15/20, 24/31, and 26/33); *Fogli volanti* (Scattered Leaves, op.
8/12); *Mélodies poétiques* (op. 29/36); Pieces (3, op. 42), *Romanza senza
parole*; and *Pièces lyriques* (op. 23). A number of his works are in the neobaroque vein: a Prelude and Fugue in E-flat major (op. 6); the Pieces (op. 13)
which consist of a Prelude, "Vecchio Menuetto," "Nenia," and a concluding
Toccata; and the Gavotte in A-flat major (op. 9). His only larger work, the
Suite (op. 16/21), is in effect a set of character pieces. The other prominent
Italian composer of piano music of the time was Giuseppe Martucci (1856–
1909), an avowed supporter of German music in general and of Wagner in
particular, as his large Fantasia (op. 51) indicates. His music for piano consists
primarily of character pieces, some with the neobaroque evident; at the beginning of his career he produced his only Sonata (op. 34, composed ca. 1876).

In Great Britain the leading native composer of piano music—since
Elgar's contributions to the repertory are both few and modest—was a disci-
ple of Mendelssohn, Sir William Sterndale Bennett (1816–1875). Bennett was
born in Cambridge, studied in Leipzig, and ultimately became director of the
Royal Conservatory of Music in London. His piano music fully accords with
what was customary in Germany in the 1840s: it includes a Sonata in F minor
(op. 13); a Suite (op. 24); *The Maid of Orleans*, a program sonata (op. 46); a
large Fantasia in A major (op. 16); a set of Variations (op. 31); and, like Schumann, a Toccata (op. 38). There are also a number of smaller works: among
them, a Capriccio in D minor (op. 2); *Musical Sketches* (3; op. 10), *Studies in
the Form of Capriccios* (6, op. 11); Impromptus (3, op. 12); Romances (3, op.
14); and the large set, Preludes and Lessons (60, op. 33), containing pieces in
all the keys. For piano duet he composed a set of character pieces, *Diversions*
(3, op. 17). Other English composers of piano works include: Samuel Sebastian Wesley (1810–1876), C. Hubert H. Parry (1848–1918), and Charles Villiers
Stanford (1852–1924).

From elsewhere in Western Europe, but few notable contributions
emerged (Spain is treated below). In Holland the two most important composers of piano music were Julius Röntgen (1855–1932), who was born in
Germany and became director of the Amsterdam Conservatory, writing a
good deal of piano music in both large and small forms, and Gerard van
Brucken-Fock (1859–1935), who trained in Germany and produced teaching
pieces. In the Balkans the relatively little activity was strongly under German
influence: two Croatian composers were Fortunatas Pintarić (1798–1867) and
Ferdo Livadić (1798–1878).

THE NATIONAL SCHOOLS

During the late nineteenth century, in Central Europe strong nationalistic
and patriotic sentiments began to develop as a result of the breaking up of the
Hapsburg Empire. This was especially true in Bohemia and Hungary but also
holds for Italy, which gradually secured its independence from both Austria

and France. In Russia there developed, in artistic matters at least, a movement highly critical of western, specifically German, influences. Thus, nationalism began to exert an influence on music in many of these countries as composers began to turn to their native cultures for materials and inspiration.

While this focus shows itself most clearly in operas and symphonic poems, it also involved piano music: composers began to exploit native songs and dances and the characteristic sounds and styles of indigenous musical instruments in all musical media. We have already noted instances of musical nationalism in Liszt and Chopin, and elements derived from folk music appear in Brahms. But Chopin cultivated his nationalism from abroad, and the same generally holds for Liszt. Here, on the other hand, we are concerned with composers living and working in their native countries, deliberately drawing on native musical resources and the national aspirations which they wish to promote. Music in the countries of western Europe, France, England, Italy, and the others, we do not ordinarily regard as displaying this kind of nationalistic preoccupation. The most important among these national schools are those in Bohemia and Russia, with the latter being of particular significance for piano music. Other such schools existed in Scandinavia and Spain (the latter mainly in the early twentieth century and hence discussed in the next chapter).

The earliest among the national schools is the Bohemian, its foremost representatives being Bedřich Smetana (1824–1884) and Antonín Dvořák (1841–1904), both of whom composed much piano music. Both cultivated the large forms of the Germanic repertory. In this vein Smetana produced a Sonata in G minor (1846); a Sonata in E minor, for two pianos each with two players (eight hands) and cast in a long continuous movement (composed 1849); and a large concert etude entitled *Na brehu morsken* (By the Seashore, op. 17, 1861). Dvořák, for his part, produced a Suite in A major ("American," DTK 184/op. 98, composed 1894).[8]

The nationalistic spirit comes out more in the character piece, which both composers emphasized. Smetana gave much attention to the artistic elaboration of the national dance of his country, the polka, producing three sets: *Polkas de salon* (3, op. 7, published 1855), *Polkas poétiques* (3, op. 8, published 1855), and *Souvenirs de Bohême* (two sets, op. 12 and 13, composed 1859–1860, published 1863); there are also two late sets entitled *Ceske tance* (Czech Dances, composed 1877–1879), the first part of which contains polkas; other polkas he published separately. Here Smetana took elements of the dance and stylized them in a fashion resembling that of his predecessors: it has been said that Smetana did for the polka what Chopin did for the mazurka. At the same time he composed conventional waltzes, bagatelles, impromptus, album leaves, *morceaux caractéristiques*, and concert studies.

In Dvořák's character pieces we see the same division. He composed many of the traditional types, including waltzes, mazurkas, impromptus, album leaves, humoresques, and eclogues; best known is the set *Poetische Stimmungsbilder* (Poetic Mood Pictures, DTK 161/op. 85, composed 1889). Yet he also emphasized the nationalistic element. We find examples of the *dumka*, both by itself (DTK 64/op. 35) and together with a *furiant* (DTK 136–137/op. 12). The *dumka* is a type of narrative poetry characterized by sudden changes from an elegiac mood to one of exuberance, while the *furiant* is a fast, excited dance in triple time. Other nationalistic pieces of Dvořák are found in his music for piano duet: the Slavonic Dances (DTK 78 and 145/op. 46 and 72); *Legends* (10, DTK 117/op. 59); and *From the Bohemian Forest* (6, DTK 133/op. 68). Among other Bohemian composers are Zdenek Fibich (1850–1900), an outspoken adherent of German Romantic music who composed a large number of character pieces; Eduard Napravnik (1839–1916); and Ottokar Nováček (1866–1900).

Of greater interest and significance for piano music generally was the situation in Russia. Here musical life for years had been in the hands of foreign-born musicians, many from Italy, others from Germany. In the eighteenth century the important Italian harpsichordist Rutini spent time in Russia, and, later, the Germans Hässler, Henselt, and Jensen all were there, as was the Irish composer and pianist John Field. But a sharp reaction against this foreign domination of musical activity broke out, doubtless in part stimulated by the Napoleonic wars. We see it clearly in Russian opera of the time. This reaction was consolidated by a group of five composers centered in St. Petersburg who were variously known as The Five, or The Mighty Handful. While the guiding spirit here was Vladimir Stasov, a literary man, the musician most active in articulating the group's ideals was Mily Balakirev (1837–1910); the other four members of The Five were Alexander Borodin (1833–1887), César Cui (1835–1918), Modest Mussorgsky (1839–1881), and Nicolas Rimsky-Korsakov (1844–1908). Most of them were amateurs in music who received informal training from Balakirev, although Rimsky-Korsakov eventually underwent a formal course of musical studies.

Apart from Balakirev and Mussorgsky, these composers did not emphasize piano music; moreover, with some important exceptions most of their music for piano is not representative of the nationalistic attitude. The work of Balakirev, himself a pianist of some ability, shows evidence of contact with the western repertory: among others are character pieces (*Novellette, Phantasiestück*, Tarantella, *Berceuse*, Capriccio, Humoresque, Nocturne, *Gondellied* [Gondola Song], and Scherzo), a toccata, an impromptu (based on themes from two of Chopin's preludes), mazurkas, nocturnes, scherzos, waltzes, and a polka; the sole nationalistic piece here is the *Dumka* in E-flat minor (1900). His Sonata in B-flat minor (1900–1905), a brilliant, demanding piece in cyclic form, is a late work. Balakirev's most celebrated piece, however, a real virtuoso composition, is *Islamey* (composed 1869, revised 1902); described as an "oriental fantasy," it is built on Caucasian and Armenian melodies, three in all, and features rhythmic drive. He also made transcriptions of orchestral pieces and excerpts from opera and composed a few pieces for piano duet. Cui composed a Suite (op. 21), a set of variations (op. 61), and a number of character pieces in which the atmosphere of the salon is evident; Borodin composed a Little Suite in C-sharp minor (op. 7) and character pieces, among them polkas. Rimsky-Korsakov appears here in a conservative light, in which a few character pieces are balanced by neobaroque pieces, among them Variations on B-A-C-H (6, op. 10), and a set of six fugues (op. 17).

Thus, far and away the most important and arresting member of The Five is Mussorgsky, whose influence transcends the limits of nationalism. Mussorgsky was an amateur musician who made his living as a civil servant. His artistic credo was derived from nonmusical sources: the novelist Chernyshevsky, the psychologist Troitzky, and the German philosopher Feuerbach. As we can see from the incomplete biographical sketch that Mussorgsky intended for Hugo Riemann's encyclopedic dictionary of music,[9] he viewed art not as an end in itself, but as a means of communication and as a means of expressing human emotions; and since speech and music are both involved with sound, they may be said to be controlled to an extent at least by the same laws, so that music also has the capacity of expressing human emotions. While such an attitude has much in common with Romanticism, Mussorgsky's compositions manifest it in an unusually direct and graphic manner, largely unfettered by traditional procedures.

Piano music occupies an important place in his musical output, and it accords with his artistic beliefs. The traditional large forms are lacking; some early sonatas have been lost, but an early Scherzo in C-sharp minor (1858) is extant. The rest of his work consists of character pieces: from the period 1859–1860 an *Impromptu passioné*, *Ein Kinderscherz* (A Children's Prank), and a Prelude *in modo classico*; from 1865 the set of two pieces *From Memories of Childhood* (*Nurse and I—First Punishment: Nurse Shuts Me in the Dark Room*), in which his involvement with psychology (terror) is evident; *Duma*, a reverie; and *La Capricieuse*; from the 1870s, a *scherzino* entitled *The Seamstress* and his magnum opus of piano music, *Pictures at an Exhibition* (composed 1874, not published until 1886); and, from the 1880s, *On the Southern Shore of the Crimea* in two parts, *Gurzuf* and *Capriccio*, and three short character pieces. Mussorgsky also completed arrangements for piano of movements from Beethoven's string quartets. For piano duet he composed the Allegro and Scherzo (parts of an unfinished sonata) and transcriptions from Balakirev, Berlioz, and others.

His most important piece of piano music, and doubtless the most important piece of piano music produced by any of The Five, is the set *Pictures at an Exhibition*. It consists of musical representations of drawings and paintings by Mussorgsky's friend Victor Hartmann, an unusual instance of the connection between works of art and musical compositions. The stimulus to Mussorgsky was a memorial exhibition of Hartmann's works in 1874 organized by Stasov. Stasov also arranged for the publication of Mussorgsky's *Pictures at an Exhibition*, for which he provided a descriptive commentary. Although Hartmann is not generally regarded as among the outstanding Russian artists of the time, his emphasis on elaborately detailed ornamentation using folk and oriental motives attracted Mussorgsky's attention. Hartmann actually was known chiefly as an architect and as a designer of stage sets; he prepared the sets for a revival of Glinka's *Russlan and Ludmilla* and *Trilbi*, a nationalistic ballet.

In February 1874 the St. Petersburg Architectural Association held a memorial exhibition in honor of Mussorgsky's friend Victor Alexandrovich Hartmann. Mussorgsky's *Pictures at an Exhibition*, inspired by Hartmann's engravings, includes "The Hut on Fowl's Legs (Baba Yaga)" and "The Great Gate of Kiev." Hartmann's design for a clock in the form of Baba Yaga's hut was described in the exhibition catalogue as being in the Russian style of the fourteenth century. The Great Gate of Kiev was never built; Hartmann's design, an entry in a competition for a ceremonial gateway, inspired the ceremonial processional in Mussorgsky's piece.

Left. Clock in the Form of Baba-Yaga's Hut
Above. The Great Gate of Kiev

Mussorgsky's *Pictures at an Exhibition*, then, is based on Hartmann's memorial exhibition. Each piece in the set represents an individual drawing or painting, preceded and connected by a Promenade that depicts the composer wandering through the gallery.[10] The Promenade theme appears within some of the pieces as well, so that Mussorgsky has also unified the set in musical terms. The set begins with "Gnomus," a gnome on awkward, deformed legs, an elaborate design for a toy nutcracker, and continues with "Il vecchio castello" (The Old Castle), a landscape depicting a medieval castle with a troubadour in the foreground. Next comes "Tuileries," children noisily at play in the famous Parisian gardens, followed by "Bydlo," a lumbering, crude Polish ox-drawn cart on enormous wheels. There follows "Ballet of the Chicks," based on a series of sketches portraying chicks in various roles and costumes, originally composed for the ballet *Trilbi*. "Samuel Goldenberg and Schmuyle," a graphic portrayal of two Polish Jews, one rich, the other poor, is next, followed by "Limoges, the Market Place," the "furious dispute," as Mussorgsky puts it, of the women at market (marginal notes on the manuscript by Mussorgsky give the dialogue, which seems more like a conversation than a dispute). The next two follow one another without a break: "Catacombae," depicting the artist viewing the catacombs by lantern light, and "Con mortuis in lingua mortua" (With the Dead in a Dead Language), which has another marginal note by the composer that reads, "the creative spirit of the immortal Hartmann leads me toward the skulls and addresses them—a pale light radiates from the interior of the skulls." There follows "The Hut on Fowl's Legs," a clock in the form of the witch Baba Yaga's hut, which is mounted on fowl's legs (the drawing provides a good example of Hartmann's detailed ornamentation). The finale is "The Great Gate of Kiev," an architectural drawing showing a massive gate in the old Russian style.

In this cycle of character pieces, the usual form is that most common in character pieces generally, the three-part arrangement. New and different, however, is Mussorgsky's way of writing music, his relative freedom from traditional methods, which produces highly individual results. The Promenade illustrates this. First, we note the constant changing of meter—at the beginning bars of 5/4 alternate with bars of 6/4. Second, the succession of harmonies, notably the avoidance of the dominant–tonic progression, is not what would have been prescribed in a harmony textbook of the time (see Ex. 6-2A). The Promenade music appears as interludes four times in varied forms as well as in "Con mortuis in lingua mortis" and "The Great Gate of Kiev." "Il vecchio castello," with its lyrical Slavic melody with a repeated pattern of figuration in the accompaniment, represents a more traditional way of writing for the piano, as does the popular and effective "Ballet of the Chicks." The latter is another contribution to the repertory of barnyard pieces, the chirping of the chicks suggested by the treble register, rapid chords, and dissonant grace-notes. On the other hand, "Bydlo" portrays its subject by heavy, awkward chords in the bass and an angular melody with wide leaps and irregular accentuations (see Ex. 6-2B); in the midsection a crescendo reaches a climax,

Example 6-2. MUSSORGSKY: *Pictures at an Exhibition*—Excerpts
    A. "Promenade"—Beginning (mm. 1–4)
    B. "Bydlo"—Beginning (mm. 1–10)

after which there is a gradual return to the quiet that prevailed at the beginning. Other unusual conceptions are "Gnomus," again with irregularity in the phrase structure and expressive use of trills in the accompaniment; "Samuel Goldenberg and Schmuyle," in which the rich Jew is depicted by a pompous long-phrased melody in octaves, while the poor Jew is put in the treble with rapidly repeated notes, staccato, the two elements contrapuntally combined in the final section. "The Hut on Fowl's Legs" is a virtuoso tour de force, virtually an octave and chord study. While sonority plays an important role throughout the set, it assumes particular importance in "Catacombae," with its long sustained chords, and in the concluding number, "The Great Gate of Kiev," emphasizing contrast in dynamic levels. Here the main theme proves to be a variant of the Promenade, while the episode is a variant of a Russian hymn.[11] Near the end Mussorgsky introduces thematic material that he also used in the coronation scene of his opera *Boris Godunov,* in both cases to represent the ringing of church bells.

On the basis of pieces like the Promenade and "Bydlo," some critics have questioned Mussorgsky's ability to write idiomatically for the piano, citing his lack of formal training in music. It has seemed to many that his conceptions suffer from the way he has actually put them into music, as in "The Great Gate of Kiev," in which the immense quantity of sound that seems appropriate is simply not producible from what Mussorgsky has written. This situation has given rise to revised editions along with different versions and arrangements of his works, whereby, ironically enough, *Pictures at an Exhibition* is better known in the orchestration by Ravel (1922) than in its original version for solo piano. It thus appears that some judicious emendation is necessary to produce a version that will sound satisfactory, but care should be taken that in the process Mussorgsky's intentions are not violated.

Although the nationalistic group, The Five, stood in the forefront of Russian musical composition in the second half of the nineteenth century, other composers with more conventional outlooks, closer to the conceptions of western European music, opposed them. This opposition was most pronounced in Anton Rubinstein (1829–1894), a former pupil of Liszt and an internationally known pianist who established the St. Petersburg Conservatory in 1862. His large output of piano music resembles that of the German composers discussed earlier in the chapter. Character pieces are the most numerous: caprices, serenades, romances, nocturnes. Along with these are *Melodies* (op. 3) in F major and B minor (of which the first is well known); two sets of Etudes (op. 23 and 81); a set of Preludes (op. 24); and a set of Preludes and Fugues (op. 53). There are also many dances. Beyond these mostly short pieces are suites of character pieces: *Kamennïy-ostrov* (op. 10), *The Ball* (op. 14), *Soirées à St. Petersbourg* (op. 44), and *Soirées musicales* (op. 109). The large forms are also present: there are four sonatas, in E major (op. 12), E minor (op. 20), F major (op. 41), and A minor (op. 100); an immense Suite (op. 38, in ten movements); a big set of Variations in G major (op. 88); and a Ballade (part of op. 93) based on a famous German narrative poem of the late eighteenth century, Bürger's *Lenore.* Among his early works are the nationalistic Fantasias on Russian Themes (2, op. 2). For piano duet he composed a set of character pieces (6, op. 50); a set of stylized dances, *Bal costumé* (op. 103); and a Sonata in D major (op. 89); along with a large Fantasia in F minor (op. 73) for two pianos. In his larger works virtuosity is stressed, while the smaller pieces are easy and ingratiating and in many cases evoke the world of the salon.

The leading Russian composer opposed to the ideals of The Five was, of course, Peter Ilyich Tchaikovsky (1840–1893). Although he composed nationalistic pieces, he was primarily oriented to the western European view, especially the Germanic. Like others discussed earlier, Tchaikovsky composed piano music only secondarily to what he did for opera or orchestra.[12] There are two large sonatas, the earlier, in C-sharp minor (op. 80, composed 1865, published 1900), and the later, in G major (op. 37, composed 1878, published 1879), both in four movements; three sets of variations, an early set in A minor, the *Pieces on a Theme* (op. 21, composed and published 1873), and the Theme and Variations in F major (op. 19 vi, composed 1873, published 1874). The rest is given over to character pieces. There are the usual types (*Scherzo à la Russe* and Impromptu, op. 1; Waltz-Caprice, op. 4; Romance in F minor, op. 5; Capriccio in G-flat major, op. 8; Nocturne and Humoresque, op. 10), among others. On the other hand, Tchaikovsky also wrote *Dumka* (op. 59, composed and published 1886), similar to Dvořák's. His best-known work for piano, however, is the suite *The Seasons* (12, op. 37b, composed 1875–1876, published 1876), a set of short pieces, one for each month, of which those for January ("At the Fireside"), April ("Snowdrops"), May ("Clear Nights"), June ("Barcarolle"), September ("Hunting Song"), and November ("Sleighbells") are particularly engaging. For piano duet Tchaikovsky published a set of fifty arrangements of Russian folk songs (1868–1869).

Two other Russian composers who remained true to western European ideals were Anatol Liadov (1855–1914) and Anton Arensky (1861–1906), both active in St. Petersburg. Both published a large amount of piano music in which the small form is dominant. In Liadov, particularly, we can discern the influence of Liszt and, even more, Chopin, as confirmed by his preludes, mazurkas, waltzes, and etudes; along with these go arabesques, bagatelles, intermezzos, miniatures, variations, and so forth. His extended *Ballad from Days of Old* in D major (op. 21, composed 1889, published 1890) shows aspects of Russian folk music. Arensky produced many character pieces in a traditional vein, but is also known for his *Essais sur des rythmes oubliés* (Essays on Forgotten Rhythms, 6, op. 28) and Pieces in All Keys (op. 36). Other Russian composers of this period are Sergei Liapunov (1859–1924), Alexander Gretchaninov (1864–1956), Alexander Glazunov (1865–1936), and Reinhold Glière (1875–1956).

The third important national school is the Scandinavian, where, as we might expect, the German influence remained strong. Although Norway was the only Scandinavian country to produce a composer of real stature in the nineteenth century (Grieg), we find activity elsewhere. In Denmark, the closest to Germany, the Germanic orientation is clear from the work of Friedrich Kuhlau (1786–1832), who became universally known for his short and simple sonatinas in the galant style; Johann Peder Emilius Hartmann (1805–1900); and, especially, Niels Willem Gade (1817–1890), the close friend and colleague of Mendelssohn. Hartmann's piano music embraces character pieces and sonatas, there being two of the latter (op. 34 and 80). Gade's work[13] reveals a close connection to that of Mendelssohn and Schumann, as is evident from his character pieces, many of which resemble Mendelssohn's *Lieder ohne Worte*, among which are *Aquareller* (Watercolors, 10, op. 19, and 4, op. 57); the *Arabeske* (op. 27); *Idyller* (4, op. 34); *Fantasiestykker* (4, op. 41). He also composed a Sonata in E minor (op. 28, composed 1840, revised and published 1854), with a recurring motto, along with music for piano duet. Except for some arrangements of folk dances and a set of character pieces for piano duet, *Nordiske Tonebilleder* (Tone Pictures of the North, 3, op. 4), Gade did not engage in nationalistic music of the type we have been considering. Two of his best-known pupils who produced piano music were August Winding (1835–1899) and Ludwig Schytte (1848–1909). Two Swedish composers of the time were Ludwig Norman (1831–1885) and Emil Sjögren (1853–1918).

The seat of activity in Scandinavian nationalistic music of this period clearly was Norway. The Germanic influence dominated the work of Ole Andreas Lindemann (1769–1857), and Halfdan Kjerulf (1815–1868), like Gade, had studied with Mendelssohn and Schumann and thus was much in the German tradition. But Kjerulf began to employ folk melodies in his works as early as 1824, also making arrangements of folk songs and dances for piano, such as his *Udvalgte norske Folkedanser* (Collection of Norwegian Folk Dances, 20, 1861) and *Norske Folkeviser* (Norwegian Folk Melodies, 1867). Another prolific composer of piano music was Agathe Backer-Grndahl (1847–1907).

The dominant figure here is, of course, Edvard Grieg (1843–1907). Again we meet with the Germanic orientation, since Grieg was trained at Leipzig and absorbed the Mendelssohn-Schumann influence; he also studied with Gade. The large forms are represented by a sonata and a ballade. An early work, the Sonata in E minor (op. 7, composed 1865, published 1866, revision published 1887), is in four movements: in most respects it is a typically Germanic production with big movements in sonata form at the beginning and end, an andante in second place, and minuet and trio in third. The Ballade in G minor (op. 24, composed 1875–1876, published 1876), perhaps Grieg's most satisfying venture into the large form, displays his nationalistic proclivities. Unlike the ballades of Chopin and most of those of Brahms, it is based on a Norwegian folk song, "E kann so mangen ein vakker sang," on which it presents fourteen variations. Grieg's other large work for piano is a suite, *Fra Holbergs tid* (From Holberg's Time, op. 40, composed 1884, published 1885), perhaps better known in Grieg's later orchestral arrangement. This is a neo-classical work (Holberg was a well-known eighteenth-century Norwegian-born writer) in five movements: Preludium, Sarabande, Gavotte (with a Musette serving as trio), Air (Andante religioso), and Rigaudon (with trio).

With the important exception of the Ballade and certain passages of the Sonata (the second movement and parts of the third), Grieg did not incorporate nationalistic elements into his large works for piano. But with the character pieces it is different: here Norwegian folk dances play a primary role, beginning with his Pieces (4, op. 1, composed 1861). Three basic types of folk dances are involved: the *springdans*, in fast triple time, often danced with singing, the melody accompanied by a drone bass; the *halling*, a leaping acrobatic dance in duple time native to the Halling Valley between Bergen and Oslo; and, of lesser importance, the *gangar*, a moderate "walking" dance in a steady, stately 6/8, the accents shifting occasionally to 3/4. These appear over and over again in Grieg's character pieces. Elements derived from them make their first appearance, perhaps rather tentatively, in his *Humoresker* (Humoresques, 4, op. 6, 1865), which despite their traditional title are dances: we find a trace of the *springdans* in the waltz (the last number), while the second is related to the *halling*. Folk-dance elements become more pronounced in the *Albumblade* (Album Leaves, 5, op. 28, composed 1864–1876, published 1878), again despite the non-nationalistic title, which Grieg composed after his first contact with Rikard Nordraak (1842–1866) who was among the first to work toward a national style for Norwegian music. We find each of the three types in the *Albumblade*: first, a *halling*, with the characteristic triplets but elaborated by chromatic harmonies and syncopations in the accompaniment; then a modified *gangar*, here in 3/4; and, finally, a *springdans*. After the *Albumblade*, however, Grieg brought this nationalistic aspect out into the open with his *Norske Folkeviser ed Danser* (Norwegian Folk Melodies and Dances, 25, op. 17, composed 1869, published 1870), the *Folkelivsbilleder* (Pictures from the Life of the People, 3, op. 19, composed 1870–1871, published 1872), the set of longer *Improvisata* on Norwegian folk melodies (2, op. 29, composed and published 1878), the *Norske Fjeldmelodier* (Norwegian Mountain Tunes, 6, composed ca. 1875, published 1875, revision published 1886), and the *Norske Folkeviser* (Norwegian Folk Melodies, 19, op. 66, composed 1896, published 1897). These Grieg himself collected and arranged for piano, setting them with extreme chromaticism as was his wont in his later works.

A notable example of Grieg's preoccupation with folk music appeared near the end of his life, the *Slåtter* (17, op. 72, composed 1901–1903, published 1903). A *slat* is any dance played on a native musical instrument. Grieg had been impressed by the *hardangenfele* (Hardanger fiddle), with eight strings, four of which sound in sympathetic resonance to those that are bowed. A Norwegian folklorist, Johan Halvorsen, fearful that the old art of the *slat* and the *hardangenfele* was dying out, collected a number of the melodies and adapted them to the modern violin. Then, to give wider currency to his work, he persuaded Grieg to arrange them for piano. This Grieg did, skillfully adapting for piano the characteristic sonority and texture of the original.

Grieg's remaining character pieces generally belong more to the Germanic tradition. Like so many of his contemporaries, he emphasized the miniature, as in the *Poetiske Tonebilleder* (Poetic Tone Pictures, 6, op. 3, composed 1863, published 1864), the *Morceaux de piano* (4, op. 1, composed and published 1865), the late *Stemninger* (Moods, 7, op. 73, composed 1903–1905, published 1905), and three posthumous pieces. Grieg's largest collection of miniatures, however, consists of the ten sets of *Lyriske Stykker* (Lyric Pieces, op. 12, 38, 43, 47, 54, 57, 62, 65, 68, and 71, composed 1867–1901, published contemporaneously). These resemble Mendelssohn's *Lieder ohne Worte*. Most are cast in the familiar and conventional three-part form, but some exhibit structures that are less common. Along with the more usual kinds of character piece (album leaf, berceuse and cradle song, elegy, papillon, melancholy, nocturne, folk song, scherzo, and march), we find nationalistic pieces. Op. 12 contains a Norwegian melody, op. 38 and 47 both have a *halling* and a *springdans*, and a *gangar* appears in op. 54, to name only a few. Especially popular are the "Voegtersang" (Watchman's Song, op. 12 iii) and the effective "Klokkeklang" (Bells Ringing, op. 54 vi), in which fifths with thirds as appoggiaturas create a striking aural image.

A school of lesser importance existed in Poland, where, in piano music, the example of Chopin remained decisive. The genres he established were taken over in the work of Josef Nowakowski (1800–1865); an older musician who had studied with Chopin, Ignacy Felix Dobryznski (1807–1867); Stanislaus Moniouszko (1819–1872); Vladislav Zeleński (1837–1921); and Sigismund von Noskowski (1846–1909). Of greater significance than these, although in a different field, was Theodor Leschetizky (1830–1915), who distinguished himself as a teacher of pianists at the Vienna Conservatory.

THE UNITED STATES

The European tradition, particularly the Germanic, exercised a dominant influence in the United States throughout the nineteenth century, as has already been observed. European, particularly German pianists, active in the United States included Charles Grobe (ca. 1817–1880); Hermann Adolf Wollenhaupt (1827–1863); Frederic Louis Ritter (1826–1891); from Alsace-Lorraine, who lived in Cincinnati and later taught at Vassar College; Richard Hoffman (1831–1909) and Sebastian Bach Mills (1838–1898), both from England; Karl Baermann (1839–1913), a pupil of Lachner in Munich; and Rafael Joseffy (1852–1915), a pianist, editor, and teacher.

At the time it was customary for native born Americans to obtain their musical education in Europe, once again especially in Germany. Among the pianists and composers of piano music to be mentioned here are William Mason (1829–1908), the son of Lowell Mason, who studied with Moscheles and Liszt and produced a well-known Toccata (op. 37, 1882) and character pieces; Dudley Buck (1839–1909); John Knowles Paine (1839–1906) from Portland, Maine, who studied in Berlin and then taught at Harvard from 1862, becoming Professor of Music, the first in the United States, there in 1875; Silas Gamaliel Pratt (1846–1916), who studied with Liszt and Dorn; Albert Ross Parsons (1847–1933), who studied with Kullak and Liszt; George Whitefield Chadwick (1854–1931); William Hall Sherwood (1854–1911), who studied with Kullak as well as with Liszt; Edward Baxter Perry (1855–1924), a blind pianist who studied with, among others, Kullak, Liszt, and Clara Schumann; Wilson George Smith (1855–1929), a pupil of Kiel and composer of many popular character pieces; and Ethelbert Nevin (1862–1901), who studied in Berlin and, after a period of teaching in Boston, returned to France and Italy where he remained for the rest of his life. Ernest Kroeger (1862–1934), on the other hand, spent his life in St. Louis. Composers of the nationalistic persuasion who used native American (Indian) melodies in their piano music were Arthur Foote (1853–1937), Henry F. Gilbert (1868–1928), and Arthur Farwell (1872–1952). Notable were two talented black pianists and composers: Thomas Greene Bethune (1849–1908), known as Blind Tom, who although a slave was able to pursue a career as a concert pianist; his best-known piece is yet another *battaglia, The Battle of Manassas* (1894); and Robert Nathaniel Dett (1882–1943), whose work emphasized the character piece, but with strong overtones from black spirituals.

The most important of these in regard to piano music are Paine and Nevin. In common with other late nineteenth-century composers, in his piano music Paine worked exclusively with the character piece under the influence of Schumann. These works include: his *Funeral March in Memory of President Lincoln* (1865); *A Christmas Gift* (op. 7); Romances (2 sets, op. 12 and 39, 1869 and 1883 respectively); Characteristic Pieces (op. 25, composed and published 1876); the set *In the Country* (op. 26, published 1876), which in particular owes much to Schumann; Piano Pieces (op. 41, published 1884); and a popular Nocturne (op. 45, published 1889). Nevin composed many character pieces, among them *Water Scenes* (op. 13), of which "Narcissus" has become familiar. He also emphasized the etude.

Easily the most colorful figure was Louis Moreau Gottschalk (1829–1869), born in New Orleans. Unlike many of his colleagues, he chose to go to Paris for his musical training, where he became acquainted with Berlioz, then returned to the United States to take up a varied career as a pianist. His tours took him all over the country, even to the islands of the Caribbean and to South America. He died in Brazil. He recorded his life and experiences in an autobiography *Notes of a Pianist* (1881).[14] His music, which emphasizes the piano, is to a large extent of the popular concert or salon type, frequently sentimental but often incorporating a good deal of virtuosity.[15] Examples include (dates are of publication) a large virtuoso *morceau de concert* consisting of variations on "God Save the Queen" or "America" (op. 41, 1861), an extremely pathétique *Marche funèbre* (op. 64, published 1874), among others, and shorter pieces, such as "The Last Hope" (op. 16, 1854, religious), Berceuse (op. 47, 1861), "The Dying Poet" (ca. 1863), and "Morte!" (She Is Dead, op. 60, 1868). More important are the pieces that incorporate elements of black, Creole, and Latin American music: "Bamboula" (op. 2, 1849); the *caprice americaine* entitled "The Banjo" (op. 15, 1854–1855), which effectively adapts the twanging sound of that instrument to the piano, much in the spirit of the earlier effort by Heinrich (see Chapter Four). Gottschalk has another piece with the same title (op. 82, 1853–1854), as well as "Souvenir de Porto Rico" in variation form (op. 31, 1857–1858); and "Ojos Criollos" (Creole Eyes, op. 37, 1859).

By far the most important American composer of the time was Edward MacDowell (1860–1908). Like most of his colleagues he was trained in Germany, under Ehlert and particularly Raff; he even taught at the conservatory in Darmstadt before returning to the United States. In 1896 he became Professor of Music at Columbia University, a post he resigned in 1904 in a dispute with the university's president. His lectures in music and music history reveal the extent of his belief in and commitment to German Romanticism. In them he described music as "a kind of soul language," "a language of the intangible," and declared "music is not art but psychological utterance."[16]

His piano music, as was typical of German composers of such music at the time, consists mostly of character pieces. As usual, the titles, given in German in the earlier pieces, indicate the inspiration and/or expressive character (dates are of publication): *Forgotten Fairy Tales* (4, op. 4, 1897) and *Fancies* (6, op. 7, 1898), published under the pseudonym of Edgar Thorn (or Thorne); *Fantasiestücke* (Fantastic Pieces, 2, op. 17, 1884); *Wald-Idyllen* (Forest Idylls, 4, op. 19, 1884); *Idylls after Goethe* (6, op. 28, 1887); *Poems after Heine* (6, op. 31, 1887); *Little Poems* (4, op. 32, 1894); *Les Orientals* (3, op. 37, 1889); *Marionettes* (6, op. 38, 1888); the familiar *Woodland Sketches* (10, op. 51, 1896), which contains his two best-known pieces, "To a Wild Rose" and "To a Water Lily"); *Sea Pieces* (8, op. 55, 1898); *Fireside Tales* (6, op. 61, 1902); and *New England Idylls* (10, op. 62, 1902). In the same vein are two sets for piano duet, *Poesien* (op. 20, 1886) and *Mondbilder* (Moon Pictures, 5, op. 21, 1886). Along with these are other sets called simply Pieces or Compositions. He also composed pieces of the etude type, some of them making virtuosic demands: *Étude de concert* (op. 36, 1889), Etudes (12, op. 39, 1890), and *Virtuoso Studies* (12, op. 46, 1894).

In the character pieces with titles, literary associations are important, as indeed would have been the case in the work of a German composer. MacDowell refers to Goethe, Heine, Hugo, Hans Christian Andersen, Shelley, and Tennyson (the latter in op. 32), and some Americana, Bre'r Rabbit (op. 51 and 61). An element common in musical nationalism also appears: the occasional use of Indian and black melodies, the former particularly in the *New England Idylls*. As was usual, in his character pieces MacDowell emphasized simple three-part form, along with its extension to five parts. He himself distinguished three varieties among his character pieces: "quaint," the quiet lyrical ones; "frisky," the lively, spirited pieces; and "dramatic," for the bigger pieces involving contrast of affect. In general, MacDowell's character pieces resemble the *Lyriske Stykker* of Grieg, whose work he admired.

MacDowell also took up the composition of piano sonatas, producing in all four works each of which bears a descriptive title (dates are of publication).

MACDOWELL'S PIANO SONATAS

Sonata tragica, G minor (op. 45, 1893)
Sonata eroica, G minor (op. 50, 1895)
Norse Sonata, D minor (op. 57, 1900)
Keltic Sonata, E minor (op. 59, 1901)

Here we again meet with literary associations. The first commemorates the passing of MacDowell's teacher, Raff; its last movement is a lamentation, since the program of the work as a whole, in MacDowell's words, was intended "to heighten the darkness of tragedy by making it fall closely on the heels of triumph." The *Sonata eroica*, related to the King Arthur legends, is similar: its four movements represent in turn the coming of Arthur, a knight surrounded by elves (Scherzo), Guinevere (the slow movement), and the passing of Arthur. The two remaining sonatas are involved with epic poetry generally, based as they are on poetic fragments by MacDowell himself. The Norse Sonata, in three movements, is prefixed by a motto that describes the recounting around the campfire at night of tales of heroic battles fought and won in bygone times, while the Keltic Sonata is connected with the chronicle of the Gaels, the cycle of the Red Branch, and the characters Deidre, Nassi, and Culchulling. MacDowell wrote that this work is a "bardic rhapsody on the subject," stating further that even if one was not familiar with the literary background, "one will easily perceive that something extremely unpleasant is happening." This sort of program he had encountered in the symphonies of his teacher, Raff, while the northern inspiration once again echoes Grieg. While these large and difficult works employ forms traditionally associated with the genre, MacDowell also makes use of cyclic form, bringing all the themes of the previous movements of a sonata together in the finale. This association of the virtuoso with the literary and the use of cyclic form testify to the influence of Liszt.[17]

Other works of MacDowell stand midway between the sets of character pieces and the sonatas. Important here are the two *Modern Suites* (op. 10 and 14, both 1883), whereby the qualification "modern" refers to the absence of the old dances traditional to the suite; while preludes and fugal movements are present, the others are simply character pieces. Here MacDowell followed the example set by Hiller and Bargiel. The neobaroque element appears elsewhere in MacDowell: there is the Prelude and Fugue (op. 13, 1883) and a later set, *Kleine Stücke nach Skizzen von J. S. Bach* (Little Pieces on Sketches by J. S. Bach, 1890).

We can regard MacDowell not only as the leading American composer of the time but also as representative of the situation of the American composer. The European traditions in which he was trained dominate his work. Not until the twentieth century did composers of art music in the United States develop their own idioms, forms, and procedures in music.

Yet a new kind of music developed in the United States around 1890 out of a different tradition—ragtime. While we do not ordinarily regard ragtime as belonging to the repertory of art or classical music, it nonetheless shares some important features with that kind of music: it was composed rather than improvised, proved itself capable of moving from the saloon to the salon, and was circulated as printed scores (later paper rolls for player pianos).

Ragtime emerged from the acculturation of the repertory of the black slaves—in which rhythm and particularly syncopation was pre-eminent—

with the repertory of the whites which was composed according to European traditions. The specific antecedents of ragtime seem to have been marches, but we can also adduce dances, particularly the cakewalk (a promenade from minstrel shows), and coon songs (songs by whites the texts of which in a stereotypical way imitate the speech of blacks). The name *rag* itself seems to have referred to the syncopated rhythms featured in this music, but other derivations have been suggested, among them the suburb of St. Louis called Shake Raggers and the ragged clothing stereotypically associated at the time with black musicians.[18]

A typical ragtime piece consists of a number of sections, called strains, each usually sixteen bars long, each stated twice but often with some reprising of strains heard earlier. Some typical schemes are shown below. Such schemes are similar to those used in marches, as those of Sousa, whereby the third strain is often in a different key and labeled trio, which helps establish the relationship with the march. Moreover, the tempo marking at the beginning frequently contains a reference to march time. In a typical ragtime piece the left hand keeps the time or beat, analogous to the drums and bass instruments in a marching band and also to the African master drummer, while the right hand provides the syncopation, featuring the so-called hot rhythm,

or some variant (see Ex. 6-3).

While we have noted isolated examples of music by whites which took over rhythmic features of black music—notably in Heinrich and Gottschalk—

Example 6-3. JOPLIN: "The Entertainer"—Introduction and Beginning of First Strain (mm. 1–8)

ragtime presents us with a large and coherent repertory. Although the first published rag was by a white—"The Mississippi Rag" by William H. Krell (published 1897)—the most important musicians associated with ragtime were blacks who lived and worked in the South and Midwest: Scott Joplin (1868–1917), Thomas Turpin (1873–1922), and James Scott (1886–1938), as well as another white, Joseph Lamb (1877–1960). Turpin, who operated a saloon, was the first black to publish a rag, "The Harlem Rag" (1897), but it was Joplin who became the leading exponent of ragtime, beginning with his classic, "The Maple Leaf Rag" (1899). We can find in his rags a number of variants to the basic scheme indicated above, among them:

AA BB A CC DD	"The Maple Leaf Rag" (1899)
	"The Figleaf Rag" (1908, strains of 32 bars)
IN AA BB A CC DD	"The Entertainer" (1902)
IN AA BB CC DD EE FF	"The Rag Time Dance"(1906)
IN AA BB A CC A CD	"Euphonic Sounds" (1909)
IN AA BB CC DD AA	"The Magnetic Rag" (1914)

NOTE: In this chart, IN = introduction; CD = coda; dates refer to publication.

Within schemes of this sort Joplin achieved great variety, incorporating unusual harmonic and rhythmic configurations, the stride bass in the left hand, strains in the minor ("Euphonic Sounds" and "The Magnetic Rag"), riffs, stop-time, and short "solo" breaks, many of which became commonplace in jazz. Joplin also produced pieces that are not strictly rags: "Bethena" (1905), a waltz, and "Solace" (1909), with Latin American rhythms, may serve as examples.

Among rags by other composers are Scott's "Frog Legs Rag" (1906) and "Ragtime Oriole" (1911) and Lamb's well-known "Sensation Rag" (1908), "Champagne Rag" (1910), in which thematic material is shared among consecutive strains, and "The Ragtime Nightingale" (1915). This last not only contains strains that work with material used earlier, but also has passages that seem less like ragtime and more like a typical character piece of the time.[19]

While ragtime lost popularity around the time of World War I—but not before influencing such composers as Debussy, Stravinsky, Milhaud, Copland, and others (see below)—it experienced a renaissance in the 1970s which in turn led such composer-pianists as William Bolcom, William Albright (for both, see Chapter Nine), Max Morath (1926–), and others to compose new pieces in the style.

LATIN AMERICA

Art music in the western European tradition took hold first in Mexico, Cuba, Brazil, and Argentina, but influences from the indigenous musical cultures of these countries made themselves evident as early as the 1840s: *musica criolla* generally, the *mestizo* music of Mexico, and the *gauchesco* music of

Argentina, along with the rhythms of the most characteristic dances, the habañera, the samba, and the tango.[20] Among the more prominent composers, most of whom were themselves pianists, were Julio Ituarte (1845–1905) and Riccardo Castro (1864–1907) of Mexico; Nicolas Ruiz Espadero (1832–1890) and Ignacio Cervantes (1847–1905) of Cuba, the latter a friend of Gottschalk; Alexander Levy (1864–1892) of Brazil, who emphasized the tango; and Alberto Williams (1862–1952) of Argentina. Teresa Carreño (1853–1917) of Venezuela, a noted pianist who was married to the famous German pianist,

An elaborate art-case Steinway grand piano, late 1890s to early 1900s.
Courtesy Steinway & Sons.

Eugen d'Albert (1864–1932)—himself a composer and editor—composed character pieces. As we will see, the amount of musical composition in Latin America increases significantly in the twentieth century.

NOTES FOR CHAPTER SIX

1. WWV numbers from J. Deathridge et al., *Wagner Werk-Verzeichnis* (Mainz: Schott, 1986).

2. See, generally, G. Puchelt, *Verlorene Klänge: Studien zur deutschen Klaviermusik 1830–1880* (Berlin-Lichterfelde: Lienau, 1969).

3. W. Irmen, *Thematisches Verzeichnis der musikalischen Werke Gabriel Josef Rheinbergers*, Studien zur Musikgeschichte des 19. Jahrhunderts 37 (Regensburg: Bosse, 1974).

4. F. Stein, *Thematisches Verzeichnis der im Druck erschienenen Kompositionen von Max Reger* (Leipzig: Breitkopf & Härtel, 1953). More recent is W. Grim, *Max Reger: A Bio-Bibliography*, Bio-Bibliographies in Music 7 (New York: Greenwood, 1988), 11–43.

5. J.-M. Nectoux, *Gabriel Urbaine Fauré: A Musical Life*, trans. R. Nichols (Cambridge: Cambridge University Press, 1991) offers a "Chronological Catalogue," pp. 525–558, which we follow here.

6. FWV numbers assigned by W. Mohr, *Caesar Franck*, 2nd ed. (Tutzing: Schneider, 1969), 220–232 (piano music).

7. V. d'Indy, *César Franck*, trans. R. Newmarch (London: Lane, 1909), 119.

8. DTK numbers assigned in J. Burghauser, *Antonín Dvořák: Thematicky Katalog* (Prague: Artia, 1960).

9. In *The Musorgsky Reader*, ed. and trans. J. Leyda and S. Bertensson (New York: Norton, 1947), 416–420; see also M. Calvocoressi, *Modest Musorgsky* (Fair Lawn, NJ: Essential Books, 1956), 2–5 (the sketch) and 84–95 (interpretation).

10. See A. Frankenstein, "Victor Hartmann and Modeste Mussorgsky," *Musical Quarterly* 25 (1939): 268–291; Frankenstein includes many reproductions of Hartmann's work.

11. L. Hübsch, *Modest Mussorgskij: Bilder einer Ausstellung*, Meisterwerke der Musik 15 (Munich: Fink, 1978), 36–39.

12. Dates according to *Systematisches Verzeichnis der Werke von Pjotr Iljitsch Tschaikowsky* (Hamburg: Sikorski, 1973), 77–86.

13. See D. Fog, *N. W. Gade-Katalog* (Copenhagen: Fog, 1986).

14. Modern ed. by J. Behrend (New York: Knopf, 1964; New York: Da Capo, 1975).

15. See J. Doyle, *Louis Moreau Gottschalk: A Bibliographical Study and Catalog of Works*, Bibliographies in Music 7 (Detroit: Information Coordinators, 1982). Dates are of composition unless otherwise indicated. His compositions, many of them published in Europe, often appeared under different opus numbers.

16. Quotations from E. MacDowell, "Origin of Song Vs. Origin of Instrumental Music," *Critical and Historical Essays*, ed. W. Baltzell (Boston: Schmidt, 1912), 28, and L. Gilman, *Edward MacDowell: A Study* (New York: Lane, 1909; New York: Da Capo, 1969), 82.

17. See D. Pesce, "MacDowell's 'Eroica Sonata' and its Lisztian Legacy," *Musical Quarterly* 49 (1988): 169–189.

18. E. Berlin, *Ragtime: A Musical and Cultural History* (Berkeley: University of California Press, 1980), 99–122 and 26–29, respectively.

19. See F. Tirro, *Jazz: A History* (New York: Norton, 1977), 97.

20. See generally G. Behágue, *Music in Latin America* (Englewood Cliffs: Prentice-Hall, 1979).

CHAPTER SEVEN

The Twentieth Century to Midcentury: France and Germany

A reaction against Germanic Romantic music provided a basic driving force in the early twentieth century, but this reaction took different forms in different places. In some cases the Germanic tradition was rejected by those who sought to produce something as different as possible, while in others elements from this tradition were taken and worked into something radically different.

Beyond this general principle, however, we find no central tendency governing the history of music in the twentieth century. Elements and trends in nineteenth-century music informed much that took place in the first half of the twentieth: the development of national musical styles and the undercurrent of interest in Baroque music that ran all through the nineteenth century, especially, as we have seen, in France. Singly and in combination these play an important part in twentieth-century music. Yet there still remained the comprehensive Germanic Romantic tradition in which a large number of composers continued to work, sometimes introducing modifications and new interpretations and sometimes not.

FRANCE

Relations between French and German music have long been problematical. In the nineteenth century, French elements were incorporated into German music, as the works of Berlioz and Meyerbeer, among others, testify. On the other hand, the music dramas of Wagner made a profound impression on French intellectual life, not only on musicians but also on writers, especially the Symbolist poets (Baudelaire, Mallarmé, Verlaine, and Rimbaud). Yet it was also in France that the first consequent reaction against the Germanic Romantic tradition of music took place. This reaction took its point of departure from impressionist painting, the aim of which was to portray the transient, shifting, and ephemeral aspects of reality, and in which the emphasis went not to clarity of design but to color, especially the use of light, shading, and texture; the painters involved include Monet, Manet, and Seurat. In music the central figure was Claude Debussy; along with him, somewhat later and with somewhat different objectives, went Maurice Ravel; another contemporary, involved in still a different way, was Erik Satie. In the work of these three we find much that became characteristic of music in the first half of the twentieth century.

Claude Debussy (1862–1918) led an outwardly uneventful life devoted to music, primarily in and around Paris except for a few years in Italy (he received the Prix de Rome) and a short stay in Russia. He led a retiring life as composer and critic, making few public appearances.

Piano music occupies a prominent position in his work as a composer, this in sharp contrast to the lesser role accorded it in the works of late nineteenth-century German composers. The old large forms, however—the sonata and variations—are absent; the emphasis is on the character piece.

DEBUSSY'S PRINCIPAL WORKS FOR PIANO

Arabesques (2, L. 61,[1] composed 1888–1891, published 1891):
    E major and G major
Suite bergamasque (4, L. 75, composed 1890–1905, published
    1905): Prélude; Menuet; "Clair de lune"; Passepied
Pour le piano (3, L. 95, composed 1894–1901, published 1901
    [Sarabande separately published 1896]): Prélude; Sarabande;
    Toccate
D'un cahier d'esquisses (From a Sketchbook, L. 99, composed
    1903, published 1904)
[Les] estampes (3, L. 100, composed and published 1903):
    "Pagodes"; "Soirée dans Grenade"; "Jardins sous la pluie"
Masques (L. 105, composed and published 1904)
L'isle joyeuse (L. 106, composed and published 1904)
Images
    Set I (3, L. 110, composed 1904–1905,[2] published 1905):
        "Reflets dans l'eau"; "Hommage à Rameau"; Mouvement
    Set II (3, L. 111, composed 1907, published 1908): "Cloches à
        travers les feuilles"; "Et la lune descend sur le temple qui
        fut"; "Poissons d'or"
Children's Corner (6, L. 113, composed 1906–1908, published
    1908): "Doctor Gradus ad Parnassum"; "Jimbo's Lullaby";
    "Serenade for the Doll"; "The Snow is Dancing"; "The Little
    Shepherd"; "Golliwog's Cakewalk"

Préludes
> Book I (12, L. 117, composed 1909–1910, published 1910):
> "Danseuses de Delphes"; "Voiles"; "Le vent dans la
> plaine"; "Les sons et les parfums tournent dans l'air du
> soir"; "Les collines d'Anacapri"; "Des pas sur la neige ";
> "Ce qu'a vu le vent d'Ouest"; "La fille aux cheveux de
> lin"; "La sérénade interrompue"; "La cathédrale engloutie";
> "La danse de Puck"; "Minstrels"
>
> Book II (12, L. 123, composed 1910–1912, published 1913):
> "Brouillards"; "Feuilles mortes") "La Puerta del Vino"; "Les
> fées sont d'exquises danseuses"; "Bruyères"; "Général
> Lavine—Eccentric"; "La terrasse des audiences au clair
> de lune"); "Ondine"; "Hommage à S. Pickwick, Esq.,
> P.P.M.P.C."; "Canope"; "Tierces alternées"; "Feux d'artifice"

Études (12, L. 136, composed 1915, published 1916)
> Set I "Pour les cinq doigts d'après M. Czerny"; "Pour les
> tierces"; "Pour les quartes"; "Pour les sixtes"; "Pour les
> octaves"; "Pour les huit doigts"
>
> Set II "Pour des degrés chromatiques"; "Pour les agréments";
> "Pour les notes répétées"; "Pour les sonorités opposées";
> "Pour les arpèges composés"; "Pour les accords"

Among the early piano pieces not shown above are a Mazurka (L. 67), a Rêverie (L. 68, both 1890), and several dances tinged somewhat with traits from Bohemia and Russia (L. 60 and 70), none of which provide much that arouses attention. Then come two sets in which Debussy clearly revealed the direction he was to follow: the *Suite bergamasque* and the set *Pour le piano*. Here we see a revival of the eighteenth-century suite, as the minuet and passepied make evident; and Debussy clearly has cast the prelude along traditional lines. The novelty comes with the slow movement, "Clair de lune" in D-flat major, his most popular piano piece—it is also the first true example of impressionist piano music. Debussy revealed his new world of sound in this new kind of nocturne: the blurring effect of the pedals, triads with added sixths, portato, the rather undefined melody with its loosely sequential meandering phrases. The title itself lies in the impressionist tradition. Two other pieces once planned for the *Suite bergamasque* were published separately: *Masques* and *L'isle joyeuse*.

In *Pour le piano* we find both the new harmonies and the neoclassical orientation, the latter evident from the genre, form, and style. All three pieces (Prelude, Sarabande, and Toccata) in fact hark back to the eighteenth century: the Prelude operates entirely with figuration but uses the whole-tone scale, the Toccata is similar but more of a virtuoso piece, and the Sarabande, which had been composed three years earlier, observes the rhythmic pattern of the dance and the old rounded binary form but emphasizes the new harmonies, especially parallel seventh-chords (parallel chords being known as planing, see Ex. 7-1). Debussy deliberately avoided, not to say circumvented, the highly charged emotional aura of the Germanic Romantic tradition in the late nineteenth century by seeking models and emotional temperature from the eighteenth century and by using harmonies that weakened the conventional props of the usual system of tonal harmonies. He thus created an art that was refined, delicate, and, at times, aloof. This spirit became prominent in twentieth-century music.

The next few piano works by Debussy are more impressionist and less neoclassic; the visual inspiration, related to impressionist painting, comes to the foreground, as indeed he suggested by his titles. Involved are *D'un cahier d'esquisses*, the set *Estampes*, and two sets of *Images*. The three pieces of *Estampes* are characteristic. The first, "Pagodes," inspired by the Balinese gamelan (gong-orchestra) that Debussy heard at the Paris International Exposition (1899), features the pentatonic scale and parallel chords using seconds and fourths which combine to create an effect of oriental exoticism. The second, "Soirée dans Grenade" (Evening in Granada), takes its inspiration from Spanish music; a nocturne that uses the characteristic *habañera* rhythm, it features contrasting sections that follow one another with but little mediation and abounds in coloristic effects, as exemplified by the use of the pedals with octaves high in the treble, *pianissimo*, and at one point imitates the guitar. The final piece in the set, "Jardins sous la pluie" (Gardens in the Rain), involves another subject dear to the impressionist painters: along with the "watery" figuration, which owes something to Liszt, and along with the new harmonies, Debussy has introduced two French nursery songs, "Do-do l'enfant do" and "Nous n'irons plus au bois."

Much the same holds for *Images*. "Reflets dans l'eau" (Reflections in the Water, Set I i), another "watery" piece, features arpeggios; bell-like effects are evident in "Cloches à travers les feuilles" (Bells through the Leaves, Set II i), with coloristic use of dissonance; "Et la lune descend sur le temple qui fut" (And the Moon Descends Over the Temple from the Past, Set II ii) is another nocturne; then there is the more virtuoso, etude-like, "Mouvement" (Set I iii), a moto perpetuo piece, and "Poissons d'or" (Goldfish, Set II iii), another oriental inspiration, capricious and somewhat discontinuous. The neoclassical element returns in "Hommage à Rameau" (Set I ii), actually a sarabande, essentially diatonic.

Two larger pieces, *Masques* and *L'isle joyeuse*, Debussy had originally planned for the *Suite bergamasque*, as we have already mentioned. The former is related to the Italian *commedia dell'arte* and the latter to a painting of Watteau (*Embarquement pour Cythère*); both are large virtuoso pieces that represent a rapprochement between the overtly impressive Germanic manner and Debussy's more characteristic reticence.

Roughly contemporary with these is the suite *Children's Corner* (all titles here originally in English), composed for the entertainment of Debussy's daughter, but, like certain pieces by Schumann and others, intended for large

Example 7-1. DEBUSSY: *Pour le Piano* (L. 95)—Excerpts
    A. Sarabande—Beginning (mm. 1–8)
    B. Toccate—Beginning (mm. 1–8)

as well as small children. Humor, a quality uncommon in European fine-art music, is prominent, first in the etude-like "Dr. Gradus ad Parnassum," in which the Clementi kind of scale exercise is interrupted by impressionistic episodes, and in "The Golliwog's Cakewalk," the popular concluding number of the suite, which draws its material from American minstrel show music. It has a riff-like figure in the accompaniment, syncopations typical of ragtime, and here and there a touch of the blues (see Ex. 7-2); toward the end comes a reference to Wagner's *Tristan und Isolde,* marked *with great emotion.* In between these numbers come "Jimbo's Lullaby," for a toy elephant (Debussy may have intended "Jumbo"); "Serenade for the Doll," capricious with rapid figuration and quartal harmony; "The Snow is Dancing"; and the lyrical "The Little Shepherd" with its cantabile line in which the augmented second is important, over a simple harmonic accompaniment.

Apart from a few isolated and relatively insignificant pieces, the remainder of Debussy's piano music is found in the two sets of Preludes, twelve in each, and the two sets of Etudes, six in each. While the preludes are essentially character pieces not principally different from his others, the etudes are concerned more with technical problems and less with the expression of affects. We recall that both genres were important in Chopin.

In the Preludes Debussy was at some pains to put the characteristic titles at the end of each piece rather than as captions at the beginning, perhaps in an effort to include them in the aura of ambiguity and ephemerality. In any case, these pieces provide a cross section, if not summation, of Debussy's pianistic art. There is the impressionistic nocturne, with parallel chords and pedal effects, in "Les sons et parfums tournent dans l'air du soir" (Sounds and Perfumes Turn in the Evening Air, Book I), a line from Baudelaire's *Harmonies du soir,* and, in "La terasse des audiences au clair de lune" (Reception

Example 7-2. Debussy: "Golliwog's Cakewalk" from *Childrens' Corner* (L. 113, vi)—Excerpt (mm. 10–17)

in the Moonlight, Book II), a scene from India. Then there are aural images of winter, "Des pas sur la neige" (Footsteps in the Snow, Book I); autumn, "Feuilles mortes" (Dead Leaves, Book II); and fog, "Brouillards" (Book II). Two pieces associated with water appear, "Voiles" (Sails, possibly Veils, Book I) and "Ondine," (Book II). Light filigrees of arpeggiation with a touch of the capricious characterize "La danse de Puck" (Book II) and "Les fées sont d'exquises danseuses" (Fairies Are Most Exquisite Dancers, Book II). Then we have the bigger and more impressive pieces that require virtuosity. From Book I there is "Le vent dans la plaine" (The Wind in the Plain) and the tumultuous "Ce qu'a vu le vent d'ouest" (What the West Wind Saw) with its striking dissonances; from Book II there is "Les tierces alternées" (Thirds in Alternation) and "Feux d'artifice" (Fireworks), which quotes "La Marseillaise" near its end; another large piece is "La cathedrale engloutie" (The Engulfed Cathedral, Book I), an impression of the legendary cathedral of Ys rising from the depths of the sea, which uses blurred ascending fourth-chords and later parallel full chords that produce a clangorous bell-like effect. Debussy has also exploited national musical idioms in the Preludes: we find Spanish elements in "La sérénade interrompue" (The Interrupted Serenade, Book I) and "La puerta del Vino" (The Gate of Wine, Book II), the latter complete with the *habañera* rhythm and even a lyrical *copla*; Scottish traits in "La fille aux cheveux de lin" (The Maid with the Flaxen Hair, Book I), with its pentatonic melody, and "Bruyères" (Heaths, Book II); Afro-American music in "Minstrels" (Book I); and an Italian tarantella in "Les collines d'Anacapri" (Book I). Debussy included two grave ceremonial dances of antique inspiration, perhaps indebted to Satie (see below): "Danseuses de Delphes" (Delphic Dancers, Book I) and "Canope" (Book II). Finally, we can identify two humorous pieces in Book II: "Général Lavine—eccentric," the awkward clown of the *Folies-Bergères*, portrayed via a discontinuous dance, "Hommage à S. Pickwick, P.P.M.P.C.," a depiction of Dickens' character replete with the impressive appearance of the British national anthem; to these we might add "Minstrels," associated in part with American minstrel show music.

The etudes eschew the expressive and impressionist and deal directly with technical problems. The first of them, "Pour les cinq doigts d'après Monsieur Czerny" (For the Five Fingers According to Mr. Czerny), clearly is a burlesque of the famous man's style of etude and, like the earlier "Dr. Gradus ad Parnassum," is humorous. The first set continues with a lyrical study in thirds and fourths; a Chopinesque exercise in sixths (resembling somewhat the midsection of Chopin's famous Etude in E major [op. 10 iii]); a waltz-like octave study; and an unusual etude, "Pour les huit doigts," featuring rapid scale patterns to be played without using the thumbs. In the second set we find a fast exercise with chromatic scales in thirds; a barcarolle-like piece with a cantabile line embellished with unusual ornaments ("Pour les agréments"); a virtuoso study in repeated notes that has some similarity to his earlier piece, *Masques*; a delicate study in arpeggios; and two pieces that exploit chordal passages and unusual sonorities, "Pour les sonorités opposées" and the concluding "Pour les accords."

While these compositions make up the bulk of Debussy's music for piano, there are two other sets, both composed at the same time as the second book of Preludes and the Etudes: the six *Epigraphes antiques* for piano duet (L. 131, composed 1914, published 1915) and the set of three pieces *En blanc et noir* for two pianos (L. 134, composed and published 1915). The first of these, originally planned to accompany poems by Debussy's friend Pierre Louÿs (his *Chansons de Bilitis*), are short, simple, and impressionistic. They include a rain picture ("Pour remercier la pluie au matin") that uses the whole-tone scale, parallel fifths, and arpeggios; an oriental piece with the augmented second prominent in its melodic line ("Pour L'Égyptienne"); the pentatonic lamentation ("Pour un tombeau sans nom"); and so forth. The other set, which Debussy originally planned to entitle *Caprices*, is both longer and more varied. Most interesting is the second, *Lent, sombre*, a solemn dirge with a military episode using fanfares and running bass figures, for which the models clearly were Chopin's famous Polonaise in A-flat major (op. 53) and Liszt's "Funérailles."

In the work of Debussy, then, we see a reaction against the German Romantic tradition. He asserted specifically French conceptions, as represented, first, by the association with impressionism, and, second, by seeking out the genres and spirit of eighteenth-century French harpsichord music. But Debussy employed other sources as well: the idiom of Spanish dances, the sounds of oriental music, and Afro-American music. He also displayed something of the experimental, antitraditional attitude of the Russian nationalist composers, Mussorgsky in particular. The ways in which all this reveals itself are many and varied: he used new and different scales, avoided the old traditional functional harmonies, devising new combinations (such as fourth-chords, triads with the added sixth, and parallel chords) to take their place. Perhaps most important, he rejected the arch-Romantic notion of the musical artwork as embodying intense passionate and subjective expression; instead he made his compositions more objective, detached, and less personal, thus setting an example for composers to come.

Associated with Debussy was Maurice Ravel (1875–1937), born in the south of France not far from the Spanish border, but trained in Paris where he spent most of his life. Like Debussy he was a pianist, but unlike him was a virtuoso performer who gave concerts and went on tours. Like Debussy he composed many important pieces for the instrument; but he ceased composing for solo piano in 1918, returning to the instrument only late in his career with two concertos, one for the left hand alone.

RAVEL'S PRINCIPAL WORKS FOR PIANO[3]

"Pavane pour une Infante défunte" (composed and published
   1899)
"Jeux d'eau" (composed and published 1901)
Sonatina, F-sharp minor (composed and published 1905)
Miroirs (5, composed 1905, published 1906): "Noctuelles";
   "Oiseaux tristes"; "Une barque sur l'océan"; "Alborada del
   gracioso"; "La vallée des cloches"
Gaspard de la nuit (3, composed and published 1908): "Ondine";
   "Le gibet"; "Scarbo"
"Menuet sur le nom de Haydn" (composed and published 1909)
Valses nobles et sentimentales (8, composed and published 1911)
Le tombeau de Couperin (6, composed 1914–1917, published
   1917): Prélude; Fugue; Forlane; Rigaudon; Menuet; Toccate

Ravel's piano music can be divided into two large groups, one impressionist, the other neoclassical, with the latter playing a larger role than it did in Debussy. It makes itself evident in the early unpublished "Sérénade grotesque" (1893), the Minuet antique (1895), and, particularly, in the famous "Pavane pour une Infante défunte" (1899). Then comes his first striking venture into impressionism, "Jeux d'eau" (Play of the Waters, composed 1901), which takes its place beside the "water" pieces of Debussy and his predecessors (see above). "Jeux d'eau" displays many features characteristic of musical impressionism: the coloristic use of dissonance, here arpeggio figurations involving simultaneous seconds along with unresolved sevenths; the loose linking of episodic passages; the use of glissandos and chromatic scale-runs; and irregularities in rhythm that disturb normal metrical order. This piece gained immediate acceptance and placed Ravel in the forefront of progressive composers of the time.

The other impressionist works of Ravel for solo piano are contained in two sets, *Miroirs* and *Gaspard de la nuit*. The *Miroirs* are on the whole similar to Debussy's *Estampes, Images*, and his later Preludes. This is most evident from the presence of the quiet mood piece abounding in unusual sonorities—chords and pedal effects—as in the vague and chromatic "Noctuelles" (Night Moths); the slow, fragmentary phrases interspersed with sudden outbursts of figuration in "Oiseaux tristes" (Sad Birds); or the lugubrious melody accompanied by bell-like chords in "La vallée des cloches" (Valley of the Bells), which may be compared with Debussy's "Cloches à travers les feuilles," from *Images*, Book II. On the other hand, there is the virtuoso etude-like "Une barque sur l'océan" (A Boat on the Ocean), which features rapid arpeggiated figuration despite the slow basic tempo, as well as a Spanish piece, "Alborada del gracioso," complete with the *seguidilla* rhythm, a lyrical refrain (the *copla*), and unexpected comic interruptions. Again we can compare this piece with Debussy's "La sérénade interrompue" from the Preludes, Book I, which, however, was composed later; thus the influence seemingly went in both directions.

While the pieces in *Miroirs* have many similarities to Debussy, the three of *Gaspard de la nuit*, although essentially impressionistic, are much larger and more difficult than what is found in Debussy, perhaps excepting *Masques* and *L'isle joyeuse*. The subject matter comes from Louis Bertrand (1807–1842), a French Romantic poet whose work emphasizes the supernatural. The first of the three pieces is "Ondine," depicting a Lorelei-like figure who lures young men to death by drowning; in it typically impressionist"water" figuration goes along with an enticing and innocent-sounding diatonic cantabile line (Debussy's version of Ondine is in his Preludes, Book II). Then comes the mournful "Le gibet" (The Gallows), in which a slow melody, sometimes stated in parallel chords, is accompanied by an ostinato bell-like figure that tolls throughout, a pedal-point being maintained all the way through as well. "Scarbo," the last piece, portrays a dwarf, an evil figure from the underworld; it is a virtuoso display piece, highly rhythmical, using short staccato motives and much figuration.

Turning to the neoclassical works, the first is "Pavane pour une Infante défunte" (1899), which has already been mentioned. It is a stately dance in a rondo-like arrangement that uses elements of Debussy's new harmonic style—parallel chords instead of the normal tonal harmonic progressions and coloristic use of unresolved dissonances. This is the first piece in which Ravel reveals his true nature. His second neoclassic venture is the Sonatina in F-sharp minor (1905)—note that in his piano music Debussy turned away from the traditional large forms—a piece based on the little or easy sonata of the eighteenth century. Ravel has cast it in the three-movement plan in the usual sequence, with sonata form in the outside movements and a minuet as the slow movement. The thematic material is primarily lyrical, with melodies consisting of balanced phrases unfolding over an accompaniment derived from eighteenth-century models but using the new harmonies. In the finale the melodic line involves irregular but clearly articulated phrases which are accompanied by rapid figuration.

Ravel's principal neoclassical work, however, is his last composition for solo piano, *Le tombeau de Couperin* (1917). Originally planned as a *suite française*, its succession of movements clearly associates it with the French harpsichord suite of the eighteenth century: Prelude, Fugue, Forlana, Rigaudon, Minuet (with a Musette as trio), and Toccata. Beyond a certain similarity in harmonic idiom, the piece shows little kinship with impressionism; the individual movements reflect the basic features of their eighteenth-century counterparts. The prelude and the concluding toccata emphasize figuration, the former in its lilting 6/8 meter and mordents, while the latter, larger and more difficult, with rapidly repeated notes and some use of the pentatonic scale. The lyrical fugue is quite correct, the tonally ambiguous impressionist harmonies tending to obscure the movement of the individual lines. The forlana is also lyrical, in dotted 6/8 and with leaps in the melody and a modal flavor in the harmonies. The rigaudon, in vigorous duple time, is bright and diatonic in its main section, but chromatic in the midsection. The minuet, however, is slow and lyrical, making use of a pedal-point and modal effects, with parallel chords in the musette. Here, then, we find less of the impressionist vagueness and suggestiveness of mood, on the one hand, and more of the virtuoso demands of *Gaspard de la nuit*, on the other.

Ravel composed a number of other pieces for piano. There are the distinctly lesser works, among them the neoclassical minuet commemorating the centenary of Haydn's death; two pieces in the style of Borodin and Chabrier (composed 1913, published 1914); and the *Valses nobles et sentimentales* (8, 1911), in which Ravel has given the Viennese waltz an impressionist twist. The inspiration here, as Ravel acknowledged, goes back to Schubert, although there are also suggestions of Schumann, Brahms, and, especially, Chopin. There are seven waltzes and an impressionist epilogue in which the themes of the previous waltzes are heard again. Ravel later made two arrangements of the set, one for two pianos, the other for orchestra, the latter used for the ballet *Adélaïde*. His only other piece for two pianos is the early *Les sites auriculaires* (composed 1895), which contains the symptomatic "Habañera" (published 1895)—his first effort in the Spanish idiom—and "Entre cloches" (unpublished). In addition he made arrangements of his two most popular orchestra works, *La valse* and Bolero, for two pianos (1921 and 1922 respectively). For piano duet he composed *Ma mère l'Oye* (Mother Goose, 1908), later orchestrated for use as a ballet, which displays both neoclassical and impressionist elements, along with oriental effects, and a single piece, "Frontispiece" (1918).

We have seen that the neoclassical attitude was important in the French reaction against the Germanic Romantic tradition: it meant that composers specifically ignored their immediate musical heritage and sought models and inspiration from an earlier historical period in which emotional and subjective expression was not central in the musical art work. We have noted this tendency in late nineteenth-century piano music and its importance for Debussy and particularly Ravel. We also encounter it, along with other elements, in the music of Erik Satie (1866–1925), a former café pianist and constant foe of Germanic Romantic music. Among his earliest piano music we find pieces that reveal his characteristic bent as a composer: Sarabandes (3, composed 1887, published 1911), *Gymnopédies* (3, composed 1888, published 1888 and 1895), and *Gnossiennes* (3, 1890, published 1913). There is a suggestion of Antiquity here—Satie in fact took his titles from ancient Greece—*Gymnopédie* from a festival and *Gnossienne* freely from Knossos, the city on Crete. In manner of composition, the three sets are similar. Satie presents a lyrical line, clear and unproblematic in its phrase structure and with many repetitions, over a spare chordal accompaniment of unusual harmonic progressions involving modal effects and unresolved dissonances (Ex. 7-3). The effect is of

Example 7-3. Satie: "Gymnopédie" No. 2—Beginning (mm. 1–12)

something grave and dignified, perhaps even liturgical, while at the same time being refined and aloof—all characteristic of the neoclassical orientation and all features that have become important in twentieth-century music. After all, Satie was the first, among the more important composers we have been considering here, to compose sarabandes. Perhaps most striking in comparison with Germanic Romantic music is the curious lack of direction that the pieces display: they seem static, they lack points of climax, they do not go anywhere, they simply *are*. The *Gnossiennes*, the most ornate of the three sets, have an oriental cast about them by virtue of the augmented seconds, florid ornamental phrases, and the free rhythm, since they lack bar lines and time signatures.

Subsequent works of Satie are similar, except that the element of satire, which had already appeared in the *Gnossiennes*, becomes more pronounced. It often—but not always—is restricted to the titles and markings. There are the three *Pièces froides* (Cold Pieces, composed 1897, published 1912) and his longest works for piano, the "three" *Morceaux en forme de poire* (Pieces in the Shape of a Pear, composed 1903, published 1911): Debussy had advised Satie to impose some definite form on his pieces and this was the answer; however, there are not three pieces, but seven. Except for the neoclassical *Prélude en tapisserie* (Prelude in Tapestry) and *Passacaille* (both 1906), Satie composed relatively little between 1897 and 1912. Thereafter come sets of humorous and satirical pieces; to name only some: *Préludes flasques* (Flabby Preludes, 1912), *Croquis et agaceries d'un gros bonhomme en bois* (Sketches and Provocations of a Big Wooden Man), and *Chapitres tournés en tous sens* (Chapters Turned in All Directions, all 1913); and *Heures séculaires et instantanées* (Moments Ancient and Instantaneous), *Valses distinguées d'un précieux dégoûté* (Distinguished Waltzes of a Disgusted Dandy), and *Sports et divertissements* (Sports and Diversions, all 1914). In these pieces we find such performance directions as the injunction to play softly "like a nightingale with a toothache," which is aimed at the serious and often equally explicit directions in German music of the time. Moreover here and there in these pieces Satie has parodied the styles of several celebrated composers: Chopin's Funeral March, which Satie identifies as "Mazurka by Schubert," in "Edriophthalma" of the *Embryons desséchés* (Dried-out Embryos, 1913); Mozart and Chabrier in *Croquis et agaceries*; and Gounod in *Vieux sequins et vieilles cuirasses* (Old Sequins and Breast Plates, 1914). The *Valses distinguées d'un precieux dégoûté* contain some bitonality. Among the twenty *Sports et divertissements* there is a satirical and dissonant treatment of a chorale-like melody, a slap at traditional instruction in part-writing, as well as an important element in large compositions of the Romantic tradition, both German and French, a movement that doubtless influenced Stravinsky's *L'histoire du soldat*. Satie's last work of any significance for piano is the set, Nocturnes (1919), in which he has restricted the satire to the titles and performance instructions, while the music resembles his other works except that the conception is larger and the writing, with its consistent use of conventional patterns of figuration, is more pianistic.

Satie was a catalyst; the effects of his work are clear in Debussy, Ravel, and others. We have seen the neoclassical orientation, particularly in his earlier work, as well as his satirical bent. All this clearly influenced Debussy, as can be witnessed in the latter's curious, serene pieces in the Preludes ("Danseuses de Delphes" and "Canopes") that suggest Antiquity, as well as in "Hommage à S. Pickwick, Esq., P.P.M.P.C.," also from the Preludes, and the "Golliwog's Cakewalk" from *Children's Corner*, among others. Ravel's "Pavane pour une Infante défunte" also seems indebted to Satie, for whose work Ravel expressed admiration.

Here, then, was the first breakthrough of a new kind of music, one that owed its inception largely to the desire to create something unlike the prevailing Germanic conceptions: either expression was replaced by suggestion and the dynamic and forthright by something veiled and aloof, or the whole traditional way was satirized. Eighteenth-century ideals were important. Otherwise, the means involved calling into question the whole system of tonal harmony. In this change, while Debussy seems to have been the most important, actual priority is difficult to establish.

The impressionist way took on central importance in French music and for modern music in general. In one way or another it dominated the outlook and work of many composers. Among the French were Gabriel Pierné (1863–1937), Charles Koechlin (1867–1950), Albert Roussel (1869–1937), Florent Schmitt (1870–1958), Déodat de Sévérac (1873–1921), Nadia Boulanger

(1887–1979), Robert Casadesus (1899–1972), and Jean Martinon (1910–1976), all of whom composed a good deal of piano music, mostly in the smaller forms. Pierné emphasized the neoclassical, especially in his Variations in C minor (op. 42, 1918). Koechlin was an ardent supporter of contemporary music who himself composed extensively in different styles, including even Schoenberg's dodecaphonic serialism (see below). Roussel's character pieces include the early set *Des heures passant* (Of Passing Hours, op. 1, 1898); the *Conte à la poupée* (Story for the Doll, 1904); *Rustiques* (op. 5, composed 1904–1906); and *L'accueil des muses* (The Gathering of the Muses, 1920), a tombeau for Debussy. In his later work, however, the neoclassical came to the fore, most impressively in the large Suite (op. 14, composed 1909–1910) in four movements (Prélude, Bourrée, Sicilienne, and Ronde); a Prelude and Fugue (op. 46, 1932–1934), which he entitled "Hommage à Bach"; and pieces (3, op. 49, 1933), the first of which is a toccata. Somewhat in this vein are the Sonatina (op. 16, 1912) and the *Petite canon perpetuel* (1913). In his piano music Schmitt dedicated himself to the character piece. Out of a great many are the two volumes of *Musiques intimes* (op. 16 and 29, composed 1890–1904), which betray both the Germanic tradition and impressionism; but *Ombres* (Shadows, 3, op. 64, composed 1913–1917) and *Mirages* (op. 70, 1920–1921) provide brilliant examples of impressionist coloring. He also composed two sets of preludes, the second (op. 5) entitled *Soirs*; and like Roussel he wrote a tombeau for Debussy (op. 70 i, 1920). He followed this with the set *Clavecin obtempérant* (Obedient Keyboard, 4, op. 107, 1945). For his part Sévérac worked almost wholly in the realm of the character piece, as his early *Le chant de la terre* (Song of the Earth, subtitled "Poème géorgique," 4, 1900), *En Languedoc* (5, 1904), or *La nymphe emué ou le faune indiscret* (The Excited Nymph or the Indiscreet Faun, 1909), with its obvious reference to Debussy, testify. Prominent in his work is the *étude pittoresque* (pictorial etude), related to the characteristic etude of the nineteenth century, notably his *Baigneuses au soleil* (Women Bathing in the Sun, 1908) and *Cerdaña* (5, 1910). Yet the large form is also represented: there is a Sonata in B-flat minor; and, for two pianos, a suite, *Le soldat de plomb* (The Lead Soldier, 1905). The last three were less well-known as composers: Boulanger, a distinguished teacher of composition, Casadesus, a famous pianist, and Martinon, a prominent conductor, all exemplified the neoclassic, but in contrast to the others Casadesus worked extensively with the large forms, especially the sonata.

Shortly after World War I in France there set in a strong reaction against the delicacy and refinement of impressionism. As for music, an important spokesman was Jean Cocteau (1889–1963), a poet, novelist, and dramatist who represented the avant-garde in the artistic world of the time. He was impressed by Satie, who he thought had dared to do the bravest thing: to be simple. Like Satie, Cocteau was opposed to the Germanic Romantic tradition. Music, for him, should be simple and clear, with melody as the central element; the composer should seek his inspiration not from the idealized and the romanticized, but from the world around him—from the music hall (and Satie had been a music hall pianist), the circus, popular songs, even jazz, and so on. While we can find some of this in Debussy and Ravel, here the new emphasis led to something different. The composers associated with Cocteau, whose works accorded with his ideals and were played together on the same concerts, were heralded in 1920 in a newspaper article by the critic Henri Collet as The Six, in obvious analogy to The Five of nineteenth-century Russia. An album of piano pieces then appeared, one piece by each member of the group, who were: Louis Durey (1888–1979), Arthur Honegger (1892–1955), Darius Milhaud (1892–1974), Germaine Tailleferre (1892–1983), Georges Auric (1899–1983), and Francis Poulenc (1899–1963). Just how much they had in common beyond their association with Cocteau and their own friendship has been disputed, with Milhaud, for one, disclaiming a common intent among the members of the group. Neither Durey nor Tailleferre continued to make reputations for themselves as composers, while Auric turned to the composition of film scores; the other three, however, emerged as important composers.

Perhaps most in accord with the ideals of Cocteau was Darius Milhaud, who lived in Paris and traveled extensively. In 1940 he came to the United States, where he taught at Mills College. After 1947 he also taught at the Paris Conservatory and elsewhere. While he composed a large amount of piano music in the large as well as small forms, it seems significant that he orchestrated many of these pieces, which suggests that his convictions concerning the piano as the proper medium for them were not strong. In any case, there is little of impressionism here. The forms are for the most part small, sharp, and clear; the textures simple; the melodies clearly phrased; the harmonies extremely dissonant, often polytonal; and the rhythmic element strong. In short, Milhaud's style can be regarded as a twentieth-century counterpart to the galant style of the eighteenth century, surely deliberate on his part and something that became an important category of twentieth-century music. Especially characteristic are his South American compositions (Spanish rhythms also appeared in Debussy and Ravel, among others). Among many are the two books of his *Saudades do Brasil* (12, op. 67, composed 1920–1921, published 1925), a souvenir of his sojourn in Brazil, which offer typical Latin dances in a dry polytonal idiom (see Ex. 7-4), and *Le printemps* (6 in two books, 1915–1920). The later *L'Automne* (3, op. 115, 1932) is a suite in recollection of a trip to Madrid. Then there is a set of pieces influenced by jazz: the *Rag-Caprices* (3, op. 78, 1922), which also exist in a version for small orchestra. Among other sets of character pieces are the *Romances sans paroles* (4, op. 129, 1933), the lively *Promenade (La tour de l'exposition)*, (composed 1933, revised 1937), the set *Une journée* (5, op. 269, composed 1946), the pieces of which represent various times of the day; *Jeu* (op. 302, composed 1950); and *Le candelabre à sept branches* (7, op. 315, composed 1951), corresponding to the seven principal religious festivals of the Jewish year.

With one exception Milhaud's works in the large forms appear early in his career, but they are not really large. There is a Suite (op. 8, composed 1913), a Sonata (op. 33, composed 1916), both neoclassical, as is the much

Example 7-4. MILHAUD: "Sumaré" from *Saudades do Brasil* (No. 9)—Beginning (mm. 1–9)
Copyright 1922 Éditions Max Eschig. Used by permission of the publisher. Sole representative U.S.A. Theodore Presser Company.

later second Sonata (op. 293, composed 1949), both demanding technically, and a Sonatina (op. 354, composed 1956). There is also the early unpublished set of variations on a theme by Cliquet (op. 23, composed 1915). Milhaud composed for two pianos, among others, the suite *Scaramouche* (op. 165b, composed 1937), which he later arranged for saxophone and orchestra, and the set *Kentuckiana* (20, op. 287, composed 1948), based on Kentucky folk songs, which he orchestrated on commission from the Louisville Orchestra. Finally, there is a set of pieces for four pianos, *Paris* (6, op. 284, composed 1948).

Arthur Honegger, a close friend of Milhaud, was a Swiss who studied in France where he spent most of his life, for some years teaching at the École normale de musique. Although associated with The Six, he was not really sympathetic to their aims as enunciated by Cocteau, retaining instead his disposition toward the Germanic Romantic tradition from which they were distancing themselves. However, while his music is more serious and expressive than theirs was apt to be, his harmonic idiom fully accords with theirs. The emphasis on large forms found in his work generally, however, is not reflected in his music for piano: there is only the early Toccata and Variations (S. 3,[4] 1916) and the *Prélude, arioso, et fughette sur le nom de Bach* (S. 72, 1932), which despite its title suggestive of Franck is a relatively short piece based on the B-A-C-H theme. His other pieces for piano are mostly short. Among others are a set of three (S. 17, 1915–1919); the *Pièces brèves* (7, S. 20,

1919–1920); the set of miniatures in *Le cahier romande* (The French-Swiss Notebook, 5, S. 43, 1921–1923); the pictorial *Scenic Railway* (S. 112, 1931), a small pianistic counterpart to his famous orchestral *Pacific 231*; *Esquisses* (2, S. 156, 1941) which employ a novel manner of notation; and *Souvenir de Chopin* (S. 161a, 1947). For two pianos he composed a Partita (S. 126, 1930).

The piano assumes more importance in the work of Poulenc, who remained more in the tradition of nineteenth-century piano music and gave prominence to the character piece, especially the elegant type associated with the salon, neglecting for the most part the larger forms. Among his character pieces the more conventional types are represented in his popular *Mouvements perpetuels* (3, composed 1918), the Pieces (3, 1928), Nocturnes (8, composed 1929–1938), Improvisations (15, 1932–1959), *Feuillets d'album* (Album Leaves, 3, 1933), and *Mélancholie* (1940), along with bagatelles, impromptus, intermezzos, novellettes, and waltzes. Of somewhat greater weight is the suite *Napoli* (1922–1925) in three movements (Pastoral, Nocturne, and "Caprice italien"), the last of which uses popular Neapolitan song melodies. Doubtless his most important composition for piano solo is the suite *Les soirées de Nazelles* (composed 1930–1936), in which a theme and eight very free variations are preceded by a Préambule and followed by a Cadenza and Finale; each variation is a musical portrait of one of Poulenc's friends, reminding us of Elgar's *Enigma* Variations. Poulenc's principal neoclassic work is the *Suite française d'après Claude Gervaise* (1935), which recreates something of Renaissance music: each dance is short, simple, and clear, and the harmonic style involves diatonic modal scales. Other neoclassic pieces are included in the sets listed above: the Toccata in the set of pieces (1928) and an Ariette and Gigue in the *Feuillets d'album*. He also wrote a children's piece, "Bourrée au pavillon d'Auvergne" (1937). His sole compositions for piano in the traditional large forms are two sonatas. The one for piano duet (1919), like much of his other piano music, is light and pleasing with a touch of humor; moreover, its three movements (Prelude, Rustique, and Finale) avoid the forms historically associated with the sonata. The other is the Sonata for two pianos (composed 1952–1953), which, in contrast, is big, dissonant, and powerful.

The light salon style that Poulenc frequently displayed, in which impressionist, neoclassical, and at times nationalistic elements are included, became a commonplace in French piano music of the time. We have already noted its presence in Milhaud. Two others are Jacques Ibert (1890–1962) and Jean Françaix (1912–), both of whom worked with small forms and strove to be simple yet witty and elegant, in short, as noted, what we may call the contemporary galant. Of the two, Ibert composed the most for piano, ranging from early impressionist pieces, like "Le vent dans les ruines" (The Wind in the Ruins) and "Matin sur l'eau" (Morning on the Water, both composed 1915)), to his main efforts, *Histoires* (10, composed 1922), a set of pictorial miniatures, the impressionist set *Les rencontres*, subtitled "a petite suite in the form of a ballet" (composed 1921–1924) and the later *Petite suite en quinze images* (1943). He also composed *Toccata sur le nom de Roussel* (1929).

Français' work is essentially similar, emphasizing dancelike pieces arranged as suites: Bagatelles (8, composed 1931); a set of *Portraits de jeunes filles* (5, 1936), here coupled with portraiture (see Poulenc as well); *Éloge de la danse* (1947), musical representations of six epigraphs of Paul Valéry (published 1947); and *Stücke für Kinder zum Spielen und Träumen* (10, 1975), a late set of pieces that depict stages in the development of a boy from infancy to young manhood. Corresponding more to the traditional genres, he composed a Scherzo (1932) and a Sonata (1960); the latter, like that of Poulenc, avoids forms historically associated with the genre. With *Bis* (5, 1965) he produced a set of brilliant pieces for use as encores. For two pianos he composed *Danses exotiques* (8, 1938).

This elegance, however, does not tell the whole story of French piano music in the first half of the twentieth century. Another group sought to affirm music as an intensely serious and deeply expressive art, and thus accorded more with the Germanic Romantic tradition. Honegger, as we have seen, has much in common with this tendency. The school that represented these ideals in the 1930s was known as Jeune France (Young France); its principal members were André Jolivet (1905–1974), Jean Yves Daniel-Lesur (1908–), Jéhan Alain (1911–1940), René Leibowitz (1913–1972) and Henri Dutilleux (1916–); Olivier Messiaen (see Chapter Nine) also belonged to this group.

Jolivet, interested in primitive forms of religion, believed in the essentially expressive value of music, thus in accord with the Romantic tradition, and sought a "rehumanization" of music. He composed but few works for piano:[5] among them a set of pieces, *Temps* (3, 1930); a set entitled *Mana* (6, composed 1935, published 1946), an oriental inspiration; *Danses rituelles* (5, 1939); an *Étude sur des modes antiques* (1944); and two sonatas (1945 and 1957), the first in memory of Bartók. For two pianos he composed *Hopi Snake Dance* (1948). Daniel-Lesur worked mostly in the tradition of The Six, as exemplified by his *Suite française* (1934), *Pastorale variée* (1947), and *Le bal* (7, 1954), although his later efforts, the Ballade (1950) and the pieces for two pianos—the Fantasy (1962) and Contra-Fugue (1970)—are bigger. Alain, principally an organist, produced a *Suite monodique* (1935) and the set *L'oeuvre de piano* (1944) in three books containing easy suites, a mixed group emphasizing etudes, and a group of concert pieces. Leibowitz, an early French supporter of Schoenberg (see below), concentrated on abstract compositions in that idiom: two sonatas (op. 1 and 43), three sets of pieces (op. 8, 1943; op. 19, 1950; and op. 28, 1952), a Fantasy (op. 27, 1952), and a brilliant Toccata (op. 62, 1964). And Dutilleux began working in the style of impressionism but then emphasized the larger forms and contrapuntal writing, as in his large Sonata (1948). The most important and influential figure here, however, is clearly Messiaen; in the next chapter we will consider his profound influence on music after World War II.

VIENNA

The dominant attitudes and aims of music in the early twentieth century developed in France, first among the impressionists and then in and around The Six: an important element shared by most of these artists was opposition to the tradition of Germanic Romantic music. In Germany and Austria during this time we also find changes, some of them radical, often modifying the Romantic tradition in the face of new aesthetic ideals in France or moving beyond this tradition in a consequent, but at times drastic, way. Because composers living in Vienna effected the most profound changes, our survey will begin there.

In the earlier part of the century a group of composers continued in the Romantic expressive tradition. The most important among them in regard to piano music were Franz Schmidt (1874–1939), Joseph Marx (1882–1964), and Hans Gál (1890–1987). Schmidt worked mostly with organ music but also composed a Toccata in D minor (1938) for piano (or harpsichord), left hand. Marx described himself openly as a romantic realist and composed typically Romantic character pieces in 1916; much the same applies to Gál.

At the same time, a far-reaching innovation was taking place. Again the essential constitution of music itself was called into question; but unlike French impressionism, this innovation was regarded by its proponents as evolutionary, as the direct, natural, and inevitable outgrowth of the traditional tonal system as it had manifested itself at the end of the nineteenth century. The principal figure here was Arnold Schoenberg (1874–1951), followed by his two pupils, friends, and colleagues, Anton Webern (1883–1945) and Alban Berg (1885–1935), neither of whom composed much piano music. The three exerted such a profound influence on the composition of music generally that they have been called the second Viennese school, to parallel the earlier trinity of Haydn, Mozart, and Beethoven. Webern's music, neglected during his lifetime, has been taken as the point of departure for much of the music composed in the decades following World War II.

The central figure, particularly for piano music, was Schoenberg, who exerted a decisive influence on twentieth-century music. Not a concert artist, he made his living mostly as a teacher, first freelance in Vienna, coming to the academy in Berlin (1925), and then settling in the United States, where he taught at the University of Southern California and later at the University of California at Los Angeles, among others. Although in number piano works do not form a major portion of his output as a composer, they nonetheless occupy a strategic position in his development, since they consistently display new procedures and ideas which he then extended to other genres of musical composition.

SCHOENBERG'S PRINCIPAL WORKS FOR PIANO[6]

Klavierstücke (3, op. 11, composed 1909, published 1910)
Kleine Klavierstücke (6, op. 19, composed 1911, published 1913)
Klavierstücke (5, op. 23, composed 1920–1923, published 1923)
Suite (op. 25, composed 1921–1923, published 1925)
Klavierstücke (2, op. 33a and b, composed 1929 and 1932,
    published 1929 and 1932)

NOTE: There are also a number of other pieces, some unfinished, as well
as arrangements for piano duet of his two chamber symphonies.

By means of the published compositions shown above we can trace most
of the stages of Schoenberg's evolution as a composer. From them it is evident that Schoenberg accepted the dominant genre of piano music of the
late nineteenth century, the character piece; the suite represents the only
departure. Like those of Brahms, his character pieces lack the explicit titles
commonly used in the standard repertory.

Schoenberg's early compositions, not represented in his published piano
music, are much in the Wagner-Mahler vein of powerful expression, at times
involving large forces. He began teaching privately in Vienna and came to
reflect on the conventions of this style of composing, with its intense chromaticism, often involving complex chords, and constant modulating, which
in his view undermined the unity of the composition. He went further and did
away with key, tonality, achieving what Leibowitz called the "the suspension
of the tonal system." In place of the major and minor scales, he advocated the
use of the twelve-tone scale to make all the pitches available to the composer at any given time. Moreover, he called into question traditional notions
of consonance and dissonance, which are now recognized as relative concepts, and began "the emancipation of the dissonance."[7] Instead of building
chords in thirds, he often built them in fourths (quartal harmony), as indeed
Debussy had also done. The resulting extremely dissonant tonic-less music
has often been labelled *atonal*; Schoenberg himself preferred the term *pan-
tonal.* It has also been associated with the artistic and literary movement
called expressionism.

His first set of piano pieces, the three Pieces (op. 11, 1909), clearly are
related to the character piece in general and to those of Brahms in particular;
the density of texture, lyricism of thematic material, contrapuntal detail in the
accompaniment, and typically pianistic patterns of figuration all bespeak this
orientation. Yet Schoenberg had indeed emancipated the dissonance and in
so doing achieved a completely new sound: the set has been characterized as
the first atonal masterpiece.[8] The second, the largest and most traditional of

the three, follows a plan common in the character piece: a lyrical beginning, a progression to a passionate climax, and then a falling off leading to a restatement of the opening material near the end—thus, ternary form. The first piece (see Ex. 7-5), variously regarded as in three- or five-part form, has been shown to have important thematic connections with Wagner's Prelude to *Tristan und Isolde*. With the third piece of the set, however, Schoenberg became more individual in that, along with abandoning tonal functions, he also abandoned theme, so that the piece has been described not only as atonal but also as athematic. Moreover, it resists being put into any of the traditional formal designs. The second and third pieces exhibit an unusually wide range of dynamics.

We can observe much the same thing in the Little Pieces (op. 19, 1911), except that Schoenberg abandoned traditional elements that he had used in the earlier set: repetition of thematic motives, melodic sequences, and set formal plans. These pieces, instead, are short, aphoristic, thus, a clear rejection of the great length so common in the late nineteenth century. The first piece seems impressionist, with the use of pedal-point to provide color; the second works chiefly with chords; a concertato effect of opposing chords is prominent in the third; the fourth, unusually short even in this context, presents virtuoso figuration; the fifth is cantabile.

Example 7-5. SCHOENBERG: Klavierstück (op. 11 i)—Beginning (mm. 1–10)
Used by permission of Belmont Music Publishers, Pacific Palisades, CA 90272.

Schoenberg evidently felt that, although the abandonment of the traditional harmonic system of tonal functions was necessary, it had created a
void; some new means of establishing order in the succession and combination of the notes of the chromatic scale had to be found to replace those that
he had discarded. This attitude may explain the extreme brevity of the Little
Pieces (op. 19) and of other works composed around the same time (1911).
In any case, he composed little in the period 1915–1923, although he continued his work as teacher and theorist (he produced his famous treatise on traditional harmony at this time). Then he came out with his third set of Piano
Pieces (op. 23, 1923), which generally seems similar to the two previous sets.
Again we encounter the new totally dissonant sound, but, harking back to op.
11, he reinstated attributes of the traditional character piece: idiomatic figuration and patterns of accompaniment, embellishment, chordal passages, and
so on. The first of them has been described as a three-part invention. But the
last of them, the Waltz, presents something new, a way of organizing the
twelve tones that, while it may have been suggested in previous pieces, now
appears as systematic. This is in fact the first dodecaphonic serial piece, based
on a series or tone row.

Schoenberg's own discussion of serial composition is in his lecture,
"Composition with Twelve Tones."[9] The system, briefly, was an outgrowth of
his advocacy of the use of all twelve pitches of the chromatic scale and, simultaneously, the abandonment of tonality. In his new method of organizing the
tones of the chromatic scale, he arranged them in an arbitrary sequence, one
designed specifically for a particular composition. This sequence is the set,
series, or row, on which the piece is to be based. In theory the pitches are to
be sounded in order, so that the restatements of the set constitute the elemental material of the piece. No pitch is to be used a second time until all the
others have been used; the original form of the set is known as prime. Moreover, Schoenberg built variations into the system: the intervals of the set may
be inverted (the *I* form), the set may be taken in retrograde (*R*), or in retrograde inversion (*RI*); finally, the set—in any of its forms—may be transposed
to any of the twelve degrees of the scale. Furthermore, the set may be
deployed either horizontally (melodically, contrapuntally) or vertically (harmonically). Still other operations may be used: the set, for instance, can be
divided into parts, one of which can provide, among other choices, the main
melodic line, while the other provides the accompaniment. Although the system can be used harmonically, as indicated, to control the chords and progression, it is primarily a polyphonic, linear method of composing; and, since
in most cases the set remains the same throughout a composition, even one
in several movements, the old principle of cyclic form with variations clearly
remains basic.

Once he had tried the new method out in a small form, the Waltz (op. 23
v, see Ex. 7-6), he soon employed it in a larger form: the first work was for
piano, not the sonata but rather the suite, an old genre to an extent associated
with contrapuntal writing and consisting of a number of small movements.
The resulting piece, the Suite (op. 25), along with its use of the serial principle, is also neoclassical: its movements, all based on the same set, he associ-

Example 7-6. SCHOENBERG: "Walzer" from *Klavierstücke* (op. 23 v)—Beginning
(mm. 1–9)

ated with Baroque types—Prelude, Gavotte (with Musette as Trio), Intermezzo, Minuet and Trio, and Gigue. Except for the Intermezzo, the writing is
appropriately simpler and leaner than in his earlier piano pieces. The Prelude
is based on imitatively treated figuration; the Gavotte, while contrapuntal,
uses balanced phrase-structure as does the Musette. While the lyrical Minuet
is a canon in retrograde motion, the Gigue, unlike its eighteenth-century
counterpart, does not feature imitation. Canonic minuets, as we have seen,
may be found in Haydn.

Schoenberg's last piano pieces are those of op. 33 a and b, which, despite
their strict serial structure, show a return to the composer's earlier preference
for what had been favored by Brahms. This conservatism applies particularly
to the first (op. 33a).

Thus Schoenberg's relatively small output for the piano reflects important
aspects of his development as a composer. Yet despite his innovations, his
attitude toward the traditions of the repertory of piano music remained conservative. In common with Germanic composers of the late nineteenth century, he neglected the large form of the sonata while emphasizing the chief
type of piano music of the nineteenth century, the character piece. This genre
served as the vehicle for his complete reorganization of the principles controlling the twelve pitches of the chromatic scale; his sole venture in a larger
form was the suite, with its neoclassical associations.

In the work of Schoenberg's closest friends and disciples, Alban Berg and Anton Webern, the relationship between old and new emerges clearly: while Berg applied Schoenberg's system to large expressive music in the Romantic tradition, Webern used it to create a new and different kind of music. Each published but one work for piano: Berg, a Sonata (op. 1, 1907–1910, published 1910), and Webern, Variations (op. 27, composed 1936, published 1937),[10] and each has some unpublished music for the instrument.

Berg's sonata, contemporary with Schoenberg's Piano Pieces (op. 11) and composed while he was still under Schoenberg's tutelage, is cast as a single movement; he originally planned a three-movement work, but decided to allow the movement to stand by itself. It is in sonata form, but variation is prominent—the entire thematic material derives from the first few bars. As in Schoenberg's works of the same period, Berg freely employs all twelve tones of the chromatic scale while at the same time establishing a basic tonality, B minor. This is a highly expressive work in the Romantic tradition. Its phrase structure is clear, melodic sequences are used extensively, and the piece has an expressive ebb and flow much like music of Brahms and Franck. Thus, the sonata appears more closely related to nineteenth-century conventions than to the contemporary pieces of Schoenberg.

With Webern's Variations, however, we are in a different musical world. Despite the title, Webern has divided the piece into three movements, while at the same time basing the whole on a single set. Moreover, Webern went beyond Schoenberg in serializing levels of dynamic intensity. While we are reminded of a small sonata or sonatina rather than variations, the musical materials and procedures are not what we would associate with these genres. The piece exhibits Webern's characteristic brevity—reinforced no doubt by Schoenberg's Little Piano Pieces (op. 19)—such that in place of phrases he uses intervals. That is, he made the expressive quality of these individual and usually dissonant intervals—their notes at times so separated by rests and range that they appear as individual tones—primary. Thus, Webern went beyond the usual conception of music and discarded the organizing power of successive melodic phrases in favor of something static, suspended, detached. His use of mirror canon here and elsewhere promotes this static effect: each subsection is so disposed that its latter half is the mirror image (*Spiegelbild*) of the first, so that the notion of progression in the music has been eliminated. In a way quite different from Satie, this music literally goes nowhere: it simply is. As we will see, Webern's music became enormously influential after World War II.

Roughly contemporary with Schoenberg's innovations were those of Joseph Matthias Hauer (1883–1959), who developed a system of arranging musical tones in set sequences or patterns (he called them tropes), which in some aspects resembles Schoenberg's. But this music has a completely different effect from Schoenberg's since Hauer avoided dissonance and remained closer to the traditional harmonic functions while still working with atonal combinations. For piano he composed several refined character pieces and etudes that share the static quality noted in Webern. A good example is provided by his Little Piano Pieces (5, op. 15).

Other Germanic composers of the time who took up Schoenberg's method of composing and have given some emphasis to piano music include the pianist Arthur Schnabel (1882–1951), Egon Wellesz (1885–1974), Paul Amadeus Pisk (1893–1990), Hermann Heiss (1897–1966), Hanns Eisler (1898–1962), Ernst Krenek (1900–1991), Hans Erich Apostel (1901–1972), Hanns Jelinek (1901–1969), Stefan Wolpe (1902–1972), Rudolph Wagner-Régeny (1903–1969), and Leopold Spinner (1906–1980). Of these the most important and productive was Krenek, whose works display all the principal trends of twentieth-century music, but since 1939 he employed the serial methods to the exclusion of everything else. He composed a good deal for piano: there are six large sonatas, a set of sonatinas, suites of different kinds, sets of character pieces, and variations.

GERMANY

Among the older conservative representatives of early twentieth-century German piano music are the eminent teacher and theorist Heinrich Lemacher (1891–1966); three associated with the conservative Munich school and its Romantic inclinations, Hans Pfitzner (1869–1949), August Reuss (1871–1935), and Joseph Haas (1879–1960); Armin Knab (1881–1951); Walther Braunfels (1882–1954), and Hermann Grabner (1886–1969). Lemacher wrote various children's pieces and was an influential teacher, and Braunfels, a pupil of Leschetizky and Thuille, became known for a set of scherzos for two pianos (op. 9) and a number of other mostly shorter pieces. We know Pfitzner primarily for his operas and for his ardent opposition to the new developments that were taking place in musical composition; he composed some piano music late in his career—a set of pieces (5, op. 47, 1941) and *Studien* (op. 51, 1943). More important is the work of Haas and Knab. Haas in particular resembles a typical secondary composer of the late nineteenth century in his extensive cultivation of piano music. He emphasized the miniature character piece, of which he published numerous sets including suites in the fashion of Schumann, such as the *Deutsche Reigen und Romanzen* (German Dances and Romances, op. 51, 1919) and *Schwänke und Idyllen* (Pranks and Idylls, op. 55, 1921). Among his relatively few excursions into the large forms are *Eulenspiegeleien* (op. 39, 1912), a set of variations on an original theme, and three sonatas (op. 46 and op. 61 i and ii). Haas' music is distinguished by lyricism and use of counterpoint, both features that derive from his teacher, Reger. The same elements dominate the much smaller output of Knab, whose conservatism is revealed in such works as the *Klavierchoräle* (Chorales for Piano, composed 1933–1934), two suites, one in G major (1937) and the other entitled *Aus alten Märchen* (From Old Fairy Tales, ca. 1939), and the *Poly-*

phone Studien (Polyphonic Studies, 1942). In a Schubertian vein are two sets of Austrian country dances, *Ländliche Tänze* (1927) and *Lindegger Ländler* (1936). The large form is represented by the Sonata in E major (1928).

Later composers of conservative orientation are Werner Egk (1901–1983), Gerhard Frommel (1906–1984), and Kurt Hessenberg (1908–). Of the three, Egk is at once the best known and least active in regard to piano music, his chief effort being the Sonata (1947). Character pieces dominate the output of Frommel and Hessenberg, the former with a set *Caprichos* (6, op. 14, 1939) and seven sonatas to his credit, while the latter's output includes Inventions (op. 1, 1930), Preludes (op. 35, 1945), Variations (op. 123, 1984), and three sonatas (op. 78, 79, and 107, 1964–1979).

Yet some departures may be found as well, often according with the French combination of new and dissonant harmonies, developed from impressionism, with neoclassicism. This combination shows itself primarily in a fundamentally linear approach to music composition, a concentration on counterpoint, and secondarily with new ways of organizing rhythm. We also see a certain objectivity and impersonality in the conception of the musical art work, which brings with it a preference for more neutral genres of composition. The four principal composers of this persuasion are Paul Hindemith (1895–1963), Boris Blacher (1903–1975), Karl Amadeus Hartmann (1905–1963), and Wolfgang Fortner (1907–1987).

Hindemith is the most important of the four. He left Germany during the Nazi era, teaching at Yale University and later also in Zurich. A theorist, teacher, and performer, he evolved his own system for relating the musical notes to one another, which he explained in a textbook, *The Craft of Musical Composition*. This is a tonal but fully chromatic system in which the different pitches of the scale are related to the tonic or fundamental in principle by their distances from it in the overtone series. He also developed a hierarchy of the intervals from the simplest to the most complex, moving from the most consonant to the most dissonant, or from the octave systematically to the tritone. The system permits polytonal combinations.

Although not professionally a pianist, Hindemith composed for the instrument.[11] The character piece, a mainstay of the traditional repertory, is not prominent. Apart from teaching pieces—the *Klaviermusik* (op. 37, which has two parts, the *Übung in drei Stücken* [1925] and the *Reihe kleiner Stücke* [1927])—he composed three sets, all early: *In einer Nacht* (In a Night, 15, op. 15, 1921), essentially rather simple but encompassing great variety; the *Kleine Klaviermusik* (1929, the fourth part of the series *Sing- und Spielmusik für Liebhaber und Musikfreunde* [Music for Singing and Playing for Amateurs and Friends of Music]), pieces composed with five tones; and the *Tanzstücke* (Dance Pieces, 8, op. 19, 1928), the first of which features jazz elements.

Otherwise Hindemith worked with the large forms. First, there is *Suite 1922* (op. 26), which consists of five movements (March, Schimmmy, Nachtstück, Boston, and Ragtime). With some of the satiric spirit of The Six, Hindemith has replaced the traditional dances of the suite with contemporary forms and the aria with a nocturne. His impersonal and objective attitude emerges in the instructions for Ragtime: "Play this piece very wildly but in strict rhythm, like a machine. Consider the piano as an interesting kind of percussion instrument and act accordingly." Hindemith somewhat later composed a toccata for player piano (op. 40, 1926, unpublished and lost), which presumably better approached his ideal of performance by a machine.

After the suite come the sonatas; apart from a very early and unpublished example (op. 17, 1917), there are the three important works of 1936: the sonatas in A, G, and B-flat. In the first and third Hindemith conceived the sonata as a large and important form, following the tradition, while the second is essentially a sonatina. The first has five movements, the second three, and the third four. The first also has a literary inspiration, the poem "Der Main" by the Romantic poet Friedrich Hölderlin, and lines from the poem fit the principal themes. Hindemith used formal plans resembling those traditionally associated with the genre: a ternary scheme suggestive of the old sonata form in the first movements, three-part form in the slow movements, rondo for the finales. But here the resemblance ends, for Hindemith's conception of music is radically different. His model, rather, comes from the eighteenth century, thus is neoclassical or, more accurately, neobaroque. The individual movements tend toward homogeneity of character, thematic material, types of figuration, and rhythm, thus resembling the Baroque *style d'un teneur*, with its singleness of affect within a movement or large sections of a movement. Hindemith's principle of melodic construction is *Fortspinnung* (spinning forth), in which a motive is used sequentially and in combination to produce a long, inherently endless melodic line; this has often led him to abandon time signatures, while keeping the same note value as the unit of pulse, as in the first movement of the first sonata. Furthermore, Hindemith frequently conceived music as linear and contrapuntal, which he even carried to the point of casting separate parts in different keys. While this orientation is evident in all three sonatas, it is particularly clear in the third: the first movement is related to the siciliano; the second, corresponding to the scherzo, has a terse, insistently repeated figure; the lyrical slow movement has a fugal midsection with a subject clearly derived from Baroque music; and, as finale, there is an impressive fugue, the second subject of which has been taken from the third movement (Ex. 7-7). Impressive sonorous passages appear in all three sonatas. In these compositions, we see no attempt to be individual or unique, as had been characteristic of nineteenth-century Romantic art. Hindemith himself remains aloof and distant, concerned only with presenting a well-crafted work. This idea, so important in the art of the twentieth century, harks back to the ideals of earlier times.

His other main composition for piano, *Ludus tonalis* (Game of Tones, 1943), represents the same ideals, only more explicitly, since it bears direct relation to two works of Bach, *The Well-Tempered Clavier* and, to a lesser extent, *The Art of Fugue*. The *Ludus tonalis* consists of twelve fugues, one in each tonality, with eleven interludes, a prelude, and a postlude. The work as a whole has been conceived as a large cyclic entity. Following *The Well-Tempered Clavier*, Hindemith used a system for the arrangement of the tonalities,

Example 7-7. HINDEMITH: Mässig schnell from Sonata No. 3—Fugue subject
(mm. 27–35)

not that of Bach but one based on his own ranking of them as explained in
his books on music theory: C–G–F–A–E–E-flat–A-flat–D–B-flat–D-flat–B–F-
sharp, whereby the interludes serve to modulate from one tonality to the
next. Moreover, the postlude is the retrograde inversion of the prelude; the
entire piece is both upside down and backward, not only in the individual
parts but in the vertical disposition of the parts. Finally, Hindemith has given
careful attention to contrast and balance in regard to the tempos and effects
of the various pieces as they follow one another.

The fugues, all in three voices, display Bach's manner and spirit, except,
of course, that the counterpoint is dissonant. But unlike the fugues of *The
Well-Tempered Clavier*, Hindemith's frequently drew on the devices of
learned counterpoint: there is a triple fugue in ricercar style (i), a rapid double fugue (iv), a very serious mirror fugue (iii), a fugue with systematic inversion (x), one with both retrograde and retrograde inversion (ix), and a lyrical
canon (xi). This emphasis on the learned connects the *Ludus tonalis* directly
with *The Art of Fugue*. In the interludes, as in Bach's preludes, we find various characteristic styles, some related to Baroque types but all characterized
by the Baroque principle of similarity and continuity throughout. For instance,
there is the small toccata or prelude type based on figuration (iv and viii), a
march (vi), a pastoral (ii), a waltz (xi), a lyric piece (ix), and so forth. The prelude is larger and sectional, corresponding to the larger toccata or fantasia, in
three parts: the first is in typical toccata style, then an arioso, and finally a fast
conclusion based on an ostinato.

Hindemith also composed for piano duet, treating this medium in accordance with the old Viennese tradition. Not only is the waltz represented, as in the set (7, op. 6, 1916), but also the large form, as in the Sonata (1938). The mixture of dances and large forms also characterizes Schubert's work in this medium. The Sonata (1942) for two pianos is another large composition in four movements, not dissimilar to the bigger among the three piano sonatas, with two contrapuntal movements, a slow canon, and an impressive fugal finale.

Like Hindemith, Blacher worked primarily with the conventional large forms as well as character pieces, displaying essentially the same intellectual-objective bias and incorporating elements of Baroque music. There are two sonatinas (op. 14, composed 1940, published 1941); Pieces (3, op. 21, published 1943); *Ornamente* (Ornaments, 7, op. 38, published 1950); a Sonata (op. 39, published 1951); the latter a small piece; and a late set of Preludes (24, published 1974). Like Hindemith, Blacher formulated a theoretical basis for his composition, one that involves rhythmic organization. This is evident from *Ornamente*, which has the subtitle, "Seven Studies in Variable Meters," the Sonata, and the Preludes. The expression "variable meters" refers to an arbitrary succession of bars with differing numbers of beats, all using the same unit of beat, a succession that is repeated over and over again throughout the piece. In the first of the *Ornamente* the succession of time signatures is 2/8, 3/8, 4/8, 5/8, 6/8, 7/8, 8/8, 9/8, and then back in reverse order to 2/8; in the second it runs from 3/8 to 9/8 and back; in subsequent pieces the patterns become less regular. This principle of rhythm provides the basic organization of the composition; the pattern remains unchanged throughout and thus regulates the phrase structure as well. Through lean textures and emphasis on dissonance, Blacher achieves a dryness and, to use the language of jazz, "coolness," that is common to much twentieth-century music.

Hartmann, who played an important role in reestablishing musical life in Germany after World War II, reveals himself in his piano music as essentially conservative, infusing traditional formal schemes with dissonant harmonies and imbuing them with strong expression. His principal work is the Sonata "27 April 1945," associated with the Nazi evacuation of prisoners from the concentration camp at Dachau prior to the arrival of Allied troops. In this sombre work he makes use of workers' songs. Earlier he composed Jazz-Toccata and Fugue (1928), a Sonatina (1931), and a Sonata (composed 1932, published 1992); two suites remain unpublished.

Fortner's work reveals many influences, among which the French neoclassical and the German neobaroque are the most pronounced. His work after 1947 is often based on Schoenberg's dodecaphonic serialism (see above). His compositions comprise a sonatina and rondo (1936), both based on Swabian folk dances, the former purely diatonic; a set entitled *Kammermusik* (Chamber Music, 1944) which is neoclassic; the set *Elegien* (7, 1950); and a set *Epigramme* (7, 1964). He shared with Hindemith the inclination toward chromatic and dissonant counterpoint.

There are many other composers to be mentioned here. Among the older generation we refer to Philipp Jarnach (1892–1982); somewhat younger are Hermann Reutter (1900–1985), Ernst Pepping (1901–1981), Wilhelm Maler (1902–1976), Günter Raphael (1903–1960), Harald Genzmer (1909–), Helmut Degen (1911–), and two pupils of Hindemith, Konrad Friedrich Noetel (1903–1947), and Siegfried Borris (1906–1987). In all we find the traditional types of piano music subjected to new modes of musical organization in which dissonant but tonally oriented counterpart is the guiding principle. Incidentally, many of these composers (Maler, Degen, Borris, and, of course, Hindemith himself) pursued studies in the history of music and, particularly, of music theory, and these studies may have influenced their way of composing. The character piece dominates the work of Jarnach; in, for example, *Das Amrumer Tagebuch* (4, op. 30, published 1947)—although he composed an unusually elaborate Sonatina (op. 18, published 1825), the suite-like set entitled *Marsch, Wiegenlied und Pastorale* (op. 32, published 1948), and a very big sonata, which he identified as his second (published 1952). Degen's work is evenly divided between his early character pieces and later sonatas, a set of four of which appeared in 1949. Pepping and Raphael devoted themselves to abstract types with emphasis on the sonata and sonatina. Reutter, on the other hand, who was trained in the tradition of the Munich school, developed strong neoclassic tendencies. Baroque forms dominate his later piano music: a Chaconne and Fugue in C-sharp minor (op. 4), *Fantasie apocalyptica* (op. 7, 1926) based on Lutheran hymns, Variations on a Chorale of Bach (op. 15), and an unusual cyclic work, *Die Passion in neun Inventionen* (The Passion in Nine Inventions, op. 25, 1930), depicting scenes from Holy Week. There is also a set of pieces (op. 28, 1828) and the Dance Suite (op. 32). For two pianos he composed the striking *Antagonismus* (Antagonism, op. 1) and another set entitled simply *Musik* (op. 42). Much the same holds for Genzmer and for Maler—Maler composed six sonatas between 1937 and 1947, and a suite, *Der Mayen* (composed 1942, published 1947), in lyrical but dissonant counterpoint.

Important to the work of some of these composers is the notion of music designed specifically for the use of particular people in particular situations. This genre was known as *Gebrauchsmusik* (music for use). It refers to compositions using the composer's special techniques and styles that are easy to perform and thus more widely accessible, and that also display an objective and therefore universal quality. Thus, this tradition has been associated with the contemporary literary and artistic movement, *die neue Sachlichkeit* (roughly, the New Objectivity). Another term used for this in Germany was *Spielmusik* (music for playing), music intended mostly for the instruction and enjoyment of the young. Hindemith composed pieces of this kind, as his *Kleine Klaviermusik* (see above) demonstrates. While Fortner and Blacher did not compose this sort of music, there are notable contributions by Maler, Borris, and Degen. Two other figures notable in this movement are Carl Orff, whose comprehensive output does not include piano music, and Paul Höffer (1895–1949), best known for his set of one hundred *Spielstücke* based on German folk songs.

We have seen, then, that composers of the twentieth century variously called into question fundamental aspects of nineteenth-century music and at times rejected them altogether. We have noted Debussy, Ravel, and Satie in France, on the one hand, and Schoenberg and his associates in Vienna. But in France as well as in Germany and Austria, many other composers continued to work largely in the nineteenth-century tradition, while still others retained elements of it but made modifications as well. It is worth emphasizing that Schoenberg and his colleagues, even in their most "progressive" work, did not change the actual repertory of piano music, the genres involved: they did not invent new genres to go along with the new musical idiom but rather continued to work with those that had come down from the past. Yet the neutral titles they chose particularly for character pieces, such as Klavierstück or Spielstück, bespeak a new aesthetic.

NOTES FOR CHAPTER SEVEN

1. L. numbers assigned by F. Lesure, *Catalogue de l'oeuvre de Claude Debussy*, Publications du Centre de Documentation Claude Debussy 3 (Geneva: Minkoff, 1977).

2. Early version composed 1894.

3. According to *Catalogue de l'oeuvre de Maurice Ravel* (Paris: Soins de la Fondation Maurice Ravel and Durand [n. d.]).

4. S numbers from G. Spratt, *Catalogue des oeuvres de Arthur Honegger*, rev. ed. (Geneva: Slatkine, 1986). Dates are of composition.

5. Dates of composition from *André Jolivet: Catalogue des oeuvres* (Paris: Billaudot [n. d.]), 15–16.

6. Dates according to J. Rufer, *The Works of Arnold Schoenberg* (New York: Free Press, 1963).

7. This expression appears frequently in Schoenberg's writings, as, among others, his "Opinion or Insight," *Style and Idea*, ed. L. Stein (Berkeley: University of California Press, 1974), 258–263. See the account of R. Leibowitz, *Schoenberg and His School* (New York: Philosophical Library, 1949; New York: Da Capo, 1970), 70 and 74.

8. A. Forte, "The Magical Kaleidoscope," *Journal of the Arnold Schoenberg Institute*, vol. 5, no. 2 (1981): 127–168.

9. In his *Style and Idea*, ed. L. Stein, 214–245.

10. H. Moldenhauer, *Anton Webern* (London: Gollancz, 1978), 716–717.

11. Dates and other information from *Paul Hindemith: Katalog seiner Werke* (Frankfurt: Städtische Musikbibliothek [1970?]). Dates are of publication.

CHAPTER EIGHT

The Twentieth Century to Midcentury: Other Countries of Europe, the New World, and Asia

Composers of piano music in France and the Germanic countries in the first half of the twentieth century ventured beyond traditions inherited from the nineteenth. When we look elsewhere we find that another important legacy from the nineteenth century underwent modifications in the twentieth: nationalism. We have already seen how national schools grew up in certain European countries—especially Bohemia, Russia, and Scandinavia—frequently rejecting the Germanic forms and in their place employing the idioms of their native cultures. The continued use of these idioms together with the development of national schools elsewhere has been an important force in twentieth-century music: from these schools, in fact, have emerged some of the most important composers of the time. After reviewing these national schools (in Hungary, Czechoslovakia, the former Soviet Union, Scandinavia, Iberia, Poland, and the Jewish tradition), we turn our attention to those countries in which a pronouncedly national style did not develop (Italy, England, the Netherlands, Belgium and Switzerland), countries whose music generally depended on that of France and/or the Germanic countries. We will then consider piano music in the United States and, finally, take a quick look at developments in Latin America and Asia.

HUNGARY

In the nineteenth century Hungarian folk music had been exploited by Liszt as well as by other composers, Brahms among them. But at the time Hungary failed to produce any composer of stature who was involved with its true folk music. Most Hungarian composers of the time had been trained in Germany and remained true to the ideals of the grand tradition: among them were István Thomán (1862–1940), Theodor Szántó (1877–1934), Albert Siklós (1878–1942), and Ernst (originally Ernö) Dohnányi, all of whom emphasized piano music, some of it tinged with features derived from Hungarian folk music but most in the manner of Brahms or Reger. Szántó attracts special interest for his *Essays and Studies* based on Japanese music (composed 1918–1922), but Dohnányi, himself a virtuoso pianist, composed a large amount of piano music, mostly character pieces but also sets of variations and some etudes.

Out of this school emerged one of the most distinctive and powerful musical talents of the twentieth century, Béla Bartók (1881–1945), who devoted himself not only to the piano and composition but also to the systematic and scientific study of folk music of Hungary and other countries. Thus in important ways he resembles Liszt; not only was he a virtuoso pianist but the piano was also basic to his composition. Of his extensive output for piano the following are the most important.

BARTÓK'S PRINCIPAL WORKS FOR PIANO[1]

Rhapsody (Sz. 26/op. 1, 1904)
Hungarian Folk Songs from Csík (3, Sz. 35a, 1907)
Bagatelles (14, Sz. 38/op. 6, 1908)
Easy Piano Pieces (10, Sz. 39, 1908)
Elegies (2, Sz. 41/op. 8b, 1908–1909)
For Children (85 in 4 vols., Sz. 42, 1908–1910; revised, 79 in 2
     vols., 1945)
Rumanian Dances (2, Sz. 43/op. 8a, 1909–1910)
Sketches (7, Sz. 44/op. 9b, 1908–1910)
Nenies (Dirges, 4, Sz. 45/op. 9a, 1909–1910)
Images (2, Sz. 46/op. 12, 1910)
Burlesques (3, Sz. 47/op. 8c, 1908–1911)
Allegro barbaro (Sz. 49, 1911)
The First Term at the Piano (Sz. 53, 1913–1929)
Sonatina Based on Transylvanian Folk Tunes (Sz. 55, 1915)
Rumanian Folk Dances (6, Sz. 56, 1915)
Rumanian Christmas Songs (20 in 2 vols., Sz. 57, 1915)
Suite (Sz. 62/op. 14, 1916)
Hungarian Folk Tunes (3, Sz. 66, 1914–1917)
Hungarian Peasant Songs (15, Sz. 71, 1914–1917)
Etudes (3, Sz. 72/op. 18, 1918)
Improvisations on Hungarian Peasant Songs (8, Sz. 74/op. 20, 1920)
Sonata (Sz. 80, 1926)
Out of Doors (5, Sz. 81, 1926)
Little Pieces (9 in 3 vols., Sz. 82, 1926)
Rondos on Folk Tunes (3, Sz. 84, 1916–1927)
Mikrokosmos (153 in 6 vols., Sz. 107, 1926–1937)

Bartók's early compositions reveal the influence of the Germanic Romantic tradition that one would expect at the time, considering the conservative training he had received at the Budapest Conservatory; among the unpublished piano pieces are a sonata and a few character pieces. In 1905 he commenced his joint work with his colleague Zoltán Kodály (1882–1967) on Hungarian folk music, which began with field trips in the summers to different regions of the country to collect native songs; over the years he continued to go on such trips, extending them to neighboring countries, eventually going as far afield as Africa. In 1907 he became Professor of Piano at the Budapest Conservatory (he never taught composition) and in 1912 he largely abandoned his career as a concert pianist, devoting himself to teaching, composing, and studying folk music, although in 1937 he presented recitals of early keyboard music. He emigrated to the United States in 1940 where, despite a research position in folk music at Columbia University, he spent his last years in poverty.

Hungarian folk music pervades his musical composition. Not only did he produce simple transcriptions and arrangements of folk dances for the piano, but he infused the idiom, melodic types, phrase patterns, rhythms, and instrumental colors of this music into the very thematic stuff of his music and manner of composing in a way that went beyond anything that the nineteenth century produced. Presumably the new sounds of Debussy's music, in particular, made it possible for him to take a radically new approach to the problem, permitting him to incorporate irregular meters, often in fast and exhilarating tempos, modal scales, and dissonant intervals (notably the tritone) and chords, the latter in part derived from the drone bass of the bagpipe (*Dudelsack*).

Bartók's direct transcriptions and arrangements for piano emphasize pieces that are simple and unassuming, the composer stands back and presents the folk tunes direct and unaltered. The most important of these are the six Rumanian Dances (op. 8a), the fifteen Hungarian Peasant Songs, and two sets of Rumanian Christmas Songs. The Peasant Songs in particular go back to melodies he had collected on his field trips; several of them reveal features that were to become important in his larger works: the slow declamatory type, which he named *parlando-rubato*, and the rapid dance type using strong, clear and periodic rhythms, which he named *tempo giusto*. Pieces of the latter type often use ostinatos, as in the last piece of the set. The central piece, however, is the Ballad, much longer than the other pieces, and cast in variation form. We have previously noted the general relation of ballads for piano to types of epic poetry and the corresponding association with strophic form, so that here Bartók is following an old tradition.

The other sets of arrangements of folk music are more elaborate, in that Bartók has used the folk melodies to form larger musical entities: the three Rondos on Hungarian Folk Tunes and the seven Improvisations on Hungarian Peasant Songs (op. 20) can serve as examples. He cast the first of the rondos in regular rondo form with two episodes that are lyrical; the other two, composed ten years later, he made not only more complex in structure but also uncompromising in their complexity of texture, use of dissonance, and driving rhythms. The Improvisations (note the use of Grieg's title) again are no simple settings but artistic works based on folk melodies yet in Bartók's advanced dissonant style. In the slow lyrical piece, full of modal harmonies, we note the prominent melodic use of the tritone, which in one place serves as the interval of canonic imitation; polytonality also appears; in the fast, vigorous dance we find ostinato figures and percussive dissonant chords, as in the second-chords (dyads) played *forte* at the extremes of the keyboard's range.

In Bartók's character pieces, which usually appear in sets and suites, he has imparted to the old form a totally new sound, much as had Debussy and Schoenberg, albeit in a very different way. In his earliest unpublished pieces (composed around 1903) he still followed the Romantic tradition, with a strong influence from Liszt, and this holds also for the two Elegies (op. 8b), a type we also encounter in Liszt. These large and rhetorical pieces include expressive unaccompanied phrases in recitative style that permit improvisation by the player and also employ coloristic pedal effects and dissonance. The second Elegy, in particular, displays Bartók's characteristic economy of means, based as it is on a five-note motive. The *Nenies* (Dirges) are shorter. In the Bagatelles (op. 6) and the Burlesques (op. 8c) Bartók has employed specifically Hungarian melodies and rhythms, yet in the *Sketches* (op. 9b), a set of seven small character pieces, he has made the folk element more explicit, including "Rumanian Folk Song" and "In Wallachian Style"; two others, the "Lento" with its ornate, rhapsodic melodic line, and the concluding two-voice "Poco lento," are related to the parlando-rubato style of folk music. The first piece of the set, "Portrait of a Girl," has some affinity with Debussy's "La fille aux cheveux de lin," from the Preludes (Book I).

Then comes an explosive piece that is truly characteristic of much of Bartók's mature work, a sudden and violent breakthrough, the famous Allegro barbaro (1911, Ex. 8-1). This is a frenetic dance featuring driving rhythms, insistent ostinatos, and sharp, percussive, dissonant chords; the melodic structure, based on short but balanced phrases, and the emphasis on the tritone point to the folk background of the piece. There is indeed something primitive and elemental about the piece, which antedates Stravinsky's famous *Le sacre du printemps* by about two years and represents a type that Bartók was to use frequently. (The French virtuoso pianist-composer Alkan, mentioned earlier, produced a piece in the same vein around 1850.)

The two remaining sets of character pieces Bartók intended to have performed as entities: a Suite (op. 14) and the group entitled *Out of Doors*. In the Suite, elements from folk music are prominent, as in the opening Allegretto and in the second and third movements that feature harsh dyads and rapid irregular ostinatos, while the last piece, "Sostenuto," at once lyrical and dissonant, reminds us of impressionism. *Out of Doors* shows Bartók at his most developed and uncompromising. The opening and closing numbers, "With Drums and Pipes" and "The Chase," are loud, fast, and percussive; the "Barcarolle" has a folklike melody over a sparse arpeggiated accompaniment, an updated version of Mendelssohn's Gondola Songs; "Musettes" is an example of Bartók's bagpipe music, with sustained chords and a drone bass. Perhaps the most notable piece here is the fourth, "Musiques nocturnes" (Nocturnal

Example 8-1. BARTÓK: *Allegro barbaro*—Beginning (mm. 1–12)
Copyright 1918 by Universal Edition; Copyright Renewed. Copyright and Renewal assigned to Boosey & Hawkes, Inc. Reprinted by permission.

Musics), a Lento. This is not the usual kind of nocturne but rather a musical impression of the sounds of night in the Hungarian countryside—it is a study in sonorities, with a slow, steadily repeated (throbbing) arpeggiated chord in the accompaniment against which isolated notes and chords, short scale-runs, and so on occur seemingly at random; there follows a folklike melody in two voices spaced three octaves apart. This represents the first appearance in Bartók's music of a type that was to figure prominently in subsequent compositions—the Music for Strings, Percussion, and Celesta; the Fourth and Fifth String Quartets; and the Third Piano Concerto. Although originally arranged by the publisher in two volumes, the sequence of tonalities (i.e., the central keynotes, E–G–A–G–E) suggests that the pieces in the set should be played in succession.

Bartók composed but two works in the old large form, the Sonatina Based on Transylvanian Folk Tunes and a Sonata (1926). The sonatina, however, since it is made up of what amounts to three character pieces, does not follow the traditions of that genre. While its first movement, "Bagpipes," provides another example of this type, the "Bear Dance" is short, simple, and less violent than might be expected, and the finale is a typical fast Hungarian dance that shows parallel phrase structure in the melody and much use of figuration. The sonata, on the other hand, is a large composition, the only piece among the piano works that can rank with Bartók's major works in other media, such as the string quartets, with which it has much in common. Here alone among the piano works, we can see how the traditional aspects of the sonata have been reinterpreted under the influence of Hungarian folk music, affecting not only the thematic material and harmony but also the very way of writing for the instrument, which emphasizes the percussive quality. There are three movements: the first an Allegro moderato in sonata form, then a Sostenuto e pesante in simple tripartite form, and last an Allegro molto in rondo form with thematic variation. The first movement immediately establishes the character of the piece: the steady pounding chords in the bass, the contrapuntally treated motivic theme with its repeated notes and its upbeat character, the irregular accentuations, and the continuously unfolding of the thematic material, all percussive and dissonant. In the development, the principal theme is presented in variation, and downwardly arpeggiated (strummed) chords produce an unusual effect; the recapitulation commences in the "wrong" key, and there is a short coda. The slow movement is a polytonal dirge in which a melody consisting of long sustained notes is accompanied by dense chords. The finale is a fast dance which again displays percussive dyads and irregular, driving rhythms. Bartók has used no real folk melodies in this work; rather, he has so completely assimilated the folk idiom that it permeates all aspects of the composition. Yet his concern for economy of means was such that he worked with few basic raw materials—highly motivic themes—that are varied and combined to produce larger entities, in a fashion no different in principle from that of Haydn and Beethoven. All in all this sonata, which has been unduly neglected, must rank among the major works of twentieth-century piano music.

A final and important group among Bartók's piano compositions comprises those for teaching. Typical of his big virtuoso manner are the Etudes (1918), the direct descendant of the concert etude of the previous century. More unusual and characteristic is the large body of music for children. Here, while pianistic technique has been simplified, Bartók has sacrificed none of his individual approach to composition. Thus they provide an excellent introduction to contemporary musical practice while developing facility in playing the piano. Bartók's pieces aimed at young children are the Easy Pieces, four volumes of *For Children*, which contain eighty-five pieces in all; *The First Term at the Piano*, and the Little Piano Pieces. The Easy Pieces, ten short pieces preceded by an introductory "Dedication," reveal the basic features of his approach to the teaching piece: while they are miniatures in the nineteenth-century sense, they use elements of Hungarian peasant music, as in "Peasant Song," the "Slovakian Boy's Dance," the two folk songs, and, particularly, the "Bear Dance," the latter being a small-scale version of the fast frenetic dance, strongly rhythmic and with percussive dissonances, that we have seen in his larger works. "Dawn" is impressionistic, while "Étude" is an outspoken if satirical finger exercise consisting of scale segments over an insistent accompaniment. *For Children* contains exclusively pieces based on folk music, Hungarian in the first set, Slovakian in the second. Noteworthy in the first volume is the dissonantly harmonized chorale which immediately suggests Satie and Stravinsky. The Little Piano Pieces, although contemporary with Bartók's large works for piano—*Out of Doors* and the sonata—remain simple children's pieces with a touch of the neoclassical. The first four numbers, called "Dialogues," are short, two-voice imitative compositions; they are followed by a Minuet, an Air, a March (called "delle bestie" [of the beasts]), Tambourine, and, last, "Preludio all'ungherese." These pieces, mostly dances, have been "Hungarianized" by the use of percussive dissonances, the prominent tritone, irregular rhythms, and counterpoint.

But Bartók's most comprehensive work of this kind is *Mikrokosmos*, a complete progressive course in piano technique that consists of 153 pieces in six volumes, composed during the latter phase of his career, from 1926 on, ranging from extremely simple one- and two-voice pieces in the early books to very difficult exercises in the later books. We can recognize five types of pieces here: easy exercises, folk songs, technical studies, compositional studies (the most important), and character pieces.[2] In its all-inclusiveness, *Mikrokosmos* illustrates all aspects of Bartók's manner of composing and thus all the techniques that have become the common property of music in the first half of the century, so that, more than his other sets of teaching pieces, it can serve as a compendium of compositional practice of the time.

COMPOSITIONAL ELEMENTS AND TECHNIQUES IN BARTÓK'S MIKROKOSMOS—EXAMPLES

NOTE: Bartók numbered the pieces of *Mikrokosmos* consecutively throughout the six books.

SCALES/MODES: the Dorian (xxxii); the Phrygian (xxxiv); the Lydian (xxxvii and lv, to name only the most obvious); the Mixolydian (xlviii); the pentatonic (lxi and lxviii); the whole-tone (cxxxvi); and what Bartók describes as "Oriental" (lviii)

NEW HARMONIC PRACTICES: polytonality (lxx, lxxxvi, cv, cx, cxxv, cxlii); harmonics (cii); tone-clusters (cvii); constant modulation (civ); opposition of major and minor in the same key (lix, cii-cxxii, cxl, cxliv, cxlvi)

NEW RHYTHMIC PROCEDURES: (lxxxii, cxxxvi, cxl, the various Bulgarian dances, cxiii, cxv)

COUNTERPOINT: imitation (xxii, xxiii, xxv, xxix); canon (xxv, xxxi, xxvii, cxli, cxlv)

NATIONAL STYLES: Hungarian (xliii, lxviii [two pianos], lxxiv), Yugoslavian (xl), Transylvanian (liii), Russian (xc), Balinese (cix)

Under rhythm we must single out the Bulgarian Dances for their incorporation of the *aksag* (limping) rhythms characteristic of that repertory, which employ such time signatures as

$$\frac{4 + 2 + 3}{8}, \frac{2 + 2 + 3}{8}, \frac{3 + 2 + 3}{8}, \text{ or } \frac{3 + 3 + 2}{8}$$

and which rank among the most difficult, brilliant pieces in the entire *Mikrokosmos.*

Naturally such an enumeration of individual elements and procedures, which is by no means complete, merely suggests what can be found in the set; it does not show the extraordinary combinations, in particular the new sonorities, that result. *Mikrokosmos* in fact may well be the greatest single achievement in the field of progressive piano courses.

Bartók's approach to composition generally shows similarities to that of Debussy and Ravel. He in effect questioned the accepted method of organizing the musical pitches and derived new procedures using models from a great variety of sources. Debussy and Ravel found models in exotic (oriental) or popular music from different countries (Spain, the United States, Asia), while Bartók, although open to much of this, drew in addition on the peasant music of his native land and of neighboring countries, with which he saturated his music, thus imparting to it a primitive crudeness and force lacking in their music. All three worked mainly with the character piece of the nineteenth century to the virtual neglect of the old large forms (Ravel composed a sonatina), so that Bartók's sonata stands out as an important exception. Moreover, all three shared a commitment to the neoclassical, although in Bartók this appears in a manner different from that of the others, since he did not make use of the old forms connected with the eighteenth-century keyboard suite (they appear only in his Little Pieces, 1926). Rather, Bartók emphasized imitative counterpoint and continuously unfolding melodic lines reminiscent of the eighteenth-century device of *Fortspinnung.* At the same time, in Debussy, Ravel, and Satie we frequently encounter a static sort of music, whereas in Bartók the organizing forces of tonality and the driving rhythms are much stronger. In the parlance of jazz, while the impressionist ideal is "cool," that of Bartók is "hot." There is also a principal difference between Bartók and the impressionists on the one hand and Schoenberg and his colleagues on the other: while Schoenberg in a logical way carried basic traditions of late nineteenth-century tonal harmony to a final point, Bartók, following the impressionists, took a completely different point of departure. Drawing on foreign conceptions, he developed novel ways of controlling the succession and combination of musical pitches.

Bartók clearly is the most important figure in twentieth-century Hungarian music and surely the outstanding representative of a national style in twentieth-century music generally. In some measure this may be attributed not only to his extraordinary talent but also to his unusually comprehensive and scholarly studies in folk music. But the similar combination of interests that we find in his colleague Zoltán Kodály did not produce results of nearly the same artistic quality. It was actually Kodály who interested Bartók in the study of folk music and, unlike Bartók, Kodály actually earned a Ph.D. in the field. Yet in his compositions a strong French influence tempered the strength of the native Hungarian materials. Moreover, unlike Bartók, he composed relatively little for the piano, and in that little the character piece is dominant—although early in his career he produced a set of Variations in C minor (1907)—and the impressionistic bias clear. The rest of his output suggests this tendency, beginning with another early piece, *Meditation on a Motive of Debussy* (1907), and continuing with the set Pieces (9, op. 3, 1909–1910), the two sets of *Zongaramuzsika* (Gypsy Music, 9, op. 9, 1901, and 7, op. 11, 1910–1918), and *Marosszéki táncok* (1927), the last consisting of dances. Like Bartók he also composed teaching pieces, including one pentatonic set to be played on the black keys.

Other Hungarian composers include Tibor Harsányi (1898–1954), Jenö Takács (1902–), Miklos Rosza (1907–), and Mátyás Seiber (1905–1960). None of these, however, remained in Hungary: Harsányi settled in France, and his work shows elements of the French music of the time (impressionism, the contemporary galant, neoclassicism, and some elements of jazz). Takács has lived in Egypt, the Philippines, and the United States; Rosza, who has composed pieces much in the nineteenth-century tradition—a set of variations, a Sonata (op. 21), and character pieces, particularly *Kaleidoscope*—is better known for his scores to Hollywood films; and Seiber, who lived in England, drew on many elements of contemporary music, the Magyar (Hungarian), the neoclassical, jazz, and even Schoenberg's dodecaphonic serialism.

THE CZECH SCHOOL

The leading European national school in the nineteenth century, the Czech, continued to exist in the twentieth, represented by composers like Josef Jiránek (1855–1940), Karel Strecker (1861–1918), Vítešlav Novák (1870–1949), Joseph Suk (1874–1935), Rudolf Karel (1880–1945), and Karel Jirák (1891–1972). The example of Dvořák loomed large, especially in the work of his pupil Novák and his son-in-law Suk. Although Suk, a violinist, emphasized Romantic and nationalistic character pieces, Novák was more comprehensive in his output, more like a typical German composer of the same time. He composed the large programmatic *Sonata eroica* (op. 24, 1900); Variations on a Theme of Schumann (op. 4, 1893); Sonatinas (6, op. 54, 1919–1920); a number of suites, among them the cyclical *Songs of Winter Nights* (4, op. 30, 1903); and character pieces both large, such as the Ballade in E minor (op. 2, 1893) and *Pan* (op. 43, published 1963), and small, such as the *Reminiscences* (4, op. 6, 1894), the Barcaroles (4, op. 10, 1896), Eclogues (op. 11, 1896), representing a genre long associated with Bohemian music, the set *Twilight* (4, op. 13, 1896), and the Bagatelles (op. 5, 1899). He also made arrangements of folk dances in *Youth* (2 vols., op. 55, 1920), intended for children. Jirák, who emigrated to the United States, emphasized the older, more abstract forms, composing two sonatas, along with sets of character pieces.

More important are Leoš Janáček (1854–1928), Bohuslav Martinů (1890–1959), and Alois Hába (1893–1973). Janáček presents an unusual case, since he passed most of his life in quiet and retiring work, suddenly bursting on the scene in 1916 via opera, becoming the country's leading composer virtually overnight. Like the impressionists as well as Schoenberg and Bartók, Janáček developed his own way of organizing musical elements which he explained in two treatises, one on the chords and their progressions, the other a complete treatise on harmony. Although he remained essentially within the chromatic but still tonal harmonic idiom of the late nineteenth century, he introduced novel features: he believed that moving from key to key should depend on rhythm and tempo and the ability of the ear to perceive the changes. In his music, then, tonality became "fluid," as he put it, avoiding traditional cadences. He even abandoned key signatures in his late work. Typically a few basic motives provided the thematic material for the entire piece through a continuous process of variation. Janáček composed only a small amount of piano music:[3] an early set of variations; three sets of character pieces—*Hudba ke krouženi kužely* (Music for Swinging Indian Clubs, published 1895), *Po zarostlém chodnicku* (By the Overgrown Tracks, 15, in two sets, composed 1902 and 1908 respectively, published 1911), and *V mlhách* (In a Mist, 4, composed and published 1913)—and a programmatic sonata *I. X. 1905* (October 1, 1905, published 1924) in two movements, "Predltucha" (Foreboding) and "Smrt" (Death), two earlier sonatas having been lost.

Martinů, who has lived and worked in Paris and the United States, stands in some contrast. His large output includes much piano music in which French conceptions, in some cases those of The Six and neoclassicism, overshadow the character and forms of Czech music.[4] This French character emerges from his Preludes (8, 1929), which include "Blues" and "Foxtrot"; *Les Ritournelles* (1932); the Fantasy and Toccata (1940); and the Etudes and Polkas (16, 1945). In his later years he produced two sonatas (1954 and 1958). Even his dances reveal a French background, as in the *Esquisses de danse* (Dance Sketches, 5, 1932) and Mazurka (1941), although there are the earlier Czech Dances (1926) and the polkas just mentioned.

Hába, a pupil of Novak and Schreker, has become known for his work with quarter-tone music, for which he designed a special piano. His piano music, which forms an important part of his output, is in two groups, those in the semitone system (the normal scale system) and those in quarter-tones. He composed in various genres: we can single out, in the semitone system, a set of Fugues (op. 1a, 1918), Variations on a Canon of Schumann (op. 1b, 1918), several character pieces, and a *Toccata quasi una fantasia* (op. 38, 1931); in the quarter-tone system, suites, fantasias (10), and two sonatas (op. 3, 1918, and op. 62, 1946–1947). While innovation of this sort does not represent a movement of significant proportions within Czech music of the time, Hába's systematic use of microtones allies him with avant-garde tendencies that became important later.

In Rumania the influential Georges Enesco (1881–1955), a pianist and teacher, composed according to the neoclassical aesthetic. The Greek Nikos Skalkottas (1904–1949) combined this tradition with a free adaptation of Schoenberg's system.

RUSSIA

As we have seen, there were two principal elements in Russian musical life of the nineteenth century: the intensely nationalistic anti-western group, The Five, and those who preferred to work in the western, principally Germanic, tradition. The latter group plainly was in the majority, as we see from the work of Vasily Ilyich Safonov (1852–1918), Sergei Taneyev (1856–1915), Vladimir Rebikov (1866–1920), Vasily Sapelnikov (1867–1941), and Nicolai Roslavets (1881–1944). While Safonov and Rebikov studied in Germany, Sapelnikov spent most of his life there; Taneyev and Rebikov, on the other hand, were trained in Russia under Rubinstein, Rimsky-Korsakov, and Tchaikovsky. Yet only Rebikov made an extensive contribution to piano music and this largely in the character piece; in his music composed after 1900 we see some influence from the impressionists in his use of coloristic dissonance ("Mélomimiques"), the whole-tone scale ("Les démons s'amusent"), and chords built in fourths. Some of his pieces have strong psychological overtones, as in op. 22, 24, and 25, which associate him with Mussorgsky. Roslavets also used dissonant harmonies in his piano music, such as the Compositions (3, 1914).

The two most important contemporaries of these were Alexander Scriabin (1872–1915) and Sergei Rachmaninov (1873–1943), both of whom worked essentially within the western European tradition. Both made their reputations primarily as pianists. Scriabin, however, was notable not only for his rapprochement with the music of the French impressionists but also for his involvement with theosophy, an occult religion in which man is envisioned as ascending through a series of incarnations to ever-higher spiritual spheres, and art serves as the ideal representation of this ascent. The grandiose design of his theosophic system led him to seek a universal sort of artistic expression in which, among others, the French notion of synesthesia, the correspondence between colors and musical pitches, was important. These ideas led him to work out what he called a mystic chord that related to these higher spheres; this chord, however, he developed in an entirely rationalistic manner, making it consist of the eighth-to-fourteenth partials of C (omitting the twelfth), which are arranged in ascending fourths, thus, C–F-sharp–B-flat–E–A–D. Scriabin developed a duodecuple scale, corresponding to the twelve-note chromatic scale but with all notes except the tonic having equal weight; he also employed the whole-tone and octatonic scales. Thus, he reduced the importance of the dominant-tonic progression; over time, his use of dissonance increased to the point that some of his music has been described as atonal.

The character piece, large and small, is important in Scriabin's work.

SCRIABIN'S PRINCIPAL CHARACTER PIECES⁵

Pieces (3, op. 2, 1893; 3, op. 45, 1905; 3, op. 49, 1906; 4, op. 51,
   and 3, op. 52, both 1911; 4, op. 56, and 2, op. 57, both 1908;
   and 2, op. 59, 1913)
Nocturnes (2, op. 5, 1893)
Impromptus (2, op. 7, 1893; 2, op. 10, 1895; 2, op. 12, and 2, op.
   14, both 1897)
Preludes (24, op. 11; 6, op. 13; 5, op. 15; 5, op. 16; and 7, op. 17,
   all 1897; 4, op. 22, 1898; 2, op. 27, 1901; 4, op. 31; 4, op. 33;
   3, op. 35; 4, op. 37; and 4, op. 39, all 1904; 4, op. 48, 1906; 2,
   op. 67, 1913; and 5, op. 74, 1914)
Mazurkas (10, op. 3, 1893; 9, op. 25, 1899; and 2, op. 40, 1904)
Poems (2, op. 32; 34 [Tragic]; op. 36 [Satanic]; and op. 41, all
   1904; op. 44, 1905; op. 61 [Nocturne]; 2, op. 63; and 2, op. 69,
   all 1913; 2, op. 71; and op. 72 [*Vers la flamme*], both 1914)

Even from this incomplete listing, the influence of Chopin is evident;
indeed Scriabin composed, as well, two waltzes and a polonaise that are not
shown. After 1907 he no longer used titles derived from Chopin. Yet along
with the small form of the character pieces (the prelude, impromptu, nocturne), Scriabin also developed a larger form, which he called the poem; to
some of the poems he gave characteristic titles (see above). The preludes in
particular afford a good opportunity to trace Scriabin's stylistic development,
since the series begins early in his career and continues up to the end. While
in the first set of twenty-four he closely followed Chopin's model, after 1907
he became more and more radical in his use of unusual scales and dissonances, the last set (op. 74) being totally chromatic, with some pieces virtually atonal. He also composed a Prelude and Nocturne for the left hand alone.
   In his work the large form is represented by the sonata, of which he composed ten.

SCRIABIN'S PIANO SONATAS

F minor (No. 1, *Fantasia*, op. 6, composed 1894, published 1895)
G-sharp minor (No. 2, *Sonate-Fantasie*, op. 19, composed
   1892–1897, published 1898)
F-sharp minor (No. 3, op. 23, composed 1897–1898, published
   1898)
F-sharp major (No. 4, op. 30, composed 1903, published 1907)
F-sharp major (No. 5, op. 53, composed 1908, published 1913)

G major (No. 6, op. 62, composed 1911, published 1912)
F-sharp major (No. 7, *White Mass*, op. 64, composed 1911,
    published 1912)
A major (No. 8, op. 66, composed 1912–1913, published 1913)
F major (No. 9, *Black Mass*, op. 68, composed 1912–1913,
    published 1913)
C major (No. 10, op. 70, composed and published 1913)

These are Romantic and programmatic sonatas, related to his theosophical beliefs. In the Sonata in F-sharp minor (op. 23), first, the soul is cast into a sea of strife; second, it flounders; third, illusory, transient rest comes to it; fourth, the ecstasy of the struggle. In the Sonata in F-sharp major (op. 53) there appears a motto, "I call you to life, / O mysterious forces, / Submerged in depths obscure. / O thou creative spirit, / Timid embryos of life, / To you I now bring courage." The expression of ecstasy was among his central aims, something not unknown in the Romantic tradition, but here in a religious sense. These are large-scale compositions, the earlier of which are divided into several movements, while the later (from No. 5, op. 53, on) are cast as long, continuous, sectional works. Frequently in a sonata individual themes stand for elements of its theosophical program, so that for Scriabin the sonata was a large cyclic work that is in effect a symphonic poem for piano, again something within the Romantic tradition (Liszt). Scriabin evidently associated the emphasis on technical display and the use of rich harmonies with the expression of ecstasy. The combination makes these works both individual and in some cases rather extreme. Related to them is the Fantasy in B minor (op. 28, 1902).

Finally, Scriabin composed a number of studies or etudes (12, op. 8; 8, op. 42; and 3, op. 65).

In contrast to Scriabin, Rachmaninov throughout his career remained true to the nineteenth-century Romantic tradition, with the emphasis on lyrical themes and rich harmonies in the traditional tonal system; Tchaikovsky, Liszt, and Chopin were dominant influences on his work as a composer. Yet in comparison with Scriabin, his output of piano music is much smaller.[6]

RACHMANINOV'S PUBLISHED CHARACTER PIECES

Pieces (5, op. 3, composed 1892, published 1893; 7, op. 10,
    composed and published 1894)
Moments musicaux (6, op. 16, composed and published 1896)
Preludes (10, op. 23, composed and published 1903; 13, op. 32,
    composed 1910, published 1911)

---

322   *Eight*

Curiously, following Chopin's model—and thus, also, Bach's—Rachmaninov composed in all twenty-four preludes, but he distributed them among three sets. The famous one in C-sharp minor appears in op. 3 ii, and there are twenty-three others in the two sets entitled Preludes to bring the number to twenty-four. Allied with the character pieces generally are the virtuoso characteristic studies, the *Études-tableaux*, in two sets (8, op. 33, composed 1911, published 1912; and 9, op. 39, composed 1916–1917, published 1917).

RACHMANINOV'S LARGE PIANO WORKS

Variations on a Theme by Chopin (op. 22, composed 1903, published 1904)
Sonata, D minor (No. 1, op. 28, composed 1907, published 1908)
Sonata, B-flat minor (No. 2, op. 36, composed 1913, published 1914; revised and republished 1931)
Variations on a Theme of Corelli (op. 42, composed 1931, published 1932)

The themes used in the variations are, respectively, Chopin's Prelude in C minor (op. 28 xx) and the famous *La Folia* (op. 5 xii), a traditional melody used but not composed by Corelli. While the former set of variations displays the traditional arrangement, the latter is divided into two parts, separated by an intermezzo and ending in a coda. The two sonatas are big and demanding works, very long, true descendants of the nineteenth-century Romantic type. Other large works are two suites for two pianos (op. 5, composed and published 1893, entitled Fantasy, and op. 17, composed and published 1901). He also produced a set of six short piano duets (op. 11, 1894).

One consequence of the Russian revolution of 1917 was that many of the wealthier Russian musicians and composers left to live elsewhere. Rachmaninov was among those who left and never returned. Others included Nicolai Medtner (1879–1951), Issay Dobroven (1894–1953), and two members of the Tcherepnin family, the father, Nicolai (1873–1945) and the son, Alexander (1899–1977). All composed piano music: Medtner and Dobroven, the latter a well-known conductor, produced sonatas and character pieces; the former composed twelve sonatas much in the nineteenth-century manner; while Alexander Tcherepnin, apart from the conventional genres, worked with folk music of his native Georgia.

By all odds the outstanding among the expatriate Russian composers was Igor Stravinsky (1882–1971), arguably among the greatest composers of all time, and one whose works had a profound effect on twentieth-century music. His innovations commenced with the three celebrated ballets for the Ballets Russes in Paris and continued unabated with the turn to neoclassicism in the early 1920s and his late adoption of Schoenberg's serial method of composing, all stamped with his own individuality. Despite his being a concert pianist himself, Stravinsky composed but a handful of works for the instrument.

STRAVINSKY'S WORKS FOR SOLO PIANO[7]

Tarantella (composed 1898, unpublished)
Scherzo, G major (1903–1904)
Sonata, F-sharp minor (1903–1904)
Etudes (4, op. 7, 1908)
Piano-Rag Music (1919)
Les cinq doigts (1921)
Sonata (1924)
Serenade in A (1925)
Tango (1940)

In addition he made arrangements for piano of orchestral compositions, *Ragtime* (1919) and of excerpts (3) from the ballet *Petrushka* (1921), which comprise a brilliant virtuoso essay; there are also the Circus Polka (1942) and the ballet *Agon* (for two pianos, 1957). He also created an Etude for player piano (1917).

The large works draw the most attention. While the earlier of the two sonatas is much in the nationalistic tradition of the nineteenth century, the second is neoclassical, a small "objective" work in three movements. Using the old succession of tempos (Fast–Slow, marked Adagietto–Fast), Stravinsky employs the usual forms for the individual movements: a small sonata form with an insignificant development, a simple ternary structure featuring a florid melody; and a driving, toccata-like finale in rondo form (two episodes, each stated twice). All in all, it is a very *sec* composition displaying the continuously driving rhythms and figuration patterns so characteristic of Baroque music. Even at the beginning of the first movement, the principal theme appears in thirds over a dissonant, rapidly moving figurative accompaniment (see Ex. 8-2). The Serenade in A exhibits similar features, but its succession of movements does not follow any particular model: a ceremonial Hymne, then Romanza, Rondoletto, and a quiet Cadenza finale. For all their relative brevity, dryness, and impersonality, these pieces are fully worthy of Stravinsky and wholly representative of his neoclassicism.

Stravinsky also composed music for piano duet and two pianos. For the former, there are easy pieces, a set of three (1915) and another set of five

Example 8-2. STRAVINSKY: First Movement from Sonata—Beginning (mm. 1–9)
Copyright 1925 by Édition Russe de Musique; Copyright Renewed. Copyright and Renewal assigned to Boosey & Hawkes, Inc. Reprinted by permission.

(1917) that contain characteristic types (Polka, March, Waltz, "Española," "Napolitana," and "Galop," among others). One part has been kept easy for the pupil, while the other provides rhythmic elaboration. For two pianos there are the Concerto for Two Solo Pianos (1936) and the Sonata (1944). The latter, similar to the earlier Serenade in A, consists of three movements: a Moderato, a theme and four variations, and a concluding Allegretto. On a small scale and neoclassical, it displays what Stravinsky himself called a "linear contrapuntal style."[8] The concerto, on the other hand, takes its place among his largest instrumental compositions. As he said, it is a "large-scale symphonic piece . . . of orchestral volumes and proportions," which he composed to serve as "a vehicle for concert tours in orchestra-less cities," played by himself and his son Soulima. It was, as he also said, the "favorite child among my purely instrumental compositions." Indeed, the concerto accords with his large instrumental works of the 1930s and 1940s, resembling especially the Symphony in Three Movements. Its four movements encompass a vigorous and percussive Con moto cast in a sectional arrangement that resembles sonata form, a lyrical Notturno, a theme with four variations, and an elaborate prelude and fugue as finale. Again the driving rhythmic figuration of Baroque music is prominent, along with sharply delineated motivic themes; this quality comes to the fore particularly in the fugue, which has as countersubject an insistent figure of rapidly repeated notes; the fugue also features inversion. Clearly, this concerto is Stravinsky's *magnum opus* of piano music.

The composers who continued to live in the USSR under the Soviet regime had to conform to artistic regulation by the Communist Party, which generally affirmed an aesthetic of art for the people, or Socialist Realism; generally this meant that since the central purpose of art was to further the aims of the Revolution and the Party, art had to be readily comprehensible to the broad mass of the population. This implied conservatism and traditionalism. In music it meant continuing the manner of The Five and Tchaikovsky, although some progressiveness in harmony was tolerated. It thus meant shunning western innovations, notably those of impressionism and serialism, which were regarded as "formalistic" and "decadent." Among a large number of composers who remained in the Soviet Union were, apart from Prokofiev and Shostakovitch, Sergei Bortikievich (1877–1952), Nicolai Miaskovsky (1881–1950), Samuel Feinberg (1890–1962), Dimitri Kabalevsky (1904–1987), and Aram Khachaturian (1903–1978). Miaskovsky, an astonishingly productive composer with a number of sonatas and character pieces in an outspokenly nineteenth-century Romantic manner to his credit, was among the most wholehearted supporters of Socialist Realism. Feinberg was more progressive, concentrating on the sonata and showing some relation to Scriabin. Kabalevsky and Khachaturian stressed nationalism, the former emphasizing music for children and the latter known for a vigorous neobaroque Toccata.

Among the most outstanding of Soviet composers of piano music was Sergei Prokofiev (1891–1953). Unlike many of his colleagues, Prokofiev spent a good deal of his life abroad, during World War I in the United States and just after the war in Paris, attracting attention as a virtuoso pianist and as a daringly progressive composer greatly under the influence of the innovations that had been taking place in France. When he returned to the Soviet Union, it was by choice, but perhaps in part because of his long sojourn in the West, he at times faced severe criticism from the authorities.

In an autobiographical sketch Prokofiev itemized the five principal elements of his musical composition:[9] 1) the classical, related specifically to Beethoven's piano sonatas; 2) the search for innovation, seeking a new harmonic idiom for strong emotional expression; 3) the toccata or motor element, involving insistently repeated rhythmic patterns; 4) the lyrical; 5) the satirical or grotesque, which he qualified as "scherzo-ness, jest, laughter, mockery." His statements on artistic matters, given in newspaper interviews, invariably emphasize his striving for simple melodic expression ("all my work is founded on melodies")—essentially a conservative position—and for the proper subordination of dissonance within a context of tonal harmony. Yet his interest in innovation led him not only to employ dissonance in his striking harmonies but also to treat the piano as a percussive instrument; the combination of these with the toccata style is among his most characteristic traits.

All this appears in genres of piano music with which we are familiar from the nineteenth century. Most prominent are the character pieces.

PROKOFIEV'S PRINCIPAL CHARACTER PIECES[10]

Pieces (4, op. 3, composed 1907–1911, published 1911; 4, op. 4, composed 1910–1911, published 1913; 10, op. 12, composed 1913, published 1914; 4, op. 32, composed 1918, published 1922; 3, op. 59, composed 1934, published 1935; 10, op. 75, composed 1937, published 1938; 3, op. 95, composed 1942, published 1943)

Toccata, D minor (op. 11, composed 1912, published 1913)

Sarcasms (5, op. 17, composed 1912–1914, published 1916)

Visions fugitives (Fleeting Visions, 20, op. 22, composed 1915–1917, published 1917)

Tales of the Old Grandmother (4, op. 31, composed 1918, published 1922

Things in Themselves (2, op. 45, composed and published 1928)

Pensées (4, op. 62, composed 1933–1934, published 1935)

The early sets of pieces contain works that indicate Prokofiev's particular bent. Especially characteristic is the well-known "Suggestion diabolique" (op. 4 iv), an extended virtuoso piece featuring coloristic use of dissonance, percussive treatment of the piano, and insistently repetitive "mechanical" rhythms, all of which produce the grotesque quality noted above. Other pieces of the set display similar features, like "Élan" (ii) and "Désespoir" (iii) with its fast ostinato, while lyricism is found in "Reminiscence" (i). The grotesque and toccata styles, as defined by Prokofiev, are also prominent in *Sarcasms*. Elsewhere we find the neoclassical (or "classical," as Prokofiev put it), as in op. 12, which contains a Gavotte (ii) and a Rigaudon (iii); op. 32, which contains, among others, a Minuet and a Gavotte; the Gavotte (op. 77); and individual pieces here and there. For the most part, however, lyricism remains the dominant impulse, as in the miniatures entitled *Visions fugitives*, the short and simple *Tales of the Old Grandmother*, the larger pieces of *Things in Themselves*, and the *Pensées*.

The Toccata, its title peculiarly symptomatic for Prokofiev, is a large virtuoso, perpetual-motion piece based on figuration, thus true to tradition and doubtless suggested by Schumann's famous example. Then there are the virtuoso etudes (particularly op. 2, composed 1909, published 1912, but also op. 3,) along with a set of teaching pieces, *Music for Children* (12, op. 65, composed 1935, published 1936). Other individual piano pieces are transcriptions of orchestral and other works: a set (6, op. 52, composed 1930–1931, published 1932), *Peter and the Wolf* (op. 67, composed and published 1937), pieces from *Romeo and Juliet* (10, op. composed 1937, published 1938), the Gavotte from the music to *Hamlet* (op. 77a, composed and published 1938), pieces from the ballet *Cinderella* (3, op. 95, 1942), and a set of waltzes (op. 96, composed 1941–1942, published 1943), the first piece of which is from *War and Peace*, the others from *Lermontov*.

Prokofiev shared the typically Russian interest in the large form of piano music, the sonata, completing—apart from early unpublished essays—nine works in the genre (a tenth remained a fragment [C minor, op. 137, 1953] and he planned yet another).

PROKOFIEV'S PIANO SONATAS

F minor (No. 1, op. 1, composed 1907–1909, published 1911)
D minor (No. 2, op. 14, composed 1912, published 1913)
A minor (No. 3, op. 28, composed 1917, published 1918)
C minor (No. 4, op. 29, composed 1907–1917, not published until 1980)
C major (No. 5, op. 38, composed 1923, published 1925; revised version, identified as op. 135, 1952–1952, published 1954)
A minor (No. 6, op. 82, composed 1939–1940, published 1941)
B-flat major (No. 7, op. 83, composed 1939–1942, published 1943)
B-flat major (No. 8, op. 84, composed 1939–1944, published 1946)
C major (No. 9, op. 103, composed 1947, published 1955)

Prokofiev composed the first two while he was a student of Glazunov in St. Petersburg. While the first, in one long movement, remains entirely within the nineteenth-century Romantic tradition, the second, in four movements and roughly contemporary with "Suggestion diabolique" and the Toccata, reveals much of his mature style: a lyrical first movement in sonata form, a grotesque Scherzo, a warmly expressive Andante, and a "mechanical" Tarantella as finale. The next three, composed while Prokofiev was abroad in the West, are varied: while No. 3 and No. 5 are big display pieces—and among the most popular of his sonatas; No. 4 emphasizes lyricism. There then ensues a long pause in Prokofiev's composition of sonatas (1925–1939), after which come in rapid succession three of his most important works in the genre, the so-called "War Sonatas," No. 6–8. These are all big works in three movements, except for No. 6, which has four. The seventh sonata is representative: its first movement, in sonata form, displays contrast among the thematic elements and features harsh dyads, insistent martial rhythms, and percussive treatment of the instrument (Ex. 8-3A), all mainstays of Prokofiev's style; there follows a lyrical slow movement in three-part form, the principal melody of which is sentimental, almost popular, but with ringing dissonant chords in its midsection; the finale again presents Prokofiev's toccata type, a perpetual motion powered by a driving ostinato in 7/8 meter (Ex. 8-3B) that attains a great climax at the end. In contrast the next sonata, also in B-flat major, emphasizes the lyrical, as does the last completed one, No. 9 in C major.

This concentration on the piano sonata seems something peculiarly Russian, since it generally does not occur to anything like this extent in the work of composers elsewhere. We have already noted the decline in importance of the genre through the nineteenth century. In the twentieth century, the sonata appears frequently as a small-scale work related to the eighteenth-century sonata or sonatina, the principal exceptions, apart from the Russians, Bartók, Hindemith (his No. 1 and 3), and possibly Stravinsky. Prokofiev thus stands out, not only in his preoccupation with the genre, but also in that he did not significantly alter either the form or the traditional Romantic expressive intent of the genre, despite the use of his individual harmonic idiom. The constraints imposed by Socialist Realism doubtless played a role in this conservatism.

The other Soviet composer to achieve wide and abiding international recognition was Dmitri Shostakovitch (1906–1975). Although best known for his symphonies and string quartets, he also produced a good deal of piano music.[11] He composed two sonatas: the first (op. 12, composed 1926) is a large, virtuoso, highly dissonant and expressionistic work in one long move-

Example 8-3. PROKOFIEV: Sonata in B-flat major (op. 83)—Excerpts
    A. Allegro inquieto—Excerpt (mm. 21–25)
    B. Precipitato—Beginning (mm. 1–4)

ment; the second, in B minor (op. 61, 1943 [originally published as op. 64]) is more moderate, in three movements with a set of variations as finale. Among the individual pieces, our attention is drawn to the preludes, the early set (8, op. 2, composed 1919–1920, five of which were published 1966) and the later and more important set (24, op. 34, composed 1932–1933, published 1933), in which Shostakovitch employs all the major and minor keys, but following Chopin's sequence, not Bach's. Yet his most significant contribution in the neobaroque vein is the set of Preludes and Fugues (24, op. 87, composed 1950–1951, published 1952), inspired by Bach's *Well-Tempered Clavier*. Here the preludes, unlike his others, often assume specific forms (sarabande, march, scherzo, passacaglia, and so forth), while the fugues not only employ striking and characteristic subjects but also revive the old learned devices of counterpoint. More like the usual kind of character piece are the Fantastic Dances (op. 1, 1922) and *Aphorisms* (10, op. 13, composed and published 1927). He also composed two sets of children's pieces.

SCANDINAVIA

Here we find for the most part continued dependence on French and, particularly, German music. Much in the vein of a Jensen or Henselt in the cultivation of the lyrical character piece in its small form are such composers as the Swedes Lennart Arvid Lundberg (1863–1931), Wilhelm Peterson-Berger (1867–1942), Wilhelm Eugen Stenhammar (1871–1927), Hugo Alfven (1872–1960), and Kurt Atterberg (1887–1974); the Finns Erkki Gustaf Melaertin (1875–1937), Selim Palmgren (1878–1951), who taught at the Eastman School of Music from 1923 to 1926, and Yrjö Kilpinen (1892–1959); the Norwegians Christian Sinding (1856–1941), Halfdan Cleve (1879–1951), David Monrad Johansen (1888–1974), and Harald Saeverud (1897–); and two Danes, members of the Langgaard family, Siegfried (1852–1914) and Rued Immanuel (1893–1952), his son. Of these, Lundberg shows some influence from impressionism. Sinding produced a notable Sonata in B minor (op. 91, ca. 1901), along with the well-known "Rustle of Spring" (op. 32 iii); Stenhammar's work shows the imprint of Brahms. Essentially the same orientation but with greater emphasis on nationalism appears in the work of Peterson-Berger, who made use of Swedish folk songs; Atterberg; and Saeverud, the latter of whom, like Grieg, composed pieces called *Slåtter* in which he adapted qualities of the Hardanger fiddle to the piano.

This essentially conservative orientation in piano music characterizes the best-known Scandinavian composer of the twentieth century, the Finn Jan Sibelius (1865–1957), in whose work piano music took a position secondary to orchestral compositions.[12] To be sure, Sibelius' work includes a substantial number of character pieces, some nationalistic, many of which are in the light and simple character of salon music—Impromptus (6, op. 5, 1893), *Pensées lyriques* (op. 40, 1912–1914), Lyric Pieces (4, op. 74, 1914), Romantic Pieces (5, op. 101, 1923), Sketches (5, op. 114), and many sets of pieces. The large form appears infrequently: the sole sonata is early (F major, op. 12, composed 1893), the only other effort being the set of sonatinas (3, op. 67, 1912). The sole piano work in which Sibelius drew on the Finnish mythological background—the epic, the *Kalevala*, that provided the inspiration for many of his orchestral works—is the set *Kyllikki* (3, op. 41, composed 1904–1906).

The situation is essentially the same in regard to the greatest Danish composer of the time, Carl Nielsen (1865–1931), who also did not give piano music a prominent place in his creative work.[13] Unlike Sibelius, however, Nielsen emphasized the larger genres: among his larger works are two suites (op. 8, *Symfoniks*, composed 1894, published 1895, and *Luciferiske*, op. 45, composed 1919–1920, published 1923), a Chaconne (op. 32, composed 1916, published 1917), and a Theme and Variations (op. 40, composed 1916, published 1920). In addition Nielsen produced sets of pieces (4, op. 3, composed 1890, published 1891; and 3, op. 59, composed and published 1928), the *Humoreske-Bagateller* (6, op. 11, composed 1894–1897, composed 1897), and a set of children's pieces (op. 53, composed and published 1930).

Among the younger composers whose work took new directions should be included the Dane Paul von Klenau (1883–1946), trained in Germany, whose early work was much in the manner of the late nineteenth century but who later adopted aspects of Schoenberg's serial method of composition, as in his Preludes and Fugues (2 vols., 1939 and 1941). The Swedes Hilding Rosenberg (1892–1985) and Lars-Erik Larsson (1908–1986) were prominent, the latter having studied with Berg in Vienna. Two other Swedes, Knudåge Riisager (1897–1974) and Karl-Birger Blomdahl (1916–1968), came under the influence of Hindemith. Most important, however, is the Dane Niels Viggo Bentzon (1919–), who embraced not only the serial principle but also much of the neoclassical spirit.[14] His extensive work for piano includes a Toccata (op. 10, 1947), a Passacaglia (op. 31, 1945), a Partita (op. 38, 1946), *Das temperierte Klavier* (op. 157, 1966), preludes and fugues in the tradition of Bach but using a sequence in which the keys ascend chromatically from C; very chromatic two-part Inventions (15, op. 159), the neoclassical *Frederiksberg* Suites (2, op. 173 and 174, 1968); thirteen outstanding sonatas, and a number of other works. Some of these compositions involve the most progressive tendencies. He thus occupies a pre-eminent position among Scandinavian composers for the piano.

IBERIA

The only other important national school emerged in Spain and Portugal.[15] Here the chief influence emanated not from Germany but from France. We have seen that elements of Spanish music appeared now and then in the work of French composers of the time. In fact the example set by the French impressionists proved decisive for Spanish composers, many of whom studied or lived in France. The two most important Spanish composers of piano music who represent the earlier generation are Isaac Albéniz (1860–1909) and Enrique Granados (1867–1916), both of whom owed their interest in their native music to their teacher Felipe Pedrell, also the teacher of Falla. Apart from their dedication to the music of their native country and to music for piano, the two present considerable contrast. Albéniz, a prodigy, was an extraordinary virtuoso pianist who spent the earlier part of his life in restless wandering, settling in Paris in 1893. Granados, however, although an excellent pianist, traveled less and lived a retiring existence. He died, however, during World War I when the boat on which he was a passenger became the victim of a torpedo attack.

During his period of concertizing Albéniz composed a large amount of piano music,[16] mostly of the showy salon variety common in France at the time, aimed at popular consumption. Among these works are the *Suites antiguas* (3, all published 1887) and the *Piezas características* (12, op. 92, 1888), which include eighteenth-century dance types. He also composed five sonatas (1883–1886), of which one has been lost. Later he turned to serious works that exploit features of native Spanish music. First we find settings of songs, *Suites españolas* (3), *Danzas españolas* (both before 1887), and *Cantos de España* (op. 232, 1896).

But his major contribution is the set of character pieces, or as Albéniz called them, "impressions," *Iberia* (four books, each consisting of three pieces, composed 1905–1907, published 1906–1909), most of which depict places in Spain. Indigenous Spanish dances are everywhere in evidence; the most characteristic type is in fast triple time with rapid subdivision of the second beat and incessant repetition of rhythmic patterns interspersed with a lyrical—originally sung—refrain, the *copla* (couplet). This may be found in two pieces based on the fandango, "Evocación" (Part I) and "Rondeña" (Part II), the latter alternating between 3/4 and 6/8 and incorporating the contrapuntal combination of the fandango and its copla near the end. In Book 4 "Málaga" and "Jerez" represent the *malagueña* and "Eritaña" the *seguidilla*, but without the copla. The *paso-doble*, a rapid dance in duple time with coplas, lies back of "Triana" (Part II), the most-played piece of the set, and "Lavapies." Specifically Andalusian dances appear in "El Puerto" (Part I): the lamenting *polo*, the lyrical *bulerías*, and the *siguiriya gitana*, this last a rapid gypsy *seguidilla*. The *polo* also dominates "El Polo" (Part III) and the *bulerías* "El Abaicín." Especially arresting is the representation of the religious procession with the march and the lyrical interlude in the middle, the *saeta* (arrow [of song]), in "Fête-Dieu à Seville" (also entitled "Corpus Christi en Sevilla," Part I). The writing for the instrument is brilliant throughout *Iberia*, suggesting now and then the art of passionate guitar playing. Albéniz provided color by the use of modal scales (Hypodorian in "Jerez," Lydian in "Almería") and of dissonance (especially "El Puerto" and "Triana"). Two unfinished late pieces, "Navarra" and "Azulejos," completed by Sévérac and Granados respectively, are in the same spirit.

Granados, on the other hand, adheres more consistently to the ideals of his teacher Pedrell in the use of native Spanish musical material in his composition. Although his work includes the Allegro de concierto, the Marche militaire, and the Valse de concert, most of his piano music consists of nation-alistic pieces such as *Capricho español*, Spanish Dances, *Jota aragonese*, and *Rapsodie aragonese*, among others. Often these are of the salon type; he occasionally gave even the more conventional types a Spanish twist, as in the Spanish waltz "Carezza" and the mazurka "Elvira," even producing a set enti-tled *Valses poéticos*. We have seen that in the German character piece the sketch or scene is common, and this holds for Granados as well: there are three sets, two of *Escenas poéticas* and another of *Escenas románticas*, and his major work for piano is related to it as well—the suite *Goyescas*, subtitled *Los majos enamorados* (The Majos in Love, 6 in 2 vols., 1911–1912, published 1912–1914), inspired by etchings of Goya. Since these etchings represent scenes of a continuous narrative, it was possible for Granados later to adapt the suite to serve as the basis for an opera with the same title. Not only does *Goyescas* have continuity of subject matter, but cyclic themes serve to provide even more coherence. This is especially important for the long, dramatic "El amor y la muerte" (Love and Death), which Granados refers to as *balada* (ballad) and the last piece, "Epilogo," subtitled "Serenata del espectro" (Ser-enade of the Ghost), in which he also quotes the "Dies irae." In common with Albéniz, Granados employed Spanish dances, as in "El fandango de Candil" and "El Pelele" (The Dummy, a separate piece related to the cycle), and a *tonadilla* tune in the first piece, but generally the two sets have little in common. *Goyescas* in fact is one of the few large and important nationalistic pieces of piano music, fully deserving a place beside Mussorgsky's *Pictures at an Exhibition*, both of which owe their inspiration to art.

Two other well-known Spanish composers are Manuel de Falla (1876–1946) and Joaquín Turina (1882–1949), both of whom, like their two prede-cessors, spent time in France and came under the spell of impressionism. Turina concentrated on piano music,[17] producing many sets of character pieces with a good deal of Spanish color, among them *Evocaciónes* (3, op. 46, published 1929) and *Miniaturas* (8, op. 52, 1930); he also composed Spanish dances. Among his efforts in the large forms are the early *Sonata romantica sur un thème espagnol* (op. 3, 1909) and *Sanlúcar de Barrameda*, subtitled *Sonata pitoresca* (op. 24, 1922); the earlier sonata is cyclic, its three move-ments based on the song "El vito." He also composed the comprehensive set, *Ciclo pianistico* (published 1930–1935), which includes "Tocata y fuga" (op. 50), Partita in C major (op. 57), "Pieza romántica" (op. 64), "El castillo do Almódovar" (op. 65), "Rincones de Sanlúcar" (op. 78), Preludios (5, op. 80), and Concierto sin orquestra (op. 88). Falla, on the other hand, composed but little for piano solo.[18] There is Nocturno (1899); a set entitled *Pièces espag-noles* (4, composed 1906, published 1909); the large and difficult virtuoso *Fantasia baetica* (composed 1919, published 1922), which smacks of the primitive and thus resembles Bartók's Allegro barbaro; and a piece in mem-ory of Dukas. His most popular piece for piano, however, is the transcription of the "Ritual Fire Dance" from the ballet *El amor brujo*.

Somewhat less conventional is the work of Federico Mompou (1893–1897), who on account of his search for a wholly individual and essentially primitive manner, may be looked upon as a counterpart to Satie. This style involves the avoidance of normal musical conventions like regular meters and time signatures, key signatures, and cadential progressions. In his many compositions miniature character pieces arranged in suites predominate, including *Impressiones intimas* (6, composed 1911–1914) and the *Cants magics* (1919). More traditional are the Variations (1921) and the Preludes (10 in 2 vols., composed 1928 and 1944 respectively), neoclassical in style.

Also among Iberian composers are the Spaniard Joaquín Nin (1879–1949), known chiefly for his editions of eighteenth-century Spanish keyboard music but who also composed Spanish dances, and the Portuguese José Vianna da Motta (1868–1948), a pupil and friend of Liszt, whose piano works he edited for the collected edition, and of Busoni. He incorporated Portuguese elements in his music, notably in the Portuguese Scenes (op. 9) and Portuguese Rhapsodies (op. 10). Two other Portuguese composers are Luis de Freitas Branco (1890–1955) and Ruy Coelho (1891–1986), both of whom were influenced by French impressionism. Freitas Branco's contribution to piano music included a number of character pieces (especially the *Mirages* [1911] and Preludes), while Coelho is known for two sets of character pieces and a sonatina. Joaquín Rodrigo (1901–), a pupil of Falla, composed little for piano. In 1930 the Grupo de los ocho (Group of Eight), consisting of composers interested in polytonality and serial composition, was formed. Of them Ernesto Halffter (1905–1989) produced both character pieces and a Sonata in D major (composed 1926–1932), in one long movement. His brother Rodolfo (1900–1987), perhaps the most important member of the group, later moved to Mexico. Roberto Gerhard (1896–1970), a pupil of Schoenberg and thus of the same persuasion but not a member of the group, settled in England; he composed the brief atonal *Apunts* (2, composed 1921–1923, published 1923) and later combined serialism with elements of Spanish folk music, as in his Impromptus (3, composed 1950, published 1955).

POLAND

Piano music in twentieth-century Poland, the only other European country that can lay claim to a national school, is greatly indebted to its leading figure of the preceding century, Chopin. Among the more important composers here are Ignace Jan Paderewski (1860–1941), the great pianist, editor and statesman; Karol Szymanowski (1882–1937); Alexandre Tansman (1897–1986); Grazyna Bacewicz (1913–1969); Witold Lutoslawski (1913–1994); and Andrei Panufnik (1914–1991). Two others, important mostly as teachers, were the Scharwenka brothers, Philipp (1847–1917) and Xaver (1850–1924). Paderewski, who had studied with Leschetizky, wrote numerous piano pieces, mostly in the small forms and very much in the nineteenth-century tradition, of which the Minuet from the First Book of his *Humoresques de concert* (op. 14) is popular. The influence of Chopin is more important in Szymanowski, with additional influence from Scriabin. A pupil of Noskowski, Szymanowski produced, among others (dates are of publication), Preludes (9, op. 1, 1900), two sets of Mazurkas (20 in 4 vols., op. 50, 1924; and 2, op. 62, 1926), two groups of character pieces, *Metopes* (3, op. 29, 1915) and *Masques* (3, op. 34, 1917), as well as Etudes (4, op. 4, 1902). But he also worked in the large forms, composing three sonatas, in C minor (op. 8, 1904), A major (op. 21, 1910), and D minor (op. 36, 1917), a Fantasia, F minor (op. 14, 1905), and several sets of variations, including two early sets, one in B-flat minor (op. 3, 1901) and the other on a Polish folk song (op. 10, 1903).

Like Chopin before him, Tansman lived most of his life in Paris, and although the influence of his great predecessor was strong, particularly in his earlier work, he later came under the influence of impressionism and then of neoclassicism. This evolution is clearly reflected in his piano music. The example of Chopin emerges in his many early character pieces: preludes, two sets of mazurkas, impromptus, three large ballads, five sonatas, and two suites, among others. Impressionistic features dominate such pieces as "Lent" from the Preludes and the two sets entitled *Impressions* (5, 1934 and 4, 1945), and neoclassicism appears in his *Suite dans le style ancien*, the *Préludes en forme de blues* (3, 1937), with explicit elements of Afro-American music, and the *Sonatina transatlantique* (1930). In *Novelettes*, pieces of moderate length and difficulty, he brought together many facets of his varied art. He also wrote several sets of teaching pieces. While Lutoslawski, a pianist, displayed nationalistic traits in his earlier work, he later embraced Schoenberg's serial method, of which he became an outstanding exponent. Panufnik became known especially for two sets entitled Miniature Studies (published 1955 and 1966).

JEWISH

The central figure is Ernest Bloch (1880–1959), born in Switzerland, trained in Germany and France, and a long-time resident of the United States. He began with French impressionism, tinged with elements of oriental music. While his most characteristic compositions are for orchestra and string quartet, some piano pieces stand out.[19] Among those that are impressionist are *Ex-Voto* (1914), the love poem *In the Night* (1922), a set entitled *Poems of the Sea* (3, 1922), *Nirvana* (1923), *Sketches in Sepia* (5, 1923), and *Visions and Prophecies* (5, arranged from his oratorio *Voice in the Wilderness*, composed 1936, published 1940). Yet Bloch appears at his best in the large form, as is clear from his single Sonata (1935), a large and powerful cyclic work in three movements—a vigorous first movement in sonata form, a lyrical pastorale, and, as finale, a march. He also has a set of children's pieces (10, 1923). In the work of another leading Jewish composer, Paul Ben-Haim (1897–1984), oriental elements are more pronounced, as in his Nocturne (op. 20), the set called Pieces (5, op. 34), and the Sonatina in A minor (op. 38, 1946); his Sonata (composed 1954, revised and published 1955) draws from the neoclassic but avoids the forms traditionally associated with the genre.

ITALY

In some countries a pronouncedly nationalistic style did not develop. In Italy during the nineteenth century, as we have seen, the German Romantic tradition of instrumental music never took a firm hold on musical life, but it nonetheless dominated what relatively little instrumental music was composed by Italians. This situation continued in the twentieth century, even though French impressionism and neoclassicism left their mark.

The most important figure in this connection is Ferruccio Busoni (1866–1924), of German-Italian parentage and trained in Leipzig, who became a virtuoso pianist in the tradition of Liszt but who after 1914 emphasized composition and teaching. Yet in his compositions he did not follow the German tradition: most of his work took its point of departure from Baroque music, especially that of Bach. And while the music of Liszt and Reger, for instance, shows important connections to the Baroque, Busoni's goes much further. He became involved with what he referred to as the Young Classical movement which stressed the essentially absolute and objective nature of any musical composition, and led back to the ideals of Bach and earlier Italian composers. His views are expressed in his *Entwurf einer neuen Ästhetik der Tonkunst* (1910).[20] Clarity, restraint, and economy characterize much of his work.

Among his earlier pieces,[21] there are *Racconti fantastici* (Fantastic Tales, 3, K. 100/op. 12, composed presumably 1878, published 1882), character pieces with literary associations in the fashion of Schumann and Liszt; six unpublished sonatas; Variations and Fugue on a Theme of Chopin (K. 213/op. 22, 1884 [second version, op. 22a], the theme taken from Chopin's Prelude in C minor [op. 28 xx]); Preludes (24, K. 181/op. 37, 1882), in which Chopin's influence is clear; Etudes (6, K. 203/op. 16, 1883); and the Etude in the Form of Variations in C-sharp minor (L. 206/op. 17, ca. 1883). Among his later sets of character pieces are the *Élégies* (7, K. 249, composed 1907, published 1908); *Nuit de Noël* (K. 251, composed 1908, published 1909), with impressionistic traits; and *Indianisches Tagebuch* (Indian Diary, 4, K. 267/op. 4, composed 1915, published 1916) which contains pieces based on American Indian themes. Still the neoclassical bent shows through here and there even in earlier works: the early set, Pieces (5, K. 71/op. 3, 1877), consists of Prelude, Minuet, Gavotte, Etude, and Gigue; Busoni continued in this neoclassic style in the *Pezzi nello stile antico* (3, K. 159/op. 10), the *Danze antichi* (4, K. 126/op. 11), and the Gavotte (K. 89/op. 25), all composed 1880–1882; and *Fantasia in modo antico* (K. 241/op. 33b iv, published 1896), *Macchiete mediovali* (Medieval Ornaments, 5, K. 194/op. 33), and a Prelude and Fugue, all composed 1882, and a set of neoclassic teaching pieces, *An die Jugend* (4, K. 254, 1909). The series of six sonatinas (composed 1910–1920)—Busoni here referred not to small sonatas but more generally to music of different kinds for piano—encompasses great variety but emphasizes thematic development, variation, and cyclic form, often incorporating dissonant harmonies and novel rhythmic configurations; No. 5 is based on Bach, No. 6 on Bizet's *Carmen.*

The major work in which Busoni reveals his bent toward the Baroque and the learned in general and Bach in particular is the large *Fantasia contrappuntistica* (K. 256, 1910–1921), for which he produced two additional versions, a short one (K. 256a) and one for two pianos (K. 256b, both composed 1921). This extended composition, representing the combination of three musical genres, is most unusual. First there is a chorale-prelude on the hymn "Allein Gott in der Höh' sei Ehr'," with toccata-like figuration that alternatively suggests both the old toccata and the manner of Liszt; then fugues on the subject of Bach's *Art of Fugue*; a set of three variations with a cadenza; and a concluding section in which Busoni brings together all the themes used in the work and combines them with the B-A-C-H theme—all in all an ambitious composition. Other late works that recall the Baroque are the Toccata (1921) and two sets of teaching pieces, each entitled *Klavierübung* (1917–1925).

Among Busoni's other contributions, those for which he is best known are the transcriptions of different works of Bach, all done in the years 1888–1902. Apart from several chorale-preludes, he arranged three large organ works for piano: the Prelude and Fugue in D major (BWV 532, K. B20); the Toccata, Adagio, and Fugue in C major (BWV 564, K. B29 i); and the Toccata and Fugue in D minor (BWV 565, K. B29 ii); he also made piano versions of the Chromatic Fantasy and Fugue in C minor (BWV 903, K. B31), originally for harpsichord, and the famous Chaconne from the Partita in D minor, for unaccompanied violin (BWV 1004, K. B24). The *Kontrapunktstudien* (K. B40 and B41), also based on music of Bach, consist of arrangements of the Fantasia and Fugue in A minor (BWV 904), and canonic variations and fugue on the theme from the *Musical Offering* (BWV 1029). In these transcriptions Busoni remains in the tradition established by Liszt. Transcriptions he made of music by other composers include the brilliant sonatina on Bizet's *Carmen* (No. 6, K. 284, 1920), already mentioned. For piano duet he composed a set of Finnish folk songs (K. 227/op. 27, 1889); and for two pianos, Improvisation on Bach's chorale "Wie wohl ist mir" (K. 271, composed and published 1916), Duettino concertante on the finale of Mozart's Piano Concerto in F major (K. 459, K. B88), and an elaborate contrapuntal fantasia. Busoni also prepared performing editions of many Bach keyboard works.

Other Italian composers of the late nineteenth and early twentieth centuries who came largely under German influence include Alessandro Longo (1864–1945), known mostly as the editor of Scarlatti's sonatas; Amilcare Zanella (1873–1949); and Ermanno Wolf-Ferrari (1876–1948). The German orientation is especially clear in the works of Zanella, who had been a student of Rheinberger, and, to a lesser extent, in those of Longo.

French influence, from impressionism and neoclassicism, is important in Ottorino Respighi (1879–1936), Gian Francesco Malipiero (1882–1973), Alfredo Casella (1883–1947), Mario Castelnuovo-Tedesco (1895–1968), and Vittorio Rieti (1898–). Of these Malipiero composed the most for piano, mostly small character pieces of various kinds using harmonies based on impressionism.[22] We may note here the *Poemetti lunari* (7, composed 1910, published 1918), *Preludi autunnali* (4, composed 1914, published 1917), *Poemi Asolani* (3, composed 1916, published 1918), *Barlumi* (5, composed 1917, published 1918), *Maschere che passano* and *Risonanze* (both composed 1918, published 1920 and 1919 respectively), *A Claudio Debussy* (composed 1920, published 1921), and *Il tarlo* (composed and published 1922); also noteworthy are the *Cavalcate* (3, composed 1921, published 1923), each of which represents an animal that can be ridden (donkey, camel, and horse), and *Hortus conclusus* (8, composed 1946, published 1949). Among Malipiero's larger works are the impressionistic *Pasqua di rissurrezione* (composed and published 1924), the neoclassical *Tre Preludi e una fuga* (composed and published 1926), the *Prélude a une fugue imaginaire: Homage à Bach* (composed and published 1932), and a Prelude and Fugue (composed 1940, published 1941); he employed Gregorian chant in his *Preludi, ritmi, e canti gregoriani* (composed and published 1937). Later works include *Studi per domani* (Studies for Tomorrow, 1959), a set of variations on a theme from Falla's ballet *El amor brujo* (1959), and *Bianchi e neri* (1964). For two pianos he composed *Dialogo* No. 2 (1955).

Respighi composed little for piano. There is a set of preludes based on Gregorian chants (3, 1921) and a set of children's pieces (6, 1926). On the other hand, Casella, Castelnuovo-Tedesco, and Rieti composed a good deal for the instrument, mostly under the influence of the French The Six, with the contemporary galant aesthetic prominent, along with elements of impressionism and the neoclassicism. Again character pieces and eighteenth-century formal types dominate. Especially characteristic are Casella's Pavan (op. 1, 1901), Variations on a Chaconne (op. 3, 1903), Toccata (op. 6, 1904), Sarabande (op. 10, 1908), and, among his later works, *Ricercari sul nome di B. A. C. H.* (2, op. 52, 1932) and the larger *Sinfonia, arioso, e toccata* (op. 59, 1936); his earlier *Nove pezzi* (9, op. 24, 1914) are expressionistic. Castelnuovo-Tedesco produced a large number of character pieces which he often grouped in sets,[23] especially *Evangelion* (28, op. 141, composed 1949), short pieces for children based on the New Testament, along with sets of canonic pieces (op. 142 and op. 156, composed 1950 and 1951), a Sonata (op. 51, composed 1928), and a Suite in the Italian Style (op. 138, composed 1947).

Other Italian composers whose work is in the impressionist vein are Domenico Alaleona (1881–1928) and Salvatore Musella (1896–), while neoclassical elements in combination with nineteenth-century Romanticism appear in Riccardo Pick-Mangiagalli (1882–1949). This Germanic orientation may also be seen in the character pieces of Ildebrando Pizzetti (1880–1968), as in his *Foglio d'Album* (composed 1906) and the set *Da un autunno già lontano* (3, composed 1911); later he produced a Sonata (1942) and Variations (1943).

The Schoenberg school had its representatives in Goffredo Petrassi (1904–) and, especially, Luigi Dallapiccola (1904–1975). The latter emerged as one of the most respected composers of the time composed two important works for piano:[24] *Sonata canonica sui capricci di Paganini* in E-flat major (composed 1942–1943, published 1946), which includes his earlier study based on Paganini's Capriccio No. 14, and the set *Quaderno musicale di Annalibera* (Music Book of Annalibera, 11, composed 1952; second version composed and published 1953); there is an early piece for three pianos, *Inni* (Hymns, 1935). Dallapiccola clearly modeled the *Quaderno musicale*, his principal work for piano, on Bach, the fugues in general and the collections for Wilhelm Friedemann and Anna Magdalena in particular. The first piece of the set employs the B-A-C-H theme in transposition. Strictly serial, the set contains fugues and canons (Dallapiccola borrowed the term *contrapunctus* from Bach's *Art of Fugue*) involving inversion and retrograde, along with interludes. Like Berg, Dallapiccola was especially concerned with the melodic and expressive potential of the set used in a composition, so that the lyrical element is uppermost in his work. Petrassi's small output for piano[25] emphasizes the neoclassic and neobaroque, his published music including a Partita (composed 1926, published 1927), a Toccata (composed 1933, published 1934), and, later, *Invenzioni* (18, composed 1944, published 1946), and Pétite pièce (composed 1950, published 1976).

GREAT BRITAIN

Here again no national tradition established itself during the nineteenth century; instead German music and musicians dominated. The influence of Mendelssohn was pronounced, resulting in an essentially Germanic repertory with traces of English folk music. Elgar, the leading English composer of the late nineteenth century, composed little for the piano. Among composers who gave some emphasis to piano music are Sir Alexander Campbell Mac-Kenzie (1847–1935); Sir Granville Bantock (1868–1946), who worked mostly with character pieces, notably *Silhouettes* and *Miniatures* (12 in each, both 1912), and two sets based on poems of Browning (1935); and John Ireland (1879–1962), whose piano music sometimes makes reference to Celtic legends and rituals, as in his *Decorations* (3, 1912–1913), Preludes (4, 1914–1915), Rhapsody, *Sarnia*, and the lone Sonata in E minor, entitled *The Darkened Valley* (composed 1919, published 1921). Others include Frank Bridge (1879–1941), who emphasized the character piece in his early career[26] but also produced a sonata in three movements (composed and published 1925); Sir Arnold Bax (1883–1953), who continued the nineteenth-century Romantic tradition in both large and small forms, adapting Celtic as well as Russian elements; Sir Eugene Goosens (1893–1962); and the Australian Arthur Benjamin (1893–1960). Gustav Holst (1874–1934) and another Australian Percy Aldridge Grainger (1882–1961), the latter a noted pianist, incorporated English folk music into their compositions and thus were more in accord with musical nationalism. Edmund Rubbra (1901–1986) and Alan Rawsthorne (1905–1971) emphasized strong expression in the Romantic tradition.

An interesting case is presented by Cyril Scott (1879–1970), a poet as well as composer, German-trained but also influenced by occult philosophy (theosophy). Scott expressed his views in several books, among them *Music:*

Its Secret Influence Through the Ages (1933). Unlike Scriabin, however, who was also a theosophist, Scott did not manifest his beliefs in his compositions but instead adhered to more traditional practices. While he followed the impressionists, he also went beyond them to the point of eliminating key signatures, time signatures, and metrical barring. His works for piano include character pieces and three sonatas.

Kaikhosru Shapurij Sorabji (originally Leon Dudley, 1892–1988) carried things much further. His compositions—often showing strong associations to mysticism—are complex and intense (he was a virtuoso pianist), at times displaying Asian rhythms, extreme dissonance, and athematicism. They are frequently very long. His principal work is the immense *Opus clavicembalisticum* (completed 1930), which consists entirely of contrapuntal pieces, thus maintaining associations with Bach and Busoni. He also produced a series of six sonatas (composed 1917–1935), which he followed with a series of six symphonies for solo piano (composed 1938–1976), some with descriptive titles. Two other works are the Prelude, Interlude, and Variation (1920–1922) and Variations and Fugue on the Dies irae.

Another group of English composers were more influenced by French impressionism, neoclassicism, and the views of The Six. The most impressionistic among them was Frederick Delius (1862–1934), who studied in Germany and lived for some years in the southern United States and then in France; however, he composed but little for piano[27]—a set of Pieces (5, composed 1922–1923, published 1925), Preludes (3, composed and published 1923), a few dances, and some early pieces that remained unpublished. Satirical in the spirit of Satie was Lord Berners (the pseudonym of Gerald Hugh Tyrwhitt-Wilson, 1883–1950), a friend of Stravinsky. This satire is evident in his *Petites marches funèbres* (3, 1914), the *Fragments psychologiques* (3, 1915), and the *Valses bourgeoises* for piano duet (1917), known for its parody of Strauss waltzes; on the other hand, *Le poisson d'or* (1919) is pure impressionism and a difficult piece at that. Lennox Berkeley (1903–1989) also worked in the spirit of The Six. Neoclassicism is again represented by the work of Sir Arthur Bliss (1891–1975) and Howard Ferguson (1908–). Ferguson, who has edited valuable anthologies of early keyboard music, composed a long Sonata in F minor (op. 8, 1938–1940) in four movements, a set of Bagatelles (5, op. 9, 1944), and an extended Partita (op. 5b, 1935–1936) for two pianos.

Elizabeth Luytens (1906–1983), on the other hand, took up the serial method of Schoenberg, among the first British composers to do so. In this she was joined by Humphrey Searle (1915–1982), who after his traditional Ballade (op. 10, composed 1947, published 1949) also adopted Schoenberg's method, as we can see in his *Vigil* (op. 3, 1944), *Threnos and Toccata* (op. 14, 1948), the latter using Baroque forms, a Sonata (op. 21, 1951), a Suite (op. 29, 1965), and a Prelude (op. 45, 1965) based on a theme of Alan Rawsthorne.

Finally, only one of the four major English composers of the first half of the century—Ralph Vaughan Williams (1872–1958), Sir William Walton (1902–), Sir Michael Tippett (1905–), and Benjamin Britten (1913–1976)—

paid much attention to the piano: Tippett. For his part, Vaughan Williams composed[28] the Suite of Six Short Pieces (published 1921), and one large work for two pianos—Introduction and Fugue (composed 1946, published 1947)—although he arranged for piano the score he had composed for the film *The Lake in the Mountains.* Walton also lacked interest in the piano, composing a set of piano duets for children. Britten[29] composed for piano only a set of Waltzes (5, op. 3, composed 1923–1925, revised 1969, published 1970), the suite *Holiday Diary* (op. 5, composed and published 1934), and the elaborate *Night Piece* (composed and published 1963), reminiscent of Bartók; in addition he composed several pieces for two pianos. Tippett, however, has concentrated on the sonata,[30] producing four notable works: the first, in G minor (composed 1936–1938, revised 1942 and 1954, published 1942 and 1954 respectively), a large work in four movements in which he replaced the traditional structure of the first movement, sonata form, by theme and variations, as indeed did Haydn, Mozart, and Beethoven, among others, before him; No. 2 (composed and published 1962) in one long continuous movement; No. 3 (composed 1972–1973, published 1975); and No. 4 (composed 1984, published 1986).

A few composers working in other countries of Europe made notable contributions to the piano repertory. In Belgium there were Desiré Pasque (1867–1939), closely associated with French music, and Marcel Poot (1901–), who was interested in the work of The Six and in whose music we find humorous irony and jazz elements. Nearby, in the Netherlands, the German influence was more pronounced, as in the work of Dirk Schäfer (1873–1931), Bernard van den Sigtenhorst Meijer (1888–1953), Willem Pijper (1894–1947), Henk Badings (1907–1987), and Hans Henkemans (1913–). Except for Schäfer, the large forms play a more important role than generally encountered elsewhere, with the neoclassical element prominent. Of these composers, Pijper wrote the most significant piano music: moving from the Romantic tradition he developed the principle of deriving melodic and harmonic materials from a single germ-cell stated at its beginning; he also emphasized bitonality. Outstanding are two sonatas (composed 1930 and 1935), the latter for two pianos; he has also composed pieces of extreme brevity, among them the early *Aphorisms* (1915) and a series of three sonatinas (1918–1925).

The more important composers of piano music in Switzerland are Emile Jaques-Dalcroze (1865–1950), Othmar Schoeck (1886–1956), Frank Martin (1890–1974), Willy Burkhard (1900–1955), and Rolf Liebermann (1910–). Jaques-Dalcroze, most famous for his eurhythmics, a system of music teaching, produced a large number of character pieces primarily for teaching. Both Schoeck and Burkhard belonged to the conservative contrapuntal tradition that took its point of departure from Reger. Burkhard emphasized the larger forms, as in his early Fantasia, two sonatinas (the second for Christmas, op. 71 i, published 1947), a Sonata (op. 66), and two sets of variations; he also produced preludes and fugues and two sets of piano pieces. More international, on the other hand, is the work of Martin, who studied in France and Italy and who adopted elements of Schoenberg's method in his later work. Yet he composed little for piano:[31] apart from the early Overture and Fox Trot for two pianos (1920), there are the set *Guitare* (4, 1933), the Preludes (8, 1947–1948), *Clair de lune* (1952), the Rhythmical Study, and *Esquisse* (both 1965), and the late Fantasy on Flamenco Rhythms (1973). The preludes, worked out with a free application of Schoenberg's serialism, are the best known and most important—in a general way they maintain features associated with the genre, being small pieces in which the same character or affect is consistently maintained. The third clearly is a nocturne, and the fifth, Vivace, is a virtuoso etude; the last two, however, are larger sectional pieces. Finally, Liebermann composed a Sonata (1951) using the serial principle.

THE UNITED STATES

The United States came of age musically in the twentieth century. In the nineteenth century musical life in the United States had been under the sway of European traditions, with the German influence of particular strength, as we have seen. In general musical life in the United States was immeasurably enriched by the many influential musicians, particularly composers, who immigrated in the wake of the political upheavals in Europe. On the other side, and just as important, was the growth of a conscious effort to produce a special American manner of composing, in part supported by the new French neoclassic aesthetic taught to a number of important composers by Nadia Boulanger.

At the beginning of the century a strong reminder of nineteenth-century practice lingered in the work of composers who lived in New England, mostly teaching at colleges and universities there. For the most part they continued in the aesthetics of the German Romantic tradition, emphasizing in particular the character piece. Important here were David Stanley Smith (1877–1949), Henry F. Gilbert (1868–1928), Frederick Converse (1871–1940), Edward Burlingame Hill (1872–1960), Daniel Gregory Mason (1873–1953), John Powell (1882–1963), Quincy Porter (1897–1966), and Richard Donovan (1891–1970). The large output of Amy (Mrs. H. H. A.) Beach (1867–1944), not an academic, emphasized character pieces.

Yet the New England academic environment played a role in the formation of one of the most unusual and characteristic figures in American music, Charles E. Ives (1874–1954) of Connecticut, a graduate of Yale and pupil of Horatio Parker and Dudley Buck. But Ives' work only partially reflects the influence of his academically oriented teachers, for Ives, somewhat like the poet Whitman, was from the beginning something of an experimenter who took nothing for granted and respected no long-standing tradition about how music should be organized. Similar in a way to Cocteau and his associates, Ives was stimulated by what he heard around him: the off-key singing of hymns by a church choir, the sound of an out-of-tune organ, the clash of dissonance as two bands, each playing a different march in a different key, passed one another on Main Street during a parade, or the quarter-tone inflections of country fiddlers at square dances. He incorporated such sounds into his music, along with passages whose tonal and rhythmic organization remained conventional. But he carried his appropriation of such elements to the point of quoting music of all varieties—hymns, marches, popular songs, classical music—in his own compositions, sometimes disguising these quotations by using only part of something and introducing much variation. In this he may have been influenced by Emerson, who, in his essay "Quotation and Originality," stressed the necessity and value of tradition in making a case for writers' using quotations from authors of the past; as he says "Next to the author of a good sentence is the first quoter of it" or "Only an inventor knows how to borrow," sentiments with which Ives presumably agreed.[32] Proper identification of these elements constitutes a fundamental aspect of understanding Ives' music.[33]

Since from the first Ives' work aroused the opposition of his teachers, he determined that he could not become a successful professional musician without abandoning his ideals of what music should be, and therefore decided to seek his livelihood in the insurance business, in which he proved very successful. Not until late in his life did his musical compositions come to be recognized as important; he received the Pulitzer Prize for music in 1947.

Piano music is not only prominent in Ives' output[34] but also represents his individual approach. He composed three sonatas: the first in order of composition (but often known as the "third") is a smaller work entitled "Three-Page Sonata" (it occupies three pages in Ives' original manuscript, composed 1905, published 1949); then the "first" (composed 1901–1909, published 1954) in seven movements, five of which are extant; and finally the "second," the celebrated "Concord Sonata" (composed 1910–1915, but mostly 1911–1912, published 1920, revised 1947) in four movements. He also composed Varied Air with Variations (supposedly 1923). Then he worked on a set of character pieces, to be called *Studies*, of which he planned twenty-seven but completed only three, leaving many others in various stages of completeness (he did some renumbering over the years): the "Anti-Abolitionist Riots" (ix), "Some Southpaw Pitching" (xxi, both composed 1908, published 1949), and a piece entitled simply "22"; several others have been reconstructed and edited. There are other pieces apart from this set, including six marches, Ragtime Dances, "New Year's Dance," and "Circus Band" (composed 1884–1887); "Take-offs" (5, composed 1906–1907, published 1977); and "The Celestial Railroad" (composed 1916), the latter in part based on earlier compositions. He composed little after 1918, but among his later work is the set *Quarter Tone Pieces* for two pianos tuned a quarter-tone apart (3, composed 1923–1924) and Improvisations (3, composed presumably 1938, published 1984).

His principal piano works are the sonatas. He made his style evident in the very first of these, the "Three-Page Sonata," with its dissonant harmonies, complex rhythms, and disregard of the conventions of formal organization associated with the genre, although we can find elements of the three-part scheme, particularly in the finale. He quotes from the hymns "Proprior Deo" and "Westminster Chimes"—and we should note that Ives worked as an organist and was familiar with the practice of improvising on hymn tunes—and also incorporates a march, a waltz, and ragtime, while using the B-A-C-H theme extensively.

In the "First" Sonata, Ives continued this practice. He quotes from two hymns in the first, third, and fifth movements: "Lebanon" (all three, but mostly in the first and last) and "Erie" (in the third, where it is joined by "Massa's in the Cold Cold Ground"). Popular songs appear in the second (the second part of which bears the title "In the Inn") and fourth: "Bringing in the Sheaves," "Happy Day," and "Welcome Voice." In addition he introduces dance rhythms (rhumba, Charleston, ragtime) and dissonant harmonies, including second chords (dyads). Yet we can note a traditional aspect here—Ives' organization of the work as a whole involves the alternation between the sacred (first, third, and fifth) and the secular (second and fourth, these two being in the nature of scherzos); moreover his use of themes in more than one movement results in cyclic form. In a note in the manuscript Ives suggests that the sonata as a whole expressed something of the character of outdoor life in Connecticut in 1880–1890.

The "Second" Sonata, entitled "Concord, Mass., 1840–1860," is just as large. Each of its four movements bears a title: "Emerson," the big opening movement; "Hawthorne," the scherzo; "The Alcotts," the slow movement; and "Thoreau," the finale, all of which confirms the association with New England Transcendentalism of the nineteenth century. In its first edition (1920), published by Ives himself, he included his *Essays Before a Sonata*,[35] in which we find his views on what music can express, the ideal aims of the composer, and his conceptions of Emerson, Hawthorne, the Alcotts, and Thoreau. Ives' association of music with philosophy puts him squarely in the tradition of German Romantic instrumental music. But his notion of the proper expression of ideas required him to seek out new ways of organizing music, to draw elements from here and there, mixing the most divergent styles and techniques, often placing one next to the other. In his *Essays* Ives called Emerson "an invader of the unknown . . . America's greatest explorer of spiritual immensities" and in the first movement of the sonatas celebrated his role in revelation; in "Hawthorne" Ives chose not the writer's fundamental preoccupation with guilt, but rather some of "his wilder, fantastical adventures in the half-childlike, half fairy-like phantastic realms"; "The Alcotts" is a souvenir of their home (Orchard House) where they dwelt in "conviction in the power of the common soul"; finally, "Thoreau" represents a day at Walden spent in meditation, in solitary contemplation of nature, forsaking the normal pursuits of everyday life. Expression, therefore, is the central aim here.

The "Concord Sonata" is a large cyclic work based on four themes or motives that are embedded in its first three bars (Ex. 8-4A).[36] Of central importance is the motive from the first movement of Beethoven's Fifth Symphony, which has features in common with two hymn tunes, the "Missionary Chant" and "Martyn." The other themes are lyrical. All are used throughout the work, often in varied form. Ives associated the Beethoven theme first with Emerson

A.

Example 8-4. IVES: Sonata No. 2 ("Concord" [First edition])—Excerpts
  A. "Emerson"—Beginning (mm. 1–9)
  B. "Hawthorne"—Excerpt (mm. 11–21)
  C. "The Alcotts"—Excerpt (mm. 7–15)

B.

C.

and his groping for revelation and then with the Alcotts, at whose house it was often played. But he quoted other music as well: "Stop that Knocking at My Door" (Ex. 8-4C), "Massa's in the Cold Cold Ground," and a march. In other respects these movements, in sectional form, bear little resemblance to traditional structural schemes. Furthermore, since Emerson wrote both prose and verse, Ives distinguished the two in music, labeling parts of the movement "prose" or "verse," the former characterized by freedom of rhythm, the latter by a greater degree of periodicity.

Just as Emerson constantly sought out the new, so did Ives in his music, and the "Concord Sonata" abounds in new and unusual procedures. Polytonality appears in "The Alcotts" and in "Emerson"; only a few parts of the various movements of the sonata contain regular time signatures ("Emerson" for the most part has none, but at times we find 7/8, 8/8, 5/8, and 7/4), and "Hawthorne" contains long passages that lack bar lines altogether. More striking are the new sounds, the result of unheard-of chordal combinations, which stand outside of the traditions of tonal harmony. A remarkable passage in "Hawthorne" requires the player to depress a group of keys with a heavy piece of wood, creating what we know as tone-clusters (Ex. 8-4B). Moreover, just as Emerson, Hawthorne, and Thoreau broke the bounds of the conventional and generally acceptable, so Ives broke the bounds of his medium to call upon additional instruments on an *ad libitum* basis—a viola at the end of "Emerson" and a flute at the end of "Thoreau." While Ives has put many performance directions into the score, at times he has left much to the discretion of the performer, as in his instruction that a certain passage be played as fast as possible.

In the late Varied Air with Variations—Ives' only other piano piece in one of the traditional large forms—the theme itself is a sort of row consisting of all twelve pitches of the chromatic scale which appears as a cantus firmus—he refers to it as "the old stone wall." Of the five variations, the second is in the style of a march and makes use of inversion, while the third is canonic. As interludes Ives includes three "Protests," passages in traditional tonal harmony that use regular meters.

The character pieces, mostly included among the *Studies*, show the same features: extensive quotations of music of all kinds, irregular formal structures, dissonance, and rhythmic complexities, which coexist with passages in traditional harmony and rhythm. "Some Southpaw Pitching," a study for the left hand—although there is plenty for the right hand as well—draws on "Down in the Cornfield," "Massa's in the Cold Cold Ground," and the hymns "Antioch" (which we know as "Joy to the World") and "All Saints New." Similarly, "The Anti-Abolitionist Riots" makes use, again, of "Massa's in the Cold Cold Ground" and the hymn "Antioch."

Three other American composers bear some similarity to Ives: Carl Ruggles (1876–1971), John Becker (1886–1961), and Henry Cowell (1897–1965). Ruggles lived a retiring life, almost unknown to the world of music generally. Like Ives, he was a New Englander, and like him he had a lofty vision of the expressive capacities of music, which motivated his search for new ways of conceiving and organizing musical materials. His two pieces for piano, both experimental, athematic, totally chromatic, and highly dissonant, are *Evocations* (4, 1937–1945) and *Polyphonic Compositions* for three pianos (1945). Becker is known for his unusual forms and highly idiosyncratic harmonies, as in *Architectural Impressions* (2, 1924), *Soundpiece No. 5* (actually a short sonata, 1937), and *Modern Dances*.

Cowell's experimental approach first manifested itself in his piano music, specifically in his character pieces composed as early as 1911 and continuing until 1935,[37] in which he explored new sound capacities of the piano: tone clusters (dyads), as in "The Trumpet of Agnus Og" (L. 399); the use of the forearm on the keyboard, as in "The Tides of Manaunaun" (L. 219/1), "Antimony" (L. 213/5), and "The Voice of Lir" (L. 354/3); strumming directly on the strings of the instrument, as in "The Harp of Life" (L. 384), "The Banshee" (L. 405, in which the strings are both plucked and played glissando), and "The Aeolian Harp" (L. 370), in which a lyric melody played on the keys is accompanied by glissandos played directly on the strings); and overtones obtained by stopping the strings by hand ("Sinister Resonance," L. 462). Cowell frequently used melodies and harmonies associated with folk song, some of which are stylized country dances ("Exultation"[L. 328] and "Lilt of the Reel" [L. 463/1a]); "The Snows of Fuji-Yama" (L. 395) is pentatonic. Cowell also modified the sound of the instrument by placing various objects on the strings—hammers, knives, coins, rubber bands, and so on. This idea was carried further by John Cage in his prepared piano (see Chapter Nine).

As has been indicated, the chief impetus to musical composition in the United States stemmed not from any indigenous tradition but from those of Europe. French conceptions, in fact, proved to be decisive. For example, Charles Tomlinson Griffes (1884–1920) composed in the manner of French impressionism despite his German training.[38] We can see this tendency in his three sets of character pieces, *Tone Pictures* (3, op. 5, composed 1910–1912, published 1915), *Fantasy Pieces* (3, op. 6, composed 1912–1914, published 1915), and *Roman Sketches* (4, op. 7, composed 1915–1916, published 1917), the first of which is the well-known "The White Peacock." His Preludes (3, composed 1919, composed 1967) were discovered much later, as was a serious character piece *De profundis* (composed 1915, published 1978). More ambitious is his intense Sonata in D major (composed 1917–1918, published 1921), in three movements, based on an oriental scale and influenced both by impressionism and Scriabin.

We encounter similar influences in the work of Dane Rudhyar (1895–1985), who was born in France but settled in the United States, and who composed intense character pieces that grew out of the same mystic theosophy that inspired Scriabin, as many of his titles make clear; for example, *Tetragrams* (9, 1920–1967) and *Pentagrams* (4, 1974), both corresponding to symbols important in this belief, and *Paens* (3, 1935), which express religious ecstasy.

Another composer whose work was closely related to French music was Virgil Thomson (1896–1989), for many years an influential critic. The examples of Satie and The Six provided models for much of his work. Beginning with a set of Two-Part Inventions (5, published 1926),[39] he continued with short sonatas (2, 1929–1940, two more remaining unpublished), two books of attractive Etudes (10, 1943–1944, and 9, 1940–1951), the set *Parson Weems and the Cherry Tree* (1975), and the series *Portraits*, over a hundred in number, in five books (composed 1927–1985); there are also some independent pieces.

Composers of somewhat more importance whose work may be related to French conceptions are Walter Piston (1894–1976), Arthur Berger (1912–), Vincent Persichetti (1915–1987), and Irving Fine (1914–1962). Piston, who belonged to the academic tradition, composed little for piano, but that little demonstrates his neoclassical tendencies.[40] Apart from an early Sonata (1926)—Piston did not take up music as a career until 1920—he composed a Passacaglia (1943) and an Improvisation (1945). Berger, like Piston, has also composed but little for piano: among his pieces are Episodes (2, 1933), Fantasy (1940), a set Bagatelles (3), a Suite (both 1946), and a Partita (1947), this last related to Stravinsky; his later work is serial. Persichetti, who was trained in the United States and who composed a good deal of piano music, was much in the spirit of what we have called the contemporary galant vein so prominent in France. Although there are character pieces,[41] among them three sets entitled *Poems* (op. 4, 5, and op. 14, 1939–1941) and another set called *Parades* (op. 57, 1952), he emphasized the sonata, of which he composed twelve. His fourth sonata is substantial; for two pianos he also composed a Sonata (op. 13, 1940) and reminiscent of Stravinsky, a Concerto (op. 56, 1952) for piano duet. Strongly neoclassical is the sole piano work of Fine, a suite simply and characteristically entitled *Music for Piano* (1947), which also belongs to the contemporary galant. The piano music of both Marion Bauer (1887–1955) and Miriam Gideon (1906–) owes much to French influence.

The leading figure here—and one of the most important and influential American composers—was Aaron Copland (1900–1990). Unlike many of his colleagues, Copland, himself a pianist, composed some of his most important works for the instrument.[42] In his earlier work the French contemporary galant is evident: apart from some early pieces, including a Sonata (1920–1921), we have "The Cat and the Mouse" (subtitled *Scherzo humoristique*, 1920, dates here being of composition), "Sentimental Melody," and two "Blues" (both 1926), all composed in Paris while he was studying with Boulanger. From the 1930s, however, Copland deliberately composed in two separate veins: one was admittedly directed to the larger pubic, while the other is serious, making no concessions to the taste of that larger public. Among his piano music, the first is represented, among others, by two children's pieces (1936), two later "Blues" (1948), "In Evening Air" (1966), "Midsummer Nocturne" (1948, revised 1977), and the "Danzon Cubana" for two pianos (1942). The artistically more significant serious works comprise the early Passacaglia (1922), the Piano Variations (1930), the Piano Sonata (1939–1941), the Piano Fantasy (1955–1957), and *Night Thoughts* (1972). His last pieces were "Midday Thoughts" and "Proclamation" (composed 1982 and 1983 respectively, published 1984).

The large pieces form the center of his piano music. While the Passacaglia testifies to a certain learnedness and involvement with the neoclassical (or neobaroque), the Piano Variations represents his first really individual essay in which he revealed his style in its essentials. The work consists of a theme, twenty variations, and a coda. The basic motive of the Piano Variations consists of four notes, presented first in declamatory fashion, monophonically, *marcato*, and *fortissimo* (Ex. 8-5A and B). These four notes provide the basis for all that follows: octave transposition is a principal device and there is also something of Schoenberg's serial method. But the sound is different. The old qualifications of homophonic and polyphonic have become virtually irrelevant: there is no melodic line, no melody and accompaniment, no contrapuntal imitation; rather, there are isolated notes and chords ranging over the extent of the keyboard, even including overtones, achieved by holding silently depressed keys in the higher register while sounding chords in the lower. Copland frequently uses conventional chords, especially triads, but in completely new relationships, contexts, and progressions (Ex. 8-5C). Furthermore, although large chord complexes are used, they are spaced: the instrument is allowed to resonate so that the full quality of the sounds created may be absorbed. Yet there is a certain sparseness or leanness, economy, about the work that is also characteristic of much of the music of the time. What is important and individual is the aloof and objective atmosphere. Stimulating an emotional response from the listener is not the aim; the dynamic quality of German Romanticism is not present. Instead, the music is presented as something there, stable, detached, well-made, and independent, thus conforming to an important quality of the neoclassical.

The same features reappear in the Piano Sonata, the Piano Fantasy, and *Night Thoughts*. Apart from the three-movement scheme, the sonata bears little relation to previous sonatas; the formal plans in the component movements are not those usually associated with the genre. In the first movement we find a sort of sonata structure, but very free and lacking thematic development in the conventional sense. The interval of the third is important, played in all ranges and in different combinations, so that once again sonority is primary. The second movement is fast with a chorale-like midsection, and the finale uses a folklike theme not unlike those of Copland's ballets. The Piano Fantasy, which follows no traditional formal plan (in the nineteenth century, as we have seen, it frequently appeared as a long work comparable to a sonata), shows the same concept of piano sound and the same preoccupation with the manipulation of intervals. While its theme forms a ten-tone succession of pitches, the two remaining tones being reserved for use in cadences, Copland has not used the serial method. Unlike the Piano Variations and Piano Sonata, the Fantasy calls for virtuoso skills from the player. *Night Thoughts* displays many of the same features.

Example 8-5. COPLAND: Piano Variations—Excerpts
    A. Theme—Beginning (mm. 1–4)
    B. Variation One—Beginning (mm. 10–14)
    C. Variation Four—Beginning (mm. 41–44)

Among the most serious and uncompromising of American composers was Roger Sessions (1896–1985), who like Copland and others received his training in Europe. For piano he composed three sonatas (1927–1930, 1946, and 1964–1965), a march, a waltz, a set of children's pieces, and two sets of character pieces. For one of them, *Pages From a Diary* (4, composed 1939–1940, published 1946), the title has given rise to some misunderstanding—all Sessions wanted to suggest was the old type, the album leaf. The other is a set of five pieces (composed 1974–1975). The sonatas typify his proclivity toward the large musical forms; they are big, intense, and complicated works conceived in an individual manner that shuns external display. In this we may detect the influence of his teacher Ernest Bloch (see above).

One of the most innovative composers to work in the atonal idiom independently of Schoenberg but incorporating some aspects of his method was Ruth Crawford Seeger (1901–1953), who, after receiving the first Guggenheim fellowship in composition ever awarded to a woman, went to study in Germany. Her music for piano consists of two groups of Preludes (5, composed 1924–1925, unpublished, and 4, composed 1927–1928, published 1928), and the "Study in Mixed Accents" (composed 1930, published 1932). Although technical preoccupations loom large here, an intense belief in the spiritual power of music informs all her work.

The composers just discussed took their point of departure either from French neoclassicism or from innovations like those of Schoenberg, which indeed in different ways dominate much twentieth-century music. Yet other composers remained true to the Romantic-expressive tradition of nineteenth-century German instrumental music: they accepted the old aesthetic of the musical art work, maintained conventional musical forms and procedures, but enlarged their harmonic vocabulary with some of the new sounds. While many American composers belong to this group, most of them did not emphasize piano music. Prominent among the earlier figures was Leo Ornstein (1892–), whose music, mostly character pieces of which we cite "Wild Man's Dance" (1915), created a sensation in the years 1910–1930 but then passed from view. Others include Ernst Toch (1887–1964), born in Austria, who composed much piano music, again mostly character pieces; Florence B. Price (1888–1953); Karol Rathaus (1895–1954); William Grant Still (1895–1978); George Antheil (1900–1959); Anis Fuleihan (1900–1970); Paul Creston (1906–1985); Ross Lee Finney (1906–), who also worked with dodecaphonic serialism; Halsey Stevens (1908–1989), who has been extraordinarily active in composing piano music for many years, his work encompassing all important genres, large and small; Howard Swanson (1909–1978); Alan Hovhaness (1911–); and Norman Dello Joio (1913–).

By all odds the outstanding composer of this persuasion—and with Copland doubtless the outstanding contemporary American composer of piano music—was Samuel Barber (1910–1981). As is typical of other contemporary composers, his reputation as a composer of piano music was based on but two works (Copland's essentially was based on three):[43] the set of character pieces, *Excursions* (4, op. 20, composed 1944), and the Sonata in E-flat minor (op. 26, 1949), although he also produced a Nocturne (op. 33, 1959), subtitled "Homage to John Field," and the late Ballade (op. 46, 1977). The *Excursions*, as Barber himself put it, represent "excursions in small classical forms into regional American idioms." The first two come from jazz, a boogie-woogie and a stylized blues; the third is a set of variations on the cowboy song "The Streets of Laredo" (which Copland used in his ballet *Billy the Kid*); and the last is a vivid suggestion of a barn dance with an energetic country fiddler. The sonata, on the other hand, commissioned by the League of Composers for its twenty-fifth anniversary, is a major work. In the traditional large form, its four movements are Allegro energico in sonata form, an Allegro vivace, an Adagio mesto, and, as finale, a brilliant fugue, Allegro con spirito. In the treatment of the forms Barber is strictly traditional. The sonata form embodies thematic contrast, the principal theme strong and motivic (see Ex. 8-6A), the secondary theme lyrical and ornamented, the development strict and powerful. Both Scherzo and Adagio display the conventional three-part scheme and the characters normally associated with such movements. The fugue, in three voices, has a lengthy figuration-based subject (see Ex. 8-6B) and a countersubject derived from a stock jazz figure. The working-out involves learned counterpoint (stretto, augmentation, inversion, motivic treatment of the subject); and the movement attains a large climax, followed by a written-out cadenza. Chromaticism and dissonance predominate (the Adagio even contains some unsystematic dodecaphonic writing). This sonata ranks among the most outstanding produced by an American.

Another group of composers consists of nationalists, composers preoccupied with the establishment of a musical art that draws its inspiration and materials from indigenous elements, similar to movements in Europe. We have already observed instances of this here and there: folk songs, barn dances, and hymn tunes in Ives, Cowell, Copland, and Barber; and jazz elements in Copland and Barber. For jazz itself, there is the well-known set Preludes (3, composed 1926, published 1927) by George Gershwin (1898–1937), of which the second is a stylized blues, the others being fast and in the style of "hot" jazz; Gershwin also made a solo piano version of his famous *Rhapsody in Blue* (1923). But generally the composers included here used what they regarded as peculiarly American to derive a set of traits from all aspects of music.

An outstanding exponent of the American nationalist manner was Roy Harris (1898–1979). His impact, while profound, has not been primarily through piano music (dates here are of composition).[44] The large form is represented in his work by the early Sonata (op. 1, 1928), an intense, serious three-movement work in cyclic form that foreshadows what he was later to achieve in the symphony; the Suite in Three Movements (1944); and the Toccata (1950). The smaller form is represented by the Little Suite (1939) and the highly characteristic set *American Ballads* (5, 1942), which are American equivalents of Bartók's folk song arrangements. Harris emphasized modal

Example 8-6. BARBER: Sonata in E-flat minor (op. 26)—Excerpts
    A. Allegro energico—Beginning (mm. 1–4)
    B. Allegro con spirito—Beginning (mm. 1–4)

scales and their related harmonies, linear texture, long and continuously flowing lines in constantly changing meters, and dissonant, often quartal, harmonies. At the same time, like the neoclassicists, he rejected nineteenth-century forms. Another composer of this persuasion is Harris' pupil William
Schuman (1910–1992), important in American musical life through his work
as director of the Juilliard School and later of Lincoln Center in New York City.
Piano music again is relatively unimportant in his output; he composed but
three works, all character pieces—*Three Score Set* (3, 1943), *Piano Moods* (3,
1950), and the cycle *Voyage* (5, 1954). Finally, there was Elie Siegmeister
(1909–1991), who composed character pieces and sonatas.

Another group of composers who worked toward the development of a
particularly American way of composing was associated with the Eastman
School of Music in Rochester. The first director of the school, Howard Han-
son (1896–1981), wrote piano music only during his early career as a composer. His way of composing remained indebted to the values of the German
Romantic tradition, and in his piano music we find the usual types of character pieces, frequently with Nordic associations that relate him to MacDowell; he also composed a sonata. Other composers associated with this group
likewise composed relatively little for the piano. Hunter Johnson (1906–) has
a single Sonata (composed 1933–1934, revised 1936 and again 1947–1948), a
work in three movements that seeks to express the spirit of the American
South. Burrill Phillips (1907–1988) composed music in which he combined
folk and jazz elements with the neoclassical: among his early pieces is *Nine
by Nine* (1942), a set of nine variations in nine-beat meter; *Informalities* (3,
1945), which contain a blues; a toccata (1946) that employs an ostinato boogie-woogie figure; the Divertimenti (3, 1946), which contain a neoclassical
"Homage to Monteverdi"; and a Sonata (1947); more recently he has composed another set of character pieces entitled *Various and Sundry* (5, 1961)
and three more sonatas. Robert Ward (1917–) produced a single piano sonata
and several character pieces, among them *Lamentation* (composed 1946,
published 1948). Ulysses Kay (1917–) also composed a piano Sonata (1941)
but otherwise emphasized the neoclassical, as in his two sets of Inventions
(1946 and 1964). Finally, Gardner Read (1913–) composed *American Circle*,
variations on a folklike melody, and several character pieces.

More prolific, at least in regard to piano music, were David Diamond
and Robert Palmer (both born 1915). Whereas Palmer was trained entirely in
the United States (apart from work at Eastman he studied with Copland and
Harris), Diamond also studied in France with Boulanger (and also with Sessions). Both have given prominence to the large form, Diamond with a Sonata
(1935) and a Concerto for Two Pianos (1941), along with an earlier Sonatina
(1935), and Palmer with three large sonatas for piano solo (the first 1938–
1946, the second 1942–1948, and the third 1979) and two others, one for two
pianos (1944), the other for piano duet (1952). Diamond also has sets of children's pieces and three extended character pieces, *A Myriologue* (1935,
revised 1949), "The Tomb of Melville" (1944–1949), both in the French tradition of the tombeau, "Gambit" (1967), and a neoclassic Prelude and Fugue

(1978). Palmer produced a set of Preludes (3, 1941); the brilliantly propulsive "Toccata ostinato" (1945); the modal nocturne "Evening Music" (1956); *Epigrams* (3, 1960); "Morning Music" (1973); and Prelude, Fantasia, and Fugue (1983).

Finally, while a number of American composers worked with Schoenberg's dodecaphonic serialism, this method of composition did not become important until around midcentury, so that—with one exception—we can defer this discussion until the next chapter. That exception is Wallingford Riegger (1885–1961). While he did not compose extensively for the piano, Riegger adopted a distinctly American experimental, perhaps pragmatic, approach to the serial method, using it freely here and there. His music for piano comprises early impressionist character pieces, the brilliant "New Dance" (op. 18, 1935) with its Latin-American rhythms; a set that comprises a compendium of compositional techniques under the title *New and Old* (12, op. 38, 1944), the last movement of which was revised and separately issued as *Toccata* (1957); and the bitonal "Petite Étude" (op. 62, 1956).

While there was much variety in American piano music of the first half of the twentieth century, its broad trends correspond to what we have observed elsewhere: the old Romantic tradition, largely Germanic; the newer French manner derived from impressionism and emphasizing the neoclassical; the nationalists; and Schoenberg's serialism. Yet the work of Cowell in particular suggests a new and radical kind of avant-garde music that was to become important only around the middle of the century and after.

CANADA

Among Canadian composers of piano music[45] are Wesley Octavius Forsyth (1859–1937), a virtuoso pianist; Clarence Lucas (1866–1947); Rudolphe Mathieu (1890–1962); and Claude Champagne (1891–1965), all of whom worked within the Romantic tradition. We find more progressive tendencies in Jean Coulthard (1908–), who oriented himself to the neoclassic; John Weinzweig (1913–), the first Canadian to take up the serial method, albeit in an individual way; and Jean Papineau-Couture (1916–), who moved from impressionism through neoclassicism to dissonant chromaticism. Two others who emphasized serialism have been Otto Joachim (1910–), who emigrated from Germany; and István Anhalt (1919–), who emigrated from Hungary. The French interest in oriental music has also been reflected in the work of Colin McPhee (1901–1964), who lived in the United States, whose *Balinese Ceremonial Music* for two pianos suggests the gamelan (Indonesian gong orchestra). Two prominent women composers have emphasized piano music: Barbara Pentland (1912–), whose extensive work has included serialism, especially as practiced by Webern; and Violet Archer (1913–), whose music is characterized by counterpoint, neoclassicism, and elements of serialism.

LATIN AMERICA AND ASIA

Here we find essentially the same picture: the overriding influence of European music associated with the effort to create individual ways of composing music based on native materials. Among the more traditional composers of Latin America are Manuel Ponce (1882–1948) of Mexico,[46] whose works include Variations and Fugue on a Theme of Handel and also *Canciónes Mexicanas* (1912); two Chileans, Alfonso Leng (1884–1974), who followed the German Romantic orientation in his set *Doloras* (4, composed 1901–1914, published 1916) in the tradition of the tombeau and a late Sonata (published 1951), and Enrique Soro (1884–1955); and the Brazilian Oscar Lorenzo Fernandez (1897–1948). Guillermo Uribe-Holguín (1880–1971) of Colombia, Pedro Umberto Allende Sarón (1885–1959) of Chile, and Teodoro Valcárcel (1900–1942) of Peru combined impressionist with nationalist elements. On the other hand, Juan Carlos Paz (1897–1972) of Argentina began using the serial method in 1934, among the first Latin-American composers to do so; this method characterizes his pieces (12, op. 30), based on a single tone row; he was followed by Rodolfo Halffter, who had moved from Spain to Mexico; José Ardévol (1911–1981), who moved from Spain to Cuba; Claudio Santoro (1919–1989) of Brazil,[47] the latter also involved with nationalism; and the Panamanian Roque Cordero (1917–). Among the many who were involved with neoclassicism, the Argentinean Roberto Garcia Morillo (1911–) and the Chileans Alfonso Letelier (1912–) and Juan Orrego-Salas (1919–) are prominent: the former produced a set of variations in F major (1948), and the latter, who emigrated to the United States, a set of variations, the character piece "Rustica," a sonata, and two suites.

Yet nationalism retained its importance: virtually all composers made at least some use of indigenous musical materials; some composers in a more pronounced way than others. Among those who emphasized indigenous materials are the Chileans Carlos Lavín (1883–1962) and Domingo de Santa Cruz (1899–1987), the latter an important figure whose large output also encompassed the neoclassic and atonality; the Peruvians Federico Gerdes (1873–1953), who used Indian materials as the basis for character pieces, and Andrés Sás (1900–1967), who emigrated from France; the Argentineans José María Castro (1892–1964), his brother Juan José Castro (1895–1968), Jacopo Ficher (1896–), who came from Russia, and Luis Gianneo (1897–1968); the Cuban Alejandro García Caturla (1906–1940); the Venezuelan Juan Bautista Plaza (1898–1964); and particularly the Brazilians Octavio Pinto (1890–1950), Francisco Mignone (1897–1986) who composed much for the piano and is known particularly for his series *Lendes brasileiras* (4, 1923–1930), and Camargo Guarnieri (1907–). A number of these subsequently moved to the international style, particularly the neoclassic. On the other hand, of the Mexican Grupo de los cuatro (Group of four) who were associated with the Aztec renaissance, only Blas Galindo-Dimas (1910–) produced much for piano, much of that neoclassic. (The Grupo de los cuatro were followers of Chavez, discussed below.) Central America is represented by the Nicaraguan Luis Delgadillo (1887–1961) and the Guatemalan Ricardo Castillo (1894–1967).

Finally, there was experimentation: Julián Carrillo (1875–1965) of Mexico worked with microtonal tunings, which he called *sonido 13* and eventually had pianos built to his specifications; and Rodolfo Holzmann (1910–), a German who emigrated to Peru, worked out a system of atonal composition using diatonic scales and quartal harmonies.

Amid all this activity, three Latin American composers of this period attained international stature: Heitor Villa-Lobos (1887–1959) of Brazil, Carlos Chávez (1899–1978) of Mexico, and Alberto Ginastera (1916–1983) of Argentina.

Villa-Lobos was typical in many respects. Curious about music, largely self-taught, open to the native music of his country (he made expeditions into the jungle to familiarize himself with the music of the native population), he also spent time in France, came under the influence of neoclassicism, and characteristically adapted these diverse aspects into his compositions. His output, in which piano music is important, was large and varied (dates are of composition except where indicated otherwise).[48] Among the neoclassical works are the *Bachianas brasileras* in which Villa-Lobos combined Brazilian and Bach-like elements; the fourth, in four movements (1930–1940), is for piano. Among the many nationalistic pieces are the early *Carnaval des criancas* (1919–1920); the three sets entitled *Prole do Bébé* (The Baby's Toys, 1918, 1921, and 1926), which along with their association with childhood are full of references to Brazilian music and, in the second set particularly, contain large, ambitious, and difficult pieces; the *Saudades das selvas brasileiras* (Memories of the Forests of Brazil, composed 1927); the *Alma brasileira* (the fifth in his series of *Choros*, composed 1925); *Amazonas* (1932); and the set *Ciclo brasileiro* (published 1937). In the "New York Skyline Melody" (composed 1939), he determined the theme by superimposing a photograph of the skyline of Manhattan on a musical staff. By far the largest of his piano works, however, is the grandiose quasi-improvisational *Rudepoema* (Rude Poem, composed 1921–1926), an extended virtuoso conception in continuous sections (related to the rhapsodic-epic-ballad tradition in European piano music) in which elements of native Brazilian music are effectively brought to expression.

Chávez and Ginastera also have been influenced by contemporary developments in music in the United States and Europe, as well as by the music of their native countries. Chávez worked with the large forms,[49] producing in all six sonatas (composed 1917–1961, not all of them published), an early Prelude and Fugue (composed 1917, unpublished), and a sonatina (composed 1924, published 1930). He also emphasized character pieces, including an early set, Waltzes (composed 1919–1921); Madrigals (7, 1921–1922); Nocturnes (4, 1922); Pieces (7, 1925–1930), some of which require virtuoso playing and which include a "Blues" and a "Fox[-trot]"; Preludes (10, 1937, published 1940); a large *Invención* (composed 1958, published 1960); and the set *Caprichos* (5, 1983). He paid particular attention to the etude, producing two sets, one early (4, 1919–1921), two late, the *Estudios* (3, 1949) and the *Nuevos*

Estudios (4, 1952, unpublished), and two individual pieces, one subtitled "Hommenaje a Chopin," the other for the pianist Artur Rubinstein. While elements of indigenous music, particularly its more primitive aspects, inform his scores, Chávez' music is very chromatic, strongly dissonant, and frequently linear, and often more international than Mexican.

Ginastera[50] composed three nationalistic pieces—the *Danzas Argentinas* (op. 2, 1937), the Pieces (op. 6), and *Malambo* (op. 7, both 1940); he also wrote *Preludios americanos* (12 in 2 vols., op. 12, 1944) in various styles, some resembling etudes, others in the styles of different countries of North and South America, still others resembling specific composers; the Creole Dance Suite (op. 15, 1946); and a Rondo on Argentine Children's Folk Tunes (op. 19, 1947). His major work, however, is his large first Sonata (op. 22, 1952). In four movements, this work generally accords with the old Romantic expressive tradition, incorporating at the same time features of Argentinean music and the new sound world of Copland's piano music. The first movement is in sonata form with a powerful declamatory and rhetorical opening; the second is the Scherzo (marked *scorrevole*), third is the rhapsodic slow movement, and the work concludes with the percussive, toccata-like finale. Ginastera subsequently composed two more sonatas (1981 and 1983).

Western art music has had different fates in the countries of Asia, in some countries making an enormous impact—in the sense that native composers began receiving training in the western style which they then adopted—in others less. It challenged the ancient traditional art music of Japan and has become a potent force in that country. Shukichi Mitsukuri (1895–1971) was among the first Japanese composers to work in the tradition of nineteenth-century German Romanticism, as evidenced, for instance, by his *Night Rhapsody* (1935). Yoritsune Matsudaira (1907–) and Kiyoshige Koyama (1914–) used Japanese musical materials much the way a European nationalistic composer would have. Still others, as we will see in the next chapter, took up impressionism and Schoenberg's serial method so that by the second half of the century the full range of western piano music finds representation.

In China, on the other hand, western music has been far less successful, mostly because of the isolationist policies of the empire, the many years of war and revolution, and finally the often difficult times of Communist rule. Western art music has yet to take hold in India or elsewhere in Asia.

NOTES FOR CHAPTER EIGHT

1. Dates of composition according to *Béla Bartók: A Complete Catalogue of His Published Works* (London: Boosey & Hawkes, 1970), and D. Yeomans, *Bartók for Piano* (Bloomington: Indiana University Press, 1988). Sz. numbers from A. Szöllösy, "Bibliographie des oeuvres musicales et écrits musicologiques de Béla Bartók," published in B. Szabolsci, *Bartók: Sa vie et son oeuvre* (Budapest: Covina; Leipzig: Breitkopf & Härtel, 1957), 299–345.

2. J. Uhde, *Bartóks Mikrokosmos: Spielanweisungen und Erläuterungen* (Regensburg: Bosse, 1952), 21.

3. Dates of composition according to J. Kratochvilová, *Dílo Leose Janáčka (1854–1928)*, Vyběrová Bibliografie č. 220 (Brno: Statni Vedecka Knihovna, 1978).

4. See B. Cervinková et al., *Bohuslav Martinů: Bibliografický Katalog* (Prague: Panton, 1990), 16–35.

5. Dates according to M. Montagu-Nathan, *Handbook to the Pianoforte Works of Alexander Scriabin* (London: Chester, 1922), and A. Swan, *Scriabin* (London: Lane, 1923). Dates are of publication unless otherwise specified.

6. See R. Palmieri, *Sergei Vasil'evich Rachmaninoff: A Guide to Research*, Garland Composer Resource Manuals 3 (New York: Garland, 1985), 7–23.

7. Dates of composition from C. Caesar, *Igor Stravinsky: A Complete Catalogue* (San Francisco: San Francisco Press, 1982).

8. I. Stravinsky with Robert Craft, *Dialogues and a Diary* (New York: Doubleday, 1963), 74–75, for this and the following quotations.

9. Summarized by D. Gutman, *Prokofiev* (London: Alderman, 1988), 13, and I. Nestycv, *Sergei Prokofiev* (New York: Knopf, 1946), 68–73.

10. Dates according to S. Schlifstein, *Sergej Prokofjew: Dokumente, Briefe, Erinnerungen*, trans. F. Loesch (Leipzig: VEB Breitkopf & Härtel, 1961), 171 ff.

11. Dates from D. Hulme, *Dimitri Shostakovich: Catalogue, Bibliography and Discography* (Muir of Ord: Kyle & Glen, 1982). Dates are of composition unless otherwise indicated.

12. Dates of composition according to E. Tanzberger, *Werkverzeichnis Jean Sibelius* (Wiesbaden: Breitkopf & Härtel, 1962).

13. Dates according to D. Fog, *Carl Nielsen: Kompositioner* (Copenhagen: Nyt Nordisk, 1965).

14. Dates of publication from K. Mllerhj, *Niels Viggo Bentzons Kompositioner* (Copenhagen: Hansen, 1980).

15. See generally L. Powell, *A History of Spanish Piano Music* (Bloomington: Indiana University Press, 1980).

16. Dates of publication according to A. Ruiz Tarazona, *Isaac Albéniz: España soñada* (Madrid: Real Musical, 1975), 51–58.

17. See J. del Busto, *Turina* (Madrid: Esposa-Calpe, 1981). Dates are of publication.

18. See R. Crichton, *Manuel de Falla: Descriptive Catalogue of His Works* (London: Chester; Copenhagen: Hansen, 1976). See also G. Chase and A. Budwig, *Manuel de Falla: A Bibliography and Research Guide*, Garland Composer Resource Manuals 4 (New York: Garland, 1986).

19. See D. Kushner, *Ernest Bloch: A Guide to Research*, Garland Research Manuals 14 (New York: Garland, 1988), 232–233.

20. English translation as *Towards a New Esthetic of Music*, trans. T. Baker (New York: Schirmer, 1911); also in *Three Classics in the Aesthetic of Music* (New York: Dover, 1962), 73–102.

21. K numbers and dates from J. Kindermann, *Thematisch-chronologisches Verzeichnis der musikalischen Werke von Ferruccio B. Busoni*, Studien zur Musikgeschichte des 19. Jahrhunderts 19 (Regensburg: Bosse, 1980). See also M. Roberge, *Ferruccio Busoni: A Bio-Bibliography*, Bio-Bibliographies in Music 34 (New York: Garland, 1991). In most cases publication followed shortly after composition.

22. Dates (up to 1950) according to G. Gatti, *L'opera di Gian Francesco Malipiero* (Treviso: Canova, 1952): 256–259; 266–267.

23. N. Rossi, *Catalogue of Works by Mario Castelnuovo-Tedesco* (New York: International Castelnuovo-Tedesco Society, 1977), 42–51.

24. Dates according to C. MacDonald, *Luigi Dallapiccola: A Complete Catalogue* (London: Boosey & Hawkes, 1978).

25. Dates according to C. Annibaldi and M. Monna, *Bibliografia e catalogo delle opere di Goffredo Petrassi* (Milan: Zerboni, 1980).

26. See P. Hindmarsh, *Frank Bridge: A Thematic Catalogue* (London: Faber, 1983).

27. Dates according to R. Threlfall, *A Catalogue of the Compositions of Frederick Delius* (London: Delius Trust, 1977), 183–193.

28. Dates according to M. Kennedy, *A Catalogue of the Work of Ralph Vaughan Williams*, rev. ed. (London: Oxford, 1982).

29. Dates according to *Benjamin Britten: A Complete Catalogue of His Published Works* (London: Faber & Faber, 1973).

30. Dates according to G. Theil, *Michael Tippett: A Bio-Bibliography*, Music Reference Collection 21 (New York: Greenwood, 1989), 43–45.

31. Dates of composition according to *Frank Martin: Liste des oeuvres* (Zurich: Schweizerisches Musik-Archiv, 1981), 33–34.

32. See *The Portable Emerson*, ed. M. van Doren (New York: Viking, 1946), 294 and 302 respectively.

33. See particularly C. Henderson, *The Charles Ives Tunebook*, Bibliographies in American Music 14 (Michigan: Harmonie Park Press, 1990), the most extensive presentation of this subject.

34. Dates according to G. Block, *Charles Edward Ives: A Bio-Bibliography*, Bio-Bibliographies in Music 14 (New York: Greenwood, 1988), 27–32.

35. See the edition by H. Boatwright (New York: Norton, 1972).

36. See A. Ghandar, "Charles Ives: Organisation in 'Emerson,'" *Musicology* [Australia] 6 (1980): 111–127.

37. L numbers and dates from W. Lichtenwanger, *The Music of Henry Cowell: A Descriptive Catalog*, ISAM Monograph 23 (Brooklyn: Institute for the Study of American Music, 1986).

38. See D. Anderson, *The Works of Charles T. Griffes: A Descriptive Catalogue*, Studies in Musicology 68 (Ann Arbor: UMI, 1983).

39. Dates of composition according to M. Meckna, *Virgil Thomson: A Bio-Bibliography*, Bio-Bibliographies in Music 4 (New York: Greenwood, 1986), 48–66.

40. See H. Pollock, *Walter Piston*, Studies in Musicology 50 (Ann Arbor: UMI, 1982), 187–193.

41. See D. and N. Patterson, *Vincent Persichetti: A Bio-Bibliography*, Bio-Bibliographies in Music 16 (New York: Greenwood, 1988), 24–37. Dates are of composition.

42. See J. Skowronski, *Aaron Copland: A Bio-Bibliography*, Bio-Bibliographies in Music 2 (New York: Greenwood, 1985), 239. Dates are of composition.

43. Dates of composition from D. Hennessee, *Samuel Barber: A Bio-Bibliography*, Bio-Bibliographies in Music 3 (Westport, CT: Greenwood, 1985).

44. See R. Strassburg, *Roy Harris: A Catalog of His Works* (Los Angeles: California State University, 1974).

45. See H. Kallmann, *A History of Music in Canada, 1534–1914* (Toronto: University of Toronto Press, 1960), and G. Proctor, *Canadian Music of the Twentieth Century* (Toronto: University of Toronto Press, 1980).

46. See D. Malmström, *Introduction to Twentieth Century Mexican Music* (Uppsala: University Press, 1974).

47. See D. Appleby, "Trends in Recent Brazilian Piano Music," *Latin American Music Review* 2 (1981): 91–102, as well as his *The Music of Brazil* (Austin: University of Texas Press, 1983).

48. See *Villa-Lobos, sua obra*, 2nd ed. ([n.p.], 1971), 150–167.

49. Dates according to [R. Halffter,] *Carlos Chávez: Cátalogo completo de sus obras* (Mexico, D.F.: Sociedad des Autores y Compositores de Musica, 1971).

50. See *Alberto Ginastera: A Catalogue of His Published Works* (London: Boosey & Hawkes, 1976), 20, 21.

CHAPTER NINE

From Mid- to Late Twentieth Century

T he years following the end of World War II appear more and more to have been a watershed, symbolic of great and thoroughgoing changes in our culture. Of profound importance has been the growth of technology. For music the recording and reproduction of sound, which began in the late nineteenth century, has become increasingly important in the twentieth. Closely related is the virtually instantaneous transmission of sound via radio and (with visual images) television. Then there is the electronic generation of sound by means of the synthesizer.

Electronic transmission of all kinds of information has fundamentally affected our lives. Anything that happens in a remote part of the world—even the moon and beyond—can be experienced almost simultaneously in one's own home. By extension, whatever human civilizations have recorded from the past can also readily be made available to us. For the composer this accessibility means that he or she can experience any sort of music that has existed at virtually any time and in virtually any place. This accessibility has affected musical composition in that the music of far-off continents, India and Asia, for instance, now has a greater impact on composers in Europe and the United States than had been true before. Concerning this situation, Leonard Meyer[1] believes that evolutionary development is no longer possible: instead we will experience a stasis in which there will be no main line of development, no central style as we have observed in the past, but rather a profusion of individual styles, as composers select elements from the universe of possibilities available to them.

Moreover, there is the international character imparted to musical life in the age of the instant transmission of knowledge and of travel at the speed of sound. Styles are no longer restricted to individual countries but rather are free to take hold and develop anywhere and everywhere. The dislocations caused by war, particularly World War II, have had much to do with this internationalism. Yet to a lesser degree the situation had existed since the early part of the century: the influence of Debussy, Schoenberg, and Stravinsky, for instance, transcended national borders. But in the second half of the century, individual national differences in musical composition have virtually disappeared. We will see, for example, that many Japanese composers have allied themselves with the most avant-garde tendencies of western art music. Along with this internationalization and universalization, many more women have taken up composition.

The developments of broadcasting, recording, and synthesized sound in particular have given rise to many questions, some of which strike at the heart of the traditional ways of making and listening to music. Broadcasting and recording, for instance, have radically changed the ways in which we can experience music. Musical performance has also been affected. In the 1920s both Stravinsky and Hindemith urged the performer rigorously to adhere to the score, to suppress individual desires as to how the piece should be performed, the logical conclusion of which leads to music produced by a machine: synthesized sound has made it possible to eliminate the performer altogether. Then there is the issue of what constitutes real musical instruments, in this context referred to as "acoustical," as opposed to synthesized sound. We will see that some composers have combined the two. A synthesized piano has also been developed and marketed, one that incorporates degrees of resistance into the action of the keys to simulate that of the conventional acoustical instrument, so that loudness depends on the force with which the keys are struck. An early example of a synthesized piano was Emerick Spielmann's Superpiano (1930), in which photoelectric cells generated the electric current that produced the tone. Since the middle 1970s many manufacturers became involved in digital electronic pianos: along with traditional firms such as Baldwin, Bösendorfer, and Yamaha, there are electronic firms such as Akai, Casio, Kawai, Kurzweil, Roland, Suzuki, and Technics.

In any case, composers continued to emphasize the piano. We will commence with a composer who gave the instrument unusual prominence in his work, a composer of overriding significance whose life virtually spans the century. His work is based on important traditions interpreted in the light of continued investigation of the materials of music and experimentation with new and different techniques of organizing them, but here associated with powerful expression. The music of French organist and composer, Olivier Messiaen (1908–1992), has had an influence both wide and deep.

Trained under Dukas and Dupré at the Paris Conservatory, Messiaen emerged in the 1930s as the most important member of the Jeune France group who called for a "rehumanization" of music and thus were ardent opponents of the neoclassic aesthetic that prevailed at the time. He continually insisted upon the emotional, even spiritual, power of music. He believed in the correspondence between music and religion, thus in the same tradition as his colleague Jolivet, the Englishman Cyril Scott, the Russian Scriabin, and the Americans Dane Rudhyar and, later, George Crumb (see below).

MESSIAEN'S PRINCIPAL WORKS FOR PIANO

Pieces (1917)
"La dame de Shalott" (1917)
"La tristesse d'un grand ciel bleu" (1925)
Preludes (8, composed 1928–1929, published 1932)
"Fantaisie burlesque" (1932)
"Pièce pour le tombeau de Paul Dukas" (composed 1935,
    published 1936)
Rondeau (1943)
Visions de l'Amen, two pianos (1943)
Regards sur l'enfant Jésus (20, composed 1944, published 1955)
Cantéyodjayâ (composed 1948, published 1953)
Études de rythme (4, composed 1948–1950, published 1951): "Ile
    de feu, I"—"Mode de valeurs et d'intensités"—"Neumes
    rythmiques"—"Ile de feu, II"[2]
Catalogue d'oiseaux (13 in 7 vols., composed 1956–1958,
    published 1964)
La fauvette des jardins (The Golden Warbler, published 1972)
Petites esquisses d'oiseaux (6, composed 1986)

In general in the pieces composed prior to World War II, Messiaen worked in traditional genres of composition—the character piece and the prelude—which show the influence of impressionism and The Six, as in "La dame de Shalott" and "La tristesse d'un grand ciel bleu"; polytonality and jazz inform the "Fantaisie burlesque." In the works composed during and after the war, however, Messiaen revealed himself to be among the most progressive composers of the time, not only on account of his compositions but also by means of his composition class at the Paris Conservatory which attracted a generation of composers from all over Europe. In his compositions an essentially Romantic conception is clear enough, with the expressive power of music heightened by the expansion of resources from within and the addition of new elements from without. Recognizing that just as chromatic notes represent alterations of or additions to the diatonic scale, Messiaen developed chromatic rhythms that make use of note values that stand in a similar relation to conventional metric relationships.[3] He took rhythmic patterns from Hindu music, specifically identifying them in his music. He also employed what he called non-retrogradable rhythms, in which the arrangement of the different note values is such that its retrograde is the same as the original. Similarly he used modes of limited transpositions, scales for which only a few transpositions involve pitches not present in the original form, such as the chromatic scale (no transposition possible) or the whole-tone scale (one transposition possible); he devised a number of others. He was also interested in natural sounds, particularly bird calls, which he systematically collected, investigated thoroughly, adapted, and incorporated into musical compositions.[4] Other natural sounds he used include bells, the wind, the sea, and so on. He also drew plainsong into his compositions. The symbolic and expressive value of these elements plays an important part in his use of them.

First among these newer works are large sets of pieces, *Visions de l'Amen* for two pianos and *Regards sur l'enfant Jésus*. Both reveal fundamental aspects of his new art: the fervent religious expression, the juxtaposition of passages embodying the greatest possible contrast, the use of themes derived from the songs of birds and plainsong, Indian rhythms (talas), non-retrogradable rhythms, modes of limited transpositions, and rhythmic canons. The combination of intense, indeed rhapsodic, expression with learned technique is fundamental to his art. Moreover, both sets involve cyclic themes to which Messiaen assigned symbolic meanings: "Amen" in *Visions de l'Amen*, "God," "Star and Cross" in *Regards sur l'enfant Jésus*. These large and intense works represent in a rough way the pianistic equivalent of a large symphony by Mahler. *Cantéyodjayâ* is a single extended piece that displays the same features but with emphasis on Indian rhythmic patterns.

In his search for new techniques Messiaen engaged aspects of Schoenberg's serial principle (he never worked with Schoenberg's techniques and aesthetics in any strict sense), applying it in an individual way to all aspects of a composition; along with controlling the pitch content of the work, the serial principle affected rhythm, dynamics, and types of articulation. This approach has been called total or integrated serialism (Stravinsky called it "totalitarian" serialism); and while we have noted something approaching it in Blacher and Wagner-Régeny, Messiaen carried the idea out in a more consequent way.

The critical piece here is the second of his *Études de rythme*, "Mode de valeurs et d'intensités." Messiaen's instructions show in order (see Ex. 9-1A): twelve different modes of attack ("attaques"), seven levels of dynamics ("intensités"), and a total of twenty-four different durations ("valeurs")— arranged progressively in what he calls "durées chromatiques" increasing incrementally by the value of a 32nd-note and organized in three "divisions." Finally, he has organized the pitches into three "divisions," each containing all twelve pitches, the first in the treble register, the second in the middle, and the third in the bass, but with each pitch rigorously bound to a particular dynamic level and type of attack.

The two pieces in the set entitled "Ile de feu"—the title refers to Papua, an island he never visited—contain episodes in which Messiaen has used twelve pitches, twelve different note values (durations), and five degrees of loudness. Thus these etudes count among the first examples of integrated serialism: the other early, actually earlier, example is by Milton Babbitt (see below). These etudes of Messiaen had an enormous impact, particularly in Europe.

Messiaen then commenced a series of compositions based on bird song which culminates in his magnum opus of piano music, the seven books of the

Catalogue d'oiseaux that contain in all thirteen pieces, two of which—"La rousserolle effarvatte" (The Reed Warbler, vii) and "Le merle de roche" (The Rock Thrush, x)—are long. In the subtitle to the set Messiaen tells us that these pieces involve "songs of birds in the provinces of France. Each one is presented in its habitat, surrounded by its landscape and the songs of other birds which live in the same region." Messiaen has also provided each piece with a description. While bird songs supply the principal thematic material of these pieces, in most cases the listener will not be able to recognize them, since Messiaen has modified them by transposition, slowing down the tempo and adapting their melodic content to the pitches available on the piano. The player, however, does not have this difficulty, since the bird songs are plainly labeled in the score (see Ex. 9-2). In other respects the pieces display features typical of Messiaen: modal and synthetic scales, dissonant harmonies, east Indian and other exotic rhythms, and sudden juxtapositions of contrasting material, all driven by great fervor. In the same spirit is his late and lengthy *La fauvette des jardins*.

Among Messiaen's pupils who have composed for the piano we can mention, apart from Boulez and Stockhausen (see below), Betsy Jolas (1926–), Jean Barraqué (1928–1973), Michel Fano (1929–), Alexander Goehr (1932–), Robert Sherlaw Johnson (1932–), and Gilbert Amy (1936–). Messiaen has also influenced the Canadians Gilles Tremblay (1932–1982) and Jacques Hétu (1938–).

Messiaen's work reveals the international character that musical life has assumed since midcentury. Six principal trends or traditions dominating piano music can be distinguished:

1. *The chromatic-dissonant tradition*, most often, but not always, atonal and serial, which emphasizes traditional formal structures and produces compositions that are serious, often large-scaled, complex, intense, and difficult if not forbidding. At its basis such music most often has an important intellectual and rationalistic component, as seen in the organization and manipulation of the tone row, series, or set, and yet, following the example of Berg, it often achieves powerful expression. This trend has dominated the composition of art music internationally from the 1950s at least until the early 1990s, so that if one had to designate a central tradition for art music in the late twentieth century, this would seem to offer the best choice.

2. *Extended techniques and new sounds*. The traditional sounds produced by the acoustical piano are supplemented or replaced by elements of noise and other sounds, sometimes synthesized, sometimes not. Important here are extended techniques by means of which the piano's strings can be played directly by the hand, either struck, plucked, or bowed, tone clusters and harmonics can be sounded, or the sounds produced by the instrument are electronically manipulated and amplified. Such sounds can also be synthesized, as already pointed out. While this sort of thing has a long history, going back to the Futurists and the early work of Henry Cowell, it became

A.

Ce morceau utilise un mode de hauteurs (36 sons), de valeurs (24 durées), d'attaques (12 attaques), et d'intensités (7 nuances). Il est entièrement écrit dans le mode.

Attaques: (avec l'attaque normale, sans signe, cela fait 12.)

Intensités: *ppp* *pp* *p* *mf* *f* *ff* *fff*
1   2   3   4   5   6   7

Sons: Le mode se partage en 3 Divisions ou ensembles mélodiques de 12 sons, s'étendant chacun sur plusieurs octaves, et croisés entre eux. Tous les sons de même nom sont différents comme hauteur, comme valeur, et comme intensité.

Valeurs:

Division I: durées chromatiques de 1 à 12

Division II: durées chromatiques de 1 à 12

Division III: durées chromatiques de 1 à 12

Au total 24 durées:

Voici le mode:

I

(la Division I est utilisée dans la portée supérieure du Piano)

II

(la Division II est utilisée dans la portée médiane du Piano)

III

(la Division III est utilisée dans la portée inférieure du Piano)

Example 9-1. MESSIAEN: "Mode de valeurs et d'intensités" from *Études de rythme*—
Excerpts
    A. Chart
    B. Beginning (mm. 1–10)

B.

important in the late 1940s. Composers of such music frequently use new and radically different kinds of musical notation.

   3. *Open form.* Among the new concepts for organizing music this has been among the most important. Here the composer leaves important aspects of the composition—in some cases the entire work—up to chance, so that the composition becomes indeterminate or aleatory (alea being the Latin word for dice). There are two basic types: one in which chance operations create the substance of the piece, the other in which chance operations affect how the piece is performed (the order of sections in the piece, for instance, having not been determined by the composer). Such music appeared in the early 1950s. Again composers have developed new means of notation for such compositions. Related to open form music is concept music, in which the score either contains or consists of instructions for what the performer is to do; not all concept music is performable in the conventional sense.

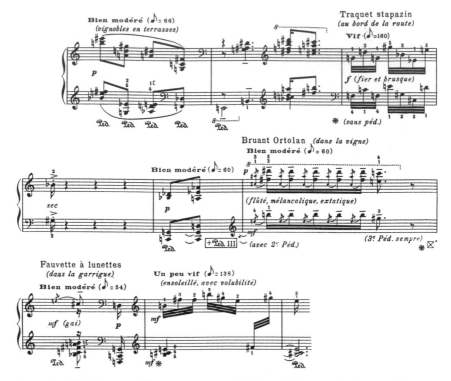

Example 9-2. Messiaen: "Le traquet stapazin" (The Black-eared Wheatear) from
Catalogue d'oiseaux (vii)—Beginning (mm. 1–9)
Courtesy of Alphonse LeDuc, Éditeurs de musique, Paris.

    4. *Minimalism,* a reductive style emphasizing constant repetition of basic figuration patterns in the context of simple tonal harmonies. This began in the 1960s but became important only several decades later.

    5. *The new tonality or new romanticism,* in which composers seem to have "rediscovered" tonal harmony and the traditional harmonic functions, which they exploit anew. This movement became important in the 1970s.

    6. *Conservatism,* involving composers who work within the system of tonal harmony and according to the aesthetics of nineteenth-century Romanticism, thus in effect continuing the tradition of composers of the first half of the century such as Prokofiev and Barber.

    These six trends will provide the basis for organizing our survey. As a cautionary note, however, we must keep in mind that many composers work in more than one of these traditions. In particular it will prove convenient for us to combine the second and third of these, new sounds and open form, since composers using one often also use the other. We conclude with separate sections devoted to piano music in Latin America and Asia.

THE CHROMATIC-DISSONANT TRADITION

Inspired by the serial methods of composition developed by Schoenberg but particularly influenced by Berg, whose music was saturated with Romantic expression in the traditional sense, this trend became dominant in the late 1940s and remained so for decades. Prominent among German composers who continued to work essentially within the limits established by Schoenberg were Giselher Klebe (1925–) and Hans Werner Henze (1926–). Neither of these has composed extensively for the piano. Klebe has composed sets of character pieces, and Henze, among the most successful composers of the time but known mostly for operas and symphonies, has produced two sets of variations (1949 and 1963), a Sonata for piano, the latter (1959) under the influence of Webern, and a Divertimento for two pianos (1964).

Elliott Carter (1908–), among the foremost composers of his time, is difficult to classify. While his music is not serial, its uncompromising intellectuality and intense expression stem from that tradition. Carter has created two important works for piano: the Sonata (composed 1945–1946) and *Night Fantasies* (1982). In two large movements, the sonata reveals conventional elements: its first movement may be associated with the old sonata structure, with two contrasting tempos. The last movement, less traditional, employs a chorale-like passage as a refrain element and features a brilliant neobaroque fugue full of driving figuration. In its sonorous conception of the piano it owes something to Copland. *Night Fantasies* is an extended piece of great complexity and difficulty.

Among other composers of the older generation is George Perle (1915–), an important theorist and explicator of the serial method of composition who has composed a significant body of works for the piano involving mostly traditional categories. He began with the neoclassical, as evidenced by such pieces as the Pantomime, Interlude, and Fugue (op. 1, 1937) and the Classical Suite (op. 3, 1940), but then adopted the serial method. Over time he developed a personal way of dealing with this method which he identified as twelve-tone tonality, in which he discarded Schoenberg's idea that all pitch classes (a term referring to the twelve pitches with no specification of their octave transposition) should have equal value. Thus his music in general operates with traditional structures and identifiable themes while displaying good grasp of the potential of the piano. Among his compositions of this type are the Short Sonata (composed 1964, published 1967), the Toccata (1969), the Suite in C (1960), Fantasy Variations (1971), the lyrical Ballade (1981), two sets of etudes (1976 and 1984), the Sonatina (published 1986), and *Lyric Intermezzo* (1987). Perle is doubtless to be reckoned among the most important composers of piano music to have emerged from the serial tradition.

Of essentially the same persuasion is Leon Kirchner (1919–) who also has not specifically been a serialist but whose work partakes of similar complexities; he has composed a Sonata (1948), a Little Suite (1949), "A Moment for Roger" (1978), and a set of pieces (5, 1980). Other composers to be grouped here include Louise Talma (1906–), Arthur Berger, Robert Moevs (1920), Lawrence Moss (1927–), Yehudi Wyner (1929–), Iain Hamilton (1922), T. J. Anderson (1928–), Thea Musgrave (1928–), Sofia Gubaidulina (1931–), Easley Blackwood (1933–), Harrison Birtwhistle (1934–), Richard Rodney Bennett (1936–), and Shulamit Ran (1949–). The great difficulties that attend much of this music, both in compositional technique and in performance, have given rise to the expression *the New Virtuosity* to characterize much of it, and symptomatically this is associated with a revival of interest in the etude.

Further development and extension of the serial principle, however, fascinated other composers, particularly Milton Babbitt (1916–), who has taught for many years at Princeton University and has become an important analyst and theorist of the serial method. The vehicle for his breakthrough proved to be the piano: the Compositions for Piano (3, composed 1947–1948, published 1957). Here the series (Babbitt prefers the term *set*) in the first of these Compositions (Ex. 9-3) is exposed in the bass (m. 1–2).[5] The set of rhythmic values is 5–1–4–2, meaning that within each hexachord (set of six notes) a group of five notes is followed by a single note and then a group of four is followed by a group of two (see mm. 1–2, each hand having a complete statement). The usual modifications apply: inversion (1–5–2–4), retrograde (2–4–5–1), and retrograde inversion (4–2–5–1). Finally, Babbitt has associated a level of dynamics with each form of the set: prime = *mp*, inversion = *f*, retrograde = *mf*, and retrograde inversion = *p*. This seems to be the earliest example of total or integrated serialism, antedating Messiaen by about one year. Again, the music is complex, exploiting the extremes of the range of the instrument, with wide

Example 9-3. Babbitt: Composition for Piano (i)—Beginning (mm. 1–6)
Copyright 1957 by Boelke-Bomart, Inc. Used by permission.

leaps and sudden shifts of register, along with discontinuities of tempo, rhythm, and dynamics. Technically the piece has some points of similarity with Messiaen's (see above), but its expressive character is entirely different.

In particular Babbitt has been associated with the view that the musical art work is something complex and esoteric, directed at those specially trained to comprehend it, with much the same appeal that a paper on sub-atomic particles might have to an audience of physicists. As he has put it:

> The time has passed when the normally well-educated man without special preparation can understand the most advanced work in, for example, mathematics, philosophy and physics. Advanced music, to the extent that it reflects the knowledge and originality of the informed composer, scarcely can be expected to appear more intelligible than these arts and sciences to the person whose music education has been even less than his background in other fields.[6]

This elitist attitude seems implicitly shared by composers working in this tradition: it may go far to explain the lack of success this music has had with the general concert-going public.

Other pieces for piano by Babbitt (dates are of composition) include Duet, Semi-Simple Variations (both 1956), Partitions (1957), Post-Partitions (1966), *Tableaux* (1972), *Reflections* for piano and tape (1975), "Minute Waltz" (1977), two pieces entitled "Playing for Time" (1977 and 1983), "My Compliments to Roger," (1978), "About Time" (1982), Canonical Form (1983), "It Takes Twelve to Tango" (1984), and *Lagniappe* (1985). More recently he has produced "Emblems" and Prelude, Interlude, and Fugue (both published 1993). For piano duet he composed "Don" (1983) and Envoi (1993).

Messiaen's breakthrough as represented in his *Études de rythme* was developed along radically different lines by Pierre Boulez (1925–), who has been preoccupied with securing rational control over all aspects of musical composition. In a provocative article,[7] Boulez criticized Schoenberg for, among other things, having in his serial method been concerned exclusively with pitch and not with rhythm and dynamics, to say nothing of form. In his own composition Boulez not only has dissociated themes from the twelve-tone set but went on to abandon traditional notions of melody and accompaniment, counterpoint, and form.

Piano music has been important in his early career as a composer. His first works were serial character pieces, the sets *Notations* (12, 1945, not published until 1985) and *Psalmodies* (3, 1945). *Notations* consists of twelve pieces each twelve bars in length, testifying to the influence of Webern; four of these he subsequently orchestrated. Thereupon Boulez turned to the large form, the sonata, of which he produced three, the first two in the late 1940s, while the third, begun in 1961, has remained unfinished. The first two sonatas reveal his preoccupation with Schoenberg's serial method, except that, following the example of Webern, he abandoned traditional means in favor of a complex arrangement of motives embedded in figuration characterized by wide leaps and unmediated contrasts, all in the context of dissonant harmony and fully exploiting the extremes of the range of the instrument, with fili-gree-like passages of great delicacy in the high treble register. Boulez not only subjects the series to constant permutation but derives short elements, cells, from it which he then employs thematically. Yet Boulez also uses detailed markings indicating dynamics and expressive character. While the first sonata (composed 1946, published 1951) is in two movements, the sec-ond (composed 1947–1948, published 1950) is in the traditional four: Boulez in fact has described it as his "Beethoven sonata." The individual movements of the second sonata in particular (see Ex. 9-4)—this is less clear in the first—may be related to the forms usually associated with the genre: sonata struc-ture in the first movement, a throughcomposed slow movement, scherzo and trio (four scherzo passages and three trios) in the third, and a complex involv-ing an introduction, fugue, rondo, and coda for the finale.[8] Thereafter he abandoned traditional structures.

Boulez followed the first two sonatas with the first book of *Structures I* for two pianos (composed 1951, published 1955–1957), which consists of three pieces, identified as "a," "b," and "c." "Ia" may provide an example.[9] While it is based on the same series that Messiaen used in his "Mode de valeurs et d'intensités," Boulez went further, creating sequences first of dura-tions that are associated with each pitch class of the series according to its position in the series, second of dynamic levels, and third of modes of attack, twelve of each. Particular forms of the various sequences are arbitrarily as-signed to either of the two pianos. Thus Boulez created true total or inte-

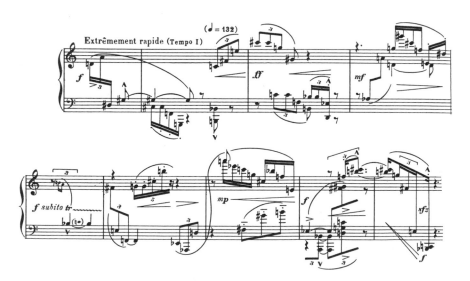

Example 9-4. Boulez: First Movement from Sonata No. 1—Beginning (mm. 1–9)
Courtesy of Alphonse LeDuc, Éditeurs de musique, Paris.

grated serialism in which all aspects of the composition are controlled by sets consisting of twelve levels. He also composed a second set entitled *Structures* (1956–1961, published 1961).

Boulez planned the third Sonata (composed 1956–1957, movements published separately 1961–1968) as a five-movement composition, each movement called *Formant*. These formants are: "Antiphonie"—"Trope"—"Constellation miroir"—"Strophe"—"Sequence," of which only the second and third have been completed. These completed movements are divided into sections and in some cases the order of their performance Boulez has left to the player, even the order in which the movements are to be played, except that once the work has been completed "Constellation miroir" must be played third. Thus Boulez has in a limited way introduced chance into the work and in this may have been influenced by Cage and Stockhausen (see below). Throughout the sonata Boulez has designated passages as either points or blocs according to their style.

Such an ultrarational approach to musical composition also characterizes the work of the German Karlheinz Stockhausen (1928), who studied with Milhaud as well as Messiaen and has also done extensive work in acoustics. His early thinking was also influenced by the Belgian Karel Goeyvaerts (1923–), whose Sonata for two pianos (op. 1, composed 1950–1951) represents yet another early essay into integrated serialism. Unlike Boulez, Stockhausen has ventured into electronic music, while also composing extensively for traditional instruments, sometimes combined with electronics; as in Boulez, the piano has been important.

In 1952 Stockhausen began a series of twenty-one piano pieces which he planned to publish, most in groups, one by itself, as follows: pieces I–IV, V–X, XI, XII–XVI, XVII–XIX, and XX–XXI; to date he has completed fourteen, but has also withdrawn V and VI; XII and XIII are arrangements of sections from his large work *Licht* (Light). These are complex works based, like Boulez' *Structures*, on the serialization of all aspects of music, often involving continuums between polarities or between abstractions, e.g., differentiation–harmonization, analysis–synthesis, static–dynamic, which he has interpreted in terms of sound and time, along with the use of numerical ratios and number series, such uses not immediately evident to the listener.

For example, Klavierstück III (composed 1952), which lasts but thirty seconds, has been regarded as based on an unordered set of five pitch classes, such that at the beginning and end the white keys of the piano are emphasized, and in the middle the black keys; it employs but four dynamic levels (*p, mf, f,* and *ff*), each applied to individual notes, the latter (*ff*) reserved for the last note which is also the highest; and a set of six rhythmic values, excluding grace-notes,

$$ \flat \quad \flat \quad \flat \flat \quad \flat \quad \quad \quad $$

the order of which is permuted during the piece (see Ex. 9-5).[10] Klavierstück IX (composed 1954–1955, revised 1961) has attained some popularity. Conceived in terms of conventional meters and thus lacking complex rhythmic

Example 9-5. Stockhausen: Klavierstück III—Beginning (mm. 1–4)

proportions while at the same time emphasizing the pitch classes of a single bitonal chord that sounds throughout, its rhythmical organization is related to the Fibonacci series (0–1–2–3–5–8–13, etc.; except at the beginning, each number is the sum of its two immediate predecessors). Klavierstück X (composed 1954–1955, revised 1961) takes its point of departure from the number seven (seven steps in a diatonic scale), so that the durations, dynamic levels, and types of attacks are also plotted on scales of seven degrees; the piece is also noted for its fast glissandos and tone clusters that are even trilled. Klavierstück XI (composed 1956), the largest of the twenty-one and the first to have been published separately, has aroused the most attention: nineteen passages of music, events, as Stockhausen has called them, are printed on a large sheet of paper (37 × 21 inches). These passages may be played in any order, but at the end of each there are instructions regarding the tempo, dynamic level, and type of attack to be used in playing the next one. When an event has been played three times the performance is considered complete. Thus, the length of the piece can vary from three events up to 38! (38 factorial, i.e., the products of all numbers between 1 and 38, the latter running into the millions).[11] Throughout the piece Stockhausen has fixed pitch and rhythm in the notation.

Stockhausen has here reached a radical reformulation of the musical art work. The notions of causality, progress, and evolution, implicit in the system of tonal harmony, and the forms and types of thematic material that were developed in that context, have been replaced by a series of events or moments the order of which has not been determined by the composer. Put another way, he has eliminated any sort of logical consequence by which one event follows another: each exists independently for itself alone so that the traditional notion of a piece of music as embodying a coherent whole, often analogous to a narrative, has been displaced by a succession of passages (moments or events), all possessing the same significance, the order of which has not been set by the composer. As Stockhausen has said: "either every moment is important or nothing is important. A moment is not simply the result of preceding moments nor the anticipation of moments to come. It is a personal, centered entity, with its own existence."[12]

Stockhausen's largest work of piano music is *Mantra* (premiered 1970, published 1975) for two pianos in which the pianists also play antique cymbals and wood blocks and one of whom operates a shortwave radio or tape recorder. Microphones, an amplifier, a ring modulator, and loudspeakers, the latter mounted on towers, are also necessary. The modulation of piano tones by sine waves using the ring modulator yields combination tones which characterize the sound world of the piece. The term *mantra* refers to basic sounds and the waveforms that cause them by means of which in India it is believed possible to communicate with different planes of existence. The long work is based on a dodecaphonic series—the mantra—each note of which forms the basis for a section of the piece. The ambience of total dissonance that is found in most of Stockhausen's other works does not obtain here: many passages are harmonious in the conventional meaning of the word.

As we have seen, the ultrarationalistic, almost scientific, attitude that underlies much of the work of Babbitt, Boulez, and Stockhausen, and that provided some of the basis for Messiaen's work, became widespread among composers from the 1950s to the late 1980s. We will deal with those composers who seem to have the most importance for piano music.

An outstanding figure who belongs to the older generation but appropriated the aesthetics of the new music is the German Bernd Aloys Zimmermann (1918–1970) who did not emerge as an important composer until after World War II. His earlier works, *Ex temporale* and *Enchiridion* (both composed 1949–1952), reveal influences from Schoenberg, Hindemith, and Bartók, as does his *Metamorphosen* (1954), which he withdrew and revised, under the influence of Stockhausen, as *Konfigurationen* (8, 1954–1956). He also produced two pieces for two pianos, *Perspektiven* (1955), examples of integrated serialism; and *Monologe* (Monologs, 1964), the latter with quotations from Mozart and Debussy.

A composer who has adopted a radically different and highly individual method of composition is the Greek-born Iannis Xenakis (1922–), who has also worked as an architect for a time associated with Le Corbusier. His formalized music, which he has described in a book,[13] is based not on serialization or indeterminacy but rather on the laws of probability, game theory, group theory, set theory, and Boolean algebra, all emphasizing stochastic (chance) processes. He has composed four pieces for piano: *Herma* (1960–1961), *Evryali* (1973), *Mists* (published 1981), and *à r (Hommage à Maurice Ravel* [1989]), all of them complex and difficult.

More directly associated with Boulez and Stockhausen is the Hungarian-born György Ligeti (1923–), who has lived in Vienna since 1956. The music he composed in Hungary before coming to the West, the Capriccios (2, 1947), Invention (1948), and the set *Musica ricercata* (11, 1951–1953) reveal particularly the influence of Bartók. *Musica ricercata* also discloses something different but fundamental to his art: setting and working out a basic compositional problem related to the raw materials of music and their control. Here a basic condition involves limiting the number of pitch classes: the first piece in the set uses mostly a single pitch class, adding a second only at the end; the second piece uses but three pitch classes, the next four, and so on until the eleventh, which uses all twelve and bears the subtitle "Omaggio a Frescobaldi," since it is related to one of that composer's ricercars; the ninth piece memoralizes Bartók, and indeed some pieces in the latter's large *Mikrokosmos* operate with small numbers of pitch classes. In any case, unlike the work of Babbitt, Boulez, and Stockhausen, Ligeti's early compositions have an organizing principle that is palpable and audible, not arcane and hidden.

Thereafter Ligeti came under the influence of Boulez and Stockhausen, particularly in the context of the summer courses instituted in Darmstadt in 1958. Yet Ligeti never adopted the serial method nor the aleatory aspects that appear in Boulez and Stockhausen; in fact one of his Bagatelles (3, 1961, published 1968) satirizes the use of chance operations. Since he has been in the West in addition to the Bagatelles Ligeti has composed the set *Monument–Selbstporträt–Bewegung* (Monument–Self-portrait–Movement, 1976) for two pianos, and the Etudes, Book I (6, 1985). These works continue the line established in *Musica ricercata*. In "Monument" Ligeti concerned himself primarily with tempo, rhythm, and dynamics, whereby he differentiated each of the pianos from one another. The thematic material, here as elsewhere in his work, consists mostly of figuration. In "Monument" the two pianos begin simultaneously but then diverge according to their differing tempos; moreover specific dynamic levels are associated with specific registers of pitch. Yet since the sounds of the two instruments blend, Ligeti has created the illusion of distance; the loud passages sound closer to the listener, the soft ones more distant. A parallel to this is provided by the illusionistic op art of his compatriot Vasarelli; there are also similarities to minimalism (see below), acknowledged by Ligeti, although harmonically, at least, Ligeti's music is more complex. "Selbstporträt mit Reich und Riley (und Chopin is auch dabei)" (Self-Portrait with Reich and Riley [and Chopin is also present]) underlines the point, although Ligeti did not know the work of Reich and Riley at the time. Here the main device, borrowed from Karl-Erik Welin and Henning Seidentopf, involves one hand silently depressing groups of keys while the other plays the same keys and those adjacent to them, thus producing complex and irregular rhythms with great accuracy, so that once again we meet with illusion: those keys that are played and sounded and those played and not sounded. Ligeti also quotes Chopin here, as suggested by his subtitle, a trace of the famous "Minute Waltz" and the Finale of the Sonata in B-flat minor (op. 35). The third piece, "Bewegung," is more like the first, but to be played legato.

Ligeti's Etudes, which are studies in compositional as well as performance technique, reveal similar preoccupations: "Désordre" (i), has the right hand playing the white keys and the left hand the black keys, the two moving in and out of phase, with irregular accentuations that produce three against five or five against three; "Cordes vides" (Open Strings, ii) involves melodic fifths in two-part counterpoint, and "Touches bloquées" (Blocked Keys, iii) uses the technique just described in "Selbstporträt" (see above and Ex. 9-6); in "Fan-

Example 9-6. LIGETI: "Touches bloquées" from Études, Volume I—Beginning (mm. 1–8)

fares" (iv) an ostinato accompanies a chordal figure based on the *aksag* rhythms of Bulgaria:

$$\frac{3 + 2 + 3}{8}$$

The last etude, "Automne à Varsovie" (Autumn in Warsaw), a lament, again involves the appearance of different tempos through shifting accentuations. These preoccupations reveal Ligeti as more closely oriented to older traditions than to those of Boulez and Stockhausen, although he has adapted these elements with great originality.

From Italy there is Luciano Berio (1925–), who studied with Dallapiccola before coming under the influence of Boulez and Stockhausen. While his early set Variations (5, composed 1952–1953) is serial, he subsequently broke away from this sort of rigidity as evidenced by his most celebrated piece for piano, *Sequenza IV* (composed 1966, published 1971). He has produced a series of pieces with this title, each for a different instrument. This is an extended virtuoso exercise emphasizing a process of chord transformation, over time gradually altering the pitches of a chord; this is one of the best-known piano pieces by a composer of this persuasion. More recently Berio has produced a series of six shorter character pieces for piano: first a group associated with the old conception of the four elements, the pair "Wasserklavier" and "Erdenklavier" (Water Keyboard and Earth Keyboard respectively, both published 1971), continuing with "Luftklavier" (Air Keyboard, published 1987), and ending with "Feuerklavier" (Fire Keyboard, published

1989); he then added the pair, "Brin" and "Leaf" (both published 1990). For two pianos he has composed Intermezzo con fantasia (composed 1965).

Three composers closely associated with Stockhausen are the Belgian Henri Pousseur (1929–), the Swede Bo Nilsson (1937–), the Englishman Brian Ferneyhough (1943–), and the German Wolfgang Rihm (1952–). Pousseur has emphasized the combination of serial manipulation and aleatory performance, the latter in evidence in his *Caractères* (Characters) I and II, the second of which is subtitled "Miroir de votre Faust" (Mirror of Your Faust, published 1967). The pages of this set contain boxed areas marked *découper*, to be cut out, allowing the player to see music printed on the preceding or following pages, the folios of pages to be arranged in any order and the passages to be played in any order, somewhat after the fashion of Stockhausen's Klavierstück XI; the second of the three pieces has an optional vocal part. His *Icari obstiné*, Volume I (1981), is also aleatory. For two pianos he has composed *Nobile* (1958). Nilsson has produced three pieces for piano, *Bewegungen* (Motions), *Schlagfiguren* (Strike Figures, both 1956) and *Quantitäten* (1958), which display the ultrarationalistic rigor associated with music from this group. Ferneyhough, who has emphasized integrated serialism, has composed *Epigrams*, a Sonata for two pianos (both 1966), a set of three pieces for piano (1971), and *Lemma-Icon Epigram* (1981). Rihm was for a time under Stockhausen's influence but broke away. He has composed a good deal for the piano, especially the series Klavierstücke (7, composed 1966–1980). These are often extreme compositions, full of violent contrasts and incorporating music theater, in which the performer's actions and gestures are specified in the score, as in the fourth of the series (op. 8c, 1971), which calls for the performer to stand up, hum, and cough, in addition to executing glissandos on and damping the strings by hand.

Two composers from the United States may be included here even though neither has been associated with Boulez and Stockhausen: Donald Martino (1931–) and Charles Wuorinen (1938–). Martino, trained at Princeton under Sessions and Babbitt, has produced a number of challenging pieces for piano, more than most composers working in this intense and complex type of composition: Fantasy (1958); *Pianissimo, a Sonata for Piano* (1970), a very large and difficult work; a set of shorter pieces; "Impromptu for Roger" (1977); Suite in Old Form: Parody Suite (1982); and the large cycle Fantasias and Impromptus (composed 1978, published 1982). Wuorinen, a pianist, has associated advanced methods of musical organization with the traditional large forms, Variations (1965) and the sonata, of which he has composed two (1969 and 1976), but has also produced character pieces.

Other composers of the chromatic-dissonant persuasion, some serial, others not, who have composed for the piano include Otto Luening (1900–), Erik Bergman (1911–), Esther Williamson Ballou (1915–1973), Ben Weber (1916–), Ruth Shaw Wylie (1916–), Seymour Shifrin (1926–1979), Jounas Kokkonen (1921–), Ralph Shapey (1921–), George T. Walker (1922–), Kasimierz Serocki (1922–1981), Lukas Foss (1922–), Finn Mortensen (1922–1983), Jean Eichelberger Ivey (1923–), Luigi Nono (1924–), Robert Starer (1924–),

André Boucourechliev (1925–), Harry Somers (1925–), Gottfried Michael König (1926–), Ton de Leeuw (1926–), John Beckwith (1927–), Salvatore Martirano (1927–), Robert Helps (1928–), Jacob Druckman (1928–), Usko Meriläinen (1930–), Cristobal Halffter (1930–), Luís de Pablo (1930–), Mauricio Kagel (1931–), Alan Stout (1932–), Miklós Kocsár (1933–), Mario Davidovsky (1934–), Peter Maxwell Davies (1934–), Zsolt Durkö (1934–), Roger Reynolds (1934–), Richard Wernick (1934–), Peter Schat (1935–), Joan Tower (1938–), Barbara Kolb (1939–), John McCabe (1939–), Tom Johnson (1939–), Alfred Fisher (1942–), Dennis Riley (1943–), Reinhard Febel (1952–), Richard Danielpour (1956–), and Edward Smaldone (1956–).

Some composers who share this orientation have used the piano in conjunction with electronic sounds recorded on tape. Among the earliest compositions of this kind, perhaps the earliest, were those by Morton Subotnick (1933–), who otherwise has published only Preludes 3 (1965) and 4 (1966) for the piano. These were followed by Davidovsky's *Synchronisms 6* (1970), in which the electronic sounds modulate those produced by the piano; this won the Pulitzer Prize for music in 1971. Other pieces include Barbara Kolb's revery-like *Solitaire* (1971) and *Spring, River, Flowers, Moon, Night* (1975) for two pianos and tape; *Music for Prince Albert on his 150th Birthday* (1971) and *Mirrors* (1973) by Elliott Schwartz (1936–); Jean Eichelberger Ivey's *Skaniadaryo* (1973); *Evening Psalm of Dr. Dracula* (1973) by Robert Moran (1937–); Milton Babbitt's *Reflections* (1975); *Dimensions II* (1974) by Barton McLean (1938–); *405* by Laszlo Vidovsky (1944–); and *Sphaera* (1985) by William Albright (1944–).[14] In Stockhausen's *Mantra*, described earlier, as in Davidovsky's *Synchronisms 6*, the piano sound is electronically modulated; later Crumb and Cage created compositions in which the piano is either amplified or accompanied by electronic sounds.

Finally, Conlon Nancarrow (1912–), born in the United States but living in Mexico, has employed such complex simultaneously sounding rhythms along with such impossibly wide reaches for the pianist's hand that he has composed them directly on piano rolls, thus eliminating the performer altogether. Earlier Henry Cowell did something similar. Nancarrow's main work is the collection of Studies for Player Piano (begun in the 1940s). He has also published music for piano played in the ordinary way, most of it recent: Prelude and Blues (1935, 1992), Sonatina (1986), "Tango?" (1990), "Canons for Ursula" (2, 1992), and "2-Part Studies" (3, 1993).

EXTENDED TECHNIQUES, NEW SOUNDS, AND OPEN FORM

Most of the music discussed up to now in this chapter uses the twelve traditional pitch classes, with electronic processing being introduced in a few cases. The music to be taken up now is at times even more radical, since the piano is in some cases made to produce sounds not attainable by playing the instrument in the ordinary way, but rather by what have been called extended techniques. Some such compositions may be notated in conventional symbols; others may contain—or even consist entirely of—instructions for the performers. As Cage, one of the most important composers involved with this sort of music, has put it, "let notations refer to what is to be done, not to what is heard, or to be heard."[15] Although the presuppositions and conditions are entirely different, this bears some similarity to the old tablature, in which the notation indicated what the player is to do to or with the instrument, not the pitch classes and rhythmic values to be realized.

The idea of using pitches that do not belong to the traditional chromatic scale and tone colors not normally obtainable on traditional instruments goes back to the early years of the twentieth century, the ideas of Busoni (which he did not put into practice), and the Futurists in Italy, who worked to create an art of noises. Similarly, Cowell specified tone clusters and playing directly on the strings of the piano in the period 1911–1930. An important figure here was Edgard Varèse, who did not compose for the piano, but whose music was profoundly influential, emphasizing percussion instruments and various noise producers and often abolishing metrical rhythm.

Such preoccupations dominate the early work of John Cage (1912–1992), a consistent leader of the musical avant-garde. Although he studied with Cowell and Schoenberg, he went far beyond them, as will become clear. In his work the piano once more occupies a critical position.

CAGE'S PRINCIPAL WORKS FOR PIANO

NOTE: Dates are of composition.

Pieces (2, 1935, revised 1974)
Metamorphosis (1938)
Bacchanale, prepared piano (1940)
Tossed As It Is Untroubled, prepared piano (1943)
The Perilous Night, prepared piano (1943–1944)
Sonatas and Interludes, prepared piano (1946–1948)
Music of Changes (1951)
Music for Piano: 1 (1952), 2 and 3 (both 1953), 4–19 and 20 (all
     1953), 21–36 (1955), 37–52 (1955), 53–68 (1956), 69–84 (1956)
Haiku (7, 1952)
34'46.776", prepared piano (1954)
Winter Music, four or five pianos (20, 1957)
TV Köln (1960)
31'57.9864", prepared piano (1960)
Etudes Australes (32, 1974–1975)
Furniture Music, Etc, two pianos (1989)
Two² (1987), two pianos
One⁵ (1990)

There are many others. We should note that the famous *4'33"*, although first performed by pianist David Tudor, is indeterminate as to performing medium, thus not specifically for piano. In its first performance Tudor placed the score on the rack and sat in front of the instrument for the period of time specified in the title.

Cage's early work, *Metamorphosis*, uses procedures that were radical for its time (1938), strictly maintaining a structural principle involving restatements of a rhythmic unit. Shortly after, he developed the prepared piano. As he described it in the instructions for the Sonatas and Interludes, "mutes of various materials are placed between the strings of the keys used, thus effecting transformations of the piano sounds with respect to all of their characteristics." These mutes include screws, bolts, erasers, and rubber bands that are to be attached to or inserted between the strings at specific distances from the bridge in accordance with a chart that is included with the score. The music is notated and the keyboard played in the ordinary way, but the sound of the instrument has been radically modified, so that it often resembles a gamelan—Asian music and thought, as we will see, have influenced Cage in other ways as well. The damper pedal is also used to great coloristic effect. On the other hand, by his own account the development of the prepared piano in the first instance was a practical matter: Cage had received a commission to provide percussive music for a ballet, but limitations of space for the performance precluded a percussion ensemble; he therefore found a solution in thus modifying the sound of the piano, and *Bacchanale* was the result.

The most important and influential works for prepared piano are the Sonatas and Interludes, a set of sixteen sonatas and four interludes, the latter coming between Sonatas 4 and 5, 8 and 9 (two are placed here, the halfway point), and 12 and 13. While the interludes are throughcomposed, the sonatas are disposed in sections that are to be repeated, the number of sections varying from one to four, their respective lengths being determined by numerical ratios based on the numbers of eighth-notes. The thematic material for the most part consists of motives based on figurative elements; there are neither conventional melodies, accompanying parts, passages in imitative counterpoint, nor the like. Most important, however, is the expressive quality of the pieces—quiet, contemplative, and detached, all fostered by the exotic sounds elicited from the piano.

Cage's next step involved *Music of Changes*, a work central in his development: it marks the start of his move to open form. Up to this point he had composed his music in a more-or-less traditional fashion. In *Music of Changes*, however, he left all aspects of the composition to chance operations: tossing three coins six times and referring the results to the table of sixty-four hexagrams in the Chinese *I Ching* (Book of Changes, tenth to twelfth centuries B.C.) which Cage musically interpreted on a set of twenty-six charts encompassing pitch classes, durations, tempos, and dynamics. A number sequence, apparently arbitrary, the sum of which is 29 5/8, determines all aspects of the structure: 3–5–6 3/4–6 3/4–5–3 1/8. The work in all consists of 29 5/8 sections—a section defined as comprising the number of measures of

A version of the prepared piano. John Cage first described the prepared piano in 1938 and wrote in the instructions for the Sonatas and Interludes (composed 1946–1948): "mutes of various materials are placed between the strings of the keys used, thus effecting transformations of the piano sounds with respect to all of their characteristics."

4/4 time before there is a change of tempo. Each section contains 29 5/8 bars.[16] Thus, Cage rigidly determined and notated everything in the conventional way, so that the performer has merely to play the score as it is printed. In style and character the music resembles, perhaps in an odd way, the integrated serialist pieces discussed in the preceding section: discontinuous and dissonant, with wide leaps, abrupt changes of tempo, long spaces of rest, and so on.

The impetus behind *Music of Changes* may be set forth something like this. Our world view has been changing from one that posits a deterministic evolutionary process based on reason, order, and causality to one based on the nonrational, chance, and the unpredictable. That an individual person, whether a creative artist or not, should assume a passive role with respect to nature and the world, should let events take their course without intervention, is common in Asian thought. We can cite C. J. Jung, who has compared the Chinese with the western view of an individual moment in time as follows:

The moment under actual observation appears to the ancient Chinese view more of a chance hit than a clearly defined result of concurring causal chain processes. The matter of interest seems to be the configuration formed by chance events in the moment of observation, and not at all the hypothetical reasons that seemingly account for the coincidence. While the Western mind carefully sifts, weighs, selects, classifies, isolates, the Chinese picture of the moment encompasses everything down to the minutest nonsensical detail, because all of the ingredients make up the observed moment.[17]

Thus two fundamental aspects of Cage's work are the new sounds of the prepared piano and the notion of indeterminacy or open form. In each his example has stimulated others. Among those interested in indeterminacy who have emphasized piano music are Morton Feldman (1926–1987), Sylvano Bussotti (1931–), Christian Wolff (1934–), and Cornelius Cardew (1936–1981). Feldman was a very prolific composer for the piano; while his early works are serial, under the influence of Cage he turned to open form, producing pieces to which he gave abstract titles, such as *Projection, Intersection, Extension,* and *III*, each designation covering a group of individual pieces. He later returned to notating his music in the traditional fashion, adopting at the same time generalized titles, such as, simply, *Piano* (1977); among these is *Triadic Memories* (1981), a very long (ninety-minute) piece, in which short figures are subtly varied. Bussotti's art is varied: at times he requires the performer to wear gloves, to use his fists, to beat his leg with his hand, and so on; some of his pieces have erotic associations. Among his works are *Musica per amici* (1957), Pieces for David Tudor (5, 1959), *Foglio d'album* (1970), *Novelletta* (1962–1973), and, for two pianos, *Tableaux vivantes* (1965). Wolff, Cage's long-time friend and colleague, began working with open forms in 1958. Up to that time his works included some for prepared piano and others that are conventionally notated but are strictly limited as to the pitch classes used: *For Piano I* (1952), for instance, uses but nine. Other early pieces use integrated serialism. Later he took up work with open form, as in his Duo II for pianists (1958), which has no score, no beginning, and no end; it makes use of his principle of cueing, so that the decisions of one performer are in part determined by the actions of another. His works composed since 1972, in contrast, exhibit a shift in attitude. He had come to regard his earlier work, as he put it, as "too specialized, too esoteric, too introverted,"[18] and thus adopted more traditional means which he associated with political messages: *Accompaniments, Bread and Roses* (both 1977), and *Hay una mujer desaparecida* (1981), based on labor songs, or, in the last instance, a Chilean revolutionary song. Cardew, an Englishman who worked with Stockhausen, emphasized indeterminacy and the prepared piano in his earlier phase (Books of Study for Pianists [composed 1959, published 1966], *February Pieces* [3, 1959–1961], *Memories of You* [1964], *Winter Potatoes* [3, composed 1959–1961, published 1965], and *Volo Solo* [1965]), while his later work shows a return to more traditional forms, as in Piano Album (1973), which included some pieces based on protest and revolutionary songs. Others associated with Cage's indeterminacy in connection with piano music are Netty Simons (1913–), the Canadian Udo Kasemets (1919–), Earle Brown (1926–), Barney Childs (1926–), Misha Mengelberg (1935–), Theodore Lucas, and László Sary (1940–). Richard Bunger (1942–) has worked extensively with the prepared piano, as has Alexandra Pierce (1934–) and the Swede Bentzon (see Chapter Eight).[19]

Other composers have made use of extended techniques entirely apart from open form. Pre-eminent here is George Crumb (1929–), a student of Finney and Blacher and member of the faculty of the University of Pennsylvania.

CRUMB'S PIANO WORKS

Piano Pieces (5, composed 1962)
Makrokosmos (4 vols.)
  I. Twelve Fantasy Pieces after the Zodiac for Amplified Piano (1972)
  II. Twelve Fantasy Pieces after the Zodiac for Amplified Piano (1973)
  IV. Celestial Mechanics: Cosmic Dances for Amplified Piano, Four Hands (1979)
Little Suite for Christmas A.D. 1979 (composed 1979)
Gnomic Variations (composed 1981)
Processional (composed 1983)
Zeitgeist, two amplified pianos (composed 1987)

NOTE: The third part of *Makrokosmos*, scored for two amplified pianos and percussion, falls outside the scope of this book.

Of primary interest here are the first two sets of *Makrokosmos*, with their rich web of associations ranging from astrology, primitive religions, mythology, and philosophical allegory to friends and colleagues of the composer, while the title itself is a variation on Bartók's. In the first two sets, Crumb has associated each of the twelve pieces both with a sign of the Zodiac and a person identified by initials. The titles are evocative (in the spirit of Debussy's Preludes, Crumb put the titles at the ends of the pieces). The following, from Volume I, indicate something of the range: "Primeval Sounds (Genesis I) *Cancer*" (i), "Pastorale (from the Kingdom of Atlantis, ca. 10,000 B.C.) *Taurus*," (iii), or "Dream Images (Love-Death Music) *Gemini*," (xi). While Crumb used traditional means of notation except for the lack of time signatures and bar lines, in every fourth piece he adapted the staff to a symbolic form—cross, circle, spiral, and so on. Not only is the piano amplified by a conventional microphone suspended above the strings, but extended techniques are required of the performer: muting the strings by hand, producing harmonics, plucking strings, playing glissandos on the strings, using a metal plectrum, or placing a chain, wire brush, or drinking glass on the strings, along with singing, chanting, moaning, and whistling (see Ex. 9-7). Occasionally Crumb has quoted from other music: the revival hymn "Will There Be Any Stars in My Crown," the Trio of Chopin's Fantasy-Impromptu, the "Dies irae," the Coronation Scene of Mussorgsky's *Boris Godunov*, and Beethoven's Sonata in B-

Example 9-7. CRUMB: "The Phantom Gondolier [Scorpio]" from *Makrokosmos*, vol. I—Beginning (m. 1)
Copyright 1974 by C. F. Peters Corporation. Used by permission.

flat major (op. 106). While precursors are easy to identify—Cowell, Cage, and Stockhausen—Crumb employs these effects to express a sense of mystery, awe, revery, dreams, as is appropriate to the subject matter, thus making a clear connection to the expressive aesthetics of the Romantic tradition. His emphasis on sonority, however, is much greater: sound itself as evocation, as incantation. This spirit informs all of Crumb's work for piano.

Other examples of extended techniques are presented by Ben Johnston (1926–), whose *Knocking Piece* for two pianos is actually a percussion piece to be played on the inside of the instruments; Ann Silsbee (1930–), in whose *Doors* (published 1976) tone clusters in the extreme treble register are accompanied by bass notes sustained by the sostenuto pedal; Zsolt Durkö, a Hungarian, who has employed strumming on the strings of the piano; and Curtis Curtis-Smith (1942–), who has developed a way of bowing the piano: in his *Rhapsodies* and *Sonorous Inventions* (both 1973) and *Unisonics* (1976) long, thin strips of nylon are passed underneath the strings and drawn back and forth. The bowed piano has been carried further by Stephen Scott (1944–).

Then there is the use of tunings involving intervals not found in the traditional system, intervals that either are smaller than a semitone or are not available in equal temperament. Ives, as we have noted, composed for two pianos tuned a quarter-tone apart, and of course such intervals are common in any music involving synthesized sound. John Eaton (1935–), however, has not only followed Ives' example in his Microtonal Fantasy for two pianos (1965) but has developed a system of microtonal tuning and a special keyboard instrument, the Syn-Ket, on which to perform them; among his pieces are Concert Piece (1966) and *Soliloquy* (1967); the earlier Variations (1958) are in a traditional style. We can refer again to Ben Johnston, who composed a Microtonal Suite (1965).

Finally, concept music may be considered a subgroup under open form. In this kind of music the score consists of a set of instructions governing what the performers are to do; these instructions are not necessarily couched in terms of conventional musical notation. While concept music generally cannot be regarded as piano music, sometimes that instrument is specified. An early example is by La Monte Young (1935–), the Piano Piece for David Tudor No. 1 (1960), which calls for a piano, some hay, and a pail of water: the assumption is that either the piano eats the hay and drinks the water, or it doesn't. This piece, then, involves undetermined sounds, as indeed do many of Cage's. In "Accidents" (1967) by Larry Austin (1930–), the pianist is instructed to make gestures but not to play the instrument in the usual way: instead shells are to be placed around on the strings and the smallest vibrations to be picked up by contact microphones, fed through a ring modulator, amplified and reproduced through loudspeakers. The Composition for Piano and Pianist (ca. 1965) by Robert Moran, to give one further example, calls for the pianist to come on stage, climb up on and sit on the strings of the piano: as the score puts it, "the piano plays him."

MINIMALISM

This term generally refers to a reductive sort of music that operates with mostly diatonic scales in the context of conventional tonal harmony and involves the incessant repetition of brief melodic, usually figurational, fragments. Thus this type of music is often known as repetitive music and in common with some forms of Asian and African music may over time produce a meditative, even hypnotic, effect on the listener, so that it has also been called trance music. Like much of the music described here, it has no sense of forward progress in time, and thus appears to lack a sense of direction, to develop no climactic points. In some forms of minimalism the patterns are gradually modified as the piece unfolds. The changes, however, are not taking place at the same time in all parts, which thus get "out of sync," as the popular expression has it. At times a piece evolves according to a pre-established scheme of permutations, so that eventually the original condition is restored and the piece can come to a resolution. This form of minimalism has been variously called process, phase, or systemic music. In its reversion to basic elements of traditional tonal music and the gradual unfolding of the changes in the context of incessant repetition, minimalist music shows a resemblance to op art, as in the work of Ligeti.

Minimalism in music originated in Berkeley, California, in the 1960s in the work of La Monte Young and Terry Riley (1935–); they were followed by Steve Reich (1936–), Philip Glass (1937–), and John Adams (1947–). Young, who in his early phase was a follower first of Schoenberg and then of Cage, and produced, as we have noted, well-known pieces of concept music, composed among others two sets of pieces for Terry Riley (1960) and *The Well-Tuned Piano* (1964). In Riley's Keyboard Studies (1963), the first piece moves gradually through fifteen thematic figures, the one giving way to the other, accompanied by a pulse, while the second uses but eight different pitches. Reich, who studied under Milhaud, Persichetti, and Berio, has emphasized process or systemic music. His *Piano Phase* for two pianos (or two marimbas, composed 1967, published 1980) in its first section is based on a series of twelve notes involving but five pitch classes, both instruments beginning in unison. After the series has been stated eighteen times Piano II speeds up and then stabilizes at the new tempo; after twelve such shifts the two instruments are back in phase (see Ex. 9-8). His other piece, *Six Pianos* (1973), involves a rhythmic pattern of eight beats using different pitch classes played by three pianos; Glass has produced relatively little for piano: "Modern Love Waltz," "Mad Rush" (1981), the set of five pieces entitled *Metamorphosis* (1988), and "Sutra Vortex" (1988). Adams' first minimalist work appeared in the piano pieces *China Gates* (1977) and *Phrygian Gates* (1978). Other minimalist composers include the Dane Per Nörgaard (1932–), who composed among others *Grooving* (1968), and the Hungarian Zóltan Jeny (1943–), who has produced a number of shorter pieces, among them *Endgame* (1973). We have noted that while some of Ligeti's work bears similarity to minimalism, he was unfamiliar at the time with the work of the composers just mentioned.

Example 9-8. REICH: Piano Phase—Beginning (mm. 1–5)

THE NEW TONALITY OR NEW ROMANTICISM

In the midst of the ultrarationality of Boulez and Stockhausen and their followers, music in open form, music based on new sounds, concept music, and minimalism, there developed a new interest in the traditional system of tonal harmony, the forms and structures associated with this system, and its potential for expression. While minimalism mostly restricted itself to the tonal system, the movement under discussion here involves elaborate and varied music resembling that of the older repertory. Here George Rochberg (1918–) is important; his long career as a composer reveals three phases, beginning with the neoclassical and the nationalistic, then in the early 1950s turning to serial composition in all its complexities and intensity, and finally, in the late 1960s, coming back to the principles of functional tonal harmony.

ROCHBERG'S PIANO WORKS[20]

Book of Contrapuntal Pieces for Keyboard Instruments
    (composed 1940–1946, published 1979)
Variations on an Original Theme (1941)
Arioso (composed 1944, revised ca. 1956, published 1957)
Preludes and Fughettas (2, 1946)
Bagatelles (12, composed 1952, published 1955)

Bartókiana (composed ca. 1956, published 1957)
Sonata-Fantasia (composed 1956, published 1958)
Nach Bach (composed 1966, published 1967)
Prelude on "Happy Birthday" for Almost Two Pianos (1969)
Carnival Music (composed 1971, published 1975)
Partita Variations (composed 1976, published 1977)
Short Sonatas (4, composed 1984, published 1986)

The background of *Bartókiana* is clear enough. Examples of his serial work are the Bagatelles and the Sonata-Fantasia. While the former are short, complex, and intense, the Sonata-Fantasia is a big piece, full of great expression, wholly atonal and rigorously serial, even quoting from Schoenberg's Piano Piece (op. 23 i). Then comes one of his best-known works, *Nach Bach* for piano or harpsichord, a fantasia in a neobaroque idiom that quotes portions of Bach's own Partita in E minor (BWV 830), and Chromatic Fantasia (BWV 903). In the Partita-Variations Rochberg has explicitly returned to the tonal system: the piece is mostly in B minor, with some movements in G major, A-flat major, and E-flat major, while still others show no key signature at all. The work begins with a Praeludium and ends with a Fugue, while in between is a series of character pieces of different sorts ("Burlesca," "Cortège," Impromptu, Nocturne, "The Deepest Carillon," for example, along with a Minuet [see Ex. 9-9] and a Canon). This tonal orientation also informs his Carnival Music and the Short Sonatas, the latter being single-movement pieces after the fashion of Scarlatti, which despite their tonal leanings have no key signatures.

Another leading exponent of this stylistic direction is David Del Tredici (1937–), who worked in the chromatic dissonant atonal tradition up to the late 1960s, composing among others the notable expressionistic *Soliloquy* (1958) along with a set Fantasy Pieces (composed 1959–1960) and a Scherzo for piano duet (1960). More recently he has turned to tonality and has extended his series of works based on Lewis Carroll's *Alice in Wonderland* to include an extended bravura essay for piano, *Virtuoso Alice* (1988), essentially variations on the folklike tune used in his orchestral *Final Alice*.

Frederic Rzewski (1938–), an eclectic composer who has been sympathetic to Stockhausen, as is evident from his piano music of the late 1950s, has produced a set of Preludes (1957), Poem (1959), a set of studies, a Sonata for two pianos (1960), and two studies (1960–1961). Although also interested in open form music and minimalism, he has composed extensively in the neotonal idiom. His chief work is the extended *The People United Will Never Be Defeated* (composed 1975, published 1979), a virtuoso set of thirty-six variations on a Chilean revolutionary song. This interest in revolutionary songs allies him with Wolff and Cardew (see above). Other works include *Falling Music*, amplified piano and tape (1971), Variations on "No Place To Go But Around" (1974), Piano Pieces (4, composed 1977, published 1981), *Squares* (1978), *North American Ballads* (4, 1979), and *A Machine*, two

Example 9-9. ROCHBERG: Minuetto from Partita-Variations—Beginning (mm. 1–6)
Copyright 1977 Theodore Presser Company. Used by permission.

pianos (1984). Other composers of this persuasion include Nicholas Maw (1935–), John Corigliano (1938–), who has composed *Etude Fantasy* (5, 1976), John Harbison (1938–), Nicholas Thorne (1950–), and Lowell Liebermann (1961–).

CONSERVATISM

Then there are those composers who remained true to a trend important in the first half of the twentieth century: the use of an essentially tonal and functional harmonic idiom but expanded to include dissonant elements, applied for the most part to forms inherited either from nineteenth-century Romanticism or from early twentieth-century neoclassicism. Outstanding among the romantics are Gottfried von Einem (1918–), William Bergsma (1921–), Karel Husa (1921–), Robert Evett (1922–1975), Ned Rorem (1923–), Benjamin Lees (1924–), Alan Hoddinott (1929–), and Robert Muczynski (1929–), all of whom have cultivated traditional genres of composition. Einem remained essentially true to the Romantic tradition, although in his Pieces (4, op. 3) and two sonatinas (op. 7) he displayed influences from jazz and neoclassicism. Bergsma has composed a number of character pieces, among them the set of Fantasies (3, 1943) and the cycle *Tangents* (8 in 2 vols., 1950). Rorem has three sonatas, full of strong expression, of which the second, with its virtuoso toccata-like finale, was published first (1953), the others later (1971); a set of brilliant Etudes (8, 1976); and several sets of character pieces. Lees too has remained aloof from the various fashions we have noted: he has produced five sonatas (1949–1963), one of them for two pianos (1951); Fantasia (1953); Toccata (1959); Ornamental Etudes (6, 1957); and Preludes

(3, 1962); along with character pieces, some of which have titles, as *Kaleidoscopes* (10, 1959), *Epigrams* (1960), and the extended *Odyssey* (1972). Muczynski has produced a large body of work, including three sonatas (op. 9, 22, and 35, 1955–1975), Sonatina in F major (op. 52, 1949), Toccata (op. 15, 1962), and sets of character pieces, among them Preludes (6, op. 6, 1961), *Diversions* (9, op. 23, 1970), *Maverick Pieces* (12, op. 37, 1976), *Masks* (op. 40, 1980), and *Dream Cycle* (op. 44, 1983). Hoddinott, an eclectic, has concentrated on the sonata. The conservative group also includes Ingolf Dahl (1912–1970), Irena Garztecka (1913–1963), the conductor Leonard Bernstein (1918–1990), Janina Garšcia (1920–), Ruth Schonthal (1924–), Einojuhani Rautavaara (1928–), Ronald Stevenson (1928–), and Philip Ramey (1939–).

The neoclassical spirit informs the work of Harold Shapero (1920–), who has composed in all four piano sonatas, a set of three (1944) that are neoclassical and a very large and demanding one in F minor (1948), a set Variations in C minor (1947), two short pieces, and another sonata for two pianos. A foreign-born composer of this persuasion is the Russian Alexei Haieff (1914–), a pupil of Boulanger, who composed three sonatas, several shorter pieces, and a Sonata for two pianos (1945) that reflects Stravinsky. Ellis Kohs (1916–) produced an extended Toccata for piano (also playable on the harpsichord, 1949), two sets of variations, one of them on *L'homme armé* (1946–1947), based on the fifteenth-century song so often employed in cyclic masses in the Renaissance, several short pieces, and a Sonata (1962) that shows some use of Schoenberg's serial method. Lou Harrison (1917–) composed, apart from three traditional sonatas, a set of six modeled on those of Domenico Scarlatti (1943), an extended Suite (1943), and some shorter pieces. Other neoclassicists are Everett Helm (1913–), Peter Mennin (1923–1983), Daniel Pinkham (1923–), André Previn (1929–), Erkii Salmenhaara (1941–), and Denise Lassimone.

Finally, some composers have incorporated styles and forms from popular music into their compositions. Salvatore Martirano (1927–), a pupil of Dallapiccola who in some respects has been a radical in his composition, has produced *Cocktail Music* (1962). Among others William Bolcom (1938–) and William Albright have composed in the ragtime tradition. Albright has produced a large sonata in this idiom (1974), as well as the earlier *Pianoagogo* (1965–1966), Chromatic Dances (5, 1976), and *Sphaera* for piano and tape (1985). Apart from ragtime pieces Bolcom has composed two sets of etudes (1964 and 1987) that display a cross section of idioms encompassing both the tonal and atonal, the popular and the classical. There is a piece by John Lennon (1940–1980), *Death Angel* (published 1983).

LATIN AMERICA AND ASIA

The international character of musical composition was much greater in the second half of the twentieth century than before. While differences of style and technique associated with national origin in effect cease to exist, the incorporation of elements from indigenous traditions can become a purely artistic decision. We have noted this, for instance, in Messiaen. Western art music has also come to the fore in Latin America and in Asia, especially in Japan.

In Latin America as elsewhere the chromatic-dissonant course has been dominant, often with the inclusion of indigenous elements. Included here are the Argentineans Guillermo Graetzer (1914–), born in Austria, and Carlos Guastavino (1914–); the Cuban Aurelio de la Vega (1925–); and the Brazilians Oswaldo Lacerda (1927–), who has composed extensively for the piano, Sérgio Oliveira de Vasconcellos Corrêa (1934–), Willy Corrêa de Oliveira (1938–), and José Antonio Almeida Prado (1943–), who studied with Messiaen. The serial method found adherents, many of whom went on to work with integrated serialism and open forms: the Brazilians César Guerra Peixe (1914–); Alcides Lanza (1929–), who composed a series called *Plectros*, one for solo piano (1962), one for piano and tape (1966), and a third for piano with synthesizer (1966); Marlos Nobre (1939–), who demonstrated the integration of serialism and open form with indigenous materials, as in his three sets each entitled *Ciclo nordestino* (op. 5, 1960; op. 13, 1963; op. 22, 1966); and Aylton Escobar (1943–); the Bolivian Atiliano Auza León (1925–); the Chileans Claudio Spies (1925–) and Leon Schidlowsky (1931–); and the Peruvian José Malsio (1924–). Serialists in the Caribbean area and Central America include the Cubans Harold Gramatges (1918–), who composed the elaborate *Movil I* (1969), and Leo Brouwer (1939–), the latter, an emigrant from Germany, having composed Sonata *piano e forte* (1970) for piano and tape involving recorded excerpts from Giovanni Gabrieli's famous piece; the Puerto Rican Héctor Campos-Parsi (1922–); and the Mexicans Manuel Enríquez (1926–), who has worked with open form, as in his *A Lápiz* (3, 1965); Manuel Jorge de Elías (1939–); and Mario Lavista (1943–), who composed the aleatory *Pieza para un(a) pianista y un piano* (1970), and has also been involved with concept music. Cage's prepared piano has also found adherents in the Argentinean Francisco Kröpfli (1928–), in his *Estudios* (1953), and the Cuban Brouwer, in his *Sonogramma* (1963).

The only other important case is presented by Japan, where an ancient culture of art music confronted that of the West, but where the latter has made an enormous impact.[21] Among the followers of the rigorous chromatic-dissonant tradition we can refer to Joji Yuasa (1929–); Tōru Takemitsu (1930–); Makato Moroi (1930–); Nachiko Koni (1932–); Akira Miyoshi (1933–); Tadasi Yamanouchi (1935–); and Maki Ishii (1936–), who studied with Stockhausen; Yugi Takahashi (1938–); and Jo Kondo (1947–), who has also involved himself with minimalism; Toshiro Mayazumi (1929–) and Toshi Ichiyanagi (1933–) have been influenced by Cage. Takemitsu, one of Japan's foremost composers, has been concerned with *ma*, the expressive force that exists between things or events separated from one another, a mystical concept beyond western empiricism; this he undertook to describe in his series of pieces *Pause interrompue* (3, composed 1952–1960), in free rhythm notated without bar lines; *Piano Distance* (1961); *Far Away* (1973); and *Les yeux clos* (1979).[22] On the other hand, Yoshino Nakada (1923–), Hajime Okumura (1925–), Akiro Yashiro (1929–1970), Akira Yuyama (1932–), and Yoshimitsu Kurokami (1933–) have adhered to the norms of tonal music but enriched with dissonant chords, while Kazuo Fukushima (1930–)—who has also been influenced by Cage—has combined western idioms with those of indigenous Japanese music, as in his *Suien* (1972).

From Korea come the traditional serialist Isang Yun (1917–), who emigrated to Germany, and Stockhausen's student Junsang Bakh (1938–), and, from China, Bright Sheng (1955–), who has emigrated to the United States and whose suite *My Song* (1988) in four movements belongs among those in which eastern and western elements are brought together.

OUTLOOK

The piano in one form or other continues to be a vital force in music, and the repertory of that music continues to be pluralistic: the many traditions and persuasions that exist create immense variety. While the infinite universe of possibilities appears to preclude the traditional notion of progress and evolution and rather to support Meyer's idea of stasis, referred to at the beginning of this chapter, there remains plenty of opportunity—unless we get too much music like the concept piece by Annea Lockwood (1939–) of New Zealand entitled *Piano Burning* (1971). It calls for a piano, preferably an upright, to be set on fire, its strings having been tuned as high as possible so that they will snap impressively under the heat; kerosene and firecrackers are optional.

NOTES FOR CHAPTER NINE

1. L. Meyer, *Music, the Arts and Ideas* (Chicago: University of Chicago Press, 1967), 87–232.

2. "Mode de valeurs et d'intensités" and "Neumes rythmiques" were originally published separately.

3. *The Technique of My Musical Language*, trans. J. Satterfield, 2 vols. (Paris: Leduc, 1956), and *Traité du rythme* (Paris: Leduc, 1954).

4. See T. Hold, "Messiaen's Birds," *Music and Letters* 52 (1971): 113–122, and M. Kurenniemi, "Messiaen, the Ornithologist," *Music Review* 41 (1980): 121–126.

5. See D. Cope, *New Directions in Music*, 5th ed. (Dubuque: Brown, 1989), 40–44.

6. M. Babbitt, "Who Cares If You Listen?" in *The American Composer Speaks*, ed. G. Chase (Baton Rouge: Louisiana State University Press, 1966), 239 (originally in *High Fidelity* [1958]); Babbitt has disclaimed the title.

7. P. Boulez, "Schoenberg is Dead," trans. H. Weinstock, in Boulez, *Notes of an Apprenticeship* (New York: Knopf, 1958), 268–279; originally in *The Score* (February 1952 in a somewhat different version).

8. A good account of Boulez' piano music in general may be found in D. Jameux, *Pierre Boulez*, trans. S. Bradshaw (Cambridge: Harvard University Press, 1991).

9. The piece has often been described and analyzed, first by G. Ligeti, "Pierre Boulez: Entscheidung und Automatik in der Struktur IA," *Die Reihe* (1958, no. 4): 38–63.

10. J. Harvey, *The Music of Stockhausen* (London: Faber and Faber, 1975), 22–26, and R. Maconie, *The Works of Stockhausen*, 2nd ed. (Oxford: Clarendon, 1990), 63–66.

11. See D. Cope, *New Directions in Music*, 5th ed., 157–158.

12. K. Stockhausen, quoted by W. Mertens, *American Minimalist Music*, trans. J. Hautekiet (London: Kahn & Averill; New York: Broude, 1983), 101–102.

13. *Formalized Music* (Bloomington: Indiana University Press, 1971; New York: Pendragon, 1992).

14. See M. Hinson, *Guide to the Pianist's Repertoire*, 2nd ed., 852, for a more complete list.

15. Quoted by M. Nyman, *Experimental Music: Cage and Beyond* (New York: Schirmer, 1974), 19.

16. See B. Simms, *Music of the Twentieth Century* (New York: Schirmer, 1980), 361–362; see also M. Bryan, "'The Book of Changes' and Music," *Music Review* 51 (1990): 1–10, and C. Weng-Chung, "Asian Concepts and Twentieth-Century Composition," *Musical Quarterly* 57 (1971): 211–219.

17. C. G. Jung, preface to R. Wilhelm's translation of the *I Ching*, reprinted in Jung's *Psyche and Symbol*, ed. V. de Laszlo (New York: Doubleday/Anchor, 1958), 227–228; also quoted by M. Nyman, *Experimental Music*, 8.

18. Quoted by J. Behrens, "Recent Piano Works of Christian Wolff," *Studies in Music* [Canada] 2 (1977): 1–7.

19. M. Hinson, *Guide to the Pianist's Repertoire*, 2nd ed., 852, gives a list of composers who have used the prepared piano.

20. Dates according to J. Dixon, *George Rochberg: A Bio-Bibliographical Guide to His Life and Works* (Stuyvesant, NY: Pendragon, 1992).

21. See generally B. Heifetz, "East-West Synthesis in Japanese Composition," *Journal of Musicology* 3 (1984): 443–455.

22. T. Koozin, "Toru Takemitsu and the Unity of Opposites," *College Music Symposium*, vol. 30, no. 1 (1990): 34–44.

Bibliography

This bibliography is selective: it is an attempt to present what has been written concerning the piano and its music in historical perspective, emphasizing the scholarly musicological literature. Thus, it does not provide a list of editions of music; for these the reader should turn to the standard dictionaries and general references in the field, notably Maurice Hinson's exhaustive guides (see the section, Bibliographies), along with that of his precursors (Friskin and Freundlich), K. Wolters' handbook, A. Heyer's *Historical Sets, Collections, and Monuments of Music: A Guide to their Contents*, 3rd. ed., 2 vols. (Chicago: American Library Association, 1980), and the standard encyclopedic dictionaries, notably *The New Grove Dictionary of Music*, ed. S. Sadie, 20 vols. (London: Macmillan, 1980), among others. Included here are only the most recent editions and their reprints.

Because this bibliography covers only books and articles dealing with the piano and its music, it does not show the following types of materials:

1. General works on the history of music, including surveys and studies of historical periods

2. General books and articles on composers, of the "life and works" type or devoted to aspects of the historical or intellectual background; some important books and articles of this type are shown in the endnotes as are bibliographical works, such as thematic catalogs

3. Guides to performance and interpretation

4. Studies in languages other than English and those of Western Europe. Where a study exists in an English translation, the original is not shown

5. Masters' theses and most D.M.A. dissertations; Ph.D. dissertations the substance of which has been incorporated into books or articles; unfinished Ph.D. dissertations.

The bibliography, which was essentially completed in the fall of 1993, is organized as follows:

    I.   General Works, Handbooks, and Surveys
    II. Bibliographies
    III. History of the Piano
    IV. Studies of Historical Periods
    V. Studies of Individual Composers.

For composers not shown in V, consult I (General Works, Handbooks, and Surveys) and the appropriate section of IV.

I. GENERAL WORKS, HANDBOOKS, AND SURVEYS

Aguettant, L. *La musique de piano, des origines à Ravel.* Paris: Michel, 1954; St. Maxime: Éditions d'aujourd'hui, 1981.

Apel, W. *Masters of the Keyboard.* Cambridge: Harvard University Press, 1947.

Bacon, E. *Notes on the Piano.* Syracuse: Syracuse University Press, 1963; Seattle: University of Washington Press, 1968.

Batel, G. *Geschichte des Klaviers und der Klaviermusik.* Musikpädagogische Bibliothek 6. Wilhelmshaven: Noetzel, 1991.

Bie, O. *History of the Pianoforte and Pianoforte Players.* London: Dent, 1899; New York: Da Capo, 1966.

Blom, E. *The Romance of the Piano.* London: Foulis, 1928; New York: Da Capo, 1969.

Borrel, E. *La sonate.* Paris: Larousse, 1951.

Bosquet, E. *La musique de clavier: et par extension de luth.* Brussels: Amis de musique, 1953.

Bruhn, S. *Die Kunst musikalischer Gestaltung am Klavier: Gestaltungsskriterien und Gestaltungsmittel in Bach'scher und klassischer Klaviermusik.* Frankfurt: Lang, 1981.

Cortot, A. *French Piano Music.* Trans. H. Andrews. London: Oxford, 1932; New York: Da Capo, 1977.

Demuth, N. *French Piano Music: A Survey with Notes on Its Performance.* London: Museum Press, 1959.

Dirksen, P., ed. *The Harpsichord and Its Repertory: Symposium Utrecht 1992.* Utrecht: STIMU Foundation, 1992.

Dubal, D. *The Art of the Piano.* New York: Summit, 1989.

Eberle, M. *Studien zur Entwicklung der Setzart für Klavier zu vier Händen.* Unpub. diss., Munich, 1922.

Eschmann, J. *Wegweiser durch die Klavierliteratur.* 7th ed. Leipzig: Hug, 1910.

Fallows-Hammond, P. *Three Hundred Years at the Keyboard: A Piano Sourcebook from Bach to the Moderns.* Berkeley: Ross, 1984.

Favre, G. *La musique française de piano avant 1830.* Paris: Didier, 1953.

Fillmore, J. *Pianoforte Music: Its History.* New York: McCoun, 1884; Boston: Longwood, 1978.

Georgii, W. *Klaviermusik.* 4th ed. Zurich and Berlin: Atlantis, 1965.

Gill, D., ed. *The Book of the Piano.* Ithaca: Cornell, 1981.

Gillespie, J. *Five Centuries of Keyboard Music.* Belmont: Wadsworth, 1965; New York: Dover, 1972.

Gradenwitz, P. *Kleine Kulturgeschichte der Klaviermusik.* Munich: List, 1986.

Hamilton, C. *Piano Music: Its Composers and Characteristics.* New York: Ditson, 1925.

Hering, H. "Übertragung und Umformung." *Die Musikforschung* 12 (1959): 274–294.

Hildebrandt, D. *A Social History of the Piano.* Trans. H. Goodman. New York: Braziller, 1988.

Hollfelder, P. *Geschichte der Klaviermusik.* 2 vols. Wilhelmshaven: Noetzel, 1987.

Hutcheson, E. *The Literature of the Piano.* 3rd ed, rev. R. Ganz. New York: Knopf, 1964; London: Hutchinson, 1974.

Kehler, G., ed. *The Piano in Concert.* 2 vols. Metuchen: Scarecrow, 1982.

Kirby, F. *A Short History of Keyboard Music.* New York: Free Press, later Schirmer Books, 1966.

Klauwell, O. *Geschichte der Sonate.* Universal-Bibliothek für Musikliteratur 18–20. Cologne and Leipzig: vom Ende, 1899.

Krehbiel, H. *The Pianoforte and Its Music.* New York: Scribners, 1910.

Kugler, M. *Die Musik für Tasteninstrumente im 15. und 16. Jahrhundert.* Taschenbücher für Musikwissenschaft 41. Wilhelmshaven: Heinrichshofen, 1975.

Lockwood, A. *Notes on the Literature of the Piano.* Ann Arbor: University of Michigan Press, 1949; New York: Da Capo, 1968.

Loesser, A. *Men, Women, and Pianos.* New York: Simon and Schuster, 1954.

Lubin, E. *The Piano Duet: A Guide for Pianists.* New York: Grossman, 1970; New York: Da Capo, 1976.

Marshall, R., ed. *Eighteenth-Century Keyboard Music.* New York: Schirmer, 1994.

Matthews, D., ed. *Keyboard Music.* New York: Praeger, 1972.

Moldenhauer, H. *Duo-Pianism: A Dissertation.* Chicago: Chicago Musical College, 1951.

Müller-Blattau, J. "Zur Geschichte und Stilistik des vierhändigen Klaviersatzes." *Jahrbuch Musikbibliothek Peters* 47 (1940): 40–58.

Niemann, W. *Das Klavierbuch: Kurze Geschichte der Klaviermusik und ihrer Meister.* 11th ed. Munich: Callwey, 1907.

Palmieri, R. *Piano Information Guide.* New York: Garland, 1989.

Phillips, L. *Piano Music by Black Composers.* Unpub. diss., Ohio State, 1977.

Powell, L. *Spanish Piano Music.* Bloomington: Indiana University Press, 1980.

Prosniz, A. *Handbuch der Clavier-Literatur.* 2nd ed. Leipzig and Vienna: Doblinger, 1908.

Rüger, C., ed. *Konzertbuch Klaviermusik A–Z.* Leipzig: VEB Deutscher Verlag für Musik, 1979.

Ruthardt, A. *Wegweiser durch die Klavierliteratur.* 10th ed. Leipzig and Zurich: Hug, 1925.

Schmitt, H. *Studien zur Geschichte und Stilistik des Satzes für 2 Klaviere zu 4 Händen.* Unpub. diss., Saarbrücken, 1965.

Schmitz, E. *Klavier, Klaviermusik, und Klavierspiel.* Leipzig: Breitkopf & Härtel, 1919.

Schneider, H. *Instrumentale Trauermusik im 19. und frühen 20. Jahrhundert dargestellt an 18 Klavierkompositionen zwischen 1797 und 1936.* Kölner Beiträge zu Musikforschung 148. Regensburg: Bosse, 1987.

Schumann, O. *Handbuch der Klaviermusik.* 2 vols. Munich: Heyne, 1982.

Schünemann, G. *Geschichte der Klaviermusik.* Berlin: Hahnefeld, 1940.

Seiffert, M. *Geschichte der Klaviermusik.* Leipzig: Breitkopf & Härtel, 1899.
Shedlock, J. *The Pianoforte Sonata: Its Origin and Development.* London: Methuen, 1895; New York: Da Capo, 1963.
Sonnedecker, D. *Cultivation and Concepts of Duets for Four Hands, One Keyboard in the Eighteenth Century.* Unpub. diss., Indiana University, 1953.
Tranchefort, F., ed. *Guide de la musique du piano et du clavecin.* Paris: Fayard, 1987.
Unger-Hamilton, C. *Keyboard Instruments.* Minneapolis: Control Data, 1981.
Weiser, B. *Keyboard Music.* Dubuque: Brown, 1971.
Weitzmann, C. *History of Pianoforte Playing and Pianoforte Literature.* Trans. H. Westerby. New York: Schirmer, 1894; New York: Da Capo, 1969.
Westerby, H. *A History of Pianoforte Music.* London and New York: Kegan Paul, Trench, Traubner, Dutton, 1924; New York: Da Capo, 1971.
Wier, A. *The Piano: Its History, Makers, Players, and Music.* New York: Longmans, Green, 1941.
Wolff, K. *Masters of the Keyboard.* Enl. ed. Bloomington: Indiana, 1989.
Wolters, K. *Handbuch der Klavierliteratur zu zwei Händen.* 3rd. ed. Zurich: Atlantis, 1985.

II. BIBLIOGRAPHIES

Alker, H. *Literatur für alte Tasteninstrumente: Versuch einer Bibliographie für die Praxis.* Wiener Abhandlungen zur Musikwissenschaft und Instrumentenkunde 4. Vienna: Geyer, 1962.
Altmann, W. *Verzeichnis von Werken für Klavier vier- und sechshändig sowie für zwei und mehr Klaviere.* Leipzig: Hofmeister, 1943.
Friskin, J., and I. Freundlich. *Music for the Piano: A Handbook of Concert and Teaching Material from 1580 to 1952.* New York: Rinehart, 1952; New York: Dover, 1974.
Fuszek, R. *Piano Music in Collections: An Index.* Detroit: Harmonie Press, 1982.
Ganzer, K., and L. Kusche. *Vierhändig.* Rev. ed. Munich: Heimeran, 1954.
Gillespie, J., and A. Gillespie. *A Bibliography of Nineteenth-Century American Piano Music.* Music Reference Collection 2. Westport: Greenwood, 1984.
Gustafson, B. *French Harpsichord Music of the Seventeenth Century: A Thematic Catalogue of Sources with Commentary.* 3 vols. Ann Arbor: UMI, 1979.
Gustafson, B., and D. Fuller. *A Catalog of French Harpsichord Music, 1699–1780.* Oxford: Clarendon, 1990.
Hinson, M. *Guide to the Pianist's Repertoire.* 2nd ed. Bloomington: Indiana University Press, 1987.
———. *Music for More than One Piano.* Bloomington: Indiana University Press, 1983.
———. *The Pianist's Guide to Transcriptions, Arrangements, and Paraphrases.* Bloomington: Indiana University Press, 1990.
———. *The Pianist's Reference Guide: A Bibliographical Survey.* Los Angeles: Alfred, 1987.
Kortsen, B. *Contemporary Norwegian Piano Music: A Catalogue.* 4th ed. Contemporary Norwegian Music 4. Bergen: Kortsen, 1973.
McGraw, C. *Piano Duet Repertoire.* Bloomington: Indiana University Press, 1981.
McRoberts, G. *An Annotated Catalog of Original Two-piano Literature.* Unpub. thesis, California State University (Long Beach), 1973.
Meggett, J. *Keyboard Music by Women Composers: A Catalog and Bibliography.* Westport: Greenwood, 1981.

Rezits, J. *The Pianist's Resource Guide*. Park Ridge, IL: Pallma, 1974.

Schulz, F. *Pianographie. Klavierbibliographie der lieferbaren Bücher und Periodica sowie Dissertationen* . . . Recklinghausen: Piano-Verlag, 1982.

Walker-Hill, H., ed. *Piano Music by Black Women Composers: A Catalog of Solo and Ensemble Works*. Music Reference Collection 35. New York: Greenwood, 1992.

III. HISTORY OF THE PIANO

Ahrens, C. "Pantaleon Hebenstreit und die Frühgeschichte des Hammerklaviers." *Beiträge zur Musikwissenschaft* 29 (1987): 37–48.

Barli, O. *La facture française du piano*. Paris: Flute de Pan, 1983.

Barry, W. "Henri Arnault de Zwolle's 'Clavicordium' and the Origin of the Chekker." *American Musical Instrument Society Journal* 11 (1985): 5–13.

Belt, P., et al. *The Piano*. New Grove Musical Instrument Series. New York: Norton, 1988.

Brinsmead, E. *A History of the Pianoforte*. London: Novello, 1879; Detroit: Information Coordinators, 1969.

Brunner, H. *Das Klavierklangideal Mozarts und die Klaviere seiner Zeit*. Augsburg: Filser, 1933.

Closson, E. *History of the Piano*. Trans. D. Ames. London: Elek, 1947; St. Clair Shores, MI: Scholarly Press, 1977.

Colt, C. *The Early Piano*. London: Stainer & Bell, 1981.

Dolge, A. *Pianos and Their Makers: A Comprehensive History*. Covina, CA: Covina, 1911–1913; New York: Dover, 1972.

Ehrlich, C. *The Piano: A History*. Rev. ed. London: Dent, 1990.

Ernst, F. *Der Flügel Joh. Seb. Bachs*. Frankfurt and New York: Peters, 1955.

Gabry, G. "Die Klaviere Beethovens und Liszts." *Studia Musicologica* 8 (1966): 379–390.

Good, E. *Giraffes, Black Dragons, and Other Pianos*. Stanford: Stanford University Press, 1982.

Grafing, K. "Alphaeus Babcock's Cast-iron Frames." *Galpin Society Journal* 27 (1974): 118–124.

Handschin, J. "Das Pedalklavier." *Zeitschrift für Musikwissenschaft* 17 (1935): 418–425.

Harding, R. *The Pianoforte: Its History to the Great Exposition of 1851*, 2nd ed. Old Woking: Gresham, 1978.

Hess, A. "The Transition from Harpsichord to Piano." *Galpin Society Journal* 6 (1953): 75–94.

Hipkins, A. *A Description and History of the Pianoforte and of the Older Stringed Keyboard Instruments*. Music Primers and Education 52. London and New York: Novello, Ewer, 1896, 1929; Detroit: Information Coordinators, 1975.

Hirt, F. *Meisterwerke des Klavierbaus = Stringed Keyboard Instruments, 1440–1850*. Trans. M. Boehme-Brown. Dietikon: Urs Graf, 1981.

Hoover, C. "The Steinways and Their Pianos in the 19th Century." *American Music Instrument Society Journal* 7 (1981): 47–89.

James, P. *Early Keyboard Instruments*. 1930. Reprint. London: Holland Press, 1960, 1967; New York: Barnes & Noble, 1970.

Maunder, R. "Mozart's Keyboard Instruments." *Early Music* 20 (1992): 207–219.

Meeus, N. "The Chekker." *Organ Yearbook* 16 (1985): 5–25.

Mobbs, K. "Stops and Other Special Effects on the Early Piano." *Early Music* 12 (1984): 471–476.

Neupert, H. *Vom Musikstab zum modernen Klavier.* 3rd ed. Berlin: Krause, 1926.
Parrish, C. "Criticisms of the Piano When It Was New." *Musical Quarterly* 30 (1944): 428–440.
———. *The Early Piano and Its Influence on Keyboard Technique and Composition in the Eighteenth Century.* Unpub. diss., Harvard, 1939.
Paul, O. *Geschichte des Claviers vom Ursprunge bis zur modernsten Form dieses Instruments.* Leipzig: Payne, 1868.
Pleasants, V. "The Early Piano in Britain (c. 1760–1800)." *Early Music* 13 (1985): 39–44.
Pollens, S. "Gottfried Silbermann's Pianos." *Organ Yearbook* 17 (1986): 103–121.
———. "The Pianos of Bartolomeo Cristofori." *American Music Instrument Society Journal* 10 (1984): 32–68.
Rattalino, P. *Storia della pianoforte.* 2nd ed. La cultura 6. Milan: Saggiatore, 1982.
Restle, K. "Mozarts Hammerflügel." In *Bericht über den Internationalen Mozart-Kongress Salzburg 1991,* ed. R. Angermüller et al., 313–318. Mozart-Jahrbuch 1991. Kassel: Bärenreiter, 1992.
Rimbault, E. *The Pianoforte: Its Origin, Progress, and Construction.* London: Cocks, 1860.
Ripin, E. "Towards an Identification of the Chekker." *Galpin Society Journal* 28 (1975): 11–25.
Ripin, E., ed. *Early Keyboard Instruments.* The New Grove Musical Instruments Series. New York: Norton, 1989.
Roell, C. *The Piano in America, 1890–1940.* Chapel Hill: University of North Carolina Press, 1991.
Russell, R. *The Harpsichord and Clavichord: An Introductory Study.* 2nd ed., rev. H. Schott. London: Faber; New York: Norton, 1973.
Sachs, C. *Das Klavier.* Handbücher des Instrumentenmuseums der Staatlichen Hochschule für Musik 1. Berlin: Baud, 1923.
Sakka, K. "Beethovens Klaviere: der Klavierbau und Beethovens künstlerische Reaktion." In *Colloquium amicorum: Joseph Schmidt-Görg zum 70. Geburtstag,* 327–337. Bonn: Beethovenhaus, 1967.
Sumner, W. *The Piano.* 1966. Reprint. London: St. Martin's, 1971.
Wainwright, D. *Broadwood by Appointment: A History.* London: Quiller, 1982.
———. *The Piano Makers.* London: Hutchinson, 1975.
Winter, R. "Striking it Rich: The Significance of Striking Points in the Evolution of the Modern Piano." *Journal of Musicology* 6 (1988): 267–292.
Wittmayr, K. "Der Flügel Mozarts." In *Bericht über den Internationalen Mozart-Kongress Salzburg 1991,* ed. R. Angermüller et al., 301–312. Mozart-Jahrbuch 1991. Kassel: Bärenreiter, 1992.
Wolters, K., and F. Jacob. *Das Klavier: Einführung in Geschichte und Bau des Instruments und in die Geschichte des Klavierspiels.* 2nd ed. Unsere Musikinstrumente 2. Mainz: Schott, 1984.

IV. STUDIES OF HISTORICAL PERIODS

A. To ca. 1750

Äpfel, E. "Ostinato und Kompositionstechnik bei den englischen Virginalisten der elisabethianischen Zeit." *Archiv für Musikwissenschaft* 19–20 (1962–1963): 29–39.
Andrews, H. "Elizabethan Keyboard Music." *Musical Quarterly* 16 (1930): 59–71.
Apel, W. *Early European Keyboard Music.* Stuttgart: Steiner, 1989.

————. *The History of Keyboard Music to 1700*. Trans. H. Tischler. Bloomington: Indiana University Press, 1972.

Auerbach, C. *Die deutsche Clavichordkunst des 18. Jahrhunderts*. 3rd ed. Kassel: Bärenreiter, 1959.

Bates, C. "French Harpsichord Music in the First Decade of the Eighteenth Century." *Early Music* 17 (1989): 184–196.

Bedbrook, G. *Keyboard Music from the Middle Ages to the Beginnings of the Baroque*. London: Macmillan, 1949; New York: Da Capo, 1973.

Bergenfeld, N. *The Keyboard Fantasy of the Elizabethan Renaissance*. Unpub. diss., New York University, 1978.

Borren, C. *Les origines de la musique de clavier dans les Pays-bas nord et sud jusq'à vers 1630*. Brussels: Breitkopf & Härtel, 1914; Westport: Greenwood, 1970; Wiesbaden: Breitkopf & Härtel, 1977.

————. *The Sources of Keyboard Music in England*. Trans. J. Matthew. London: Novello, 1914; Westport: Greenwood, 1970.

Bosquet, E. "Origine et formation de la sonate allemande pour clavecin de 1698 à 1742." *Revue internationale de la musique* 1 (1939): 853–862.

Bradshaw, M. "The Influence of Vocal Music on the Venetian Toccata." *Musica Disciplina* 42 (1988): 157–198.

————. *The Origin of the Toccata*. Musical Studies and Documents 28. Rome: American Institute of Musicology, 1972.

Brunold, P. *Traité des signes et agréments employés par les clavecinistes français des XVIIe et XVIIIe siècles*. 2nd ed. Lyons: Janin, 1965.

Buch, D. "The Influence of the 'Ballet de cour' in the Genesis of the Baroque Suite." *Acta Musicologica* 57 (1985): 94–109.

Burns, J. *Neapolitan Keyboard Music from Valente to Frescobaldi*. Unpub. diss., Harvard, 1953.

Caldwell, J. *English Keyboard Music Before the 19th Century*. New York: Praeger, 1973; New York: Dover, 1986.

Clercx, S. "Les clavecinistes belges." *Revue musicale* 20 (no. 192, 1939): 11–22.

————. "Le toccate, principe du style symphonique." In *La musique instrumentale de la renaissance*, ed. J. Jacquot, 313–326. Paris: Centre national de la recherche scientifique, 1955.

Cooper, B. *English Solo Keyboard Music of the Middle and Late Baroque*. New York: Garland, 1990.

Deffner, O. *Über die Entwicklung der Fantasie für Tasteninstrumente (bis J. P. Sweelinck)*. Kiel: Mühlau, 1928.

Denison, W. *Recitative in Baroque Keyboard Music*. Unpub. diss., Florida State University, 1969.

Douglass, R. *The Keyboard Ricercar in the Baroque Era*. Unpub. diss., North Texas State University, 1963.

Eggebrecht, H. "Terminus 'ricercar.'" *Archiv für Musikwissenschaft* 9 (1952): 137–147.

Eitner, R. "Die Sonate: Vorstudien zur Entstehung der Form." *Monatshefte für Musikgeschichte* 20 (1888): 163–170, 179–185.

Epstein, E. *Der französische Einfluss auf die deutsche Klaviersuite im 17. Jahrhundert*. Würzburg: Triltsch, 1940.

Faisst, I. "Beiträge zur Geschichte der Claviersonate von ihren ersten Anfängen bis auf C. P. Emanuel Bach." *Neues Beethoven-Jahrbuch* 1 (1924): 7–85 (orig. *Caecilia* 25-26 [1846–1847]).

Fischer, K. "Chaconne und Passacaglia: ein Versuch." *Revue Belge de musicologie* 12 (1958): 19–34.

Flotzinger, R. "Die Klavierbücher der Anna Franziska von Spitzenberg (1725)." *Händel-Jahrbuch* 24 (1988): 71–107.

Fuller, D. "Accompanied Keyboard Music." *Musical Quarterly* 60 (1974): 222–245.

———. *Eighteenth-Century French Harpsichord Music.* Unpub. diss., Harvard, 1965.

Glyn, M. *About Elizabethan Virginal Music and Its Composers.* Rev. ed. London: Reeves, 1934.

Göllner, T. *Formen früher Mehrstimmigkeit in deutschen Handschriften des späten Mittelalters.* Münchener Veröffentlichungen zur Musikgeschichte 6. Tutzing: Schneider, 1961.

Gombosi, O. "Zur Vorgeschichte der Tokkata." *Acta Musicologica* 6 (1934): 49–53.

Gress, R. *Die Entwicklung der Klaviervariation von Andrea Gabrieli bis Johann Sebastian Bach.* Stuttgart: Zechnall, 1929.

Harding, R. "The Earliest Pianoforte Music." *Music and Letters* 13 (1932): 194–199.

Harris, C. *Keyboard Music in Vienna During the Reign of Leopold I (1658–1705).* Unpub. diss., University of Michigan, 1967.

Hering, H. "Das Tokkatische." *Die Musikforschung* 7 (1954): 277–294.

Hibberd, L. *The Early Keyboard Prelude.* Unpub. diss., Harvard, 1940.

Hoffmann-Erbrecht, L. *Deutsche und italienische Klaviermusik zur Bachzeit.* Jenaer Beiträge zur Musikforschung 1. Leipzig: VEB Breitkopf & Härtel, 1954.

Horsley, I. "The 16th-Century Variation: A New Historical Survey." *Journal of the American Musicological Society* 12 (1959): 118–132.

Howell, A. "Paired Imitation in Sixteenth-Century Spanish Keyboard Music." *Musical Quarterly* 53 (1967): 377–396.

Hudson, R. *Passacaglia and Ciaccona: From Guitar Music to Italian Keyboard Variations in the 17th Century.* Studies in Musicology 37. Ann Arbor: UMI, 1981.

Jacobs, C. *La interpretación de la musica española del siglo XVI para instrumentos de teclado.* Musica en Compostela 2. Madrid: Dirección General de Relaciónes Culturales, 1959. Jacquot, J. "Sur quelques formes de la musique de clavier elisabethaine." In *La musique instrumentale de la renaissance*, 241–258. Paris: Centre nationale de la recherche scientifique, 1955.

Johnsson, B. "Eighteenth-Century Catalan Keyboard Music." *Dansk årbog for musikforskning* 15 (1984): 39–113.

Judd, R. "Repeat Problems in Keyboard Settings of canzoni alla francese." *Early Music* 17 (1989): 198–214.

Kämper, D. "Zur Vorgeschichte der Fantasie Sweelincks." In *Bericht über den internationalen musikwissenschaftlichen Kongress Berlin 1974*, 275–276. Kassel: Bärenreiter, 1980.

Kastner, M. *The Interpretation of Sixteenth- and Seventeenth-Century Iberian Keyboard Music.* Stuyvesant, NY: Pendragon, 1987.

———. "Parallels and Discrepancies between English and Spanish Keyboard Music of the 16th and 17th Centuries." *Annuario musical* 7 (1952): 77–115.

Kenyon, M. *Harpsichord Music: A Survey of Virginals, Spinet, and Harpsichord.* London: Cassel, 1949; St. Clair Shores, MI: Scholarly Press, 1978.

Kinkeldey, O. *Orgel und Klavier in der Musik des 16. Jahrhunderts.* Leipzig: Breitkopf & Härtel, 1910; New York: Da Capo, 1978.

Kirkendale, W. "Ciceronians versus Aristotelians on the Ricercar as Exordium, from Bembo to Bach." *Journal of the American Musicological Society* 23 (1979): 1–44.

Klakowich, R. *Keyboard Sources in Mid 17th-Century England and the French Aspect of English Keyboard Music.* Unpub. diss., Buffalo, 1985.

Kraemer, U. *Die Courante in der deutschen Orchester- und Klaviermusik des 17. Jahrhunderts.* Unpub. diss., Hamburg, 1967.

Kugler, M. *Die Tasteninstrumentenmusik im Codex Faenza.* Münchener Veröffentlichungen zur Musikgeschichte 21. Tutzing: Schneider, 1972.

Launay, D. "La fantaisie en France jusqu'au milieu de XVIIe siècle." In *La musique instrumentale de la Renaissance,* ed. J. Jacquot, 327–338. Paris: Centre national de la recherche scientifique, 1955.

Ledbetter, D. *Harpsichord and Lute Music in 17th-Century France.* Bloomington: Indiana University Press; London: Macmillan, 1987.

Maas, M. *Seventeenth-Century English Keyboard Music.* Unpub. diss., Yale, 1968.

Marco, G. "The Alberti Bass Before Alberti." *Music Review* 20 (1959): 93–103.

Martin, M. *French Harpsichord Music: 1687–1713.* Unpub. diss., University of California, Los Angeles, 1991.

Mereaux, A. *Les clavecinistes de 1627 à 1790.* Paris: Heugel, 1867.

Merian, W. *Der Tanz in den deutschen Tabulaturbüchern.* Leipzig: Breitkopf & Härtel, 1927.

Miller, H. "The Earliest Keyboard Duets." *Musical Quarterly* 29 (1943): 438–457.

Monroe, J. *Italian Keyboard Music in the Interim Between Frescobaldi and Pasquini.* Unpub. diss., Michigan, 1959.

Monson, C. "Elena Malvezzi's Keyboard Manuscript: A New Sixteenth-Century Source." *Early Music History* 9 (1990): 73–128.

Montagonier, J. "La fugue pour clavecin en France vers 1700–1730." *Revue de Musicologie* 76 (1990): 173–186.

Murphy, R. *Fantasia and Ricercare in the Sixteenth Century.* Unpub. diss., Yale, 1954.

Naylor, E. *An Elizabethan Virginal Book.* London: Dent, 1905.

Nelson, R. *The Technique of Variation: A Study of the Instrumental Variation from Cabezon to Bach.* University of California Publications in Music 3. Berkeley: University of California Press, 1948.

Neudenberger, L. *Die Variationstechnik der Virginalisten im Fitzwilliam Virginal Book.* Berlin: Triltsch & Huther, 1937.

Newman, W. *The Sonata in the Baroque Era.* 2nd ed. New York: Norton, 1972.

Niemann, W. *Die Virginalmusik.* Leipzig: Breitkopf & Härtel, 1919.

Nordenfelt-Aberg, E. "The Harpsichord in Eighteenth-Century Sweden." *Early Music* 9 (1981): 47–54.

Pannain, G. *Le origini e lo sviluppo dell'arte pianistica in Italia dal 1500 al 1730 circa.* Naples: Izzo, 1917.

Parker, M. "Some Speculations on the French Keyboard Suites of the 17th and Early 18th Centuries." *International Review of the Aesthetics and Sociology of Music,* vol. 7, no. 2 (1976): 203–217.

Pestelli, G. "Bach, Handel, D. Scarlatti, and the Toccata of the Late Baroque." In *Bach, Handel, and Scarlatti: Tercentenary Essays,* ed. P. Williams, 277–291. Cambridge: Cambridge University Press, 1985.

Pirro, A. *Les clavecinistes.* Paris: Laurens, 1925; St. Maxime: Éditions d'aujourd'hui: 1984.

Plamenac, D. "The Codex Faenza, Biblioteca Communale 117." *Journal of the American Musicological Society* 4 (1951): 179–201.

Podolsky, S. *The Variation Canzona for Keyboard Instruments in Italy, Austria, and Southern Germany in the Seventeenth Century.* Unpub. diss., Boston University, 1954.

Prévost, P. *Le prélude non mensuré pour clavecin (France 1650–1700).* Collection d'études musicologiques 75. Baden-Baden: Koerner, 1987.

Reimann, M. *Untersuchungen zur Formgeschichte der französischen Klaviersuite.* 1941. Reprint. Regensburg: Bosse, 1968.

————. "Zur Deutung des Begriffs 'fantasia.'" *Archiv für Musikwissenschaft* 10 (1953): 253–274.

————. "Zur Entwicklungsgeschichte des Double." *Die Musikforschung* 5 (1952): 317–32; 6 (1953): 97–111.

————. "Zur Spielpraxis der Klaviervariationen des 16. bis 18. Jahrhunderts." *Die Musikforschung* 7 (1954): 457–459.

Riedel, F. "Der Einfluss der italienischen Klaviermusik des 17. Jahrhunderts auf die Entwicklung der Musik für Tasteninstrumente in Deutschland während der ersten Hälfte des 18. Jahrhunderts." *Analecta Musicologica* 5 (1968): 18–33.

————. *Quellenkundliche Beiträge zur Geschichte der Musik für Tasteninstrumente in der 2. Hälfte des 17. Jahrhunderts.* 2nd ed. Musikwissenschaftliche Schriften 22. Munich: Katzbichler, 1990.

Rumohr, E. *Der Nürnbergische Tasteninstrumentenstil im 17. Jahrhundert.* Münster: Hermer, 1939.

Sandberger, A. "Zur italienischen Klaviermusik des 17. und 18. Jahrhunderts." In *Ausgewählte Aufsätze zur Musikgeschichte*, vol. 1, 169–180. Munich: Drei Masken, 1921.

Schierning, L. *Die Überlieferung der deutschen Orgel- und Klaviermusik aus der 1. Hälfte des 17. Jahrhunderts.* Schriften des Landesinstituts für Musikforschung Kiel 12. Kassel: Bärenreiter, 1961.

Schrade, L. "Ein Beitrag zur Geschichte der Tokkata." *Zeitschrift für Musikwissenschaft* 8 (1925–1926): 610–635.

————. *Die handschriftliche Überlieferung der ältesten Instrumentalmusik.* Lahr: Schauenburg, 1931.

Schuler, M. "Zur Frühgeschichte der Passacaglia." *Die Musikforschung* 16 (1963): 121–126.

Silbiger, A. *Italian Manuscript Sources of 17th-Century Keyboard Music.* Studies in Musicology 18. Ann Arbor: UMI, 1980.

Slim, H. *The Keyboard Ricercar and Fantasy in Italy, ca. 1500–1550.* Unpub. diss., Harvard, 1961.

Southern, E. "Some Keyboard Basse Danses of the 15th Century." *Acta musicologica* 35 (1963): 114–124.

Stilz, E. *Die Berliner Klaviersonate zur Zeit Friedrichs des Grossen.* Saarbrücken: Saarbrücker Druckerei, 1930.

Sumner, F. *The Instrumental Canzone Prior to 1600.* Unpub. diss., Rutgers, 1973.

Teepe, D. *Die Entwicklung der Fantasie für Tasteninstrumente im 16. und 17. Jahrhundert.* Kieler Schriften zur Musikwissenschaft 36. Kassel: Bärenreiter, 1990.

Torrefranca, F. *Le origini italiane del romanticismo musicali: I primitivi della sonata moderna.* Turin: Bocca, 1930.

Tuttle, S. *A Study of the History of English Keyboard Music to 1623.* Unpub. diss., Harvard, 1941.

Valentin, E. *Die Entwicklung der Tokkata im 17. und 18. Jahrhundert (bis J. S. Bach).* Universitas-Archiv 45, Musikwissenschaftliche Abteilung 6. Münster: Helios, 1930.

Vendrix, P. "Il 'tombeau' in musica nel periodo barocco." *Nuova rivista musicale italiana* 23 (1989): 325–341.

Walker, T. "Ciaccona and Passacaglia: Remarks on Their Origin and Early History." *Journal of the American Musicological Society* 21 (1968): 300–320.

Ward, J. "The 'dolfull domps.'" *Journal of the American Musicological Society* 4 (1951): 111–121.

————. "Les sources de la musique pour clavier en Angleterre." In *La musique instru-*

mentale de la Renaissance, ed. J. Jacquot, 225–236. Paris: Centre national de la recherche scientifique, 1955.

Whittaker, W. "Byrd and Bull's Walsingham Variations." *Music Review* 3 (1942): 270–279.

Williams, P. "'Figurae' in the Keyboard Works of Scarlatti, Handel, and Bach: An Introduction." In *Bach, Handel and Scarlatti: Tercentenary Essays*, ed. P. Williams, 327–346. Cambridge: Cambridge University Press, 1985.

Wuellner, G. "The Fitzwilliam Virginal Book: Textural Procedures of the English Virginalists." *Music Review* 32 (1971): 326–348.

Young, W. "Keyboard Music to 1600." *Musica Disciplina* 16 (1962): 115–150; 17 (1963): 163–193.

B. The Classic Period

Badura-Skoda, E. "Die 'Clavier'-Musik in Wien zwischen 1750 und 1770." *Studien zur Musikwissenschaft* 35 (1984): 65–88.

Becker, C. "Zur Geschichte der Hausmusik in früheren Jahrhunderten 1. Die Klaviersonate in Deutschland." *Neue Zeitschrift für Musik* 7 (1837): 25–26, 29–30, 33–34.

Climent, J. "La musica española para tecla en el siglo XVIII." *Revista de musicologia* 8 (1985): 15–21.

Franzova, T. "Die Entwicklung der böhmischen Cembalomusik in der zweiten Hälfte des 18. Jahrhunderts." In *Zur Entwicklung der Kammermusik in der zweiten Hälfte des 18. Jahrhunderts*, 50–52. Michaelstein and Blankenburg: Kultur- und Forschungsstätte Michaelstein, 1986.

Grimm, H. "Frei und gezügelte Phantasie: zur Ästhetik einer Gattung des achtzehnten Jahrhunderts und ihre Zurücknahme." *Musik und Gesellschaft* 35 (1985): 592–597.

Halski, C. "Murky: A Polish Musical Freak." *Music and Letters* 39 (1958): 35–37.

Heuschneider, K. *Contributions to the Development of the Piano Sonata*, 2 vols. Capetown: Balkema, 1967–1970.

Kahl, W. "Frühe Lehrwerke für das Hammerklavier." *Archiv für Musikwissenschaft* 9 (1952): 231–245.

Kamien, R. "Style Change in the Mid-18th-Century Keyboard Sonata." *Journal of the American Musicological Society* 19 (1966): 37–58.

Korisheli, W. *Die Entstehung und Geschichte der vierhändigen Klavierliteratur bis zu Schubert und seinen Zeitgenossen*. Unpub. diss., Freiburg, 1975.

Lange, M. *Beiträge zur Entstehung der südwestdeutschen Klaviersonate im 18. Jahrhundert*. Berlin: Lankewitzer Anzeige, 1930.

Marks, F. *The Sonata: Its Meaning and Form as Exemplified in the Sonatas of Mozart*. London: Reeves, 1921.

McCarthy, M. "Two-Piano Music Around Beethoven's Time." *College Music Symposium* 17 (1977): 131–143.

Michel, H. *La sonate pour clavier avant Beethoven*. Amiens: Yvert & Tellier, 1907.

Newman, W. *The Sonata in the Classic Era*. 2nd ed. New York: Norton, 1972.

Pilkova, Z. "Charakteristische Züge im Klavierschaffen der tschechischen Komponisten um die Wende des 18. zum 19. Jahrhundert." In *Bericht über den Internationalen musikwissenschaftlichen Kongress Bonn 1970*, 531–533. Kassel: Bärenreiter, 1977.

Pollack, C. *Viennese Solo Keyboard Music, 1740–1770*. Unpub. diss., Brandeis, 1984.

Reeser, E. *De Klaviersonate met Vioolbegleiding in het Parijsche Muziekleben ten Tijde van Mozart*. Rotterdam: [n. p.] 1939.

Sanders, D. *The Keyboard Sonatas of Giustini, Paradisi, and Rutini.* Unpub. diss., University of Kansas, 1983.
Schleuning, P. *Die freie Fantasie.* Groppinger akademische Beiträge 76. Groppingen: Kummerle, 1973.
Stone, D. *The Italian Keyboard Sonata for Harpsichord and Piano in the Eighteenth Century (1730–1790).* 3 vols. Unpub. diss., Harvard, 1952.
Wolverton, B. *Keyboard Music and Musicians in the Colonies and United States of America Before 1830.* Unpub. diss., Indiana University, 1966.

C. The Romantic Period

Augustini, F. *Die Klavieretüde im 19. Jahrhundert.* Duisburg: Gilles & Franke, 1986.
Ballstaedt, A., and T. Widmaier. *Salonmusik: zur Geschichte und Funktion einer bürgerlichen Musikpraxis.* Beihefte des Archiv für Musikforschung 28. Wiesbaden: Steiner, 1989.
Berlin, E. *Ragtime: A Musical and Cultural History.* Berkeley: University of California Press, 1980.
Biget, M. *La geste pianistique: essai sur l'écriture du piano entre 1800 et 1930.* L'artisanat furieux 1. Rouen: Université de Rouen, 1986.
Brody, E., and J. LaRue. "Trois nouvelles études (Moscheles' 'Méthode des méthodes')." *Musical Quarterly* 72 (1986): 1–15.
Clark, J. *The Dawning of American Keyboard Music.* New York: Greenwood, 1988.
Dale, K. *Nineteenth-Century Piano Music.* London: Oxford, 1954; New York: Da Capo, 1972.
———. "The Three C's (Clementi, Czerny, Cramer): Pioneers of Pianoforte Playing." *Music Review* 6 (1945): 138–148.
Egert, P. *Die Klaviersonate im Zeitalter der Romantik.* Berlin and Johannistal: Self-published, 1934.
Ellis, M. *The French Piano Character Piece of the 19th and Early 20th Centuries.* Unpub. diss., Indiana University, 1969.
Finlow, S. *The Piano Study from 1820 to 1850.* Unpub. diss., Cambridge, 1986.
Friedland, M. *Zeitstil und Persönlichkeitsstil in den Variationenwerken der musikalischen Romantik.* Sammlung musikwissenschaftlicher Einzeldarstellungen 14. Leipzig: Breitkopf & Härtel, 1930.
Ganz, P. *The Development of the Etude for Piano.* Unpub. diss., Northwestern, 1960.
Glusman, E. *The Early 19th-Century Lyric Piece.* Unpub. diss., Columbia, 1969.
Golos, G. "Some Slavic Precursors of Chopin." *Musical Quarterly* 46 (1960): 437–447.
Gruhn, W. "'Dolente'–'Scherzante': Poesie und Charakter in den Polonaisen von Franz Schubert und Robert Schumann." In *Florilegium musicologium: Helmut Federhofer zum 75. Geburtstag,* ed. C. Mahling, 121–131. Tutzing: Schneider, 1988.
Hering, H. "Orchestrale Klaviermusik." *Acta Musicologica* 56 (1974): 76–91.
———. "Satzstrukturen der Klaviermusik im 18. und 19. Jahrhundert." *Die Musikforschung* 17 (1964): 234–244.
Horton, C. *Serious Art and Concert Music for Piano in the 100 Years from Alexander Reinagle to Edward MacDowell.* Unpub. diss., University of North Carolina, 1965.
Jasen, D., and T. Tichenor. *Rags and Ragtime: A Musical History.* New York: Seabury, 1978; New York: Dover, 1989.
Kämper, D. *Die Klaviersonate nach Beethoven: von Schubert bis Skrjabin.* Darmstadt: Wissenschaftliche Buchgesellschaft, 1987.
Kretzschmar, H. "Die Klaviermusik seit Robert Schumann." In *Gesammelte Aufsätze,* vol. 1, 87–135. Leipzig: Breitkopf & Härtel, 1910.

Krueger, W. *Das Nachtstück: ein Beitrag zur Entwicklung des einsätzigen Pianoforte-stücks im 19. Jahrhundert.* Schriften zur Musik 9. Giebing: Katzbichler, 1971.

Leikin, A. *The Dissolution of Sonata Structure in Romantic Piano Music.* Unpub. diss., University of California, Los Angeles, 1986.

Newman, W. *The Sonata Since Beethoven.* 3rd rev. ed. New York: Norton, 1972.

Niemann, W. *Die nordische Klaviermusik.* Leipzig: Breitkopf & Härtel, 1918.

Parker, J. *The Clavier Fantasia from Mozart to Liszt.* Unpub. diss., Stanford, 1974.

Presser, D. "Die Opernbearbeitungen des 19. Jahrhunderts." *Archiv für Musikwissenschaft* 12 (1955): 227–238.

Pruett, L. "Napoleonic Battles in Keyboard Music of the Nineteenth Century." *Early Keyboard Journal* 6 (1991): 73–90.

Puchelt, G. *Variationen für Klavier im 19. Jahrhundert: Blüte und Verfall einer Kunstform.* Hildesheim: Ohm, 1973.

———. *Verlorene Klänge: Studien zur deutschen Klaviermusik 1830 bis 1880.* Berlin: Lienau, 1969.

Salmen, W. *Geschichte der Rhapsodie.* Zurich: Atlantis, 1966.

Schafer, W., and J. Riedel. *The Art of Ragtime.* Baton Rouge: Louisiana State University Press, 1973; New York: Da Capo, 1977.

Schubert, G. "'Vibrierende Gedanken' und 'Katasterverfahren' der Analyse: Zu den Klaviersonaten von Dukas und d'Indy." In *Das musikalische Kunstwerk:Festschrift Carl Dahlhaus zum 60. Geburtstag,* ed. H. Danuser et al., 619–634. Laaber, 1988.

Schwab, H. "Das lyrische Klavierstück und der nordische Ton." In *Gattung und Werk in der Musikgeschichte Norwegens und Skandinaviens,* ed. F. Krummacher, 136–153. Kieler Studien zu Musikwissenschaft 26. Kassel: Bärenreiter, 1982.

Stegemann, M. "Immanenz und Transzendenz: Chopin, Skrjabin, Szymanowski und die pianistische Ornamentik." In *Frydryk Chopin,* 80–108. Musik-Konzepte 45. Munich: text & kritik, 1985.

Stenger, G. *Studien zur Geschichte des Klavierwalzers.* Europäische Hochschulschriften. Musikwissenschaft, ser. 36, vol. 1. Frankfurt: Lang, 1978.

Suttoni, C. *Piano and Opera: A Study of the Piano Fantasias Written on Opera Themes in the Romantic Era.* Unpub. diss., New York University, 1973.

Thäle, D. *Die Klaviersonate bei Mendelssohn-Bartholdy, Chopin, Schumann, und Liszt.* 2 vols. Unpub. diss., Halle, 1973.

Todd, R., ed. *Nineteenth-Century Piano Music.* New York: Schirmer, 1990.

Turrill, P. *The Piano Ballade in the Romantic Era.* Unpub. diss., University of Southern California, 1977.

Vidor, M. *Zur Begriffs-Bestimmung des musikalischen Charakterstücks für Klavier.* Unpub. diss., Leipzig, 1924.

Vogel, J. "Die böhmischen Klassiker:Einige Bemerkungen zu ihrer Klaviermusik." *Musica* 27 (1973): 124–129.

Wagner, G. *Die Klavierballade um die Mitte des 19. Jahrhunderts.* Berliner musikwissenschaftliche Arbeiten 76. Munich: Katzbichler, 1976.

———. *Klaviermusik im 19. Jahrhundert.* Unpub. diss., Berlin (Technical University), 1978.

Waldo, T. *This is Ragtime.* New York: Hawthorn, 1976; New York: Da Capo, 1984.

Wangermée, R. "Tradition et innovation dans la virtuosité romantique." *Acta Musicologica* 42 (1970): 5–32.

Wehmeyer, G. "Klavierabende." *Concerto,* vol. 4, no. 4 (1984): 58–65.

Westphal, K. "Die romantische Sonate als Formproblem." *Schweizerische Musikzeitung* 74 (1934): 45–49, 117–122, 189–192.

D. The Twentieth Century to 1950

Albrecht, A. *Die Klaviervariation im 20. Jahrhundert.* Unpub. diss., Cologne, 1961.
Baas, P. "Dutch Twentieth-Century Piano Music in Development." *Key Notes* 13 (1981): 28–37; 14 (1982): 30–43.
Baecker, C. *Die Poetik des lyrischen Klavierstücks um 1900.* Europäische Hochschulschriften, ser. 36, vol. 42. Frankfurt: Lang, 1991.
Bennighof, J. "'Heliotrope Bouquet' and the Critical Analysis of American Music." *American Music* 10 (1992): 411–433.
Borris, S. "Die Krise der Sonate im 20. Jahrhundert." In *Musa–Mens–Musici: Im Gedenken an Walter Vetter,* ed. H. Wegener, 361–378. Leipzig: Deutscher Verlag für Musik, 1969.
Burge, D. *Twentieth-Century Piano Music.* New York: Schirmer, 1990.
Butler, S., ed. *Guide to the Best in Contemporary Piano Music.* 2 vols. Metuchen: Scarecrow, 1973.
Chapman, N. *Piano Music by Canadian Composers, 1940–1965.* Unpub. diss., Case Western Reserve University, 1973.
Dorfmüller, J. *Studien zur norwegischen Klaviermusik der ersten Hälfte des 20. Jahrhunderts.* Marburger Beiträge zur Musikforschung 4. Kassel: Bärenreiter, 1969.
Fritz, T. *The Development of Russian Piano Music as Seen in the Literature of Mussorgsky, Rachmaninoff, Scriabin, and Prokofiev.* Unpub. diss., University of Southern California, 1959.
Grandela, I. "La musica chilena para piano de la generación joven (1925)." *Revista musical chilena* 25 (no. 113–114, 1971): 35–54.
Hegman, S. *The Latin-American Piano Sonata in the Twentieth Century.* Unpub. diss., Indiana University, 1975.
Herrmann, K. *Die Klaviermusik der letzten Jahre.* Leipzig and Zurich: Atlantis, 1934.
Hildreth, J. *Keyboard Works of Selected Black Composers.* Unpub. diss., Northwestern, 1978.
King, I. *Neoclassical Tendencies in Seven American Piano Sonatas (1925–1945).* Unpub. diss., Washington University (St. Louis), 1971.
Knieser, V. *Tonality and Form in Selected French Piano Sonatas, 1900–1950.* Unpub. diss., Ohio State University, 1977.
Roberts, P. *Aspects of Modernism in Russian Piano Music: Skriabin, Prokofiev, and Their Russian Contemporaries.* Russian Music Studies. Bloomington: Indiana University Press, 1993.
Schulte-Bernet, D. *Die deutsche Klaviersonate des 20. Jahrhunderts.* Regensburg: Bosse, 1963.
Schulz, H. *Musikalischer Impressionismus und impressionistischer Klavierstil.* Würzburg: Triltsch, 1938.
Sims, D. "An Analysis and Comparison of Piano Sonatas by George Walker and Howard Swanson." *Black Perspectives in Music* 4 (1976): 70–81.
Teichmüller, R., and K. Hermann. *Internationale moderne Klaviermusik: Ein Wegweiser und Berater.* Leipzig and Zurich: Hug, 1927.
Vogel, J. "Die Wiederbelebung der Klaviersonate: deutscher Klassizimus im 20. Jahrhundert." *Musica* 39 (1985): 353–359.
Wolf, H. *The Twentieth-Century Piano Sonata.* Unpub. diss., Boston University, 1957.
Wolters, K. "Schweizerische Klaviermusik des 20. Jahrhunderts." *Schweizerische Musikzeitung* 104 (1964): 85–89.

E. The Twentieth Century Since 1950

Appleby, D. "Trends in Recent Brazilian Piano Music." *Latin American Music Review* 2 (1981): 91–102.

Bailey, B. *A Historical and Stylistic Study of American Piano Music Published from 1956 through 1976.* Unpub. diss., Northwestern, 1980.

De la Motte Haber, H. "Ausdrucksreduktion und Klangvielfalt in der Klaviermusik des 20. Jahrhunderts." *Musica* 43 (1989): 306–314.

Descaves, L. "[France:] La musique pour piano." *La face cachée de la musique française contemporaine: Revue musicale* 70 (no. 316–318, 1978): 125–133.

Tawaststjerna, E. *Finnish Piano Music since 1945.* Unpub. diss., New York University, 1982.

Toop, R. "Messiaen, Goeyvaerts, Fano/Stockhausen, Boulez." *Perspectives of New Music* 13, 1 (1974): 141–169.

V. STUDIES OF INDIVIDUAL COMPOSERS

ALBÉNIZ

Franco, E. "La suite Iberia di Albéniz." *Nuova rivista musicale italiana* 7 (1973): 51–74.

Iglesias, A. *Isaac Albéniz: Su obra para piano.* Madrid: Al puerto, 1985.

Mast, P. *Style and Structure in "Iberia" by Isaac Albéniz.* Unpub. diss., University of Rochester, 1974.

ALBERO

Powell, L. "The Keyboard Music of Sebastian Albero." *Early Keyboard Journal* 5 (1986–1987): 9–28.

ALBERTI

Wörmann, W. "Die Klaviersonate Domenico Albertis." *Acta musicologica* 27 (1955): 84–107.

ALKAN

Bellamann, H. "The Piano Works of C. V. Alkan." *Musical Quarterly* 10 (1924): 252–262.

Schilling, B. *Virtuose Klaviermusik des 19. Jahrhunderts am Beispiel von Charles Valentin Alkan.* Kölner Beiträge zur Musikforschung 145. Regensburg: Bosse, 1985.

Searle, H. "A Plea for Alkan." *Music and Letters* 18 (1937): 276–279.

Smith, R. *Alkan.* 2 vols. London: Kahn & Averill, 1987.

White, J. "The Alkan Centenary: A Time for Recognition." *Music Review* 49 (1988): 161–168.

BABBITT

Barkin, E. "A Simple Approach to Milton Babbitt's Semi-Simple Variations." *Music Review* 28 (1967): 316–322.

Wintle, C. "Milton Babbitt's Semi-Simple Variations." *Perspectives on New Music* 15 (1976): 111–154.

BACH, C. P. E.

Barford, P. *The Keyboard Music of C. P. E. Bach.* London: Barrie & Rockliff; New York: October House: 1965.

Berg, D. "Carl Philipp Emanuel Bach's Character Pieces and His Friendship Circle." In *C. P. E. Bach Studies,* ed. S. Clark, 1–32. Oxford: Clarendon Press, 1988.

———. "Carl Philipp Emanuel Bachs Umarbeitungen seiner Claviersonaten." *Bach-Jahrbuch* 74 (1988): 123–161.

———. *The Keyboard Sonatas of C. P. E. Bach: An Expression of the Mannerist Principle.* Unpub. diss., State University of New York, Buffalo, 1975.

———. "Towards a Thematic Catalogue of the Keyboard Sonatas of C. P. E. Bach." *Journal of the American Musicological Society* 32 (1979): 276–303.

Canave, P. *A Re-Evaluation of the Role Played by Carl Philipp Emanuel Bach in the Development of the Clavier Sonata.* Washington, D.C.: Catholic University Press, 1956.

Chrysander, F. "Eine Klavierphantasie von Karl Philipp Emanuel Bach mit nachträglich von Gerstenberg eingefügten Gesangsmelodien mit zwei verschiedenen Texten." *Vierteljahrsschrift für Musikwissenschaft* 7 (1891): 1–25.

Clercx, S. "La forme du rondo chez Carl Philipp Emanuel Bach." *Revue de musicologie* 19 (1935): 148–166.

Cohen, P. *Theorie und Praxis der Clavierästhetik Carl Phillipp Emanuel Bachs.* Hamburger Beiträge zur Musikwissenschaft 13. Hamburg: Wegner, 1974.

Edler, A. "Das Charakterstück Carl Philipp Emanuel Bachs und die französische Tradition." In *Aufklärungen*, ed. W. Birtel and C. Mahling, vol. 2, 209–218. Heidelberg: Winter, 1986.

Fischer, K. "Carl Philipp Emanuel Bachs Variationswerke." *Revue belge de musicologie* 6 (1952): 190–218.

Fox, P. *Melodic Nonconstancy in the Keyboard Sonatas of C. P. E. Bach.* Unpub. diss., University of Cincinnati, 1983.

Gonnermann, W. "Carl Philipp Emanuel Bach: einige Gedanken zur Zeit, zur Persönlichkeit und zum Klavierschaffen des Meisters." In *Carl-Philipp-Emanuel-Bach-Konzepte*, ed. H. Otterberg, 30–52. Frankfurt: Neuer Tag, 1983.

Häussler, R. "Carl Philipp Emanuel Bach: Rondos für 'Kenner und Liebhaber.'" In *Beiträge zur musikalischen Analyse*, 9–35. Musikreflektionen 1. Basel: Amadeus, 1987.

Helm, E. "The 'Hamlet' Fantasia and the Literary Element in C. P. E. Bach's Music." *Musical Quarterly* 58 (1972): 277–296.

Horn, W. *Carl Philipp Emanuel Bach: Frühe Klaviersonaten.* Hamburg: Wagner, 1988.

Jurisch, H. *Principien der Dynamik im Klavierwerk Philipp Emanuel Bachs.* Unpub. diss., Tübingen, 1959.

Lee, D. "Bach and the Free Fantasia." In *C. P. E. Bach Studies*, ed. S. Clark, 177–184. Oxford: Clarendon Press, 1988.

Müller, W. *Das Ausdrucksproblem in der Klaviermusik Carl Philipp Emanuel Bachs.* Unpub. diss., Saarbrücken, 1959.

Poos, H. "Harmoniestruktur und Hermeneutik in C. Ph. E. Bachs Fis-Moll Fantasie." In *Bericht über den Internationalen Musikwissenschaftlichen Kongress Berlin 1974*, 319–323. Kassel: Bärenreiter, 1980.

———. "Nexus vero est poeticus: zur Fis-moll Fantasie Carl Philipp Emanuel Bachs." *Jahrbuch des Staatlichen Instituts für Musikforschung Preussischer Kulturbesitz 1983-1984.* Berlin: Merseburger, 1984: 83–114.

Salzer, F. "Über die Bedeutung der Ornamente in Philipp Emanuel Bachs Klavierwerken." *Zeitschrift für Musikwissenschaft* 13 (1929–1930): 398–418.

Schenker, H. *Ein Beitrag zur Ornamentik, als Einführung zu Philipp Emmanuel Bachs Klavierwerken.* Vienna: Universal, 1903.

Schering, A. "Carl Philipp Emanuel Bach und das redende Prinzip der Musik." *Jahrbuch der Musikbibliothek Peters* 45 (1938): 13–29.

Serwer, H. "C. P. E. Bach, J. C. F. Rellstab, and the Sonatas with Varied Reprises." In *C. P. E. Bach Studies*, ed. S. Clark, 233–243. Oxford: Clarendon Press, 1988.

Wagner, G. "Die Entwicklung der Klaviersonate bei C. Ph. E. Bach." In *Carl Philipp Emanuel Bach und die europäische Musikkultur des mittleren 18. Jahrhunderts*, 231–243. Veröffentlichungen der Joachim Jungius-Gesellschaft der Wissenschaft Hamburg 62. Göttingen: Vandenhoeck & Rupprecht, 1990.

———. "Originalgenie oder Publikumsgeschmack als bestimmende Grösse? Die Klaviersonaten Carl Philipp Emanuel Bachs." *Die Musikforschung* 41 (1988): 331–348.

Wiemer, W. "C. P. E. Bachs Fantasie in c-moll: Ein Lamento auf den Tod des Vaters." *Bach Jahrbuch* 74 (1988): 163–177.

Wyler, R. *Form- und Stiluntersuchungen zum ersten Satz der Klaviersonaten Carl Philipp Emanuel Bachs*. Biel: Schuler, 1960.

BACH, J. C.

Baierle, I. *Die Klavierwerke von Johann Christian Bach*. Vienna: Verband der wissenschaftlichen Gesellschaften Österreichs, 1974.

Maunder, R. "J. C. Bach and the Early Pianoforte in London." *Journal of the Royal Musical Association* 116 (1991): 201–210.

Mekota, B. *The Solo and Ensemble Keyboard Works of Johann Christian Bach*. Unpub. diss., University of Michigan, 1969.

Roe, S. *The Keyboard Music of J. C. Bach*. New York: Garland, 1991.

BACH, J. S.

Adams, C. "Organization in the Two-Part Inventions of J. S. Bach." *Bach*, vol. 13, no. 2 (1982): 6–16; and no. 3 (1982): 12–19.

Badura-Skoda, P., and A. Clayton. *Interpreting Bach at the Keyboard*. New York: Oxford University Press, 1993.

Bergel, E. *Johann Sebastian Bach, Die Kunst der Fuge*. Bonn: Brockhaus, 1980.

Bergner, C. *Studien zur Form der Präludien des Wohltemperierten Klaviers von J. S. Bach*. Tübinger Beiträge zur Musikwissenschaft 11. Stuttgart: Hänssler, 1986.

Besseler, H. "Bach als Wegbereiter." *Archiv für Musikwissenschaft* 12 (1955): 1–39.

Bitsch, M. *The Art of the Fugue by J. S. Bach*. Paris: Durand, 1967.

Bodky, E. *The Interpretation of Bach's Keyboard Works*. Cambridge: Harvard, 1960; Westport: Greenwood, 1976.

Breckoff, W. *Zur Entstehungsgeschichte des zweiten Wohltemperierten Klaviers von Johann Sebastian Bach*. Unpub. diss., Tübingen, 1965.

Breig, W. "Bach's Goldberg-Variationen als zyklisches Werk." *Archiv für Musikwissenschaft* 32 (1975): 243–265.

———. "Bachs 'Kunst der Fuge': zur instrumentalen Bestimmung und zum zyklischen Charakter." *Bach-Jahrbuch* 68 (1982): 103–124.

Brokaw, J. "The Genesis of the Prelude in C major, BWV 870." In *Bach Studies*, ed. D. Franklin, 225–239. Cambridge: Cambridge University Press, 1989.

———. "Recent Researches on the Sources and Genre of Bach's 'Well-Tempered Clavier.'" *Bach*, vol. 16, no. 3 (1985): 17–35.

Buchmayer, C. "Cembalo oder Pianoforte." *Bach-Jahrbuch* 5 (1908): 64–93.

Butler, G. "Neues zu Datierung der Goldberg-Variationen." *Bach-Jahrbuch* 74 (1988): 219–222.

———. "Ordering Problems in J. S. Bach's Art of Fugue Resolved." *Musical Quarterly* 69 (1983): 44–61.

Byrt, J. *Improvisation and Style in the Works of Sebastian Bach and Emanuel Bach*. Unpub. diss., Oxford, 1969.

Constantini, F. "Zur Typusgeschichte von Johann Sebastian Bachs Wohltemperierten Klavier." *Bach-Jahrbuch* 55 (1969): 31–45.

Corten, W. "Clefs numériques dans L'Art de la fugue de J. S. Bach." *Revue belge de musicologie* 42 (1988): 199–221.

Czaczkes, L. *Analyse des Wohltemperierten Klaviers: Form und Aufbau der Fuge bei Bach*. 3rd ed. 2 vols. Vienna: Österreichischer Bundesverlag, 1985.

Dammann, R. *Johann Sebastian Bachs "Goldberg Variationen."* Mainz: Schott, 1986.

———. "Bachs Capriccio B dur." In *Analysen: Beiträge zu einer Problemgeschichte des Komponierens: Festschrift für Hans Heinrich Eggebrecht*, 158–179. Beihefte zum Archiv für Musikwissenschaft 23. Wiesbaden: Steiner, 1984.

David, H. "The Art of Fugue." *Bach*, vol. 1, no. 3 (1970): 5–21.

———. *Bach's Musical Offering: History, Interpretation, and Analysis*. 1945. Reprint. New York: Schirmer, 1972.

———. "Die Gestalt von Bachs Chromatischer Fantasie." *Bach-Jahrbuch* 23 (1926): 23–67.

David, J. *Das wohltemperierte Klavier: Versuch einer Synopsis*. Göttingen: Vandenhoeck & Rupprecht, 1962.

Dehnhard, W. "Beobachtungen am Autograph von Bachs 'Wohltemperierten Klavier.'" In *Bachstunden*, ed. W. Dehnhard, 92–106. Frankfurt: Evangelischer Presseverband, 1978.

Derr, E. "The Two-Part Inventions: Bach's Composers' Vade Mecum." *Music Theory Spectrum* 3 (1981): 26–48.

Dürr, A. "The Historical Background of the Composition of Johann Sebastian Bach's Clavier Suites." *Bach* 16, no. 1 (1985): 53–68.

———. "Neue Forschungen zu Bachs 'Kunst der Fuge.'" *Die Musikforschung* 32 (1979): 153–158.

———. "Das Präludium Es-dur BWV 852 aus dem Wohltemperierten Klavier I." In *Studien zur Instrumentalmusik: Lothar Hoffmann-Erbrecht zum 60. Geburtstag*, ed. A. Bingmann et al., 93–101. Tutzing: Schneider, 1988.

———. "Tastenumfang und Chronologie in Bachs Klavierwerk." In *Festschrift Georg von Dadelsen zum 60. Geburtstag*, ed. T. Kohlhase, et al., 73–88. Stuttgart: Hänssler, 1978.

———. *Zur Frühgeschichte des Wohltemperierten Klaviers I von Johann Sebastian Bach*. Nachrichten der Akademie der Wissenschaften in Göttingen. I. Philologisch-Historische Klasse. Göttingen: Vandenhoeck & Rupprecht, 1984.

Eggebrecht, H. *Bachs "Kunst der Fuge": Erscheinung und Deutung*. Munich and Zurich: Piper, 1984.

Eppstein, H. "Chronologieprobleme in Johann Sebastian Bachs Suiten für Soloinstrumente." *Bach-Jahrbuch* 62 (1976): 35–57.

———. "J. S. Bach und der galante Stil." In *Aufklärungen*, ed. M. Birtel and C. Mahling, 209–218. Heidelberg: Winter, 1986.

Ernst, F. *Bach und das Pianoforte*. 2nd ed. Das Musikinstrument 6. Frankfurt: Musikinstrument, 1980.

Feldmann, F. "Untersuchungen zur Courante als Tanz, insbesondere im Hinblick auf die Klaviersuiten-Couranten J. S. Bachs." *Deutsches Jahrbuch für Musikwissenschaft* 6 (1961): 40–57.

Flindell, E. "A propos Bach's Inventions." *Bach*, vol. 14, no. 4 (October 1983): 3–14; vol. 15, no. 1 (January 1984): 3–16; vol. 15, no. 2 (April 1984): 3–17.

Franke, E. "Themenmodelle in Bachs Klaviersuiten." *Bach-Jahrbuch* 52 (1966): 72–98.

Fuller-Maitland, J. *The Keyboard Suites of J. S. Bach*. London: Oxford, 1925.

Göllner, T. "J. S. Bach and the Tradition of Keyboard Transcriptions." In *Studies in Eighteenth-Century Music: A Tribute to Karl Geiringer*, 253–260. New York: Oxford, 1970.

Graeser, W. "Bachs Kunst der Fuge." *Bach Jahrbuch* 21 (1924): 1–104.

Hahn, H. *Symbol und Glaube im 1. Teil des Wohltemperierten Klaviers von Johann Sebastian Bach.* Wiesbaden: Breitkopf & Härtel, 1973.

———. *Das vielfältige Formenmosaik J. S. Bachs in den kleinen Präludien und Fugen für Klavier.* Hamburg: Wagner, 1986.

Hawthorne, W. *J. S. Bach's Inventions and Sinfonias: An Analysis.* Unpub. diss., University of Cincinnati, 1980.

Hering, H. "Bachs Klavierübertragungen." *Bach-Jahrbuch* 45 (1958): 94–113.

———. "Spielerische Elemente in J. S. Bachs Klaviermusik." *Bach-Jahrbuch* 60 (1974): 44–69.

Hermelink, S. "Das Präludium in Bachs Klaviermusik." In *Jahrbuch des Staatlichen Instituts für Musikforschung Preussischer Kulturbesitz*, 7–80. Berlin: Merseburger, 1977.

Hoke, H. "Neue Studien zur 'Kunst der Fuge.'" *Beiträge zur Musikwissenschaft* 17 (1975): 95–115.

Husmann, H. "'Die Kunst der Fuge' als Klavierwerk: Besetzung und Anordnung." *Bach-Jahrbuch* 35 (1938): 1–61.

Jenne, N. "Bach's Use of Dance Rhythms in Fugues." *Bach*, vol. 4, no. 1 (1973): 18–26; vol. 5, no. 1 (1974): 3–8; and no. 2 (1974): 3–21.

Johnson, T. *An Analytical Survey of the Fifteen Two-Part Inventions by J. S. Bach.* Lanham, MD: University Press of America, 1982.

Kaussler, I. *Die Goldberg-Variationen von J. S. Bach.* Stuttgart: Freies Geistesleben, 1985.

Keller, H. *Die Klavierwerke Bachs.* Leipzig: Breitkopf & Härtel, 1950.

Kirkendale, U. "The Source for Bach's 'Musical Offering': The 'Institutio oratoria' of Quintilian." *Journal of the American Musicological Society* 33 (1980): 88–141.

Klein, H. *Der Einfluss der Vivaldischen Konzertform im Instrumentalwerk Johann Sebastian Bachs.* Sammlung musikwissenschaftlicher Abhandlungen 54. Strassburg: Heitz, 1970.

Kolneder, W. *Die Kunst der Fuge: Mythen des 20. Jahrhunderts.* Taschenbücher zur Musikwissenschaft 42–45. Wilhelmshaven: Heinrichshofen, 1977.

Kreft, R. *Johann Sebastian Bach: "Die Kunst der Fuge" und ihre B-A-C-H Elemente.* Tutzing: Schneider, 1977.

Krüger, E. *Stilistische Untersuchungen zu ausgewählten Klavierfugen J. S. Bachs.* Hamburger Beiträge zur Musikwissenschaft 2. Hamburg: Wagner, 1970.

Kunze, S. "Gattungen der Fuge in Bachs Wohltemperierten Klavier." In *Bach-Interpretationen*, ed. M. Geck, 74–93. Göttingen: Vanderhoeck, 1969.

Ladewig, J. "Bach and the 'prima prattica.'" *Journal of Musicology* 9 (1991): 358–375.

Leonhardt, G. *"The Art of Fugue": Bach's Last Harpsichord Work.* The Hague: Nijhoff, 1952.

Louwenaari-Lueck, K. "The Sequence of Sarabande and Air in Bach's Keyboard Partitas." *Bach*, vol. 23, no. 1 (1992): 38–50.

Martin, B. *Untersuchungen zur Struktur der "Kunst der Fuge" J. S. Bachs.* Regensburg: Bosse, 1941.

Metzger, K., ed. *Johann Sebastian Bach: das spekulative Spätwerk.* Musik-Konzepte 17–18. Munich: text & kritik, 1981.

Metzger, K., and R. Riehn, eds. *Johann Sebastian Bach: Goldberg-Variationen.* Musik-Konzepte 42. Munich: text & kritik, 1985.

Pfingsten, I. "Formale Aspekte der Fuge in D-moll aus dem 1. Teil des Wohltemperierten Klaviers von Johann Sebastian Bach." In *Alte Musik als ästhetische Gegenwart*, ed. D. Birke and D. Hanemann, vol. 1, 342–348. Kassel: Bärenreiter, 1987.

Plath, W. *Das Klavierbüchlein für Wilhelm Friedemann Bach.* Unpub. diss., Tübingen, 1958.

Riedel, H. *Recognition and Re-cognition: Bach and the Well-Tempered Clavier.* Unpub. diss., University of California (Berkeley), 1970.

Rivera, B. "Bach's Use of Hitherto Unrecognized Types of Countersubjects in the 'Art of Fugue.'" *Journal of the American Musicological Society* 31 (1978): 344–362.

Sachs, K. "Das späte 'Clavier'-Schaffen Bachs." In *Johann Sebastian Bachs Spätwerk und dessen Umfeld*, 176–187. Kassel: Bärenreiter, 1988.

Schleuning, P. "Diese Fantasie ist einzig . . . Das Recitativ in Bach's 'Chromatischer Fantasie.'" In *Bach-Interpretationen*, ed. M. Geck, 57–73. Göttingen: Vanderhoeck & Ruprecht, 1969.

Schlötter-Traimer, R. *Bach: "Die Kunst der Fuge."* Meisterwerke der Musik 4. Munich: Fink, 1964.

Schmalzriedt, S. "Über Zwischenspiele in den Fugen des 'Wohltemperierten Klaviers.'" In *Festschrift Georg von Dadelsen zum 60. Geburtstag*, ed. T. Kohlhase, 284–299. Stuttgart: Hänssler, 1978.

Schulenberg, D. *The Keyboard Music of J. S. Bach.* New York: Schirmer, 1992.

Schulze, H. "The French Influence in Bach's Instrumental Music." *Early Music* 13 (1985): 180–184.

Schwebsch, E. *J. S. Bach und die Kunst der Fuge*, 3rd ed. Stuttgart: Geistesleben, 1987.

Siegele, U. *Kompositionsweise und Bearbeitungstechnik in der Instrumentalmusik Johann Sebastian Bachs.* Tübinger Beiträge zur Musikwissenschaft 3. Neuhausen-Stuttgart: Hänssler, 1975.

———. "Zu Bachs Fugenkomposition." *Bach Studien* 9 (1986): 19–24.

Siegmund-Schultze, W. "Bachs Inventionen und Sinfonien." In *Bachforschung und Bachinterpretationen heute*, ed. R. Brinkmann, 146–151. Leipzig: Neue Bachgesellschaft, 1981.

Stauffer, G. "'This Fantasia . . . Never Had Its Like:' On the Enigma and Chronology of Bach's Chromatic Fantasia and Fugue in D minor, BWV 903." In *Bach Studies*, ed. D. Franklin, 160–182. Cambridge: Cambridge University Press, 1989.

Street, A. "The Rhetorico-Musical Structure of the Goldberg Variations: Bach's Clavier-Übung IV and the Institutio oratorio of Quintilian." *Music Analysis* 6 (1987): 89–131.

Tovey, D. *A Companion to the Art of Fugue.* London: Oxford, 1931.

Traub, A. *Johann Sebastian Bach: "Goldberg-Variationen" BWV 988.* Meisterwerke der Musik 38. Munich: Fink, 1983.

Vidal, P. *L'origine thématique de "L'Art de la Fugue" et ses incidences.* Paris: Flute de Pan, 1984.

Wagner, G. "Concerto-Elemente in Bachs zweistimmigen Inventionen." *Bach-Jahrbuch* 65 (1979): 37–44.

Werker, W. *Studien über die Symmetrie im Bau der Fugen und motivische Zusammengehörigkeit der Präludien und Fugen des Wohltemperierten Claviers.* Abhandlungen des Sächsischen staatlichen Forschungsinstituts zu Leipzig. Forschungen des Instituts für Musikwissenschaft 3. Leipzig: Breitkopf & Härtel, 1922; Wiesbaden: Sändig, 1969.

White, A. "The Prelude and Fugue from Bach's Well-Tempered Clavier (Book I): Notes on the Compositional Process." *Bach*, vol. 23, no. 2 (1992): 47–60.

Wiemer, W. *Die Wiederhergestellte Ordnung in Johann Sebastian Bachs "Kunst der Fuge."* Wiesbaden: Breitkopf & Härtel, 1977.

Wolff, C. *Bach.* Cambridge: Harvard, 1991.

Zacher, G. "Befremdendes bei Bach: die Unterschrift in der cis-moll Fuge des Wohltemperierten Klaviers I." *Musiktheorie* 3 (1988): 243–247.

BACH, W. F.

Bohnert, A. *Studien zum Klavierwerk Wilhelm Friedemann Bachs.* Unpub. diss., Heidelberg, 1991.

BARBER

Carter, S. *The Piano Music of Samuel Barber.* Unpub. diss., Texas Technical University, 1980.

Heist, D. "Harmonic Organization and Sonata Form: The First Movement of Samuel Barber's Sonata, op. 26." *Journal of the American Liszt Society* 27 (1990): 25–31.

Tischler, H. "Barber's Piano Sonata Opus 26." *Music and Letters* 33 (1952): 352–354.

BARRAQUÉ

Durand, J. "La sonate pour piano de Jean Barraqué." *Entretemps* 5 (1987): 89–117.

BARTÓK

Agawu, V. "Analytical Issues Raised by Bartók's Improvisations for Piano." *Journal of Musicological Research* 5 (1984): 131–164.

Breuer, J. "Kolinda Rhythm in the Music of Bartók." *Studia Musicologica* 17 (1975): 39–58.

Chazelle, T. "En plein air, suite pour piano de Béla Bartók." *Analyse musicale*, vol. 7, no. 2 (1987): 56–61.

Child, P. "Structural Unities in a Work of Bartók: 'Boating,' from 'Mikrokosmos,' Vol. 5." *College Music Symposium*, vol. 30, no. 1 (1990): 103–114.

Engelmann, J. *Béla Bartóks Mikrokosmos: Versuch einer Typologie "neuerer Musik."* Literaturhistorische-musikwissenschaftliche Abhandlungen. Würzburg: Triltsch, 1953.

Fenyo, T. *The Piano Music of Béla Bartók.* Unpub. diss., University of California, Los Angeles, 1956.

Hundt, T. *Bartóks Satztechnik in den Klavierwerken.* Kölner Beiträge zur Musikforschung 63. Regensburg: Bosse, 1971.

Josephson, N. "Zur Entstehungsgeschichte von Bartóks Klaviersonate (1926)." *Die Musikforschung* 33 (1980): 487–489.

Parks, D. "Harmonic Resources in Bartók's 'Fourths.'" *Journal of Music Theory*, vol. 25, no. 2 (1981): 245–274.

Somfai, L. "Nineteenth-Century Ideas Developed: Bartók's Piano Notation in the Years 1907–1914." *Nineteenth Century Music* 11 (1987): 73–91.

Souchoff, B. *Guide to Bartók's "Mikrokosmos."* Rev. ed. London: Boosey & Hawkes, 1971.

Uhde, J. *Bartók's Mikrokosmos: Spielanweisungen und Erläuterungen.* Regensburg: Bosse, 1952.

———. "Zur Neubewertung von Béla Bartóks 'Mikrokosmos.'" *Studia Musicologica* [Hungary] 24, Supplementum (1982): 9–20.

Vinton, J. "Towards a Chronology of the Mikrokosmos." *Studia musicologica* [Hungary] 8 (1966): 41–69.

Weissmann, J. "La musique de piano de Bartók: L'évolution d'une écriture." *Revue musicale*, no. 224 (1955): 171–222.

Yeomans, D. *Bartók for Piano*. Bloomington: Indiana University Press, 1988.

BAUER

Stewart, N. *The Solo Piano Music of Marion Bauer*. Unpub. diss., University of Cincinnati, 1990.

BEETHOVEN

Abraham, L. "Trivalität und Persiflage in Beethovens Diabelli-Variationen." In *Neue Wege der musikalischen Analyse*, 7–17. Veröffentlichungen des Instituts für neue Musik und Musikerziehung Darmstadt 6. Berlin: Merseburger, 1967.

Albrecht, T. "Beethoven and Shakespeare's 'Tempest': New Light on an Old Allusion." In *Beethoven Forum*, vol. 1, ed. C. Reynolds, 81–92. Lincoln: University of Nebraska Press, 1992.

Badura-Skoda, P., and J. Demus. *Die Klaviersonaten von Ludwig van Beethoven*. Wiesbaden: Brockhaus, 1970.

Barford, P. "Beethoven's Last Sonata." *Music and Letters* 35 (1954): 319–331.

Barth, G. *The Pianist as Orator: Beethoven and the Transformation of Keyboard Style*. Ithaca, NY: Cornell University Press, 1992.

Bazzana, K. "The First Movement of Beethoven's Op. 109." *Canadian Universities Music Review* 12 (1992): 1–36.

Bernary, P. "Sonata quasi una fantasia: zu Beethoven's opus 27." *Musiktheorie* 2 (1987): 129–136.

Bockholdt, R. "Beethovens zweiundzwanzigste Diabelli Variation." In *Beiträge zu Beethovens Kammermusik*, ed. S. Brandenburg and H. Loos, 225–253. Veröffentlichungen des Beethovenhauses in Bonn, ser. 4, vol. 10. Munich: Henle, 1988.

Cone, E. "Beethoven's Experiments in Composition: The Late Bagatelles." *Beethoven Studies*, vol. 2, ed. A. Tyson, 84–105. London: Oxford, 1977.

Cooper, B. *Beethoven and the Creative Process*. Oxford: Clarendon, 1990.

———. "Beethoven's Portfolio of Bagatelles." *Journal of the Royal Academy of Music* 112 (1987): 208–228.

Coren, D. "Structural Parallels Between op. 28 and op. 36." In *Beethoven Studies*, vol. 2, ed. A. Tyson, 66–83. London: Oxford, 1977.

Dahlhaus, C. "Eine wenig beachtete Formidee: zur Interpretation einiger Beethoven-Sonaten." In *Analysen: Beiträge zu einer Problemgeschichte des Komponierens. Festschrift für Hans Heinrich Eggebrecht*, 248–256. Beihefte zum Archiv für Musikwissenschaft 23. Wiesbaden: Steiner, 1984.

———. "Zur Formidee von Beethovens d-moll Klaviersonate op. 31, 2." *Die Musikforschung* 33 (1980): 310–312.

Danuser, H. "Beethoven als Klassiker der Klaviersonate." In *Gattungen der Musik und ihre Klassiker*, ed. H. Danuser, 119–219. Laaber, 1988.

Derr, E. "Beethoven's Long-Term Memory of C. P. E. Bach's Rondo in E-flat, W. 61." *Musical Quarterly* 70 (1984): 45–76.

Der Zanden, J. "Beethovens 'Bagatellen' op. 126: Bemerkungen zu ihrer Entstehung." *Die Musikforschung* 39 (1986): 13–17.

Drabkin, W. *A Study of Beethoven's op. 111 and Its Sources*. Unpub. diss., Princeton, 1977.

Dreyfus, K. "Beethoven's Last Five Piano Sonatas." *Beethoven Jahrbuch* 9 (1973–1977): 37–45.

Federhofer, H. "Analyse des zweiten Satzes von Ludwig van Beethovens Klaviersonate Op. 10 Nr. 3." In *Festschrift Jens Peter Larsen*, 339–350. Copenhagen: Hansen, 1972.

Feurich, H. "L. v. Beethoven: Klaviersonate in f-moll op. 57." In *Werkanalyse in Beispielen*, ed. S. Helms and H. Hopf, 112–122. Regensburg: Bosse. 1986.

Finscher, L. "Beethovens Klaviersonate op. 31, 3. Versuch einer Interpretation." In *Festschrift für Walter Wiora zum 31. Dezember 1966*, 385–396. Kassel: Bärenreiter, 1967.

Forte, A. *The Compositional Matrix*. Cincinnati: Music Teachers National Association, 1961; New York: Da Capo, 1974.

Frohlich, M. *Beethoven's 'Appassionata' Sonata*. Oxford: Clarendon, 1991.

Geiringer, K. "The Structure of Beethoven's Diabelli Variations." *Musical Quarterly* 50 (1964): 496–503.

Guardia, E. de la. *Las sonatas para piano de Beethoven*, 3rd ed. Buenos Aires: Ricordi, 1947.

Heinemann, M. "'Altes' und 'Neues' in Beethovens 'Eroica'-Variationen." *Archiv für Musikwissenschaft* 49 (1992): 38–45.

Hoyt, R. "Rhythmic Practices in the Scherzo of Beethoven's Sonata op. 110." *Indiana Theory Review* 9 (1988): 99–133.

Kaiser, J. *Beethovens 32 Klaviersonaten und ihre Interpreten*. Frankfurt: Fischer, 1976.

Kalisch, V. "Beethovens Klaviersonate e-moll op. 90." *Studien zur Musikwissenschaft* 35 (1984): 89–123.

Kamien, R. "Chromatic Details in Beethoven's Piano Sonata in E-flat major, op. 7." *Music Review* 35 (1974): 149–156.

———. "Subtle Enharmonic Connections, Modal Mixture, and Tonal Plan in the First Movement of Beethoven's Piano Sonata in C major, Opus 53 ('Waldstein')." In *Beethoven Forum*, vol. 1, ed. C. Reynolds, 93–110. Lincoln: University of Nebraska Press, 1992.

Katz, M. "Über Beethovens Klaviersonate opus 110." *Die Musikforschung* 22 (1969): 481–485.

Kidd, J. "Wit and Humor in Tonal Syntax." *Current Musicology* 21 (1976): 70–82.

Kinderman, W. *Beethoven's Diabelli Variations*. London: Oxford, 1987.

———. "Integration and Narrative Design in Beethoven's Piano Sonata in A♭ major, Opus 110." In *Beethoven Forum*, vol. 1, ed. C. Reynolds, 111–145. Lincoln: University of Nebraska Press, 1992.

———. "Thematic Contrast and Parenthetical Closure in the Piano Sonatas op. 109 and 111." In *Zu Beethoven: Aufsätze und Dokumente*, vol. 3, ed. H. Goldschmidt, 43–59. Berlin: Neue Musik, 1988.

Klein, R. "Beethoven's 'gebundener Stil' in Opus 106." *Beethoven Jahrbuch* 9 (1973–1977): 185–199.

Knab, A. "Zur Einheit der Beethovenschen Klaviersonate in As-Dur op. 110." *Zeitschrift für Musikwissenschaft* 1 (1918–1919): 388–399.

Kunze, S. "Die 'wirklich gantz neue Manier' in Beethovens Variationen op. 34 und op. 35." *Archiv für Musikwissenschaft* 29 (1972): 124–149.

Löw, H. *Improvisation im Klavierwerk L. van Beethovens*. Unpub. diss., Saarbrücken, 1962.

Marston, N. "Schenker and Forte Reconsidered: Beethoven's Sketches for the Piano Sonata in E, Op. 109." *Nineteenth Century Music* 10 (1986–1987): 24–42.

Matthews, D. *Beethoven Piano Sonatas*. BBC Music Guides. London: BBC, 1967; London: Ariel, 1986.

Mies, P. ". . . Quasi una fantasia . . ." In *Colloquium amicorum: Joseph Schmidt-Görg zum 70. Geburtstag*, 239–249. Bonn: Beethovenhaus, 1967.

Münster, A. *Studien zu Beethovens Diabelli-Variationen*. Schriften zur Beethovenforschung 8. Munich: Henle, 1982.

Newman, W. *Beethoven on Beethoven: Playing His Piano Music His Way.* New York: Norton, 1988.

Oppel, R. "Über Beziehungen Beethovens zu Mozart und Ph. Em. Bach." *Zeitschrift für Musikwissenschaft* 5 (1922–1923): 30–39.

Pollack, H. "Umfangs- und Strukturfragen in Beethovens Klaviersonaten." *Beiträge zu Musikwissenschaft* 12 (1970): 333–338. Reprinted in *Ludwig van Beethoven.* Ed. L. Finscher. Darmstadt: Wissenschaftliche Buchgesellschaft, 1983.

Poniatowska, I. "Der Klaviersatz bei Beethoven." In *Bericht über den internationalen musikwissenschaftlichen Kongress Bonn 1970,* 536–539. Kassel: Bärenreiter, 1973.

Porter, D. "The Structure of Beethoven's 'Diabelli' Variations." *Music Review* 31 (1970): 295–301.

Reti, R. *Thematic Patterns in Sonatas of Beethoven.* New York: Macmillan, 1967.

Reynolds, C. "Beethoven's Sketches for the Variations in E-flat, Op. 35." In *Beethoven Studies,* vol. 3, ed. A. Tyson, 47–79. London: Cambridge University Press, 1982.

Ringer, A. "Beethoven and the London Pianoforte School." *Musical Quarterly* 56 (1970): 742–758.

Rosenberg, R. *Die Klaviersonaten Ludwig van Beethovens: Studien über Form und Vortrag.* 2 vols. Olton: Urs Graf, 1957.

Sakka, K. "Beethovens Klaviere: der Klavierbau und Beethovens künstlerische Reaktion." In *Colloquium amicorum: Joseph Schmidt-Görg zum 70. Geburtstag,* 327–337. Bonn: Beethovenhaus, 1967.

Schenker, H. [Beethoven] *Die letzten Sonaten.* Ed. O. Jonas. 4 vols. Vienna: Universal, 1971.

———. "Beethoven: Sonata Opus 57." *Tonwille* 4 (1924; Hildesheim: Ohm 1990): 3–33.

Timbrell, C. "Notes on the Sources of Beethoven's op. 111." *Music and Letters* 58 (1977): 204–215.

Uhde, J. *Beethovens Klaviermusik.* 3 vols. Stuttgart: Reclam, 1968–1974.

Voss, E. "Zu Beethovens Klaviersonate As-dur op. 110." *Die Musikforschung* 23 (1970): 256–268.

Walker, E. "The [Beethoven] Pianoforte Sonatas: Some Textural Problems." *Music and Letters* 8 (1927): 11–18.

Weber, F. *Harmonischer Aufbau und Stimmführung in den Sonatensätzen der Klaviersonaten Beethovens.* Studien zur musikalischen Kultur- und Stilgeschichte 7. Schriftenreihe des Musikwissenschaftlichen Seminars der Universität München. Würzburg: Triltsch, 1940.

Westerby, H. *Beethoven and His Piano Works.* London: Reeves, 1931.

Wiora, W. "Klaviersonaten Beethovens mit 'anhaftendem Gehalt.'" In *Florilegium musicologium: Helmut Federhofer zum 75. Geburtstag,* ed. C. Mahling, 493–500. Tutzing: Schneider, 1988.

Uhde, J. "Reflexionen zu Beethovens op. 120." *Zeitschrift für Musiktheorie,* vol. 7, no. 1 (1976): 30–53.

Zenk, M. "Rezeption von Geschichte in Beethovens 'Diabelli-Variationen.'" *Archiv für Musikwissenschaft* 37 (1980): 61–75.

BENNETT, R. R.

Marston, M. *The Serial Keyboard Music of Richard Rodney Bennett.* Unpub. diss., Wisconsin, 1968.

BENNETT, W. S.

Bush, G. "Sterndale Bennett: The Piano Works." *Proceedings of the Royal Musical Association* 91 (1964–1965): 85.

BERG

Stephan, R. "Alban Berg als Schüler Arnold Schönbergs: Auf dem Weg zur Sonate op. 1." In *Die Wiener Schule in der Musikgeschichte des 20. Jahrhunderts*, ed. R. Stephan and S. Wiesmann, 22–30. Publikationen der Internationalen Schönberg-Gesellschaft 2. Vienna: Lafite, 1986.

BIZET

Muller, M. *L'oeuvre pianistique originale de Georges Bizet.* Unpub. diss., Neuchatel, 1976.

BOULEZ

DeYoung, L. "Pitch Order and Duration Order in Boulez' 'Structures Ia.'" *Perspectives of New Music*, vol. 16, no. 2 (1978): 27–34.

Eckart-Backer, U. "Pierre Boulez: Structure I pour 2 pianos." In *Werkanalyse in Beispielen*, ed. S. Helms and H. Hopf, 390–399. Regensburg: Bosse, 1986.

Grimm, J. "Formaspekte der 2. Klaviersonate von Boulez." *Revue musicale Suisse* 112 (1972): 201–205.

Hirsbrunner, T. "Pierre Boulez' Weg zum Serialismus." *Musiktheorie* 2 (1987): 3–13.

Jedrzejewski, F. "La mise en oeuvre du principe dodecaphonique dans la 1er sonate de Pierre Boulez." *Analyse musicale*, vol. 7, no. 2 (1987): 69–76.

Ligeti, G. "Pierre Boulez: Entscheidung und Automatik in der Struktur IA." *Die Reihe* 4 (1958): 38–63.

———. "Zur III. Klaviersonate von Boulez." *Die Reihe* 5 (1959): 38–40.

Piret, A. "Pierre Boulez: Troisième Sonate pour piano." *Analyse musicale* 29 (Nov. 1992): 61–74.

Stahnke, M. *Struktur und Ästhetik bei Boulez: Untersuchungen zum Formanten 'Trope' der 3. Klaviersonate.* Hamburger Jahrbücher für Musikwissenschaft 21. Hamburg: Wegner, 1979.

Stoianowa, I. "La troisième sonate de Boulez et le projet mallarméen du livre." *Musique en jeu* 16 (1974): 9–28.

Trenkamp, A. "The Concept of 'Alea' in Boulez's 'Constellation-miroir.'" *Music and Letters* 57 (1976): 1–10.

BRAHMS

Bernstein, J. "An Autograph of the Brahms 'Handel Variations.'" *Music Review* 34 (1973): 272–281.

Bozarth, G. "Brahms's 'Lieder ohne Worte' and 'Poetic' Andantes of the Piano Sonatas." In *Brahms Studies: Analytical and Historical Studies*, 345–378. Oxford: Clarendon, 1990.

Brodbeck, D. "'Primo' Schubert, 'Secondo' Schumann: Brahms' Four-Hand Waltzes, op. 39." *Journal of Musicology* 7 (1989): 58–80.

Budde, E. "Johannes Brahms' Intermezzo Op. 117, No. 2." In *Analysen: Beiträge zu einer Formgeschichte des Komponierens. Festschrift für Hans Heinrich Eggebrecht*, 324–337. Beihefte des Archiv für Musikforschung 23. Wiesbaden: Steiner, 1984.

Cai, C. "Was Brahms a Reliable Editor? Changes Made in Opus 116, 117, 118, and 119." *Acta Musicologica* 61 (1989): 83–101.

Danuser, H. "Aspekte der Hommage-Komposition: zu Brahms' Schumann-Variationen op. 9." In *Brahms-Analysen*, ed. F. Krummacher and W. Steinbeck, 91–106. Kieler Schriften zur Musikwissenschaft 28. Kassel: Bärenreiter, 1984.

Evans, E. *Handbook to the Pianoforte Works of Johannes Brahms.* New York: Scribner; London: Reeves, 1936.

Floros, C. "Studien zu Brahms Klaviermusik." *Brahms Studien* 5 (1983): 25–63.

Horne, W. "Brahms' Düsseldorf Suite Study and His Intermezzo, Opus 116, No. 2." *Musical Quarterly* 73 (1989): 249–283.

Hübler, K. "Die Kunst, ohne Einfälle zu komponieren: dargestellt an Johannes Brahms' späten Intermezzi." In *Aimez-vous Brahms "The Progressive."* ed. H. Metzger and R. Riehm, 24–40. Musik-Konzepte 65. Munich: text & kritik, 1989.

Kirsch, W. "Die Klavierwalzer op. 39 von Johannes Brahms und ihre Tradition." In *Jahrbuch des Staatlichen Instituts für Musikforschung Preussischer Kulturbesitz*, 38–67. Berlin: Gruyter, 1970.

Konold, W. "Mendelssohn und Brahms: Beispiele schöpferischer Rezeption im Lichte der Klaviermusik." In *Brahms-Analysen*, ed. F. Krummacher and W. Steinbeck, 91–106. Kieler Schriften zur Musikwissenschaft 28. Kassel: Bärenreiter, 1984.

Kraus, D. *Johannes Brahms: Composer for the Piano*. Trans. L. Lim. Wilhelmshaven: Noetzel, 1988.

Mason, C. "Brahms' Piano Sonatas." *Music Review* 5 (1944): 112–118.

Matthews, D. *Brahms Piano Music*. BBC Music Guides. Seattle: University of Washington Press, 1978; London: Ariel, 1986.

Mies, P. "Herders Edvard-Ballade bei Johannes Brahms." *Zeitschrift für Musikwissenschaft* 2 (1919–1920): 225–232.

———. "Zu Werdegang und Strukturen der Paganini-Variationen." *Studia musicologica* [Hungary] 11 (1969): 323–332.

Murdoch, W. *Brahms: With an Analytical Study of the Complete Pianoforte Works*. New York: Sears, 1933.

Nagel, W. *Die Klaviersonaten von Johannes Brahms*. Stuttgart: Groninger, 1915.

Neighbour, O. "Brahms and Schumann: Two Opus Nines and Beyond." *Nineteenth Century Music* 7 (1984): 266–270.

Newbould, B. "A New Analysis of Brahms' Intermezzo in B minor, op. 119, no. 1." *Music Review* 38 (1977): 33–43.

Pascall, R. "Unknown Gavottes by Brahms." *Music and Letters* 57 (1976): 404–411.

Schädler, S. "Technik und Verfahren in den 'Studien für Pianoforte: Variationen über ein Thema von Paganini' op. 35 von Brahms." In *Aimez-vous Brahms "The Progressive."* ed. H. Metzger and R. Riehn, 3–23. Musik-Konzepte 65. Munich: text & kritik, 1989.

Schuhmacher, G. "Historische Dimensionen in den Händel-Variationen op. 24 von Johannes Brahms." In *Alte Musik als ästhetische Gegenwart*, ed. D. Berke and D. Hannemann, 72–77. Kassel: Bärenreiter, 1987.

Webster, J. "Schubert's Sonata Form and Brahms' First Maturity." *Nineteenth Century Music* 2 (1978): 18–35; 3 (1979): 52–71.

BREUNICH

Riedel, F. "Die Klavierkompositionen von Johann Michael Breunich (1699–1755)." In *Studien zur Instrumentalmusik: Lothar Hoffmann-Erbrecht zum 60. Geburtstag*, ed. A. Bingmann et al., 159–165. Tutzing: Schneider, 1988.

BULL

Cunningham, W. *The Keyboard Music of John Bull*. Studies in Musicology 71. Ann Arbor: UMI, 1984.

Henry, L. *Dr. John Bull*. 1937. Reprint. New York: Da Capo, 1968.

Mellers, W. "John Bull and English Keyboard Music." *Musical Quarterly* 40 (1954): 364–383, 548–571.

BUONO

Carapezza, P. "Le quattordici sonate di cimbalo di Giovanni Pietro del Buono." *Analecta musicologica* 22 (1984): 131–147.

BUSONI
• Beaumont, A. *Busoni the Composer.* London: Faber; Bloomington: Indiana University Press, 1985.
Meyer, H. *Die Klaviermusik Busonis.* Wolfenbüttel: Moseler, 1969.
Prinz, U. *Feruccio Busoni als Klavierkomponist.* Unpub. diss., Heidelberg, 1970.
Sitsky, L. *Busoni and the Piano.* Contributions to the Study of Music and Dance 7. Westport: Greenwood, 1986.

BUXTEHUDE
Buszin, W. "Buxtehude: On the Tercentenary of His Birth." *Musical Quarterly* 23 (1937): 465–490.
Lorenz, H. "Die Klaviermusik Dietrich Buxtehudes." *Archiv für Musikwissenschaft* 11 (1954): 238–251.

BUUS
Sutherland, G. "The Ricercari of Jacques Buus." *Musical Quarterly* 31 (1945): 448–463.

BYRD
Neighbour, O. *The Consort and Keyboard Music of William Byrd.* London: Faber & Faber, 1978.

CABEZÓN
Carpenter, H. *The Works of Antonio de Cabezón.* Unpub. diss., University of Chicago, 1957.
Dart, T. "Cavazzoni and Cabezón." *Music and Letters* 36 (1955): 2–6.
Howell, A. "Cabezón: An Essay in Structural Analysis." *Musical Quarterly* 50 (1964): 18–30.
Hughes, J. *The Tientos, Fugas, and Diferencias in Antonio de Cabezón's Obras de musica para tecla, harpa y vihuela.* Unpub. diss., Florida State University, 1961.
Jeppesen, K.,"Cavazzoni-Cabezón." *Journal of the American Musicological Society* 8 (1955): 81–85.

CAGE
Cage, J. "To Describe the Process of Composition Used in 'Music of Changes' and 'Imaginary Landscape No. 4' [and . . .] 'Music for Piano 21–52.'" In *Silence*, 57–61. Middletown, CT: Wesleyan University Press, 1961.
Fürst-Heidtmann, M. *Das präparierte Klavier des John Cage.* Kölner Beiträge zur Musikwissenschaft 97. Regensburg: Bosse, 1979.
Kluppelholz, W. "Schlüsselwerke der experimentellen Musik: 'Music of Changes' von John Cage." *MusikTexte 15* (1986): 34–39.

CARTER
Below, R. "Elliott Carter's Piano Sonata." *Music Review* 34 (1973): 282–293.
Warburton, T. "A Literary Approach to Carter's 'Night Fantasies.'" *Music Review* 51 (1990): 208–220.

CHABRIER
Roberts, W. "The Pianoforte Works of Chabrier." *Music and Letters* 4 (1923): 133–143.

CHÁVEZ
Nordyke, D. *The Piano Works of Carlos Chávez.* Unpub. diss., Texas Tech, 1982.

CHOPIN
Abraham, G. *Chopin's Musical Style.* 1939. Reprint. London: Oxford, 1960.
Agawu, V. "Concepts of Closure and Chopin's Opus 28." *Music Theory Spectrum* 9 (1987): 1–17.

Bibliography

Barbag-Drexler, I. "Die Impromptus von Fryderyk Chopin." *Chopin–Jahrbuch* 3 (1970): 25–108.

Belotti, G. "Il problema delle date dei preludi di Chopin." *Rivista italiana di musicologia* 5 (1970): 159–215.

Branson, D. *John Field and Chopin.* London: St. Martin's, 1972.

Bronarski, L. *Études sur Chopin,* 2nd ed. 2 vols. in 1. Lausanne: La Concorde, 1947–1948.

Dammeier-Kirpal, U. *Der Sonatensatz bei Frederic Chopin.* Wiesbaden: Breitkopf & Härtel, 1973.

Dunn, J. *Ornamentation in the Works of Chopin.* London: Novello, 1921.

Egert, P. *Friedrich Chopin.* Potsdam: (Self-published), 1936.

Eibner, F. "Über die Form der Ballade op. 23 von Fr. Chopin." *Annales Chopin* 3 (1958): 107–112.

Eigeldinger, J. "The 24 Preludes of Chopin." In *Chopin Studies,* ed. J. Samson, 167–193. Cambridge: Cambridge University Press, 1988.

Griffel, L. "The Sonata Design in Chopin's Ballades." *Current Musicology* 36 (1983): 125–136.

Guignard, S. *Frederic Chopins Walzer.* Sammlung musikwissenschaftlicher Abhandlungen 70. Baden-Baden: Koerner, 1986.

Higgins, T. "Tempo and Character in Chopin." *Musical Quarterly* 59 (1973): 106–120.

Higgins, T., ed. *Frederic Chopin: Preludes, op. 28.* Norton Critical Scores. New York: Norton, 1973.

Holcman, J. "The Labyrinth of Chopin Ornamentation." *Juilliard Review,* vol. 5, no. 2 (1958): 23–41.

Jonson, G. *A Handbook to Chopin's Works.* London: Reeves, 1905; London: Ayer, 1972; Boston: Longwood, 1978.

Kaiser, J. "Chopin und die Sonate." In *Fryderyk Chopin,* 3–16. Musik-Konzepte 45. Munich: text & kritik, 1985.

Kallberg, J. *The Chopin Sources: Variants and Versions in Later Manuscripts.* Unpub. diss., University of Chicago, 1982.

———. "Chopin's Last Style." *Journal of the American Musicological Society* 38 (1985): 264–315.

———. "Compatibility in Chopin's Multipartite Publications." *Journal of Musicology* 4 (1983): 391–417.

———. "The Rhetoric of Genre: Chopin's Nocturne in G minor." *Nineteenth Century Music* 11 (1988): 238–261.

Kinzler, H. *Frederic Chopin: Über den Zusammenhang von Satztechnik und Klavierspiel.* Freiburger Schriften zur Musikwissenschaft 9. Munich: Katzbichler, 1977.

Koscewski, A. "Das Walzerelement im Schaffen Chopins." *Deutsches Jahrbuch für Musikwissenschaft* 5 (1960): 58–66.

———. "Das Wienerische in Chopins Walzer." *Chopin-Jahrbuch 1963:* 27–52.

Leichtentritt, H. *Analyse der Chopin'schen Klavierwerke.* Berlin: Hesse, 1921–1922.

Lissa, Z. "Die Chopinsche Harmonik aus der Perspektive der Klangtechnik des 20. Jahrhunderts." *Deutsches Jahrbuch für Musikwissenschaft* 2 (1957): 68–84; 3 (1958): 74–91.

Lissa, Z., ed. *Book of the First Musicological Congress Devoted to the Works of Frederic Chopin.* Warsaw: Polish Scientific Publishers, 1963.

Meister, E. *Stilelemente und die geschichtliche Grundlage der Klavierwerke Friedrich Chopins.* Hamburg: Holler, 1936.

Nowik, W. "Chopins Mazurka F-moll op. 68, Nr. 4: die letzte Inspiration des Meisters." *Archiv für Musikforschung* 30 (1973): 109–127.

Opiénski, H. "Chopin's Sonaten und ihr Verhältnis zum Beethovenschen Stil." In *Kongressbericht der Beethoven-Zentenarfeier*, 140. Vienna: Universal, 1927.

Oster, E. "The Fantaisie-Impromptu—A Tribute to Beethoven." *Musicology* 1 (1947): 407–429.

Ottich, M. *Chopins Klavierornamentik.* Wolfenbüttel and Berlin: Kallmeyer, 1938.

Parakilas, J. *Ballads without Words: Chopin and the Tradition of the Instrumental Ballade.* Portland, OR: Amadeus, 1992.

Pestelli, G. "Sul Preludio di Chopin op. 28 n. 1." *Acta musicologica* 63 (1991): 98–114.

Revue de musicologie, vol. 75, no. 2 (1989) [Chopin issue].

Rink, J. "Un siècle et demi d'analyse des 'Ballades' de Chopin." *Analyse musicale*, vol. 27, no. 2 (1992): 65–75.

Rogers, N. "Chopin: Prelude in A minor, Op. 28, No. 2." *Nineteenth Century Music* 4 (1981): 244–250.

Rosen, C. "Rehearings: The First Movement of Chopin's Sonata in B-flat minor, op. 35." *Nineteenth Century Music* 14 (1990): 60–66.

Salzer, F. "Chopin's Nocturne in C♯ minor, Op. 27, No. 1." *Music Forum* 2 (1970): 283–297.

Samson, J. *The Music of Chopin.* London: Routledge and Kegan Paul, 1985.

Sudolski, Z. "La poésie romantique polonaise et la musique de Chopin." *Revue de musicologie* 75 (1989): 171–184.

Swartz, A. "Folk Dance Elements in Chopin's Mazurkas." *Journal of Musicological Research* 4 (1983): 417–426.

Thomas, B. *Harmonic Materials and Treatment of Dissonance in the Pianoforte Music of F. Chopin.* Unpub. diss., University of Rochester, 1963.

Toncitch, V. "Regards sur les préludes de Chopin." *Revue musicale suisse* 114 (1975): 78–86.

Zaccagnini, G. "Field e Chopin." *Nuova rivista musicale italiana* 24 (1990): 47–71.

CIMAROSA

Ferrari Barassi, E. "Cimarosa clavicembalista." In *Scritti in onore di Luigi Ronga,* 191–209. Milan: Ricciardi, 1973.

CLEMENTI

Allorto, R. *Le sonate per pianoforte di Muzio Clementi.* Historiae musicae cultores biblioteca 12. Florence: Olschki, 1959.

Badura-Skoda, E. "Clementi's 'Musical Characteristics.'" *Studies in Eighteenth-Century Music: A Tribute to Karl Geiringer*, 53–67. New York: Oxford, 1970.

Barford, P. "Formalism in Clementi's Pianoforte Sonatas." *Monthly Musical Record* 82 (1952): 205–208, 238–241.

Graue, J. *Muzio Clementi and the Development of Pianoforte Music in Industrial England.* Unpub. diss., University of Illinois, 1971.

Plantinga, L. "Clementi, Virtuosity, and the German Manner." *Journal of the American Musicological Society* 25 (1972): 303–330.

Ringer, A. "Clementi and the Eroica." *Musical Quarterly* 47 (1961): 454–468.

Stauch, M. *Muzio Clementis Klaviersonaten im Verhältnis zu den Sonaten von Haydn, Mozart, und Beethoven.* Bonn: Doppen, 1930.

Stoelzel, M. *Die Anfänge vierhändiger Klaviermusik: Studien zur Satztypik in den Sonaten Muzio Clementis.* Europäische Hochschulschriften ser. 36, vol. 7. Frankfurt: Lang, 1984.

COELHO
Kastner, M. *Musica hispanica: O estilo musical do Padre R. Coelho.* Lisbon: Atica, 1936.

COPLAND
Young, D. "[Copland:] The Piano Music." *Tempo* 95 (1971): 15–22.

CORDERO
Filos Gooch, R. *El piano en los obras de Roque Cordero.* Tibas, Costa Rica: LIL, 1985.

COUPERIN, F.
Beaussant, P. *François Couperin.* Trans. A. Land. Portland: Amadeus, 1990.
Hofmann, S. *L'oeuvre de clavecin de François Couperin.* Paris: Picard, 1961.
Mélanges François Couperin. La vie musicale en France sous les rois Bourbons 13. Paris: Picard, 1968.
Mellers, W. *François Couperin and the French Classical Tradition,* new version. London and Boston: Faber & Faber, 1987.
Tessier, A. "Les Pièces de clavecin de Couperin." *Revue de musicologie,* vol. 6, no. 7 (1923): 123–138.
Tiersot, J. *Les Couperins.* Paris: Alcan, 1926; Paris: Musique d'aujourd'hui, 1975.

COUPERIN, L.
Kitchen, J. *Harpsichord Music in Seventeenth-Century France.* Unpub. diss., Cambridge, 1979.

CRAMER
Schlesinger, T. *John Baptist Cramer und seine Klaviersonaten.* Munich: Knorr & Hirt, 1928.

CRUMB
Bass, R. "Sets, Scales and Symmetries: The Pitch-Structural Basis of George Crumb's 'Makrokosmos' I and II." *Music Theory Spectrum* 13 (1991): 1–20.
Lusk, L. "[Crumb:] Makrokosmos Vol. 1." *Notes* 31 (1974–1975): 157–158.
Terse, P. "[Crumb:] Makrokosmos I, 12." In *Amerikanische Musik seit Charles Ives,* ed. H. Danuser et al., 191–199. Laaber, 1987.
Weber, H. "George Crumb: Amplified Piano—Amplified Tradition." In *Das Projekt Moderne und die Postmoderne,* ed. W. Gruhn, 197–210. Regensburg: Bosse, 1989.

CZERNY
Sheets, R. "Carl Czerny Reconsidered: Romantic Elements in His Sonata op. 7." *Journal of the American Liszt Society* 16 (1984): 54–71.

DANDRIEU
Beechey, G. "The Harpsichord Music of Jean-François Dandrieu." *Consort* 45 (1989): 18–42.
Brunold, P. "Trois livres de Pièces de Clavecin de Jean-François Dandrieu." *Revue de musicologie* 16 (1932): 147–151.

D'ANGLEBERT
Scheibert, B. *Jean-Henri D'Anglebert and the 17th-Century Clavecin School.* Bloomington: Indiana University Press, 1986.

DAVIES
Griffiths, P. "Maxwell Davies' Piano Sonata." *Tempo* 40 (1982): 5–9.

DEBUSSY
Charru, P. "Une analyse des 24 preludes pour le piano de Claude Debussy." *Analyse musicale* 12 (July 1988): 63–86.

Dawes, F. *Debussy Piano Music*. BBC Music Guides. London: BBC, 1969.
Freundlich, I. "Random Thoughts on the Preludes of Claude Debussy." *Current Musi-
. cology* 13 (1972): 48–57.
Gatti, G. "The Piano Music of Claude Debussy." *Musical Quarterly* 7 (1921): 418–460.
Howat, R. "Debussy, 'Masques,' 'L'isle joyeuse,' and a Lost Sarabande." *Musicology
Australia* 10 (1987): 16–30.
———. "Debussy, Ravel, and Bartók: Towards Some New Concepts of Form." *Music
and Letters* 58 (1977): 285–293.
Jacobik, A. *Die associative Harmonik in den Klavierwerken Debussys*. Würzburg:
Triltsch, 1940.
Koptchewski, N. "'Children's Corner' von Claude Debussy." *Jahrbuch Peters: Aufsätze
zur Musik* 1 (1979): 173–209.
Nadeau, R. "[Debussy's] Brouillards: A Tonal Music." *Cahiers Debussy: Nouvelle série*
4–5 (1980–1981): 38–50.
Perrachio, L. *L'opera pianistica di Claude Debussy*. Milan: Bottega di poesia, 1924.
Porten, M. *Zum Problem der Form bei Debussy: Untersuchungen am Beispiel der
Klavierwerke*. Unpub. diss., Zurich, 1972.
Schmitz, E. *The Piano Works of Debussy*. New York: Duell, Sloan, & Pierce, 1950;
Westport: Greenwood, 1970; New York: Da Capo, 1984.
Schnebel, D. "Brouillards—Tendencies in Debussy." *Die Reihe* 6 (1964): 30–35.
Storb, I. *Untersuchungen zur Auflösung der funktionellen Harmonik in den Klavier-
werken von Claude Debussy*. Unpub. diss., Cologne, 1967.

DOHNÁNYI
Hallman, M. "Ernö von Dohnányi's Piano Works." *Journal of the American Liszt Society* 17 (1985): 48–54.

DURANTE
Paribene, G. "Francesco Durante cembalista." *Il Pianoforte* 2 (1921): 303–307.

DUSSEK
Grossmann, O. *The Piano Sonatas of Jan Ladislav Dussek*. Unpub. diss., Yale, 1975.
Schiffer, L. *Johann Ladislaus Dussek: seine Sonaten und seine Konzerte*. Borna: Noske,
1914; New York: Da Capo, 1972.

EBERL
White, A. *The Piano Works of Anton Eberl*. Unpub. diss., University of Wisconsin,
1971.

EDELMANN
Benton, R. "Jean-Frederic Edelmann, a Musical Victim of the French Revolution." *Musical Quarterly* 50 (1964): 165–187.

EISLER
Münch, S. "Hanns Eislers Klaviersonate op. 1 und die 4 Klavierstücke op. 3." *Die
Musikforschung* 39 (1986): 37–44.

FALLA
Chase, G. "Falla's Music for Solo Piano." *The Chesterian* 21 (1940): 41–46.
Koppers, M. "Tonal Elements of Andalusian Folk Music in Manuel de Falla's 'Fantasia
baetica' (1919)." *South African Journal of Musicology* 6 (1986): 41–49.

FARNABY
Marlow, R. "The Keyboard Music of Giles Farnaby." *Proceedings of the Royal Musical
Association* 92 (1965–1966): 107–120.

FIELD
Hibbard, T. "John Field's Rondeaux on 'Speed the Plow.'" *Music Review* 24 (1963): 139–146.
———. "The Slow Movements in the Sonatas of John Field." *Music Review* 23 (1961): 89–93.

FISCHER
Plotinsky, A. *The Keyboard Works of Johann Kaspar Ferdinand Fischer.* Unpub. diss., City University of New York, 1978.

FRANCK, E.
Bittner, J. *Die Klaviersonaten Eduard Francks (1817–1893) und anderer Kleinmeister.* Unpub. diss., Hamburg, 1968.

FRESCOBALDI
Hammond, F. *Girolamo Frescobaldi.* Cambridge: Harvard, 1983.
———. "Girolamo Frescobaldi and the Hypothesis of Neapolitan Influence." In *La musica a Napoli durante il seicento,* ed. D. d'Alessandro and A. Zino, 217–236. Rome: Torre d'Orfeo, 1987.
Harper, J. *The Instrumental Canzonas of Girolamo Frescobaldi.* Unpub. diss., University of Birmingham, 1975.
Klein, H. *Die Tokkaten Girolamo Frescobaldis.* Mainz: Schott, 1990.
Ladewig, J. *Frescobaldi's "Recercari, et Canzoni francese" (1615).* Unpub. diss., University of California, Berkeley, 1978.
Machabey, A. *Gerolamo Frescobaldi Ferrarensis.* Paris: La Colombe, 1952; Paris: Billaudot, 1981.
Newcomb, A. "Frescobaldi's Toccatas and Their Stylistic Ancestry." *Proceedings of the Royal Musical Association* 111 (1984–1985): 28–44.
Ronga, L. *Girolamo Frescobaldi.* Turin: Bocca, 1930.
Silbiger, A., ed. *Frescobaldi Studies.* Durham: Duke University Press, 1987.
Zacher, G. "Frescobaldi und die instrumentale Redekunst." *Musik und Kirche* 45 (1975): 54–64.

FROBERGER
Bauer, E. *Die Klaviersuite Johann Jakob Frobergers.* Unpub. diss., Saarbrücken, 1962.
Seidler, K. *Untersuchungen zur Biographie und Klavierstil Johann Jacob Frobergers.* Unpub. diss., Königsberg, 1930.
Siedentopf, H. *Studien zur Kompositionstechnik Johann Jakob Frobergers.* Tübingen: (Self-published), 1978.
Somer, A. *The Keyboard Music of Johann Jacob Froberger.* Unpub. diss., University of Michigan, 1962.
Starke, D. *Frobergers Suitentänze.* Darmstadt: Tonus, 1972.

FUX
Riedel, F. "Französischer Einfluss in der Klaviermusik von Johann Joseph Fux." In *Aufklärungen,* ed. W. Birtel and C. Mahling, vol. 2, 200–207. Heidelberg: Winter, 1986.

GADE
Brix, L. "Niels W. Gade als Klavierkomponist." *Die Musikforschung* 26 (1973): 22–36.

GALUPPI
Sartori, C. "Le sonate per cembalo di Baldassare Galuppi." In *Galuppiana 1985: Studi e ricerche,* ed. M. Muraro and F. Rossi, 327–334. Quaderni della Rivista italiana di musicologia 13. Florence: Olschki, 1986.

GASPARINI

Levarie, S. "Composizioni per clavicembalo o organo di Francesco Gasparini." In *Francesco Gasparini*, ed. F. della Seta and F. Piperna, 157–162. Quaderni della Rivista italiana di musicologica 6. Florence: Olschki, 1981.

GERSHWIN

Wyatt, R. "The Seven Jazz Preludes of George Gershwin." *American Music* 7 (1989): 68–85.

GIBBONS

Hendrie, G. "The Keyboard Music of Orlando Gibbons (1583–1625)." *Proceedings of the Royal Musical Association* 89 (1962–1963): 1–15.

GIUSTINI

Botti-Caselli, A. "Le sonate da cimbalo di piano e forte di Lodovico Giustini." *Nuova rivista musicale italiana* 12 (1978): 34–66.

Frum, B. "An Early Example of Dramatic Periods in 18th-Century Keyboard Music." *Musical Quarterly* 56 (1970): 230–246.

Harding, R. "The Earliest Pianoforte Music." *Music and Letters* 13 (1932): 194–199.

GOTTSCHALK

Smith, P. "Gottschalk's 'The Banjo, op. 15' and the Banjo in the Nineteenth Century." *Current Musicology*, no. 50 (1992): 47–61.

GRAUPNER

Hoffmann-Erbrecht, L. "Alte und neue Erkenntnisse zum Klavierschaffen Graupners." In *Christoph Graupner*, ed. O. Bill, 308–333. Mainz: Schott, 1987.

————. "Johann Christoph Graupner als Klavierkomponist." *Archiv für Musikwissenschaft* 10 (1953): 140–152.

GRECO

Lippmann, F. "Sulle composizione per cembalo di Gaetano Greco." In *La musica a Napoli durante il seicento*, ed. A. D'Alessandro and A. Zino, 285–306. Miscellanea Musicologica 22. Rome: Torre d'Orfeo, 1987.

GRIEG

Fischer, K. *Griegs Harmonik und die nordländische Folklore*. Berner Veröffentlichungen zur Musikforschung 12. Bern and Leipzig: Haupt, 1938.

Hong, B. "Gade Models for Grieg's Symphony and Piano Sonata." *Dansk årbog for musikforskning* 15 (1984): 27–38.

Horton, J. "Grieg's Slaater for Piano." *Music and Letters* 26 (1945): 229–235.

Schjelderup, G. "Edvard Grieg als Klavierkomponist." *Der Kunstwart* 18 (1904): 72–77.

Skyllstad, K. "Thematic Structure in Relation to Form in Edvard Grieg's Cyclical Works." *Studia Musicologica Norvegica* 3 (1977): 75–94.

HÁBA

Vyslouzil, J. "Hábas Musik für Vierteltonklänge." *Musicologica-Slovaco* 7 (1968): 107–116.

HANDEL

Abraham, G. "Handel's Clavier Music." *Music and Letters* 16 (1935): 278–285.

Best, T. "Die Chronologie von Händels Klaviermusik." *Händel-Jahrbuch* 27 (1981): 79–87.

————. "Handel's Keyboard Music." *Musical Times* 112 (1971): 845–848.

Kahle, F. *Georg Friedrich Händels Cembalosuiten*. Unpub. diss., Berlin, 1928.

Mies, P. "Die Chaconne (Passacaille) bei Händel." *Händel-Jahrbuch* 2 (1929): 13–24.

Pauly, P. *Georg Friedrich Händels Klavierfugen.* Unpub. diss., Saarbrücken, 1961.
Roth, H. "[Handel:] Bemerkungen zum Sondercharakter der ersten Klaviersuiten-sammlung." *Händel-Jahrbuch* 2 (1929): 41–49.
Seiffert, M. "Zu Händels Klavierwerken." *Sammelbände der Internationalen Musikgesellschaft* 1 (1899–1900): 131–141.

HARTMANN, J.
Brix, L. *Die Klaviermusik von Johann Peter Emilius Hartmann.* Unpub. diss., Göttingen, 1971.

HAYDN
Abert, H. "Joseph Haydns Klaviersonaten" [and] "Klavierwerke." *Zeitschrift für Musikwissenschaft* 2 (1919–1920): 553–573; 3 (1920–1921): 535–552.
Andrews, H. *Tonality and Structure in the First Movements of Haydn's Solo Keyboard Sonatas.* Unpub. diss., University of North Carolina, 1967.
Brown, A. *Joseph Haydn's Keyboard Music: Sources and Style.* Bloomington: Indiana University Press, 1986.
Feder, G. "Probleme einer Neuordnung der Klaviersonaten Haydns." In *Festschrift Friedrich Blume,* ed. A. Abert and W. Pfannkuch, 92–103. Kassel: Bärenreiter, 1963.
Fillion, M. "Sonata-Exposition Procedures in Haydn's Keyboard Sonatas." In *Haydn Studies,* ed. J. Larsen et al., 475–481. Proceedings of the International Haydn Conference, Washington, D.C., 1975. New York: Norton, 1981.
Graue, J. "Haydn and the London Pianoforte School." In *Haydn Studies,* ed. J. Larsen, 422–431. Proceedings of the International Haydn Congress, Washington, D.C., 1975. New York and London: Norton, 1981.
Leisinger, U. *Joseph Haydn und die Entwicklung des klassischen Klavierstils (1760–1784).* Unpub. diss., Heidelberg, 1992.
Moss, L. "Haydn's Sonata Hob. 52 (ChL62) in E-flat major: An Analysis of the First Movement." In *Haydn Studies,* ed. J. Larsen et al., 496–501. Proceedings of the International Haydn Congress, Washington, D.C., 1975. New York: Norton, 1981.
Parrish, C. "Haydn and the Piano." *Journal of the American Musicological Society* 1 (1948): 27–34.
Pollack, H. "Some Thoughts on 'Clavier' in Haydn's Solo Sonatas." *Journal of Musicology* 9 (1991): 74–91.
Ripin, E. "Haydn and the Keyboard Instruments of His Time." *Haydn Studies* 5 (1981): 302–308.
Rutmanowitz, L. *The Expositions and Developments of the First Movements of Haydn's Keyboard Sonatas.* Unpub. diss., Columbia, 1987.
Schenker, H. "Haydn: Sonate [52] Es-dur." *Der Tonwille* 3 (1923): 2–21.
Schmid, E. "Joseph Haydn und C. P. E. Bach." *Zeitschrift für Musikwissenschaft* 14 (1931–1932): 299–312.
Shangar, B. "Rhythmic Interplay in the Retransitions of Haydn's Piano Sonatas." *Journal of Musicology* 3 (1984): 55–68.
Somfai, L. *The Keyboard Sonatas of Joseph Haydn.* Trans. L. Somfai and C. Greenspan. Chicago: University of Chicago Press, in press.
Tovey, D. "Haydn: Pianoforte Sonata in E flat, No. 1." In *Essays in Musical Analysis: Chamber Music,* 93–105. London: Oxford, 1944.
Vignal, M. "L'oeuvre pour piano seul de Haydn." *Revue musicale,* Carnet critique, 249 (1961): 7–20.
Wackernagel, B. *Joseph Haydns frühe Klaviersonaten.* Tutzing: Schneider, 1975.

HELLER
Müller-Kersten, U. *Stephen Heller: ein Kleinmeister der Romantik.* Europäische Hoch-schulschriften, ser. 36, vol. 16. Frankfurt: Lang, 1986.

HENSELT
Davis, R. "Henselt, Balakirev, and the Piano." *Music Review* 28 (1967): 173–208.

HINDEMITH
Billeter, B. "Die kompositorische Entwicklung Hindemiths am Beispiel seiner Klavier-werke." *Hindemith Jahrbuch* 6 (1976): 104–121.
Neumeyer, D. "The Genesis and Structure of Hindemith's 'Ludus tonalis.'" *Hindemith Jahrbuch* 7 (1978): 72–103.
Tischler, H. "Hindemith's 'Ludus tonalis' and Bach's 'Well-Tempered Clavier.'" *Music Review* 20 (1959): 217–227.

HÜLLMANDEL
Benton, R. "Nicolas-Joseph Hüllmandel." *Revue de musicologie* 47 (1961): 177–194.

HUMMEL
Davis, R. "The Music of J. N. Hummel: Its Derivations and Development." *Music Review* 26 (1965): 169–191.

HÜNTEN
Zöllner, G. *Franz Hünten: Sein Leben und seine Werke.* Beiträge zur rheinischen Musikgeschichte 34. Cologne: Volk, 1959.

IVES
Alexander, M. *The Evolving Keyboard Style of Charles Ives.* New York: Garland, 1989.
Boatwright, H. "Ives' Quarter-Tone Impressions." *Perspectives of New Music*, vol. 3, no. 2 (Spring–Summer, 1965): 22–31.
Bruderer, C. *The Studies of Charles Ives.* Unpub. diss., Indiana University, 1968.
Clark, S. "The Element of Choice in Ives's 'Concord Sonata.'" *Musical Quarterly* 60 (1974): 167–186.
Ghandar, A. "Charles Ives: Organisation in 'Emerson.'" *Musicology* [Australia] 6 (1980): 111–127.
Henderson, J. *Die "Concord Sonata" von Charles Ives.* Unpub. diss., Berlin (Freie Uni-versität), 1991.
Joyce, M. *The Three-Page Sonata of Charles Ives.* Unpub. diss., Washington University (St. Louis), 1970.
Rosenfield, P. "Ives' Concord Sonata." *Modern Music* 16 (1939): 109–112.
Schubert, G. "Die Concord-Sonate von Charles Ives." *Aspekte der musikalischen Inter-pretation. Sava Savoff zum 70. Geburtstag*, ed. H. Danuser and C. Keller, 121–138. Hamburg: Wegner, 1980.
Toncitch, V. "Charles Ives' Three-Page Sonata pour piano." *Revue musicale de Suisse Romande*, vol. 22, no. 3 (1969): 3–5.

JANÁČEK
Jiranek, J. "Janáčeks Klavierkompositionen vom Standpunkt ihrer dramatischen Char-akter." *Archiv für Musikwissenschaft* 39 (1982): 179–197.
Uhde, J. "Ein musikalisches Monument: Zu Leoš Janáčeks Klaviersonate Fragment." *Zeitschrift für Musiktheorie* 6 (1975): 89–95.

JOPLIN
Gammond, P. *Scott Joplin and the Ragtime Era.* New York: St. Martin's, 1975.

KALKBRENNER

Nautsch, H. *Friedrich Kalkbrenner: Wirkung und Werke.* Hamburger Beiträge zur Musikwissenschaft 25. Hamburg: Wegner, 1983.

KIRCHNER

Sietz, R. *Theodor Kirchner: Ein Klaviermeister der deutschen Romantik.* Studien zur Musikgeschichte des 19. Jahrhunderts 21. Regensburg: Bosse, 1971.

KLENGEL

Jäger, R. *August Alexander Klengel und seine "Kanons und Fugen."* Unpub. diss., Leipzig, 1929.

KOECHLIN

McGuire, T. *The Piano Works of Charles Koechlin (1867–1950).* Unpub. diss., University of North Carolina, 1975.

KRENEK

Huetteman, A. *Ernst Krenek's Theories of the Sonata and Their Relations to His Six Piano Sonatas.* Unpub. diss., Iowa, 1968.

KUHLAU

Beimfohr, J. *Das C-dur Klavierkonzert opus 7 und die Klaviersonaten von Friedrich Kuhlau.* Hamburg: Wegner, 1971.

Dawe, E. *Three Piano Sonatas by Friedrich Kuhlau.* Unpub. diss., University of British Columbia, 1988.

KUHNAU

Bruno, S. *The Published Keyboard Works of Johann Kuhnau.* Unpub. diss., University of Connecticut, 1986.

Clercx, S. "Johann Kuhnau et la sonate." *Revue musicale* 16 (1935): 89–110.

LEBÈGUE

Gillespie, J. *The Harpsichord Works of Nicholas LeBègue.* Unpub. diss., University of Southern California, 1951.

Tessier, A. "L'oeuvre de clavecin de Nicolas LeBègue." *Revue de musicologie* 6, 7 (1925): 106–112.

LETELIER

Grebe, M. "Las Variaciónes en Fa para piano de Alfonso Letelier." *Revista musical chilena* 23 (no. 109, 1969): 33–46.

LIADOV

Lissa, Z. "Über den Einfluss Chopins auf Ljadov." *Deutsches Jahrbuch für Musikwissenschaft* 13 (1968): 5–42.

LIGETI

Bouliane, D. "Les six études pour piano de György Ligeti." *Canadian Universities Music Review* 9 (1989): 36–83.

Floros, C. "Versuch über Ligetis jüngste Werke." In *Für György Ligeti: Die Referate des Ligeti-Kongresses Hamburg 1988*, 335–348. Hamburger Jahrbücher für Musikwissenschaft 11. Laaber, 1991.

Kinzler, H. "György Ligeti: Decision and Automatism in 'Désordre, Ire Étude, Premier Livre.'" *Interface* 20 (1991): 89–124.

Ligeti, G. "Mes Études pour piano (premier livre): Polyrythme et création." *Analyse musicale* 11 (April 1988): 44–45.

Svard, L. *Illusion in Selected Keyboard Works of Györgi Ligeti.* Unpub. diss., Johns Hopkins University, 1991.

LISZT

Arminsky, H. *Die ungarischen Phantasien von Franz Liszt.* Unpub. diss., Vienna, 1929.

Arnold, B. "Recitative in Liszt's Solo Piano Music." *Journal of the American Liszt Society* 24 (1988): 3–22.

Backus, J. "Liszt's 'Harmonies poétiques et religieuses': Inspiration and Challenge to Musical Form." *Journal of the American Liszt Society* 24 (1988): 45–73.

———. "Liszt's 'Sposalizio': A Study in Musical Perspective." *Nineteenth Century Music* 12 (1988): 173–183.

Becker, R. *"Offenheit" und "Geschlossenheit" instrumentaler Formen des 19. Jahrhunderts—exemplifiziert an Liszts H-moll Sonate.* Unpub. diss., Marburg, 1980.

Biget, M. "Étude comparative de geste pianistique chez Liszt et chez Debussy." *Revue musicale,* no. 405–407 (1987): 155–163.

Bollard, D. "An Introduction to Liszt's 'Weinen Klagen' Variations." *Studies in Music* (Australia) 22 (1988): 48–64.

Diercks, J. "[Liszt:] The Consolations." *Journal of the American Liszt Society* 3 (June 1978): 19–24.

Döhring, S. "Reminiscences: Liszts Konzeption der Klavierparaphrase." In *Heinz Becker zum 60. Geburtstag,* ed. J. Schlader, 131–151. Laaber, 1982.

Fowler, A. "Motive and Program in Liszt's 'Vallée d'Obermann.'" *Journal of the American Liszt Society* 29 (1991): 3–11.

Friedheim, P. "The Piano Transcriptions of Liszt." *Studies in Romanticism* 1 (1962): 83–96.

Gardonyi, Z., and S. Mauser, eds. *Virtuosität und Avantgarde: Untersuchungen zum Klavierwerk Franz Liszts.* Schriften der Hochschule für Musik Würzburg. Mainz: Schott, 1988.

Goudet, G. "Une analyse thématique de la sonate en si mineur de Franz Liszt." *Analyse musicale,* vol. 7, no. 2 (1987): 49–55.

Grew, E. " Liszt's Dante Sonata." *The Chesterian* 21 (1940): 21–40.

Hilmar, E. "Kritische Beiträge zu Liszts Transkriptionen von Liedern von Franz Schubert." In *Liszt Studien: 1. Kongressbericht Eisenstadt 1975,* ed. W. Suppan, 115–123. Graz: Akademische Verlagsanstalt, 1977.

Huschke, W. "Anmerkungen zu Franz Liszts 'Freischütz Fantasia.'" *Studia musicologica* [Hungary] 28 (1986): 261–271.

Kabisch, T. *Liszt und Schubert.* Berliner musikwissenschaftliche Arbeiten 23. Munich and Salzburg: Katzbichler, 1984.

———. "Struktur und Form im Spätwerk Franz Liszts: Das Klavierstück 'Unstern' (1886)." *Archiv für Musikwissenschaft* 42 (1985): 178–199.

Kokai, R. *Franz Liszt in seinen frühen Klavierwerken.* Leipzig: Wagner, 1933; Kassel: Bärenreiter, 1969.

Kroó, G. "'La Ligne intérieure': The Years of Transformation and the 'Album d'un voyageur.'" *Studia musicologica* 28 (1986): 249–260.

Lee, R. *Some Little-Known Late Piano Works of Liszt (1869–1886).* Unpub. diss., University of Washington, 1970.

Longyear, R. "Liszt's B minor Sonata: Precedents for a Structural Analysis." *Music Review* 34 (1973): 198–209.

——— "The Text of Liszt's B minor Sonata." *Musical Quarterly* 60 (1974): 435–450.

Pesce, D. "Liszt's 'Années de pèlerinage,' Book 3: A Hungarian Cycle?" *Nineteenth Century Music* 13 (1990): 207–229.
Presser, D. "Liszts 'Années de pèlerinage.'" In *Liszt Studien: 1. Kongressbericht Eisenstadt 1975*, ed. W. Suppan, 137–153. Graz: Akademische Verlagsanstalt, 1977.
Redepfennig, D. *Das Spätwerk Franz Liszts: Bearbeitungen einiger Kompositionen.* Hamburger Beiträge zur Musikwissenschaft 27. Hamburg: Wegner, 1984.
Reich, N. "Liszt's Variations on the March from Rossini's Siège de Corinth." *Fontes artes musicae* 23 (1976): 102–106
Rexroth, D. "Zum Spätwerk Franz Liszts: Material und Form in dem Klavierstück 'Unstern.'" In *Bericht über den internationalen Kongress Bonn 1970*, 544–547. Kassel: Bärenreiter, 1973.
Riethmüller, A. "Franz Liszts 'Reminiscences de Don Juan.'" In *Analysen: Beiträge zu einer Problemgeschichte des Komponierens. Festschrift für Hans Heinrich Eggebrecht*, 276–291. Beihefte zum Archiv für Musikwissenschaft 23. Wiesbaden: Steiner, 1984.
Rüsch, W. *Franz Liszts Années de pèlerinage: Beiträge zur Geschichte seiner Persönlichkeit und seines Stiles.* Bellinzona: Leins and Vescovi, 1934.
Saffle, M. "Liszt's Sonata in B minor." *Journal of the American Liszt Society* 11 (1982): 28–39.
Schenkman, W. "Liszt's Reminiscences of Bellini's 'Norma.'" *Journal of the American Liszt Society* 9 (June 1981): 55–64.
———. "The Venezia e Napoli Tarantella: Genesis and Metamorphosis." *Journal of the American Liszt Society* 4 (December 1979): 10–24; 5 (June 1980): 47–58; 7 (June 1980): 35–41.
Stenzl, J. "L'énigme Franz Liszt: prophéties et conventions dans les oeuvres tardes." *Revue musicale*, no. 405–407 (1987): 127–135.
Szasz, T. "Liszt's Symbols for the Divine and Diabolical: Their Revelation of a Program for the B minor Sonata." *Journal of the American Liszt Society* 15 (1984): 39–95.
Torkewitz, D. "Anmerkungen zu Liszts Spätstil." *Archiv für Musikwissenschaft* 35 (1978): 231–236.
Walker, A. "Liszt and the Schubert Song Transcriptions." *Musical Quarterly* 67 (1981): 50–63.
Westerby, H. *Liszt: Composer and His Piano Works.* London: Reeves, 1936; West Newfield, CT: Longwood, 1977.
Wilson, K. *A Historical Study and Stylistic Analysis of Franz Liszt's "Années de pèlerinage."* Unpub. diss., University of North Carolina, 1977.
Winklhofer, S. "Liszt, Marie d'Agoult, and the 'Dante' Sonata." *Nineteenth Century Music* 1 (1977): 15–32.
———. *Liszt's Sonata in B minor.* Studies in Musicology 29. Ann Arbor: UMI, 1980.
Wuellner, G. "Franz Liszt's 'Liebestraum' No. 3: A Study of 'O Lieb' and Its Piano Transcription." *Journal of the American Liszt Society* 24 (1988): 45–73.

LOEILLET
Priestman, B. "The Keyboard Works of John Loeillet." *Music Review* 16 (1955): 89–95.

LOEWE
Salmon, J. *The Piano Sonatas of Carl Loewe.* Unpub. diss., University of North Texas, 1988.

LÖHLEIN
Wilson, D. "Löhlein's 'Klavierschule': Toward an Understanding of the Galant Style." *International Review of the Aesthetics and Sociology of Music* 12 (1981): 103–115.

LOPEZ

Gillespie, J. "The Keyboard Sonatas of Felix Maxime Lopez." In *Studies in Eighteenth-Century Music: A Tribute to Karl Geiringer*, ed. H. Robbins Landon, 243–252. New York: Oxford, 1970.

MACDOWELL

Brancaleone, F. *The Short Piano Works of Edward MacDowell*. Unpub. diss., City University of New York, 1982.

———. "Edward MacDowell and Indian Motives." *American Music* 7 (1989): 359–381.

Pesce, D. "MacDowell's 'Eroica Sonata' and Its Lisztian Legacy." *Music Review* 49 (1988): 169–189.

———. "The Other Sea in MacDowell's 'Sea Pieces.'" *American Music* 10 (1992): 391–410.

MARTINI

Tagliavini, L. "Le sonate per organo e cembalo di Martini." In *Padre Martini*, ed. A. Pompilio, 295–303. Quaderni della Rivista italiana de musicologia 12. Florence: Olschki, 1987.

MARTINO

Klumpenhouwer, H. "Aspects of New Structure and Harmony in Martino's Impromptu No. 6." *Perspectives of New Music*, vol. 29, no. 2 (1991): 318–354.

MATTHESON

Scares, M. "Johann Mattheson as a Keyboard Composer." *Studies in Music* [Australia] 22 (1988): 1–12.

MEDTNER

Gerstle, H. "Piano Music of Nicholas Medtner." *Musical Quarterly* 10 (1924): 500–510.

Keller, C. *The Piano Sonatas of Nicolas Medtner*. Unpub. diss., Ohio State University, 1971.

Truscott, H. "Medtner's Sonata in G minor, op. 22." *Music Review* 22 (1961): 112–123.

MENDELSSOHN, F.

Fellerer, K. "Mendelssohn in der Klaviermusik seiner Zeit." In *Das Problem Mendelssohn*, ed. C. Dahlhaus, 195–200. Studien zur Musikgeschichte des 19. Jahrhunderts 41. Regensburg: Bosse, 1974.

Godwin, J. "Early Mendelssohn and Late Beethoven." *Music and Letters* 55 (1974): 272–285.

Jost, C. *Mendelssohns Lieder ohne Worte*. Frankfurter Beiträge zur Musikwissenschaft 14. Tutzing: Schneider, 1988.

Kahl, W. "Zu Mendelssohns Lieder ohne Worte." *Zeitschrift für Musikwissenschaft* 3 (1920–1921): 459–469.

Siebenkäs, D. "Zur Vorgeschichte der 'Lieder ohne Worte' von Mendelssohn." *Die Musikforschung* 15 (1962): 171–173.

Tischler, H., and L. "Mendelssohn's Songs Without Words." *Musical Quarterly* 33 (1947): 1–16.

Vitercik, G. *The Early Works of Felix Mendelssohn: A Study in the Early Romantic Sonata*. Philadelphia: Gordon & Breach, 1992.

MERULO

Meier, B. "Die Modi der Toccaten von Merulo." *Archiv für Musikwissenschaft* 34 (1977): 180–198.

Völkl, G. *Die Toccaten Claudio Merulos*. Unpub. diss., Munich, 1969.

MESSIAEN

Hirsbrunner, T. "Olivier Messiaen: 'sehr schwer einzuordnen.'" *Die Musikforschung* 42 (1989): 222–232.

Schweizer, K. "Olivier Messiaens Klavieretüde 'Mode de valeurs et d'intensités.'" *Archiv für Musikwissenschaft* 30 (1973): 128–146.

MOZART, L.

Schmid, M. "Zu den Klaviersonaten von Leopold Mozart." *Mozart-Jahrbuch* 1989–1990: 23–30.

MOZART, W.

Badura-Skoda, P., and E. *Interpreting Mozart at the Keyboard.* Trans. L. Black. New York: St. Martin's, 1962.

Bass, R. "The Second Theme Problem and Other Issues in Mozart's Sonata K. 457." *Indiana Theory Review* 9 (1988): 3–22.

Beach, D. "The First Movement of Mozart's Piano Sonata in A minor (K. 310)." *Journal of Musicological Research* 7 (1987): 157–179.

Broder, N. "Mozart and the Clavier." *Musical Quarterly* 27 (1941): 422–432.

Burde, W. *Studien zu Mozarts Klaviersonaten.* Schriften zu Musik 1. Giebing: Katzbichler, 1969.

Buslau, O. *Mozarts Klaviersonaten.* Unpub. diss., Cologne, 1991.

Croll, G. "Zu Mozarts Largo und Allegro in Es-dur für 2 Klaviere." *Mozart-Jahrbuch* 1964: 28–37.

Delfausse, R. *The Roles of Symmetrical Measure Groups in Mozart's Sonatas.* Unpub. diss., City University of New York, 1988.

Dennerlein, H. *Der unbekannte Mozart: Die Welt seiner Klavierwerke.* 2nd ed. Leipzig: Breitkopf & Härtel, 1955.

Ferguson, H. "Mozart's Duets for One Pianoforte." *Proceedings of the Royal Musical Association* 73 (1946–1947): 35–44.

Fischer, K. "Mozarts Klaviervariationen." In *Hans Albrecht In Memoriam*, 168–173. Kassel: Bärenreiter, 1962.

Flothuis, M. "Mozarts Fantasie und Sonate in C-moll: ein Wendepunkt." In *Über das Klassische*, ed. R. Bockholdt, 276–287. Frankfurt: Suhrkamp, 1987.

Flotzinger, R. "Die Klaviervariationen W. A. Mozarts in der Tradition des 18. Jahrhunderts." *Mitteilungen der Internationalen Stiftung Mozarteum*, vol. 23, no. 3–4 (1975): 13–27.

Gerstenberg, W. "Über Mozarts Klaviersatz." *Archiv für Musikwissenschaft* 16 (1959): 108–116.

Haefeli, A. "Wolfgang Amadé Mozarts Sonate in D für zwei Klaviere." In *Beiträge zur musikalischen Analyse*, 37–62. Musikreflektionen 1. Basel: Amadeus, 1987.

Hortschansky, K. "Zu Mozarts 'Lindor'-Variationen, KV 354." In *Liedstudien: Wolfgang Osthoff zum 60. Geburtstag*, ed. M. Just and R. Wiesend, 203–228. Tutzing: Schneider, 1989.

Johde, F. "Die Thematik der Klaviersonaten Mozarts." *Mozart-Jahrbuch* 2 (1924): 7–53.

King, A. "Mozart's Piano Music." *Music Review* 5 (1944): 163–191.

Komlos, K. "Fantasia and Sonata K. 475/457 in Contemporary Context." In *Bericht über den Internationalen Mozart-Kongress Salzburg 1991*, ed. R. Angermüller et al., 816–823. Mozart-Jahrbuch 1991. Kassel: Bärenreiter, 1992.

Lorenz, F. *W. A. Mozart als Klavierkomponist.* Breslau: Leuckart, 1866.

Mason, W. "Melodic Unity in Mozart's Piano Sonata, K. 333." *Music Review* 22 (1961): 28–33.

Mercado, M. *The Evolution of Mozart's Pianistic Style*. Carbondale, IL: Southern Illinois Press, 1992.

Neumann, H. "The Two Versions of Mozart's Rondo K. 494." *Music Forum* 1 (1967): 3–34.

Parrish, G. "Multi-level Unification in Mozart's Piano Sonata K. 333 (315c)." In *Bericht über den Internationalen Mozart-Kongress Salzburg 1991*, ed. R. Angermüller et al., 1039–1049. Mozart-Jahrbuch 1991. Kassel: Bärenreiter, 1992.

Ratner, L. "Topical Content in Mozart's Keyboard Sonatas." *Early Music* 19 (1991): 615–619.

Reijen, P. *Vergleichende Studien zur Klaviervariationstechnik von Mozart und seinen Zeitgenossen*. Keyboard Studies 8. Buren: Knuf, 1988.

Rosenberg, R. *Die Klaviersonaten Mozarts*. Hofheim: Hofmeister, 1972.

Russell, J. "Mozart and the Pianoforte." *Music Review* 1 (1940): 226–244.

Schenker, H. "Mozart: Sonate a-moll." *Der Tonwille* 2 (1922): 7–24.

Somfai, L. "Mozart's First Thoughts: The Two Versions of the Sonata in D major, K. 284." *Early Music* 19 (1991): 601–613.

Stoelzel, M. "Mozarts letzte vierhändige Sonate C-dur KV 521." In *Bericht über den Internationalen Mozart-Kongress Salzburg 1991*, ed. R. Angermüller et al., 716–723. Mozart-Jahrbuch 1991. Kassel: Bärenreiter, 1992.

Wolf, E. "The Rediscovered Autograph of Mozart's Fantasia and Sonata, K. 475/457." *Journal of Musicology* 10 (1992): 3–47.

Wolff, C. "'Musikalische Gedankenfolge' und 'Einheit des Stoffes': Zu Mozarts Klaviersonate F-dur (KV 533 und 494)." In *Das musikalische Kunstwerk: Festschrift Carl Dahlhaus zum 60. Geburtstag*, ed. H. Danuser et al., 441–453. Laaber, 1988.

MUFFAT, G. OR T.

Adler, G. "I 'Componimenti musicali per il cembalo' di Teofilo Muffat." *Rivista Musicale Italiana* 3 (1896): 1–35.

Knöll, J. *Die Klavier- und Orgelwerke von Theophil Muffat*. Unpub. diss., Vienna, 1916.

Wollenberg, S. *Viennese Keyboard Music in the Reign of Karl VI, 1712–40: Gottlieb Muffat and His Contemporaries*. Unpub. diss., Oxford, 1970.

———. "The Keyboard Suites of Gottlieb Muffat." *Proceedings of the Royal Music Association* 102 (1975–1976): 83–91.

MÜLLER

Haupt, G. *August Eberhard Müllers Leben und Klavierwerke*. Leipzig: (Self-published?), 1926.

MUSSORGSKY

Frankenstein, A. "Victor Hartmann and Modeste Musorgsky." *Musical Quarterly* 25 (1939): 268–291.

Hübsch, L. *Modest Musorgskij: Bilder einer Ausstellung*. Meisterwerke der Musik 15. Munich: Fink, 1978.

MÜTHEL

Hoffmann-Erbrecht, L. "Sturm und Drang in der deutschen Klaviermusik von 1753–1763." *Die Musikforschung* 10 (1957): 466–479.

NANCARROW

Carlsen, P. *The Player-Piano Music of Conlon Nancarrow*. Institute for the Study of American Music Monograph 26. Brooklyn: Brooklyn College Conservatory, 1988.

Fürst-Heidtmann, M., and J. Tenney. "Conlon Nancarrow's 'Studies for Player Piano.'" *Melos* 46 (1984): 104–137.

NIELSEN

Miller, M. "Carl Nielsen's Tonal Language: An Examination of the Piano Music." *College Music Symposium* 22 (1982): 32–45.

PAISIELLO

Hunt, J. "The Keyboard Works of Giovanni Paisiello." *Musical Quarterly* 61 (1975): 212–232.

PASQUINI, B.

Haynes, M. *The Keyboard Works of Bernardo Pasquini.* Unpub. diss., Indiana University, 1960.

Heimrich, W. *Die Orgel- und Cembalowerke Bernardo Pasquinis (1637–1710).* Unpub. diss., Berlin (Freie Universität), 1958.

PEPPING

Hamm, W. *Studien über Ernst Peppings drei Klaviersonaten 1937.* Literaturhistorische-musikwissenschaftliche Abhandlungen 12. Würzburg: Triltsch, 1955.

PERSICHETTI

Farrell, L. *Vincent Persichetti's Piano Sonatas from 1943 to 1965.* Unpub. diss., University of Rochester, 1976.

PETRASSI

Stone, O. "Goffredo Petrassi's Toccata for Pianoforte." *Music Review* 37 (1976): 45–51.

PLATTI

Torrefranca, F. *Giovanni Benedetto Platti e la sonata moderna.* Instituzione e monumenti dell'arte musicale italiana, Nuova seria 2. Milan: Ricordi, 1963.

PLEYEL

Hornick, M. *Ensemble and Keyboard Works of Ignaz Pleyel Originally Composed for Keyboard.* Unpub. diss., New York University, 1987.

POGLIETTI

Riedel, F. "Ein Skizzenbuch von Alessandro Poglietti." In *Essays in Musicology*, ed. H. Tischler, 145–152. Bloomington: School of Music, Indiana University, 1968.

POULENC

Davies, L. "The Piano Music of Poulenc." *Music Review* 33 (1972): 195–203.

Nelson, J. *The Piano Music of Francis Poulenc.* Unpub. diss., University of Washington, 1978.

PROKOFIEV

Brown, M. "Prokofiev's Eighth Piano Sonata." *Tempo* 70 (1964): 9–15.

Merrick, F. "Prokofiev's Piano Sonatas." *Proceedings of the Royal Musical Association* 75 (1948–1949): 13–21.

PURCELL

Ferguson, H. "Purcell's Harpsichord Music." *Proceedings of the Royal Musical Association* 91 (1964–1965): 1–9.

RAMEAU

Hendrie, G. "Some Reflections on the Keyboard Music of Jean-Philippe Rameau (1683–1764)." *Studies in Music* [Australia] 22 (1988): 13–38.

Klitenic, Z. *The Clavecin Works of Jean-Philippe Rameau.* Unpub. diss., University of Pennsylvania, 1955.

RAVEL

Akeret, K. *Studien zum Klavierwerk von Maurice Ravel.* Zurich: Hug, 1941.

Hirsbrunner, T. "'Gaspard de la nuit' von Maurice Ravel." *Archiv für Musikwissenschaft* 44 (1987): 268–281.

Sannemüller, G. *Das Klavierwerk von Maurice Ravel.* Unpub. diss., Kiel, 1961.

Teboul, J. *Ravel: Le langage musical de l'oeuvre pour piano.* Paris: Leopard d'or, 1987.

RAWSTHORNE

Allison, R. *The Piano Works of Alan Rawsthorne (until 1968).* Unpub. diss., University of Washington, 1970.

REGER

Dejmek, G. *Der Variationszyklus bei Max Reger.* Essen: (Self-published), 1930.

Hopkins, W. *The Short Piano Compositions of Max Reger.* Unpub. diss., Indiana University, 1971.

Schmidt, C. "Von Satztypen Regerscher Charakterstücke." *Reger-Studien* 2 (1986): 105–113.

Sievers, G. "Die Klavierkompositionen von Max Reger." *Mitteilungen Max Reger Institut.* Sonderheft 1973: 37–43.

Weiss-Aigner, G. *Max Reger: Mozart-Variationen.* Meisterwerke der Musik 52. Munich: Fink, 1989.

Wünsch, G. *Die Entwicklung des Klaviersatzes bei Max Reger.* Unpub. diss., Vienna, 1950.

———. "Spielformen in Regers Klaviermusik." *Mitteilungen des Max Reger Instituts* 18 (1971): 16–29.

REICH

Epstein, P. "Pattern Structure and Process in Steve Reich's 'Piano Phase.'" *Musical Quarterly* 72 (1986): 494–502.

REICHARDT

Dennerlein, H. *Johann Friedrich Reichardt und seine Klavierwerke.* Universitas-Archiv 4. Münster: Helios, 1930.

REINAGLE

Krohn, E. "Alexander Reinagle as Sonatist." *Musical Quarterly* 18 (1932): 140–149.

REUBKE

Songayllo, R. "A Neglected Masterpiece: Reubke Piano Sonata in B-flat minor." *Journal of the American Liszt Society* 18 (1985): 122–128.

RIES

Lamkin, K. *The Solo Piano Sonatas of Franz Ries.* Unpub. diss., Northwestern, 1981.

RIHM

Mauser, S. "Primäre Ausdrucksformen: Anmerkungen zum Klavierstück Nr. 7 von Wolfgang Rihm." In *Der Komponist Wolfgang Rihm*, ed. D. Rexroth, 153–159. Mainz: Schott, 1985.

ROSSI

Silbiger, A. "Michelangelo Rossi and His Toccate e Correnti." *Journal of the American Musicological Society* 36 (1983): 18–38.

ROUSSEL

Cortot, A. "L'oeuvre pianistique d'Albert Roussel." *Revue musicale*, no. 177 (1937): 293–308.

Gil-Marchex, H. "La musique de piano d'Albert Roussel." *Revue musicale*, no. 400–401 (1987): 35–53.

RUBBRA

Dawney, M. "Edmund Rubbra and the Piano." *Music Review* 31 (1970): 214–248.

RUBINSTEIN, A.

MacLean, C. "Rubinstein as Composer for the Piano." *Proceedings of the Royal Musical Association* 39 (1913): 129–151.

RUGGLES

Faulkner, S. *Carl Ruggles and His Evocations for Piano.* Unpub. diss., American University (Washington, D.C.), 1975.

Gilbert, S. "The Twelve-Tone System of Carl Ruggles: A Study of the 'Evocations' for Piano." *Journal of Music Theory* 14 (1970): 68–91.

SAINT-SÄENS

Ratner, S. *The Piano Works of Camille Saint-Säens.* Unpub. diss., University of Michigan, 1972.

SATIE

Danckert, W. "Der Klassizismus Erik Saties und seine geistesgeschichtliche Stellung." *Zeitschrift für Musikwissenschaft* 12 (1929–1930): 105–114.

Gillmore, A. "Musico-poetic Form in Satie's 'Humoristic' Piano Suites." *Canadian University Music Review* 8 (1987): 1–44.

Orledge, R. "Satie's Approach to Composition in His Later Years." *Proceedings of the Royal Musical Association* 111 (1984–1985): 155–179.

SCARLATTI, A.

Pestelli, G. "Le toccate per strumento a tastiera di Alessandro Scarlatti." In *Studien zur deutsch-italienischen Musikgeschichte*, ed. F. Lippmann, vol. 8, 169–172. Analecta musicologica 12. Cologne: Volk, 1973.

Shedlock, J. "The Harpsichord Music of Alessandro Scarlatti." *Sammelbände der Internationalen Musikgesellschaft* 6 (1904–1905): 160–178, 418–422.

SCARLATTI, D.

Benton, R. "Form in the Sonatas of Domenico Scarlatti." *Music Review* 13 (1952): 264–273.

Bogianckino, M. *The Harpsichord Music of Domenico Scarlatti.* Trans. J. Tickner. Rome: De Santis, 1967.

Choi, S. *Newly Found 18th-Century Manuscripts of Domenico Scarlatti's Sonatas.* Unpub. diss., University of Wisconsin, 1974.

Dale, K. "Domenico Scarlatti: His Unique Contribution to Keyboard Literature." *Proceedings of the Royal Musical Association* 74 (1947–1948): 33–44.

Domenico Scarlatti. Musik-Konzepte 47. Munich: text & kritik, 1986.

Gerstenberg, W. *Die Klavierkompositionen Domenico Scarlattis.* Forschungsarbeiten des musikwissenschaftlichen Instituts der Universität Leipzig. 1933. Reprint. Regensburg: Bosse, 1969.

Hautus, L. "Beiträge zur Datierung der Klavierwerke Domenico Scarlattis." *Die Musikforschung* 26 (1973): 59–61.

Keller, H. *Domenico Scarlatti: Ein Meister des Klaviers.* Leipzig: Peters, 1957.

Kirkpatrick, R. *Domenico Scarlatti.* 1953. Princeton: Princeton University Press, 1983.

Pestelli, G. *Le sonate di Domenico Scarlatti: Proposta di un ordinamento cronologico.* Turin: Giappichelli, 1967.

Sheveloff, J. "Domenico Scarlatti: Tercentary Frustrations." *Musical Quarterly* 71 (1985): 399–436; 72 (1986): 90–118.

Siccardi, H. *Domenico Scarlatti a través de sus sonatas.* Buenos Aires: Editorial Argentina, 1945.

SCHOBERT

Turrentine, H. *Johann Schobert and French Clavier Music from 1700 to the Revolution.* Unpub. diss., University of Iowa, 1962.

SCHOENBERG

Barkin, E. "A View of Schoenberg's op. 23/1." In *Perspectives of New Music*, vol. 12, no. 1–2 (1973–1974): 99–127.

Boulez, P. "Schoenberg's Piano Works." In *Notes of an Apprenticeship*, trans. H. Weinstock, 371–376. New York: Knopf, 1958.

Brinkmann, R. *Arnold Schönberg: Drei Klavierstücke op. 11.* Beihefte des Archiv für Musikwissenschaft 7. Wiesbaden: Steiner, 1969.

Christensen, T. "Schoenberg's op. 11, no. 1: A Parody of Pitch-Cells from 'Tristan.'" *Journal of the Arnold Schoenberg Institute* 10 (1987): 38–44.

Forte, A. "The Magical Kaleidoscope: Schoenberg's First Atonal Masterwork, op. 11, no. 1." *Journal of the Arnold Schoenberg Institute*, vol. 5, no. 2 (1981): 127–168.

Friedberg, R. "The Solo Keyboard Works of Arnold Schoenberg." *Music Review* 23 (1962): 39–50.

Grandjean, W. "Form in Schoenberg's op. 19, no. 2." *Zeitschrift für Musiktheorie* 8, 1 (1977): 15–18.

Graziano, J. "Serial Procedures in Schoenberg's Opus 23." *Current Musicology* 13 (1972): 58–63.

Krieger, G. *Schönbergs Werke für Klavier.* Göttingen: Vandenhoeck & Ruprecht, 1968.

Kurth, R. "Mosaic Polyphony: Formal Balance, Imbalance, and Phrase Structure in the Prelude of Schoenberg's Suite, Op. 25." *Music Theory Spectrum* 14 (1992): 188–108.

Maegard, J. "A Study of the Chronology of Op. 23–26 by Arnold Schoenberg." *Dansk årbog for musikforskning* 1962: 93–115.

Massow, A. von. "Abschied und Neuorientierung—Schönberg's Klavierstück op. 19, 6." *Archiv für Musikwissenschaft* 50 (1993): 187–195.

Morrison, C. "Syncopation as Motive in Schoenberg's op. 19, nos. 2, 3, and 4." *Music Analysis* 11 (1992): 75–93.

Oesch, H. "Schönberg im Vorfeld der Dodekaphonie." *Melos* 41 (1974): 330–339; *Zeitschrift für Musiktheorie*, vol. 5, no. 1 (1974): 2–10.

Reible, J. *"Tristan" Romanticism and the Expression of the Three Piano Pieces, op. 11, of Arnold Schoenberg.* Unpub. diss., Washington University (St. Louis), 1980.

Rogge, W. *Das Klavierwerk Arnold Schönbergs.* 1964. Reprint. Regensburg: Bosse, 1977.

Tuttle, T. "Schoenberg's Compositions for Piano Solo." *Music Review* 18 (1957): 300–318.

Wittich, G. "Interval Set Structure in Schoenberg's op. 11, no. 1." *Perspectives of New Music*, vol. 13, no. 1 (1974): 41–55.

SCHUBERT

Bisogni, F. "Rilevi filologici sulle sonate della maturità di Franz Schubert." *Rivista italiana di musicologia* 11 (1976): 71–105.

———. "Rilevi filologici sulle sonate giovanili di Franz Schubert (1815–1817)." *Rivista italiana di musicologia* 2 (1968): 453–472.

·Cervone, G. "Franz Schubert: le sonate per pianoforte degli anni 1815–1818." *Nuova rivista musicale italiana* 18 (1984): 10–51.

Chusid, M. "A Suggested Redating of Schubert's Piano Sonata in E-flat, op. 122." In *Schubert-Kongress Wien 1978: Bericht*, ed. O. Brusatti, 37–44. Graz: Akademische, 1979.

Cone, E. "Schubert's Beethoven." *Musical Quarterly* 56 (1970): 779–793.

Denny, T. "Schubert as Self-Critic: The Problematic Case of the Unfinished Sonata in C major, D. 840." *Journal of Musicological Research* 8 (1988): 91–117.

Dürr, W. "'Wer vermag nach Beethoven noch etwas zu machen.'" *Beethoven Jahrbuch* 9 (1973–1977): 48–67.

Fisk, C. "Rehearing the Moment and Hearing In-the-Moment: Schubert's First Two 'Moments musicaux.'" *College Music Symposium*, vol. 30, no. 2 (1990): 1–18.

Godel, A. *Schuberts letzte drei Klaviersonaten.* Sammlung musikwissenschaftlicher Abhandlungen 69. Baden-Baden: Körner, 1985.

Goldberger, D. "An Unexpected New Source for Schubert's A minor Sonata." *Nineteenth Century Music* 6 (1982): 3–9.

Hill, W. "The Genesis of Schubert's Posthumous Sonata in B-flat." *Music Review* 12 (1951): 269–278.

Kahl, W. "Das lyrische Klavierstück Schuberts und seine Vorgänger bis 1810." *Archiv für Musikwissenschaft* 3 (1921): 54–82, 99–122.

Költzsch, H. *Franz Schubert in seinen Klaviersonaten.* Sammlung musikwissenschaftlicher Einzeldarstellungen 7. Leipzig: Breitkopf & Härtel, 1927; Hildesheim: Ohm, 1976.

Komma, K. "Franz Schuberts Klaviersonate a-moll op. posth. 164 (D. 537)." *Zeitschrift für Musiktheorie*, vol. 3, no. 1 (1972): 2–15.

Krause, A. *Die Klaviersonaten Franz Schuberts: Form–Gattung–Ästhetik.* Kassel: Bärenreiter, 1992.

Kuhn, C. "Zur Themenbildung Franz Schuberts: Sechs Annäherungen." In *Das musikalische Kunstwerk: Festschrift Carl Dahlhaus zum 60. Geburtstag*, ed. H. Danuser et al., 503–515. Laaber, 1988.

McCreless, P. "Schubert's 'Moment musical' No. 2." *In Theory Only* 3–4 (1977): 3–11.

Porter, E. *Schubert's Piano Works.* London: Dobson, 1980.

Radcliffe, P. *Schubert Piano Sonatas.* BBC Music Guides. Seattle: University of Washington Press, 1971.

Siegel, L. *Schubert's Harmonic Geometry: Structural Means in the First Movement of the B-flat Piano Sonata, D. 960.* Unpub. diss., Brandeis, 1988.

Truscott, H. "Schubert's Unfinished Piano Sonata in C (1825)." *Music Review* 18 (1957): 114–137.

————. "The Two Versions of Schubert's op. 122." *Music Review* 14 (1953): 89–106.

Tusa, M. "Why Did Schubert Revise His op. 122?" *Music Review* 45 (1984): 208–219.

Whaples, M. "On Structural Integration in Schubert's Instrumental Works." *Acta Musicologica* 40 (1968) 186–195.

————. "Style in Schubert's Piano Music from 1817 to 1818." *Music Review* 35 (1974): 260–280.

SCHUMANN, C.

Susskind, P. *Clara Wieck Schumann as Pianist and Composer.* Unpub. diss., Berkeley, 1977.

SCHUMANN, R.

Appel, B. *Schumanns Humoreske für Klavier op. 20.* Unpub. diss., Saarbrücken, 1981.

Beaufils, M. *La musique de piano de Robert Schumann*. Paris: Phebus, 1979.

Becker, C. "A New Look at Schumann's Impromptus." *Musical Quarterly* 67 (1981): 568–586.

Boetticher, W. *Robert Schumanns Klavierwerke: Neue biographische und textkritische Untersuchungen*. 2 vols. Quellenkataloge zur Musikgeschichte 9–10A. Wilhelmshaven: Heinrichshofen, 1976–1984.

————. "Zur Zitatpraxis in R. Schumanns frühen Klavierwerk." In *Speculum musicae artis: Festgabe für Heinrich Husmann zum 60. Geburtstag*, ed. H. Becker and R. Gerlach, 63–73. Munich: Fink, 1970.

Bolzan, C. "Il velo Iside ovvero Schumann di fronte a Kreisler." *Nuova rivista musicale italiana* 22 (1988): 423–440.

Bracht, H. "Schumanns 'Papillons' und die Ästhetik der Frühromantik." *Archiv für Musikwissenschaft* 50 (1993): 71–84.

Chailley, J. *Carnaval de Schumann*. 2nd ed. Paris: Leduc, 1975.

————. "Zum Symbolismus bei Robert Schumann mit besonderer Berücksichtigung der 'Papillons' op. 2." In *Robert Schumann—ein romantisches Erbe in neuer Forschung*, 57–66. Mainz: Schott, 1984.

Chissell, J. *Schumann Piano Music*. BBC Music Guides. Seattle: University of Washington Press, 1972; London: Ariel, 1986.

Dadelsen, G. "Robert Schumann und die Musik Bachs." *Archiv für Musikwissenschaft* 14 (1957): 46–59.

Daverio, J. "Reading Schumann by Way of Jean Paul and His Contemporaries." *College Music Symposium*, vol. 30, no. 2 (1990): 28–45.

——. "Schumann's 'Im Legendenton' and Friedrich Schlegel's Arabeske." *Nineteenth Century Music* 11 (1987): 150–163.

Dietel, G. *"Eine neue poetische Zeit": Musikanschauung und stilistische Tendenzen im Klavierwerk Robert Schumanns*. Kassel: Bärenreiter, 1991.

Dill, H. "Romantic Irony in the Works of Robert Schumann." *Musical Quarterly* 73 (1989): 172–195.

Draheim, J. "Schumann's Jugendwerk: acht Polonaisen, op. 3." In *Schumanns Werke: Text und Interpretation*, ed. O. Mayeda and K. Niemöller, 179–191. Mainz: Schott, 1987.

Eggebrecht, H. "'Töne sind höhere Worte': Robert Schumanns poetische Klaviermusik." In *Robert Schumann*, vol. 1, 105–115. Musik-Konzepte (Sonderband 4). Munich: text & kritik, 1981.

Erhardt, D. "Les 'Etudes symphoniques' de Robert Schumann: Projet d'integration des variations posthumes." *Revue de musicologie* 78 (1992): 289–306.

Fowler, A. "Robert Schumann and the 'Real' Davidsbündler." *College Music Symposium*, vol. 30, no. 2 (1990): 19–27.

Fuller-Maitland, J. *Schumann's Pianoforte Works*. Musical Pilgrim 16. London: Oxford, 1927.

Gertler, R. *Robert Schumann in seinen frühen Klavierwerken*. Leipzig: Radelli & Hille, 1931.

Gieseler, W. "Schumanns frühe Klavierwerke im Spiegel der literarischen Romantik." In *Robert Schumann: Universalgeist der Romantik*, ed. J. Alf et al., 62–87. Düsseldorf: Droste, 1981.

Gruber, G. "Robert Schumanns 'Fantasie' op. 17, 1. Satz: Versuch einer Interpretation." *Musicologica Austriaca* 4 (1984): 101–130.

Harwood, G. "Robert Schumann's Sonata in F-sharp minor." *Current Musicology* 29 (1980): 17–30.

Hering, H. "Das Variative in Schumann's früher Klaviermusik." *Melos/Neue Zeitschrift für Musik*, vol. 1, no. 5 (1975): 347–354.

Hohenemser, R. "Formale Eigentümlichkeiten in Robert Schumanns Klaviermusik." In *Festschrift zum 50. Geburtstage Adolf Sandberger*, 21–50. Munich: Zierfuss, 1918.

Hopf, H. *Stilistische Voraussetzungen der Klaviermusik Robert Schumanns*. Unpub. diss., Göttingen, 1958.

———. "R. Schumann: Träumerei." In *Werkanalyse in Beispielen*, ed. S. Helms and H. Hopf, 151–156. Regensburg: Bosse, 1986.

Jacobs, R. "Schumann and Jean Paul." *Music and Letters* 30 (1949): 250–258.

Jensen, E. "A New Manuscript of Robert Schumann's 'Waldszenen' op. 82." *Journal of Musicology* 3 (1984): 69–89.

Jost, P. *Schumann's "Waldszenen op. 82."* Saarbrücken: Saar-Druckerei, 1989.

Kaminsky, P. "Principles of Formal Structure in Schumann's Early Piano Cycles." *Music Theory Spectrum* 11 (1989): 207–225.

Katzenberger, G. "Robert Schumann, Klassiker des Lyrischen Klavierstücks?" In *Gattungen der Musik und ihre Klassiker*, ed. H. Danuser, 251–270. Laaber, 1988.

Knechtges-Obrecht, I. *Robert Schumann im Spiegel seiner späten Klavierwerke*. Kölner Beiträge zur Musikforschung 142. Regensburg: Bosse, 1985.

Kollen, J. "Tema, op. 13, Robert Alexander Schumann (1810–1856)." In *Notations and Editions: A Book in Honor of Louise Cuyler*, ed. E. Boroff, 163–171. Dubuque: Brown, 1974.

König, T. "Robert Schumanns 'Kinderszenen' op. 15." In *Robert Schumann*, vol. 2, 299–342. Musik-Konzepte (Sonderband). Munich: text & kritik, 1982.

Kötz, H. *Der Einfluss Jean Pauls auf Robert Schumann*. Weimar: Böhlau, 1933.

Liszt, F. "Robert Schumanns Klavierkompositionen op. 5, 11, und 14." In *Gesammelte Schriften*, vol. 2, 99–107. Leipzig: Breitkopf & Härtel, 1881.

MacDonald, C. "Schumann's Earliest Compositions." *Journal of Musicological Research* 7 (1987): 259–283.

Marston, N. "'Im Legendenton': Schumann's 'Unsong Voice.'" *Nineteenth Century Music* 16 (1993): 227–241.

———. *Schumann: 'Fantasie,' op. 17*. Cambridge Music Handbooks. Cambridge: Cambridge University Press, 1992.

Münch, S. "'Fantasiestücke in Kreislers Manier': Robert Schumanns Kreisleriana op. 16 und die Musikanschauung E. T. A. Hoffmanns." *Die Musikforschung* 45 (1992): 255–275.

Nejgauz, G. "Schumanns Klaviersonate in f-moll op. 14 und ihre Überlieferung." In *Robert und Clara Schumann und ihre Zeit*, ed. G. Muller, 53–58. Zwickau: Rat der Stadt, 1989.

Parrott, I. "A Plea for Schumann's op. 11." *Music and Letters* 33 (1952): 55–58.

Polansky, R. "The Rejected 'Kinderscenen' of Robert Schumann's op. 15." *Journal of the American Musicological Society* 31 (1978): 126–131.

Reti, R. "Schumanns 'Kinderszenen': Quasi Thema mit Variationen." In *Robert Schumann*, vol. 2, 275–298. Musik-Konzepte (Sonderband). Munich: text & kritik, 1982.

Roesner, L. "The Autograph of Schumann's Piano Sonata in F minor, op. 14." *Musical Quarterly* 61 (1975): 98–130.

———. "Schumann's 'Parallel' Forms." *Nineteenth Century Music* 14 (1991): 265–278.

———. "Schumann's Revisions in the First Movement of the Piano Sonata in G minor, op. 22." *Nineteenth Century Music* 1 (1977): 97–109.

————. "The Sketches for Schumann's 'Davidsbündlertänze,' op. 6." In *Mendelssohn and Schumann*, ed J. Finson et al., 53–70. Durham: Duke University Press, 1984.

Schwarz, W. *Robert Schumann und die Variation*. Königsberger Studien zur Musikwissenschaft 15. Kassel: Bärenreiter, 1932.

Taylor, T. "Aesthetic and Cultural Issues in Schumann's 'Kinderszenen.'" *International Review of the Aesthetics and Sociology of Music* 21 (1990): 161–178.

Wörner, K. "Schumanns 'Kreisleriana.'" *Sammelbände der Robert Schumann Gesellschaft* 2 (1966, published 1967): 58–65.

SCOTT

Darson, T. *The Solo Piano Works of Cyril Scott*. Unpub. diss., New York University, 1979.

SCRIABIN

Baker, J. *Music of Alexander Scriabin*. New Haven: Yale, 1986 (Composers of the 20th Century).

Hull, A. "Survey of the Pianoforte Works of Scriabin." *Musical Quarterly* 2 (1916): 601–614.

Mauser, S. "Harmonik im Aufbruch: Anmerkungen zu Skrjabins 'Preludes' op. 74." In *Aleksandr Skrjabin und die Skrjabinisten*, vol. 2, 53–60. Musik-Konzepte 37–38. Munich: text & kritik, 1984.

Montagu-Nathan, M. *Handbook to the Pianoforte Works of Scriabin*. 1916. Reprint. London: Chester, 1922.

Reise, J. "Late Skryabin: Some Principles Behind the Style." *Nineteenth Century Music* 6 (1983): 220–231.

Schmidt, M. *Ekstase als musikalisches Symbol in den Klavierpoèmes Alexander Skrjabins*. Musikwissenschaftliche Studien 6. Pfaffenweiller: Centaurus, 1989.

————. "Komposition als Symbol: Überlegungen zu Skrjabins Fünfter Sonate op. 53." In *Aleksandr Skrjabin*, vol. 2, 44–52. Musik-Konzepte 37–38. Munich: text & kritik, 1984.

Steger, H. *Materialstrukturen in den fünf späten Klaviersonaten Alexander Skrjabins*. Regensburger Beiträge zur Musikwissenschaft 3. Regensburg: Bosse, 1977.

————. *Der Weg der Klaviersonate bei Alexander Skrjabin*. Musikbuch. Reihe 1. Munich: Wollenweber, 1979.

SEIXAS

Heimes, K. "Carl Seixas: zum Quellenstudium seiner Klaviersonaten." *Archiv für Musikwissenschaft* 28 (1971): 205–216.

Kastner, M. *Carlos de Seixas*. Coimbra: Coimbra Editora, 1947.

SERTORI

Pestelli, G. "Sei sonate per cembalo di Girolamo Sertori (1785)." *Rivista italiana de musicologia* 2 (1967): 131–139.

SHOSTAKOVITCH

Biesold, M. *Dimitrij Schostakowitsch: Klaviermusik der neuen Sachlichkeit*. Beiträge zur Klaviermusik 3. Wittmund: Musica et claves, 1988.

Burde, T. *Die Klaviermusik von Dimitri Shostakowitsch*. Unpub. diss., Halle, 1982.

SIBELIUS

Tawaststjerna, E. *The Pianoforte Compositions of Sibelius*. Helsinki: Kustannusosakeyhtiö Otava, 1957.

SMETANA

Goebel, A. "Friedrich Smetanas 'Das Brautpaar.' Ein Beitrag zum Charakterstück im 19. Jahrhundert." *Musik und Bildung* 14 (1982): 12–19.

SMITH, J.

Beechey, G. "The Keyboard Suites of John Christopher Smith (1712–1795)." *Revue belge de musicologie* 24 (1970): 52–80.

SOLER

Dieckow, A. *A Stylistic Analysis of the Solo Keyboard Sonatas of Antonio Soler.* Unpub. diss., Washington University (St. Louis), 1971.

SOMERS

Butler, G. "Harry Somers: The Culmination of a Pianistic Style in the Third Piano Sonata." *Studies in Music* [Canada] 9 (1984): 124–132.

SORABJI

Gula, R. "Kaikhosru Shapurji Sorabji (1892–[sic]): The Published Piano Works." *Journal of the American Liszt Society* 12 (1982): 38–51.

SORGE

Miller, F. *The Keyboard Music of Georg Andreas Sorge (1703–1778).* Unpub. diss., Michigan State University, 1974.

STEIBELT

Müller, G. *Daniel Steibelt.* Collection d'études musicologiques 10. Strassburg: Heitz, 1933.

STOCKHAUSEN

Henck, H. "Karlheinz Stockhausens Klavierstück IX." In *Musik und Zahl,* ed. G. Schnitzler, 171–200. Orpheus 17. Bonn: Verlag für systematische Musikwissenschaft, 1978.
––––––. *Karlheinz Stockhausen's Piano Piece X.* Trans. D. Richards. Cologne: Neuland, 1980.
Müller, A. *Karlheinz Stockhausens Klavierstücke.* Unpub. diss., Saarbrücken, 1991.

STÖLZEL

Schmidt-Weiss, W. *Gottfried Heinrich Stölzel (1690–1749) als Instrumentalkomponist.* Schriftenreihe des musikwissenschaftlichen Seminars der Universität München 4. Würzburg: Triltsch, 1939.

STRAVINSKY

Boettcher, B. *A Study of Stravinsky's "Sonate pour piano" (1924) and "Serenade en la."* Lewiston, NY: Mellen, 1992.
Joseph, C. *Stravinsky and the Piano.* Ann Arbor: UMI, 1983.

SWEELINCK

Bradshaw, M. "The Toccatas of Jan Pieterzoon Sweelinck." *Tijdschrift der Vereniging voor nederlandsche Muziekgeschiedenis* 25 (1975): 38–60.
Curtis, A. *Sweelinck's Keyboard Music: A Study of English Elements in 17th-Century Dutch Composition.* 3rd ed. Leiden: Brill, 1987.

SZYMANOWSKI

Barroll, R. "The Keyboard Style of Karol Szymanowski: I. The Early Style." *Journal of the American Liszt Society* 19 (1986): 49–66.
Cruz-Perez, H. *The Piano Sonatas of Karol Szymanowski.* Unpub. diss., Northwestern, 1987.

TAKEMITSU

Koozin, T. "Octatonicism in Recent Piano Works of Toru Takemitsu." *Perspectives of New Music*, vol. 29, no. 1 (1991): 124–140.

———. "Toru Takemitsu and the Unity of Opposites." *College Music Symposium* 30, 1 (1990): 34–44.

TELEMANN

Schaefer-Schmuck, K. *Georg Philipp Telemann als Klavierkomponist.* Borna and Leipzig: Noske, 1934.

THOMSON

Tommasini, A. "The Musical Portraits of Virgil Thomson." *Musical Quarterly* 70 (1984): 234–247.

VALENTE

Burns, J. "Antonio Valente, Neapolitan Keyboard Primitive." *Journal of the American Musicological Society* 12 (1959): 133–143.

Caravaglios, N. "Una nuova 'Intavolatura di cimbalo' di Antonio Valente cieco." *Rivista musicale italiana* 23 (1916): 491–508.

VANHALL

Dewitz, M. *Jean Baptiste Vanhal: Leben und Klavierwerke.* Munich: Salesianische Offizin, 1933.

VOLKMANN

Hopkins, W. "The Solo Piano Works of Robert Volkmann."In *Music East and West: Essays in Honor of Walter Kaufmann*, ed. T. Noblitt, 327–328. New York: Pendragon, 1981.

VOŘÍŠEK

DeLong, K. "The Piano Rhapsodies of J. H. Voříšek." *Journal of the American Liszt Society* 26 (1989): 12–28.

WAGENSEIL

Hausswald, G. "Der Divertimentobegriff bei Georg Christoph Wagenseil." *Archiv für Musikwissenschaft* 9 (1952): 45–50.

WAGNER

Breithaupt, R. "Richard Wagners Klaviermusik." *Die Musik* 3 (1903–1904): 103–134.

WEBER

Georgii, W. *Karl Maria von Weber als Klavierkomponist.* Leipzig: Breitkopf & Härtel, 1914.

WEBERN

Maurer-Zenck, C. "Der Sinn von Weberns Variationen." In *Anton Webern*, vol. 2, 342–353. Musik-Konzepte (Sonderband). Munich: text & kritik, 1984.

Schnebel, D. "[Webern:] Die Variationen für Klavier op. 27." In *Anton Webern*, vol. 2, 162–217. Musik-Konzepte (Sonderband). Munich: text & kritik, 1984.

WELLESZ

Greiman, J. *The Solo Piano Music of Egon Wellesz.* Unpub. diss., University of Maryland, 1988.

WOLFF

Behrens, J. "Recent Piano Works of Christian Wolff, 1972–1976." *Studies in Music* [Canada] 2 (1977): 1–7.

WÖLFL
Baum, R. *Joseph Wölfl (1773–1812)*. Kassel: Bärenreiter, 1918.

WOLPE
Brody, M. "Sensibility Defined: Set Projection in Stefan Wolpe's 'FORM' for Piano." *Perspectives of New Music* 15 (1977): 3–22.

ZIMMERMANN
Imhoff, A. *Untersuchungen zum Klavierwerk Berndt Aloys Zimmermanns (1918–70)*. Kölner Beiträge zur Musikforschung 83. Regensburg: Bosse, 1976.

ZIPOLI
Erickson-Bloch, S. *The Keyboard Music of Domenico Zipoli*. Unpub. diss., Cornell, 1975.

Index of Names and Terms